THE 2020-21 NBA PREVIEW ALMANAC

by

Richard Lu

Credits:

Additional Scouting and Editing:
Alan Lu

Stats and Information:
Basketball-Reference.com
Synergy Sports
Spotrac
RealGM
probasketballtransactions.com/basketball
NBA.com/stats
82games.com
addmorefunds.com/nba/wowy
hoopsrumors.com Two-Way Tracker

Cover:
Hayley Faye, fayefayedesigns on fiverr.com
Cover photo based on the following trading card, 1993-94 Fleer Ultra NBA All-Defense #4 Scottie Pippen

Back Cover photo by:
Josh Springer
The Candid Crow, joshspringerphotography.com

For all comments, questions and requests, you can reach the author by email at lurv82@gmail.com or you can find him on Twitter as @rvlhoops.

For all of the author's other work, please go to: www.amazon.com/author/rvlhoops

TABLE OF CONTENTS

Welcome to The 2020-21 NBA Preview Almanac

To everybody that has read any of my previous books, welcome back and I hope you like this preview of the upcoming 2020-21 NBA season. If this is your first time reading any of my work, thanks for giving this a chance. Anyway, this version of the preview almanac is going to be similar to the last two editions because this book will provide you with valuable information backed by years of intensive research to give you a better idea of what to expect for this upcoming season. To be specific, I use my own proprietary forecasting system to break down and project the future performance of players and teams. From there, I'll discuss the results to help you understand the general expectations of all 30 teams and gain insight into the potential productivity level of any given individual player this season. Typically, this book is less writing intensive than my annual draft almanac because there's more data to sort through, which makes the turn-around time much shorter in a normal offseason cycle. Given the events of the current coronavirus pandemic, the time to produce this is much more compressed. As a result, the individual player projections are usually explained with bullet-pointed notes instead of detailed prose to keep things concise. Also, I wanted to avoid some unnecessary rehashing because we're mostly dealing with established NBA players instead of unknown draft prospects. In addition to this, the shortened offseason didn't allow me to flesh out a detailed preview of each team. Therefore, the analysis of each team is also presented in bullet point form. If you already know how my general process works, you can skip ahead and enjoy the rest of this preview almanac. Otherwise, if you're a new reader or if you need a quick refresher on my basic methods, the following answers to the most common questions will give you a better sense of what to expect.

1. *Who are you and what is your background?*

I've been conducting research on the NBA for more than a decade. This accumulation of knowledge gave me the expertise needed to provide analytic consulting services for the Phoenix Suns and Chicago Bulls. My primary specialty is the NBA Draft, so this can help to explain why I write a separate book to break down and disseminate that information. With the Similarity Based Projection Model that I still use to evaluate draft prospects, I made the recommendation for the Bulls to use of one of their first round picks in 2011 to take Jimmy Butler. In the time since that draft, Butler has gone on to become a five-time All-Star and a three-time All-NBA team selection. Before that, I primarily performed advanced analysis of lineups to assist the Suns in their Western Conference Finals run in 2010. My main contribution was that I helped to identify a key defensive switch in the team's first round series against Portland that altered the momentum in favor of the Suns. Based on data from prior matchups, I suggested that the Suns should utilize Grant Hill as Andre Miller's primary defender instead of Jason Richardson. The team went through with the switch and Miller's effectiveness was basically neutralized after the first game. In addition to that, Richardson broke out offensively to the point where he averaged more than 25 points-per-game in the last five games of the series because he was freed from the difficult defensive responsibility of guarding Miller. With this past experience, I can draw upon it to give my readers a greater insight into the finer points of the NBA by providing you with the same high-level analysis that I applied to assist front office personnel

2. *Please explain your forecasting system. What it is and how does it work?*

After I had some success with my draft system, I utilized a similar method to build this forecasting system that projects the future performance of NBA players and teams. It has had several different names and acronyms over the years, but I've settled on calling it the **S**ystematized **C**omparison **H**euristic **R**ationalizing **E**mpirically **M**ethodical **P**erformance **F**orecasts, or SCHREMPF, named after former Seattle SuperSonics forward and two-time Sixth Man of the Year, Detlef Schrempf. With that out of the way, here are the basics on how the system works. The system takes a weighted average of an established NBA veteran player's stats over the most recent three-year period and uses statistical similarity to compare these numbers against all player seasons from the 1979-80 season to the present. I also project the performance of incoming college rookies and other newcomers from overseas by using a combination of forecasted metrics from my draft system and translated stats based on researched international league strength values, whenever it applies. After initially comparing the given player against the database, the system generates a baseline forecast of future performance based on a set of historical comparables. Most of the projected metrics are rate statistics because raw counting stats are fairly dependent on subjective factors like coaching decisions that can be hard to accurately quantify. Then, based on a best estimate of the expected roles of various players and the team's potential playing time distribution, the system uses the forecasted baselines of players to produce a base rating of the talent levels of various teams. In prior years, I've attempted to apply other calculations to the base rating to project win totals. However, I haven't found a reliable way to accurately account for all of the different variables that come into play in a quantifiable way. For example, the effect of any given player changing teams is not uniform because every player is their own unique case. Instead of trying to overfit the data to get a relatively unreliable win total, I chose to post each team's base rating and then break down its potential legitimacy using all of the information at my disposal to get a reasonable estimate for any given team's regular season record. This forecasting system isn't perfect by any means, but these projections are useful to sort through the various stats to give you a better idea of what to expect for this season.

This is basically how everything works in this book. The next page will explain the different metrics and abbreviations that you'll see on the projection pages, if you don't already know what those are. If you're familiar with the material on the projection pages, then you can just go ahead and read through the forecasts. As a simple reminder or disclaimer, I'm not claiming that every projection is going to be perfectly correct. After all, the future is difficult to predict and even the best forecasting models can get things wrong. However, I assure you that you will gain a more complete and deeper understanding of the season ahead by giving you insights into the possible performance of every current NBA player along with some general breakdowns of all 30 teams. If you would like an enhanced knowledge of the NBA and higher level of enjoyment of the game of basketball for the 2020-21 season, turn the page and immerse yourself in The 2020-21 NBA Preview Almanac.

Explaining the Player Projection Pages

Right now, I'm going to quickly explain the set of metrics and abbreviations that you will see on the projection page of any given NBA player. For this, I will walk you through a sample projection to show you everything that you will see on the page. If you have picked up either of the last two preview almanacs and you already know how this all works, then you can skip ahead and dive into the rest of this book.

Player A [1]	Height	Weight	Cap #	Years Left
	6'0"	175	$$$$	##

Similar at Age 30

	[2]	Season	SIMsc
1	Tim Hardaway	1996-97	908.3
2	Bobby Jackson	2003-04	901.4
3	Jason Terry	2007-08	900.0
4	Monta Ellis	2015-16	895.0
5	Chris Paul	2015-16	894.6
6	Kyle Lowry	2016-17	892.8
7	David Wesley	2000-01	886.4
8	Mookie Blaylock	1997-98	883.6
9	Lou Williams	2016-17	882.4
10	Nick Van Exel	2001-02	881.9

Baseline Basic Stats [3]

MPG	PTS	AST	REB	BLK	STL
33.0	16.4	5.4	3.4	0.2	1.5

Advanced Metrics [4]

USG%	3PTA/FGA	FTA/FGA	TS%	eFG%	3PT%
24.5	0.374	0.243	0.535	0.492	0.360
AST%	**TOV%**	**OREB%**	**DREB%**	**STL%**	**BLK%**
21.0	11.5	3.6	12.2	2.4	0.8
PER	**ORTG**	**DRTG**	**WS/48**	**VOL**	
18.30	108.0	103.3	0.145	0.358	

[1] – This top row gives you some basic information like the player's name, listed height, weight, current cap number and the number of years left on the player's contract after this season.

[2] – This list is the set of the ten most statistically similar players at any given age. The number on the right, abbreviated as SIMsc, is the Similarity Score. This tells you how similar the listed comparable is to the player. These Similarity Scores are taken out of 1000, so a score of 900 would represent a 90% degree of similarity. I used 1000 instead of 100 to make the differences between players more noticeable. An asterisk signifies that the comparable is in the Hall of Fame.

[3] – This row is a weighted average of the projected basic per-game stats based on a composite of the comparables used by the system. The measured composite consists of more data points than the ten players listed on the projection page.

[4] – These three rows are the player's projected advanced stats. Here is what each abbreviation and metric means.

USG%, Usage Percentage – An estimate of the percentage of team plays used by the player while he's on the floor.

3PTA/FGA, Three-Point Attempts per Field Goal Attempt

FTA/FGA, Free Throw Attempts per Field Goal Attempt

TS%, True Shooting Percentage – A measure of shooting efficiency that accounts for field goals, threes and free throws

eFG%, Effective Field Goal Percentage – A measure of field goal shooting efficiency that accounts for the additional point value of a three-pointer

3PT%, Three-Point Percentage

AST%, Assist Percentage – An estimate of the percentage of teammate field goals a player assisted on while he was on the floor

TOV%, Turnover Percentage – An estimate of turnover per 100 plays

OREB%, Offensive Rebound Percentage – An estimate of the percentage of offensive rebounds a player grabbed while he was on the floor

DREB%, Defensive Rebound Percentage – An estimate of the percentage of defensive rebounds a player grabbed while he was on the floor

STL%, Steal Percentage – An estimate of the percentage of opponent possessions that end in a steal by the player while he was on the floor

BLK%, Block Percentage – An estimate of the percentage of opponent two-point field goal attempts blocked by the player while he was on the floor

PER, Player Efficiency Rating – A linear weights rating developed by John Hollinger that sums up all of a player's positive box score accomplishments, subtracts the negative ones and returns a per-minute rating of a player's performance. The built-in average is 15.

ORTG, Offensive Rating – An estimation of points produced per 100 possessions

DRTG, Defensive Rating – An estimation of points allowed per 100 possessions

WS/48, Win Shares per 48 Minutes – An estimate of the number of wins contributed by the player per 48 minutes. The league average is approximately 0.100.

VOL, Volatility Rating – My personal metric to measure the level of variability within a given projection. A lower number means that the performances of the comparables are within a reasonable range of the projected metrics. A higher value means that the performance of the comparables vary considerably and they are either significant higher or lower than the projected metrics. A value above 0.400 would be considered volatile.

Below the metrics, there are a series of bullet points that will provide you with a quick scouting report on the player. The idea behind this is to give you a better grasp on who any given player is and what you could reasonably expect from him this season. More or less, this is how the projection pages work. Therefore, we can move on to the page and look at a new way to quantify defensive matchups as well as on-ball defense. From there, we will get into previewing the 2020-21 NBA season, starting with the Eastern Conference.

Introducing Defensive Degree of Difficulty and Points Prevented

The analytics movement in basketball has really helped to enhance the understanding of various nuances of the game, but when it comes to evaluating defense at the individual level, there's still a long way to go. There's no better evidence of this than the discourse around last season's Defensive Player of the Year voting. On the one hand, the winner, Giannis Antetokounmpo led the NBA in every advanced defensive metric and he was the most impactful defender on the league's best defensive team in the regular season. However, critics would point that though he has the extraordinary athleticism and versatility to defend all positions, he was mainly utilized as a roamer and typically, he didn't defend elite players on a regular basis. Those detractors would usually point to an established rim protecting big man like Anthony Davis or Rudy Gobert as a better candidate for the award due to their strong performance in standard metrics like Blocks per Game or Steals per Game.

This discussion raises some questions because the modern game has de-emphasized the traditional center in favor of greater spacing and mobility on the perimeter. This would theoretically place more value on perimeter defense in today's NBA, but the voting for the Defensive Player of the Year Award still favors interior defenders to a disproportionate degree. In fact, 17 of the last 20 Defensive Player of the Year Award winners were big men. Very rarely is a perimeter defender considered for this kind of award. This is mainly because most of the readily available metrics inherently skew towards big men. Counting stats like rebounds or blocks tend to be accumulated by big men because those events usually happen around the basket. Then, a lot of advanced metrics account for defense as being when possessions end, so this tends to favor rebounders rather than the individual that forces the initial miss. Therefore, perimeter defense is still a gray area because there are more factors to consider than the current set of metrics allow us to see. Fortunately, the information to help us quantify on-ball perimeter defense is available through the NBA's website. Specifically, the league's Advanced Stats Player Tracking system lists the individuals that a defender guards and how those players performed against that specific defender. Everything is just tedious to go through and it's not really summed up in a simple manner. Normally, I wouldn't have time to figure this out because the turn-around time to produce these books is tight due to the placement of events in a traditional schedule. However, the pandemic temporarily halted events to open up some available time for me to create a couple of new metrics to place a player's ability to play on-ball defense in a proper context. These new stats are called Defensive Degree of Difficulty and Points Prevented.

Defensive Degree of Difficulty

We'll start with Defensive Degree of Difficulty and what it measures is self-explanatory. The way it does this is that I first assigned a strength value to every player in the NBA based on scoring efficiency, usage and playing time. The idea is that higher usage and efficiency scorers are theoretically harder to defend than lower usage or efficiency ones. Then, I went through any given defender's list of matchups and took a weighted average of the strength values of each matchup to get an overall Defensive Degree of Difficulty value. The result is a simple number that measures how tough that player's matchups are on average and the ranges of these values break down like so.

- 0.500 and above – normally guards elite players
- 0.400 to 0.499 – guards starting level players
- 0.300 to 0.399 – guards second unit level players
- Below 0.300 – typically plays in garbage time, guards end of the roster players

To see this metric in action, we'll quickly look at the players that drew the toughest assignments last season. This is a brief list of the players that had the highest Defensive Degree of Difficulty ratings among those that played 500 or more minutes in 2019-20

	Team	DDD Value
Torrey Craig	DEN	0.611
Dorian Finney-Smith	DAL	0.596
Wesley Matthews	MIL	0.574
Luguentz Dort	OKC	0.572
Jrue Holiday	NOP	0.564
Ben Simmons	PHI	0.562
Trevor Ariza	SAC/POR	0.559
Royce O'Neale	UTA	0.556
Terrance Ferguson	OKC	0.553
Rodney Hood	POR	0.551

At first glance, you can see that Torrey Craig drew the toughest assignments in the league last season. His list of matchups from NBA.com back this up because eight of his ten most frequent matchups were All-Stars in the 2019-20 season. The rest of list consists of various three-and-D types or players with solid defensive reputations. The most interesting name on this is Wesley Matthews because his role can help to illuminate the flaws in many of the current metrics that we use for evaluating defense on a broad level. To illustrate this, we can look at the Defensive Degree of Difficulty values for the Milwaukee Bucks to get a sense of Matthews' level of defensive responsibility in relation to the rest of his team's main rotation players.

	MP	DDD VAL
Wesley Matthews	1635	0.574
Eric Bledsoe	1646	0.470
George Hill	1271	0.450
Khris Middleton	1853	0.424
Brook Lopez	1817	0.413
Giannis Antetokounmpo	1917	0.400
Donte DiVincenzo	1520	0.400
Ersan Ilyasova	986	0.352
Pat Connaughton	1243	0.349
Robin Lopez	958	0.320
Kyle Korver	960	0.248

Based on this information, we can see that Matthews drew difficult assignments by a wide margin, but the impact of this isn't really reflected in any of his defensive stats. After all, he doesn't have the luxury of being able to help and make plays off the ball because his main job is to neutralize the opponent's best perimeter scorer, so he's not able to accumulate traditional stats like steals, blocks or defensive rebounds. His performance in plus-minus may not fully capture his effect because these metrics tend to inadvertently measure multiple variables at the same time. Namely, the minutes of most players that are designed as their team's defensive specialist are matched to those of the opposition's top player. Matthews was mostly deployed in this manner by Milwaukee. Specifically, he tended to come off the floor at the same time as his main assignment. In addition to this, the Bucks' second unit often out-performed their opponent's bench in the regular season, so the plus-minus numbers for somebody like Matthews could be deflated to a degree. His real value, as evidenced by the earlier table, is that he capably soaked up the toughest matchups on a consistent basis, so his teammates can make a greater impact on both ends of the floor. Matthews' presence on the floor often allowed Khris Middleton to take on lower stress matchups. This gave Middleton the ability to concentrate more on his offense and he ended up having his most productive season. Matthews' effectiveness as an on-ball defender against top players allowed the other players, namely Giannis Antetokounmpo, to have more freedom to roam and help off the ball. This enabled the Bucks to be one of the league's best teams at preventing points around the rim last season. In the playoffs, the Heat discombobulated Milwaukee's overall defensive strategy in the first game of their series when Jimmy Butler scored 40 points with Matthews as his main defender. Miami, through the performance of Butler, repeatedly showed that they could break Milwaukee's first line of defense, Matthews, which meant that the Bucks needed to adjust their defense. However, Matthews was really the only member of the Bucks that took on difficult defensive responsibilities. Therefore, the Bucks were caught in a bind because their choices were to either continue with a flawed strategy of using Matthews to guard Butler or switch to defenders that were sub-optimal. As a result, the Bucks lost the series and they may have to re-think their defensive schemes to try to move forward. Namely, they will have to figure out if it makes sense to continue to have one player assume such a large workload on the defensive end. This idea is tough to see without tangible metrics, so that's where this kind of Defensive Degree of Difficulty metric can be helpful. Specifically, it allows us to understand the level of responsibility that a player has on defense in a way that's similar to Usage Percentage on offense. This way, we can figure out ways to optimize a player's defensive performance by seeing where he fits on some kind of a defensive spectrum.

Points Prevented

Defensive Degree of Difficulty provides insight into the difficulty level of any given defender's matchups. From here, we need to measure an on-ball defender's level of effectiveness when he handles these assignments. To do this, I created a metric called Points Prevented, or more specifically, Points Prevented per 100 Partial Possessions. The basic idea behind this metric is that we measure the actual performance of any given defender's set of matchup against their expected level of production. Specifically, this metric goes through a defender's list of matchups and calculated an expected point value of each assignment based that player's True Shooting Percentage and the number of field goal and free throw attempts that were taken against the defender over the course of the season. After that, this expected point value is subtracted by the value of points allowed to get the raw Points Prevented total. Then, that raw Points Prevented total is divided by the total of Partial Possessions, as listed by NBA.com, and multiplied by 100 to get an unadjusted Points Prevented value. These unadjusted values were still skewed towards valuing big men because there was no real way to parse out other factors like double teams or other help defense. To account for this in the best way that I could, I looked at the unadjusted values by a player's position, as listed by Basketball-Reference. I essentially found that it was tougher to prevent points from the perimeter, which makes sense because a defender is more likely to be on an island rather than receiving help in a weak side situation. So, the final step in creating this metric is that I incorporate a position adjustment to get the final Points Prevented metric. With this in mind, we can get a sense of how this metric works by once again looking at the defenders that had the most difficult assignments in the league last season. Here are the Points Prevented numbers for the top ten in

Defensive Degree of Difficulty value in 2019-20. As a note, a player qualified for this leaderboard if he played at least 500 or more minutes last season and a number in parentheses represents a negative number.

	Team	DDD Value	Points Prevented
Torrey Craig	DEN	0.611	(0.588)
Dorian Finney-Smith	DAL	0.596	2.008
Wesley Matthews	MIL	0.574	2.936
Luguentz Dort	OKC	0.572	3.245
Jrue Holiday	NOP	0.564	2.631
Ben Simmons	PHI	0.562	2.072
Trevor Ariza	SAC/POR	0.559	0.642
Royce O'Neale	UTA	0.556	(0.482)
Terrance Ferguson	OKC	0.553	0.376
Rodney Hood	POR	0.551	(1.322)

Based on the table above, most of the players that drew the toughest assignments in the league last season were effective at holding their matchup to less than their expected level of production. However, a few players, Craig, Royce O'Neale and Rodney Hood, were probably over-extended and not quite able to handle this high difficulty level because they tended to allow their opponent to score more than average. Thus, their respective teams might be better served by either adding another high leverage defender to ease their workload or move them into lower stress matchups. From here, we can look at the sub-set of players that generally drew the toughest assignments to get a better idea of which ones played the best on-ball defense last season. The following is a list of the ten highest Points Prevented values among players that had a Defensive Degree Value of 0.500 or higher.

	Team	DDD Value	Points Prevented
Luguentz Dort	OKC	0.572	3.245
Avery Bradley	LAL	0.538	3.240
Wesley Matthews	MIL	0.574	2.936
Elfrid Payton	NYK	0.532	2.822
Jrue Holiday	NOP	0.564	2.631
Patrick Beverley	LAC	0.519	2.306
Kawhi Leonard	LAC	0.505	2.231
Jimmy Butler	MIA	0.511	2.108
Josh Richardson	PHI	0.515	2.105
Ben Simmons	PHI	0.562	2.072

The composition of this list shouldn't be too surprising because most of these players have strong defensive reputations. The only name that sticks out is Elfrid Payton because he played on a bad Knicks team, so he didn't get a lot of attention for his defense. However, he took on a lot of tough point guard assignments and according to this metric, he was one of the league's better on-ball defenders last season. For example, he allowed Bradley Beal to score ten points on 16 field goal attempts. Also, Donovan Mitchell was only able to score six points on eight field goal attempts last season. Even so, Payton's presence on the list points out that the effect of one strong perimeter defender has limits. Even if a team is helped by a defender's ability to successfully guard his opponent, it can be undone by simply being bad in the other facets of the game. On the other hand, getting a more accurate understanding of this component of defense is important because a team's top perimeter defender is the first line of defense. If an opponent breaks this first line, it can sometimes be more harmful to a team in this era because it can lead to a lot of open threes and it's harder to bring help. Therefore, teams can still gain a lot of value from having an elite on-ball perimeter defender on their team. This list shows it because two of the top three defenders, Avery Bradley and Wesley Matthews, were on teams that had the best record in their respective conference. In addition to that, eight of the top ten came from teams that made the playoffs, so quality perimeter defenders are important to helping a team win.

A metric like Points Prevented can help to give defenders proper credit for their contributions. As for awards, the NBA would benefit from creating a separate award to honor the performance of top perimeter defenders. The main reason for this is that it would encourage everyone in the basketball world to pay as much attention to the defensive side of the ball as they do on offense. This way, top perimeter defenders would get more respect for the value they create in preventing scores. Ideally, this new award would be called the Scottie Pippen Award in honor of Pippen, who is widely regarded as one of the NBA's greatest perimeter defenders, but he never earned Defensive Player of the Year honors because the stats weren't really good enough to fully capture his value. If this award were to exist last season, the three finalists would be as follows:

- Ben Simmons, Philadelphia – 10th in Points Prevented, multi-positional versatility, led the NBA in Steals per game
- Wesley Matthews, Milwaukee – 3rd in Points Prevented, best on-ball defender on the NBA's best defensive team
- Luguentz Dort, Oklahoma City – 1st in Points Prevented, best per-possession on-ball defender in the NBA

Each one of these candidates has a compelling case, with Dort and Simmons have the strongest arguments in their favor. Dort established himself as an elite defender in a short amount of time, routinely holding some of the league's top scorers to below average levels of efficiency. His excellent defense on James Harden in the playoffs convincingly validates his overall candidacy for this theoretical award. On the other hand, Simmons has a more well-rounded profile because he was effective on a per-possession basis and he did well the traditional metrics, as he led the league in Steals per Game. With that in mind, this hypothetical Scottie Pippen Award would be presented to Ben Simmons for being the best perimeter defender in the NBA in 2019-20.

Hypothetical awards aside, metrics like Defensive Degree of Difficulty and Points Prevented help to clarify and define a player's defensive value, particularly as an on-ball defender. These metrics will be featured in this preview almanac from here on out. For the sake of this book, I created these metrics at different junctures of the pandemic, so each one is going to be presented differently for this particular edition. Because I came up with this metric first, I included Defensive Degree of Difficulty values on every player page to provide a better insight into that player's defensive role. Points Prevented was created towards the end of last season, so I was only able to post a basic leaderboard, which will come at the end of this write-up. Anyway, these metrics are two new pieces that give you a more complete picture of any given player's defensive ability, which help to provide a more in-depth overall understanding of that player's performance from last season.

2019-20 Points Prevented Leaders

These are the Points Prevented stats for all qualifying players during the 2019-20 NBA season. A player qualified if he played 500 or more minutes. As stated in the previous article, Points Prevented is technically Points Prevented per 100 Partial Possessions and a number in parentheses represents a negative value.

- Defensive Degree of Difficulty ratings that are 0.500 or above and have positive Points Prevented values

	POS	MP	Team	DDD VAL	PTS Prevented
Luguentz Dort	SG	820	OKC	0.572	3.245
Avery Bradley	SG	1186	LAL	0.538	3.240
Wesley Matthews	SG	1635	MIL	0.574	2.936
Elfrid Payton	PG	1246	NYK	0.532	2.822
Jrue Holiday	SG	2117	NOP	0.564	2.631
Patrick Beverley	PG	1342	LAC	0.519	2.306
Kawhi Leonard	SF	1848	LAC	0.505	2.231
Jimmy Butler	SF	1959	MIA	0.511	2.108
Josh Richardson	SG	1693	PHI	0.515	2.105
Ben Simmons	PG	2017	PHI	0.562	2.072
Dorian Finney-Smith	PF	2120	DAL	0.596	2.008
LaMarcus Aldridge	C	1754	SAS	0.502	1.986
Malcolm Brogdon	PG	1666	IND	0.507	1.769
Marcus Smart	SG	1919	BOS	0.506	1.522
Gary Harris	SG	1780	DEN	0.532	1.099
Bruce Brown	SG	1634	DET	0.513	1.093
Cory Joseph	PG	1759	SAC	0.515	1.004
Josh Okogie	SG	1547	MIN	0.525	0.801
OG Anunoby	SF	2066	TOR	0.509	0.718
Trevor Ariza	SF	1493	SAC/POR	0.559	0.642
Derrick White	SG	1677	SAS	0.517	0.390
Terrance Ferguson	SF	1257	OKC	0.553	0.376
Paul George	SF	1419	LAC	0.502	0.152
Dillon Brooks	SG	2112	MEM	0.549	(0.094)
Royce O'Neale	PF	2049	UTA	0.556	(0.482)
Torrey Craig	SF	1072	DEN	0.611	(0.588)
Danny Green	SG	1687	LAL	0.543	(0.608)
Dejounte Murray	PG	1687	SAS	0.524	(0.652)
Tony Snell	SF	1641	DET	0.535	(0.830)
Kris Dunn	PG	1269	CHI	0.520	(1.184)
Rodney Hood	SF	619	POR	0.551	(1.322)
Evan Fournier	SG	2076	ORL	0.509	(1.388)
Jae Crowder	SF	1875	MEM/MIA	0.508	(1.654)
Maurice Harkless	SF	1427	LAC/NYK	0.534	(1.887)
Glenn Robinson III	SF	1786	GSW/PHI	0.542	(2.207)

- Defensive Degree of Difficulty ratings that are between 0.400 and 0.499

	POS	MP	Team	DDD VAL	PTS Prevented
Rudy Gobert	C	2333	UTA	0.457	7.754
Ivica Zubac	C	1326	LAC	0.472	6.556
Eric Gordon	SF	1016	HOU	0.414	5.471
Deandre Ayton	C	1236	PHO	0.448	5.429
Anthony Davis	PF	2131	LAL	0.445	5.165
Brook Lopez	C	1817	MIL	0.413	4.746
Derrick Jones Jr.	SF	1375	MIA	0.494	4.164
Jarrett Allen	C	1852	BRK	0.450	4.151
Giannis Antetokounmpo	PF	1917	MIL	0.400	3.963
Alex Len	C	970	ATL/SAC	0.420	3.303
Jonathan Isaac	SF	980	ORL	0.464	3.259
Hassan Whiteside	C	2008	POR	0.423	3.023
Kristaps Porzingis	PF	1814	DAL	0.420	2.968
Serge Ibaka	C	1485	TOR	0.415	2.819
Matisse Thybulle	SG	1287	PHI	0.482	2.805
Daniel Theis	C	1566	BOS	0.456	2.728
Eric Bledsoe	PG	1646	MIL	0.470	2.626
Fred VanVleet	PG	1928	TOR	0.475	2.587
LeBron James	PG	2316	LAL	0.422	2.581
Clint Capela	C	1279	HOU/ATL	0.455	2.551
Justin Holiday	SG	1826	IND	0.403	2.533
Domantas Sabonis	PF	2159	IND	0.404	2.484
Bam Adebayo	PF	2417	MIA	0.471	2.460
Hamidou Diallo	SF	896	OKC	0.401	2.401
Jerami Grant	PF	1892	DEN	0.424	2.291
Maxi Kleber	C	1890	DAL	0.425	2.206
Reggie Jackson	PG	743	DET/LAC	0.435	2.135
Joel Embiid	C	1506	PHI	0.420	2.120
Kyle Anderson	PF	1330	MEM	0.412	2.014
Aaron Gordon	PF	2017	ORL	0.480	1.909
Josh Hart	SF	1755	NOP	0.448	1.754
Ja Morant	PG	2074	MEM	0.428	1.715
James Harden	SG	2483	HOU	0.423	1.611
Pascal Siakam	PF	2110	TOR	0.440	1.547
Rondae Hollis-Jefferson	SF	1122	TOR	0.442	1.528
Norman Powell	SG	1479	TOR	0.414	1.433
Bismack Biyombo	C	1029	CHH	0.405	1.360
Gordon Hayward	SF	1740	BOS	0.418	1.335
Tim Hardaway Jr.	SG	2091	DAL	0.496	1.334
Draymond Green	PF	1222	GSW	0.466	1.296
Miles Bridges	SF	1995	CHH	0.483	1.244
Willie Cauley-Stein	C	1097	DAL	0.464	1.225
Jonas Valanciunas	C	1845	MEM	0.413	1.195
Alex Caruso	PG	1175	LAL	0.450	1.178
Zach LaVine	SG	2085	CHI	0.469	1.151
Tristan Thompson	C	1721	CLE	0.494	1.147
Richaun Holmes	C	1242	SAC	0.439	1.127
Khris Middleton	SF	1853	MIL	0.424	1.101
Al Horford	C	2025	PHI	0.429	1.080
Aaron Holiday	PG	1617	IND	0.420	1.022
George Hill	PG	1271	MIL	0.450	1.012

- Defensive Degree of Difficulty ratings that are between 0.400 and 0.499 (continued)

	POS	MP	Team	DDD VAL	PTS Prevented
Nicolas Batum	SF	505	CHH	0.456	0.980
Mikal Bridges	SF	2042	PHO	0.480	0.945
Marc Gasol	C	1161	TOR	0.427	0.924
Derrick Favors	C	1243	NOP	0.459	0.906
Garrett Temple	SG	1730	BRK	0.470	0.894
Spencer Dinwiddie	SG	1994	BRK	0.468	0.845
Steven Adams	C	1680	OKC	0.432	0.812
Taurean Prince	SF	1857	BRK	0.469	0.789
Dwayne Bacon	SG	687	CHH	0.403	0.782
Kyle Lowry	PG	2098	TOR	0.436	0.752
Dennis Schroder	PG	1999	OKC	0.400	0.709
Kyrie Irving	PG	658	BRK	0.440	0.679
Lonzo Ball	PG	2025	NOP	0.467	0.678
Cody Martin	SF	903	CHH	0.434	0.643
Rodney McGruder	SG	871	LAC	0.406	0.639
Joe Ingles	SF	2137	UTA	0.450	0.559
Damian Lillard	PG	2474	POR	0.407	0.537
Russell Westbrook	PG	2049	HOU	0.415	0.537
Jaylen Brown	SF	1934	BOS	0.473	0.471
Kemba Walker	PG	1742	BOS	0.426	0.446
Kentavious Caldwell-Pope	SG	1762	LAL	0.477	0.427
Devin Booker	SG	2512	PHO	0.446	0.399
Julius Randle	PF	2080	NYK	0.445	0.390
Shai Gilgeous-Alexander	SG	2428	OKC	0.422	0.372
Dewayne Dedmon	C	774	SAC/ATL	0.403	0.281
Will Barton	SF	1916	DEN	0.457	0.260
Jeremy Lamb	SG	1291	IND	0.464	0.212
Langston Galloway	SG	1702	DET	0.408	0.209
Cam Reddish	SF	1551	ATL	0.451	0.167
Kenrich Williams	PF	832	NOP	0.409	0.147
Nikola Jokic	C	2336	DEN	0.420	0.128
Myles Turner	C	1826	IND	0.437	0.071
Jayson Tatum	PF	2265	BOS	0.441	0.065
Donte DiVincenzo	SG	1520	MIL	0.400	0.043
Kent Bazemore	SG	1688	POR/SAC	0.486	0.012
Eric Paschall	PF	1654	GSW	0.400	(0.002)
P.J. Tucker	PF	2467	HOU	0.471	(0.055)
Lauri Markkanen	PF	1492	CHI	0.432	(0.064)
JaVale McGee	C	1130	LAL	0.450	(0.084)
T.J. Warren	SF	2202	IND	0.468	(0.088)
CJ McCollum	SG	2556	POR	0.451	(0.134)
Alec Burks	SG	1754	GSW/PHI	0.413	(0.188)
Danilo Gallinari	PF	1834	OKC	0.410	(0.225)
De'Andre Hunter	SF	2018	ATL	0.460	(0.271)
Jamal Murray	PG	1904	DEN	0.419	(0.295)
Dario Saric	PF	1632	PHO	0.417	(0.314)
Dennis Smith Jr.	PG	537	NYK	0.411	(0.339)
Treveon Graham	SG	929	MIN/ATL	0.456	(0.347)
Dwight Powell	C	1061	DAL	0.473	(0.358)
Caris LeVert	SG	1330	BRK	0.404	(0.412)

- Defensive Degree of Difficulty ratings that are between 0.400 and 0.499 (continued)

	POS	MP	Team	DDD VAL	PTS Prevented
Gary Trent Jr.	SG	1332	POR	0.403	(0.432)
Trey Lyles	PF	1271	SAS	0.438	(0.434)
Landry Shamet	SG	1452	LAC	0.429	(0.565)
Marcus Morris	PF	1936	NYK/LAC	0.464	(0.618)
Tomas Satoransky	PG	1878	CHI	0.438	(0.619)
Donovan Mitchell	SG	2364	UTA	0.414	(0.652)
Danuel House	SF	1913	HOU	0.448	(0.667)
Karl-Anthony Towns	C	1187	MIN	0.440	(0.719)
Taj Gibson	C	1025	NYK	0.448	(0.758)
Cedi Osman	SF	1910	CLE	0.466	(0.951)
Kelly Oubre Jr.	SF	1933	PHO	0.489	(1.079)
Bradley Beal	SG	2053	WAS	0.458	(1.083)
Victor Oladipo	SG	528	IND	0.426	(1.083)
Tobias Harris	PF	2469	PHI	0.430	(1.091)
Jaren Jackson Jr.	C	1622	MEM	0.427	(1.201)
Carmelo Anthony	PF	1902	POR	0.401	(1.228)
Terry Rozier	PG	2164	CHH	0.437	(1.232)
DeAndre' Bembry	SG	915	ATL	0.470	(1.261)
Buddy Hield	SG	2216	SAC	0.435	(1.290)
Ky Bowman	PG	1015	GSW	0.417	(1.320)
Markelle Fultz	PG	1996	ORL	0.461	(1.343)
Nikola Vucevic	C	1998	ORL	0.415	(1.388)
Paul Millsap	PF	1240	DEN	0.439	(1.403)
Brandon Ingram	PF	2104	NOP	0.426	(1.404)
Andrew Wiggins	SG	1858	GSW	0.463	(1.460)
Wendell Carter Jr.	C	1256	CHI	0.405	(1.471)
Thaddeus Young	PF	1591	CHI	0.405	(1.526)
Frank Ntilikina	PG	1187	NYK	0.486	(1.625)
Harrison Barnes	PF	2482	SAC	0.469	(1.685)
Bryn Forbes	SG	1579	SAS	0.482	(1.725)
Sekou Doumbouya	SF	754	DET	0.422	(1.876)
Darius Garland	PG	1824	CLE	0.426	(1.886)
Shabazz Napier	PG	1344	MIN/WAS	0.435	(1.894)
De'Aaron Fox	PG	1634	SAC	0.455	(1.928)
Kendrick Nunn	SG	1962	MIA	0.440	(1.983)
Ian Mahinmi	C	808	WAS	0.477	(2.118)
Patrick McCaw	SF	908	TOR	0.468	(2.140)

- Defensive Degree of Difficulty ratings that are between 0.400 and 0.499 (continued)

	POS	MP	Team	DDD VAL	PTS Prevented
James Johnson	PF	619	MIA/MIN	0.440	(2.232)
DeMar DeRozan	SF	2316	SAS	0.456	(2.388)
Reggie Bullock	SG	684	NYK	0.486	(2.456)
Isaac Bonga	SF	1250	WAS	0.449	(2.484)
Collin Sexton	SG	2143	CLE	0.447	(2.513)
RJ Barrett	SG	1704	NYK	0.449	(2.573)
Michael Carter-Williams	SG	833	ORL	0.456	(2.593)
Kevin Huerter	SG	1760	ATL	0.411	(2.642)
Andre Drummond	C	1879	DET/CLE	0.414	(2.651)
Ricky Rubio	PG	2016	PHO	0.420	(2.694)
Rui Hachimura	PF	1444	WAS	0.450	(2.696)
Troy Brown Jr.	SG	1782	WAS	0.400	(2.769)
D'Angelo Russell	PG	1452	MIN	0.408	(2.978)
Thomas Bryant	C	1147	WAS	0.421	(2.979)
Robert Covington	C	2137	MIN/HOU	0.470	(3.020)
James Ennis	SF	1265	PHI/ORL	0.409	(3.148)
Damion Lee	SG	1423	GSW	0.433	(3.196)
De'Anthony Melton	PG	1167	MEM	0.468	(3.266)
Meyers Leonard	C	1034	MIA	0.427	(3.451)
Aron Baynes	C	934	PHO	0.464	(3.603)
Cody Zeller	C	1341	CHH	0.403	(3.934)
Damian Jones	C	887	ATL	0.411	(7.605)

- Defensive Degree of Difficulty ratings below 0.400

	POS	MP	Team	DDD VAL	PTS Prevented
DeAndre Jordan	C	1234	BRK	0.337	5.088
Robin Lopez	C	958	MIL	0.320	4.806
Skal Labissiere	PF	567	POR/ATL	0.317	4.708
Montrezl Harrell	C	1749	LAC	0.378	3.500
John Henson	PF	600	CLE/DET	0.355	2.815
Christian Wood	PF	1325	DET	0.373	2.721
Gorgui Dieng	C	1096	MIN/MEM	0.382	2.437
D.J. Augustin	PG	1420	ORL	0.344	2.219
Pat Connaughton	SG	1243	MIL	0.349	2.187
Abdel Nader	SF	867	OKC	0.322	2.142
John Collins	PF	1363	ATL	0.399	2.141
Chris Boucher	PF	819	TOR	0.299	2.125
Brandon Clarke	PF	1300	MEM	0.357	1.938
Grant Williams	PF	1043	BOS	0.351	1.864
Vince Carter	SF	876	ATL	0.340	1.836
Anthony Tolliver	PF	872	POR/SAC/MEM	0.385	1.832
Terence Davis	SG	1209	TOR	0.333	1.768
Nerlens Noel	C	1127	OKC	0.396	1.680
Jordan McRae	SG	784	WAS/DEN/DET	0.365	1.647
Darius Bazley	PF	1130	OKC	0.288	1.528
Patrick Patterson	PF	776	LAC	0.383	1.395
Mo Bamba	C	878	ORL	0.283	1.327
Bogdan Bogdanovic	SG	1766	SAC	0.365	1.319
Wesley Iwundu	SF	953	ORL	0.387	1.295
Jordan Clarkson	SG	1705	CLE/UTA	0.340	1.280
Patty Mills	PG	1485	SAS	0.374	1.262
Furkan Korkmaz	SG	1559	PHI	0.353	1.247
Jakob Poeltl	C	1171	SAS	0.367	1.241
Justin Jackson	PF	1045	DAL	0.335	1.235
Tyus Jones	PG	1232	MEM	0.341	1.195
Rodions Kurucs	PF	684	BRK	0.345	1.160
Daniel Gafford	C	609	CHI	0.336	1.130
Enes Kanter	C	983	BOS	0.370	1.120
Monte Morris	PG	1636	DEN	0.335	1.089
Lonnie Walker	SG	988	SAS	0.390	1.069
Goran Dragic	PG	1663	MIA	0.328	1.018
Jordan McLaughlin	PG	590	MIN	0.320	1.018
Ersan Ilyasova	PF	986	MIL	0.352	0.980
Troy Daniels	SG	532	LAL/DEN	0.289	0.931
Wilson Chandler	SF	734	BRK	0.377	0.931
Jerome Robinson	SG	979	LAC/WAS	0.336	0.921
Jake Layman	PF	505	MIN	0.374	0.873
Quinn Cook	PG	508	LAL	0.361	0.835
Matthew Dellavedova	PG	821	CLE	0.380	0.813
Jevon Carter	PG	945	PHO	0.371	0.765
Lou Williams	SG	1864	LAC	0.321	0.686
Tyler Johnson	SG	709	PHO/BRK	0.355	0.657
Luke Kennard	SG	922	DET	0.355	0.650
Luka Doncic	PG	2047	DAL	0.389	0.637
Tyler Herro	SG	1508	MIA	0.315	0.603
Zion Williamson	PF	668	NOP	0.388	0.473
T.J. McConnell	PG	1326	IND	0.305	0.459

- Defensive Degree of Difficulty ratings below 0.400 (continued)

	POS	MP	Team	DDD VAL	PTS Prevented
Timothe Luwawu-Cabarrot	SG	853	BRK	0.355	0.433
Rajon Rondo	PG	984	LAL	0.370	0.429
JaMychal Green	PF	1307	LAC	0.347	0.397
P.J. Washington	PF	1759	CHH	0.391	0.361
Jarrett Culver	SG	1506	MIN	0.377	0.356
Kyle Korver	SF	960	MIL	0.248	0.320
Sterling Brown	SF	767	MIL	0.326	0.299
Nassir Little	PF	573	POR	0.343	0.251
Derrick Rose	PG	1298	DET	0.392	0.246
E'Twaun Moore	SG	1020	NOP	0.355	0.117
Grayson Allen	SG	718	MEM	0.380	0.045
Austin Rivers	SG	1594	HOU	0.392	0.007
Marco Belinelli	SG	883	SAS	0.289	(0.013)
Wayne Ellington	SG	558	NYK	0.332	(0.034)
Chris Paul	PG	2208	OKC	0.384	(0.037)
Duncan Robinson	SG	2166	MIA	0.381	(0.044)
Gary Clark	PF	567	HOU/ORL	0.305	(0.049)
Emmanuel Mudiay	PG	850	UTA	0.305	(0.157)
Damyean Dotson	SG	836	NYK	0.325	(0.206)
Bojan Bogdanovic	SF	2083	UTA	0.393	(0.222)
Mike Scott	PF	1207	PHI	0.352	(0.227)
Ryan Arcidiacono	PG	930	CHI	0.337	(0.233)
Kyle Kuzma	PF	1526	LAL	0.385	(0.237)
Marvin Williams	PF	1129	CHH/MIL	0.362	(0.239)
Jordan Poole	SG	1274	GSW	0.340	(0.286)
Semi Ojeleye	PF	1011	BOS	0.378	(0.327)
Marquese Chriss	PF	1196	GSW	0.393	(0.363)
Tony Bradley	C	663	UTA	0.293	(0.403)
Frank Jackson	PG	797	NOP	0.370	(0.423)
Mitchell Robinson	C	1412	NYK	0.355	(0.457)
Devonte' Graham	PG	2211	CHH	0.389	(0.526)
Trae Young	PG	2120	ATL	0.388	(0.534)
Terrence Ross	SG	1889	ORL	0.303	(0.582)
Anfernee Simons	SG	1449	POR	0.333	(0.648)
Omari Spellman	PF	886	GSW/MIN	0.333	(0.681)
Kevin Knox	SF	1166	NYK	0.317	(0.691)
Delon Wright	SG	1570	DAL	0.387	(0.737)
Trey Burke	PG	520	PHI/DAL	0.370	(0.804)
Svi Mykhailiuk	SF	1265	DET	0.360	(0.882)
Ish Smith	PG	1787	WAS	0.367	(0.914)
Malik Beasley	SG	1209	DEN/MIN	0.368	(0.939)
Jeff Green	C	960	UTA/HOU	0.367	(0.955)
Seth Curry	SG	1576	DAL	0.358	(0.986)
Thon Maker	C	776	DET	0.389	(1.018)
Keita Bates-Diop	SF	744	MIN/DEN	0.341	(1.092)
Malik Monk	SG	1169	CHH	0.299	(1.159)
Brad Wanamaker	PG	1369	BOS	0.347	(1.162)
Mike Conley	PG	1363	UTA	0.387	(1.173)
Jalen Brunson	PG	1022	DAL	0.370	(1.251)
Rudy Gay	PF	1461	SAS	0.389	(1.285)
Jeff Teague	PG	1464	MIN/ATL	0.375	(1.337)

- Defensive Degree of Difficulty ratings below 0.400 (continued)

	POS	MP	Team	DDD VAL	PTS Prevented
Ben McLemore	SG	1619	HOU	0.377	(1.337)
Khem Birch	C	922	ORL	0.343	(1.344)
Mario Hezonja	PF	871	POR	0.381	(1.411)
Davis Bertans	PF	1583	WAS	0.349	(1.452)
Doug McDermott	PF	1372	IND	0.275	(1.468)
Markieff Morris	PF	1187	DET/LAL	0.374	(1.509)
J.J. Redick	SG	1581	NOP	0.314	(1.510)
Michael Porter Jr.	PF	903	DEN	0.323	(1.555)
Mike Muscala	C	572	OKC	0.314	(1.647)
Bobby Portis	C	1393	NYK	0.340	(1.667)
Joe Harris	SF	2123	BRK	0.372	(1.746)
Raul Neto	PG	668	PHI	0.331	(1.845)
Dwight Howard	C	1306	LAL	0.356	(2.003)
Chandler Hutchison	SF	527	CHI	0.391	(2.102)
Kevin Love	PF	1780	CLE	0.374	(2.140)
Bruno Fernando	C	713	ATL	0.393	(2.172)
Coby White	SG	1674	CHI	0.311	(2.574)
Larry Nance Jr.	C	1472	CLE	0.364	(2.605)
Solomon Hill	SF	1088	MEM/MIA	0.353	(2.638)
Yogi Ferrell	PG	530	SAC	0.287	(2.687)
Shake Milton	SG	805	PHI	0.392	(2.778)
Jabari Parker	PF	917	ATL/SAC	0.399	(2.942)
Jaxson Hayes	C	1080	NOP	0.345	(2.989)
Cameron Johnson	PF	1255	PHO	0.336	(2.995)
Alfonzo McKinnie	SF	593	CLE	0.324	(3.044)
Nickeil Alexander-Walker	SG	591	NOP	0.303	(3.406)
Blake Griffin	PF	512	DET	0.382	(3.555)
Georges Niang	PF	923	UTA	0.275	(3.729)
Nemanja Bjelica	PF	2011	SAC	0.376	(3.734)
Mason Plumlee	C	1057	DEN	0.330	(4.113)
Kevin Porter Jr.	SF	1162	CLE	0.385	(4.123)
Juan Hernangomez	PF	833	DEN/MIN	0.371	(4.174)
Luke Kornet	C	559	CHI	0.379	(4.464)
Frank Kaminsky	C	777	PHO	0.366	(4.547)
Kelly Olynyk	C	1300	MIA	0.320	(4.750)
Elie Okobo	PG	719	PHO	0.372	(4.815)
Nicolo Melli	C	1042	NOP	0.332	(5.478)
Moritz Wagner	C	835	WAS	0.344	(6.000)
Harry Giles	PF	667	SAC	0.375	(7.973)

PREVIEWING THE EASTERN CONFERENCE

SCHREMPF Rankings:

1. Brooklyn Nets
2. Philadelphia 76ers
3. Milwaukee Bucks
4. Toronto Raptors
5. Boston Celtics
6. Miami Heat
7. Indiana Pacers
8. Atlanta Hawks
9. Orlando Magic (10th)
10. Washington Wizards (9th)
11. Chicago Bulls
12. Cleveland Cavaliers
13. Detroit Pistons
14. Charlotte Hornets
15. New York Knicks

Rosters are accurate as of December 2, 2020. For my official 2020-21 NBA predictions, turn to page 500. The SCHREMPF rankings listed above did not account for the trade involving Russell Westbrook and John Wall because the trade happened just as the book was being finalized. The adjustments that reflect this trade are in parentheses.

BROKLYN NETS

Last Season: 35 – 37, Lost 1st Round to Toronto (0 – 4)

Offensive Rating: 108.9, 22nd in the NBA

Defensive Rating: 109.5, 9th in the NBA

Primary Executive: Sean Marks, General Manager

Head Coach: Steve Nash

Key Roster Changes

Subtractions
Dzanan Musa, trade
Garrett Temple, free agency
Wilson Chandler, free agency

Additions
Landry Shamet, trade
Bruce Brown, trade
Jeff Green, free agency

Roster

Likely Starting Five

1. *Kyrie Irving*
2. Joe Harris
3. *Caris LeVert*
4. *Kevin Durant*
5. *DeAndre Jordan*

Other Key Rotation Players
Jarrett Allen
Spencer Dinwiddie
Taurean Prince
Landry Shamet
Jeff Green
Bruce Brown

* Italics denotes that a player is likely to be on the floor to close games

Remaining Roster

- Timothe Luwawu-Cabarrot
- Rodions Kurucs
- Nicolas Claxton
- Tyler Johnson
- Jeremiah Martin, 24, 6'3", 185, Memphis (Two-Way)
- Reggie Perry, 20, 6'10", 250, Mississippi State (Exhibit 10)
- Jordan Bowden, 24, 6'5", 193, Tennessee (Exhibit 10)
- Elie Okobo, 23, 6'3", 190, France (Exhibit 10)
- Chris Chiozza, 25, 5'11", 175, Florida (Exhibit 10)
- Nate Sestina, 23, 6'9", 234, Kentucky (Exhibit 10)

SCHREMPF Base Rating: 42.8 (72-game season)

Strengths

- Elite front-end talent and offensive firepower
- Deep rotation that features at least 10 or 11 quality NBA players

Question Marks

- Potential combustibility or chemistry concerns
- No established defensive stopper on the roster
- No coach on the current staff has demonstrated a proven ability to make adjustments on the fly

Outlook

- Potentially the most talented team in the East, will likely finish somewhere in the top six seeds

Veterans

Kevin Durant

Height	Weight	Cap #	Years Left
6'10"	240	$40.109M	1 + PO

Similar at Age 31

		Season	SIMsc
1	Al Horford	2017-18	903.5
2	Carmelo Anthony	2015-16	894.4
3	LeBron James	2015-16	889.5
4	Chris Bosh	2015-16	886.2
5	Dirk Nowitzki	2009-10	883.5
6	LaMarcus Aldridge	2016-17	876.1
7	Paul Millsap	2016-17	873.5
8	Larry Bird*	1987-88	868.5
9	Chris Webber	2004-05	863.8
10	Tim Duncan*	2007-08	862.5

Baseline Basic Stats

MPG	PTS	AST	REB	BLK	STL
33.1	20.3	4.0	7.4	0.9	0.8

Advanced Metrics

USG%	3PTA/FGA	FTA/FGA	TS%	eFG%	3PT%
27.2	0.282	0.326	0.610	0.559	0.376

AST%	TOV%	OREB%	DREB%	STL%	BLK%
22.7	11.5	2.9	19.1	1.0	2.8

PER	ORTG	DRTG	WS/48	VOL
22.94	118.3	108.7	0.202	0.519

- Missed the entire 2019-20 season while recovering from a torn Achilles'
- MVP level player before the injury, one of the best overall players in the league when healthy
- Dynamic offensive talent that excelled in every offensive situation in 2018-19
- Excellent one-on-one player that can efficiently create shots in the post or on isolation plays
- Highly efficient shooter that moves well off the ball, posted a True Shooting Percentage above 60% in nine of the previous ten seasons
- Has become a very good playmaker, excels in pick-and-roll situations as both the screener and ball handler
- 2018-19 Defensive Degree of Difficulty: 0.484
- Typically guarded starting level players, tasked to defend elite players at times
- Effective on-ball defender that possesses the versatility to guard perimeter and post players
- Above average team defender, solid on pick-and-rolls, can sometimes be late when closing out on perimeter shooters
- Very good as an off-ball roamer, good defensive rebounder, excellent weak side shot blocker

Kyrie Irving	Height	Weight	Cap #	Years Left
	6'2"	195	$33.460M	1 + PO

	Similar at Age	27	
		Season	SIMsc
1	Eric Bledsoe	2016-17	900.6
2	Damian Lillard	2017-18	899.9
3	Mike James	2017-18	893.3
4	Reggie Jackson	2017-18	891.4
5	Sam Cassell	1996-97	889.2
6	Jeff Teague	2015-16	888.9
7	Lester Hudson	2011-12	885.6
8	Jordan Farmar	2013-14	882.9
9	John Wall	2017-18	880.1
10	C.J. Watson	2011-12	876.2

Baseline Basic Stats

MPG	PTS	AST	REB	BLK	STL
32.2	19.3	5.9	3.8	0.3	1.2

Advanced Metrics

USG%	3PTA/FGA	FTA/FGA	TS%	eFG%	3PT%
28.0	0.383	0.258	0.581	0.534	0.383
AST%	**TOV%**	**OREB%**	**DREB%**	**STL%**	**BLK%**
32.9	12.0	2.8	11.6	1.8	1.0
PER	**ORTG**	**DRTG**	**WS/48**	**VOL**	
22.25	116.2	109.8	0.195	0.694	

- Regular starter for Brooklyn when healthy, missed most of last season due to injuries to his right shoulder, right hamstring and right knee
- Highly effective as the team's primary ball handler when he was in the lineup, had the highest Usage Percentage of his career last season
- Excelled at creating shots in isolation situations and as a pick-and-roll ball handler
- Great playmaker that cut his turnover rate significantly
- Efficient outside shooter that has made over 39% of his threes in each of the last four seasons
- More effective at making shots off the dribble and in spot-up situations, struggled a bit when shooting off screens
- 2019-20 Defensive Degree of Difficulty: 0.440, tends to guard starting level players
- Effort has been inconsistent in previous seasons, played solid on-ball defense in a limited amount of games last season
- Good pick-and-roll defender that can funnel his man into help
- Will fight through screens off the ball, can be late when closing out in spot-up situations
- Gets steals at a fairly high rate, effective at playing passing lanes, has been a solid defensive rebounder over the last two seasons

Caris LeVert

Height	Weight	Cap #	Years Left
6'6"	205	$16.204M	2

	Similar at Age	**25**	
		Season	**SIMsc**
1	Dion Waiters	2016-17	939.8
2	George McCloud	1992-93	927.2
3	Tim Hardaway	2017-18	917.6
4	Derek Smith	1986-87	915.5
5	Jordan Clarkson	2017-18	915.4
6	Brandon Roy	2009-10	914.0
7	Kareem Rush	2005-06	913.3
8	Kobe Bryant*	2003-04	913.2
9	Chris Carr	1999-00	911.7
10	Anfernee Hardaway	1996-97	910.7

Baseline Basic Stats

MPG	PTS	AST	REB	BLK	STL
30.0	15.7	3.2	3.8	0.3	1.0

Advanced Metrics

USG%	3PTA/FGA	FTA/FGA	TS%	eFG%	3PT%
25.3	0.356	0.262	0.532	0.493	0.358
AST%	**TOV%**	**OREB%**	**DREB%**	**STL%**	**BLK%**
21.0	12.0	3.4	10.9	1.8	0.7
PER	**ORTG**	**DRTG**	**WS/48**	**VOL**	
16.02	106.4	110.2	0.077	0.446	

- Missed the start of the season while recovering from surgery to his right thumb
- Played as a starter for most of the season, utilized in a primary scoring role, named to the All-Seeding Games second team in August 2020
- Scored in volume as an isolation player and pick-and-roll ball handler
- Effective when scoring at the rim, drew fouls at a higher rate last season, made threes at a rate above the league average
- Better at taking quick pull-up jumpers off the dribble, was below average in spot-up situations
- Energetic athlete that excels in transition, highly effective on dribble hand-off plays
- Very good playmaker that limits turnovers
- 2019-20 Defensive Degree of Difficulty: 0.404
- Tends to guard lower leverage starters or higher end second unit players
- Solid perimeter defender that can capably defend multiple positions, struggles at times to defend stronger wings in the post
- Average pick-and-roll defender, can be too aggressive when fighting over screens, can allow his man to turn the corner
- Consistently closes out on perimeter shooters, will occasionally get caught on screens off the ball
- Continues to post fairly high Steal Percentages, solid defensive rebounder, Block Percentage is still somewhat consistent with his career average

Joe Harris	Height	Weight	Cap #	Years Left
	6'6"	220	$16.071M	3

	Similar at Age	28	
		Season	**SIMsc**
1	Quentin Richardson	2008-09	939.6
2	J.R. Smith	2013-14	937.2
3	Wesley Matthews	2014-15	928.3
4	Jason Richardson	2008-09	927.1
5	Bojan Bogdanovic	2017-18	927.0
6	Sam Mack	1998-99	918.7
7	Roger Mason	2008-09	916.8
8	Jared Dudley	2013-14	914.7
9	Dennis Scott	1996-97	910.7
10	Wesley Person	1999-00	908.8

Baseline Basic Stats

MPG	PTS	AST	REB	BLK	STL
26.7	10.6	1.7	3.3	0.2	0.8

Advanced Metrics

USG%	3PTA/FGA	FTA/FGA	TS%	eFG%	3PT%
17.2	0.571	0.156	0.581	0.561	0.407
AST%	**TOV%**	**OREB%**	**DREB%**	**STL%**	**BLK%**
10.3	10.7	2.6	11.5	1.2	0.7
PER	**ORTG**	**DRTG**	**WS/48**	**VOL**	
12.55	111.6	109.5	0.100	0.357	

- Second consecutive year as a full-time starter for Brooklyn
- Maintained his effectiveness as an off-ball shooter in a low volume role
- Made over 40% of his threes for the third straight season, excellent spot-up shooter that can also run off screens
- Very good at using the screen on dribble hand-off plays to free himself, good at cutting to take advantage of defenders that overplay his shot
- Not really able to create his own shot, rarely used on isolation plays or in pick-and-rolls
- Shows some playmaking skills, cut his turnover rate to a career low last season
- 2019-20 Defensive Degree of Difficulty: 0.372
- Generally hidden in lower leverage matchups
- Not tested very often, but played solid on-ball defense in a limited number of isolation possessions
- Average pick-and-roll defender, good on switches, tends to go under screens to allow open outside shots
- Solid team defender that will fight through screens off the ball and close out on perimeter shooters
- Plays a stay-at-home style, rarely gets steals or blocks, fairly solid defensive rebounder for his size

DeAndre Jordan	Height	Weight	Cap #	Years Left
	6'11"	265	$10.376M	2

	Similar at Age	31	
		Season	**SIMsc**
1	Erick Dampier	2006-07	927.8
2	Tyson Chandler	2013-14	879.2
3	Dwight Howard	2016-17	875.9
4	James Donaldson	1988-89	872.5
5	Will Perdue	1996-97	872.0
6	Marcin Gortat	2015-16	868.1
7	Aron Baynes	2017-18	866.1
8	Benoit Benjamin	1995-96	860.6
9	Brendan Haywood	2010-11	860.1
10	Ervin Johnson	1998-99	860.0

Baseline Basic Stats

MPG	PTS	AST	REB	BLK	STL
22.7	6.9	0.8	7.6	1.0	0.3

Advanced Metrics

USG%	3PTA/FGA	FTA/FGA	TS%	eFG%	3PT%
13.8	0.009	0.518	0.636	0.615	0.157
AST%	**TOV%**	**OREB%**	**DREB%**	**STL%**	**BLK%**
8.8	19.0	11.6	29.5	0.7	3.2
PER	**ORTG**	**DRTG**	**WS/48**	**VOL**	
16.65	119.9	104.9	0.156	0.453	

- Mostly came off the bench in his first season with Brooklyn, became a starter after the coaching change was made
- Very effective in his role as a low volume, rim runner
- Still a vertical threat to catch lobs, almost 60% of his made field goals were dunks
- Very good roll man and cutter, will run the floor in transition, great offensive rebounder that scores on a high volume of put-backs
- Historically has been a poor free throw shooter, improved over the last two seasons by making almost 70% of his free throws
- Improved his passing, posted another career high in Assist Percentage, still a bit turnover prone
- 2019-20 Defensive Degree of Difficulty: 0.337
- Tended to guard second unit level big men, played a role as a rim protector when he was on the floor
- Very good rim protector, still a good shot blocker, excellent defensive rebounder
- Very effective post defender last season, played with more discipline, displayed solid mobility to defend in space on isolation plays
- Played good pick-and-roll defense, excelled at defending screeners in drop coverages, could also switch onto ball handlers for a few dribbles
- Consistently closed out on perimeter shooters off the ball

Jarrett Allen	Height	Weight	Cap #	Years Left
	6'11"	237	$3.910M	RFA

	Similar at Age	21	
		Season	**SIMsc**
1	Andris Biedrins	2007-08	936.9
2	Deyonta Davis	2017-18	920.1
3	Bam Adebayo	2018-19	910.7
4	Steven Adams	2014-15	903.7
5	Jonas Valanciunas	2013-14	900.0
6	DeAndre Jordan	2009-10	899.1
7	Al Horford	2007-08	891.1
8	Ed Davis	2010-11	890.9
9	Thomas Bryant	2018-19	890.7
10	Nenad Krstic	2004-05	890.2

Baseline Basic Stats

MPG	PTS	AST	REB	BLK	STL
27.1	10.8	1.4	8.9	1.3	0.6

Advanced Metrics

USG%	3PTA/FGA	FTA/FGA	TS%	eFG%	3PT%
16.0	0.024	0.522	0.616	0.590	0.156
AST%	**TOV%**	**OREB%**	**DREB%**	**STL%**	**BLK%**
9.0	13.5	11.9	24.3	1.1	3.3
PER	**ORTG**	**DRTG**	**WS/48**	**VOL**	
18.36	123.1	105.7	0.172	0.289	

- Regular starter for Brooklyn for the second consecutive season
- Continued to improve, overall production increased for the third straight season
- Excelled in his role as a low volume rim runner, made almost 75% of his shots inside of three feet
- Plays with high energy, great athlete that is a vertical threat to catch lobs, excellent roll man and cutter
- Active offensive rebounder that scores on a high volume of put-backs, runs hard down the floor in transition
- Improving as a passer, has continued to cut his turnover rate, has no real shooting range outside of three feet
- 2019-20 Defensive Degree of Difficulty: 0.450
- Typically guards starting level big men, served as Brooklyn's main rim protector
- Great rebounder and shot blocker, average rim protector, can be overpowered inside due to a lack of strength
- Average on-ball defender, can be bullied inside a bit in the post, has trouble defending in space for prolonged stretches
- Middling pick-and-roll defender, better in drop coverages, has staying with ball handlers
- Plays with high effort, will fight through screens off the ball, consistently closes out in spot-up situations

Spencer Dinwiddie	Height	Weight	Cap #	Years Left
	6'5"	215	$11.454M	Player Option

	Similar at Age	26	
		Season	SIMsc
1	Isaiah Rider	1997-98	914.8
2	Mitch Richmond*	1991-92	912.0
3	Rodney Stuckey	2012-13	906.9
4	Reggie Jackson	2016-17	901.2
5	Deron Williams	2010-11	900.7
6	Tim Hardaway	2018-19	898.8
7	Chauncey Billups	2002-03	897.1
8	O.J. Mayo	2013-14	896.4
9	Arron Afflalo	2011-12	895.5
10	Randy Foye	2009-10	895.3

Baseline Basic Stats

MPG	PTS	AST	REB	BLK	STL
30.7	16.9	4.1	3.2	0.2	0.8

Advanced Metrics

USG%	3PTA/FGA	FTA/FGA	TS%	eFG%	3PT%
27.0	0.336	0.364	0.538	0.478	0.353
AST%	**TOV%**	**OREB%**	**DREB%**	**STL%**	**BLK%**
27.4	12.3	2.0	9.1	1.2	0.7
PER	**ORTG**	**DRTG**	**WS/48**	**VOL**	
16.63	109.0	111.4	0.109	0.266	

- Initially came off the bench as a sixth man, but was elevated to the starting lineup when Kyrie Irving was out due to injuries
- Had his most productive NBA season, often served as Brooklyn's primary ball handler
- Great at driving to the rim as a pick-and-roll ball handler and isolation player, excellent finisher at the rim, drew fouls at a high rate
- Also good at attacking aggressive close-outs to get to the basket
- Moves well off the ball, good cutter, can curl to the rim off screens
- Has been a below break-even three-point shooter over the last three seasons, much better in the corners
- Very good playmaker that maintains a good Assist-to-Turnover Ratio
- 2019-20 Defensive Degree of Difficulty: 0.468
- Matched up against starting level players, sometimes will be tasked to defend top-level guards
- Fairly solid on-ball defender, capable of defending both guard spots
- Above average pick-and-roll defender, good on switches, can allow his man to turn the corner by being too aggressive when going over the screen
- Average off-ball defender, occasionally gets caught on screens, can be late when closing out in spot-up situations
- Stay-at-home defender, Steal Percentage has been below his career average for the last two seasons, decent defensive rebounder

Taurean Prince	Height	Weight	Cap #	Years Left
	6'7"	218	$12.250M	1

	Similar at Age	25	
		Season	SIMsc
1	Mike Miller	2005-06	932.2
2	Tracy Murray	1996-97	931.2
3	Solomon Hill	2016-17	929.0
4	Jarvis Hayes	2006-07	928.6
5	Vladimir Radmanovic	2005-06	925.3
6	Allen Crabbe	2017-18	924.1
7	Kyle Korver	2006-07	922.1
8	Carlos Delfino	2007-08	921.9
9	Morris Peterson	2002-03	921.8
10	Bojan Bogdanovic	2014-15	921.5

Baseline Basic Stats

MPG	PTS	AST	REB	BLK	STL
25.0	10.5	1.6	3.6	0.3	0.7

Advanced Metrics

USG%	3PTA/FGA	FTA/FGA	TS%	eFG%	3PT%
19.8	0.533	0.180	0.537	0.505	0.370
AST%	**TOV%**	**OREB%**	**DREB%**	**STL%**	**BLK%**
10.4	12.6	2.7	14.9	1.5	1.0
PER	**ORTG**	**DRTG**	**WS/48**	**VOL**	
11.71	103.0	110.4	0.053	0.400	

- Regular starter in his first season with Brooklyn
- Predominantly played off the ball in a spot-up role, production decreased significantly, had his worst season as a pro
- Rated as average or worse in almost every offensive situation
- Three-Point Percentage fell to just above break-even, historically has been better in the corners, made almost 43% of his corner threes in the previous three seasons with Atlanta
- Struggled to finish shots at the rim last season, Field Goal Percentage inside of three feet dropped by almost 15% last season
- Mostly a catch-and-shoot player, shows some passing skills, good at limiting turnovers
- 2019-20 Defensive Degree of Difficulty: 0.469
- Usually guards starting level players, will handle tougher defensive assignments at times
- Decent on-ball defender, capable of defending both forward positions
- Average pick-and-roll defender, fairly good on switches, can be too aggressive when fighting over the screen
- Solid team defender that will fight through screens off the ball and close out on perimeter shooters
- Played more of a stay-at-home style, steal and block rates are down from his career averages
- Good defensive rebounder, set a career high in Defensive Rebound Percentage last season

Landry Shamet	Height	Weight	Cap #	Years Left
	6'4"	188	$2.090M	Team Option

	Similar at Age	22	
		Season	SIMsc
1	Daniel Gibson	2008-09	912.7
2	J.J. Redick	2006-07	905.2
3	Malik Beasley	2018-19	902.2
4	Doron Lamb	2013-14	901.5
5	Wayne Ellington	2009-10	890.8
6	J.R. Bremer	2002-03	885.7
7	Luke Kennard	2018-19	882.1
8	Terrence Ross	2013-14	881.7
9	Evan Fournier	2014-15	880.4
10	Donte DiVincenzo	2018-19	880.0

Baseline Basic Stats

MPG	PTS	AST	REB	BLK	STL
22.2	8.3	1.6	2.0	0.1	0.5

Advanced Metrics

USG%	3PTA/FGA	FTA/FGA	TS%	eFG%	3PT%
15.3	0.603	0.183	0.565	0.533	0.395
AST%	**TOV%**	**OREB%**	**DREB%**	**STL%**	**BLK%**
10.6	8.6	1.2	7.6	1.0	0.5
PER	**ORTG**	**DRTG**	**WS/48**	**VOL**	
10.51	113.8	112.2	0.088	0.379	

- Regular rotation player for the Clippers when healthy, missed a month due to a sprained left ankle
- Used as a low volume shooter off the ball, has made over 40% of his threes in two seasons in the NBA
- Excellent spot-up shooter that can also shoot off screens, effective screener on pick-and-pops
- Good pick-and-roll ball handler, less effective at making pull-up jumpers, better at using the threat of his shot to drive to the rim
- Mostly a catch-and-shoot player, shows some passing skills, rarely turns the ball over
- 2019-20 Defensive Degree of Difficulty: 0.429
- Tends to guard higher-end second unit players, sometimes draws tougher point guard assignments
- Solid on-ball defender that can defend both guard spots, better against bigger wing players in the post
- Decent pick-and-roll defender, good at containing ball handlers, had some trouble against bigger player on switches
- Tends to be too aggressive when closing out on perimeter shooters, can get caught on screens off the ball
- Stay-at-home defender, does not really get steals or blocks, below average defensive rebounding guard

Jeff Green	Height	Weight	Cap #	Years Left
	6'8"	235	$1.621M	UFA

	Similar at Age	33	
		Season	SIMsc
1	Sam Perkins	1994-95	933.5
2	Matt Barnes	2013-14	926.1
3	Richard Jefferson	2013-14	910.6
4	Caron Butler	2013-14	907.2
5	Rodney Rogers	2004-05	906.8
6	Anthony Tolliver	2018-19	905.6
7	Carmelo Anthony	2017-18	901.3
8	Mike Dunleavy, Jr.	2013-14	901.0
9	Luol Deng	2018-19	898.8
10	Bryon Russell	2003-04	898.4

Baseline Basic Stats

MPG	PTS	AST	REB	BLK	STL
22.5	8.4	1.3	3.5	0.4	0.6

Advanced Metrics

USG%	3PTA/FGA	FTA/FGA	TS%	eFG%	3PT%
16.9	0.534	0.250	0.569	0.531	0.347
AST%	**TOV%**	**OREB%**	**DREB%**	**STL%**	**BLK%**
7.9	10.1	3.0	13.1	1.3	1.6
PER	**ORTG**	**DRTG**	**WS/48**	**VOL**	
12.48	111.4	109.6	0.101	0.362	

- Regular rotation player for Utah last season, waived in December 2019, signed by Houston in February 2020
- Played a role in Houston's rotation as a lower volume, stretch big
- Made threes at around the league average, fairly good at knocking down spot-up jumpers
- Could occasionally attack the rim on aggressive close-outs, very good at running the floor in transition
- Effective rim runner, good at rolling to the rim and cutting off the ball
- Very good at limiting turnovers, showed solid passing skills in Houston
- 2019-20 Defensive Degree of Difficulty: 0.367
- Tended to guard higher-end second unit players or lower leverage starters
- Effective at protecting the rim, not really a shot blocker, good at staying vertical to contest shots, middling defensive rebounder
- Decent on-ball defender, good at using length to contest outside shots, has trouble in staying with quicker perimeter players, can be backed down inside by stronger post players
- Solid pick-and-roll defender, can switch onto ball handlers for a few dribbles, good at covering the roll man inside
- Consistently comes out to contest perimeter shots in spot-up situations

Bruce Brown

	Height	Weight	Cap #	Years Left
Bruce Brown	6'4"	202	$1.664M	RFA

Similar at Age 23

		Season	SIMsc
1	Thabo Sefolosha	2007-08	924.3
2	Tyrone Wallace	2017-18	920.8
3	Eric Washington	1997-98	920.1
4	Anthony Peeler	1992-93	917.6
5	MarShon Brooks	2011-12	914.4
6	Willie Green	2004-05	914.2
7	Sindarius Thornwell	2017-18	913.3
8	E'Twaun Moore	2012-13	912.6
9	Greg Buckner	1999-00	912.0
10	Austin Rivers	2015-16	911.1

Baseline Basic Stats

MPG	PTS	AST	REB	BLK	STL
22.8	8.0	2.1	2.9	0.3	0.8

Advanced Metrics

USG%	3PTA/FGA	FTA/FGA	TS%	eFG%	3PT%
16.1	0.314	0.224	0.517	0.481	0.339
AST%	**TOV%**	**OREB%**	**DREB%**	**STL%**	**BLK%**
15.0	13.1	3.5	12.3	1.8	1.3
PER	**ORTG**	**DRTG**	**WS/48**	**VOL**	
11.63	105.9	109.4	0.074	0.345	

- Regular starter for Detroit in his second season in the NBA
- Utilized on offense in a low volume role as a secondary ball handler
- More than doubled his Assist Percentage from his rookie season, was slightly more turnover prone
- Improved to become an above break-even three-point shooter, much better in the corners in his two-year career
- Rated as average or worse in most offensive situations, tends to settle for too many mid-range shots
- Improved his ability to finish at the rim, will occasionally crash the offensive boards to score on put-backs
- 2019-20 Defensive Degree of Difficulty: 0.513
- Usually takes on tougher defensive assignments
- Very good on-ball defender, has the versatility to defend guards and wing players
- Good at defending pick-and-rolls, can contain ball handlers and switch to handle the roll man
- Good at staying attached to shooters off the ball, consistently closes out in spot-up situations
- Active weak side defender, good rebounding guard, increased his steals rate, can use his length to occasionally block shots

Timothé Luwawu-Cabarrot	Height	Weight	Cap #	Years Left
	6'7"	210	$1.824M	UFA

	Similar at Age	24	
		Season	SIMsc
1	Martell Webster	2010-11	946.0
2	Dahntay Jones	2004-05	932.6
3	Danuel House	2017-18	928.7
4	James Ennis	2014-15	925.3
5	Kyle Korver	2005-06	924.8
6	Eric Piatkowski	1994-95	923.9
7	Cartier Martin	2008-09	923.3
8	Antoine Wright	2008-09	923.0
9	Hollis Thompson	2015-16	921.4
10	Bobby R. Jones	2007-08	918.4

Baseline Basic Stats

MPG	PTS	AST	REB	BLK	STL
21.8	8.1	1.2	2.9	0.3	0.6

Advanced Metrics

USG%	3PTA/FGA	FTA/FGA	TS%	eFG%	3PT%
16.8	0.550	0.230	0.566	0.528	0.380
AST%	**TOV%**	**OREB%**	**DREB%**	**STL%**	**BLK%**
7.5	10.3	2.9	12.4	1.3	0.8
PER	**ORTG**	**DRTG**	**WS/48**	**VOL**	
11.37	109.9	111.4	0.083	0.388	

- Started the season on a Two-Way contract, was later signed to a standard contract in February 2020
- Became a regular rotation player for Brooklyn last season
- Primarily used as a low volume spot-up shooter, made almost 39% of his threes last season
- Good spot-up shooter, especially from the corners, made almost 45% of his corner threes
- Moves well without the ball, can run off screens, very good cutter as well
- Runs the floor hard in transition to get layups or draw shooting fouls, will opportunistically crash the offensive boards to score on put-backs
- Mostly a catch-and-shoot player, not really a passer, rarely turns the ball over
- 2019-20 Defensive Degree of Difficulty: 0.355
- Typically guards second unit level players
- Below average on-ball defender, struggled to stay with opposing perimeter players in isolation situations
- Average pick-and-roll defender, can go too far under screens to allow open outside shots
- Can get caught on screens off the ball, will close out too aggressively to allow driving lanes to the rim
- Stay-at-home defender, does not get steals or blocks at a high rate, fairly solid defensive rebounder

Rodions Kurucs

	Height	Weight	Cap #	Years Left
Rodions Kurucs	6'9"	228	$1.780M	Team Option

Similar at Age 21

		Season	SIMsc
1	Vladimir Radmanovic	2001-02	938.8
2	Juan Hernangomez	2016-17	935.3
3	OG Anunoby	2018-19	927.5
4	JaKarr Sampson	2014-15	923.8
5	Shawne Williams	2007-08	921.5
6	Omri Casspi	2009-10	911.8
7	Sasha Pavlovic	2004-05	908.4
8	Mario Hezonja	2016-17	907.3
9	Trey Lyles	2016-17	905.4
10	Omari Spellman	2018-19	905.1

Baseline Basic Stats

MPG	PTS	AST	REB	BLK	STL
22.0	8.7	1.3	3.8	0.3	0.7

Advanced Metrics

USG%	3PTA/FGA	FTA/FGA	TS%	eFG%	3PT%
17.1	0.320	0.236	0.544	0.515	0.338
AST%	**TOV%**	**OREB%**	**DREB%**	**STL%**	**BLK%**
9.9	14.6	4.0	15.4	1.6	0.9
PER	**ORTG**	**DRTG**	**WS/48**	**VOL**	
11.38	104.2	109.2	0.072	0.355	

- Fringe rotation player for Brooklyn in his second season, played a few games for the Long Island Nets in the G-League
- Mainly used as a low volume, spot-up shooter with Brooklyn
- Shot above the league average on threes overall, much better in the corners throughout his career, made almost 40% of his corner threes over the last two seasons
- Can move without the ball, decent cutter, will sometimes crash inside to score on put-backs, runs hard down the floor in transition
- Good finisher at the rim, made over 64% of his shots inside of three feet last season, effective on dribble hand-offs
- Passing improved slightly, was a bit turnover prone last season
- 2019-20 Defensive Degree of Difficulty: 0.345
- Generally guarded second unit level players
- Middling as an on-ball defender, passably guards multiple positions, better against perimeter players
- Fairly good pick-and-roll defender, good on switches
- Solid team defender that will fight through screens off the ball, consistently closes out in spot-up situations
- Solid defensive rebounder, steals rate increased, Block Percentage went down significantly

Nicolas Claxton

	Height	Weight	Cap #	Years Left
Nicolas Claxton	6'11"	215	$1.518M	1

Similar at Age **20**

		Season	SIMsc
1	Jermaine O'Neal	1998-99	890.0
2	Chris Wilcox	2002-03	881.3
3	Brandan Wright	2007-08	880.8
4	Christian Wood	2015-16	879.0
5	Kevon Looney	2016-17	878.9
6	Skal Labissiere	2016-17	861.8
7	Ivan Rabb	2017-18	861.4
8	Andray Blatche	2006-07	860.2
9	T.J. Leaf	2017-18	859.0
10	Jonas Valanciunas	2012-13	858.3

Baseline Basic Stats

MPG	PTS	AST	REB	BLK	STL
18.3	6.4	0.7	4.6	0.9	0.4

Advanced Metrics

USG%	3PTA/FGA	FTA/FGA	TS%	eFG%	3PT%
16.6	0.098	0.372	0.555	0.537	0.190
AST%	**TOV%**	**OREB%**	**DREB%**	**STL%**	**BLK%**
9.6	13.0	10.4	15.3	0.7	3.3
PER	**ORTG**	**DRTG**	**WS/48**	**VOL**	
15.02	113.7	108.7	0.118	0.346	

- Played sparingly in his rookie season with Brooklyn, missed games due to injuries to his left hamstring and left shoulder
- Had surgery on his left shoulder in June 2020, is expected to be ready for the start of the 2020-21 season
- Primarily utilized as a low volume rim runner in his limited minutes in the NBA
- Made 80% of his shots inside of three feet, very efficient as a roll man and cutter, great offensive rebounder
- Great athlete when healthy, vertical threat to catch lobs, runs hard down the floor in transition
- Tries to take outside shots, shot is still inconsistent right now, shot below 20% on threes and below 55% on free throws
- Showed solid passing skills, good at limiting turnovers
- 2019-20 Defensive Degree of Difficulty: 0.300
- Mostly served as a roaming rim protector that guarded lower leverage second unit players
- Effective rim protector in limited minutes, blocked shots at a fairly high rate
- Sometimes would be out of position to go for blocks, below average defensive rebounder
- Below average pick-and-roll, had trouble staying with ball handlers on switches
- Rarely tested on the ball, effective in a small sample of post-up and isolation possessions
- Usually would close out to contest perimeter shots

Tyler Johnson

	Height	Weight	Cap #	Years Left
Tyler Johnson	6'3"	190	$1.621M	UFA

Similar at Age **27**

		Season	SIMsc
1	Brandon Knight	2018-19	953.0
2	Luther Head	2009-10	937.8
3	Jerryd Bayless	2015-16	935.4
4	E'Twaun Moore	2016-17	933.6
5	Ian Clark	2018-19	929.1
6	Toney Douglas	2013-14	928.4
7	Craig Hodges	1987-88	926.4
8	Malcolm Delaney	2016-17	924.9
9	Terry Dehere	1998-99	924.8
10	Leandro Barbosa	2009-10	918.5

Baseline Basic Stats

MPG	PTS	AST	REB	BLK	STL
23.1	9.0	2.3	2.2	0.1	0.7

Advanced Metrics

USG%	3PTA/FGA	FTA/FGA	TS%	eFG%	3PT%
18.3	0.491	0.193	0.522	0.488	0.356
AST%	**TOV%**	**OREB%**	**DREB%**	**STL%**	**BLK%**
15.7	11.4	2.1	9.2	1.4	0.8
PER	**ORTG**	**DRTG**	**WS/48**	**VOL**	
11.45	105.4	111.6	0.069	0.332	

- Fringe rotation player for Phoenix, was later waived, signed by Brooklyn to play as a regular rotation player in the Orlando bubble
- Used as a lower volume, spot-up shooter for both Phoenix and Brooklyn last season
- Struggled to efficiently make shots in Phoenix, shot much better for Brooklyn in the restart
- Made almost 39% of his threes in the eight seeding games in Orlando, showed some ability to make shots off screens
- Below average pick-and-roll ball handler, can make perimeter shots off the dribble, struggles to get to the rim and finish efficiently
- Fairly solid secondary playmaker that consistently limits his turnovers
- 2019-20 Defensive Degree of Difficulty: 0.355
- Typically is tasked to defend second unit level players
- Rarely tested in isolation situations, played solid on-ball defense against both guard positions in a small sample of possessions
- Below average at guarding pick-and-rolls, tends to go too far under screens, will allow open perimeter shots
- Good off-ball defender that stays attached to shooters, consistently closes out in spot-up situations
- Steal and Block Percentage declined significantly last season, still a decent defensive rebounder

PHILADELPHIA 76ERS

Last Season: 43 – 30, Lost 1st Round to Boston (0 – 4)

Offensive Rating: 111.3, 13th in the NBA

Defensive Rating: 109.0, 8th in the NBA

Primary Executive: Daryl Morey, President of Basketball Operations

Head Coach: Doc Rivers

Key Roster Changes

Subtractions
Al Horford, trade
Josh Richardson, trade
Zhaire Smith, trade
Alec Burks, free agency
Glenn Robinson III, free agency
Kyle O'Quinn, free agency
Norvel Pelle, free agency
Raul Neto, free agency

Additions
Tyrese Maxey, draft
Isaiah Joe, draft
Danny Green, trade
Terrance Ferguson, trade
Seth Curry, trade
Tony Bradley, trade
Dwight Howard, free agency

Roster

Likely Starting Five

1. *Ben Simmons*
2. Matisse Thybulle
3. *Danny Green*
4. *Tobias Harris*
5. *Joel Embiid*

Other Key Rotation Players
Seth Curry
Dwight Howard
Shake Milton
Furkan Korkmaz
Terrance Ferguson

* Italics denotes that a player is likely to be on the floor to close games

Remaining Roster

- Tyrese Maxey
- Mike Scott
- Tony Bradley
- Ryan Broekhoff
- Derrick Walton, Jr.
- Isaiah Joe
- Dakota Mathias, 25, 6'4", 197, Purdue (Two-Way)
- Paul Reed, 21, 6'9", 220, DePaul (Two-Way)
- Justin Anderson, 27, 6'6", 230, Virginia (Exhibit 10)
- Lamine Diane, 23, 6'7", 205, Cal State Northridge (Exhibit 10)
- Justin Robinson, 23, 6'1", 195, Virginia Tech (Exhibit 10)

SCHREMPF Base Rating: 41.0 (72-game season)

Strengths

- Length, athleticism and defensive versatility
- Improved spacing around Simmons and Embiid

Question Marks

- No perimeter player on the roster has a proven ability to create his own offense against elite defenders
- Depth beyond their top seven players and the durability of their two stars

Outlook

- Contender in the Eastern Conference, could finish anywhere within the top six seeds

Veterans

Ben Simmons

	Height	Weight	Cap #	Years Left
Ben Simmons	6'10"	230	$30.559M	4

	Similar at Age	23 Season	SIMsc
1	Danny Manning	1989-90	914.7
2	Magic Johnson*	1982-83	895.5
3	Blake Griffin	2012-13	888.4
4	Josh Smith	2008-09	887.0
5	Derrick Coleman	1990-91	881.9
6	Charles D. Smith	1988-89	879.2
7	Greg Anderson	1987-88	876.8
8	Drew Gooden	2004-05	875.0
9	Tom Gugliotta	1992-93	874.9
10	Rasheed Wallace	1997-98	873.3

Baseline Basic Stats

MPG	PTS	AST	REB	BLK	STL
34.3	17.2	4.4	7.9	1.0	1.4

Advanced Metrics

USG%	3PTA/FGA	FTA/FGA	TS%	eFG%	3PT%
22.4	0.026	0.430	0.591	0.555	0.232
AST%	**TOV%**	**OREB%**	**DREB%**	**STL%**	**BLK%**
27.3	17.4	6.7	19.0	2.3	1.8
PER	**ORTG**	**DRTG**	**WS/48**	**VOL**	
20.81	115.0	105.0	0.173	0.113	

- Made the All-NBA 3rd Team last season, named to the All-Defensive 1st Team in 2019-20
- Missed games due to a lower back injury and dislocated kneecap
- Excelled as Philadelphia's primary ball handler, one of the NBA's best playmakers, somewhat turnover prone
- Good at attacking the rim on isolations and on pick-and-rolls to score inside or draw fouls
- Effective cutter off the ball, solid at crashing the offensive boards to score on put-backs
- Good at pushing the ball in transition to set up teammates or score at the rim, can sometimes be out of control
- Can post up smaller players, rarely takes shots outside of ten feet
- 2019-20 Defensive Degree of Difficulty: 0.562
- Had the 6th toughest set of matchups among players that played 500 or more minutes
- Solid on-ball defender that can guard multiple positions, had some trouble against quicker guards
- Good pick-and-roll defender that can effectively switch, pretty disciplined when making his rotations
- Can be out of position off the ball, tends to ball-watch or gamble for steals
- Very active help defender, led the NBA in Steals per Game, good defensive rebounder
- Good rim protector despite declining block rates, stays vertical to contest shots

Joel Embiid	Height	Weight	Cap #	Years Left
	7'0"	250	$29.542M	2

Similar at Age 25

		Season	SIMsc
1	DeMarcus Cousins	2015-16	887.8
2	Tim Duncan*	2001-02	886.9
3	Amar'e Stoudemire	2007-08	866.0
4	Mehmet Okur	2004-05	865.7
5	Benoit Benjamin	1989-90	863.0
6	Hakeem Olajuwon*	1987-88	856.1
7	Zach Randolph	2006-07	854.7
8	Brad Daugherty	1990-91	848.2
9	Alex Len	2018-19	847.0
10	Andrew Bogut	2009-10	846.9

Baseline Basic Stats

MPG	PTS	AST	REB	BLK	STL
33.6	21.0	2.9	10.3	1.8	0.9

Advanced Metrics

USG%	3PTA/FGA	FTA/FGA	TS%	eFG%	3PT%
30.4	0.198	0.465	0.577	0.515	0.354
AST%	**TOV%**	**OREB%**	**DREB%**	**STL%**	**BLK%**
16.9	13.6	8.7	29.2	1.3	3.8
PER	**ORTG**	**DRTG**	**WS/48**	**VOL**	
23.90	111.2	103.0	0.178	0.251	

- Made his third All-Star team in 2019-20, missed games due to a series of minor injuries
- Maintained his level of play in his role as Philadelphia's primary interior scorer
- Arguably the NBA's best post player, led the NBA in total points in Post-Up possessions
- Great rim running potential, can be effective at rolling to the rim and cutting off the ball, effort level can be inconsistent
- Very good offensive rebounder that scores on put-backs, draws fouls at a high rate
- Below break-even three-point shooter for his career, better in the corners
- Most effective as a stationary spot-up shooter, has trouble shooting on the move
- Very good passing big man that consistently avoids turnovers
- <u>2019-20 Defensive Degree of Difficulty</u>: 0.420
- Guards starting level big men, takes on tougher assignments against elite centers
- Great defensive rebounder and shot blocker, Block Percentage has steadily declined, not quite the rim protector that he was in previous seasons
- Solid on-ball defender, good at using his length to contest shots in the post, mobile enough to defend in space
- Good pick-and-roll defender, good in drop coverages, can switch onto ball handlers
- Usually comes out to contest perimeter shots in spot-up situations

Tobias Harris	Height	Weight	Cap #	Years Left
	6'8"	235	$34.359M	3

Similar at Age **27**

		Season	SIMsc
1	Jeff Green	2013-14	944.7
2	Marcus Morris	2016-17	936.3
3	Jamal Mashburn	1999-00	931.3
4	LaPhonso Ellis	1997-98	927.2
5	Danny Granger	2010-11	918.4
6	Wilson Chandler	2014-15	913.0
7	Terry Mills	1994-95	912.5
8	Dennis Scott	1995-96	911.8
9	Chuck Person	1991-92	909.5
10	Wally Szczerbiak	2004-05	908.9

Baseline Basic Stats

MPG	PTS	AST	REB	BLK	STL
32.7	16.2	2.5	5.6	0.4	0.8

Advanced Metrics

USG%	3PTA/FGA	FTA/FGA	TS%	eFG%	3PT%
23.2	0.342	0.214	0.547	0.512	0.373
AST%	**TOV%**	**OREB%**	**DREB%**	**STL%**	**BLK%**
13.8	9.3	3.6	17.7	1.1	1.0
PER	**ORTG**	**DRTG**	**WS/48**	**VOL**	
16.24	109.9	109.3	0.105	0.358	

- Regular starter in his first full season with Philadelphia
- Maintained his production in his role as a moderate volume scoring wing
- Solid three-point shooter throughout his career, good spot-up shooter that can shoot off screens
- Effective screener on pick-and-pops, solid at setting up for trail threes in transition
- Good at using an on-ball screen to get to the rim or make outside shots on dribble hand-offs
- Can post up smaller perimeter players, good at making floaters in the lane on pick-and-rolls
- Struggles to make shots off the dribble, moves well without the ball, good at making backdoor cuts
- Become a solid secondary playmaker that can make interior passes, rarely turns the ball over
- 2019-20 Defensive Degree of Difficulty: 0.430
- Tends to guard starter level players, sometimes takes on tougher defensive assignments
- Fairly solid on-ball defender that can guard multiple positions, better at guarding bigger players in the post
- Solid pick-and-roll defender, good at switching, sometimes allows ball handlers to turn the corner
- Can get caught on screens off the ball, tends to be too aggressive when closing out in spot-up situations
- Good defensive rebounder, stay-at-home defender, does not really get steals or blocks

Danny Green	Height	Weight	Cap #	Years Left
	6'6"	215	$15.366M	UFA

Similar at Age 32

		Season	SIMsc
1	Dan Majerle	1997-98	956.9
2	J.R. Smith	2017-18	937.9
3	Alan Anderson	2014-15	924.4
4	Garrett Temple	2018-19	909.3
5	Trevor Ariza	2017-18	903.5
6	Jud Buechler	2000-01	902.9
7	Kyle Korver	2013-14	902.8
8	Nick Anderson	1999-00	902.0
9	P.J. Tucker	2017-18	901.8
10	Anthony Parker	2007-08	901.6

Baseline Basic Stats

MPG	PTS	AST	REB	BLK	STL
26.2	8.2	1.8	3.7	0.4	0.9

Advanced Metrics

USG%	3PTA/FGA	FTA/FGA	TS%	eFG%	3PT%
14.0	0.684	0.130	0.562	0.544	0.379
AST%	**TOV%**	**OREB%**	**DREB%**	**STL%**	**BLK%**
9.8	11.9	2.7	13.1	1.8	1.5
PER	**ORTG**	**DRTG**	**WS/48**	**VOL**	
11.12	109.1	108.1	0.092	0.248	

- Full-time starter for the Lakers in his first season with the team
- Has been a low volume, spot-up shooter throughout his career, has made 40% of his career threes
- Mainly used as a stationary spot-up shooter last season, not as effective at shooting off screens as he was in previous seasons
- Rated as average or worse in almost every other offensive situation last season
- Strictly a catch-and-shoot player, sticks to making safe passes on the perimeter, does not really turn the ball over
- 2019-20 Defensive Degree of Difficulty: 0.543
- Had the 12th toughest set of matchups among players that played 500 or more minutes
- Solid on-ball defender in previous seasons, over-matched against top perimeter players
- Fairly solid pick-and-roll defender, good at switching onto screeners and guarding side pick-and-rolls, had trouble making rotations in the middle of the floor
- Stays attached to shooters off the ball, consistently closes out in spot-up situations
- Solid defensive rebounder, steals rates are still fairly high, Block Percentage has been declining for the last couple of seasons

Matisse Thybulle

	Height	Weight	Cap #	Years Left
	6'5"	200	$2.711M	2 Team Options

Similar at Age **22**

		Season	SIMsc
1	Chris Robinson	1996-97	888.8
2	Bruce Brown	2018-19	883.7
3	Josh Richardson	2015-16	881.1
4	Kyle Weaver	2008-09	876.2
5	Ben McLemore	2015-16	869.7
6	Allen Crabbe	2014-15	864.3
7	Josh Hart	2017-18	861.9
8	Iman Shumpert	2012-13	859.8
9	Mikal Bridges	2018-19	858.8
10	Malcolm Lee	2012-13	857.3

Baseline Basic Stats

MPG	PTS	AST	REB	BLK	STL
24.8	8.8	2.0	3.5	0.4	1.0

Advanced Metrics

USG%	3PTA/FGA	FTA/FGA	TS%	eFG%	3PT%
15.4	0.469	0.178	0.548	0.524	0.364
AST%	**TOV%**	**OREB%**	**DREB%**	**STL%**	**BLK%**
11.1	13.5	3.5	9.4	2.8	2.1
PER	**ORTG**	**DRTG**	**WS/48**	**VOL**	
12.17	107.3	107.0	0.090	0.417	

- Regular rotation player for Philadelphia in his rookie season, started several games in 2019-20
- Used as a low volume, spot-up shooter, made threes at around the league average
- Almost strictly a stationary spot-up shooter, limited ability to shoot on the move or off the dribble
- Can attack aggressive close-outs if his shot is falling, excellent cutter off the ball
- Good at running down the wings to get dunks in transition
- Does not really create his own shot, willing to make the extra pass, slightly turnover prone
- 2019-20 Defensive Degree of Difficulty: 0.482
- Mostly a second unit player, takes on tough defensive assignments when he is on the floor
- Good on-ball defender that can guard multiple positions
- Fairly good pick-and-roll defender, good against the high pick-and-roll, has some trouble defending side pick-and-rolls
- Stays attached to shooters off the ball, good at closing out on spot-up shooters
- Active help defender that excels at roaming off the ball, gets steals and blocks at a high rate, below average defensive rebounder at this stage

Seth Curry

	Height	Weight	Cap #	Years Left
Seth Curry	6'2"	185	$7.834M	2

Similar at Age 29

		Season	SIMsc
1	Craig Hodges	1989-90	934.6
2	E'Twaun Moore	2018-19	927.1
3	Tony Delk	2002-03	926.9
4	Patty Mills	2017-18	926.4
5	Steve Kerr	1994-95	917.7
6	Charlie Bell	2008-09	916.2
7	Brian Roberts	2014-15	914.9
8	Eldridge Recasner	1996-97	913.1
9	Eddie House	2007-08	912.8
10	Jerryd Bayless	2017-18	912.7

Baseline Basic Stats

MPG	PTS	AST	REB	BLK	STL
22.4	9.2	2.2	1.9	0.1	0.7

Advanced Metrics

USG%	3PTA/FGA	FTA/FGA	TS%	eFG%	3PT%
18.2	0.503	0.168	0.588	0.559	0.415
AST%	**TOV%**	**OREB%**	**DREB%**	**STL%**	**BLK%**
12.7	10.4	1.7	7.9	1.4	0.5
PER	**ORTG**	**DRTG**	**WS/48**	**VOL**	
13.55	114.8	112.4	0.108	0.260	

- Regular rotation player for Dallas last season, started some games in the regular season
- Primarily a low volume shooter off the ball, currently leads all active players in Three-Point Percentage
- Excellent spot-up shooter, good at coming off screens, will set up for trail threes in transition
- Effective as a pick-and-roll ball handler and isolation player, can shoot off the dribble, good finisher at the rim
- Has made over 48% of his corner threes in his career
- Mainly a catch-and-shoot player, has some secondary playmaking skills, rarely turns the ball over
- 2019-20 Defensive Degree of Difficulty: 0.358
- Tends to guard second unit level players, hidden sometimes in favorable matchups against lower leverage players
- Below average on-ball defender last season, decent lateral quickness to defend drives, lack of length allows taller players to shoot over him
- Solid pick-and-roll defender, can funnel his man into help, can capably switch to guard screeners
- Stays attached to shooters off the ball, can sometimes be late when closing out
- More of a stay-at-home defender, steals rate is down from his career average, below average defensive rebounder

Dwight Howard	Height	Weight	Cap #	Years Left
	6'10"	265	$1.621M	UFA

	Similar at Age	34	
		Season	SIMsc
1	Erick Dampier	2009-10	900.4
2	Nene	2016-17	866.9
3	Chris Andersen	2012-13	860.1
4	Mark West	1994-95	851.2
5	Artis Gilmore*	1983-84	845.3
6	Elton Brand	2013-14	842.1
7	Alan Henderson	2006-07	838.4
8	Rick Mahorn	1992-93	831.9
9	Joel Anthony	2016-17	830.7
10	Reggie Evans	2014-15	825.3

Baseline Basic Stats

MPG	PTS	AST	REB	BLK	STL
21.6	7.3	0.7	6.7	1.2	0.4

Advanced Metrics

USG%	3PTA/FGA	FTA/FGA	TS%	eFG%	3PT%
15.5	0.011	0.627	0.634	0.632	0.320
AST%	**TOV%**	**OREB%**	**DREB%**	**STL%**	**BLK%**
4.8	17.4	13.2	27.0	1.0	4.9
PER	**ORTG**	**DRTG**	**WS/48**	**VOL**	
17.01	117.2	104.8	0.154	0.562	

- Began 2019-20 on a non-guaranteed contract, became a regular rotation player for the Lakers
- Had his most efficient shooting season in his role as a low volume, rim runner
- Made over 81% of his shots inside of three feet last season, excelled as a roll man and cutter
- Very good offensive rebounder that can efficiently score on put-backs, drew fouls at a very high rate
- Good at running hard down the floor in transition to get dunks, could bully smaller defenders in the post
- No consistent shooting range outside of three feet, not really a passer, somewhat turnover prone
- 2019-20 Defensive Degree of Difficulty: 0.356, tends to guard second unit big men
- Good rim protector, excellent defensive rebounder, good shot blocker, fairly foul prone
- Solid post defender that holds position inside, mobile enough to defend big men in space on isolations
- Decent pick-and-roll defender, good in drop coverages, can switch onto ball handlers for a few dribbles, tends to be late to recognize pick-and-pops
- Willing to come out to the perimeter to contest shots, tends to be too aggressive on his close-outs

Shake Milton

	Height	Weight	Cap #	Years Left
	6'5"	207	$1.702M	1 + TO

	Similar at Age	**23**	
		Season	**SIMsc**
1	Timothe Luwawu-Cabarrot	2018-19	937.1
2	Orlando Johnson	2012-13	933.7
3	Damyean Dotson	2017-18	927.9
4	Tyrone Wallace	2017-18	924.4
5	Reggie Williams	2009-10	924.2
6	Tim Hardaway, Jr.	2015-16	924.0
7	Arron Afflalo	2008-09	921.0
8	Anthony Morrow	2008-09	919.9
9	Sterling Brown	2018-19	917.2
10	Roger Mason	2003-04	915.9

Baseline Basic Stats

MPG	PTS	AST	REB	BLK	STL
22.2	8.6	1.5	2.9	0.2	0.6

Advanced Metrics

USG%	3PTA/FGA	FTA/FGA	TS%	eFG%	3PT%
17.8	0.502	0.184	0.561	0.535	0.383
AST%	**TOV%**	**OREB%**	**DREB%**	**STL%**	**BLK%**
12.9	10.4	2.7	10.9	1.4	1.0
PER	**ORTG**	**DRTG**	**WS/48**	**VOL**	
12.64	111.7	110.9	0.094	0.368	

- Fringe rotation player for most of 2019-20, became a starter for Philadelphia towards the end of last season
- Improved his effectiveness in his role as a low volume shooter and secondary ball handler
- Made 43% of his threes last season, excellent spot-up shooter, can make pull-up jumpers on pick-and-rolls
- Good at using an on-ball screen to make outside shots on dribble hand-offs
- Good at cutting off the ball to score at the rim or draw fouls
- Solid secondary playmaker that can hit the roll man inside, good at limiting turnovers
- 2019-20 Defensive Degree of Difficulty: 0.392
- Tended to guard higher-end second unit players or lower leverage starters
- Below average on-ball defender, struggled to stay with opposing guards
- Struggled overall as a team defender, below average at guarding pick-and-rolls
- Tended to get caught on screens off the ball, consistently closed out on perimeter shoots but was too aggressive at times
- Decent defensive rebounding guard, Steal and Block Percentages decreased last season

Furkan Korkmaz

Height	Weight	Cap #	Years Left
6'7"	190	$1.763M	UFA

Similar at Age 22

		Season	SIMsc
1	Tony Snell	2013-14	939.2
2	Terrence Ross	2013-14	934.3
3	Sasha Vujacic	2006-07	931.3
4	Caris LeVert	2016-17	930.3
5	Kyle Korver	2003-04	922.1
6	Evan Fournier	2014-15	921.9
7	Luke Kennard	2018-19	915.6
8	Kevin Martin	2005-06	914.7
9	Malik Beasley	2018-19	913.3
10	Ben McLemore	2015-16	913.0

Baseline Basic Stats

MPG	PTS	AST	REB	BLK	STL
23.0	9.4	1.6	2.7	0.2	0.7

Advanced Metrics

USG%	3PTA/FGA	FTA/FGA	TS%	eFG%	3PT%
18.4	0.547	0.201	0.554	0.523	0.376
AST%	**TOV%**	**OREB%**	**DREB%**	**STL%**	**BLK%**
10.1	9.2	1.8	11.5	1.6	0.8
PER	**ORTG**	**DRTG**	**WS/48**	**VOL**	
12.32	109.2	110.7	0.093	0.318	

- Regular rotation player for Philadelphia in his third NBA season
- Utilized as a low volume shooter off the ball, made over 40% of his threes last season
- Excellent spot-up shooter that also shoot off screens, effective screener on pick-and-pop plays
- Good at making backdoor cuts if defenders overplay his shot, good at running down the wings to get layups in transition
- Lacks the ball handling ability to consistently create his own shot, rarely gets to the rim
- Catch-and-shoot player right now, flashes some passing skills, rarely turns the ball over
- 2019-20 Defensive Degree of Difficulty: 0.353, tends to guard second unit level players
- Average on-ball defender, struggles to stay with quicker guards, can be backed down in the post by stronger players
- Solid pick-and-roll defender that can fight over screens or funnel ball handlers into help
- Consistently closes out on perimeter shooters, tends to get caught on screens off the ball
- Solid defensive rebounder, gets steals at a moderate rate

Terrance Ferguson	Height	Weight	Cap #	Years Left
	6'6"	190	$3.944M	RFA

	Similar at Age	21	
		Season	**SIMsc**
1	Landry Shamet	2018-19	910.1
2	Patrick McCaw	2016-17	907.6
3	Rashad Vaughn	2017-18	894.9
4	Evan Fournier	2013-14	894.2
5	Sasha Vujacic	2005-06	892.5
6	Dante Exum	2016-17	891.2
7	Nik Stauskas	2014-15	891.2
8	Terrence Ross	2012-13	886.1
9	Jerome Robinson	2018-19	877.3
10	Kelly Oubre, Jr.	2016-17	874.7

Baseline Basic Stats

MPG	PTS	AST	REB	BLK	STL
22.4	7.8	1.3	2.4	0.2	0.6

Advanced Metrics

USG%	3PTA/FGA	FTA/FGA	TS%	eFG%	3PT%
12.5	0.477	0.142	0.523	0.500	0.332
AST%	**TOV%**	**OREB%**	**DREB%**	**STL%**	**BLK%**
7.1	11.1	1.8	7.4	1.2	0.8
PER	**ORTG**	**DRTG**	**WS/48**	**VOL**	
7.19	104.0	112.5	0.050	0.449	

- Regular rotation player for most of last season, started some games, playing time greatly reduced after the emergence of Luguentz Dort
- Used throughout his career as a very low volume, spot-up shooter, struggled to shoot efficiently in 2019-20
- Break-even three-point shooter for his career, made almost 39% of his corner threes in his career, shooting percentages dropped across the board last season
- Rated as average or worse in most offensive situations, only effective at moving off the ball
- Able to make some shots off screens, good cutter that can be a vertical lob threat due to his great athleticism
- Strictly a catch-and-shoot player, limited as a playmaker, good at avoiding turnovers
- 2019-20 Defensive Degree of Difficulty: 0.553
- Had the 9th toughest set of matchups among players that played 500 minutes or more
- Solid on-ball defender that guards multiple positions, tends to be over-aggressive when crowding his man, can allow driving lanes to the rim
- Fairly solid pick-and-roll defender, good at containing ball handlers, can be targeted in the post by bigger screeners on switches
- Stays attached to shooters off the ball, closes out in spot-up situations
- Stay-at-home defender, rarely gets steals, blocks or defensive rebounds

Mike Scott	Height	Weight	Cap #	Years Left
	6'7"	237	$5.005M	UFA

	Similar at Age	31	
		Season	SIMsc
1	Wally Szczerbiak	2008-09	935.3
2	Anthony Tolliver	2016-17	928.7
3	Mirza Teletovic	2016-17	924.1
4	Dennis Scott	1999-00	922.8
5	Wilson Chandler	2018-19	920.6
6	Richard Jefferson	2011-12	919.6
7	Jared Dudley	2016-17	916.1
8	Ed Nealy	1991-92	910.9
9	Jonas Jerebko	2018-19	907.2
10	Andres Nocioni	2010-11	907.2

Baseline Basic Stats

MPG	PTS	AST	REB	BLK	STL
17.1	5.6	0.9	2.9	0.2	0.4

Advanced Metrics

USG%	3PTA/FGA	FTA/FGA	TS%	eFG%	3PT%
14.2	0.611	0.148	0.557	0.534	0.380
AST%	**TOV%**	**OREB%**	**DREB%**	**STL%**	**BLK%**
7.4	9.1	3.9	16.3	1.0	0.9
PER	**ORTG**	**DRTG**	**WS/48**	**VOL**	
10.77	112.7	110.2	0.085	0.416	

- Regular rotation player for Philadelphia in his first full season with the team
- Mainly a low volume, shooting specialist, solid three-point shooter throughout his career
- Primarily a spot-up shooter, can shoot off screens and set up for trail threes in transition
- Effective as the screener on a small sample of pick-and-pops
- Below average in every other offensive situation last season
- Catch-and-shoot player, showed some passing skills in previous seasons, rarely turns the ball over
- 2019-20 Defensive Degree of Difficulty: 0.352, tends to guard second unit level players
- Played good on-ball defense, could capably defend both forward positions
- Decent pick-and-roll defender, good at covering the roll man, has some trouble containing ball handlers
- Sometimes gets caught on screens off the ball, good at closing out on perimeter shooters
- Stay-at-home defender, good defensive rebounder, does not really get blocks or steals at this stage of his career

Tony Bradley	Height	Weight	Cap #	Years Left
	6'10"	248	$3.542M	RFA

	Similar at Age	22	
		Season	SIMsc
1	Mitch McGary	2014-15	930.8
2	Rick Mahorn	1980-81	920.6
3	Kyle O'Quinn	2012-13	912.7
4	Nick Fazekas	2007-08	912.6
5	Jordan Hill	2009-10	907.9
6	Clint Capela	2016-17	902.0
7	Scott Williams	1990-91	901.1
8	Richaun Holmes	2015-16	896.0
9	Charles Shackleford	1988-89	895.1
10	Jeremy Tyler	2013-14	894.3

Baseline Basic Stats

MPG	PTS	AST	REB	BLK	STL
21.1	8.7	1.0	6.7	1.0	0.6

Advanced Metrics

USG%	3PTA/FGA	FTA/FGA	TS%	eFG%	3PT%
18.3	0.012	0.266	0.587	0.565	0.387
AST%	**TOV%**	**OREB%**	**DREB%**	**STL%**	**BLK%**
6.7	13.3	15.5	24.2	1.4	3.5
PER	**ORTG**	**DRTG**	**WS/48**	**VOL**	
19.01	116.8	104.9	0.165	0.468	

- Became a regular rotation player for Utah in his third NBA season
- Utilized as a low volume rim runner, made over 74% of his shots inside of three feet last season
- Plays with a high motor, dives hard to the rim as a roll man and cutter off the ball
- Excellent offensive rebounder that efficiently scores on put-backs,
- Good at running the floor in transition to get dunks or draw shooting fouls
- Limited skill at this stage, not really a post player, does not have consistent shooting range outside of three feet
- Not really much of a passer, cut his Turnover Percentage last season
- 2019-20 Defensive Degree of Difficulty: 0.293
- Tended to guard lower leverage second unit players, used as a roaming rim protector
- Good rim protector, very good shot blocker and defensive rebounder, highly foul prone
- Below average on-ball defender, can be bullied inside by stronger big men, has trouble guarding quicker players in isolation situations
- Average at guarding pick-and-rolls, can switch onto ball handlers for a few dribbles, tends to be late to cover the screener
- Consistently comes out to contest perimeter shots in spot-up situations

Ryan Broekhoff

Height	Weight	Cap #	Years Left
6'6"	215	$1.446M	RFA

Similar at Age 29

		Season	SIMsc
1	Mickael Pietrus	2011-12	921.1
2	DeShawn Stevenson	2010-11	909.9
3	C.J. Miles	2016-17	902.2
4	Quentin Richardson	2009-10	899.3
5	James Jones	2009-10	895.2
6	Dorell Wright	2014-15	894.6
7	Cartier Martin	2013-14	893.8
8	Mickael Gelabale	2012-13	893.6
9	James Posey	2005-06	888.8
10	Matt Bullard	1996-97	887.5

Baseline Basic Stats

MPG	PTS	AST	REB	BLK	STL
20.1	6.4	1.0	2.7	0.2	0.6

Advanced Metrics

USG%	3PTA/FGA	FTA/FGA	TS%	eFG%	3PT%
14.7	0.713	0.152	0.557	0.531	0.373
AST%	**TOV%**	**OREB%**	**DREB%**	**STL%**	**BLK%**
7.9	9.7	2.4	15.6	1.3	1.3
PER	**ORTG**	**DRTG**	**WS/48**	**VOL**	
10.88	109.9	110.1	0.083	0.646	

- Played sparingly for Dallas last season, waived in February 2020
- Signed by Philadelphia in July 2020, did not play in the Orlando bubble due to concerns over COVID-19
- Low volume shooting specialist in his limited two-year career, has made over 40% of his threes
- Very good spot-up shooter that can run off screens
- Offensive role has been very limited, has not been able to contribute in other offensive situations at a high enough volume
- Flashed the ability to be effective as a cutter in 2018-19, made all three of his shots as a pick-and-roll ball handler last season
- Improving as a passer, rarely turns the ball over
- 2019-20 Defensive Degree of Difficulty: 0.293, only played 180 minutes last season
- Tends to either guard second unit players or play in garbage time
- Played average on-ball defense in a small sample of possessions, had trouble against quicker players, better in the post against bigger wing players
- Middling pick-and-roll defender, can funnel ball handlers into help, struggled to cover the screener
- Tended to be late when closing out on perimeter shooters
- Very good defensive rebounder, typically does not get steals or blocks at a high rate

Derrick Walton, Jr.	Height	Weight	Cap #	Years Left
	6'0"	189	$1.621M	RFA

	Similar at Age	24	
		Season	SIMsc
1	Patty Mills	2012-13	896.2
2	Isaiah Canaan	2015-16	889.3
3	Shawn Respert	1996-97	885.1
4	Travis Diener	2006-07	882.7
5	Mario Chalmers	2010-11	877.8
6	Fred VanVleet	2018-19	877.6
7	Ryan Arcidiacono	2018-19	876.9
8	Dee Brown	2008-09	874.1
9	Chris Quinn	2007-08	871.8
10	Yogi Ferrell	2017-18	869.4

Baseline Basic Stats

MPG	PTS	AST	REB	BLK	STL
21.6	8.6	2.6	2.0	0.1	0.8

Advanced Metrics

USG%	3PTA/FGA	FTA/FGA	TS%	eFG%	3PT%
14.4	0.572	0.227	0.568	0.525	0.403
AST%	**TOV%**	**OREB%**	**DREB%**	**STL%**	**BLK%**
18.5	9.2	1.3	8.9	1.8	0.5
PER	**ORTG**	**DRTG**	**WS/48**	**VOL**	
12.62	120.8	109.7	0.127	0.522	

- Played sparingly for the L.A. Clippers, traded to Atlanta in February, then waived
- Used as a very low volume, spot-up shooter and secondary ball handler
- Has made 41.5% of his career threes in a limited number of attempts, most effective at making threes above the break
- Primarily a spot-up shooter, does not really shoot off the dribble or on the move
- Lacks the explosive quickness to create his own offense
- Decent playmaker that can find open teammates, rarely turns the ball over
- 2019-20 Defensive Degree of Difficulty: 0.337, tends to defend second unit level guards
- Lacks ideal defensive tools, average wingspan and lateral quickness for his size
- Rarely tested in isolation situations, struggled to stay with opposing guards
- Middling pick-and-roll defender, bigger players can target him on switches, not quite quick enough to contain ball handlers
- Had trouble getting around screens on dribble hand-off plays, high effort defender that will consistently close out on spot-up shooters
- Stay-at-home defender with the L.A. Clippers, below average defensive rebounding guard, can opportunistically get steals

Newcomers

Tyrese Maxey

Height	Weight	Cap #	Years Left
6'3"	198	$2.479M	1 + 2 TO

Baseline Basic Stats

MPG	PTS	AST	REB	BLK	STL
19.8	8.2	2.3	2.1	0.1	0.6

Advanced Metrics

USG%	3PTA/FGA	FTA/FGA	TS%	eFG%	3PT%
20.3	0.342	0.227	0.492	0.457	0.331

AST%	TOV%	OREB%	DREB%	STL%	BLK%
19.1	13.7	1.9	10.0	1.6	0.6

PER	ORTG	DRTG	WS/48	VOL
11.72	97.5	105.6	0.037	N/A

- Drafted by Philadelphia with the 21st overall pick
- Named to the All-SEC 2nd Team in his freshman season
- Shifty ball handler that can create his own shot, effective pick-and-roll ball handler
- Has great speed, great at pushing the ball up the floor in transition, tends to play too wildly
- Can make long range shots, shot selection is questionable, made less than 30% of his threes at Kentucky
- Tends to rush up shots, mechanics can easily get thrown off in the flow of a game
- More of a secondary playmaker, limited to making simple reads, rarely moves off the ball
- Aggressive on-ball defender, actively contests shots, good at pressuring opposing ball handlers
- Fairly solid team defender, good at containing ball handlers on pick-and-rolls, fights through screens off the ball
- More of a stay-at-home defender, can occasionally rotate from the weak side to block a shot, solid defensive rebounder

Isaiah Joe

Height	Weight	Cap #	Years Left
6'5"	180	$0.898M	2

Baseline Basic Stats

MPG	PTS	AST	REB	BLK	STL
17.7	7.1	1.7	2.1	0.2	0.6

Advanced Metrics

USG%	3PTA/FGA	FTA/FGA	TS%	eFG%	3PT%
18.7	0.536	0.181	0.506	0.477	0.328
AST%	**TOV%**	**OREB%**	**DREB%**	**STL%**	**BLK%**
13.1	10.7	2.4	9.9	1.7	0.6
PER	**ORTG**	**DRTG**	**WS/48**	**VOL**	
11.79	100.0	104.8	0.037	N/A	

- Drafted by Philadelphia with the 49th overall pick
- Solid three-point shooter at Arkansas, efficiency decreased due to excess volume, suited to a complementary role in the NBA
- Mostly a stationary spot-up shooter, struggles to shoot on the move
- Can use the threat of his shot to sometimes get to the basket, decent at using an on-ball screen to make jumpers as a pick-and-roll ball handler
- Catch-and-shoot player, limited to making simple passes on the perimeter
- Solid on-ball defender that can potentially defend both guard spots
- Good team defender, effective at containing pick-and-roll ball handlers, stays attached to shooters off the ball
- Good at playing passing lanes, gets steals at a high rate, fairly decent defensive rebounder

MILWAUKEE BUCKS

Last Season: 56 – 17, Lost 2nd Round to Miami (1 – 4)

Offensive Rating: 112.4, 8th in the NBA

Defensive Rating: 102.9, 1st in the NBA

Primary Executive: Jon Horst, General Manager

Head Coach: Mike Budenholzer

Key Roster Changes

Subtractions
Eric Bledsoe, trade
George Hill, trade
Robin Lopez, free agency
Wesley Matthews, free agency
Sterling Brown, free agency
Kyle Korver, free agency
Ersan Ilyasova, waived
Marvin Williams, retired

Additions
Jordan Nwora, draft
Sam Merrill, draft
Jrue Holiday, trade
D.J. Augustin, free agency
Bobby Portis, free agency
Torrey Craig, free agency
Bryn Forbes, free agency

Roster

Likely Starting Five

1. *Jrue Holiday*
2. *Khris Middleton*
3. Torrey Craig
4. *Giannis Antetokounmpo*
5. *Brook Lopez*

Other Key Rotation Players
Donte DiVincenzo
Pat Connaughton
D.J. Augustin
Bobby Portis
Bryn Forbes

* Italics denotes that a player is likely to be on the floor to close games

Remaining Roster

- D.J. Wilson
- Thanasis Antetokounmpo
- Jordan Nwora
- Sam Merrill
- Jaylen Adams, 24, 6'2", 190, St. Bonaventure (Two-Way)
- Mamadi Diakite, 24, 6'9", 224, Virginia (Two-Way)
- E.J. Montgomery, 21, 6'10", 228, Kentucky (Exhibit 10)
- Nik Stauskas, 27, 6'6", 205, Michigan (Exhibit 10)
- Treveon Graham, 27, 6'5", 219, VCU (Exhibit 10)
- Justin Patton, 23. 6'11", 241, Creighton (Exhibit 10)

SCHREMPF Base Rating: 40.3 (72-game season)

Strengths

- Efficient offense that blends Giannis' ability to attack the rim with solid three-point shooting
- Effective defense that relies on sound rim protection

Question Marks

- No truly reliable shot creator in a half-court set against elite defenses
- No proven wing stopper on the roster to neutralize Kevin Durant, Jayson Tatum or Jimmy Butler
- Coaching staff's ability to make adjustments to appropriately counter opponents in the playoffs

Outlook

- Contender in the East, could finish anywhere in the top six seeds

Veterans

Giannis Antetokounmpo	**Height**	**Weight**	**Cap #**	**Years Left**
	6'11"	242	$27.528M	UFA

	Similar at Age	**25** Season	**SIMsc**
1	DeMarcus Cousins	2015-16	898.7
2	Amar'e Stoudemire	2007-08	850.2
3	Tim Duncan*	2001-02	846.5
4	LeBron James	2009-10	845.9
5	Blake Griffin	2014-15	843.4
6	Alonzo Mourning*	1995-96	837.8
7	Derrick Coleman	1992-93	837.3
8	Christian Laettner	1994-95	834.6
9	Nikola Vucevic	2015-16	834.6
10	Vin Baker	1996-97	834.5

Baseline Basic Stats

MPG	PTS	AST	REB	BLK	STL
34.0	22.7	4.0	9.9	1.4	1.1

Advanced Metrics

USG%	3PTA/FGA	FTA/FGA	TS%	eFG%	3PT%
32.0	0.204	0.449	0.601	0.558	0.334
AST%	**TOV%**	**OREB%**	**DREB%**	**STL%**	**BLK%**
26.8	13.1	7.1	28.6	1.5	3.0
PER	**ORTG**	**DRTG**	**WS/48**	**VOL**	
27.57	115.7	101.4	0.231	0.351	

- Named MVP for the 2nd straight season, also named Defensive Player of the Year in 2019-20
- Led the NBA in Usage Percentage, excelled as Milwaukee's primary scorer and ball handler
- Excellent at driving downhill in transition, on isolations or as a pick-and-roll ball handler
- Made almost 78% of his shots inside of three feet last season, good post-up player that usually scores on the left block
- Excellent rim runner, vertical lob threat, great as a roll man or cutter, good offensive rebounder that scores on put-backs
- Jump shot is still a work-in-progress, posted a career low in Free Throw Percentage, made just over 30% of his threes
- Good playmaker that finds open shooters, good at limiting turnovers prone
- 2019-20 Defensive Degree of Difficulty: 0.400
- Tended to guard lower leverage starters, used mostly a roaming weak side help defender
- Good rim protector that can rotate from the weak side to block shots, gets steals at a solid rate, great defensive rebounder
- Not tested as frequently on the ball, played solid on-ball defense, capable of guarding multiple positions
- Solid pick-and-roll defender, good on switches, occasionally gives up pull-up jumpers to ball handlers
- Consistently closes out on perimeter shooters, occasionally gets caught on screens off the ball

Khris Middleton

	Height	Weight	Cap #	Years Left
	6'7"	222	$33.052M	2 + PO

Similar at Age **28**

		Season	SIMsc
1	Joe Johnson	2009-10	922.2
2	Glen Rice	1995-96	919.2
3	Tyreke Evans	2017-18	917.6
4	Richard Jefferson	2008-09	915.4
5	Andres Nocioni	2007-08	914.9
6	Caron Butler	2008-09	914.9
7	Lamond Murray	2001-02	914.1
8	Danny Granger	2011-12	913.2
9	Al Harrington	2008-09	912.2
10	Luol Deng	2013-14	911.3

Baseline Basic Stats

MPG	PTS	AST	REB	BLK	STL
32.4	16.6	2.7	4.6	0.3	0.9

Advanced Metrics

USG%	3PTA/FGA	FTA/FGA	TS%	eFG%	3PT%
23.4	0.391	0.238	0.572	0.532	0.389
AST%	**TOV%**	**OREB%**	**DREB%**	**STL%**	**BLK%**
16.4	11.1	2.7	14.6	1.4	0.5
PER	**ORTG**	**DRTG**	**WS/48**	**VOL**	
16.95	111.7	106.9	0.135	0.291	

- Made his 2nd consecutive All-Star team, had a career best season in 2019-20
- Thrived in his role as a high volume, scoring wing player
- Great improved ball handling skills, became a very good pick-and-roll ball handler and isolation
- Can make pull-up jumpers and get to the rim, good at posting up smaller perimeter players
- Solid playmaker that find open shooters, good at limiting turnovers
- Made 41.5% of his threes last season, excellent in the corners, career percentage on corner threes is 43.5%
- Good spot-up shooter that can now shoot off screens, good at setting up for trail threes in transition
- Good at using the screen on dribble hand-offs to make outside shots or get to the rim
- 2019-20 Defensive Degree of Difficulty: 0.424
- Tends to guard starting level players, occasionally draws tougher assignments
- Can defend multiple positions, average on-ball defender this season, had trouble in the post against bigger players, better in previous seasons
- Good pick-and-roll defender, good at containing ball handlers, effective on switches
- Stays attached to shooters off the ball, consistently closes out in spot-up situations
- Becoming more of a stay-at-home defender, Steal Percentage has been declining for the last two seasons, good defensive rebounder

Jrue Holiday	Height	Weight	Cap #	Years Left
	6'3"	205	$25.906M	Player Option

Similar at Age 29

		Season	SIMsc
1	Baron Davis	2008-09	938.3
2	Deron Williams	2013-14	926.7
3	Jarrett Jack	2012-13	923.9
4	Jeff Hornacek	1992-93	920.8
5	Eric Bledsoe	2018-19	915.8
6	Gilbert Arenas	2010-11	907.9
7	Voshon Lenard	2002-03	905.1
8	Raymond Felton	2013-14	903.4
9	Mike James	2004-05	901.8
10	Bobby Phills	1998-99	901.0

Baseline Basic Stats

MPG	PTS	AST	REB	BLK	STL
31.3	14.6	5.3	3.3	0.3	1.2

Advanced Metrics

USG%	3PTA/FGA	FTA/FGA	TS%	eFG%	3PT%
22.9	0.322	0.221	0.537	0.503	0.346
AST%	**TOV%**	**OREB%**	**DREB%**	**STL%**	**BLK%**
27.2	14.2	2.9	10.3	2.0	1.3
PER	**ORTG**	**DRTG**	**WS/48**	**VOL**	
16.26	107.9	110.9	0.091	0.333	

- Regular starter for New Orleans last season, missed the end of the Orlando restart due to a right elbow injury
- Per-minute production declined slightly, still effective in his role as New Orleans' primary ball handler
- Very good playmaker that can kick the ball out to shooters, good at avoiding turnovers
- Made threes at around the league average, solid spot-up shooter, solid at making backdoor cuts when defenders try to crowd him
- Less effective as a pick-and-roll ball handler, settled for tough floaters in the paint, drew fewer fouls
- More effective on dribble hand-offs, can make outside shots or use the screen to get to the rim
- 2019-20 Defensive Degree of Difficulty: 0.564
- Had the 5th toughest set of matchups in the league last season
- Very good on-ball defender that can guard multiple positions
- Solid pick-and-roll defender, good on switches, occasionally allows ball handlers to turn the corner
- Good at closing out on perimeter shooters, gambles a bit too much when chasing shooters off screens
- Active help defender, consistently gets steals, Block Percentage has steadily risen in the last four seasons, solid defensive rebounder

Brook Lopez	Height	Weight	Cap #	Years Left
	7'0"	270	$12.698M	2

Similar at Age 31

		Season	SIMsc
1	Pero Antic	2013-14	835.1
2	Channing Frye	2014-15	834.3
3	Marc Gasol	2015-16	821.7
4	Rasho Nesterovic	2007-08	821.1
5	JaVale McGee	2018-19	817.2
6	Bill Laimbeer	1988-89	815.2
7	Al Horford	2017-18	814.1
8	Dave Corzine	1987-88	813.5
9	Marvin Williams	2017-18	811.5
10	Benoit Benjamin	1995-96	808.2

Baseline Basic Stats

MPG	PTS	AST	REB	BLK	STL
23.0	9.7	1.5	4.6	1.0	0.5

Advanced Metrics

USG%	3PTA/FGA	FTA/FGA	TS%	eFG%	3PT%
18.4	0.495	0.195	0.553	0.520	0.335
AST%	**TOV%**	**OREB%**	**DREB%**	**STL%**	**BLK%**
9.0	10.0	3.4	15.9	1.0	5.6
PER	**ORTG**	**DRTG**	**WS/48**	**VOL**	
14.12	107.9	103.9	0.116	0.552	

- Regular starter for Milwaukee in his second season with the team
- Mainly used in a low volume role as a stretch big, shooting efficiency dropped last season
- Three-Point Percentage fell below break-even, average at making spot-up jumpers, more effective as the screener on pick-and-pops
- Posted up more, still an effective post player, good at making hook shots on the left block
- Slides into open spaces inside as a rim runner, good on rolls to the rim and cuts off the ball
- Mainly a catch-and-shoot big man, still a decent passer, rarely turns the ball over
- 2019-20 Defensive Degree of Difficulty: 0.413, tends to guard starting level big men
- Named to the All-Defensive 2nd team last season
- Good rim protector, posted a career high in Block Percentage for the second straight season
- Boxes his man out to allow others to get defensive boards, middling defensive rebounder right now
- Below average on-ball defender, has trouble in space due to mobility limitations
- Solid pick-and-roll defender, decent in drop coverages, can occasionally switch onto ball handlers
- Consistently comes out to contest perimeter shots in spot-up situations

Torrey Craig	Height	Weight	Cap #	Years Left
	6'7"	215	$1.621M	UFA

	Similar at Age	29 Season	SIMsc
1	Mickael Gelabale	2012-13	913.0
2	Scott Burrell	1999-00	911.9
3	Wesley Johnson	2016-17	911.8
4	Mickael Pietrus	2011-12	908.1
5	Jamario Moon	2009-10	904.8
6	Keith Askins	1996-97	904.3
7	Devean George	2006-07	900.0
8	Eric Piatkowski	1999-00	899.3
9	Lance Thomas	2017-18	899.3
10	Morris Peterson	2006-07	899.0

Baseline Basic Stats

MPG	PTS	AST	REB	BLK	STL
18.1	4.8	0.8	2.8	0.4	0.5

Advanced Metrics

USG%	3PTA/FGA	FTA/FGA	TS%	eFG%	3PT%
12.3	0.500	0.151	0.522	0.503	0.330
AST%	**TOV%**	**OREB%**	**DREB%**	**STL%**	**BLK%**
6.4	10.6	5.2	12.7	1.3	2.5
PER	**ORTG**	**DRTG**	**WS/48**	**VOL**	
9.22	107.7	110.9	0.075	0.182	

- Regular rotation player for Denver in his third NBA season
- Slightly improved last season in his role as a low volume spot-up shooter
- Three-Point Percentage increased slightly, but still below break-even, good at making spot-up jumpers late in the shot clock
- Excellent cutter off the ball, fairly good offensive rebounding wing that scores on put-backs
- Strictly a catch-and-shoot player, limited playmaker and shot creator, rarely turns the ball over
- <u>2019-20 Defensive Degree of Difficulty</u>: 0.611, almost exclusively guarded top players
- Had the toughest set of matchups among players that played 500 minutes or more
- Good on-ball perimeter defender that can guard multiple positions, struggles against bigger post players inside
- Decent pick-and-roll defender, good at covering the roll man, has some trouble containing shiftier ball handlers
- Could be late to close out on perimeter shooters, tended to get caught on screens off the ball
- Solid defensive rebounder, good shot blocking wing, Steal Percentage is still consistent with his career average

Donte DiVincenzo

Height	Weight	Cap #	Years Left
6'4"	203	$3.044M	Team Option

Similar at Age **23**

		Season	SIMsc
1	C.J. McCollum	2014-15	925.2
2	Matthew Dellavedova	2013-14	916.3
3	Josh Richardson	2016-17	915.2
4	Josh Hart	2018-19	913.8
5	Orlando Johnson	2012-13	913.3
6	Iman Shumpert	2013-14	913.2
7	Wayne Ellington	2010-11	912.3
8	Voshon Lenard	1996-97	911.8
9	Austin Rivers	2015-16	908.2
10	Courtney Lee	2008-09	907.2

Baseline Basic Stats

MPG	PTS	AST	REB	BLK	STL
22.4	8.7	1.8	2.8	0.2	0.8

Advanced Metrics

USG%	3PTA/FGA	FTA/FGA	TS%	eFG%	3PT%
17.9	0.530	0.184	0.544	0.516	0.341
AST%	**TOV%**	**OREB%**	**DREB%**	**STL%**	**BLK%**
13.3	12.2	3.5	12.6	2.0	1.0
PER	**ORTG**	**DRTG**	**WS/48**	**VOL**	
13.04	107.9	106.2	0.103	0.387	

- Became a regular rotation player for Milwaukee in his second NBA season
- Mostly used as a low volume, spot-up shooter, made threes at just above a break-even rate
- Primarily a stationary spot-up shooter right now, struggles to shoot on the move or off the dribble
- Good at attacking the rim if his shot is falling, can drive against aggressive close-outs, makes outside shots on dribble hand-off plays
- Effective at making backdoor cuts if defenders try to crowd him
- Solid secondary playmaker that finds cutter or open shooters, fairly solid at limiting turnovers
- 2019-20 Defensive Degree of Difficulty: 0.400
- Tended to guard second unit level players or lower leverage starters
- Fairly solid on-ball defender, good at keeping players away from the basket, can sometimes give up too much space for his man to take jump shots
- Good pick-and-roll defender, fights over screens to contain ball handlers, effective at switching
- Gambles a bit too much when chasing shooters off screens, tries to shoot the gap, tends to be late when closing out on perimeter shooters
- Active help defender, posted a pretty high Steal Percentage last season, can occasionally rotate inside to block a shot

Pat Connaughton	Height	Weight	Cap #	Years Left
	6'5"	209	$4.938M	1 + PO

	Similar at Age	27	
		Season	SIMsc
1	Rodney McGruder	2018-19	925.4
2	Richie Frahm	2004-05	913.1
3	Tony Snell	2018-19	912.9
4	Torrey Craig	2017-18	908.4
5	Roger Mason	2007-08	902.7
6	James Ennis	2017-18	900.4
7	Kyle Korver	2008-09	900.3
8	Keith Bogans	2007-08	897.4
9	Mickael Pietrus	2009-10	896.8
10	Thabo Sefolosha	2011-12	896.6

Baseline Basic Stats

MPG	PTS	AST	REB	BLK	STL
22.0	6.7	1.4	3.0	0.4	0.6

Advanced Metrics

USG%	3PTA/FGA	FTA/FGA	TS%	eFG%	3PT%
12.8	0.624	0.131	0.557	0.539	0.359
AST%	**TOV%**	**OREB%**	**DREB%**	**STL%**	**BLK%**
10.2	11.3	3.7	13.8	1.2	1.7
PER	**ORTG**	**DRTG**	**WS/48**	**VOL**	
10.98	112.9	107.9	0.110	0.329	

- Regular rotation player for Milwaukee in his second season with the team
- Maintained his effectiveness in his role as a low volume, spot-up shooter
- Made threes at a rate just below break-even, somewhat streaky, can attack aggressive close-outs if his shot is falling
- Great finisher at the rim, made over 70% of his shots inside of three feet
- Effective as a cutter off the ball, good at crashing the offensive glass to score on put-backs, can score on dribble hand-off plays
- Decent secondary playmaker that has been solid at avoiding turnovers
- 2019-20 Defensive Degree of Difficulty: 0.349, tends to guard second unit level players
- Fairly solid on-ball defender in 2019-20, effective at contesting shots on the perimeter and in the post
- Average pick-and-roll defender, tends to go too far under screens
- Consistently closes out on perimeter shooters, tends to get caught on screens away from the ball
- Good defensive rebounder for his size, set a career high in Block Percentage last season, became a solid weak side shot blocker

D.J. Augustin	Height	Weight	Cap #	Years Left
	5'11"	183	$6.667M	2

	Similar at Age	32	
		Season	SIMsc
1	Chucky Atkins	2006-07	929.2
2	Mark Price	1996-97	921.9
3	Jason Williams	2007-08	909.6
4	Damon Stoudamire	2005-06	909.0
5	Greg Anthony	1999-00	907.7
6	John Crotty	2001-02	904.8
7	Joe Dumars*	1995-96	903.5
8	Travis Best	2004-05	903.0
9	Dana Barros	1999-00	900.7
10	Jameer Nelson	2014-15	898.0

Baseline Basic Stats

MPG	PTS	AST	REB	BLK	STL
23.0	9.1	3.5	1.9	0.0	0.7

Advanced Metrics

USG%	3PTA/FGA	FTA/FGA	TS%	eFG%	3PT%
18.2	0.474	0.294	0.559	0.505	0.366
AST%	**TOV%**	**OREB%**	**DREB%**	**STL%**	**BLK%**
25.6	14.2	1.6	7.7	1.4	0.1
PER	**ORTG**	**DRTG**	**WS/48**	**VOL**	
14.00	112.9	112.8	0.094	0.317	

- Played a regular role as Orlando's backup point guard after starting for the previous two seasons
- Still effective as a low volume, pass-first backup, good ball control point guard that consistently limits turnovers
- Solid playmaker that can find open perimeter shooters and cutters
- Better as a pick-and-roll ball handler, doesn't quite have the quickness to get to the rim, can make pull-up jumpers
- Three-Point Percentage dropped last season, good three-point shooter throughout his career
- Still effective as a spot-up shooter that can shoot off screens
- Good at using the screen on dribble hand-offs to make outside shots
- 2019-20 Defensive Degree of Difficulty: 0.344, tends to guard second unit level players
- Hidden in favorable matchups, played solid on-ball defense against lower leverage offensive players
- Fairly solid pick-and-roll defender, good at fighting over screens to contain ball handlers, can be targeted by bigger players on switches
- Stays attached to shooters off the ball, good at closing out on perimeter shooters
- Below average defensive rebounder, Steal Percentage is still consistent with his career average

Bobby Portis

	Height	Weight	Cap #	Years Left
Bobby Portis	6'10"	246	$3.623M	Player Option

Similar at Age 24

		Season	SIMsc
1	Henry Sims	2014-15	931.7
2	Markieff Morris	2013-14	924.0
3	Marreese Speights	2011-12	915.2
4	Channing Frye	2007-08	914.6
5	Jon Leuer	2013-14	911.7
6	Joffrey Lauvergne	2015-16	911.4
7	Anthony Tolliver	2009-10	911.3
8	Ryan Anderson	2012-13	911.1
9	Andrew Nicholson	2013-14	910.3
10	Austin Croshere	1999-00	909.9

Baseline Basic Stats

MPG	PTS	AST	REB	BLK	STL
23.1	10.2	1.3	5.2	0.4	0.6

Advanced Metrics

USG%	3PTA/FGA	FTA/FGA	TS%	eFG%	3PT%
21.7	0.323	0.188	0.534	0.502	0.379

AST%	TOV%	OREB%	DREB%	STL%	BLK%
10.8	10.1	6.7	20.5	1.2	1.4

PER	ORTG	DRTG	WS/48	VOL
15.51	107.9	109.9	0.084	0.382

- Regular rotation player in his first season for New York
- Per-minute production decreased in a moderate volume role as a stretch big
- Solid stationary shooter that can knock down spot-up jumpers, made threes at around the league average last season
- Took a lot of mid-range shots, made them at an above average rate, got to the rim with less frequency
- Limited action at the rim made him less effective as a cutter and roll man
- Solid transition player that runs hard down the floor and set up for an occasional trail three
- Has become a fairly decent passing big man that limits turnovers
- 2019-20 Defensive Degree of Difficulty: 0.340, tends to guard second unit level players
- Solid rebounder, good at protecting the rim, not really a shot blocker, good at staying vertical to contest shots
- Fairly solid post defender that can push opponents off the block, has some trouble defending in space on isolations
- Above average pick-and-roll defender, good in drop coverage, has difficulty handling quicker guards on switches
- Does not always close out on perimeter shooters in spot-up situations

Bryn Forbes	Height	Weight	Cap #	Years Left
	6'2"	190	$2.337M	Player Option

Similar at Age 26

		Season	SIMsc
1	J.J. Redick	2010-11	934.1
2	Seth Curry	2016-17	930.4
3	Matt Maloney	1997-98	925.1
4	Troy Daniels	2017-18	917.3
5	Ian Clark	2017-18	917.1
6	Mike Penberthy	2000-01	914.6
7	Craig Hodges	1986-87	912.9
8	A.J. Price	2012-13	911.3
9	James Robinson	1996-97	908.3
10	Daniel Gibson	2012-13	908.1

Baseline Basic Stats

MPG	PTS	AST	REB	BLK	STL
22.6	9.1	2.1	2.0	0.1	0.6

Advanced Metrics

USG%	3PTA/FGA	FTA/FGA	TS%	eFG%	3PT%
18.3	0.541	0.148	0.561	0.535	0.394
AST%	**TOV%**	**OREB%**	**DREB%**	**STL%**	**BLK%**
12.5	9.7	1.2	8.5	1.2	0.2
PER	**ORTG**	**DRTG**	**WS/48**	**VOL**	
11.88	109.9	113.9	0.067	0.337	

- Regular starter for San Antonio when healthy, missed the Orlando restart due to a right quadriceps injury
- Mainly used as a low volume shooting specialist, has made 40% of his career threes
- Very good spot-up shooter, excellent at shooting off screens, has made over 48% of his career corner threes
- Effective ball handler on side pick-and-rolls, can make pull-up jumpers on the right side
- Good at getting to the rim on dribble hand-offs, good at running down the wing for layups in transition
- Decent secondary playmaker that can hit cutters, rarely turns the ball over
- 2019-20 Defensive Degree of Difficulty: 0.482
- Guards starting level players, took on tougher defensive assignments last season
- Played below average on-ball defense, over-matched against elite perimeter players
- Middling pick-and-roll defender, effective at defending side pick-and-rolls, can be targeted by bigger screeners on switches
- Gets caught on screens off the ball, tends to be either late or too aggressive when closing out on perimeter shooters
- Stay-at-home defender, middling defensive rebounder, rarely gets steals or blocks

D.J. Wilson	Height	Weight	Cap #	Years Left
	6'10"	231	$4.548M	RFA

	Similar at Age	23 Season	SIMsc
1	Trey Lyles	2018-19	910.6
2	Tyler Cavanaugh	2017-18	909.8
3	Sam Dekker	2017-18	909.7
4	Matt Freije	2004-05	907.7
5	Luke Babbitt	2012-13	907.2
6	Marcus Morris	2012-13	904.1
7	Perry Jones	2014-15	901.4
8	Doug McDermott	2014-15	901.0
9	Bostjan Nachbar	2003-04	900.7
10	Keita Bates-Diop	2018-19	900.6

Baseline Basic Stats

MPG	PTS	AST	REB	BLK	STL
18.4	6.8	1.0	3.5	0.3	0.5

Advanced Metrics

USG%	3PTA/FGA	FTA/FGA	TS%	eFG%	3PT%
16.5	0.532	0.187	0.548	0.528	0.358
AST%	**TOV%**	**OREB%**	**DREB%**	**STL%**	**BLK%**
8.6	10.7	4.4	17.9	1.0	1.3
PER	**ORTG**	**DRTG**	**WS/48**	**VOL**	
11.98	108.8	108.5	0.108	0.400	

- Playing time decreased significantly in his third NBA season, out of the rotation for the bulk of 2019-20
- Mainly utilized as a low volume, stretch big, struggled to shoot efficiently last season
- Three-Point Percentage fell below 25% last season, used more on pick-and-pops, struggled to shoot on the move
- Better as a stationary spot-up shooter throughout his career, career percentage on corner threes in 43.5%
- Decent rim runner in limited opportunities, solid cutter off the ball, decent at rolling to the rim on pick-and-rolls
- Improving as a passer, solid at avoiding turnovers
- 2019-20 Defensive Degree of Difficulty: 0.247
- Tended to either guard second unit level players or play in garbage time
- Solid on-ball defender in a small sample of possessions, effective post defender, mobile enough to guard in space
- Good at guarding pick-and-rolls, effective on switches, good at defending the roll man inside
- Consistently came out to contest perimeter shots
- Good defensive rebounder, good at protecting the rim, not really a shot blocker, stays vertical to contest shots

Thanasis Antetokounmpo

Height	Weight	Cap #	Years Left
6'6"	205	$1.702M	RFA

Similar at Age 27

		Season	SIMsc
1	Anthony Frederick	1991-92	896.8
2	Derek Smith	1988-89	894.9
3	George McCloud	1994-95	893.6
4	Laron Profit	2004-05	890.9
5	Marquis Daniels	2007-08	890.2
6	Harold Ellis	1997-98	890.2
7	Anthony Jones	1989-90	889.8
8	Pat Durham	1994-95	881.8
9	Lionel Simmons	1995-96	879.0
10	Gerald Paddio	1992-93	879.0

Baseline Basic Stats

MPG	PTS	AST	REB	BLK	STL
20.2	9.2	1.5	3.0	0.3	0.8

Advanced Metrics

USG%	3PTA/FGA	FTA/FGA	TS%	eFG%	3PT%
21.2	0.266	0.290	0.519	0.504	0.216
AST%	**TOV%**	**OREB%**	**DREB%**	**STL%**	**BLK%**
14.4	14.9	6.2	10.4	2.1	1.2
PER	**ORTG**	**DRTG**	**WS/48**	**VOL**	
13.16	102.5	106.3	0.076	0.563	

- Played sparingly for Milwaukee in 2019-20 after spending the previous two seasons in the Greek A1 League
- Utilized as an energy player off the bench, rated as average or worse in most offensive situations last season
- Very athletic, very effective at cutting off the ball to get dunks, almost 46% of his made field goals last season were dunks
- Limited half-court skills, fairly solid secondary playmaker, can be turnover prone
- Has struggled to shoot efficiently at the NBA level, missed all 11 of his Three-Point Attempts, makes less than 50% of his free throws
- <u>2019-20 Defensive Degree of Difficulty</u>: 0.270, mainly plays in garbage time
- Played good on-ball defense in limited minutes, has the potential to guard multiple positions
- Below average pick-and-roll defender, still learning NBA level defensive concepts and rotations
- Fights through screens off the ball, tends to be late when closing out on perimeter shooters
- Active help defender, gets steals and blocks at a high rate, decent overall rebounder, better on the offensive glass

Newcomers

Jordan Nwora	**Height**	**Weight**	**Cap #**	**Years Left**
	6'7"	225	$0.898M	1

Baseline Basic Stats

MPG	PTS	AST	REB	BLK	STL
19.1	7.1	1.0	3.2	0.2	0.6

Advanced Metrics

USG%	3PTA/FGA	FTA/FGA	TS%	eFG%	3PT%
17.2	0.314	0.226	0.517	0.485	0.338
AST%	**TOV%**	**OREB%**	**DREB%**	**STL%**	**BLK%**
7.4	11.2	5.0	14.3	1.4	0.8
PER	**ORTG**	**DRTG**	**WS/48**	**VOL**	
11.94	103.1	103.7	0.050	N/A	

- Drafted by Milwaukee with the 45th overall pick
- Named to the All-ACC 1st Team in 2019-20, represented Nigeria in the 2019 FIBA World Cup qualifiers
- Will likely be a complementary player, non-dribbling plays accounted for 87.2% of his offense in 2019-20
- Not a dynamic ball handler, struggles to get all the way to the rim, not really a natural playmaker
- Mostly a catch-and-shoot player, made over 39% of his career threes at Louisville
- Very good spot-up shooters, can occasionally shoot off screens, effective as a screener on pick-and-pops in a small sample of possessions
- Good athlete, vertical lob threat, rolls hard to the rim as the screener on pick-and-rolls, good cutter off the ball, great at running down the wings in transition
- Solid physical tools to defend multiple positions in the NBA, very good length and quickness
- Fairly good on-ball defender, will pressure perimeter players, actively contests shots
- Has some trouble against bigger players in the post, may need to get a bit stronger
- Solid pick-and-roll defender, fights over screens to contain ball handler, effective at switching onto to the screener
- Generally stayed attached to shooters off the ball, good at getting through off-ball screens, consistently closed out on perimeter shooters
- More of a stay-at-home defender, does not really go for steals, occasionally can rotate from the weak side to block shots, good defensive rebounder

Sam Merrill	**Height**	**Weight**	**Cap #**	**Years Left**
	6'5"	205	$0.898M	1

Baseline Basic Stats

MPG	PTS	AST	REB	BLK	STL
15.6	5.5	1.3	2.0	0.1	0.5

Advanced Metrics

USG%	3PTA/FGA	FTA/FGA	TS%	eFG%	3PT%
16.6	0.480	0.219	0.503	0.471	0.342

AST%	TOV%	OREB%	DREB%	STL%	BLK%
13.6	11.2	2.6	10.3	1.5	0.5

PER	ORTG	DRTG	WS/48	VOL
11.34	100.0	101.9	0.036	N/A

- Drafted by New Orleans with the 60th overall pick, traded to Milwaukee
- Made the All-Mountain West 1st Team last season, named MVP of the Mountain West Conference Tournament
- Great three-point shooter, made 42% of his career threes
- Excellent spot-up shooter, good at making shots off screens, improved ability to shoot off the dribble
- Lacks ideal athleticism, crafty ball handler that can change speeds
- More effective as a pick-and-roll ball handler and isolation player in his senior season at Utah State
- Willing passer that can find open perimeter shooters, good at making backdoor cuts if defenders try to crowd him
- Does not have ideal physical tools on defense, high effort defender that was adequate at the college level
- Effective in isolation situations last season, could steer his man into help or inefficient scoring areas
- Average pick-and-roll defender, good at preventing drives to the rim, tended to go too far under screens
- Sometimes a step slow when fighting through screens off the ball, consistently closed out in spot-up situations
- More of a stay-at-home defender, can opportunistically play passing lanes to get steals, solid defensive rebounder

TORONTO RAPTORS

Last Season: 53 – 19, Lost 2nd Round to Boston (3 – 4)

Offensive Rating: 111.1, 14th in the NBA

Defensive Rating: 105.0, 2nd in the NBA

Primary Executive: Masai Ujiri, Team President

Head Coach: Nick Nurse

Key Roster Changes

Subtractions
Marc Gasol, free agency
Serge Ibaka, free agency
Malcolm Miller, free agency
Rondae Hollis-Jefferson, free agency

Additions
Malachi Flynn, draft
Aron Baynes, free agency
Alex Len, free agency
DeAndre' Bembry, free agency

Roster

Likely Starting Five

1. *Kyle Lowry*
2. *Fred VanVleet*
3. *OG Anunoby*
4. *Pascal Siakam*
5. Aron Baynes

Other Key Rotation Players
Norman Powell
Terence Davis
Chris Boucher
Patrick McCaw

* Italics denotes that a player is likely to be on the floor to close games

Remaining Roster

- Alex Len
- DeAndre' Bembry
- Matt Thomas
- Malachi Flynn
- Stanley Johnson
- Paul Watson, 26, 6'7", 215, Fresno State (Two-Way)
- Jalen Harris, 22, 6'5", 195, Nevada (Two-Way)
- Alize Johnson, 24, 6'7", 212, Missouri State (Exhibit 10)
- Yuta Watanabe, 26, 6'8", 215, George Washington (Exhibit 10)
- Henry Ellenson, 24, 6'10", 240, Marquette (Exhibit 10)
- Oshae Brissett, 22, 6'7", 210, Syracuse (Exhibit 10)

SCHREMPF Base Rating: 39.2 (72-game season)

Strengths

- Creative defensive schemes that maximize their personnel
- Chemistry and cohesiveness as a unit on both ends
- Solid coaching staff that will consistently make timely adjustments

Question Marks

- Limited offensive firepower, may be lacking the front-end talent to compete with the other elite teams
- Not much proven depth beyond their top eight players

Outlook

- Elite team in the East, will probably finish somewhere in the top six seeds

Veterans

Pascal Siakam

Height	Weight	Cap #	Years Left
6'9"	230	$30.559M	3

Similar at Age 25

		Season	SIMsc
1	Tim Thomas	2002-03	935.6
2	Al Harrington	2005-06	931.8
3	Josh Smith	2010-11	921.3
4	Ersan Ilyasova	2012-13	919.9
5	Juwan Howard	1998-99	919.1
6	Austin Croshere	2000-01	918.8
7	Michael Beasley	2013-14	917.7
8	Tobias Harris	2017-18	917.3
9	Danny Granger	2008-09	916.9
10	David West	2005-06	914.7

Baseline Basic Stats

MPG	PTS	AST	REB	BLK	STL
32.7	16.6	2.4	6.0	0.6	1.0

Advanced Metrics

USG%	3PTA/FGA	FTA/FGA	TS%	eFG%	3PT%
23.8	0.287	0.274	0.559	0.517	0.356
AST%	**TOV%**	**OREB%**	**DREB%**	**STL%**	**BLK%**
14.4	11.3	4.5	16.8	1.5	1.7
PER	**ORTG**	**DRTG**	**WS/48**	**VOL**	
17.12	109.8	106.4	0.123	0.289	

- Made his first All-Star team last season, named to the All-NBA 2nd Team in 2019-20
- Thrived in his new role as Toronto's primary scoring option
- Good transition player that can run the floor for dunks or set up for trail threes
- Could drive by slower big men on isolations to score at the rim or draw shooting fouls
- Made threes at above the league average, solid spot-up shooter, effective screener on pick-and-pops
- Very good cutter off the ball, good playmaking big man that can hit cutters or find open shooters, good at avoiding turnovers
- 2019-20 Defensive Degree of Difficulty: 0.440
- Usually guarded starting level players, sometimes drew tougher defensive assignments
- Good on-ball defender that has the versatility to guard multiple positions
- Good pick-and-roll defender, can guard the screener or switch onto ball handlers
- Stays attached to shooters off the ball, good at closing out on spot-up shooters
- Solid defensive rebounder, Steal and Block Percentages are still consistent with his career averages
- Average rim protector last season, does not quite have the length to contest shots from taller big men inside

Kyle Lowry	Height	Weight	Cap #	Years Left
	6'0"	196	$30.500M	UFA

	Similar at Age	33 Season	SIMsc
1	Chris Paul	2018-19	905.2
2	Terry Porter	1996-97	894.6
3	Raymond Felton	2017-18	890.6
4	David Wesley	2003-04	889.3
5	Derek Fisher	2007-08	885.3
6	Tim Hardaway	1999-00	880.2
7	Byron Scott	1994-95	878.1
8	Chauncey Billups	2009-10	876.6
9	Andre Miller	2009-10	876.3
10	Jon Barry	2002-03	871.6

Baseline Basic Stats

MPG	PTS	AST	REB	BLK	STL
28.3	11.9	4.9	3.0	0.2	1.0

Advanced Metrics

USG%	3PTA/FGA	FTA/FGA	TS%	eFG%	3PT%
20.4	0.542	0.295	0.555	0.503	0.352
AST%	**TOV%**	**OREB%**	**DREB%**	**STL%**	**BLK%**
28.1	15.7	1.9	11.8	1.9	0.8
PER	**ORTG**	**DRTG**	**WS/48**	**VOL**	
15.56	111.2	106.6	0.134	0.315	

- Made his sixth consecutive All-Star team in 2019-20, missed almost a month due to a fractured left thumb
- Maintained his normal level of effectiveness in his role as Toronto's primary ball handler
- Very good playmaker that can find open shooters, slightly turnover prone last season
- Effective pick-and-roll ball handler and isolation player that can get to the rim, draw fouls and make pull-up jumpers
- Good three-point shooter throughout his career, makes spot-up jumpers, good at setting up for trail threes in transition
- Solid at using an on-ball screen to get to the rim on dribble hand-offs
- 2019-20 Defensive Degree of Difficulty: 0.436
- Tends to guard starting level players, will take on some tougher defensive assignments
- Good on-ball defender that can defend both guard spots
- Fairly solid pick-and-roll defender, good at switching onto screeners, generally contains ball handlers, but occasionally allows them to get to the rim
- Stays attached to shooters off the ball, consistently closes out on perimeter shooters
- Good defensive rebounder, gets steals at a high rate, maintained his Block Percentage from the season before

Fred VanVleet	Height	Weight	Cap #	Years Left
	6'1"	195	$21.250M	2 + PO

Similar at Age **25**

		Season	SIMsc
1	Jason Williams	2000-01	927.6
2	Raymond Felton	2009-10	922.9
3	Earl Watson	2004-05	922.5
4	Cory Alexander	1998-99	921.7
5	Mario Chalmers	2011-12	918.8
6	Chauncey Billups	2001-02	918.2
7	Mo Williams	2007-08	916.9
8	Mike Bibby	2003-04	916.8
9	David Wesley	1995-96	915.6
10	Jameer Nelson	2007-08	913.6

Baseline Basic Stats

MPG	PTS	AST	REB	BLK	STL
28.1	11.1	4.6	2.7	0.2	1.1

Advanced Metrics

USG%	3PTA/FGA	FTA/FGA	TS%	eFG%	3PT%
20.1	0.449	0.227	0.535	0.494	0.370
AST%	**TOV%**	**OREB%**	**DREB%**	**STL%**	**BLK%**
26.7	13.4	1.5	9.3	2.0	0.7
PER	**ORTG**	**DRTG**	**WS/48**	**VOL**	
14.84	109.9	108.7	0.112	0.357	

- Played his first season as a full-time starter for Toronto, missed some games due to a series of minor injuries
- Had his most productive season while serving as an additional moderate volume ball handler
- Made 39% of his threes last season, good spot-up shooter that can also run off screens
- Effective at making pull-up jumpers as a pick-and-roll ball handler, good at making backdoor cuts if defenders overplay his shot
- Draws fouls, not quick enough to regularly drive by defenders in one-on-one situations
- Good playmaker that can find open shooters and control the ball to avoid turnovers
- 2019-20 Defensive Degree of Difficulty: 0.475
- Guards starter level players, takes on tougher defensive assignments against top guards
- Solid on-ball defender that can defend both guard spots, occasionally can get beat off the dribble by quicker guards
- Solid team defender that makes sound rotations, closes out on perimeter shooters, usually stays attached to shooters off the ball
- Good pick-and-roll defender that can guard ball handlers or switch onto screeners
- Solid defensive rebounder, gets steals at a fairly high rate, Block Percentage is still consistent with his career average

OG Anunoby	Height	Weight	Cap #	Years Left
	6'7"	232	$3.872M	RFA

	Similar at Age	22 Season	SIMsc
1	Jae Crowder	2012-13	926.9
2	Jaylen Brown	2018-19	926.1
3	Chris Singleton	2011-12	922.4
4	Kedrick Brown	2003-04	916.4
5	Omri Casspi	2010-11	913.7
6	Sam Dekker	2016-17	913.3
7	Lamond Murray	1995-96	912.7
8	Kawhi Leonard	2013-14	910.3
9	Jumaine Jones	2001-02	904.1
10	Hollis Thompson	2013-14	901.2

Baseline Basic Stats

MPG	PTS	AST	REB	BLK	STL
24.1	9.5	1.5	4.2	0.4	0.9

Advanced Metrics

USG%	3PTA/FGA	FTA/FGA	TS%	eFG%	3PT%
16.9	0.398	0.215	0.573	0.550	0.368
AST%	**TOV%**	**OREB%**	**DREB%**	**STL%**	**BLK%**
8.5	11.4	4.4	13.4	2.0	1.6
PER	**ORTG**	**DRTG**	**WS/48**	**VOL**	
13.32	110.5	106.4	0.116	0.384	

- Full-time starter for Toronto in his third NBA season
- Had his most productive season in a role as a low volume, spot-up shooter
- Made 39% of his threes last season, mainly a spot-up shooter, good at setting up for trail threes in transition
- Does not quite have the ball handling skills to create his own shot, can make pull-up jumpers on pick-and-rolls
- Good off the ball, scores on a high volume of cuts, selectively crashes the offensive boards to score on put-backs
- Catch-and-shoot player, limited playmaking skills, effective at limiting turnovers
- <u>2019-20 Defensive Degree of Difficulty</u>: 0.509
- Generally takes on tough defensive assignments against top wing players
- Very good on-ball defender that guards multiple positions
- Good pick-and-roll defender that can guard ball handlers and switch onto screeners
- Usually fights through screens off the ball, tends to be late when closing out on perimeter shooters
- More active as a help defender last season, set career highs in Steal and Block Percentage, fairly good defensive rebounder

Aron Baynes	Height	Weight	Cap #	Years Left
	6'10"	260	$7.000M	1

	Similar at Age	33	
		Season	SIMsc
1	Sean Marks	2008-09	891.6
2	Joe Kleine	1994-95	888.4
3	Amar'e Stoudemire	2015-16	881.2
4	Al Jefferson	2017-18	876.8
5	David Lee	2016-17	871.6
6	Danny Ferry	1999-00	871.0
7	Drew Gooden	2014-15	869.8
8	Channing Frye	2016-17	869.3
9	Pat Burke	2006-07	868.7
10	Joe Smith	2008-09	867.6

Baseline Basic Stats

MPG	PTS	AST	REB	BLK	STL
16.0	5.7	0.9	3.9	0.4	0.3

Advanced Metrics

USG%	3PTA/FGA	FTA/FGA	TS%	eFG%	3PT%
17.1	0.290	0.232	0.548	0.516	0.317
AST%	**TOV%**	**OREB%**	**DREB%**	**STL%**	**BLK%**
9.0	13.3	8.6	18.9	0.8	2.5
PER	**ORTG**	**DRTG**	**WS/48**	**VOL**	
12.96	109.4	107.3	0.093	0.476	

- Mostly a starter for Phoenix when healthy, missed games due to a series of minor injuries mainly to his hip
- Fairly productive in his role as a moderate volume stretch big, made threes at around the league average last season
- Effective screener on pick-and-pop plays, good spot-up shooter
- Efficient shooter from ten feet and in, can slide into openings inside as a roll man and cutter
- Good at bullying smaller players on post-ups last season
- Decent passing big man, set a career high in Assist Percentage, good at avoiding turnovers
- 2019-20 Defensive Degree of Difficulty: 0.464
- Usually guarded starting level players, took on tougher assignments against top big men
- Below average rim protector last season, highly foul prone, shot blocking rates were down, solid defensive rebounder
- Strong post defender that holds position inside, may be lacking the mobility to defend in space on isolations
- Middling pick-and-roll defender, tended to be late to cover the roll man, better at switching onto ball handlers for a few dribbles
- Tended to sag into the paint, sometimes was late to close out on perimeter shooters

Norman Powell	Height	Weight	Cap #	Years Left
	6'3"	215	$10.866M	Player Option

	Similar at Age	26 Season	SIMsc
1	Gary Neal	2010-11	929.2
2	Shelvin Mack	2016-17	925.4
3	Eric Gordon	2014-15	924.4
4	Anthony Peeler	1995-96	923.2
5	Voshon Lenard	1999-00	922.2
6	O.J. Mayo	2013-14	919.3
7	Marcus Thornton	2013-14	915.8
8	Malcolm Brogdon	2018-19	914.2
9	Fred Jones	2005-06	912.4
10	Wesley Matthews	2012-13	911.4

Baseline Basic Stats

MPG	PTS	AST	REB	BLK	STL
24.7	10.8	2.2	2.6	0.2	0.8

Advanced Metrics

USG%	3PTA/FGA	FTA/FGA	TS%	eFG%	3PT%
20.4	0.457	0.207	0.567	0.533	0.383
AST%	**TOV%**	**OREB%**	**DREB%**	**STL%**	**BLK%**
12.6	11.4	1.9	10.5	1.7	1.0
PER	**ORTG**	**DRTG**	**WS/48**	**VOL**	
13.80	108.6	108.2	0.103	0.269	

- Regular rotation player for Toronto when healthy, missed games due to a left shoulder subluxation and a fractured left hand
- Had his most productive season as a moderate volume shooter off the bench
- Made almost 40% of his threes last season, good spot-up shooter that can shoot off screens
- Effective at making pull-up jumpers as a pick-and-roll ball handler, can get to the rim on dribble hand-offs
- Good transition player that can run down the wings to get layups or draw shooting fouls, solid at setting up trail threes in transition
- Very good at making backdoor cuts to catch defenders off guard
- Fairly decent secondary playmaker that is willing to make the extra pass, generally limits turnovers
- 2019-20 Defensive Degree of Difficulty: 0.414
- Tends to guard starting level players, occasionally takes on tougher defensive assignments
- Good on-ball defender that can effectively guard multiple positions
- Middling pick-and-roll defender, tends to go too far under screens, can be targeted by bigger screeners on switches
- Generally stays attached to shooters, occasionally gets caught on screens off the ball, consistently closes out in spot-up situations
- Solid defensive rebounder, Steal Percentage is consistent with his career average, set a career high in Block Percentage last season

Terence Davis	Height	Weight	Cap #	Years Left
	6'4"	205	$1.518M	RFA

	Similar at Age	**22**	
		Season	**SIMsc**
1	Reggie Jackson	2012-13	926.2
2	Jodie Meeks	2009-10	917.6
3	Donte DiVincenzo	2018-19	917.2
4	Luke Kennard	2018-19	917.1
5	Chris Carr	1996-97	914.5
6	Josh Hart	2017-18	913.7
7	Norman Powell	2015-16	907.2
8	Gary Harris	2016-17	907.1
9	Wayne Ellington	2009-10	905.5
10	Malik Beasley	2018-19	903.9

Baseline Basic Stats

MPG	PTS	AST	REB	BLK	STL
24.2	10.2	2.0	2.8	0.2	0.8

Advanced Metrics

USG%	3PTA/FGA	FTA/FGA	TS%	eFG%	3PT%
19.2	0.477	0.177	0.576	0.545	0.393
AST%	**TOV%**	**OREB%**	**DREB%**	**STL%**	**BLK%**
13.8	12.3	3.3	12.3	1.7	0.8
PER	**ORTG**	**DRTG**	**WS/48**	**VOL**	
13.97	111.2	107.9	0.114	0.288	

- Regular rotation player for Toronto in his rookie season, made the All-Rookie 2nd Team in 2019-20
- Used as a low volume ball handler and spot-up shooter
- Made almost 39% of his threes in 2019-20, made over 47% of his corner threes last season
- Mostly a stand-still shooter at this stage, has trouble shooting off the dribble or on the move
- Good at making back-door cuts, can selectively hit the offensive glass to score on put-backs
- Uses his quickness to drive by defenders on isolation plays or as a pick-and-roll ball handler
- Fairly solid secondary playmaker that finds open shooters, solid at limiting turnovers
- 2019-20 Defensive Degree of Difficulty: 0.333, tends to guard second unit players
- Below average on-ball defender, had trouble staying with opposing perimeter players
- Average at guarding pick-and-rolls, tends to go too far under screens
- Stays attached to shooters off the ball, consistently closes out on spot-up shooters
- Good defensive rebounding guard, gets steals and blocks at a moderate rate

Chris Boucher	Height	Weight	Cap #	Years Left
	6'9"	200	$6.500M	1

	Similar at Age	27 Season	SIMsc
1	Darius Miles	2008-09	835.7
2	Stromile Swift	2006-07	826.6
3	Bill Walton*	1979-80	825.2
4	Mark Strickland	1997-98	823.4
5	Charles Jones	1984-85	820.3
6	Travis Outlaw	2011-12	810.7
7	Pervis Ellison	1994-95	810.2
8	Gus Gerard	1980-81	809.7
9	Nikola Mirotic	2018-19	808.1
10	Derrick Gervin	1990-91	806.0

Baseline Basic Stats

MPG	PTS	AST	REB	BLK	STL
20.4	7.6	0.9	4.8	1.0	0.6

Advanced Metrics

USG%	3PTA/FGA	FTA/FGA	TS%	eFG%	3PT%
18.8	0.323	0.266	0.531	0.495	0.287
AST%	**TOV%**	**OREB%**	**DREB%**	**STL%**	**BLK%**
5.6	9.4	9.3	24.3	1.4	5.3
PER	**ORTG**	**DRTG**	**WS/48**	**VOL**	
15.38	109.6	101.7	0.111	0.737	

- Played his first season as a regular rotation player for Toronto
- Effective in his role as a low volume, stretch big and rim runner
- Below break-even three-point shooter in his career, mostly a stationary shooter, can set up for trail threes in transition
- High energy big man, dives hard to the rim as a roll man and cutter off the ball, draws fouls at a fairly high rate
- Active offensive rebounder that scores on a high volume of put-backs, runs hard down the floor in transition
- Catch-and-shoot or catch-and-finish player, limited passing skills rarely turns the ball over
- 2019-20 Defensive Degree of Difficulty: 0.299, tends to guard second unit big men
- Good rim protector, excellent shot blocker, good defensive rebounder
- Average on-ball defender, using length to contest shots, can be bullied inside by stronger post players due to his thin frame, highly foul prone
- Middling pick-and-roll defender, mobile enough to defend in space, tends to sag into the paint to allow open perimeter shots
- Consistently comes out to contest perimeter shots in spot-up situations

Patrick McCaw	Height	Weight	Cap #	Years Left
	6'7"	185	$4.000M	UFA

	Similar at Age	24	
		Season	SIMsc
1	Keith Askins	1991-92	913.6
2	Kim English	2012-13	900.2
3	Rudy Fernandez	2009-10	897.1
4	Sasha Vujacic	2008-09	892.2
5	E'Twaun Moore	2013-14	891.2
6	John Salmons	2003-04	889.2
7	Calvin Garrett	1980-81	888.0
8	Francisco Garcia	2005-06	887.0
9	Elliot Williams	2013-14	886.0
10	Solomon Hill	2015-16	884.7

Baseline Basic Stats

MPG	PTS	AST	REB	BLK	STL
17.7	6.1	1.5	2.1	0.2	0.7

Advanced Metrics

USG%	3PTA/FGA	FTA/FGA	TS%	eFG%	3PT%
14.0	0.431	0.199	0.527	0.491	0.349
AST%	**TOV%**	**OREB%**	**DREB%**	**STL%**	**BLK%**
12.2	14.0	2.2	10.0	1.9	0.7
PER	**ORTG**	**DRTG**	**WS/48**	**VOL**	
10.08	105.8	109.2	0.077	0.333	

- Regular rotation player for Toronto, missed games due to a left knee injury and a fractured nose
- Mainly used as a low volume, spot-up shooter, made threes at a below break-even rate last season
- Better in the corners throughout his career, has made over 37% of his career corner threes
- Primarily a stationary spot-up shooter, struggles to shoot on the move or off the dribble
- Rated as average or worse in most offensive situations last season
- Good at making backdoor cuts if defenders aren't paying attention to him
- Mostly a catch-and-shoot player, has some secondary playmaking skills, decent at avoiding turnovers
- 2019-20 Defensive Degree of Difficulty: 0.468
- Drew tougher defensive assignments in his minutes as a second unit player
- Played below average on-ball defense, over-matched against top perimeter players
- Average pick-and-roll defender, better at guarding side pick-and-rolls, tends to allow ball handlers to turn the corner
- Stays attached to shooters off the ball, good at closing out in spot-up situations
- Below average defensive rebounder, gets steals at a fairly high rate

Alex Len

	Height	Weight	Cap #	Years Left
Alex Len	7'0"	250	$2.258M	UFA

	Similar at Age	26	
		Season	SIMsc
1	Cody Zeller	2018-19	914.1
2	Will Perdue	1991-92	908.0
3	Alton Lister	1984-85	907.3
4	Chris Mihm	2005-06	907.3
5	Spencer Hawes	2014-15	906.8
6	Festus Ezeli	2015-16	904.8
7	Todd MacCulloch	2001-02	901.6
8	Chris Kaman	2008-09	900.8
9	Jordan Hill	2013-14	900.4
10	Raef LaFrentz	2002-03	899.2

Baseline Basic Stats

MPG	PTS	AST	REB	BLK	STL
21.4	9.2	1.1	6.1	1.0	0.5

Advanced Metrics

USG%	3PTA/FGA	FTA/FGA	TS%	eFG%	3PT%
19.9	0.115	0.314	0.569	0.540	0.290
AST%	**TOV%**	**OREB%**	**DREB%**	**STL%**	**BLK%**
8.6	13.9	10.2	22.7	1.1	3.6
PER	**ORTG**	**DRTG**	**WS/48**	**VOL**	
16.91	110.7	108.2	0.112	0.372	

- Regular rotation player for Atlanta and Sacramento, traded to Sacramento in February 2020
- Effective in his role as a low volume rim runner, made almost 70% of his shots inside of three feet last season
- Efficient at finishing around the rim as a roll man and cutter, good offensive rebounder that can score on put-backs
- Shot more perimeter shots in Atlanta, outside shot is still not reliable at this stage
- Made less than 30% of his threes, solid mid-range shooter last season
- Catch-and-shoot player, limited passing skills, decent at avoiding turnovers
- 2019-20 Defensive Degree of Difficulty: 0.420
- Guards second unit players, occasionally takes on tougher defensive assignments
- Solid rim protector, good defensive rebounder and shot blocker
- Below average on-ball defender, tends to commit fouls in the post, has trouble defending in space on isolations
- Solid pick-and-roll defender, good in drop coverages, can switch out onto ball handlers for a few dribbles
- Tends to be late when closing out in spot-up situations

DeAndre' Bembry

Height	Weight	Cap #	Years Left
6'5"	210	$1.737M	1

Similar at Age 25

		Season	SIMsc
1	Mitchell Butler	1995-96	935.3
2	Kent Bazemore	2014-15	933.3
3	Iman Shumpert	2015-16	920.4
4	Thabo Sefolosha	2009-10	912.7
5	Lance Stephenson	2015-16	910.7
6	Nando De Colo	2012-13	910.6
7	Shaquille Harrison	2018-19	908.2
8	John Salmons	2004-05	905.0
9	Aaron McKie	1997-98	901.4
10	Keith Bogans	2005-06	900.5

Baseline Basic Stats

MPG	PTS	AST	REB	BLK	STL
20.2	5.8	1.7	3.0	0.3	0.9

Advanced Metrics

USG%	3PTA/FGA	FTA/FGA	TS%	eFG%	3PT%
14.9	0.305	0.223	0.509	0.483	0.284
AST%	**TOV%**	**OREB%**	**DREB%**	**STL%**	**BLK%**
12.8	16.6	3.2	13.8	2.5	1.4
PER	**ORTG**	**DRTG**	**WS/48**	**VOL**	
10.34	99.4	109.1	0.039	0.380	

- Regular rotation player for Atlanta, missed some games due to a right hand and abdominal injury
- Utilized as a low volume, spot-up shooter with limited effectiveness
- Rated as average or worse in every offensive situation
- Has difficulty making shots outside of three feet, Free Throw Percentage is below 60%, Three-Point Percentage is below 30%
- Decent passer, tends to commit turnovers at a fairly high rate
- 2019-20 Defensive Degree of Difficulty: 0.470
- Tends to take on tougher defensive assignments in limited minutes, flashes the ability to guard multiple positions
- May be over-extended in this role, struggled to keep opposing players in front of him in isolation and pick-and-roll situations
- Willing to fight through screens, but can be late to close out on spot-up shooters
- Effective help defender that has increased his Steal Percentage every year
- Solid defensive rebounder for his size that can also rotate inside to occasionally block shots

Matt Thomas	Height	Weight	Cap #	Years Left
	6'4"	190	$1.518M	1

	Similar at Age	25 Season	SIMsc
1	Troy Daniels	2016-17	908.5
2	Damon Jones	2001-02	903.3
3	Bryn Forbes	2018-19	901.6
4	Quinn Cook	2018-19	897.6
5	Wayne Ellington	2012-13	892.5
6	Joe Young	2017-18	891.1
7	Alex Abrines	2018-19	890.5
8	Jeff McInnis	1999-00	889.8
9	E'Twaun Moore	2014-15	888.1
10	Seth Curry	2015-16	887.7

Baseline Basic Stats

MPG	PTS	AST	REB	BLK	STL
19.6	7.6	1.7	1.8	0.1	0.4

Advanced Metrics

USG%	3PTA/FGA	FTA/FGA	TS%	eFG%	3PT%
16.9	0.652	0.134	0.592	0.572	0.417
AST%	**TOV%**	**OREB%**	**DREB%**	**STL%**	**BLK%**
12.2	9.1	1.6	10.2	0.9	0.2
PER	**ORTG**	**DRTG**	**WS/48**	**VOL**	
12.60	115.1	111.6	0.112	0.489	

- Fringe rotation player for Toronto in his rookie season, missed over month due to a fractured finger
- Utilized as a low volume, shooting specialist, made 47.5% of his threes last season
- Very good all-around shooter, knocks down spot-up jumpers, good at running off screens
- Good at making pull-up jumpers as a pick-and-roll ball handler
- Effective at using an on-ball screen to get to the rim or make outside shots on dribble hand-offs
- Good transition player that run down the wings for layups or set up for trail threes in transition
- Not really able to create his own offense, rarely gets to the rim or draws fouls
- Catch-and-shoot player, limited playmaking skills, rarely turns the ball over
- 2019-20 Defensive Degree of Difficulty: 0.287
- Tends to either guard second unit players or play in garbage time
- Below average on-ball defender, lacks the lateral quickness to stay opposing perimeter players
- Fairly solid pick-and-roll defender, fights over screens to contain ball handlers
- Good at closing out on perimeter shooters, tends to get caught on screens off the ball
- Stay-at-home defender, solid defensive rebounder, does not really get steals or blocks

Stanley Johnson	Height	Weight	Cap #	Years Left
	6'6"	245	$3.804M	UFA

Similar at Age 23

		Season	SIMsc
1	Carlos Delfino	2005-06	909.1
2	Justin Anderson	2016-17	904.7
3	Jerald Honeycutt	1997-98	894.9
4	Cleanthony Early	2014-15	891.0
5	James Johnson	2010-11	889.3
6	Wayne Selden	2017-18	889.0
7	Dion Glover	2001-02	886.3
8	Lamond Murray	1996-97	884.8
9	James Anderson	2012-13	883.6
10	Luke Harangody	2010-11	881.4

Baseline Basic Stats

MPG	PTS	AST	REB	BLK	STL
20.4	7.5	1.4	3.5	0.4	0.8

Advanced Metrics

USG%	3PTA/FGA	FTA/FGA	TS%	eFG%	3PT%
19.0	0.419	0.213	0.507	0.479	0.315
AST%	**TOV%**	**OREB%**	**DREB%**	**STL%**	**BLK%**
12.4	13.3	4.0	17.0	2.1	1.6
PER	**ORTG**	**DRTG**	**WS/48**	**VOL**	
11.81	100.3	106.6	0.054	0.654	

- Missed over a month due to a left groin injury, played sparingly for Toronto in his first season with the team
- Utilized as a higher volume secondary ball handler and spot-up shooter
- Has struggled to make outside shots in his career, inconsistent from beyond three feet, has made less than 30% of his career threes
- Rated as below average or worse in most offensive situations last season
- Had some success in a small sample of isolations, made a few no dribble jumpers, could occasionally get to the rim
- Became a fairly solid playmaker that could find open shooters, slightly turnover prone last season
- 2019-20 Defensive Degree of Difficulty: 0.248, only played 150 NBA minutes in 2019-20
- Tended to either guard second unit player or play in garbage time
- Played solid on-ball defense, can potentially guard multiple positions at the NBA level
- Solid team defender that made sound rotations, good pick-and-roll defender that can guard ball handlers and switch onto screeners
- Stays attached to shooters off the ball, good at closing out in spot-up situations
- Active help defender, good defensive rebounder, gets steals at a high rate, Block Percentage spiked to a career high last season

Newcomers

Malachi Flynn	**Height**	**Weight**	**Cap #**	**Years Left**
	6'1"	185	$1.951M	1 + 2 TO

Baseline Basic Stats

MPG	PTS	AST	REB	BLK	STL
18.4	7.1	3.0	1.8	0.1	0.7

Advanced Metrics

USG%	3PTA/FGA	FTA/FGA	TS%	eFG%	3PT%
19.1	0.362	0.233	0.495	0.459	0.329

AST%	TOV%	OREB%	DREB%	STL%	BLK%
25.8	13.9	2.1	8.4	1.9	0.4

PER	ORTG	DRTG	WS/48	VOL
13.32	100.3	100.6	0.067	N/A

- Drafted by Toronto with the 29th overall pick
- Named Mountain West Player and Defensive Player of the Year in 2019-20
- Good ball handler, uses shifty moves to create his own offense on pick-and-rolls or isolations
- Solid playmaker that can find open teammates, controls the ball well to avoid turnovers
- Solid all-around shooter at San Diego State, great spot-up shooter that can run off screens, good at making pull-up jumpers off the dribble
- Lacks ideal length and athleticism, taller players could shoot over him
- Has solid enough lateral quickness to effectively defend smaller guards in isolation situations
- Solid pick-and-roll defender, good at fighting over screens to contain ball handlers, stays in solid position when covering screeners on switches
- Good defensive rebounding guard, led the Mountain West Conference in Steal Percentage and Steals per Game in 2019-20
- Tends to gamble too much, gets caught out of position trying to shoot the gap when covering shooters off the ball

BOSTON CELTICS

Last Season: 48 – 24, Lost in Conference Finals to Miami (2 – 4)

Offensive Rating: 113.3, 4th in the NBA

Defensive Rating: 107.0, 4th in the NBA

Primary Executive: Danny Ainge, President of Basketball Operations

Head Coach: Brad Stevens

Key Roster Changes

Subtractions
Enes Kanter, trade
Vincent Poirier, trade
Gordon Hayward, sign-and-trade
Brad Wanamaker, free agency

Additions
Aaron Nesmith, draft
Payton Pritchard, draft
Tristan Thompson, free agency
Jeff Teague, free agency

Roster

Likely Starting Five

1. *Kemba Walker*
2. *Marcus Smart*
3. *Jayson Tatum*
4. *Jaylen Brown*
5. Daniel Theis

Other Key Rotation Players
Tristan Thompson
Jeff Teague
Grant Williams
Aaron Nesmith

* Italics denotes that a player is likely to be on the floor to close games

Remaining Roster

- Robert Williams
- Semi Ojeleye
- Romeo Langford
- Payton Pritchard
- Carsen Edwards
- Javonte Green
- Tremont Waters, 23, 5'10", 175, LSU (Two-Way)
- Tacko Fall, 25, 7'5", 311, Central Florida (Two-Way)
- Amile Jefferson, 27, 6'9", 222, Duke (Exhibit 10)

SCHREMPF Base Rating: 38.8 (72-game season)

Strengths

- Defensive versatility, front-end talent level and sound team structure
- Chemistry and playoff experience

Question Marks

- Depth beyond their top eight players
- The growth of Tatum and Brown as potential leaders of a championship team

Outlook

- Contender in the Eastern Conference, can finish anywhere within the top six seeds

Veterans

Jayson Tatum

Height	Weight	Cap #	Years Left
6'8"	204	$9.897M	5

Similar at Age **21**

		Season	SIMsc
1	Josh Jackson	2018-19	929.6
2	Paul George	2011-12	918.8
3	Rudy Gay	2007-08	917.5
4	Klay Thompson	2011-12	916.5
5	Wilson Chandler	2008-09	909.0
6	Gordon Hayward	2011-12	906.6
7	Gerald Green	2006-07	904.0
8	Mike Miller	2001-02	901.4
9	Andrew Wiggins	2016-17	897.3
10	Kobe Bryant*	1999-00	895.4

Baseline Basic Stats

MPG	PTS	AST	REB	BLK	STL
32.6	16.3	2.7	5.1	0.6	1.1

Advanced Metrics

USG%	3PTA/FGA	FTA/FGA	TS%	eFG%	3PT%
23.7	0.266	0.256	0.548	0.506	0.365
AST%	**TOV%**	**OREB%**	**DREB%**	**STL%**	**BLK%**
14.2	11.8	3.1	15.5	1.8	1.6
PER	**ORTG**	**DRTG**	**WS/48**	**VOL**	
16.00	107.3	107.6	0.104	0.262	

- Made his first All-Star team last season, named to the All-NBA 3rd Team in 2019-20
- Signed a five-year maximum extension this offseason
- Excelled in his role as Boston's primary scoring option
- Very good one-on-one player that drive to the rim and make pull-up jumpers as a pick-and-roll ball handler and isolation player
- Improving playmaker that can find open shooter and cutters inside, good at avoiding turnovers
- Has made over 40% of his threes in his career, very good spot-up shooter, good screener on pick-and-pops
- Not as effective at moving without the ball, does not really run off screens, rarely cuts off the ball
- 2019-20 Defensive Degree of Difficulty: 0.441
- Tends to guard starter level players, occasionally takes on tougher defensive assignments
- Fairly solid on-ball defender that can capably guard multiple positions
- Great team defender that makes solid rotations, good against pick-and-rolls, effective at switching
- Stays attached to shooters off the ball, consistently closes out on perimeter shooters
- Active help defender, good defensive rebounder, play passing lanes to get steals, fairly good at rotating from the weak side to block shots

Kemba Walker	Height	Weight	Cap #	Years Left
	6'0"	172	$34.379M	1 + PO

	Similar at Age	29 Season	SIMsc
1	Mike Conley	2016-17	920.5
2	Kyle Lowry	2015-16	912.1
3	Mark Price	1993-94	902.9
4	Ish Smith	2017-18	897.9
5	Darren Collison	2016-17	896.7
6	Nick Van Exel	2000-01	894.2
7	John Lucas	2011-12	889.7
8	Jason Terry	2006-07	888.8
9	Eric Bledsoe	2018-19	887.7
10	Tyronn Lue	2006-07	885.6

Baseline Basic Stats

MPG	PTS	AST	REB	BLK	STL
30.6	18.2	5.6	3.4	0.3	1.1

Advanced Metrics

USG%	3PTA/FGA	FTA/FGA	TS%	eFG%	3PT%
27.3	0.466	0.289	0.559	0.507	0.371
AST%	**TOV%**	**OREB%**	**DREB%**	**STL%**	**BLK%**
28.4	12.2	2.0	10.8	1.5	1.0
PER	**ORTG**	**DRTG**	**WS/48**	**VOL**	
19.32	112.6	110.3	0.136	0.509	

- Named to his fourth All-Star in his first season with Boston, missed games due to a sore left knee
- Had his most efficient scoring season in a high usage role as one of Boston's main ball handlers
- Excellent pick-and-roll ball handler that can get to the rim, make pull-up jumpers and make plays for others
- Good at creating his offense on isolation plays, can use an on-ball screen to get to the rim on dribble hand-offs
- Good three-point shooter, made over 38% of his threes last season
- Good spot-up shooter that can shoot off screens and set up for trail threes in transition
- Tends to stand idly on the perimeter without the ball, rarely looks to cut off the ball
- 2019-20 Defensive Degree of Difficulty: 0.426
- Tends to guard starter level players, usually is hidden in lower leverage assignments
- Played solid on-ball defense, quick enough to stay in front of his man, taller players can shoot over him
- Average pick-and-roll defender, funnels his man into help, sometimes goes too far under screens
- Good at closing out on spot-up shooters, tends to get caught on screens off the ball
- Solid defensive rebounder for his size, more of a stay-at-home defender in Boston
- Steal Percentage is down from his career average, set a career high in Block Percentage last season

Jaylen Brown	Height	Weight	Cap #	Years Left
	6'6"	223	$23.735M	3

	Similar at Age	23	
		Season	SIMsc
1	J.R. Smith	2008-09	946.1
2	Quentin Richardson	2003-04	938.0
3	Michael Redd	2002-03	930.6
4	Justin Anderson	2016-17	930.5
5	Jason Richardson	2003-04	925.2
6	C.J. Miles	2010-11	923.6
7	Corey Maggette	2002-03	922.3
8	Tyreke Evans	2012-13	921.7
9	Nick Anderson	1990-91	917.4
10	Kyle Kuzma	2018-19	916.2

Baseline Basic Stats

MPG	PTS	AST	REB	BLK	STL
29.9	15.0	2.3	4.7	0.4	1.0

Advanced Metrics

USG%	3PTA/FGA	FTA/FGA	TS%	eFG%	3PT%
23.8	0.378	0.278	0.562	0.527	0.364
AST%	**TOV%**	**OREB%**	**DREB%**	**STL%**	**BLK%**
11.5	10.5	3.5	14.5	1.7	1.0
PER	**ORTG**	**DRTG**	**WS/48**	**VOL**	
16.48	109.2	107.7	0.115	0.512	

- Had his most productive season in 2019-20, missed a few games due to a series of minor injuries
- Increased his efficiency in a higher volume scoring role, posted his highest True Shooting Percentage in 2019-20
- Made over 38% of his threes last season, has made over 43% of his corner threes in his career
- Good spot-up shooter that improved his ability to shoot off screens
- Drives hard to the rim, good at using an on-ball screen on pick-and-rolls or dribble hand-offs to get to the basket or draw fouls
- Very good transition player that can push the ball up the floor or run down the wings to get easy layups
- Catch-and-shoot player, shows some passing ability, good at avoiding turnovers
- 2019-20 Defensive Degree of Difficulty: 0.473
- Usually guards starter level players, sometimes takes on tougher defensive assignments
- Solid on-ball defender that can capably defend multiple positions
- Fairly good pick-and-roll defender, good at making hard switches, sometimes goes too far under screens
- Occasionally gets caught on screens off the ball, good at closing out on spot-up shooters
- Good defensive rebounder, Steal and Block Percentages are still consistent with his career averages

Marcus Smart	Height	Weight	Cap #	Years Left
	6'3"	227	$13.446M	1

	Similar at Age	25	
		Season	SIMsc
1	Eric Gordon	2013-14	905.3
2	Fred Jones	2004-05	895.9
3	Wesley Matthews	2011-12	889.2
4	Carlos Delfino	2007-08	884.4
5	Khalid Reeves	1997-98	883.0
6	Beno Udrih	2007-08	882.5
7	Jerryd Bayless	2013-14	881.7
8	Norman Powell	2018-19	881.6
9	Jeremy Lin	2013-14	881.0
10	Alonzo Gee	2012-13	877.8

Baseline Basic Stats

MPG	PTS	AST	REB	BLK	STL
27.5	11.0	3.3	3.0	0.3	1.0

Advanced Metrics

USG%	3PTA/FGA	FTA/FGA	TS%	eFG%	3PT%
18.2	0.524	0.230	0.538	0.498	0.357
AST%	**TOV%**	**OREB%**	**DREB%**	**STL%**	**BLK%**
19.9	13.8	2.2	9.8	2.2	1.1
PER	**ORTG**	**DRTG**	**WS/48**	**VOL**	
13.30	108.8	107.5	0.095	0.292	

- Made the All-Defensive 1st Team for the second consecutive season in 2019-20
- Increased his overall production in a role as a low volume, spot-up shooter on offense
- Above break-even three-point shooter last season, decent spot-up shooter
- More effective at making pull-up jumpers as a pick-and-roll ball handler or using an on-ball screen to make shots on dribble hand-offs
- Shot can be streaky, inconsistent in other areas, rated as average in most offensive situations in 2019-20
- Improving as a playmaker, better at controlling the ball, cut his Turnover Percentage last season
- 2019-20 Defensive Degree of Difficulty: 0.506
- Took on tougher defensive assignments against top players across multiple positions
- Good on-ball defender, handles bigger players in the post
- Tends to be too aggressive when guarding perimeter players, prone to committing fouls
- Decent pick-and-roll defender, can contain ball handlers on the perimeter, sometimes goes too far under screens
- Tends to close out too aggressively in spot-up situations, gambles too much when chasing shooters off screens
- Active help defender, consistently gets steals at a high rate, set a career high in Block Percentage last season, solid defensive rebounder

Daniel Theis

	Height	Weight	Cap #	Years Left
Daniel Theis	6'8"	215	$5.000M	UFA

	Similar at Age	27	
		Season	**SIMsc**
1	James Singleton	2008-09	911.6
2	Taj Gibson	2012-13	902.6
3	Amir Johnson	2014-15	899.7
4	Maxi Kleber	2018-19	893.6
5	Cliff Levingston	1987-88	893.5
6	John Henson	2017-18	891.2
7	Louis Amundson	2009-10	890.8
8	David Benoit	1995-96	890.1
9	Brandan Wright	2014-15	889.7
10	Pervis Ellison	1994-95	887.8

Baseline Basic Stats

MPG	PTS	AST	REB	BLK	STL
22.6	8.1	1.2	5.5	1.0	0.6

Advanced Metrics

USG%	3PTA/FGA	FTA/FGA	TS%	eFG%	3PT%
15.4	0.220	0.286	0.588	0.557	0.359
AST%	**TOV%**	**OREB%**	**DREB%**	**STL%**	**BLK%**
9.4	12.2	9.1	18.2	1.3	3.6
PER	**ORTG**	**DRTG**	**WS/48**	**VOL**	
15.68	119.7	105.4	0.154	0.447	

- Became a full-time starter for Boston in his third NBA season
- Increased his production in his role as a low volume, rim runner and stretch big
- Energetic, high motor big man, dives hard to the rim as a roll man and cutter off the ball
- Good offensive rebounder that scores on put-backs, made almost 73% of his shots inside of three feet last season
- Makes threes at just above a break-rate for his career, became a solid mid-range shooter last season
- Decent spot-up shooter, more effective as a screener on pick-and-pops
- Solid passing big man that generally avoids turnovers
- 2019-20 Defensive Degree of Difficulty: 0.456
- Guards other starting big men, typically takes on tougher assignments against elite big men
- Good rim protector, very good shot blocker throughout his career, solid defensive rebounder
- Decent on-ball defender, has the mobility to defend in space, tends to commit fouls in the post
- Average pick-and-roll defender, good at switching, tends to be late to cover the screener in other coverages
- Consistently comes out to contest perimeter shots in spot-up situations

Tristan Thompson

	Height	Weight	Cap #	Years Left
	6'9"	238	$9.258M	1

	Similar at Age	28	
		Season	**SIMsc**
1	Jordan Hill	2015-16	937.3
2	Jayson Williams	1996-97	935.0
3	Kris Humphries	2013-14	929.3
4	Lawrence Funderburke	1998-99	927.2
5	Othella Harrington	2001-02	924.7
6	Kenyon Martin	2005-06	918.0
7	Marcin Gortat	2012-13	917.0
8	Tony Massenburg	1995-96	912.2
9	Gary Trent	2002-03	910.6
10	Trevor Booker	2015-16	909.3

Baseline Basic Stats

MPG	PTS	AST	REB	BLK	STL
23.6	8.7	1.1	6.7	0.7	0.6

Advanced Metrics

USG%	3PTA/FGA	FTA/FGA	TS%	eFG%	3PT%
16.8	0.034	0.297	0.539	0.512	0.278
AST%	**TOV%**	**OREB%**	**DREB%**	**STL%**	**BLK%**
8.8	13.3	12.4	22.1	1.1	2.2
PER	**ORTG**	**DRTG**	**WS/48**	**VOL**	
15.55	111.3	109.3	0.094	0.340	

- Regular starter for Cleveland in his ninth season in the NBA
- Posted a highly effective season in his main role as a low volume, rim runner
- Has been one of the best offensive rebounders in the NBA, career Offensive Rebound Percentage ranks second among all active players
- Energetic big man, scores on a high volume of cuts off the ball and rolls to the rim
- Runs hard down the floor to either get dunks or draw shooting fouls
- No real shooting range outside of three feet, below average post-up player
- Has become a decent passing big man, fairly good at limiting turnovers
- 2019-20 Defensive Degree of Difficulty: 0.494
- Consistently took on tougher interior assignments while serving as a rim protector
- Good rim protector last season, more than doubled his Block Percentage from a season ago, solid defensive rebounder
- Played solid on-ball defense, used length to contest shots inside, improved mobility to guard players in space
- Average pick-and-roll defender, good in drop coverages, had some trouble against ball handlers on switches
- Consistently closed out on perimeter shooters, but could be too aggressive, can allow driving lanes to the rim at times

Jeff Teague

	Height	Weight	Cap #	Years Left
Jeff Teague	6'3"	195	$1.621M	UFA

Similar at Age **31**

		Season	SIMsc
1	Anthony Johnson	2005-06	944.6
2	Byron Scott	1992-93	933.0
3	Brad Davis	1986-87	932.0
4	Deron Williams	2015-16	923.5
5	Jarrett Jack	2014-15	923.4
6	Terry Porter	1994-95	921.8
7	Mike James	2006-07	920.7
8	Ramon Sessions	2017-18	920.1
9	Joe Dumars*	1994-95	912.8
10	Beno Udrih	2013-14	911.9

Baseline Basic Stats

MPG	PTS	AST	REB	BLK	STL
23.2	8.8	3.8	2.1	0.1	0.8

Advanced Metrics

USG%	3PTA/FGA	FTA/FGA	TS%	eFG%	3PT%
18.9	0.262	0.328	0.545	0.485	0.357
AST%	**TOV%**	**OREB%**	**DREB%**	**STL%**	**BLK%**
28.3	16.2	1.6	8.3	1.6	0.8
PER	**ORTG**	**DRTG**	**WS/48**	**VOL**	
14.28	110.0	112.2	0.093	0.394	

- Regular rotation player for Minnesota and Atlanta last season
- Playing time decreased after the trade to Atlanta in January 2020
- Had to adapt to a lower usage backup point guard role for the Hawks
- Still has solid playmaking skills, but can be somewhat turnover prone
- More effective as a pick-and-roll ball handler in Minnesota, could get to the rim and make a few shots off the dribble
- Above average spot-up shooter, made almost 38% of his threes for Minnesota, but was only break-even for Atlanta
- 2019-20 Defensive Degree of Difficulty: 0.375
- Mostly guarded higher-end second unit players or lower leverage starters
- More of a team defender at this stage, susceptible to giving up drives to quicker guards as an on-ball defender
- Good pick-and-roll defender that can fight through screens or funnel opposing players into help
- Generally stays attached to shooters, consistently will close out in spot-up situations
- More of a stay-at-home defender now, steal and block rates have dropped, Defensive Rebound Percentage increased last season

Grant Williams	Height	Weight	Cap #	Years Left
	6'6"	236	$2.499M	2 Team Options

	Similar at Age	21	
		Season	SIMsc
1	Kirk Snyder	2004-05	877.0
2	Omari Spellman	2018-19	874.4
3	OG Anunoby	2018-19	873.0
4	Timothe Luwawu-Cabarrot	2016-17	869.8
5	Mickael Pietrus	2003-04	869.6
6	Shawne Williams	2007-08	869.0
7	K.J. McDaniels	2014-15	867.1
8	Casey Jacobsen	2002-03	863.8
9	JaKarr Sampson	2014-15	860.8
10	Sylvester Gray	1988-89	859.5

Baseline Basic Stats

MPG	PTS	AST	REB	BLK	STL
19.6	6.8	1.3	3.4	0.4	0.7

Advanced Metrics

USG%	3PTA/FGA	FTA/FGA	TS%	eFG%	3PT%
14.1	0.325	0.266	0.528	0.490	0.289
AST%	**TOV%**	**OREB%**	**DREB%**	**STL%**	**BLK%**
10.5	15.0	5.4	13.1	1.7	1.9
PER	**ORTG**	**DRTG**	**WS/48**	**VOL**	
10.56	107.5	107.1	0.093	0.367	

- Regular rotation player for Boston in his rookie season
- Utilized as a low volume, stretch big on offense, struggled to make outside shots, made only 25% of his threes last season
- Rated as average or worse in most offensive situations last season
- Most effective at posting up smaller players or crashing the offensive boards to score on put-backs
- Dives hard to the rim on cuts off the ball or rolls to the rim, draws fouls at a solid rate, does not have the lift to finish in traffic
- Shows some passing skills, somewhat turnover prone as a rookie
- 2019-20 Defensive Degree of Difficulty: 0.351
- Tended to guard second unit player, occasionally drew some tougher assignments
- Played below average on-ball defense, fairly foul prone
- Quicker players could drive by him on isolations, longer big men could shoot over him in the post
- Solid team defender that usually makes sound rotations, good at guarding pick-and-rolls, effective at making hard switches
- Consistently closes out on perimeter shooters, tends to get caught on screens off the ball
- Decent defensive rebounder, good weak side shot blocker, gets steals at a moderate rate

Robert Williams	Height	Weight	Cap #	Years Left
	6'8"	237	$2.030M	Team Option

	Similar at Age	22	
		Season	SIMsc
1	Quincy Acy	2012-13	841.2
2	Hassan Whiteside	2011-12	839.5
3	Montrezl Harrell	2015-16	837.6
4	Sam Williams	1981-82	833.4
5	Sean Williams	2008-09	833.2
6	Deyonta Davis	2018-19	830.5
7	Don Reid	1995-96	828.1
8	Michael Stewart	1997-98	827.5
9	Jeff Ayres	2009-10	826.5
10	Chuck Hayes	2005-06	826.0

Baseline Basic Stats

MPG	PTS	AST	REB	BLK	STL
16.3	5.4	0.7	4.5	1.0	0.5

Advanced Metrics

USG%	3PTA/FGA	FTA/FGA	TS%	eFG%	3PT%
13.5	0.010	0.327	0.666	0.654	0.079
AST%	**TOV%**	**OREB%**	**DREB%**	**STL%**	**BLK%**
7.3	14.8	10.8	20.7	1.7	6.5
PER	**ORTG**	**DRTG**	**WS/48**	**VOL**	
18.90	127.2	102.5	0.203	0.526	

- Missed two months due to a sore left hip, regular rotation player for Boston in the playoffs
- Highly efficient in his role as a low volume rim runner, posted a True Shooting Percentage of almost 73%
- Active rim runner, dives hard to the rim, very good roll man and cutter off the ball
- Good offensive rebounder that efficiently scores on put-backs, draws fouls at a high rate
- Flashed some ability to make mid-range shots, solid percentage from mid-range in a small sample of attempts
- Improving to become a decent passing big man, slightly turnover prone at this stage
- 2019-20 Defensive Degree of Difficulty: 0.343, tends to guard second unit big men
- Very good defensive rebounder and shot blocker, gets steals at a high rate
- Average rim protector, highly foul prone, undisciplined with his positioning
- Played solid on-ball defense, strong post defender, shows enough mobility to defend in space on isolations
- Below average pick-and-roll defender, still learning NBA defensive schemes, gets confused when making rotations
- Good at closing out on perimeter shooters in spot-up situations

Semi Ojeleye

	Height	Weight	Cap #	Years Left
Semi Ojeleye	6'6"	235	$1.753M	UFA

	Similar at Age	25	
		Season	SIMsc
1	Treveon Graham	2018-19	931.6
2	Joe Harris	2016-17	925.7
3	Abdel Nader	2018-19	921.7
4	Yakhouba Diawara	2007-08	909.4
5	Chase Budinger	2013-14	902.1
6	Glenn Robinson III	2018-19	901.5
7	Luke Babbitt	2014-15	897.6
8	Derrick Williams	2016-17	895.4
9	Sam Mack	1995-96	893.7
10	Danuel House	2018-19	892.9

Baseline Basic Stats

MPG	PTS	AST	REB	BLK	STL
17.9	5.9	0.9	2.5	0.2	0.4

Advanced Metrics

USG%	3PTA/FGA	FTA/FGA	TS%	eFG%	3PT%
12.8	0.615	0.173	0.566	0.541	0.373
AST%	**TOV%**	**OREB%**	**DREB%**	**STL%**	**BLK%**
6.9	9.1	3.5	11.8	1.1	0.7
PER	**ORTG**	**DRTG**	**WS/48**	**VOL**	
9.82	113.2	112.3	0.082	0.406	

- Regular rotation player for Boston in his third NBA season
- Predominantly a very low volume, spot-up shooter in his career, made almost 38% of his threes last season
- Almost strictly a stationary spot-up shooter, flashed some ability to be an effective screener on pick-and-pops
- Decent rim runner, good at rolling to the rim, scores on a relatively high volume of cuts, runs hard down the floor in transition
- Does not create his own offense, limited playmaking skills, rarely turns the ball over
- 2019-20 Defensive Degree of Difficulty: 0.378
- Tends to guard second unit players, occasionally draws tougher defensive assignments
- Solid on-ball defender, good at guarding wing players, has some trouble guarding bigger post players
- Below average at guarding pick-and-rolls last season, struggled to stay with quicker ball handlers
- Fights through screens off the ball, tended to be late when closing out on perimeter shooters
- Stay-at-home defender, does not really get blocks or steals, solid defensive rebounder

Romeo Langford	Height	Weight	Cap #	Years Left
	6'4"	216	$3.631M	2 Team Options

Similar at Age 20

		Season	SIMsc
1	Josh Okogie	2018-19	891.3
2	Gary Harris	2014-15	888.8
3	Austin Rivers	2012-13	870.4
4	Frank Jackson	2018-19	866.0
5	DeShawn Stevenson	2001-02	865.5
6	Jordan Adams	2014-15	863.2
7	Hamidou Diallo	2018-19	862.3
8	Derrick Jones, Jr.	2017-18	860.2
9	Xavier Henry	2011-12	856.2
10	Kentavious Caldwell-Pope	2013-14	854.2

Baseline Basic Stats

MPG	PTS	AST	REB	BLK	STL
20.1	6.7	1.4	2.4	0.2	0.6

Advanced Metrics

USG%	3PTA/FGA	FTA/FGA	TS%	eFG%	3PT%
14.7	0.341	0.268	0.513	0.472	0.308
AST%	**TOV%**	**OREB%**	**DREB%**	**STL%**	**BLK%**
9.0	11.3	3.9	8.9	1.3	1.3
PER	**ORTG**	**DRTG**	**WS/48**	**VOL**	
9.78	105.6	111.1	0.062	0.753	

- Fringe rotation player for Boston in his rookie season
- Missed games due to a strained right adductor, underwent surgery on his right wrist in September 2020
- Used as a spot-up shooter in a very low volume role, struggled to shoot efficiently
- Rated as below average or worse in most offensive situations, made less 20% of his threes last season
- Most effective in off-ball situations, showed some ability to cut off the ball, good at crashing the offensive boards to score on put-backs
- Limited playmaking skills at this stage, good at avoiding turnovers
- 2019-20 Defensive Degree of Difficulty: 0.292
- Tended to either guard second unit players or play in garbage time
- Decent on-ball defender, has the potential to guard multiple positions
- Good at playing pick-and-roll defense, can funnel his man into help or fight over screens to contain the ball handler
- Good at closing out on perimeter shooters, tends to get caught on screens off the ball
- Middling defensive rebounder, does not really get steals, good at rotating from the weak side to block shots

Carsen Edwards

	Height	Weight	Cap #	Years Left
	5'11"	200	$1.518M	1 + TO

	Similar at Age	21 Season	SIMsc
1	Shannon Brown	2006-07	874.1
2	Jerome Robinson	2018-19	873.7
3	Malik Beasley	2017-18	870.1
4	Jawun Evans	2017-18	869.9
5	William Avery	2000-01	866.5
6	Khalid El-Amin	2000-01	866.3
7	Elie Okobo	2018-19	861.4
8	Shane Larkin	2013-14	860.2
9	Terrence Ross	2012-13	854.0
10	Rashad Vaughn	2017-18	853.9

Baseline Basic Stats

MPG	PTS	AST	REB	BLK	STL
20.8	8.2	2.0	2.4	0.2	0.7

Advanced Metrics

USG%	3PTA/FGA	FTA/FGA	TS%	eFG%	3PT%
17.0	0.429	0.182	0.510	0.482	0.354
AST%	**TOV%**	**OREB%**	**DREB%**	**STL%**	**BLK%**
12.1	10.4	1.9	10.4	1.8	0.7
PER	**ORTG**	**DRTG**	**WS/48**	**VOL**	
9.99	104.1	109.2	0.077	0.574	

- Fringe rotation player for Boston in his rookie season
- Used as a lower volume shooter off the bench, struggled to shoot efficiently
- Made threes at a below break-even rate, less effective as a catch-and-shoot player
- Better at shooting off screens and making pull-up jumpers as a pick-and-roll ball handler
- Below average or worse in most offensive situations as a rookie
- Struggled to finish shots at the rim, rarely drew fouls
- Mainly a catch-and-shoot player in the NBA, not really a playmaker, rarely turned the ball over
- 2019-20 Defensive Degree of Difficulty: 0.272
- Tended to either guard second unit players or play in garbage time
- Played decent on-ball defense, quick enough to stay with opposing guards, taller perimeter players could shoot over him
- Average pick-and-roll defender, tended to go too far under screens to allow open outside shots
- Stays attached to shooters off the ball, good at closing out in spot-up situations
- Good defensive rebounding guard, gets steals and blocks at a fairly solid rate

Javonte Green	Height	Weight	Cap #	Years Left
	6'4"	220	$1.518M	RFA

	Similar at Age	26	
		Season	SIMsc
1	David Nwaba	2018-19	937.2
2	Jud Buechler	1994-95	928.9
3	Adrian Griffin	2000-01	921.9
4	Alonzo Gee	2013-14	917.5
5	Brandon Paul	2017-18	901.4
6	Thabo Sefolosha	2010-11	900.7
7	Greg Buckner	2002-03	900.7
8	Sam Young	2011-12	896.3
9	Kenny Battle	1990-91	895.3
10	Larry Stewart	1994-95	894.7

Baseline Basic Stats

MPG	PTS	AST	REB	BLK	STL
16.5	4.6	1.0	2.5	0.2	0.7

Advanced Metrics

USG%	3PTA/FGA	FTA/FGA	TS%	eFG%	3PT%
13.7	0.285	0.236	0.555	0.529	0.312
AST%	**TOV%**	**OREB%**	**DREB%**	**STL%**	**BLK%**
8.3	13.6	4.5	13.3	2.3	1.3
PER	**ORTG**	**DRTG**	**WS/48**	**VOL**	
11.78	109.6	106.4	0.091	0.377	

- Fringe rotation player for Boston in his rookie season
- Used in a low volume role as an energy guard off the bench
- Very good transition player that can push the ball up the floor and run the wings to get layups or draw fouls
- Less effective in a half court set, rated as below average or worse in most offensive situations as a rookie
- Not really an outside shooter, made less than 30% of his threes last season, more comfortable from mid-range in a small sample of shots
- Catch-and-shoot player at this stage, limited playmaking skills, good at avoiding turnovers
- 2019-20 Defensive Degree of Difficulty: 0.317, tends to guard second unit level players
- Decent on-ball defender that flashes the ability to defend multiple positions
- Below average pick-and-roll defender, tends to go too far under screens, has trouble guarding bigger players on switches
- Stays attached to shooters off the ball, consistently closes out in spot-up situations
- Active help defender, good defensive rebounder, gets steals and blocks at a fairly high rate

Newcomers

Aaron Nesmith	**Height**	**Weight**	**Cap #**	**Years Left**
	6'6"	213	$3.458M	1 + 2 TO

Baseline Basic Stats

MPG	PTS	AST	REB	BLK	STL
20.1	7.9	1.3	2.6	0.2	0.7

Advanced Metrics

USG%	3PTA/FGA	FTA/FGA	TS%	eFG%	3PT%
19.3	0.455	0.212	0.538	0.508	0.367
AST%	**TOV%**	**OREB%**	**DREB%**	**STL%**	**BLK%**
9.3	11.2	3.4	10.9	1.6	1.1
PER	**ORTG**	**DRTG**	**WS/48**	**VOL**	
12.91	102.4	106.1	0.051	N/A	

- Drafted by Boston with the 14th overall pick
- Missed most of the 2019-20 due to a stress fracture in his right foot
- Excellent all-around shooter at Vanderbilt, made 41% of his career threes
- Great spot-up shooter, can shoot off screens, sets up for trail threes in transition, good at making side-step threes off a pump fake
- Mostly a catch-and-shoot player, ball handling and playmaking skills are limited
- Only can attack the rim if defenders close too aggressively, willing to absorb contact to draw fouls
- Good physical tools on defense, solid length and athleticism, still unpolished defensively
- Solid on-ball defender that can guard multiple positions, solid against pick-and-rolls, will fight over screens to contain ball handlers
- Good at roaming on the weak side, gets steals and blocks at a solid rate, fairly good defensive rebounder
- Tends to gamble off the ball, loses focus at times, can get caught ball watching

Payton Pritchard

Height	Weight	Cap #	Years Left
6'2"	190	$2.036M	1 + 2 TO

Baseline Basic Stats

MPG	PTS	AST	REB	BLK	STL
15.7	6.1	2.2	1.6	0.1	0.6

Advanced Metrics

USG%	3PTA/FGA	FTA/FGA	TS%	eFG%	3PT%
19.9	0.409	0.217	0.499	0.467	0.343

AST%	TOV%	OREB%	DREB%	STL%	BLK%
22.7	14.9	2.2	8.9	1.9	0.4

PER	ORTG	DRTG	WS/48	VOL
12.57	98.9	102.8	0.055	N/A

- Drafted by Boston with the 26th overall pick
- Consensus 1st Team All-American, named Pac-12 Player of the Year in 2019-20
- Good all-around shooter at Oregon, has deep range, solid shooter off the dribble, good spot-up shooter that can also shoot off screens
- Improving playmaker throughout his career, plays with a score-first mindset, does not always see the whole floor
- Lacks ideal quickness and ball handling skills to create his own shot in the NBA, crafty finisher, may be able to create his own offense in short bursts
- Hidden in zones for chunks of his career, may be physically limited on defense
- Also hidden in favorable matchups when playing man defense, middling on-ball defender
- Average pick-and-roll defender, tends to go too far under screens to allow open outside shots
- Can get caught on screens off the ball, tends to be late when closing out on perimeter shooters
- Good at playing passing lanes to get steals, solid defensive rebounding guard

MIAMI HEAT

Last Season: 44 – 29, Lost NBA Finals to L.A. Lakers (2 – 4)

Offensive Rating: 112.5, 7th in the NBA

Defensive Rating: 109.5, 11th in the NBA

Primary Executive: Pat Riley, Team President

Head Coach: Erik Spoelstra

Key Roster Changes

Subtractions
Jae Crowder, free agency
Derrick Jones, Jr., free agency
Solomon Hill, free agency

Additions
Precious Achiuwa, draft
Avery Bradley, free agency
Maurice Harkless, free agency

Roster

Likely Starting Five

1. *Goran Dragic*
2. Avery Bradley
3. *Jimmy Butler*
4. Duncan Robinson
5. *Bam Adebayo*

Other Key Rotation Players
Tyler Herro
Kendrick Nunn
Andre Iguodala
Kelly Olynyk
Meyers Leonard
Maurice Harkless

* Italics denotes that a player is likely to be on the floor to close games

Remaining Roster

- Precious Achiuwa
- KZ Okpala
- Chris Silva
- Udonis Haslem
- Gabe Vincent, 24, 6'3", 200, UC Santa Barbara (Two-Way)
- Breein Tyree, 23, 6'2", 195, Mississippi (Exhibit 10)
- Paul Eboua, 20, 6'8", 214, Cameroon (Exhibit 10)
- Max Strus, 24, 6'6", 215, DePaul (Exhibit 10)
- B.J. Johnson, 25, 6'7", 200, LaSalle (Exhibit 10)

SCHREMPF Base Rating: 38.3 (72-game season)

Strengths

- Sound system that deploys talent to its fullest capabilities
- Effectively utilizes creative defensive tactics and movement-based schemes on offense
- Strong continuity and winning culture

Question Marks

- Consistent secondary scoring to ease the burden on Jimmy Butler in critical situations
- Health effects related to the quick turnaround from the last NBA Finals to the start of the 2020-21 season

Outlook

- Contender in the Eastern Conference, could finish anywhere within the top six seeds

Veterans

Jimmy Butler

	Height	Weight	Cap #	Years Left
	6'7"	230	$34.379M	1 + PO

	Similar at Age	30 Season	SIMsc
1	Clyde Drexler*	1992-93	907.8
2	Paul Pierce	2007-08	902.5
3	James Worthy*	1991-92	889.8
4	Stephen Jackson	2008-09	887.8
5	Glenn Robinson	2002-03	882.6
6	Scottie Pippen*	1995-96	881.9
7	Matt Harpring	2006-07	881.2
8	Jerry Stackhouse	2004-05	880.2
9	Manu Ginobili	2007-08	878.5
10	Bryon Russell	2000-01	876.4

Baseline Basic Stats

MPG	PTS	AST	REB	BLK	STL
34.2	18.9	4.0	5.6	0.4	1.4

Advanced Metrics

USG%	3PTA/FGA	FTA/FGA	TS%	eFG%	3PT%
24.7	0.208	0.461	0.566	0.491	0.315
AST%	**TOV%**	**OREB%**	**DREB%**	**STL%**	**BLK%**
21.2	11.1	5.3	14.1	2.3	1.2
PER	**ORTG**	**DRTG**	**WS/48**	**VOL**	
20.58	116.5	107.1	0.175	0.403	

- Made his fifth All-Star team last season, named to the All-NBA 3rd Team in 2019-20
- Increased his production in his role as Miami's primary scoring option
- Aggressively drives to the basket as a pick-and-roll ball handler and isolation player
- Made 65.5% of his shots inside of three feet last season, drew fouls at a very high rate
- Good at bullying smaller perimeter players in the post, prefers to post up on the right block
- Very good cutter off the ball, great at running down the wings to score in transition
- Good playmaker, set a career high in Assist Percentage, consistently avoids turnovers
- Struggled to make jump shots in 2019-20, made less than 25% of his threes last season
- 2019-20 Defensive Degree of Difficulty: 0.511
- Tends to draw tough assignments against top perimeter players
- Good on-ball defender that can guard multiple positions
- Solid pick-and-roll defender, good at switching, occasionally will go too far under screens
- Generally stays attached to shooters and contests perimeter shots, had trouble defending dribble hand-offs last season
- Active help defender, good rebounder that consistently gets steals at a high rate, posted a career high in Block Percentage last season

Bam Adebayo	Height	Weight	Cap #	Years Left
	6'9"	255	$5.115M	5

	Similar at Age	22	
		Season	SIMsc
1	Brian Grant	1994-95	920.6
2	Al Horford	2008-09	917.6
3	Derrick Favors	2013-14	914.9
4	Julius Randle	2016-17	914.7
5	Carlos Boozer	2003-04	912.8
6	Terrence Jones	2013-14	905.7
7	Al Jefferson	2006-07	891.9
8	Karl Malone*	1985-86	891.6
9	Nene	2004-05	891.0
10	Victor Alexander	1991-92	890.3

Baseline Basic Stats

MPG	PTS	AST	REB	BLK	STL
31.4	15.9	2.5	8.8	1.0	0.8

Advanced Metrics

USG%	3PTA/FGA	FTA/FGA	TS%	eFG%	3PT%
21.7	0.037	0.440	0.599	0.556	0.313
AST%	**TOV%**	**OREB%**	**DREB%**	**STL%**	**BLK%**
17.5	14.9	8.6	22.4	1.4	3.0
PER	**ORTG**	**DRTG**	**WS/48**	**VOL**	
20.37	116.5	105.5	0.167	0.489	

- Made his first All-Star team last season, named to the All-Defensive 2nd Team in 2019-20
- Excelled in his role as a moderate volume rim runner, made almost 73% of his shots inside of three feet last season
- Dives hard to the rim as a roll man and cutter off the ball, draws fouls at a high rate
- Solid offensive rebounder that can score on put-backs, runs hard down the floor in transition
- Has become one of the NBA's best passing big men, great at hitting cutters or finding open shooters, slightly turnover prone
- More effective at making shorter mid-range shots, inconsistent shooter from beyond 16 feet
- 2019-20 Defensive Degree of Difficulty: 0.471, draws tough assignments against top big men
- Good defensive rebounder and shot blocker, fairly solid rim protector
- Good on-ball defender, great at holding position in the post, mobile enough to defend in space
- Fairly solid pick-and-roll defender, better at defending side pick-and-rolls, good at switching, sometimes can be late to rotate back to the screener
- Willing to contest perimeter shots, tends to be either late or too aggressively when closing out

Goran Dragić	Height	Weight	Cap #	Years Left
	6'3"	190	$18.000M	Team Option

	Similar at Age	**33**	
		Season	**SIMsc**
1	Terry Porter	1996-97	933.4
2	Byron Scott	1994-95	928.1
3	Chauncey Billups	2009-10	915.2
4	Sam Cassell	2002-03	911.6
5	Kirk Hinrich	2013-14	909.7
6	Dell Curry	1997-98	909.2
7	Mike James	2008-09	908.9
8	Tony Parker	2015-16	907.7
9	John Lucas	1986-87	905.3
10	Vernon Maxwell	1998-99	904.2

Baseline Basic Stats

MPG	PTS	AST	REB	BLK	STL
24.9	11.0	3.6	2.3	0.1	0.8

Advanced Metrics

USG%	3PTA/FGA	FTA/FGA	TS%	eFG%	3PT%
22.6	0.387	0.280	0.538	0.494	0.363
AST%	**TOV%**	**OREB%**	**DREB%**	**STL%**	**BLK%**
24.5	13.5	2.0	9.4	1.5	0.5
PER	**ORTG**	**DRTG**	**WS/48**	**VOL**	
14.70	107.4	109.3	0.098	0.375	

- Had a bounce-back season after playing as Miami's sixth man during the regular season
- Used as a high volume scoring guard, maintained his effective when he became a starter in the playoffs
- Good one-on-one player that can change speeds to get to the rim or create space to take pull-up jumpers, drew fouls at a higher rate
- Good at making outside shots or driving to the rim on dribble hand-offs, good cutter off the ball
- Solid three-point shooter throughout his career, good spot-up shooter that can also run off screens
- Very good playmaker that avoids turnovers, better at making interior passes
- 2019-20 Defensive Degree of Difficulty: 0.328, tended to guard second unit level players
- Decent on-ball defender, solid against opposing guards, taller perimeter players could post him up inside
- Solid at guarding pick-and-rolls, good at going over screens to contain ball handlers, could sometimes be targeted by bigger screeners on switches
- Generally stays attached to shooters off the ball and contests shots, had some trouble preventing open jumpers on dribble hand-offs
- Stay-at-home defender, fairly solid defensive rebounder, Steal Percentage was down to a career low last season

Duncan Robinson	Height	Weight	Cap #	Years Left
	6'7"	215	$1.664M	RFA

	Similar at Age	25 **Season**	**SIMsc**
1	Danuel House	2018-19	930.9
2	Tony Snell	2016-17	922.3
3	Bojan Bogdanovic	2014-15	918.4
4	Chase Budinger	2013-14	914.1
5	Jason Kapono	2006-07	913.1
6	Steve Novak	2008-09	912.1
7	Joe Harris	2016-17	911.3
8	Antoine Wright	2009-10	908.8
9	Sam Mack	1995-96	905.5
10	Allen Crabbe	2017-18	904.9

Baseline Basic Stats

MPG	PTS	AST	REB	BLK	STL
22.7	8.7	1.2	2.9	0.2	0.5

Advanced Metrics

USG%	3PTA/FGA	FTA/FGA	TS%	eFG%	3PT%
16.4	0.696	0.143	0.574	0.551	0.376
AST%	**TOV%**	**OREB%**	**DREB%**	**STL%**	**BLK%**
7.0	9.2	1.6	11.4	1.2	0.7
PER	**ORTG**	**DRTG**	**WS/48**	**VOL**	
10.75	109.1	111.9	0.079	0.396	

- Became a full-time starter for Miami in his second NBA season
- Greatly increased his production in his role as a low volume shooting specialist
- Excellent all-around shooter, made almost 45% of his threes last season
- Great spot-up shooter that can also run off screens, good at setting up for trail threes in transition
- Good on dribble hand-offs, can make stationary outside jumpers or use the screen to get to the rim
- Can make pull-up jumpers as a pick-and-roll ball handler, good at making backdoor cuts if defenders overplay his shot
- Limited ability to create his own shot or make plays for others, rarely turns the ball over
- 2019-20 Defensive Degree of Difficulty: 0.381
- Tends to be hidden in favorable matchups against lower leverage players
- Average on-ball defender, has trouble staying with quicker players, better against bigger players in the post
- Below average at guarding pick-and-rolls, generally struggled to make effective rotations, can be exposed in space by better ball handlers
- Stays attached to shooters off the ball, consistently closes out in spot-up situations
- Stay-at-home defender, solid defensive rebounder, does not really get steals or blocks

Avery Bradley	Height	Weight	Cap #	Years Left
	6'3"	180	$5.635M	Team Option

	Similar at Age	29	
		Season	SIMsc
1	Eldridge Recasner	1996-97	944.0
2	Charlie Bell	2008-09	939.7
3	E'Twaun Moore	2018-19	935.4
4	George Hill	2015-16	926.9
5	C.J. Watson	2013-14	925.6
6	Matt Maloney	2000-01	923.6
7	Brian Roberts	2014-15	921.8
8	Rex Chapman	1996-97	920.2
9	Eddie House	2007-08	918.5
10	Jerryd Bayless	2017-18	917.9

Baseline Basic Stats

MPG	PTS	AST	REB	BLK	STL
21.8	8.1	2.3	1.9	0.1	0.7

Advanced Metrics

USG%	3PTA/FGA	FTA/FGA	TS%	eFG%	3PT%
17.2	0.402	0.124	0.528	0.506	0.374
AST%	**TOV%**	**OREB%**	**DREB%**	**STL%**	**BLK%**
13.2	12.1	2.0	8.2	1.6	0.4
PER	**ORTG**	**DRTG**	**WS/48**	**VOL**	
10.47	104.3	109.8	0.076	0.297	

- Starter for the Lakers when healthy, missed a month due to a right leg injury, opted out of the Orlando bubble
- Mainly used as a low volume, spot-up shooter, made threes at above the league average last season
- Mostly a stationary spot-up shooter, average at shooting off screens
- Good at getting to the rim on dribble hand-offs, effective at running down the wings in transition
- Rated as average or worse in most offensive situations last season
- Catch-and-shoot player at this stage, decent passer in previous seasons, avoids turnovers
- 2019-20 Defensive Degree of Difficulty: 0.538
- Had the 14th toughest set of matchups among players that played 500 or more minutes
- Solid on-ball defender that can defend both guard spots, had a little bit of trouble against quicker guards
- Solid at guarding pick-and-rolls, good at containing ball handlers, can be targeted by bigger screeners on switches
- Stays attached to shooters off the ball, consistently closes out in spot-up situations
- Stay-at-home defender, decent defensive rebounder, Steal and Block Percentages are still consistent with his career averages

Tyler Herro	Height	Weight	Cap #	Years Left
	6'5"	200	$3.822M	2 Team Options

	Similar at Age	20 Season	SIMsc
1	Daequan Cook	2007-08	936.8
2	Malik Monk	2018-19	918.0
3	Emmanuel Mudiay	2016-17	917.9
4	Ben McLemore	2013-14	909.8
5	Jamal Murray	2017-18	909.7
6	Zach LaVine	2015-16	901.1
7	Malik Beasley	2016-17	900.3
8	D'Angelo Russell	2016-17	899.0
9	Frank Jackson	2018-19	895.5
10	Martell Webster	2006-07	893.5

Baseline Basic Stats

MPG	PTS	AST	REB	BLK	STL
25.9	12.0	2.1	2.9	0.2	0.7

Advanced Metrics

USG%	3PTA/FGA	FTA/FGA	TS%	eFG%	3PT%
22.5	0.475	0.169	0.549	0.518	0.397
AST%	**TOV%**	**OREB%**	**DREB%**	**STL%**	**BLK%**
13.5	11.0	1.6	12.3	1.2	0.6
PER	**ORTG**	**DRTG**	**WS/48**	**VOL**	
13.14	105.2	111.3	0.072	0.274	

- Played in Miami's regular rotation as a rookie, named to the All-Rookie 2nd Team in 2019-20
- Productive in his role as a moderate volume, shooting specialist off the bench
- Made almost 39% of his threes as a rookie, made almost 47% of his corner threes
- Good all-around shooter, knocks down spot-up jumpers, can run off screens, good at making outside shots off dribble hand-offs
- Inconsistent shooter off the dribble, can be streaky, prone to taking wild shots
- Not quite as effective off the ball when not directly involved in the play, rarely cuts to the rim
- Decent secondary playmaker, willing to make the extra pass, good at limiting turnovers
- 2019-20 Defensive Degree of Difficulty: 0.315, tends to guard second unit level players
- Tended to be hidden in favorable matchups, played decent on-ball defense
- Solid team defender that makes sound rotations, fairly good at going over screens on pick-and-rolls
- Stays attached to shooters off the ball, consistently contests perimeter shots in spot-up situations
- Stay-at-home defender, solid defensive rebounder, rarely gets blocks or steals

Kendrick Nunn

Height	Weight	Cap #	Years Left
6'2"	190	$1.664M	RFA

	Similar at Age	24 Season	SIMsc
1	Daniel Gibson	2010-11	954.9
2	Brandon Knight	2015-16	934.4
3	Toney Douglas	2010-11	933.6
4	Avery Bradley	2014-15	928.6
5	Leandro Barbosa	2006-07	926.3
6	Ben Gordon	2007-08	925.4
7	Terry Rozier	2018-19	924.7
8	Jimmer Fredette	2013-14	920.0
9	George Hill	2010-11	917.6
10	Evan Fournier	2016-17	913.8

Baseline Basic Stats

MPG	PTS	AST	REB	BLK	STL
26.2	12.5	3.0	2.7	0.2	0.8

Advanced Metrics

USG%	3PTA/FGA	FTA/FGA	TS%	eFG%	3PT%
23.1	0.423	0.169	0.543	0.511	0.359
AST%	**TOV%**	**OREB%**	**DREB%**	**STL%**	**BLK%**
19.5	11.1	1.6	9.5	1.5	0.7
PER	**ORTG**	**DRTG**	**WS/48**	**VOL**	
14.25	106.5	111.7	0.079	0.452	

- Named to the All-Rookie 1st Team, runner-up for the Rookie of the Year award in 2019-20
- Fairly effective in his role as a higher volume ball handler for Miami
- Very good pick-and-roll ball handler that can make pull-up jumpers, drive to the rim and set up others
- Solid playmaker that can kick the ball out to open shooters, good at limiting turnovers
- Fairly solid three-point shooter that made threes around the league average
- Knocks down spot-up jumpers, good at shooting off screens or dribble hand-offs
- Has difficulty driving by defenders on his own in isolation situations, shot selection can be questionable at times
- 2019-20 Defensive Degree of Difficulty: 0.440, tends to guard starting level players
- Decent on-ball defender, good against smaller guards, taller players can shoot over him
- Below average pick-and-roll defender, tends to go too far under screens, can be targeted by bigger screeners on switches
- Can get caught on screens off the ball, tends to either be late or too aggressive when closing out
- Stay-at-home defender, middling defensive rebounder, gets steals at a moderate rate

Andre Iguodala

	Height	Weight	Cap #	Years Left
	6'6"	215	$15.000M	Team Option

	Similar at Age	36 Season	SIMsc
1	Anthony Parker	2011-12	893.8
2	Rasual Butler	2015-16	890.0
3	Dan Majerle	2001-02	881.9
4	Robert Horry	2006-07	869.3
5	Brian Shaw	2002-03	868.2
6	Michael Finley	2009-10	867.6
7	Jose Calderon	2017-18	860.8
8	Eddie Jones	2007-08	858.5
9	Vince Carter	2012-13	856.5
10	Shawn Marion	2014-15	855.5

Baseline Basic Stats

MPG	PTS	AST	REB	BLK	STL
21.1	6.3	2.3	3.1	0.4	0.7

Advanced Metrics

USG%	3PTA/FGA	FTA/FGA	TS%	eFG%	3PT%
13.6	0.509	0.192	0.518	0.505	0.309
AST%	**TOV%**	**OREB%**	**DREB%**	**STL%**	**BLK%**
16.1	15.8	3.8	14.1	1.6	2.9
PER	**ORTG**	**DRTG**	**WS/48**	**VOL**	
11.34	107.1	108.8	0.065	0.877	

- Held out for most of 2019-20 while under contract for Memphis, traded to Miami in February 2020
- Played in Miami's regular rotation after the trade, used as a low volume, spot-up shooter and secondary ball handler
- Solid playmaker that can hit cutters and find open shooters, fairly turnover prone last season
- Good at making backdoor cuts when defenders aren't paying attention
- Struggled to shoot efficiently from beyond three feet, made less than 30% of threes in 2019-20
- Break-even three-point shooter for his career, shoots slightly better from the corners
- 2019-20 Defensive Degree of Difficulty: 0.403
- Tended to guard second unit players in the regular season, drew tougher assignments in the playoffs
- Good on-ball defender that guard multiple positions, better against perimeter players
- Pretty solid when guarding pick-and-rolls, had some issues when going over screens
- Stays attached to shooters off the ball, good at closing out to contest perimeter shots
- Very solid defensive rebounder, Steal Percentages have been down for the last few seasons, blocked shots at a very high rate in fewer minutes last season

Kelly Olynyk	Height	Weight	Cap #	Years Left
	6'11"	240	$12.598M	UFA

	Similar at Age	28 Season	SIMsc
1	Nemanja Bjelica	2016-17	927.9
2	Markieff Morris	2017-18	922.0
3	Brad Lohaus	1992-93	909.5
4	Troy Murphy	2008-09	905.5
5	Vladimir Radmanovic	2008-09	903.0
6	Raef LaFrentz	2004-05	900.6
7	Channing Frye	2011-12	899.7
8	Gorgui Dieng	2017-18	898.8
9	Austin Croshere	2003-04	898.4
10	Mehmet Okur	2007-08	895.9

Baseline Basic Stats

MPG	PTS	AST	REB	BLK	STL
23.2	9.0	1.6	5.3	0.5	0.6

Advanced Metrics

USG%	3PTA/FGA	FTA/FGA	TS%	eFG%	3PT%
16.9	0.611	0.214	0.589	0.557	0.388
AST%	**TOV%**	**OREB%**	**DREB%**	**STL%**	**BLK%**
11.4	12.9	4.3	20.8	1.4	1.8
PER	**ORTG**	**DRTG**	**WS/48**	**VOL**	
13.68	112.3	107.8	0.115	0.213	

- Regular rotation player for Miami in his seventh NBA season
- Utilized as a low volume, stretch big, made almost 41% of his threes last season
- Most effective at making spot-up jumpers, good at setting up for trail threes in transition
- Mixed results when shooting on the move, solid at shooting off screens, average as the screener on pick-and-pops
- Solid rim runner, slides into open spaces inside to score on rolls to the rim or cuts off the ball
- Good at using an on-ball screen to get to the rim on dribble hand-offs, draws fouls at a decent rate
- Solid passing big man that can hit cutters or find open shooters, solid at avoiding turnovers
- 2019-20 Defensive Degree of Difficulty: 0.320, tends to guard second unit big men
- Fairly solid rim protector, stays vertical to contest shots, not really a shot blocker, good defensive rebounder
- Below average on-ball defender, has trouble against stronger post players, not quite mobile enough to defend in space, tends to commit shooting fouls
- Below average pick-and-roll defender, struggles to guard ball handlers on switches, decent in drop coverages
- Stays attached to shooters off the ball, good at closing out in spot-up situations

Meyers Leonard

	Height	Weight	Cap #	Years Left
	7'0"	260	$9.400M	Team Option

Similar at Age 27

		Season	SIMsc
1	Nemanja Bjelica	2015-16	890.6
2	Spencer Hawes	2015-16	882.6
3	Walter McCarty	2001-02	877.1
4	Kosta Koufos	2016-17	870.0
5	Mike Muscala	2018-19	869.8
6	Michael Doleac	2004-05	865.6
7	Channing Frye	2010-11	864.9
8	Kelly Olynyk	2018-19	864.9
9	Matt Bonner	2007-08	864.3
10	Brian Scalabrine	2005-06	859.7

Baseline Basic Stats

MPG	PTS	AST	REB	BLK	STL
18.9	6.8	1.2	4.2	0.4	0.5

Advanced Metrics

USG%	3PTA/FGA	FTA/FGA	TS%	eFG%	3PT%
14.5	0.539	0.166	0.602	0.584	0.409

AST%	TOV%	OREB%	DREB%	STL%	BLK%
9.8	11.9	4.9	21.4	1.1	1.5

PER	ORTG	DRTG	WS/48	VOL
13.13	116.7	108.8	0.123	0.275

- Regular rotation player for Miami in his first season with the team, started most of his games
- Utilized as a low volume, stretch big, good three-point shooter, has made 39% of his career threes
- Good spot-up shooter, very effective as the screener on pick-and-pop plays
- Plays with a high motor, dives hard to the rim as a roll man and cutter off the ball
- Good transition players, consistently runs hard down the floor, good at setting up for trail threes
- Strictly a catch-and-shoot big man, shows some passing skills, consistently limits turnovers
- 2019-20 Defensive Degree of Difficulty: 0.427, guards starting level big men
- Below average rim protector, mobility is limited, not really a shot blocker, good defensive rebounder
- Average post defender, can be beaten to spots inside, tends to commit shooting fouls
- Solid pick-and-roll defender, good in drop coverages, effective at switching onto ball handlers for a few dribbles
- Consistently will close out on perimeter shooters, tends to be too aggressive on his close-outs, can allow driving lanes to the rim

Maurice Harkless	Height	Weight	Cap #	Years Left
	6'7"	220	$3.623M	UFA

Similar at Age 26

		Season	SIMsc
1	James Ennis	2016-17	927.7
2	Alonzo Gee	2013-14	925.6
3	Devean George	2003-04	918.5
4	Robert Horry	1996-97	916.1
5	Jud Buechler	1994-95	912.8
6	Andre Roberson	2017-18	910.0
7	Wesley Johnson	2013-14	909.4
8	Chase Budinger	2014-15	909.0
9	Ryan Bowen	2001-02	906.8
10	Shane Battier	2004-05	904.3

Baseline Basic Stats

MPG	PTS	AST	REB	BLK	STL
23.6	7.1	1.2	3.9	0.5	0.8

Advanced Metrics

USG%	3PTA/FGA	FTA/FGA	TS%	eFG%	3PT%
12.9	0.380	0.230	0.554	0.532	0.348
AST%	**TOV%**	**OREB%**	**DREB%**	**STL%**	**BLK%**
7.4	12.3	4.9	12.9	1.8	2.2
PER	**ORTG**	**DRTG**	**WS/48**	**VOL**	
11.38	110.9	107.2	0.101	0.319	

- Regular starter for the L.A. Clippers and New York last season, traded to New York in February 2020
- Mostly used as a low volume, spot-up shooter
- Shot better with the Clippers, Three-Point Percentage was just above break-even overall
- Mainly a stationary shooter at this stage, does not really run off screens
- Excellent cutter off the ball in New York, drew fouls at a higher rate, good finisher at the rim overall, made two-thirds of his shots inside of three feet
- Catch-and-shoot right now, limited as a shot creator, not really a passer, good at avoiding turnovers
- 2019-20 Defensive Degree of Difficulty: 0.534
- Consistently took on tough assignments against elite perimeter players
- Good on-ball defender that can guard multiple positions
- Fairly good pick-and-roll defender that can fight over screens to contain ball handlers
- Stays attached to shooters off the ball, consistently closes out in spot-up situations
- Active help defender, posts fairly high steal and block rates, solid defensive rebounder

KZ Okpala

Height	Weight	Cap #	Years Left
6'8"	215	$1.518M	1

Similar at Age **20**

		Season	SIMsc
1	Julian Wright	2007-08	870.4
2	Kedrick Brown	2001-02	864.2
3	Jonathan Isaac	2017-18	857.9
4	Maurice Harkless	2013-14	851.2
5	Kevon Looney	2016-17	848.5
6	Gerald Wallace	2002-03	842.7
7	Chris McCullough	2015-16	841.6
8	Travis Outlaw	2004-05	836.6
9	Paul George	2010-11	835.7
10	Jordan Adams	2014-15	834.8

Baseline Basic Stats

MPG	PTS	AST	REB	BLK	STL
19.5	6.9	1.1	4.2	0.7	0.9

Advanced Metrics

USG%	3PTA/FGA	FTA/FGA	TS%	eFG%	3PT%
14.9	0.212	0.339	0.580	0.565	0.146
AST%	**TOV%**	**OREB%**	**DREB%**	**STL%**	**BLK%**
7.4	13.4	6.1	15.5	2.9	2.7
PER	**ORTG**	**DRTG**	**WS/48**	**VOL**	
14.68	111.4	105.0	0.124	0.402	

- Played sparingly for Miami as a rookie, missed parts of the season due to an Achilles injury
- Used in a low volume as an energy wing off the ball
- Made 60% of his field goals, mainly effective at scoring from ten feet and in
- Effective at cutting off the ball and running down the wings to score in transition or draw fouls
- Outside shooting ability is uncertain, missed his only three, did not attempt a two-point shot beyond ten feet
- Mostly a catch-and-shoot player right now, limited passing skills, solid at avoiding turnovers
- 2019-20 Defensive Degree of Difficulty: 0.529, only played 26 NBA minutes
- Spent most of his minutes guarding Buddy Hield and De'Aaron Fox
- True defensive ability is uncertain, not tested in most situations
- Did not have to defend in any one-on-one situation or against a pick-and-roll
- May be good at ball denial, did not allow Fox to take a shot against him
- Had trouble defending off the ball, allowed Hield, Nemanja Bejlica and Bogdan Bogdanovic to make threes in six spot-up possessions
- Played active help defense in limited minutes, grabbed four defensive rebounds, got two steals and a block in 26 minutes

Chris Silva	Height	Weight	Cap #	Years Left
	6'8"	230	$1.518M	Team Option

	Similar at Age	23 Season	SIMsc
1	Chris Wright	2011-12	868.7
2	Stephen Howard	1993-94	864.5
3	Alexander Johnson	2006-07	859.1
4	Solomon Jones	2007-08	849.8
5	Andrew DeClercq	1996-97	848.8
6	Audie Norris	1983-84	848.0
7	Anthony Miller	1994-95	846.6
8	David Vaughn	1996-97	845.8
9	Leon Powe	2006-07	845.3
10	Scott Williams	1991-92	844.5

Baseline Basic Stats

MPG	PTS	AST	REB	BLK	STL
17.2	6.0	0.8	4.7	0.7	0.5

Advanced Metrics

USG%	3PTA/FGA	FTA/FGA	TS%	eFG%	3PT%
16.5	0.025	0.599	0.602	0.563	0.000
AST%	**TOV%**	**OREB%**	**DREB%**	**STL%**	**BLK%**
8.3	20.1	14.8	20.1	1.5	3.9
PER	**ORTG**	**DRTG**	**WS/48**	**VOL**	
15.73	114.0	104.5	0.150	0.637	

- Had his Two-Way contract converted to a standard contract in January 2020, played as a fringe rotation player as a rookie
- Effective in his role as a low volume rim runner, made 75.5% of his shots inside of three feet
- Excellent offensive rebounder that creates second chance opportunities and scores on put-backs
- High energy athlete, dives hard to the rim as a roll man and cutter, draws fouls at a very high rate
- Flashed some ability to make mid-range shots, but his outside shot is still inconsistent
- Skill level is limited right now, shows some passing ability, highly turnover prone
- 2019-20 Defensive Degree of Difficulty: 0.280
- Tended to either guard second unit players or play in garbage time
- Good defensive rebounder and shot blocker, below average rim protector, undisciplined with his positioning, extremely foul prone
- Rarely tested on the ball, decent post defender that holds position inside, had trouble defending in space
- Still learning how to make proper defensive rotations in the NBA, had difficulties playing pick-and-roll defense
- Does not always come out to contest shots on the perimeter

Udonis Haslem

	Height	Weight	Cap #	Years Left
	6'8"	235	$1.621M	UFA

	Similar at Age	39	
		Season	SIMsc
1	Danny Schayes	1998-99	840.9
2	Paul Pierce	2016-17	837.8
3	Sam Perkins	2000-01	827.4
4	Clifford Robinson	2005-06	813.8
5	Rick Mahorn	1997-98	812.9
6	James Edwards	1994-95	812.4
7	Juwan Howard	2012-13	804.4
8	Grant Hill	2011-12	804.2
9	Vince Carter	2015-16	795.3
10	Earl Cureton	1996-97	794.2

Baseline Basic Stats

MPG	PTS	AST	REB	BLK	STL
17.3	5.5	0.7	3.3	0.3	0.4

Advanced Metrics

USG%	3PTA/FGA	FTA/FGA	TS%	eFG%	3PT%
14.1	0.143	0.246	0.467	0.429	0.337
AST%	**TOV%**	**OREB%**	**DREB%**	**STL%**	**BLK%**
6.1	12.5	4.6	25.3	0.6	0.8
PER	**ORTG**	**DRTG**	**WS/48**	**VOL**	
7.22	95.0	108.3	0.019	0.191	

- Has only played 580 minutes over the last five seasons
- Mainly on the roster to provide veteran leadership and guidance for young players
- Used as a low volume, stretch big in very limited action, went 1-for-3 (33.3%) on threes last season
- Mostly a mid-range spot-up shooter when he was younger, inconsistent three-point shooter in his career
- Plays with a high motor, occasionally can cut to the rim to draw fouls, no longer has the lift to consistently finish shots inside
- 2019-20 Defensive Degree of Difficulty: 0.214, only played 44 minutes last season
- Average rim protector when he was younger, not really a shot blocker, stayed vertical when contesting shots, good defensive rebounder
- Still a solid team defender that makes sound rotations, decent at guarding pick-and-rolls, willing to close out on perimeter shots
- Strong enough to handle bigger post players inside, lacks the mobility to defend quicker and more athletic players

Newcomers

Precious Achiuwa	**Height**	**Weight**	**Cap #**	**Years Left**
	6'9"	225	$2.582M	1 + 2 TO

Baseline Basic Stats

MPG	PTS	AST	REB	BLK	STL
18.4	7.0	0.9	4.2	0.7	0.5

Advanced Metrics

USG%	3PTA/FGA	FTA/FGA	TS%	eFG%	3PT%
19.3	0.101	0.332	0.481	0.443	0.289

AST%	TOV%	OREB%	DREB%	STL%	BLK%
7.3	13.1	8.8	16.7	1.4	2.9

PER	ORTG	DRTG	WS/48	VOL
13.70	95.8	96.4	0.066	N/A

- Drafted by Miami with the 20th overall pick
- Made the All-AAC 1st Team, named AAC Rookie and Player of the Year in 2019-20
- High energy rim runner at Memphis, dives hard to the rim as a roll man or cutter off the ball
- Active offensive rebounder that keeps possessions alive, runs hard down the floor in transition, draws fouls at a high rate
- Skill level still raw, does not possess many advanced post moves, limited as a passer, somewhat turnover prone
- Flashed some stretch potential, just below break-even three-point shooter, stroke still not repeatable
- Potentially can defend multiple positions at the NBA level, strong post defender that holds position inside
- Showed good lateral quickness when defending perimeter players in space on isolations
- Effective rim protector, good shot blocker and rebounder, uses active hands to deflect passes and get steals
- Struggled to defend pick-and-rolls at Memphis, tended to be indecisive when making rotations

INDIANA PACERS

Last Season: 45 – 28, Lost 1st Round to Miami (0 – 4)

Offensive Rating: 110.0, 19th in the NBA

Defensive Rating: 108.0, 6th in the NBA

Primary Executive: Kevin Pritchard, President of Basketball Operations

Head Coach: Nate Bjorkgren

Key Roster Changes

Subtractions
T.J. Leaf, trade
Alize Johnson, free agency

Additions
Jalen Lecque, trade
Kelan Martin, free agency

Roster

Likely Starting Five

1. *Malcolm Brogdon*
2. *Victor Oladipo*
3. *T.J. Warren*
4. *Domantas Sabonis*
5. *Myles Turner*

Other Key Rotation Players
Jeremy Lamb
Justin Holiday
Aaron Holiday
Doug McDermott
T.J. McConnell

* Italics denotes that a player is likely to be on the floor to close games

Remaining Roster

- JaKarr Sampson
- Goga Bitadze
- Edmond Sumner
- Jalen Lecque
- Kelan Martin
- Brian Bowen II, 22, 6'6", 190, La Lumiere HS – LaPorte, IN (Two-Way)
- Cassius Stanley, 21, 6'6", 193, Duke (Two-Way)
- Amida Brimah, 26, 6'10", 230, Connecticut (Exhibit 10)
- Rayshaun Hammonds, 22, 6'9", 235, Georgia (Exhibit 10)
- Naz Mitrou-Long, 27, 6'3", 218, Iowa State (Exhibit 10)

SCHREMPF Base Rating: 36.8 (72-game season)

Strengths

- Sound overall defensive team that steers opponents into the inefficient areas of the floor
- Excellent continuity because all of their main rotation players are returning
- Solid depth to handle a compressed schedule

Question Marks

- Lacking offensive firepower due to less than ideal front-end talent
- No proven defensive stopper on the wings to neutralize elite players
- Fit between their main starters is questionable because the Pacers have rarely been at full strength

Outlook

- Solid playoff team, not quite as good as the contenders, likely will participate in the play-in tournament

Veterans

Domantas Sabonis

Height	Weight	Cap #	Years Left
6'11"	240	$19.800M	3

Similar at Age 23

		Season	SIMsc
1	Jeff Ruland	1981-82	916.3
2	Julius Randle	2017-18	914.8
3	Nikola Vucevic	2013-14	910.3
4	Richard Anderson	1983-84	906.4
5	Derrick Coleman	1990-91	904.5
6	Blake Griffin	2012-13	904.2
7	Brad Daugherty	1988-89	903.5
8	Carlos Boozer	2004-05	903.0
9	Charlie Villanueva	2007-08	902.0
10	Jason Thompson	2009-10	900.8

Baseline Basic Stats

MPG	PTS	AST	REB	BLK	STL
31.1	16.6	2.5	8.8	0.8	0.8

Advanced Metrics

USG%	3PTA/FGA	FTA/FGA	TS%	eFG%	3PT%
24.1	0.068	0.372	0.587	0.548	0.322
AST%	**TOV%**	**OREB%**	**DREB%**	**STL%**	**BLK%**
17.2	13.8	9.1	25.6	1.2	1.6
PER	**ORTG**	**DRTG**	**WS/48**	**VOL**	
20.80	113.8	105.8	0.164	0.232	

- Made his first All-Star team in his first season as a full-time starter for Indiana in 2019-20
- Excelled in his role as a moderate volume post-up player and rim runner
- Very good roll man on pick-and-rolls, can go to the rim to finish inside, good at making mid-range shots as the screener on pick-and-pops
- Active big man, scores on a high volume of cuts off the ball, fairly solid offensive rebounder that scores on put-backs
- Solid post-up player, mostly scores on the right block, more efficient on the left block
- Excellent passing big man that hits cutters and kicks the ball out to shooters, cut his turnover rate last season
- 2019-20 Defensive Degree of Difficulty: 0.404
- Utilized as a roamer or rim protector, tends to take on lower leverage assignments
- Good rim protector, not really a shot blocker, stays vertical to contest shots, great defensive rebounder
- Fairly decent on-ball defender, effective post defender, has some trouble defending in space
- Average pick-and-roll defender, can switch onto ball handlers for a few dribbles, can slow to make rotations
- Consistently comes out to contest shots on the perimeter

Malcolm Brogdon

	Height	Weight	Cap #	Years Left
	6'5"	229	$20.700M	2

	Similar at Age	27 Season	SIMsc
1	Arron Afflalo	2012-13	922.5
2	Mitch Richmond*	1992-93	920.9
3	Gerald Henderson	2014-15	909.5
4	Isaiah Rider	1998-99	903.7
5	Sean Kilpatrick	2016-17	903.5
6	O.J. Mayo	2014-15	901.2
7	Lance Stephenson	2017-18	900.8
8	Khris Middleton	2018-19	895.1
9	Gordan Giricek	2004-05	895.0
10	Gary Neal	2011-12	894.8

Baseline Basic Stats

MPG	PTS	AST	REB	BLK	STL
26.2	12.4	2.7	3.2	0.2	0.7

Advanced Metrics

USG%	3PTA/FGA	FTA/FGA	TS%	eFG%	3PT%
22.8	0.343	0.251	0.535	0.488	0.358

AST%	TOV%	OREB%	DREB%	STL%	BLK%
21.6	12.7	2.7	11.9	1.3	0.5

PER	ORTG	DRTG	WS/48	VOL
14.80	107.3	110.5	0.105	0.275

- Regular starter in his first season with Indiana, missed some games due to an assortment of minor injuries
- Maintained his effectiveness in a higher volume as the team's primary ball handler
- Effective as a pick-and-roll ball handler and isolation player, could make pull-up jumpers and drive to the rim, drew fouls at a higher rate
- Outside shooting efficiency decreased with higher volume, made threes at a below break-even rate last season, took fewer assisted shots
- Typically, a solid spot-up shooter that can occasionally shoot off screens
- Excellent playmaker that can hit cutters and kick the ball out to shooters, great at controlling the ball to avoid turnovers
- 2019-20 Defensive Degree of Difficulty: 0.507
- Usually takes on tougher assignments against top perimeter players
- Fairly solid on-ball defender against wing players
- Above average pick-and-roll defender that fights over screens to contain ball handlers, has some trouble against bigger players on switches
- Generally stays attached to shooters off the ball, consistently closes out, occasionally gets caught on screens going to the shooter's left
- Stay-at-home defender, rarely goes for steals or blocks, posted the highest Defensive Rebound Percentage of his career last season

T.J. Warren

Height	Weight	Cap #	Years Left
6'8"	215	$12.000M	1

Similar at Age 26

		Season	SIMsc
1	Tracy Murray	1997-98	931.6
2	Glen Rice	1993-94	927.5
3	Rodney Hood	2018-19	925.2
4	Josh Howard	2006-07	925.1
5	Chris King	1995-96	924.8
6	Ken Norman	1990-91	920.4
7	Mark Alarie	1989-90	918.8
8	Wilson Chandler	2013-14	918.2
9	Vince Carter	2002-03	917.3
10	Jalen Rose	1998-99	916.1

Baseline Basic Stats

MPG	PTS	AST	REB	BLK	STL
30.7	15.4	2.1	4.5	0.4	0.9

Advanced Metrics

USG%	3PTA/FGA	FTA/FGA	TS%	eFG%	3PT%
22.9	0.267	0.224	0.569	0.534	0.385
AST%	**TOV%**	**OREB%**	**DREB%**	**STL%**	**BLK%**
10.4	8.8	3.4	11.8	1.5	1.2
PER	**ORTG**	**DRTG**	**WS/48**	**VOL**	
16.46	110.9	110.8	0.105	0.439	

- Had his most productive season as a full-time starter for Indiana, made the All-Bubble 1st Team in August 2020
- Increased his efficiency in his role as a higher volume scorer on the wing
- Has become a very good overall shooter, made over 40% of his threes last season
- Good at making spot-up jumpers, can run off screens, gets to the rim on dribble hand-offs
- Very effective cutter off the ball, great at running the floor in transition to get layups or draw fouls
- Effective at making quick pull-up jumpers as a pick-and-roll ball handler, very good overall mid-range shooter
- Mostly a catch-and-shoot player at this stage, limited as a playmaker, rarely turns the ball over
- 2019-20 Defensive Degree of Difficulty: 0.468
- Tends to defend starter level players, sometimes is tasked to guard top wing players
- Below average on-ball defender, can be over-matched against top players, has trouble staying in front of his man on isolation plays
- Better team defender, good against pick-and-rolls, can switch or funnel his man into help
- Consistently closes out on perimeter shooters, usually fights through screens off the ball
- Steal and Block Percentages are consistent with his career averages, solid defensive rebounder

Myles Turner

	Height	Weight	Cap #	Years Left
	6'11"	250	$18.000M	2

	Similar at Age	23	
		Season	**SIMsc**
1	Raef LaFrentz	1999-00	910.6
2	Benoit Benjamin	1987-88	903.7
3	Samuel Dalembert	2004-05	890.4
4	Mehmet Okur	2002-03	888.5
5	Herb Williams	1981-82	883.9
6	Richaun Holmes	2016-17	881.9
7	Terrence Jones	2014-15	880.9
8	JaVale McGee	2010-11	879.8
9	Mike Gminski	1982-83	878.3
10	Channing Frye	2006-07	875.7

Baseline Basic Stats

MPG	PTS	AST	REB	BLK	STL
27.2	11.0	1.2	7.1	1.8	0.6

Advanced Metrics

USG%	3PTA/FGA	FTA/FGA	TS%	eFG%	3PT%
18.7	0.247	0.293	0.568	0.533	0.358
AST%	**TOV%**	**OREB%**	**DREB%**	**STL%**	**BLK%**
6.8	12.3	6.9	20.0	1.2	5.5
PER	**ORTG**	**DRTG**	**WS/48**	**VOL**	
16.46	109.7	104.4	0.127	0.315	

- Regular starter for Indiana in his fifth season in the NBA
- Production declined in a reduced role as a lower volume, rim runner and stretch big
- Effective rim runner, good at rolling to the rim on pick-and-rolls, scores on a high volume of cuts off the ball
- Took more threes and fewer long twos, maintained his shooting efficiency from the season before
- Three-Point Percentage dropped to just above break-even with more attempts
- Mainly a stationary spot-up shooter, only average shooter on pick-and-pops
- Good post-up player that can go strong to the rim on the left block
- Mainly a catch-and-shoot or catch-and-finish big man, limited passing skills, good at limiting turnovers
- 2019-20 Defensive Degree of Difficulty: 0.437
- Tends to guard starting level big men, takes on tougher big man assignments
- Very good rim protector, solid defensive rebounder, excellent shot blocker
- Good on-ball defender, plays strong post defense, shows good mobile to defend in space
- Above average pick-and-roll defender, solid on switches, can be late to get back to cover the screener
- Tends to sag into the paint, does not always come out to contest perimeter shots

Victor Oladipo	Height	Weight	Cap #	Years Left
	6'4"	210	$21.000M	UFA

	Similar at Age	27 Season	SIMsc
1	O.J. Mayo	2014-15	940.6
2	Tyreke Evans	2016-17	928.8
3	Sean Kilpatrick	2016-17	927.0
4	Marcus Thornton	2014-15	923.4
5	Lester Hudson	2011-12	921.6
6	Shannon Brown	2012-13	919.5
7	Anthony Peeler	1996-97	919.2
8	Randy Foye	2010-11	917.4
9	Reggie Jackson	2017-18	914.1
10	Fred Hoiberg	1999-00	911.4

Baseline Basic Stats

MPG	PTS	AST	REB	BLK	STL
26.6	11.9	2.8	3.0	0.2	0.9

Advanced Metrics

USG%	3PTA/FGA	FTA/FGA	TS%	eFG%	3PT%
23.2	0.455	0.226	0.533	0.494	0.363
AST%	**TOV%**	**OREB%**	**DREB%**	**STL%**	**BLK%**
18.2	12.4	2.1	12.8	1.8	0.6
PER	**ORTG**	**DRTG**	**WS/48**	**VOL**	
14.30	104.6	109.4	0.067	0.478	

- Missed most of last season while recovering from a ruptured right quadricep tendon
- Regular starter for Indiana when healthy, struggled to play at his previous levels when he returned
- Still played a high volume scoring role, was more of a secondary ball handler
- Still effective as a pick-and-roll ball handler, can get to the rim and pass to the open roll man inside
- Struggled to make shots in the high-yield parts of the rim, below break-even last season on threes, made less than 50% of his shots inside of three feet
- Good at making mid-range jumpers, good at making outside shots on dribble hand-off plays
- Assist Percentage dropped with less ball handling responsibility, effective at limiting turnovers
- 2019-20 Defensive Degree of Difficulty: 0.426
- Usually guarded starting level players, took on tougher assignments in the past
- Fairly solid on-ball defender that can capably defend both guard spots
- Good pick-and-roll defender that fights over screens to contain ball handlers, not quite as effective on switches
- Stays attached to shooters off the ball, consistently closes out in spot-up situations
- More of a stay-at-home defender due to his injuries, Defensive Rebound, Block and Steal Percentages were all down from his career averages

Jeremy Lamb

	Height	Weight	Cap #	Years Left
Jeremy Lamb	6'5"	185	$10.500M	1

Similar at Age 27

		Season	SIMsc
1	Justin Holiday	2016-17	934.0
2	Jordan McRae	2018-19	929.7
3	Rex Chapman	1994-95	927.1
4	Alec Burks	2018-19	926.1
5	Derek Anderson	2001-02	924.9
6	Rodney Buford	2004-05	919.1
7	E'Twaun Moore	2016-17	918.5
8	Kent Bazemore	2016-17	916.5
9	Marco Belinelli	2013-14	913.5
10	Cuttino Mobley	2002-03	913.2

Baseline Basic Stats

MPG	PTS	AST	REB	BLK	STL
28.2	11.9	2.5	3.4	0.3	1.0

Advanced Metrics

USG%	3PTA/FGA	FTA/FGA	TS%	eFG%	3PT%
19.9	0.391	0.220	0.543	0.504	0.363
AST%	**TOV%**	**OREB%**	**DREB%**	**STL%**	**BLK%**
12.8	9.5	2.3	13.6	1.9	1.1
PER	**ORTG**	**DRTG**	**WS/48**	**VOL**	
14.38	108.6	108.0	0.103	0.336	

- Regular starter for Indiana when healthy, tore the ACL in his left knee in February 2020
- Had to adapt to a lower volume role as a shooter off the ball, still maintained his usual level of effectiveness
- Break-even three-point shooter, but very good from mid-range
- Knocks down spot-up jumpers, can run off screens, good at getting to the rim on dribble hand-offs
- Good pick-and-roll ball handler that can make quick pull-up jumpers or drive to the rim
- Effective cutter off the ball, can occasionally crash inside to score on put-backs
- Fairly decent secondary playmaker, rarely turns the ball over
- 2019-20 Defensive Degree of Difficulty: 0.464
- Tends to guard starting level players, occasionally takes on tougher assignments
- Below average on-ball defender, has trouble keeping opposing players in front of him on drives, had more success against bigger players in the post
- Average pick-and-roll defender, solid at switching onto the screener, tended to allow ball handlers to turn the corner
- Stays attached to shooters off the ball, good at closing out in spot-up situations
- Steal Percentage continues to rise, Block Percentage is still consistent with his career average, good defensive rebounder

Justin Holiday	Height	Weight	Cap #	Years Left
	6'6"	181	$5.720M	2

	Similar at Age	30	SIMsc
		Season	SIMsc
1	Garrett Temple	2016-17	926.6
2	Courtney Lee	2015-16	904.1
3	Francisco Garcia	2011-12	897.3
4	Craig Ehlo	1991-92	893.9
5	Hubert Davis	2000-01	891.6
6	Trevor Ariza	2015-16	890.1
7	Danny Green	2017-18	889.1
8	DeMarre Carroll	2016-17	888.5
9	Kyle Korver	2011-12	886.8
10	Jud Buechler	1998-99	886.4

Baseline Basic Stats

MPG	PTS	AST	REB	BLK	STL
28.7	9.9	2.5	3.5	0.4	1.2

Advanced Metrics

USG%	3PTA/FGA	FTA/FGA	TS%	eFG%	3PT%
14.9	0.594	0.162	0.554	0.528	0.374
AST%	**TOV%**	**OREB%**	**DREB%**	**STL%**	**BLK%**
10.4	10.5	2.0	12.0	2.3	1.6
PER	**ORTG**	**DRTG**	**WS/48**	**VOL**	
11.98	109.2	108.2	0.088	0.137	

- Regular rotation player in his first season with Indiana in 2019-20
- Mainly a low volume, spot-up shooter, made 40.5% of his threes last season
- Mostly a spot-up shooter, can sometimes shoot off screens
- Effective at using an on-ball screen to make outside shots or get to the rim on dribble hand-offs
- Good cutter off the ball, good at running on the wings to get layups in transition
- Cut his Turnover Percentage to a career low last season, has shown some passing skills in the past
- 2019-20 Defensive Degree of Difficulty: 0.403, tends to guard second unit level players
- Average on-ball defender, better against bigger players in the post, struggled to stay with perimeter players on isolations
- Average at guarding pick-and-rolls, effective on switches, can allow ball handlers to turn the corner
- Consistently closes out on perimeter shooters, occasionally gets caught on screens off the ball
- Active help defender, posted fairly high Steal and Block Percentages last season, good defensive rebounder

Aaron Holiday	Height	Weight	Cap #	Years Left
	6'0"	185	$2.346M	Team Option

	Similar at Age	23 Season	SIMsc
1	Yogi Ferrell	2016-17	962.5
2	Fred VanVleet	2017-18	943.3
3	Isaiah Canaan	2014-15	941.8
4	Trey Burke	2015-16	940.3
5	Mo Williams	2005-06	933.9
6	Jordan Farmar	2009-10	926.3
7	Eddie House	2001-02	924.0
8	Salim Stoudamire	2005-06	923.9
9	Frank Mason	2017-18	922.2
10	J.J. Barea	2007-08	919.8

Baseline Basic Stats

MPG	PTS	AST	REB	BLK	STL
21.3	8.5	2.9	2.1	0.1	0.7

Advanced Metrics

USG%	3PTA/FGA	FTA/FGA	TS%	eFG%	3PT%
19.8	0.447	0.176	0.523	0.490	0.364
AST%	**TOV%**	**OREB%**	**DREB%**	**STL%**	**BLK%**
21.2	11.9	1.4	9.6	1.7	0.8
PER	**ORTG**	**DRTG**	**WS/48**	**VOL**	
12.97	106.0	109.2	0.081	0.374	

- Regular rotation player for Indiana in his second season in the NBA, started some games last season
- Mainly used as a low volume, secondary ball handler and spot-up shooter
- Made over 39% of his threes last season, good spot-up shooter that can also run off screens
- Good at using an on-ball screen to get to the basket on dribble hand-offs
- Average pick-and-roll ball handler, can get to the rim and find open teammates, not as effective at shooting off the dribble
- Very good secondary playmaker, good at avoiding turnovers
- 2019-20 Defensive Degree of Difficulty: 0.420
- Defended starter level guards, got some tough matchups against top offensive guards
- Fairly solid on-ball defender, occasionally got beat to the rim on drives, good at contesting jump shots
- Solid pick-and-roll defender, fights over screens to contain ball handler or funnels his man into help, fairly good at switching
- Closes out on perimeter shooters in spot-up situations, occasionally gets caught on screens off the ball
- Solid defensive rebounder for his size, Steal Percentage increased slightly last season

Doug McDermott	Height	Weight	Cap #	Years Left
	6'7"	225	$7.333M	UFA

Similar at Age 28

		Season	SIMsc
1	Sam Mack	1998-99	939.2
2	Jared Dudley	2013-14	934.0
3	Jarvis Hayes	2009-10	926.9
4	Quentin Richardson	2008-09	922.3
5	Tracy Murray	1999-00	922.1
6	Bojan Bogdanovic	2017-18	919.7
7	Ryan Broekhoff	2018-19	911.2
8	Dennis Scott	1996-97	909.6
9	Luke Babbitt	2017-18	909.4
10	Cartier Martin	2012-13	909.1

Baseline Basic Stats

MPG	PTS	AST	REB	BLK	STL
22.5	9.0	1.2	2.7	0.2	0.5

Advanced Metrics

USG%	3PTA/FGA	FTA/FGA	TS%	eFG%	3PT%
17.2	0.562	0.160	0.593	0.568	0.413
AST%	**TOV%**	**OREB%**	**DREB%**	**STL%**	**BLK%**
8.0	8.8	2.1	11.0	0.9	0.5
PER	**ORTG**	**DRTG**	**WS/48**	**VOL**	
12.55	113.8	110.6	0.101	0.406	

- Regular rotation player for Indiana last season, had his best season as a pro in 2019-20
- Thrived as a lower volume shooter off the ball, made 43.5% of his threes last season
- Excellent all-around shooter that can make spot-up jumpers, run off screens and set up for trail threes in transition
- Good on dribble hand-offs, can use the on-ball screen to make outside shots or drive to the rim
- Very good at making backdoor cuts if defenders overplay his shot
- Mostly a catch-and-shoot player, Assist Percentage is steadily increasing, rarely turns the ball over
- 2019-20 Defensive Degree of Difficulty: 0.275
- Tends to be hidden in favorable matchups against lower leverage second unit players
- Below average on-ball defender, stronger players can back him down in the post, tends to allow his man to get extra space to take jump shots on isolation plays
- Middling pick-and-roll defender, tends to go too far under screens, not especially effective on switches
- Stays attached to shooters off the ball, consistently closes out in spot-up situations
- Stay-at-home defender, solid defensive rebounder, rarely gets blocks or steals

T.J. McConnell

Height	Weight	Cap #	Years Left
6'1"	190	$3.500M	UFA

Similar at Age **27**

		Season	SIMsc
1	Eric Snow	2000-01	919.0
2	Jacque Vaughn	2002-03	918.3
3	Moochie Norris	2000-01	906.7
4	Bobby Jackson	2000-01	906.4
5	Mark Jackson	1992-93	905.0
6	Anthony Carter	2002-03	904.5
7	Earl Watson	2006-07	903.8
8	Will Bynum	2009-10	902.3
9	Gary Grant	1992-93	901.9
10	Raymond Felton	2011-12	901.3

Baseline Basic Stats

MPG	PTS	AST	REB	BLK	STL
24.6	8.5	4.7	2.4	0.1	1.0

Advanced Metrics

USG%	3PTA/FGA	FTA/FGA	TS%	eFG%	3PT%
17.5	0.124	0.167	0.522	0.493	0.315
AST%	**TOV%**	**OREB%**	**DREB%**	**STL%**	**BLK%**
31.7	18.0	2.7	10.1	2.1	0.5
PER	**ORTG**	**DRTG**	**WS/48**	**VOL**	
14.24	107.4	109.5	0.086	0.367	

- Regular rotation player in his first season with Indiana in 2019-20
- Mainly used as a low volume, game managing backup point guard
- Good playmaker that can make interior passes and kick the ball out to shooters, tends to turnover prone
- Good pick-and-roll ball handler that can probe the defense and occasionally get to the rim
- Inconsistent outside shooter, career Three-Point Percentage is almost break-even, made less than 30% of his threes last season
- Better at corner threes, percentages tend to fluctuate from year-to-year
- Rated as below average in every off-ball shooting situation last season
- 2019-20 Defensive Degree of Difficulty: 0.305
- Tends to guard second unit level players, hidden in favorable matchups most of the time
- Below average on-ball defender, has trouble staying with quicker guards in isolation situations
- Solid pick-and-roll defender that can funnel his man into help, effective on switches
- Stays attached to shooters off the ball, consistently closes out in spot-up situations
- Good defensive rebounder for his size, has active hands, consistently gets steals at a high rate

JaKarr Sampson	Height	Weight	Cap #	Years Left
	6'7"	215	$1.621M	UFA

	Similar at Age	26	
		Season	SIMsc
1	Rod Higgins	1985-86	908.1
2	Rodney Carney	2010-11	906.8
3	Quincy Acy	2016-17	904.5
4	Chucky Brown	1994-95	903.6
5	David Benoit	1994-95	902.2
6	Kelenna Azubuike	2009-10	901.2
7	Linton Johnson	2006-07	900.8
8	Ira Newble	2000-01	898.5
9	Cartier Martin	2010-11	898.0
10	Toby Knight	1981-82	897.6

Baseline Basic Stats

MPG	PTS	AST	REB	BLK	STL
18.9	6.3	1.0	3.7	0.4	0.5

Advanced Metrics

USG%	3PTA/FGA	FTA/FGA	TS%	eFG%	3PT%
15.4	0.200	0.267	0.576	0.539	0.256
AST%	**TOV%**	**OREB%**	**DREB%**	**STL%**	**BLK%**
6.9	11.5	5.1	17.5	1.4	2.0
PER	**ORTG**	**DRTG**	**WS/48**	**VOL**	
13.43	112.6	108.6	0.108	0.554	

- Fringe rotation player for Indiana in 2019-20, playing increased towards the end of the season
- Mainly played off the ball in a low volume role as a rim running wing player
- Made over 77% of his shots inside of three feet last season, draws fouls at a fairly solid rate
- Very effective cutter and roll man, great athlete, runs hard down the wing to get dunks or draw fouls in transition
- No real shooting range outside of ten feet, limited passing skills, rarely turns the ball over
- 2019-20 Defensive Degree of Difficulty: 0.381
- Tended to guard higher-end second unit players or lower leverage starters
- Average on-ball defender, good at using his length to guard bigger players in the post, struggled to stay with perimeter players on isolations
- Decent pick-and-roll defender, good at covering the screener, had trouble containing ball handlers on the perimeter
- Consistently closes out on perimeter shooters, gambles a bit too much, tends to try to shoot the gap when chasing shooters off screens
- Active weak side defender, good at rotating inside to block shots, gets steals at a moderate rate, good defensive rebounder

Goga Bitadze	Height	Weight	Cap #	Years Left
	6'11"	245	$2.958M	2 Team Options

	Similar at Age	20 Season	SIMsc
1	Darko Milicic	2005-06	914.7
2	Mohamed Bamba	2018-19	911.2
3	Andray Blatche	2006-07	890.4
4	Deyonta Davis	2016-17	884.7
5	Myles Turner	2016-17	882.4
6	J.J. Hickson	2008-09	874.2
7	Robert Swift	2005-06	871.9
8	Trey Lyles	2015-16	870.8
9	Domantas Sabonis	2016-17	869.2
10	Zach Collins	2017-18	869.0

Baseline Basic Stats

MPG	PTS	AST	REB	BLK	STL
23.7	9.9	1.2	5.7	1.4	0.6

Advanced Metrics

USG%	3PTA/FGA	FTA/FGA	TS%	eFG%	3PT%
19.2	0.263	0.233	0.546	0.517	0.300
AST%	**TOV%**	**OREB%**	**DREB%**	**STL%**	**BLK%**
8.0	13.3	6.5	18.6	1.2	4.9
PER	**ORTG**	**DRTG**	**WS/48**	**VOL**	
14.42	104.9	106.2	0.095	0.340	

- Fringe rotation player for Indiana in his rookie season
- Utilized as a low volume, rim runner and stretch big
- More effective as a rim runner, solid at rolling to the rim and cutting off the ball
- Made almost 77.5% of his shots inside of three feet, did most of his damage from ten feet and in
- Good at opportunistically crashing the offensive glass to score on put-backs
- Outside shot is inconsistent at this stage, above average mid-range shooter, made less than 20% of his threes
- Mostly a stationary spot-up shooter, less effective as the screener on pick-and-pops
- Catch-and-shoot player at this stage, not really a passer at the NBA level, good at limiting turnovers
- 2019-20 Defensive Degree of Difficulty: 0.272
- Tends to play either in garbage time or against lower leverage second unit players
- Good rim protector, excellent shot blocker and solid defensive rebounder
- Below average on-ball defender, stronger big men can back him down in the post, highly foul prone
- Good pick-and-roll defender, good in drop coverages, can switch onto ball handlers for a few dribbles
- Consistently comes out to contest perimeter shots in spot-up situations

Edmond Sumner	Height	Weight	Cap #	Years Left
	6'4"	176	$2.160M	Team Option

	Similar at Age	24 Season	SIMsc
1	Ian Clark	2015-16	913.6
2	Milton Doyle	2017-18	904.0
3	Quincy Douby	2008-09	898.5
4	Markel Brown	2015-16	897.8
5	Greg Graham	1994-95	896.0
6	Cameron Payne	2018-19	895.5
7	Lance Blanks	1990-91	894.2
8	Shaquille Harrison	2017-18	893.7
9	Ben McLemore	2017-18	892.2
10	Elliot Williams	2013-14	891.7

Baseline Basic Stats

MPG	PTS	AST	REB	BLK	STL
19.1	7.5	2.0	2.4	0.3	0.7

Advanced Metrics

USG%	3PTA/FGA	FTA/FGA	TS%	eFG%	3PT%
18.2	0.357	0.234	0.544	0.514	0.320
AST%	**TOV%**	**OREB%**	**DREB%**	**STL%**	**BLK%**
14.8	10.9	2.3	12.6	1.8	1.4
PER	**ORTG**	**DRTG**	**WS/48**	**VOL**	
13.54	109.7	108.7	0.103	0.536	

- Missed over a month with a fractured right hand, fringe rotation player for Indiana when healthy
- Used in a low volume role as a spot-up shooter and secondary ball handler
- Mostly effective at scoring at the rim, made 72.5% of his shots inside of three feet last season
- Good at pushing the ball up the floor in transition or running on the wings to get layups
- Struggled to score efficiently in a half-court set, True Shooting Percentage was below 50%
- Inconsistent shooter, made less than 30% of his threes throughout his career
- Rated as below average or worse in every half-court offensive situation last season
- Solid secondary playmaker, good at making interior passes, good at limiting turnovers
- 2019-20 Defensive Degree of Difficulty: 0.357, tends to guard second unit level players
- Not tested very often in isolation situations, played below average on-ball defense in a small sample of possessions
- Below average pick-and-roll defender, tended to be indecisive when making rotations
- Stays attached to shooters off the ball, usually closes out in spot-up situations
- Active help defender, gets blocks and steals at a fairly high rate, decent on the defensive boards

Jalen Lecque

Height	Weight	Cap #	Years Left
6'3"	185	$1.518M	1 + TO

Similar at Age 19

		Season	SIMsc
1	Anfernee Simons	2018-19	885.1
2	Zhaire Smith	2018-19	877.8
3	Lou Williams	2005-06	847.0
4	Marquis Teague	2012-13	844.4
5	Tyus Jones	2015-16	843.7
6	Malik Monk	2017-18	838.1
7	Dajuan Wagner	2002-03	830.9
8	Frank Ntilikina	2017-18	830.0

Baseline Basic Stats

MPG	PTS	AST	REB	BLK	STL
15.7	5.9	1.4	1.5	0.1	0.5

Advanced Metrics

USG%	3PTA/FGA	FTA/FGA	TS%	eFG%	3PT%
17.2	0.330	0.222	0.508	0.464	0.189
AST%	**TOV%**	**OREB%**	**DREB%**	**STL%**	**BLK%**
13.5	13.9	0.9	8.8	1.2	0.3
PER	**ORTG**	**DRTG**	**WS/48**	**VOL**	
7.87	98.4	114.7	0.000	0.598	

- Played sparingly for Phoenix in his rookie season, spent most of 2019-20 in the G-League with the Northern Arizona Suns
- Utilized as a high volume scoring guard in the G-League, struggled to shoot efficiently
- True Shooting Percentage was below 50% in the G-League, made less than 25% of his threes
- Did not really get to the rim, made less than 50% of his two-point shots
- Showed decent playmaking skills, fairly turnover prone in the G-League
- Not really effective in any half-court situation in limited NBA minutes
- 2019-20 Defensive Degree of Difficulty: 0.227, only played 32 NBA minutes
- Mostly played in garbage time, sample size of NBA possessions is limited
- Did not defend an isolation last season, forced a turnover in his only post-up possession
- Allowed a made two-pointer and forced three misses in four pick-and-roll possessions
- Committed a shooting foul and forced a miss in two possessions when guarding shooters off screens
- Allowed Kyle Korver to make a three, forced two misses and committed a shooting foul in four possession when defending spot-up jumpers
- Solid defensive rebounder for his size, got steals at a middling rate in the G-League

Kelan Martin	Height	Weight	Cap #	Years Left
	6'5"	235	$1.446M	RFA

	Similar at Age	24	
		Season	SIMsc
1	Justin Anderson	2017-18	915.3
2	Josh Davis	2004-05	906.3
3	Wayne Selden	2018-19	902.3
4	Abdel Nader	2017-18	897.8
5	Orlando Johnson	2013-14	896.1
6	Lazar Hayward	2010-11	894.6
7	Luke Babbitt	2013-14	892.9
8	Semi Ojeleye	2018-19	885.5
9	Marcus Landry	2009-10	880.4
10	Jarell Martin	2018-19	880.0

Baseline Basic Stats

MPG	PTS	AST	REB	BLK	STL
14.3	4.9	0.6	2.3	0.2	0.4

Advanced Metrics

USG%	3PTA/FGA	FTA/FGA	TS%	eFG%	3PT%
16.4	0.589	0.175	0.527	0.489	0.304
AST%	**TOV%**	**OREB%**	**DREB%**	**STL%**	**BLK%**
6.8	10.5	2.8	16.1	0.9	1.1
PER	**ORTG**	**DRTG**	**WS/48**	**VOL**	
9.23	103.2	112.5	0.045	0.426	

- Played on a Two-Way contract last season, became a regular rotation player for Minnesota after spending some time in the G-League with the Iowa Wolves
- Used as a low volume, spot-up shooter, played a higher volume role in the G-League
- Made almost 38% of his G-League threes, made only 26% of his NBA threes
- Mostly was a spot-up shooter, flashed some ability to shoot off screens
- Good at making backdoor cuts in a small sample of possessions, made almost 73% of his shots inside of three feet in the NBA
- Pretty much a catch-and-shoot player, limited passing skills, did not turn the ball over
- 2019-20 Defensive Degree of Difficulty: 0.383
- Tended to guard second unit level players or lower leverage starters
- Below average on-ball defender, had trouble staying in front of perimeter players on isolations
- Average pick-and-roll defender, could fight over the screen to guard ball handlers, struggled to guard bigger players on switches
- Good at staying attached to shooters off the ball, consistently closed out in spot-up situations
- Good defensive rebounder, did not really get steals, posted a fairly high Block Percentage last season

ATLANTA HAWKS

Last Season: 20 – 47, Missed the Playoffs

Offensive Rating: 107.2, 26th in the NBA

Defensive Rating: 114.8, 27th in the NBA

Primary Executive: Travis Schlenk, Head of Basketball Operations and General Manager

Head Coach: Lloyd Pierce

Key Roster Changes

Subtractions
Dewayne Dedmon, trade
DeAndre' Bembry, free agency
Skal Labissiere, free agency
Damian Jones, free agency
Jeff Teague, free agency
Treveon Graham, free agency
Vince Carter, retired

Additions
Onyeka Okongwu, draft
Tony Snell, trade
Danilo Gallinari, free agency
Bogdan Bogdanovic, free agency
Kris Dunn, free agency
Rajon Rondo, free agency
Solomon Hill, free agency

Roster

Likely Starting Five

1. *Trae Young*
2. *Bogdan Bogdanovic*
3. *Danilo Gallinari*
4. John Collins
5. *Clint Capela*

Other Key Rotation Players
Kris Dunn
Rajon Rondo
Onyeka Okongwu
De'Andre Hunter
Tony Snell

* Italics denotes that a player is likely to be on the floor to close games

Remaining Roster

- Kevin Huerter
- Cam Reddish
- Solomon Hill
- Bruno Fernando
- Brandon Goodwin
- Skylar Mays, 23, 6'4", 205, LSU (Two-Way)
- Nathan Knight, 23, 6'10", 253, William and Mary (Two-Way)

SCHREMPF Base Rating: 36.1 (72-game season)

Strengths

- Outside shooting and increased offensive firepower around Trae Young
- Potentially a deep rotation with at least 10 solid players

Question Marks

- Defense due to a limited number of proven defenders on the roster
- Roster imbalance and overlapping skill sets
- Lack of front-end talent, may only have one true All-Star in their rotation

Outlook

- Greatly improved, will likely end up with one of the spots in the play-in tournament

Veterans

Trae Young	Height	Weight	Cap #	Years Left
	6'1"	180	$6.572M	Team Option

	Similar at Age	21	
		Season	SIMsc
1	Stephon Marbury	1998-99	905.8
2	Kyrie Irving	2013-14	899.1
3	Dennis Schroder	2014-15	884.6
4	Kemba Walker	2011-12	881.4
5	Tony Parker	2003-04	880.7
6	Chris Paul	2006-07	879.6
7	D.J. Augustin	2008-09	878.5
8	Mike Conley	2008-09	878.2
9	Brandon Jennings	2010-11	872.5
10	Brandon Knight	2012-13	866.6

Baseline Basic Stats

MPG	PTS	AST	REB	BLK	STL
33.5	19.0	6.6	3.3	0.2	1.3

Advanced Metrics

USG%	3PTA/FGA	FTA/FGA	TS%	eFG%	3PT%
28.3	0.256	0.353	0.558	0.500	0.336
AST%	**TOV%**	**OREB%**	**DREB%**	**STL%**	**BLK%**
39.2	15.8	2.0	9.2	1.8	0.3
PER	**ORTG**	**DRTG**	**WS/48**	**VOL**	
19.51	110.8	112.7	0.123	0.315	

- Made his first All-Star team last season
- Improved across the board, increased his scoring efficiency significantly in a very high volume role
- Very good pick-and-roll ball handler and isolation player
- Shoots with deep range, can also attack the rim, drew fouls at a much higher rate last season
- Excellent spot-up shooter, but generally middling in other areas as an off-ball player
- Not as effective at running off screens or scoring on hand-off plays, rarely looks to cut without the ball
- 2019-20 Defensive Degree of Difficulty: 0.388
- Generally hidden in favorable matchups against lower leverage offensive players
- Struggles as an on-ball defender, doesn't always stay in front of his man and taller perimeter players can shoot over the top of him
- Middling pick-and-roll defender, but showed an improved ability to handle bigger players on switches
- Improved his discipline off the ball, good at staying attached to spot-up shooters, did a better job of fighting through screens
- More active as a help defender, increased his Defensive Rebound and Steal Percentages last season

Danilo Gallinari	Height	Weight	Cap #	Years Left
	6'10"	233	$19.500M	2

Similar at Age 31

		Season	SIMsc
1	Chris Bosh	2015-16	937.1
2	Mike Dunleavy, Jr.	2011-12	914.0
3	Jeff Green	2017-18	908.9
4	Tim Thomas	2008-09	908.8
5	Al Harrington	2011-12	898.8
6	Peja Stojakovic	2008-09	894.1
7	Jonas Jerebko	2018-19	893.1
8	Marvin Williams	2017-18	892.9
9	DeMarre Carroll	2017-18	880.8
10	Dave Robisch	1980-81	876.7

Baseline Basic Stats

MPG	PTS	AST	REB	BLK	STL
24.7	12.0	1.4	4.0	0.3	0.6

Advanced Metrics

USG%	3PTA/FGA	FTA/FGA	TS%	eFG%	3PT%
22.0	0.515	0.317	0.593	0.538	0.404
AST%	**TOV%**	**OREB%**	**DREB%**	**STL%**	**BLK%**
9.1	9.2	2.2	15.7	1.1	0.8
PER	**ORTG**	**DRTG**	**WS/48**	**VOL**	
16.37	115.1	111.2	0.118	0.487	

- Fairly good starter in his first season with Oklahoma City
- Highly efficient shooter in a fairly high volume role, rated as very good or better in every offensive situation last season
- Made 40.5% of his threes last season, very good spot-up shooter that can run off screens
- Excellent screener on pick-and-pops, good at making quick no dribble jumpers on isolations
- Good at posting up smaller players, very good on dribble hand-offs at getting to the rim or making outside shots
- Effective pick-and-roll ball handler that can get to the rim or pass to open shooters, draws fouls at a high rate, rarely commits turnovers
- 2019-20 Defensive Degree of Difficulty: 0.410, tends to guard starting level players
- Fairly solid on-ball defender, good against perimeter players, can be bullied inside by stronger post players
- Below average pick-and-roll defender, tends to go too far under screens, has trouble containing ball handlers on the perimeter
- Fights through screens off the ball, tends to be either late or too aggressive when closing out on perimeter shooters
- Solid defensive rebounder, does not really get steals or blocks at this stage of his career

Bogdan Bogdanović	Height	Weight	Cap #	Years Left
	6'6"	220	$18.000M	2 + PO

	Similar at Age	27	
		Season	**SIMsc**
1	C.J. Miles	2014-15	937.9
2	Sam Mack	1997-98	936.6
3	Carlos Delfino	2009-10	932.8
4	Kareem Rush	2007-08	924.5
5	Jason Richardson	2007-08	923.8
6	Khris Middleton	2018-19	923.0
7	Mickael Pietrus	2009-10	922.8
8	Bojan Bogdanovic	2016-17	922.0
9	Gordan Giricek	2004-05	921.8
10	O.J. Mayo	2014-15	918.2

Baseline Basic Stats

MPG	PTS	AST	REB	BLK	STL
28.5	13.0	2.1	3.5	0.2	0.9

Advanced Metrics

USG%	3PTA/FGA	FTA/FGA	TS%	eFG%	3PT%
21.0	0.544	0.171	0.551	0.525	0.384
AST%	**TOV%**	**OREB%**	**DREB%**	**STL%**	**BLK%**
15.0	10.4	1.9	11.4	1.7	0.7
PER	**ORTG**	**DRTG**	**WS/48**	**VOL**	
14.16	108.9	111.2	0.089	0.369	

- Part-time starter for Sacramento in his third NBA season
- Had his most effective season in his role as a moderate volume shooter off the bench
- Good three-point shooter throughout his career, very good spot-up shooter that can run off screens
- Can set up for trail threes in transition, good at making pull-up jumpers as a pick-and-roll ball handler and isolation player
- Effective at using an on-ball screen to go to the rim on dribble hand-offs
- Good at making backdoor cuts, runs down the wing to get layups in transition
- Good secondary playmaker that hits cutters, consistently avoids turnovers
- 2019-20 Defensive Degree of Difficulty: 0.365, tends to guard second unit players
- Decent on-ball defender that can competently guard wings, has some trouble against quicker players
- Middling pick-and-roll defender, tends to allow ball handlers to turn the corner, struggles to guard screeners on switches
- Gets caught on screens off the ball, tends to close out too aggressively
- Solid defensive rebounder, Steal and Block Percentages are still consistent with his career averages

John Collins

Height	Weight	Cap #	Years Left
6'9"	235	$4.137M	RFA

Similar at Age 22

		Season	SIMsc
1	Trey Lyles	2017-18	913.0
2	Ersan Ilyasova	2009-10	906.6
3	Kris Humphries	2007-08	905.3
4	Clint Capela	2016-17	903.8
5	Darrell Arthur	2010-11	903.4
6	Andray Blatche	2008-09	898.4
7	Rasheed Wallace	1996-97	897.2
8	Terrence Jones	2013-14	896.8
9	Brandon Bass	2007-08	893.8
10	Jonas Valanciunas	2014-15	893.7

Baseline Basic Stats

MPG	PTS	AST	REB	BLK	STL
25.4	12.5	1.4	7.0	0.8	0.7

Advanced Metrics

USG%	3PTA/FGA	FTA/FGA	TS%	eFG%	3PT%
22.0	0.213	0.257	0.604	0.571	0.360
AST%	**TOV%**	**OREB%**	**DREB%**	**STL%**	**BLK%**
9.6	10.4	8.8	21.3	1.3	2.8
PER	**ORTG**	**DRTG**	**WS/48**	**VOL**	
20.61	117.7	108.9	0.154	0.420	

- Suspended in November 2019 for 25 games after testing positive for a growth hormone
- Improved his scoring efficiency in a moderately high volume role
- Outside shooting improved significantly, made over 40% of his threes last season
- Excelled as a spot-up shooter and as the screener on pick-and-pop plays
- Highly productive throughout his career as a rim runner
- Very good at rolling to the rim on pick-and-rolls, will crash the offensive glass to score on put-backs, runs the floor well in transition
- Excellent in a small sample of one-on-one possessions, can post up smaller players and drive by opposing big men on isolations
- Flashes some passing skills, cut his turnover rate last season
- 2019-20 Defensive Degree of Difficulty: 0.399
- Hidden in favorable matchups against lower leverage offensive players, used more as a roaming help defender
- Showed improvement as a rim protector, solid rebounder that posted a career high in Blocks Percentage
- Better at defending in space, could adequately switch onto a ball handler for a few dribbles
- Had difficulty guarding interior players in the post, prone to committing shooting fouls

Clint Capela	Height	Weight	Cap #	Years Left
	6'10"	240	$16.000M	2

	Similar at Age	25 Season	SIMsc
1	Miles Plumlee	2013-14	923.9
2	Ed Davis	2014-15	920.0
3	Kris Humphries	2010-11	919.9
4	Samaki Walker	2001-02	907.2
5	Clemon Johnson	1981-82	905.5
6	Taj Gibson	2010-11	903.6
7	Jelani McCoy	2002-03	901.4
8	Ben Wallace	1999-00	901.3
9	Emeka Okafor	2007-08	900.7
10	Marcin Gortat	2009-10	896.9

Baseline Basic Stats

MPG	PTS	AST	REB	BLK	STL
24.8	9.3	1.0	8.0	1.2	0.6

Advanced Metrics

USG%	3PTA/FGA	FTA/FGA	TS%	eFG%	3PT%
16.9	0.000	0.343	0.599	0.589	0.069
AST%	**TOV%**	**OREB%**	**DREB%**	**STL%**	**BLK%**
6.2	13.0	12.5	26.7	1.2	3.9
PER	**ORTG**	**DRTG**	**WS/48**	**VOL**	
19.41	119.1	104.2	0.170	0.399	

- Missed parts of last season due to a right heel injury
- Efficient, low volume rim runner, just over half of his made field goals last seasons were dunks
- Primarily scores off lobs and rolls to the rim, also scores on a high volume of cuts
- Excellent offensive rebounder, runs hard down the floor in transition
- Limited passing skills, consistently avoids turnovers
- No real shooting range outside of three feet, struggles to make free throws
- 2019-20 Defensive Degree of Difficulty: 0.455
- Solid pick-and-roll defender, good at covering roll men in drop coverages and can capably switch out on ball handlers
- Fairly effective at defending in space, held up very well in isolation situations
- Average post defender, can be undisciplined with his positioning
- Excellent rebounder and shot blocker, can sometimes sacrifice positioning to go for blocks
- Prone to allowing open perimeter shots, does not always close out on spot-up shooters

Kris Dunn	Height	Weight	Cap #	Years Left
	6'3"	205	$4.767M	Player Option

Similar at Age **25**

		Season	SIMsc
1	Jamaal Tinsley	2003-04	906.8
2	Erick Strickland	1998-99	902.7
3	John Starks	1990-91	902.3
4	Shaquille Harrison	2018-19	901.9
5	Khalid Reeves	1997-98	901.1
6	Jerryd Bayless	2013-14	898.8
7	Doug Christie	1995-96	896.7
8	Nando De Colo	2012-13	895.6
9	T.J. McConnell	2017-18	895.0
10	Ronnie Price	2008-09	894.5

Baseline Basic Stats

MPG	PTS	AST	REB	BLK	STL
23.2	9.3	3.5	2.8	0.2	1.2

Advanced Metrics

USG%	3PTA/FGA	FTA/FGA	TS%	eFG%	3PT%
18.7	0.288	0.232	0.511	0.476	0.327
AST%	**TOV%**	**OREB%**	**DREB%**	**STL%**	**BLK%**
23.1	15.0	2.2	12.2	2.9	1.0
PER	**ORTG**	**DRTG**	**WS/48**	**VOL**	
13.32	104.3	107.5	0.075	0.378	

- Regular rotation player for Chicago last season, started most games
- Could miss the start of the 2020-21 while recovering from a sprained right MCL
- Mainly used as a secondary ball handler in a low volume role, fairly good playmaker, somewhat turnover prone
- Has trouble scoring efficiently in a half court set, has not become a reliable outside shooter, percentages below break-even for his career on threes
- Can use his quickness to drive to the rim on isolation plays, made almost 65% of his shots inside of three feet, doesn't drive as frequently
- Rarely moves off the ball, has not shown that he can be a threat without the ball
- 2019-20 Defensive Degree of Difficulty: 0.520
- Tends to take on difficult assignments against top perimeter players
- Has become a good on-ball defender that can capably defend quicker guards and wings, better against guards
- Solid pick-and-roll defender that can fight over screens, fairly good on switches
- Generally closes out on perimeter shooters, can gamble too much, will get caught out of position trying to shoot the gap when chasing shooters off screens
- Led the NBA in Steal Percentage last season, good defensive rebounding guard

Rajon Rondo	Height	Weight	Cap #	Years Left
	6'1"	186	$7.500M	1

	Similar at Age	33 Season	SIMsc
1	Haywoode Workman	1998-99	922.7
2	Charlie Ward	2003-04	915.6
3	Mark Jackson	1998-99	911.1
4	Raymond Felton	2017-18	907.1
5	Mike James	2008-09	906.3
6	Terry Porter	1996-97	903.2
7	Jameer Nelson	2015-16	903.1
8	Anthony Carter	2008-09	902.8
9	Mark Price	1997-98	901.5
10	Bobby Jackson	2006-07	901.3

Baseline Basic Stats

MPG	PTS	AST	REB	BLK	STL
23.0	7.5	4.5	2.7	0.1	0.8

Advanced Metrics

USG%	3PTA/FGA	FTA/FGA	TS%	eFG%	3PT%
16.8	0.401	0.120	0.498	0.481	0.350
AST%	**TOV%**	**OREB%**	**DREB%**	**STL%**	**BLK%**
28.9	18.8	2.5	11.8	1.9	0.3
PER	**ORTG**	**DRTG**	**WS/48**	**VOL**	
12.22	104.3	108.7	0.067	0.475	

- Missed games due to a series of minor injuries, regular rotation player for the Lakers when healthy
- Used as a low volume, pass-first backup point guard
- Still an excellent playmaker that can find open shooters or hit cutters, fairly turnover prone
- Struggled to shoot efficiently, True Shooting Percentage was below 50% for the second straight season
- Rated as average or worse in almost every offensive situation last season, most effective as a pick-and-roll ball handler
- Below break-even three-point shooter for his career, shot much better in the playoffs in 2019-20
- 2019-20 Defensive Degree of Difficulty: 0.370
- Usually guards second unit players, will take on some tough assignments against top guards
- Decent on-ball defender, had trouble against quicker guards, defended better against bigger guards in the post
- Solid pick-and-roll defender, good at guarding ball handlers and switching onto screens, sometimes goes too far under screens
- Stays attached to shooters off the ball, good at closing out in spot-up situations
- Good defensive rebounder, Steal Percentage has been in decline for the last few seasons

De'Andre Hunter	Height	Weight	Cap #	Years Left
	6'7"	225	$7.422M	2 Team Options

	Similar at Age	**22**	
		Season	**SIMsc**
1	Dillon Brooks	2017-18	944.5
2	Chase Budinger	2010-11	939.1
3	Mike Miller	2002-03	935.1
4	Khris Middleton	2013-14	930.3
5	Jaylen Brown	2018-19	925.9
6	Omri Casspi	2010-11	925.5
7	Jarvis Hayes	2003-04	922.2
8	Wilson Chandler	2009-10	921.1
9	Justise Winslow	2018-19	918.0
10	Lamond Murray	1995-96	917.4

Baseline Basic Stats

MPG	PTS	AST	REB	BLK	STL
26.7	11.2	1.6	3.9	0.4	0.8

Advanced Metrics

USG%	3PTA/FGA	FTA/FGA	TS%	eFG%	3PT%
18.9	0.397	0.224	0.540	0.506	0.369
AST%	**TOV%**	**OREB%**	**DREB%**	**STL%**	**BLK%**
9.4	11.3	2.7	13.2	1.3	0.9
PER	**ORTG**	**DRTG**	**WS/48**	**VOL**	
11.64	104.5	112.5	0.053	0.449	

- Regular starter for Atlanta during his rookie season
- Mainly used as a low volume, spot-up shooter, made threes at around the league average
- Mixed results when asked to play off the ball
- Struggled to make shots off screens, but was effective as a cutter and was good at scoring on put-backs
- Scored on a fairly high volume of transition plays, runs the floor well, can hit trail threes
- Effective at driving to the rim on isolations and pick-and-rolls, had trouble making shots off the dribble
- Mostly a catch-and-shoot player, limited ability to make plays for others, effective at limiting turnovers
- 2019-20 Defensive Degree of Difficulty: 0.460
- Typically tasked with defending the opponent's top wing scorer
- Solid on-ball defender, very good at defending in isolation situations last season
- Average pick-and-roll defender, better at guarding drives to the rim, prone to giving up open perimeter shots
- Had some difficulty chasing shooters off screen, was sometimes late to close out in spot-up situations
- Very good defensive rebounder, stay-at-home defender, does not really get blocks or steals

Tony Snell	Height	Weight	Cap #	Years Left
	6'6"	213	$12.179M	UFA

	Similar at Age	28 Season	SIMsc
1	Iman Shumpert	2018-19	913.5
2	Bobby Simmons	2008-09	907.2
3	Jared Dudley	2013-14	906.8
4	Sam Mack	1998-99	906.8
5	Mickael Pietrus	2010-11	903.3
6	Thabo Sefolosha	2012-13	899.3
7	Danny Green	2015-16	898.0
8	Keith Bogans	2008-09	897.1
9	Ryan Broekhoff	2018-19	896.9
10	Torrey Craig	2018-19	896.7

Baseline Basic Stats

MPG	PTS	AST	REB	BLK	STL
20.7	6.7	1.2	2.3	0.3	0.6

Advanced Metrics

USG%	3PTA/FGA	FTA/FGA	TS%	eFG%	3PT%
12.8	0.707	0.116	0.555	0.535	0.375
AST%	**TOV%**	**OREB%**	**DREB%**	**STL%**	**BLK%**
8.9	8.3	1.5	9.5	1.3	1.1
PER	**ORTG**	**DRTG**	**WS/48**	**VOL**	
9.47	112.1	111.0	0.078	0.288	

- Full-time starter in his first season with Detroit
- Has been a low volume, spot-up shooter throughout his career, has made over 40% of his threes over the last four seasons
- Primarily a spot-up shooter, will set up trail threes in transition can occasionally shoot off screens
- Effective last season at using an on-ball screen to make outside shots on pick-and-rolls
- Good at getting to the rim on dribble hand-offs
- Cannot really create his own shot, passing skills improved last season, set a career high in Assist Percentage, rarely turns the ball over
- 2019-20 Defensive Degree of Difficulty: 0.535
- Usually has primary responsibility to guard the opposing team's top perimeter player
- Good on-ball defender that guards multiple positions, had some trouble with bigger players in the post
- Not as effective at guarding pick-and-rolls last season, still solid on switches, indecisive when making rotations
- Tends to fight through screens and close out on perimeter shooters, had some lapses off the ball last season
- Stay-at-home defender, does not really get steals or blocks, Defensive Rebound Percentage declined last season

Kevin Huerter

Height	Weight	Cap #	Years Left
6'7"	190	$2.762M	Team Option

Similar at Age **21**

		Season	SIMsc
1	Patrick McCaw	2016-17	926.5
2	Sasha Vujacic	2005-06	921.6
3	Luke Kennard	2017-18	915.4
4	Ben McLemore	2014-15	914.0
5	Martell Webster	2007-08	913.2
6	Evan Fournier	2013-14	911.3
7	Klay Thompson	2011-12	911.1
8	Dante Exum	2016-17	910.2
9	Lonzo Ball	2018-19	904.6
10	Furkan Korkmaz	2018-19	904.5

Baseline Basic Stats

MPG	PTS	AST	REB	BLK	STL
25.1	10.2	1.9	3.0	0.3	0.8

Advanced Metrics

USG%	3PTA/FGA	FTA/FGA	TS%	eFG%	3PT%
16.9	0.381	0.160	0.536	0.509	0.368

AST%	TOV%	OREB%	DREB%	STL%	BLK%
14.3	12.5	2.0	10.8	1.6	0.9

PER	ORTG	DRTG	WS/48	VOL
11.09	106.2	113.4	0.065	0.311

- Regular starter for Atlanta for the last two seasons
- Continued his role as a lower volume, spot-up shooter, incrementally improved across the board
- Excellent at making spot-up threes, shot above 38% and made over 43% of his corner threes over the last two seasons
- Can occasionally make shots off the dribble, but struggles to shoot on the move and has trouble getting all the way to the rim on drives
- Improved his playmaking skills, increased his Assist Percentage and cut his turnover rate
- 2019-20 Defensive Degree of Difficulty: 0.411
- Usually guards lower end starters or higher level second unit players
- Below average on-ball defender, has trouble keeping his man in front of him
- Below average pick-and-roll defender, can be late to close out on shooters, can get caught on screens
- Showed an improved ability to handle bigger players in a small sample of post-up possessions
- Played more actively as a help defender, became a solid defensive rebounder and increased his Block Percentage slightly, steals rate held fairly steady

Cam Reddish	Height	Weight	Cap #	Years Left
	6'8"	208	$4.458M	2 Team Options

	Similar at Age	20 Season	SIMsc
1	Paul George	2010-11	943.8
2	Rodions Kurucs	2018-19	938.5
3	Mario Hezonja	2015-16	928.3
4	Martell Webster	2006-07	926.8
5	Harrison Barnes	2012-13	926.2
6	DerMarr Johnson	2000-01	925.3
7	Al-Farouq Aminu	2010-11	925.2
8	Nicolas Batum	2008-09	924.5
9	Maurice Harkless	2013-14	918.3
10	Mike Miller	2000-01	914.7

Baseline Basic Stats

MPG	PTS	AST	REB	BLK	STL
25.9	10.8	1.8	4.0	0.4	0.8

Advanced Metrics

USG%	3PTA/FGA	FTA/FGA	TS%	eFG%	3PT%
20.2	0.459	0.216	0.527	0.490	0.368
AST%	**TOV%**	**OREB%**	**DREB%**	**STL%**	**BLK%**
10.3	12.5	2.8	13.0	1.7	1.2
PER	**ORTG**	**DRTG**	**WS/48**	**VOL**	
11.77	101.3	111.9	0.045	0.468	

- Played mostly as a starter during his rookie season, came off the bench at the end of the year
- Predominantly a lower volume, spot-up shooter, struggled to shoot efficiently
- Pretty much a break-even three-point shooter, shot slightly better in the corners
- Effective in flashes as an off-ball player, good at shooting off screens in a small sample of possessions
- Fairly good cutter, had some success getting to the rim on dribble hand-off plays
- Struggled in on-ball situations, had trouble driving by defenders
- Playmaking skills are limited at this stage, more of a catch-and-shoot player, solid at limiting turnovers
- 2019-20 Defensive Degree of Difficulty: 0.451
- Typically guarded starting level players, had some responsibility to handle tougher assignments
- Fairly solid on-ball defender, could contain the drive and contest jump shots, prone to committing shooting fouls
- Showed enough versatility to defend smaller guards and taller wing players
- Decent pick-and-roll defender, but could be a bit too aggressive, sometimes gave up driving lanes to the rim
- Generally closed out on shooters in spot-up situations, average at chasing shooters off screens
- Solid defensive rebounder, posts fairly good Steal and Block Percentages

Solomon Hill	Height	Weight	Cap #	Years Left
	6'6"	225	$1.621M	UFA

	Similar at Age	28 Season	SIMsc
1	Keith Bogans	2008-09	917.7
2	Mickael Pietrus	2010-11	916.3
3	Jarvis Hayes	2009-10	916.0
4	Iman Shumpert	2018-19	915.7
5	Jared Dudley	2013-14	915.4
6	Cartier Martin	2012-13	912.6
7	Lance Thomas	2016-17	912.5
8	Quentin Richardson	2008-09	912.2
9	Torrey Craig	2018-19	908.6
10	Kelly Tripucka	1987-88	908.4

Baseline Basic Stats

MPG	PTS	AST	REB	BLK	STL
20.5	6.8	1.3	2.8	0.2	0.7

Advanced Metrics

USG%	3PTA/FGA	FTA/FGA	TS%	eFG%	3PT%
13.9	0.600	0.193	0.534	0.507	0.359
AST%	**TOV%**	**OREB%**	**DREB%**	**STL%**	**BLK%**
10.4	13.0	3.2	12.7	1.7	1.0
PER	**ORTG**	**DRTG**	**WS/48**	**VOL**	
10.17	106.5	109.9	0.067	0.432	

- Traded from Memphis to Miami in February 2020, regular rotation player for Memphis, playing time decreased after the trade
- Used by both teams as a low volume, spot-up shooter, made almost 37% of his threes last season
- Shot more efficiently with Memphis, made less than 30% of his threes with Miami
- Almost strictly a stationary spot-up shooter, does not really shoot on the move or off the dribble
- Rated as average or worse in most offensive situations last season
- Catch-and-shoot player, decent secondary playmaker that can make the extra pass, solid at avoiding turnovers
- 2019-20 Defensive Degree of Difficulty: 0.353, tends to guard second unit players
- Solid on-ball defender that can capably defend multiple positions
- Below average pick-and-roll defender, struggled to contain ball handlers, effective at switching onto the screener
- Fights through screens off the ball, tends to either be late or too aggressive when closing out on perimeter shooters
- Solid defensive rebounder, Steal and Block Percentages were above his career averages, more active help defender in Miami last season

Bruno Fernando	Height	Weight	Cap #	Years Left
	6'9"	233	$1.518M	1

Similar at Age 21

		Season	SIMsc
1	Kris Humphries	2006-07	919.6
2	Donnell Harvey	2001-02	919.3
3	Ivan Rabb	2018-19	918.4
4	Darrell Arthur	2009-10	913.3
5	Samaki Walker	1997-98	912.4
6	Patrick Patterson	2010-11	910.9
7	Noah Vonleh	2016-17	910.8
8	Cedric Simmons	2006-07	907.0
9	Shawne Williams	2007-08	903.9
10	Rasheed Wallace	1995-96	900.0

Baseline Basic Stats

MPG	PTS	AST	REB	BLK	STL
18.6	6.7	0.8	4.8	0.6	0.5

Advanced Metrics

USG%	3PTA/FGA	FTA/FGA	TS%	eFG%	3PT%
16.3	0.086	0.293	0.528	0.505	0.242
AST%	**TOV%**	**OREB%**	**DREB%**	**STL%**	**BLK%**
8.8	14.9	9.9	19.0	1.3	2.0
PER	**ORTG**	**DRTG**	**WS/48**	**VOL**	
12.61	106.3	109.6	0.065	0.340	

- Fringe rotation player for Atlanta during his rookie season
- Mostly used as a low volume rim runner, scored on a high volume of cuts, fairly good at rolling to the rim on pick-and-rolls
- Very good offensive rebounder that could score on put-backs, runs hard down the floor in transition
- Average post-up player, more effective at flashing to the middle and scoring from the left block
- Struggled to make shots outside of three feet, flashes some passing skills, slightly turnover prone
- 2019-20 Defensive Degree of Difficulty: 0.393, tended to defend higher-end second unit players
- Solid post defender, has good enough strength to hold position inside, good at covering the roll man in drop coverages
- Has difficulty defending in space, struggles to contain quicker guards on switches on either pick-and-rolls or isolation plays
- Below average rim protector, can be out of position at times, highly foul prone
- Fairly solid defensive rebounder that can occasionally block shots
- Has active hands to sometimes get steals

Brandon Goodwin

Height	Weight	Cap #	Years Left
6'0"	180	$1.702M	RFA

Similar at Age **24**

		Season	SIMsc
1	Frank Mason	2018-19	917.2
2	Salim Stoudamire	2006-07	912.0
3	Jannero Pargo	2003-04	907.3
4	A.J. Price	2010-11	905.4
5	Lionel Chalmers	2004-05	903.8
6	Nolan Smith	2012-13	902.9
7	Dan Dickau	2002-03	902.4
8	Quincy Douby	2008-09	902.1
9	Shabazz Napier	2015-16	897.3
10	Bobby Brown	2008-09	896.5

Baseline Basic Stats

MPG	PTS	AST	REB	BLK	STL
15.8	6.4	2.3	1.5	0.1	0.4

Advanced Metrics

USG%	3PTA/FGA	FTA/FGA	TS%	eFG%	3PT%
21.6	0.379	0.241	0.492	0.441	0.335
AST%	**TOV%**	**OREB%**	**DREB%**	**STL%**	**BLK%**
24.4	12.4	2.3	9.4	1.1	0.3
PER	**ORTG**	**DRTG**	**WS/48**	**VOL**	
11.79	104.7	113.8	0.045	0.296	

- Began the 2019-20 season on a Two-Way contract, but was later signed by Atlanta to a standard contract in February 2020
- Received consistently playing time towards the end of the season, mainly used as a scoring guard off the bench
- Most effective with the ball in his hands, could make pull-up jumpers or get to the rim as either an isolation player or pick-and-roll ball handler
- Generally limited turnovers and flashed decent playmaking skills
- Below average outside shooter at this stage, Three-Point Percentage is below break-even
- More comfortable taking longer mid-range shots right now
- 2019-20 Defensive Degree of Difficulty: 0.302
- Generally guarded lower leverage second unit players, rarely tested on the ball
- Had difficulty keeping opposing players in front of him as an on-ball defender in a small sample size
- Better at fighting through screens, defended fairly well on hand-offs, could funnel his man into help on pick-and-rolls
- Tended to get caught on screens, could also be too aggressive when closing out, prone to giving up driving lanes to the rim
- More of a stay-at-home defender, middling steal and block rates, very good defensive rebounder for his size

Newcomers

Onyeka Okongwu	**Height**	**Weight**	**Cap #**	**Years Left**
	6'9"	245	$5.814M	1 + 2 TO

Baseline Basic Stats

MPG	PTS	AST	REB	BLK	STL
21.5	8.4	1.0	5.3	0.9	0.6

Advanced Metrics

USG%	3PTA/FGA	FTA/FGA	TS%	eFG%	3PT%
18.3	0.045	0.370	0.522	0.489	0.265

AST%	TOV%	OREB%	DREB%	STL%	BLK%
7.6	12.5	10.0	17.9	1.5	3.8

PER	ORTG	DRTG	WS/48	VOL
16.22	104.7	98.5	0.105	N/A

- Drafted by Atlanta with the 6th overall pick
- Led the Pac-12 in PER last season, named to the All-Pac 12 1st Team in 2019-20
- Great rim runner at USC, high motor, vertical lob threat, great length and leaping ability
- Dives hard to the rim as a roll man and cutter, excellent offensive rebounder that scores on put-backs
- Bullied smaller defenders as a post player in college, still needs to refine his post moves to be effective in the NBA, draws fouls at a high rate
- Limited shooting range right now, has flashed the potential to make mid-range shots
- Decent passer, can hit cutters and pass out of double teams, limits turnovers
- Lacks ideal height for an NBA center, has great length and athleticism to make up for it
- Great shot blocker, good at keeping his blocks inbounds, great rim protector in college
- Can be too aggressive when going for blocks, sacrifices positioning, could be better on the defensive boards
- Average post defender, can be overpowered by stronger players inside
- Middling pick-and-roll defender, solid in drop coverages, struggled to defend quicker ball handlers in space
- Did not always come out to contest perimeter shots, tended to stay planted in the paint

ORLANDO MAGIC

Last Season: 33 – 40, Lost 1st Round to Milwaukee (1 – 4)

Offensive Rating: 108.5, 23rd in the NBA

Defensive Rating: 109.5, 10th in the NBA

Primary Executive: Jeff Weltman, President of Basketball Operations

Head Coach: Steve Clifford

Key Roster Changes

Subtractions
D.J. Augustin, free agency
Wesley Iwundu, free agency
Melvin Frazier, free agency

Additions
Cole Anthony, draft
Chuma Okeke, signed 2019 draft pick
Dwayne Bacon, free agency

Roster

Likely Starting Five

1. *Markelle Fultz*
2. *Evan Fournier*
3. James Ennis
4. *Aaron Gordon*
5. *Nikola Vucevic*

Other Key Rotation Players
Terrence Ross
Gary Clark
Al-Farouq Aminu
Mo Bamba
Khem Birch

* Italics denotes that a player is likely to be on the floor to close games

Remaining Roster

- Jonathan Isaac (recovering from a torn left ACL, will likely miss the entire season)
- Chuma Okeke
- Cole Anthony
- Michael Carter-Williams
- Dwayne Bacon
- Jordan Bone, 23, 6'3", 180, Tennessee (Two-Way)
- Karim Mane, 20, 6'5", 185, Vanier College (Two-Way)
- Devin Cannady, 24, 6'2", 183, Princeton (Exhibit 10)
- Robert Franks, 24, 6'7", 225, Washington State (Exhibit 10)
- Jon Teske, 23, 7'1", 265, Michigan (Exhibit 10)

SCHREMPF Base Rating: 33.8 (72-game season)

Strengths

- Solid defensive unit that protects the rim and forces turnovers
- High degree of continuity may allow them to get off to a faster than normal start

Question Marks

- Limited ability to generate efficient offense due to lack of consistent shooting
- Lacks the front-end talent to legitimately compete with the top teams in the East
- Unclear pathway to escape their current state of mediocrity

Outlook

- Essentially the same team as last season, could compete for a spot in the play-in tournament

Veterans

Nikola Vučević	Height	Weight	Cap #	Years Left
	6'11"	260	$26.000M	2

	Similar at Age	29	
		Season	SIMsc
1	Al Jefferson	2013-14	917.7
2	Kevin Love	2017-18	899.4
3	Mehmet Okur	2008-09	890.0
4	Al Horford	2015-16	889.9
5	Troy Murphy	2009-10	886.6
6	Carlos Boozer	2010-11	881.7
7	LaMarcus Aldridge	2014-15	876.1
8	Tim Duncan*	2005-06	871.8
9	Mike Gminski	1988-89	871.6
10	Nene	2011-12	871.2

Baseline Basic Stats

MPG	PTS	AST	REB	BLK	STL
30.8	16.8	2.5	8.7	1.0	0.7

Advanced Metrics

USG%	3PTA/FGA	FTA/FGA	TS%	eFG%	3PT%
25.3	0.201	0.193	0.545	0.515	0.353
AST%	**TOV%**	**OREB%**	**DREB%**	**STL%**	**BLK%**
17.0	9.1	7.5	27.2	1.3	2.5
PER	**ORTG**	**DRTG**	**WS/48**	**VOL**	
20.86	110.9	104.1	0.149	0.384	

- Continued his near All-Star level play in his eighth season with Orlando
- Utilized as Orlando's primary scoring option as a low post scorer
- Scored on a high volume of post-ups at an average level of efficiency
- Fairly solid outside shooter, good from mid-range, break-even on threes
- Makes spot-up jumpers, effective as a screener on pick-and-pops, sometimes comes off screens
- Effective rim runner that slides into open spaces inside on cuts off the ball and rolls to the rim
- Excellent passing big man, cut his Turnover Percentage to a career low last season
- 2019-20 Defensive Degree of Difficulty: 0.415, tends to guard starting level big men
- Good rim protector despite a declining blocks rate, excellent defensive rebounder
- Below average on-ball defender, lacks the mobility to guard quicker players
- Solid pick-and-roll defender, good in drop coverages, fairly good at hedging out on ball handlers
- Tends to stay in the paint, does not always come out to contest perimeter shots

Aaron Gordon	Height	Weight	Cap #	Years Left
	6'8"	220	$18.136M	1

	Similar at Age	24 Season	SIMsc
1	Luol Deng	2009-10	940.6
2	Al Thornton	2007-08	930.9
3	Travis Outlaw	2008-09	930.3
4	Tobias Harris	2016-17	930.3
5	Mike Miller	2004-05	924.4
6	Mike Dunleavy, Jr.	2004-05	923.0
7	Pascal Siakam	2018-19	918.9
8	Danny Granger	2007-08	917.1
9	Rudy Gay	2010-11	916.7
10	Devean George	2001-02	916.2

Baseline Basic Stats

MPG	PTS	AST	REB	BLK	STL
32.7	15.4	2.6	5.7	0.6	0.9

Advanced Metrics

USG%	3PTA/FGA	FTA/FGA	TS%	eFG%	3PT%
22.0	0.317	0.269	0.531	0.494	0.337
AST%	**TOV%**	**OREB%**	**DREB%**	**STL%**	**BLK%**
15.5	10.9	4.9	17.5	1.3	1.5
PER	**ORTG**	**DRTG**	**WS/48**	**VOL**	
15.63	107.5	109.1	0.098	0.267	

- Full-time starter for Orlando in his sixth NBA season
- Production was consistent with his career averages in an undefined, moderate volume role
- Handled the ball more last season, not as effective in these situations, struggles to shoot off the dribble
- Best used as a rim runner, explosive vertical lob threat, very good at rolling to the rim and cutting off the ball
- Great at running by his man in transition to get dunks, fairly decent offensive rebounder that scores on put-backs
- Below break-even three-point shooter for his career, above break-even in the corners
- Effective screener on pick-and-pops, can sometimes knock down spot-up jumpers
- Good passer that has increased his Assist Percentage each season, good at avoiding turnovers
- 2019-20 Defensive Degree of Difficulty: 0.480
- Guards starting level players, takes on tougher defensive assignments
- Good on-ball defender that can guard multiple front-court positions
- Average pick-and-roll defender, can over-commit when making rotations
- Good at closing out on perimeter shooters, sometimes gets caught on screens off the ball
- Good at protecting the rim, stays vertical to contest shots, can occasionally block shots on the weak side, solid defensive rebounder

Evan Fournier	Height	Weight	Cap #	Years Left
	6'7"	205	$17.150M	UFA

	Similar at Age	27	
		Season	SIMsc
1	Klay Thompson	2017-18	945.1
2	Khris Middleton	2018-19	942.3
3	Voshon Lenard	2000-01	929.1
4	Bojan Bogdanovic	2016-17	925.2
5	Eric Piatkowski	1997-98	923.1
6	Steve Smith	1996-97	923.0
7	Sean Elliott	1995-96	922.7
8	Nick Anderson	1994-95	922.2
9	Sam Mack	1997-98	921.8
10	C.J. Miles	2014-15	921.5

Baseline Basic Stats

MPG	PTS	AST	REB	BLK	STL
31.2	16.4	2.4	3.6	0.3	0.9

Advanced Metrics

USG%	3PTA/FGA	FTA/FGA	TS%	eFG%	3PT%
23.0	0.461	0.220	0.570	0.535	0.389
AST%	**TOV%**	**OREB%**	**DREB%**	**STL%**	**BLK%**
15.1	10.7	1.7	9.7	1.5	0.7
PER	**ORTG**	**DRTG**	**WS/48**	**VOL**	
15.41	109.9	110.5	0.099	0.396	

- Regular starter for Orlando, had his most productive season as an NBA player in 2019-20
- Effective as a moderate volume shooter and secondary ball handler
- Made almost 40% of his threes last season, very good spot-up shooter that can run off screens
- Good at using the screen on dribble hand-offs to make outside shots, effective at making pull-up jumpers as a pick-and-roll ball handler
- Good at making backdoor cuts if defenders overplay his shot, can selectively hit the offensive glass to score on put-backs
- Solid secondary playmaker that hits open cutters, consistently limits his turnovers
- 2019-20 Defensive Degree of Difficulty: 0.509
- Takes on tougher defensive assignments against top perimeter players
- Played below average on-ball defense, over-matched against elite perimeter players
- Below average pick-and-roll defender, tended to allow ball handlers to turn the corner, could be targeted by bigger screeners on switches
- Good at closing out on perimeter shooters, tends to get caught on screens off the ball
- Steal and Block Percentages were higher than his career averages last season, middling defensive rebounder

Markelle Fultz

	Height	Weight	Cap #	Years Left
	6'3"	200	$12.289M	RFA

	Similar at Age	21 Season	SIMsc
1	Dennis Smith, Jr.	2018-19	939.2
2	Austin Rivers	2013-14	936.6
3	Jay Williams	2002-03	930.7
4	Elfrid Payton	2015-16	920.8
5	Deron Williams	2005-06	918.0
6	Emmanuel Mudiay	2017-18	913.0
7	Bradley Beal	2014-15	912.5
8	Raymond Felton	2005-06	911.9
9	Jerryd Bayless	2009-10	905.0
10	Javaris Crittenton	2008-09	903.0

Baseline Basic Stats

MPG	PTS	AST	REB	BLK	STL
23.4	9.7	3.6	2.5	0.2	0.9

Advanced Metrics

USG%	3PTA/FGA	FTA/FGA	TS%	eFG%	3PT%
19.7	0.147	0.267	0.509	0.469	0.286
AST%	**TOV%**	**OREB%**	**DREB%**	**STL%**	**BLK%**
26.2	15.0	3.0	9.7	2.0	0.5
PER	**ORTG**	**DRTG**	**WS/48**	**VOL**	
13.17	104.5	110.7	0.062	0.440	

- Regular starter for Orlando in his first full season with the team
- Solidly effective in his role as the team's point guard and primary ball handler
- Good playmaker that consistently hit the roll man and found open shooters, fairly good at limiting turnovers
- Good slashing guard that can get to the rim as a pick-and-roll ball handler
- Pretty good at pushing the ball at full speed in transition, effective cutter off the ball
- Healthy for the first time in his career, outside shot is a work-in-progress
- Fairly good mid-range shooter last season, career Three-Point Percentage is below 30%
- Better at shooting in rhythm off screens, less effective as a stationary spot-up shooter
- 2019-20 Defensive Degree of Difficulty: 0.461
- Tends to defend other starters, sometimes takes on tougher assignments against top point guards
- Middling on-ball defender at this stage, over-matched when defending elite ball handlers
- Good pick-and-roll defender, good at going over screens, does not allow ball handlers to turn the corner
- Fights through screens off the ball, tends to late when closing out on perimeter shooters
- Fairly good defensive rebounding guards, has active hands, gets steals at a fairly high rate

James Ennis	Height	Weight	Cap #	Years Left
	6'6"	210	$3.300M	UFA

Similar at Age 29

		Season	SIMsc
1	Gordan Giricek	2006-07	930.4
2	Ime Udoka	2006-07	930.4
3	Vincent Askew	1995-96	922.5
4	Mickael Pietrus	2011-12	915.9
5	Devean George	2006-07	914.6
6	C.J. Miles	2016-17	913.7
7	Cartier Martin	2013-14	912.9
8	Mike Sanders	1989-90	911.1
9	Eric Piatkowski	1999-00	910.8
10	Keith Askins	1996-97	910.7

Baseline Basic Stats

MPG	PTS	AST	REB	BLK	STL
20.8	7.2	1.2	2.6	0.3	0.6

Advanced Metrics

USG%	3PTA/FGA	FTA/FGA	TS%	eFG%	3PT%
15.1	0.463	0.241	0.556	0.518	0.347
AST%	**TOV%**	**OREB%**	**DREB%**	**STL%**	**BLK%**
7.7	11.1	4.2	12.0	1.4	1.2
PER	**ORTG**	**DRTG**	**WS/48**	**VOL**	
11.14	110.5	109.5	0.083	0.257	

- Regular rotation player for Philadelphia, traded to Orlando in February 2020, became a starter for Orlando after the trade
- Utilized by both teams as a low volume, spot-up shooter, below break-even three-point shooter last season, shot better with Philadelphia
- Mainly a stationary spot-up shooter, better in the corners, has made almost 39% of his corner threes in his career
- Most effective as a cutter off the ball, made almost 65% of his shots inside of three feet last season, draws fouls at a decent rate
- Primarily a catch-and-shoot player, limited as a playmaker, solid at avoiding turnovers
- 2019-20 Defensive Degree of Difficulty: 0.409
- Tended to guard second unit level players, sometimes got tougher defensive assignments
- Decent on-ball defender that can capably guard multiple positions, played better on-ball defense in Philadelphia
- Solid pick-and-roll defender, good at containing ball handlers, effective at switching onto screeners
- Fights through screens off the ball, tended to be late when closing out on perimeter shooters
- Stay-at-home defender, good defensive rebounder, gets steals and blocks at a moderate rate

Terrence Ross	Height	Weight	Cap #	Years Left
	6'6"	206	$13.500M	2

Similar at Age 28

		Season	SIMsc
1	C.J. Miles	2015-16	951.7
2	George McCloud	1995-96	945.2
3	Justin Holiday	2017-18	926.3
4	Wesley Matthews	2014-15	921.7
5	Randy Foye	2011-12	919.6
6	Jason Richardson	2008-09	919.0
7	Eric Piatkowski	1998-99	918.8
8	Klay Thompson	2018-19	917.6
9	Courtney Lee	2013-14	916.8
10	Gerald Green	2013-14	916.2

Baseline Basic Stats

MPG	PTS	AST	REB	BLK	STL
25.1	10.7	1.5	3.0	0.3	0.8

Advanced Metrics

USG%	3PTA/FGA	FTA/FGA	TS%	eFG%	3PT%
19.9	0.617	0.176	0.539	0.508	0.364
AST%	**TOV%**	**OREB%**	**DREB%**	**STL%**	**BLK%**
8.2	8.4	1.5	11.6	1.8	1.0
PER	**ORTG**	**DRTG**	**WS/48**	**VOL**	
12.45	105.3	108.6	0.077	0.364	

- Highly productive in 2019-20 in his role as Orlando's sixth man off the bench
- Used as higher volume scoring guard, fairly good three-point shooter throughout his career
- Very good at shooting off screens, solid spot-up shooter, can also make pull-up jumpers as the ball handler on pick-and-rolls
- Great athlete that can run down the wing in transition to finish plays above the rim
- Good at getting to the rim on dribble hand-offs, effective cutter off the ball
- Doesn't have the ball handling skills to drive by defenders on isolations
- Catch-and-shoot player, shows some passing skills, rarely turns the ball over
- 2019-20 Defensive Degree of Difficulty: 0.303
- Tends to be hidden in favorable matchups against lower leverage players
- Below average on-ball defender, tends to give up extra space for his man to take jump shots, can be bullied inside by stronger post players
- Average pick-and-roll defender, tends to go too far under screens
- Tends to be late when closing out on perimeter shooters, can get caught on screens off the ball
- Solid defensive rebounder, Block Percentage is still consistent with his career average, gets steals at a fairly good rate

Gary Clark

	Height	Weight	Cap #	Years Left
Gary Clark	6'6"	225	$2.000M	1

	Similar at Age	25 Season	SIMsc
1	Treveon Graham	2018-19	902.1
2	Abdel Nader	2018-19	877.6
3	Jaron Blossomgame	2018-19	877.5
4	Alex Abrines	2018-19	872.5
5	Shawne Williams	2011-12	863.5
6	Joe Harris	2016-17	859.0
7	Justin Anderson	2018-19	858.5
8	Glenn Robinson III	2018-19	857.0
9	Luke Babbitt	2014-15	856.4
10	James Jones	2005-06	856.3

Baseline Basic Stats

MPG	PTS	AST	REB	BLK	STL
17.8	6.1	0.8	2.6	0.3	0.4

Advanced Metrics

USG%	3PTA/FGA	FTA/FGA	TS%	eFG%	3PT%
13.0	0.721	0.121	0.562	0.541	0.369
AST%	**TOV%**	**OREB%**	**DREB%**	**STL%**	**BLK%**
5.8	7.5	4.9	12.9	1.0	2.3
PER	**ORTG**	**DRTG**	**WS/48**	**VOL**	
11.12	115.8	111.9	0.093	0.577	

- Waived by Houston in January 2020, later signed by Orlando, became a regular rotation player at the end of the season
- Used as a very low volume, spot-up shooter throughout his career, made threes at close to the league average last season
- Almost exclusively a stationary shooter, does not shoot on the move or off the dribble
- Effective cutter off the ball that can occasionally catch defenders off guard
- Not really a playmaker, rarely turns the ball over
- 2019-20 Defensive Degree of Difficulty: 0.305
- Tended to guard second unit level players, occasionally got tougher defensive assignments
- Played fairly good on-ball defense, has the potential to guard multiple positions
- Solid pick-and-roll defender, fights over screens to contain ball handlers, effective at switching onto screeners
- Can get caught on screens off the ball, tends to be late when closing out on perimeter shooters
- Good at protecting the rim despite being undersized, good shot blocker that stays vertical and has good timing
- Solid defensive rebounder that consistently boxes his man out, does not really get steals

Al-Farouq Aminu

Height	Weight	Cap #	Years Left
6'8"	220	$9.721M	1

Similar at Age **29**

		Season	SIMsc
1	Devean George	2006-07	934.3
2	David Benoit	1997-98	919.2
3	Jamario Moon	2009-10	913.5
4	Lance Thomas	2017-18	900.9
5	Pete Chilcutt	1997-98	900.5
6	Quincy Pondexter	2017-18	899.4
7	Jared Dudley	2014-15	898.4
8	Vladimir Radmanovic	2009-10	897.1
9	Cartier Martin	2013-14	894.0
10	P.J. Tucker	2014-15	891.1

Baseline Basic Stats

MPG	PTS	AST	REB	BLK	STL
19.1	4.6	1.0	3.3	0.4	0.6

Advanced Metrics

USG%	3PTA/FGA	FTA/FGA	TS%	eFG%	3PT%
12.1	0.462	0.226	0.478	0.441	0.306
AST%	**TOV%**	**OREB%**	**DREB%**	**STL%**	**BLK%**
7.1	11.8	5.1	17.8	1.7	1.6
PER	**ORTG**	**DRTG**	**WS/48**	**VOL**	
9.43	102.1	107.1	0.071	0.269	

- Missed most of last season due to a right knee injury that required surgery
- Regular rotation player when healthy, used as a low volume stretch big and rim runner
- Struggled to shoot efficiently in limited action with Orlando, rated as below average or worse in every offensive situation last season
- Was a league average three-point shooter in previous seasons with Portland
- Effective spot-up shooter that could also be a screener on pick-and-pops
- Solid as a rim runner in the past, can slide into open spaces as a cutter off the ball or roll man on pick-and-rolls
- Catch-and-shoot or catch-and-finish player, limited playmaking skills, good at avoiding turnovers
- 2019-20 Defensive Degree of Difficulty: 0.380
- Tended to guard higher-end second unit players or lower leverage starters
- Good at protecting the rim, stays vertical to contest shots, not really an on-ball shot blocker
- Active hands, gets steals at a high rate for an interior player, solid defensive rebounder
- Solid on-ball defender that can guard multiple positions
- Fairly solid pick-and-roll defender, solid at switching, sometimes doesn't get out to cover the screener on pick-and-pops
- Consistently closes out to contest perimeter shots

Mo Bamba	Height	Weight	Cap #	Years Left
	7'0"	241	$5.969M	Team Option

Similar at Age 21

		Season	SIMsc
1	Zach Collins	2018-19	889.9
2	Jason Smith	2007-08	880.9
3	Myles Turner	2017-18	880.0
4	JaVale McGee	2008-09	874.7
5	Deyonta Davis	2017-18	873.8
6	Sean Williams	2007-08	868.1
7	Darko Milicic	2006-07	861.7
8	Yi Jianlian	2008-09	861.7
9	Alex Len	2014-15	859.0
10	Andray Blatche	2007-08	857.8

Baseline Basic Stats

MPG	PTS	AST	REB	BLK	STL
23.2	8.5	0.9	6.0	1.7	0.6

Advanced Metrics

USG%	3PTA/FGA	FTA/FGA	TS%	eFG%	3PT%
16.6	0.169	0.249	0.533	0.513	0.343
AST%	**TOV%**	**OREB%**	**DREB%**	**STL%**	**BLK%**
6.9	14.2	10.0	21.5	1.3	5.7
PER	**ORTG**	**DRTG**	**WS/48**	**VOL**	
14.65	106.1	104.7	0.102	0.549	

- Regular rotation player for Orlando in his second NBA season
- Utilized more as a low volume stretch big, made almost 35% of his threes last season
- Shooting stroke is still inconsistent, Free Throw Percentage is improving but still under 65% for his career
- Average spot-up shooter, can sometimes make shots as the screener on pick-and-pops
- Effective rim runner and vertical lob threat, good cutter off the ball, active offensive rebounder that scores on put-backs
- Not as effective on rolls to the rim last season, not really a major post-up threat at this stage
- Shows some passing skills, fairly good at limiting turnovers
- 2019-20 Defensive Degree of Difficulty: 0.283
- Tends to guard lower leverage second unit players
- Very good rim protector, excellent shot blocker, good defensive rebounder, can be a bit foul prone
- Fairly solid on-ball interior defender, uses length to contest shots in the post, shows some mobility to defend in space
- Pretty good pick-and-roll defender, good in drop coverages, can switch onto ball handlers for a few dribbles
- Consistently closes out on perimeter shooters, can close out too aggressively at times

Khem Birch	Height	Weight	Cap #	Years Left
	6'9"	233	$3.000M	UFA

	Similar at Age	27 Season	SIMsc
1	Michael Smith	1999-00	931.9
2	John Shumate	1979-80	926.5
3	Lavoy Allen	2016-17	919.4
4	Ed Davis	2016-17	918.2
5	Adam Keefe	1997-98	912.1
6	Mark Madsen	2002-03	911.0
7	Major Jones	1980-81	910.8
8	Tod Murphy	1990-91	909.0
9	Mitch Kupchak	1981-82	905.9
10	Samaki Walker	2003-04	905.9

Baseline Basic Stats

MPG	PTS	AST	REB	BLK	STL
16.9	5.0	0.7	4.6	0.5	0.4

Advanced Metrics

USG%	3PTA/FGA	FTA/FGA	TS%	eFG%	3PT%
13.0	0.009	0.498	0.560	0.520	0.011
AST%	**TOV%**	**OREB%**	**DREB%**	**STL%**	**BLK%**
7.3	13.9	11.4	19.2	1.3	2.2
PER	**ORTG**	**DRTG**	**WS/48**	**VOL**	
13.86	117.0	107.4	0.125	0.298	

- In and out of Orlando's rotation, started half of his games in 2019-20
- Used as a very low volume rim runner, made almost 71% of his shots inside of three feet last season
- Scores on a high volume of rolls to the rim and cuts off the ball, has some trouble finishing the first shot attempt
- Good offensive rebounder that consistently scores on put-backs, runs hard down the floor in transition, draws fouls at a high rate
- Limited shooting range outside of three feet, shows some passing lanes, good at avoiding turnovers
- 2019-20 Defensive Degree of Difficulty: 0.343, tends to guard second unit big men
- Good rim protector, stays vertical to contest shots, effective shot blocker
- Decent defensive rebounder, Defensive Rebound Percentage has steadily declined
- Solid on-ball defender, strong enough to handle post players, has the mobility to defend in space
- Fairly solid pick-and-roll defender, good at switching onto ball handlers, sometimes can be late to get back to cover the roll man
- Tends to stay in the paint, does not always come out to contest perimeter shots

Michael Carter-Williams	Height	Weight	Cap #	Years Left
	6'5"	190	$3.300M	1

Similar at Age 28

		Season	SIMsc
1	Lorenzo Brown	2018-19	900.3
2	Kent Bazemore	2017-18	894.8
3	Toney Douglas	2014-15	892.3
4	Kevin McKenna	1986-87	892.0
5	Garrett Temple	2014-15	891.6
6	Micheal Ray Richardson	1983-84	891.5
7	Lucious Harris	1998-99	891.1
8	Bob Sura	2001-02	890.1
9	Doc Rivers	1989-90	889.3
10	Anthony Johnson	2002-03	889.0

Baseline Basic Stats

MPG	PTS	AST	REB	BLK	STL
23.6	9.2	3.1	3.2	0.3	1.2

Advanced Metrics

USG%	3PTA/FGA	FTA/FGA	TS%	eFG%	3PT%
18.0	0.323	0.317	0.514	0.462	0.300
AST%	**TOV%**	**OREB%**	**DREB%**	**STL%**	**BLK%**
19.8	12.6	4.5	12.7	2.5	1.7
PER	**ORTG**	**DRTG**	**WS/48**	**VOL**	
14.28	108.0	107.2	0.103	0.380	

- Regular rotation player for Orlando when healthy, missed games due to a series of minor injuries
- Used as a low volume, secondary playmaker on offense, consistently good playmaker that limits turnovers
- Most effective at scoring around the rim, no consistent shooting range from outside of three feet
- Effective cutter in a half-court set, draws fouls at a high rate, good at pushing the ball up the floor in transition
- Solid at using the screen on dribble hand-offs to get to the rim last season
- Has struggled to shoot from outside throughout his career, has made less than 30% of his career threes
- 2019-20 Defensive Degree of Difficulty: 0.456
- Took on tougher defensive assignments in his role as a second unit player
- Played average on-ball defender, quicker guards gave him some trouble, effective in the post against stronger wing players
- Good pick-and-roll defender that can contain ball handlers and switch to cover roll men
- Tends to late when closing out on perimeter shooters, gambles a bit too much when chasing shooters off screens
- Active help defender, gets steals and blocks at a high rate, good defensive rebounder

Dwayne Bacon

	Height	Weight	Cap #	Years Left
	6'6"	221	$1.679M	1

Similar at Age 24

		Season	SIMsc
1	Jarvis Hayes	2005-06	948.3
2	Sasha Pavlovic	2007-08	941.2
3	Kareem Rush	2004-05	939.6
4	Lazar Hayward	2010-11	935.2
5	Jeffery Taylor	2013-14	933.7
6	Chase Budinger	2012-13	929.0
7	Brian Evans	1997-98	928.8
8	Jud Buechler	1992-93	926.8
9	Orlando Johnson	2013-14	926.7
10	Wayne Selden	2018-19	925.7

Baseline Basic Stats

MPG	PTS	AST	REB	BLK	STL
18.8	7.1	1.2	2.7	0.2	0.6

Advanced Metrics

USG%	3PTA/FGA	FTA/FGA	TS%	eFG%	3PT%
18.3	0.348	0.207	0.497	0.467	0.351

AST%	TOV%	OREB%	DREB%	STL%	BLK%
10.8	10.5	2.9	13.4	1.5	0.5

PER	ORTG	DRTG	WS/48	VOL
10.09	100.7	112.2	0.027	0.373

- Fringe rotation player for Charlotte in his third season, spent some time with the Greensboro Swarm in the G-League
- Predominantly a low volume, spot-up shooter, really struggled to make shots in general at the NBA level
- Rated as average or worse in every offensive situation last season
- Has had the most success at making spot-up corner threes in his career, career percentage on corner threes is 40.4%
- Showed improved playmaking skills, set a career high in Assist Percentage, consistently good at avoiding turnovers
- 2019-20 Defensive Degree of Difficulty: 0.403
- Primarily guarded second unit level players, occasionally rotated onto top perimeter players
- Fairly solid on-ball defender that can guard multiple positions
- Very good at guarding pick-and-rolls, particularly when fighting over the screen
- Great at getting around screens to stay attached to shooters off the ball, effectively used his length to contest shots on close-outs
- Solid defensive rebounder, Steal Percentage doubled from the previous season

Jonathan Isaac

Height	Weight	Cap #	Years Left
6'11"	210	$7.363M	RFA

Similar at Age 22

		Season	SIMsc
1	Austin Daye	2010-11	905.4
2	Eddie Griffin	2004-05	890.5
3	Jonathan Bender	2002-03	887.9
4	Travis Outlaw	2006-07	880.6
5	Donyell Marshall	1995-96	874.3
6	Tyrus Thomas	2008-09	873.1
7	Maurice Harkless	2015-16	873.0
8	Marcus Camby	1996-97	872.6
9	Donte Greene	2010-11	871.5
10	Mike Dunleavy, Jr.	2002-03	871.4

Baseline Basic Stats

MPG	PTS	AST	REB	BLK	STL
25.4	10.3	1.4	5.0	1.0	0.8

Advanced Metrics

USG%	3PTA/FGA	FTA/FGA	TS%	eFG%	3PT%
19.2	0.295	0.228	0.533	0.499	0.381
AST%	**TOV%**	**OREB%**	**DREB%**	**STL%**	**BLK%**
8.6	11.5	5.3	17.4	1.9	4.5
PER	**ORTG**	**DRTG**	**WS/48**	**VOL**	
15.33	104.6	104.4	0.109	0.433	

- Missed most of the 2019-20 season due to a left knee injury, tore the ACL in his left knee in the Orlando bubble, will miss the entire 2020-21 season
- Had his most productive season as a pro, effective as a low volume, spot-up shooter
- Made threes at an above break-even rate overall in 2019-20, made over 39% of his corner threes last season
- Decent spot-up shooter, effective as the screener on pick-and-pops, can occasionally make pull-up jumpers on isolations or pick-and-rolls
- Good rim runner, effective at rolling to the rim and cutting off the ball
- Good at running the floor in transition to get dunks or set up for trail threes
- Catch-and-shoot player, improving as a passer, good at avoiding turnovers
- 2019-20 Defensive Degree of Difficulty: 0.464
- Guards starting level players, sometimes takes on tougher assignments
- Fairly good on-ball defender, good against perimeter players, can be bullied inside by stronger post players
- Decent pick-and-roll defender, good at switching onto the screener, has some trouble staying with opposing ball handlers
- Stays attached to shooters off the ball, good at using his length to contest perimeter shots
- Active help defender that can protect the rim, excellent weak side shot blocker, gets steals at a high rate, solid defensive rebounder

Newcomers

Chuma Okeke	**Height**	**Weight**	**Cap #**	**Years Left**
	6'8"	230	$3.121M	1 + 2 TO

Baseline Basic Stats

MPG	PTS	AST	REB	BLK	STL
24.1	9.3	1.6	4.6	0.6	0.9

Advanced Metrics

USG%	3PTA/FGA	FTA/FGA	TS%	eFG%	3PT%
17.6	0.256	0.256	0.515	0.484	0.322

AST%	TOV%	OREB%	DREB%	STL%	BLK%
11.1	12.4	6.9	14.2	2.0	2.0

PER	ORTG	DRTG	WS/48	VOL
13.88	104.0	101.8	0.076	N/A

- Drafted by Orlando with the 16th overall pick in 2019
- Missed the entire 2019-20 season due to a torn left ACL
- Lower volume player at Auburn, non-dribbling situations accounted for almost 97% of his offense in 2018-19
- Made almost 39% of his career threes at the college level, good spot-up shooter
- More of a stationary shooter, struggles to shoot off screens
- Good cutter off the ball, will pick his spots to crash the offensive glass, runs hard down the floor in transition
- Solid at posting up smaller players, unselfish player that can make the extra pass
- Not especially quick, ball handling skills are limited, not likely to be a shot creator at the NBA level
- Solid on-ball defender at the college level, has good length and quick feet
- Active weak side help defender at Auburn, solid defensive rebounder, posted high steal and block rates
- Can be undisciplined with his positioning, tends to gamble too much
- Tends to back off his man quite a bit, will give up extra space to allow shooters to get cleaner looks

Cole Anthony

Height	Weight	Cap #	Years Left
6'3"	190	$3.285M	1 + 2 TO

Baseline Basic Stats

MPG	PTS	AST	REB	BLK	STL
21.3	9.1	2.8	2.1	0.1	0.7

Advanced Metrics

USG%	3PTA/FGA	FTA/FGA	TS%	eFG%	3PT%
22.0	0.326	0.260	0.495	0.455	0.337

AST%	TOV%	OREB%	DREB%	STL%	BLK%
22.3	14.9	2.0	10.1	1.8	0.5

PER	ORTG	DRTG	WS/48	VOL
12.61	97.2	106.8	0.039	N/A

- Drafted by Orlando with the 15th overall pick
- Made the All-ACC 3rd Team in 2019-20, missed games due to a partially torn meniscus in his right knee
- High volume shooter at North Carolina, outside shot can be streaky, tends to force up questionable shots
- Good all-around shooter if he's under control, makes spot-up jumpers, runs off screens, can hit pull-ups off the dribble
- Effective driver if his shot is falling, lacks explosive quickness to regularly beat NBA defenders off the dribble
- More of a secondary playmaker, can only find open teammates in his direct field of vision
- Still learning to play off the ball, does not move unless he's directly involved in the play action
- Lacks ideal physical tools on defense, hidden in favorable matchups at North Carolina
- Effective defender against lower leverage players, quick enough to stay with his man on isolations, can funnel his man into help on pick-and-rolls
- Gets caught on screens off the ball, tends to late when closing out on perimeter shooters
- Active help defender, good defensive rebounder, can jump passing lanes to get steals
- Gambles too much, tends to get caught out of position when going for steals

WASHINGTON WIZARDS

Last Season: 25 – 47, Missed the Playoffs

Offensive Rating: 110.9, 15th in the NBA

Defensive Rating: 115.5, 30th in the NBA

Primary Executive: Tommy Sheppard, General Manager

Head Coach: Scott Brooks

Key Roster Changes

Subtractions
Admiral Schofield, trade
John Wall, trade
Ian Mahinmi, free agency
Shabazz Napier, free agency
Gary Payton II, free agency

Additions
Deni Avdija, draft
Russell Westbrook, trade
Robin Lopez, free agency
Raul Neto, free agency
Anthony Gill, free agency

Roster

Likely Starting Five
1. *Russell Westbrook*
2. *Bradley Beal*
3. *Deni Avdija*
4. *Rui Hachimura*
5. Thomas Bryant

Other Key Rotation Players
Davis Bertans
Robin Lopez
Troy Brown, Jr.
Ish Smith

* Italics denotes that a player is likely to be on the floor to close games

Remaining Roster

- Jerome Robinson
- Isaac Bonga
- Moritz Wagner
- Raul Neto
- Anthony Gill
- Anzejs Pasecniks
- Garrison Mathews, 24, 6'5", 215, Lipscomb (Two-Way)
- Cassius Winston, 22, 6'1", 205, Michigan State (Two-Way)
- Caleb Homesley, 24, 6'6", 205, Liberty (Exhibit 10)
- Yoeli Childs, 23, 6'8", 225, BYU (Exhibit 10)
- Marlon Taylor, 23, 6'5", 209, LSU (Exhibit 10)

SCHREMPF Base Rating: 35.1 (72-game season)

Strengths

- Efficient offense led by the dynamic shot creating skills of Beal and good complimentary shooting

Question Marks

- Overall defensive performance
- Development of young players in a potential turbulent environment

Outlook

- On the fringes of a playoff spot, good enough to compete for a spot in the play-in tournament

Veterans

Bradley Beal	Height	Weight	Cap #	Years Left
	6'3"	207	$28.752M	1 + PO

	Similar at Age	26 Season	SIMsc
1	Damian Lillard	2016-17	943.9
2	Chauncey Billups	2002-03	921.2
3	Kobe Bryant*	2004-05	914.3
4	Deron Williams	2010-11	910.0
5	Ray Allen*	2001-02	906.8
6	CJ McCollum	2017-18	900.1
7	Derrick Rose	2014-15	899.7
8	Jarrett Jack	2009-10	896.8
9	Kirk Hinrich	2006-07	894.9
10	Baron Davis	2005-06	894.5

Baseline Basic Stats

MPG	PTS	AST	REB	BLK	STL
35.9	23.3	5.3	4.2	0.3	1.1

Advanced Metrics

USG%	3PTA/FGA	FTA/FGA	TS%	eFG%	3PT%
30.6	0.378	0.309	0.575	0.520	0.370
AST%	**TOV%**	**OREB%**	**DREB%**	**STL%**	**BLK%**
26.5	10.9	2.4	10.9	1.6	0.9
PER	**ORTG**	**DRTG**	**WS/48**	**VOL**	
21.83	114.2	112.8	0.140	0.214	

- Missed the Orlando restart due to a right rotator cuff injury, produced at an All-Star level despite not making the actual All-Star team
- Had his most productive NBA season as Washington's primary scorer and ball handler
- Very good at creating offense for himself and others as a pick-and-roll ball handler and isolation player
- Very good playmaker that finds open shooter and hits cutter, good at limiting turnovers
- Regularly gets to the rim, draws fouls at a high rate, makes pull-up jumpers
- Solid three-point shooter that makes spot-up jumpers, good at setting up for trail threes in transition
- Effective on dribble hand-offs, can make outside shots and drive to the basket
- 2019-20 Defensive Degree of Difficulty: 0.458
- Guards starting level players, occasionally draws tougher assignments
- Middling on-ball defender, struggles against quicker guards, better at guarding bigger players in the post
- Average pick-and-roll defender, solid on switches, tends to allow ball handlers to turn the corner
- Good at closing out on perimeter shooters, tends to get caught on screens off the ball
- Solid defensive rebounder, Steal and Block Percentages are still consistent with his career averages

Russell Westbrook	Height	Weight	Cap #	Years Left
	6'3"	200	$41.359M	1 + PO

Similar at Age 31

		Season	SIMsc
1	Kobe Bryant*	2009-10	886.7
2	Jason Kidd*	2004-05	884.6
3	Baron Davis	2010-11	878.7
4	Mike Newlin	1979-80	877.0
5	Jarrett Jack	2014-15	874.7
6	Ricky Sobers	1983-84	873.3
7	Sam Cassell	2000-01	872.3
8	Dwyane Wade	2012-13	870.0
9	World B. Free	1984-85	861.5
10	Chauncey Billups	2007-08	861.0

Baseline Basic Stats

MPG	PTS	AST	REB	BLK	STL
33.9	19.2	6.4	4.9	0.3	1.4

Advanced Metrics

USG%	3PTA/FGA	FTA/FGA	TS%	eFG%	3PT%
29.8	0.219	0.319	0.533	0.483	0.314
AST%	**TOV%**	**OREB%**	**DREB%**	**STL%**	**BLK%**
35.1	15.0	3.9	17.5	2.1	0.8
PER	**ORTG**	**DRTG**	**WS/48**	**VOL**	
20.21	107.5	107.4	0.118	0.388	

- Made the All-NBA 3rd Team in his first season with Houston
- Increased his scoring efficiency in a high volume role as a ball handler in Houston's offense
- Good playmaker that can kick the ball out to shooters, a little bit turnover prone
- Explosive athlete, drove to the rim more frequently, very good at attacking the basket on isolations and pick-and-rolls
- Great at pushing the ball up the floor, scores at a high volume in transition
- Not really a great outside shooter, Three-Point Percentage has been below 30% in five of the last six seasons
- Takes a lot of quick mid-range shots, makes them at an above average rate
- 2019-20 Defensive Degree of Difficulty: 0.415, tends to guard starting level players
- Solid on-ball defender that can defend both guard spots
- Good pick-and-roll defender, fights over screens to contain ball handler, good at switching onto the screener
- Can lose focus off the ball, late to close out in spot-up situations, can lose his man when going around screens
- Great rebounding guard, still gets steals at a high rate, Block Percentage is consistent with his career average

Thomas Bryant	Height	Weight	Cap #	Years Left
	6'10"	248	$8.333M	1

Similar at Age 22

		Season	SIMsc
1	Richaun Holmes	2015-16	915.9
2	Terrence Jones	2013-14	913.7
3	Clint Capela	2016-17	912.7
4	Trey Lyles	2017-18	912.4
5	Al Horford	2008-09	911.7
6	Ante Zizic	2018-19	905.4
7	Raef LaFrentz	1998-99	904.1
8	Greg Smith	2012-13	897.3
9	Markieff Morris	2011-12	896.0
10	Kyle O'Quinn	2012-13	894.9

Baseline Basic Stats

MPG	PTS	AST	REB	BLK	STL
23.6	10.6	1.2	6.5	1.1	0.6

Advanced Metrics

USG%	3PTA/FGA	FTA/FGA	TS%	eFG%	3PT%
19.0	0.169	0.303	0.608	0.581	0.411

AST%	TOV%	OREB%	DREB%	STL%	BLK%
9.5	10.1	8.5	22.8	1.1	3.8

PER	ORTG	DRTG	WS/48	VOL
19.75	120.3	107.9	0.166	0.294

- Missed some games due to injuries to his right foot, regular starter for Washington when healthy
- Used as a low volume, rim runner and stretch big, posted a True Shooting Percentage of almost 65% last season
- Good rim runner that dives hard to the rim as a roll man and cutter
- Solid offensive rebounder that efficiently scores on put-backs, runs hard down the floor in transition
- Made almost 41% of his threes last season, mostly a spot-up shooter, occasionally sets up for trail threes in transition
- Fairly good passing big man that can kick the ball out to shooters, good at avoiding turnovers
- 2019-20 Defensive Degree of Difficulty: 0.421, tends to guard starting level big men
- Good defensive rebounder and shot blocker, average rim protector, undisciplined with his positioning
- Below average on-ball defender, can be beaten to spots in the post, struggles to defend quicker players in space on isolations
- Middling pick-and-roll defender, tends to sag back in his coverages, can allow open outside shots
- Does not always come out to contest perimeter shots, can be too aggressive when he does close out

Rui Hachimura

	Height	Weight	Cap #	Years Left
Rui Hachimura	6'8"	230	$4.693M	2 Team Options

Similar at Age **21**

		Season	SIMsc
1	Tobias Harris	2013-14	951.2
2	Omri Casspi	2009-10	934.5
3	Aaron Gordon	2016-17	921.5
4	Jabari Parker	2016-17	921.3
5	Joe Johnson	2002-03	918.2
6	Chase Budinger	2009-10	916.7
7	Michael Kidd-Gilchrist	2014-15	915.4
8	Thaddeus Young	2009-10	914.2
9	Al Harrington	2001-02	913.8
10	Jumaine Jones	2000-01	911.6

Baseline Basic Stats

MPG	PTS	AST	REB	BLK	STL
29.5	13.0	1.7	5.2	0.5	0.8

Advanced Metrics

USG%	3PTA/FGA	FTA/FGA	TS%	eFG%	3PT%
19.2	0.149	0.269	0.534	0.490	0.307
AST%	**TOV%**	**OREB%**	**DREB%**	**STL%**	**BLK%**
9.5	9.3	5.2	15.6	1.4	0.7
PER	**ORTG**	**DRTG**	**WS/48**	**VOL**	
13.85	109.2	111.9	0.086	0.340	

- Regular starter for Washington in his rookie season, missed games due to groin and right quadriceps injuries
- Solidly productive in his role as a low volume, rim runner and stretch big
- Made over 68% of his shots inside of three feet, drew fouls at a decent rate
- Effective rim runner that scores on a high volume of cuts off the ball, solid at rolling to the rim
- Good transition player that runs the floor to get dunks, occasionally sets up for trail threes
- Can drive by slower big men on isolations, selectively hits the offensive glass to score on put-backs
- Outside shot is still a work-in-progress, made less than 30% of his threes last season
- 2019-20 Defensive Degree of Difficulty: 0.450
- Tends to guard starter level players, sometimes draws tougher defensive assignments
- Decent on-ball defender, good at guarding perimeter players, had some trouble against stronger post players
- Middling when guarding pick-and-rolls, good in drop coverages, tends to go too far under screens to give up open outside shots
- Generally fights through screens off the ball, tends to be late when closing out on perimeter shooters
- Stay-at-home defender, good defensive rebounder, does not really get blocks or steals

Dāvis Bertāns	Height	Weight	Cap #	Years Left
	6'10"	225	$15.000M	3 + PO

	Similar at Age	27 Season	SIMsc
1	Nikola Mirotic	2018-19	916.5
2	Vladimir Radmanovic	2007-08	913.5
3	Luke Babbitt	2016-17	913.2
4	Jon Leuer	2016-17	913.1
5	Marvin Williams	2013-14	909.0
6	Patrick Patterson	2016-17	907.8
7	James Jones	2007-08	906.8
8	Doug McDermott	2018-19	906.5
9	Mike Muscala	2018-19	906.2
10	Walter Herrmann	2006-07	905.8

Baseline Basic Stats

MPG	PTS	AST	REB	BLK	STL
19.4	7.3	1.0	3.0	0.3	0.5

Advanced Metrics

USG%	3PTA/FGA	FTA/FGA	TS%	eFG%	3PT%
16.6	0.704	0.202	0.586	0.554	0.406
AST%	**TOV%**	**OREB%**	**DREB%**	**STL%**	**BLK%**
8.2	8.8	2.7	14.7	1.1	1.3
PER	**ORTG**	**DRTG**	**WS/48**	**VOL**	
12.81	115.2	112.5	0.090	0.329	

- Regular rotation player for Washington in his first season with the team
- Utilized as a low volume, shooting specialist off the bench, has made over 42% of his threes in each of the last two seasons
- Very good all-around shooter, knocks down spot-up jumpers, can shoot off screens
- Effective screener on pick-and-pop plays, good at setting up for trail threes in transition
- Good at making backdoor cuts when defenders overplay his shot, runs the floor to get layups in transition
- Unselfish, willing to make the extra pass, rarely turns the ball over
- 2019-20 Defensive Degree of Difficulty: 0.349, usually guards second unit players
- Solid rim protector, stays vertical contest shots, decent defensive rebounder, can occasionally block shots
- Played solid on-ball defense, holds position in the post, mobile enough to defend on the perimeter
- Below average pick-and-roll defender, struggled to guard screeners, quicker ball handlers could drive by him on switches
- Stays attached to shooters off the ball, good at closing out in spot-up situations

Robin Lopez

	Height	Weight	Cap #	Years Left
	7'0"	275	$7.300M	UFA

Similar at Age **31**

		Season	SIMsc
1	Rasho Nesterovic	2007-08	881.0
2	Chris Kaman	2013-14	864.3
3	Aron Baynes	2017-18	862.5
4	Brendan Haywood	2010-11	850.4
5	Luc Longley	1999-00	848.7
6	Timofey Mozgov	2017-18	848.1
7	Marc Jackson	2005-06	847.9
8	Jason Smith	2017-18	846.0
9	Pero Antic	2013-14	844.5
10	James Donaldson	1988-89	843.3

Baseline Basic Stats

MPG	PTS	AST	REB	BLK	STL
19.4	7.3	0.9	4.5	0.9	0.3

Advanced Metrics

USG%	3PTA/FGA	FTA/FGA	TS%	eFG%	3PT%
17.1	0.215	0.195	0.559	0.539	0.346
AST%	**TOV%**	**OREB%**	**DREB%**	**STL%**	**BLK%**
7.3	14.9	7.6	13.1	0.7	3.8
PER	**ORTG**	**DRTG**	**WS/48**	**VOL**	
12.56	105.6	108.8	0.079	0.485	

- Regular rotation player in his first season in Milwaukee
- Used as a rim runner by other teams in the past, played a role as a low volume stretch big with Milwaukee
- Primarily a stationary spot-up shooter, made threes at a break-even rate overall last season
- Much better at making corner threes, shot over 36% on corner threes last season
- Effective rim runner that can slide into open spaces inside as the roll man on pick-and-rolls
- Fairly good post-up player last season, good at scoring over his left shoulder on the left block
- Mostly a catch-and-shoot player, limited passing skills, slightly turnover prone last season
- 2019-20 Defensive Degree of Difficulty: 0.320, tended to guard second unit level big men
- Good rim protector that blocks shots at a fairly high rate, boxes out to allow others to grab rebounds, below average defensive rebounder on his own
- Played good on-ball defense, good post defender that can hold position inside, shows enough mobility to defend in space
- Good pick-and-roll defender, effective in drop coverages, can switch out onto ball handlers for a few dribbles
- Consistently comes out to contest perimeter shots in spot-up situations

Troy Brown, Jr.	Height	Weight	Cap #	Years Left
	6'6"	215	$3.373M	Team Option

	Similar at Age	**20**	
		Season	**SIMsc**
1	Quentin Richardson	2000-01	921.5
2	J.R. Smith	2005-06	917.9
3	Jaylen Brown	2016-17	909.5
4	Harrison Barnes	2012-13	909.3
5	C.J. Miles	2007-08	908.7
6	Al-Farouq Aminu	2010-11	906.2
7	Paul George	2010-11	905.9
8	Joe Johnson	2001-02	905.9
9	Xavier Henry	2011-12	905.0
10	Martell Webster	2006-07	904.0

Baseline Basic Stats

MPG	PTS	AST	REB	BLK	STL
25.1	10.1	1.8	3.9	0.3	0.9

Advanced Metrics

USG%	3PTA/FGA	FTA/FGA	TS%	eFG%	3PT%
18.9	0.361	0.208	0.527	0.495	0.369
AST%	**TOV%**	**OREB%**	**DREB%**	**STL%**	**BLK%**
13.1	10.4	4.2	15.5	1.8	0.6
PER	**ORTG**	**DRTG**	**WS/48**	**VOL**	
13.53	108.6	111.3	0.077	0.248	

- Regular rotation player for Washington in his second NBA season, started some games in 2019-20
- Increased his effectiveness in his role as a low volume shooter off the ball
- Made threes at an above break-even rate last season, has made almost 44% of his career corner threes
- Mainly a spot-up shooter, can set up for trail threes, does not really shoot off the dribble or on the move
- Good cutter off the ball, can crash the offensive glass to score on put-backs, draws fouls at a solid rate
- Solid passer that can make interior passes, consistently avoids turnovers
- 2019-20 Defensive Degree of Difficulty: 0.400
- Tends to guard higher-end second unit players or lower leverage starters
- Below average on-ball defender, has trouble against quicker perimeter players, can be backed down in the post by stronger post players
- Middling pick-and-roll defender, tends to allow ball handlers to turn the corner, can be late to rotate back to cover the roll man
- Gambles too much off the ball, usually is out of position to contest perimeter shots
- Active help defender, good defensive rebounder, gets steals at a high rate

Ish Smith

	Height	Weight	Cap #	Years Left
Ish Smith	6'0"	175	$6.000M	UFA

Similar at Age **31**

		Season	SIMsc
1	J.J. Barea	2015-16	929.1
2	Nick Van Exel	2002-03	919.1
3	Bimbo Coles	1999-00	916.7
4	Mo Williams	2013-14	915.7
5	Luke Ridnour	2012-13	914.1
6	Sherman Douglas	1997-98	909.7
7	Larry Drew	1989-90	909.7
8	Aaron Brooks	2015-16	909.3
9	Mike Evans	1986-87	907.6
10	David Wesley	2001-02	905.3

Baseline Basic Stats

MPG	PTS	AST	REB	BLK	STL
22.2	8.7	3.6	1.9	0.1	0.7

Advanced Metrics

USG%	3PTA/FGA	FTA/FGA	TS%	eFG%	3PT%
19.3	0.266	0.156	0.515	0.491	0.385
AST%	**TOV%**	**OREB%**	**DREB%**	**STL%**	**BLK%**
26.3	12.6	1.7	9.8	1.5	0.9
PER	**ORTG**	**DRTG**	**WS/48**	**VOL**	
13.55	107.2	112.6	0.065	0.334	

- Regular rotation player for Washington last season, started some games in 2019-20
- Used as a low volume, game managing backup point guard
- Good playmaker that can make interior passes and control the ball to avoid turnovers
- Made threes at above the league average in 2019-20, below break-even three-point shooter for his career
- Mainly a spot-up shooter, can be streaky, good at attacking aggressive close-outs if his shot is falling
- Gets to the rim on dribble hand-offs, good in short shot clock situations on isolation plays last season
- 2019-20 Defensive Degree of Difficulty: 0.367, tends to guard second unit players
- Below average on-ball defender, struggles to stay in front of opposing guards
- Below average at guarding pick-and-roll, really had trouble defending side pick-and-rolls, better in the middle of the floor
- Gets caught on screens off the ball, tends to be late when closing out on perimeter shooters
- Solid defensive rebounder, Steal and Block Percentages are mostly consistent with his career averages

Jerome Robinson	Height	Weight	Cap #	Years Left
	6'4"	190	$3.738M	Team Option

Similar at Age 22

		Season	SIMsc
1	Donte DiVincenzo	2018-19	925.9
2	Allan Ray	2006-07	922.6
3	C.J. McCollum	2013-14	922.4
4	Chris Robinson	1996-97	922.2
5	Jodie Meeks	2009-10	922.1
6	Darius Morris	2012-13	920.8
7	J.J. Redick	2006-07	919.6
8	Keyon Dooling	2002-03	916.7
9	Daniel Gibson	2008-09	916.4
10	Cameron Payne	2016-17	913.6

Baseline Basic Stats

MPG	PTS	AST	REB	BLK	STL
19.4	7.3	1.6	2.4	0.2	0.7

Advanced Metrics

USG%	3PTA/FGA	FTA/FGA	TS%	eFG%	3PT%
17.2	0.455	0.184	0.524	0.498	0.349
AST%	**TOV%**	**OREB%**	**DREB%**	**STL%**	**BLK%**
12.3	11.5	2.1	11.4	1.6	1.0
PER	**ORTG**	**DRTG**	**WS/48**	**VOL**	
10.65	103.9	110.7	0.060	0.328	

- Traded from the Clippers to Washington in February 2020, became a regular part of Washington's rotation after the trade
- Used by both teams as a low volume, spot-up shooter and secondary ball handler
- Below break-even three-point shooter in two NBA seasons, made threes at an above break-even rate with Washington
- Effective spot-up shooter that can also shoot off screens
- Average pick-and-roll ball handler, can sometimes get to the rim, struggles to shoot off the dribble
- Fairly solid secondary playmaker that can find open shooters and hit cutters, good at limiting turnovers
- <u>2019-20 Defensive Degree of Difficulty</u>: 0.336, tends to guard second unit players
- Below average on-ball defender, has trouble staying with opposing guards
- Average pick-and-roll defender, tends to allow ball handlers to turn the corner
- Good at closing out on perimeter shooters, sometimes gets caught on screens off the ball
- Solid defensive rebounding guard, Steal and Block Percentages are consistent with his career averages

Isaac Bonga	Height	Weight	Cap #	Years Left
	6'8"	180	$1.664M	RFA

	Similar at Age	20 Season	SIMsc
1	Trevor Ariza	2005-06	878.8
2	DerMarr Johnson	2000-01	876.9
3	Paul George	2010-11	872.8
4	Gordon Hayward	2010-11	872.2
5	Nicolas Batum	2008-09	871.9
6	Maurice Harkless	2013-14	867.7
7	Shaun Livingston	2005-06	862.1
8	Derrick Jones, Jr.	2017-18	858.1
9	Otto Porter	2013-14	856.6
10	Al-Farouq Aminu	2010-11	855.8

Baseline Basic Stats

MPG	PTS	AST	REB	BLK	STL
22.1	7.9	1.7	3.5	0.4	0.9

Advanced Metrics

USG%	3PTA/FGA	FTA/FGA	TS%	eFG%	3PT%
15.6	0.320	0.325	0.533	0.482	0.304
AST%	**TOV%**	**OREB%**	**DREB%**	**STL%**	**BLK%**
11.6	13.9	5.4	13.0	2.3	1.5
PER	**ORTG**	**DRTG**	**WS/48**	**VOL**	
12.42	108.4	109.1	0.080	0.504	

- Regular rotation player for Washington in his second NBA season, started most of his games
- Used as a very low volume, spot-up shooter and energy wing player
- Made threes at around the league average last season, made over 44% of his corner threes
- Strictly a stationary spot-up shooter, does not really shoot on the move or off the dribble
- Good transition player that runs the floor to get dunks or draw shooting fouls
- Good cutter off the ball, crashes the offensive boards to score on put-backs
- Showed some passing skills as a rookie, fairly turnover prone in his second season
- 2019-20 Defensive Degree of Difficulty: 0.449
- Tended to guard starting level players, sometimes drew tougher defensive assignments
- Middling on-ball defender, uses length to contest jump shots, quicker players can drive by him, can be bullied inside by stronger players in the post
- Very good pick-and-roll defender that can guard ball handlers and switch onto screeners
- Tends to get caught on screens off the ball, very good at closing out on perimeter shooters
- Solid defensive rebounder, posted fairly solid Steal and Block Percentages last season

Moritz Wagner

	Height	Weight	Cap #	Years Left
	6'11"	245	$2.162M	Team Option

Similar at Age 22

		Season	SIMsc
1	Markieff Morris	2011-12	917.1
2	Greg Foster	1990-91	916.3
3	Charlie Villanueva	2006-07	914.8
4	Kelly Olynyk	2013-14	909.0
5	Henry Ellenson	2018-19	908.2
6	James Johnson	2009-10	906.9
7	Raef LaFrentz	1998-99	904.4
8	Skal Labissiere	2018-19	903.9
9	Brad Miller	1998-99	902.2
10	Richaun Holmes	2015-16	900.0

Baseline Basic Stats

MPG	PTS	AST	REB	BLK	STL
19.6	8.2	1.1	4.8	0.7	0.5

Advanced Metrics

USG%	3PTA/FGA	FTA/FGA	TS%	eFG%	3PT%
20.0	0.237	0.287	0.557	0.514	0.280
AST%	**TOV%**	**OREB%**	**DREB%**	**STL%**	**BLK%**
9.4	14.5	7.2	19.5	1.4	2.5
PER	**ORTG**	**DRTG**	**WS/48**	**VOL**	
14.39	106.0	108.3	0.084	0.353	

- Missed almost two months due to a sprained left ankle, regular rotation player for Washington when healthy
- Utilized as a low volume, stretch big and rim runner
- Below break-even three-point shooter in his career, made 38.5% of his corner threes last season
- Middling spot-up shooter, can be effective as a screener on pick-and-pops
- Better rim runner, made almost 78% of his shots inside of three feet last season
- High motor big man, dives hard to the rim as a roll man and cutter off the ball
- Effective at posting up smaller players in a small sample of possessions
- Improving as a passer, still a bit turnover prone
- 2019-20 Defensive Degree of Difficulty: 0.344, tends to guard second unit big men
- Good defensive rebounder, can block shots, average rim protector, highly foul prone
- Solid post defender that holds position inside, has trouble defending in space
- Below average at guarding pick-and-rolls, tends to sag into the paint, gives up open outside shots
- Tends to either be late or too aggressive when closing out on perimeter shooters

Raul Neto

	Height	Weight	Cap #	Years Left
	6'1"	179	$1.621M	UFA

Similar at Age **27**

		Season	SIMsc
1	Lynn Greer	2006-07	930.9
2	Brian Roberts	2012-13	925.0
3	Mo Williams	2009-10	922.5
4	Sebastian Telfair	2012-13	921.6
5	John Crotty	1996-97	921.6
6	Shabazz Napier	2018-19	918.7
7	Negele Knight	1994-95	918.6
8	James Robinson	1997-98	918.5
9	Bryce Drew	2001-02	918.3
10	Jannero Pargo	2006-07	918.0

Baseline Basic Stats

MPG	PTS	AST	REB	BLK	STL
20.9	8.2	3.0	1.9	0.1	0.7

Advanced Metrics

USG%	3PTA/FGA	FTA/FGA	TS%	eFG%	3PT%
18.8	0.417	0.223	0.539	0.498	0.359
AST%	**TOV%**	**OREB%**	**DREB%**	**STL%**	**BLK%**
23.2	14.8	1.7	9.2	1.7	0.6
PER	**ORTG**	**DRTG**	**WS/48**	**VOL**	
12.88	107.4	110.2	0.074	0.402	

- Fringe rotation player for Philadelphia in his first season with the team
- Filled a role as a low volume, game managing, backup point guard
- Decent playmaker that can find open perimeter shooters, can be somewhat turnover prone
- Fairly effective pick-and-roll ball handler, can make pull-up jumpers, can sneak by defenders on drives if his shot is falling
- Made almost 39% of his threes last season, good spot-up shooter, makes outside jumpers on dribble hand-offs
- Not really quick enough to drive by defenders on his own on isolation plays
- 2019-20 Defensive Degree of Difficulty: 0.331, tended to defend second unit guards
- Played decent on-ball defense, good at staying with guards on the perimeter, bigger guards could shoot over him in the post
- Average pick-and-roll defender, tended to allow ball handlers to turn the corner
- Stays attached to shooters off the ball, good at closing out on spot-up shooters
- Fairly decent defensive rebounder for his size, Steal Percentage is getting closer to his career average

Anžejs Pasečņiks	Height	Weight	Cap #	Years Left
	7'1"	220	$1.518M	1

	Similar at Age	24	
		Season	SIMsc
1	Lorenzen Wright	1999-00	916.2
2	Olden Polynice	1988-89	909.6
3	Richard Washington	1979-80	908.5
4	Semih Erden	2010-11	908.3
5	William Bedford	1987-88	907.1
6	Stuart Gray	1987-88	905.9
7	Granville Waiters	1984-85	905.3
8	Eddie Lee Wilkins	1986-87	904.7
9	Tom LaGarde	1979-80	904.5
10	Randy Breuer	1984-85	904.2

Baseline Basic Stats

MPG	PTS	AST	REB	BLK	STL
17.7	6.5	1.0	4.4	0.6	0.4

Advanced Metrics

USG%	3PTA/FGA	FTA/FGA	TS%	eFG%	3PT%
17.6	0.022	0.419	0.534	0.500	0.186
AST%	**TOV%**	**OREB%**	**DREB%**	**STL%**	**BLK%**
8.2	14.2	9.0	19.1	1.0	2.2
PER	**ORTG**	**DRTG**	**WS/48**	**VOL**	
12.68	106.8	112.6	0.059	0.401	

- Spent the early part of 2019-20 in the G-League with the Capital City Go-Go, became a regular rotation player for Washington late in the season
- Mainly used as a low volume, rim runner at the NBA level
- Made 74.5% of his shots inside of three feet last season, drew fouls at a high rate
- Effective at rolling to the rim and cutting off the ball, runs hard down the floor in transition
- Good offensive rebounder that gets second chance opportunities, decent at scoring on put-backs
- Limited skill at this point, no real shooting range outside of three feet, not really a passer, solid at limiting turnovers
- 2019-20 Defensive Degree of Difficulty: 0.346, tends to guard second unit big men
- Below average rim protector, highly foul prone, undisciplined with his positioning
- Decent shot blocker, middling defensive rebounder
- Fairly solid post defender that can hold position inside, struggles to guard quicker players in space
- Decent at guarding pick-and-rolls, solid in drop coverages, quicker ball handlers can drive by him on the perimeter
- Consistently closes out on perimeter shooters in spot-up situations

Newcomers

Deni Avdija	**Height**	**Weight**	**Cap #**	**Years Left**
	6'9"	220	$4.469M	1 + 2 TO

Baseline Basic Stats

MPG	PTS	AST	REB	BLK	STL
23.1	8.8	1.5	4.0	0.5	0.7

Advanced Metrics

USG%	3PTA/FGA	FTA/FGA	TS%	eFG%	3PT%
17.7	0.340	0.252	0.539	0.508	0.335

AST%	TOV%	OREB%	DREB%	STL%	BLK%
11.8	13.9	5.1	15.8	1.6	1.6

PER	ORTG	DRTG	WS/48	VOL
12.17	106.4	110.9	0.071	N/A

- Drafted by Washington with the 9th overall pick
- Played for Maccabi Tel Aviv in the Israeli Premier League, named Israeli League MVP in 2019-20
- Good playmaker with great court vision, occasionally forces passes into tight spaces
- Moves well without the ball, can occasionally shoot off screens, good cutter
- Solid ball handler, quick enough to get to the rim, willing to absorb contact to draw fouls, can post up smaller players inside
- Inconsistent shooter, makes less than 60% of his free throws, stroke not repeatable at this stage
- Around a break-even three-point shooter, better as a stationary spot-up shooter
- Lacks ideal tools on defense, has short arms for his size, not especially quick
- Played solid defense overseas, sound position defender, avoids getting beat off the dribble
- Holds position well against bigger post players, has good timing to block shots, solid defensive rebounder
- Active hands allow him to play passing lanes, gets steals at a decent rate
- Tends to get caught ball watching, will gamble a bit too much

Anthony Gill		Height	Weight	Cap #	Years Left
		6'8"	230	$0.898M	1

Baseline Basic Stats

MPG	PTS	AST	REB	BLK	STL
17.2	5.9	0.8	4.0	0.4	0.5

Advanced Metrics

USG%	3PTA/FGA	FTA/FGA	TS%	eFG%	3PT%
14.8	0.484	0.170	0.602	0.579	0.400
AST%	**TOV%**	**OREB%**	**DREB%**	**STL%**	**BLK%**
8.6	12.4	8.8	20.1	1.2	2.0
PER	**ORTG**	**DRTG**	**WS/48**	**VOL**	
12.21	120.1	120.6	0.072	N/A	

- Went undrafted in 2016, played last season with BC Khimki in the EuroLeague
- Rim running interior player in college at Virginia, plays with high energy, draws fouls at a fairly high rate
- Dives hard to the rim as a roll man or cutter off the ball, will attack the offensive boards to score on put-backs
- Has become a good three-point shooter overseas, made 43% of his threes last season
- Mostly a stationary spot-up shooter, does not really shoot off the dribble or on the move
- Will attack aggressive close-out with straight-line drives to the rim, good athleticism allows him to finish strong at the rim
- More of a catch-and-shoot player, limited as a playmaker, good at avoiding turnovers
- High effort defender, athletic enough to be a competent defender at the NBA level
- Lacks elite lateral quickness to take on tougher defensive assignments
- Solid team defender that generally makes sound rotations
- Active on the weak side, good at rotating inside to block shots, plays passing lanes to get steals, good defensive rebounder

CHICAGO BULLS

Last Season: 22 – 43, Missed the Playoffs

Offensive Rating: 106.7, 27th in the NBA

Defensive Rating: 109.8, 12th in the NBA

Primary Executive: Arturas Karnisovas, Executive Vice President of Basketball Operations

Head Coach: Billy Donovan

Key Roster Changes

Subtractions
Kris Dunn, free agency
Shaquille Harrison, free agency

Additions
Patrick Williams, draft
Garrett Temple, free agency

Roster

Likely Starting Five

1. Zach LaVine
2. Tomas Satoransky
3. Otto Porter
4. Lauri Markkanen
5. Wendell Carter, Jr.

Other Key Rotation Players
Coby White
Thaddeus Young
Garrett Temple
Patrick Williams

* Italics denotes that a player is likely to be on the floor to close games

Remaining Roster

- Denzel Valentine
- Daniel Gafford
- Ryan Arcidiacono
- Chandler Hutchison
- Luke Kornet
- Cristiano Felicio
- Adam Mokoka, 22, 6'5", 190, France (Two-Way)
- Devon Dotson, 21, 6'2", 185, Kansas (Two-Way)
- Noah Vonleh, 25, 6'10", 257, Indiana (Exhibit 10)
- Zach Norvell, 23, 6'5", 206, Gonzaga (Exhibit 10)
- Simi Shittu, 21, 6'10", 240, Vanderbilt (Exhibit 10)

SCHREMPF Base Rating: 33.5 (72-game season)

Strengths

- Length and defensive versatility could make them an effective unit that creates turnovers

Question Marks

- Ability to generate efficient offense because the team lacks a sound offensive system
- Lack of ideal front-end talent to compete with the contenders in the East
- Potentially ill-fitting pieces and a lack of a cohesive rotation

Outlook

- On the fringes of a playoff spot, talented enough to be in the hunt for a spot in the play-in tournament

Veterans

Zach LaVine	Height	Weight	Cap #	Years Left
	6'6"	181	$19.500M	1

Similar at Age 24

		Season	SIMsc
1	Evan Fournier	2016-17	913.9
2	Richard Hamilton	2002-03	904.7
3	Jamal Crawford	2004-05	902.0
4	Flip Murray	2003-04	900.9
5	Brandon Knight	2015-16	898.9
6	Ricky Davis	2003-04	896.2
7	Kyrie Irving	2016-17	895.7
8	Jordan Clarkson	2016-17	893.7
9	Tyler Johnson	2016-17	893.2
10	Larry Hughes	2002-03	892.8

Baseline Basic Stats

MPG	PTS	AST	REB	BLK	STL
33.5	17.3	3.7	3.8	0.3	1.2

Advanced Metrics

USG%	3PTA/FGA	FTA/FGA	TS%	eFG%	3PT%
27.2	0.360	0.295	0.555	0.504	0.365
AST%	**TOV%**	**OREB%**	**DREB%**	**STL%**	**BLK%**
21.4	12.0	2.0	12.1	1.9	0.9
PER	**ORTG**	**DRTG**	**WS/48**	**VOL**	
18.06	108.8	111.2	0.115	0.300	

- Regular starter for the Bulls, led the team in scoring last season
- Had his most productive season in the NBA in his sixth year, played a high usage role as the team's primary scoring option
- Good isolation player and pick-and-roll ball handler, good shooter off the dribble
- Solid spot-up shooter, made 38% of his threes last season, good at making shots off screens
- Excellent athleticism makes him a dynamic threat in transition, also effective as a cutter off the ball
- Solid playmaker that limits turnovers
- 2019-20 Defensive Degree of Difficulty: 0.469
- Primarily guards starting level players, occasionally takes on tougher defensive assignments
- Improving as an on-ball defender, solid in isolation situations, can be pushed around inside by bigger wing players in the post
- Good pick-and-roll defender that can funnel his man into help, good on switches
- Fights through screens off the ball, but tends to be late when closing out on perimeter shooters
- More engaged as a help defender, posted the highest Steal and Block Percentages of his career
- Solid defensive rebounding guard

Wendell Carter, Jr.	Height	Weight	Cap #	Years Left
	6'9"	259	$5.449M	Team Option

	Similar at Age	20	
		Season	SIMsc
1	Jackie Butler	2005-06	919.9
2	J.J. Hickson	2008-09	918.2
3	John Collins	2017-18	915.3
4	Bam Adebayo	2017-18	914.1
5	Al Jefferson	2004-05	911.8
6	Derrick Favors	2011-12	903.1
7	Samaki Walker	1996-97	903.0
8	Jared Sullinger	2012-13	894.8
9	Kwame Brown	2002-03	894.1
10	Ivica Zubac	2017-18	892.7

Baseline Basic Stats

MPG	PTS	AST	REB	BLK	STL
24.9	11.1	1.2	7.4	0.9	0.6

Advanced Metrics

USG%	3PTA/FGA	FTA/FGA	TS%	eFG%	3PT%
19.8	0.074	0.346	0.577	0.536	0.307
AST%	**TOV%**	**OREB%**	**DREB%**	**STL%**	**BLK%**
8.4	13.6	10.1	23.3	1.3	2.5
PER	**ORTG**	**DRTG**	**WS/48**	**VOL**	
17.61	112.7	106.9	0.124	0.253	

- Regular starter for Chicago when healthy, missed over a month due to a high right ankle sprain
- Mostly used as a low volume rim runner, aggressive player inside, draws fouls at a high rate
- Scores on a high volume of cuts and rolls to the rim, good offensive rebounder that will score on put-backs
- Runs hard down the floor in transition, average post-up player, better on the left block
- Inconsistent shooter from outside, flashed solid passing skills as a rookie, generally good at avoiding turnovers
- 2019-20 Defensive Degree of Difficulty: 0.405
- Typically guards starting level players, serves as a primary rim protector for Chicago
- Good defensive rebounder and shot blocker, can be undisciplined with his positioning at times, highly foul prone
- Average on-ball defender, has enough strength to defend in the post, but tends to bite on fakes, has trouble with shiftier guards on isolation plays
- Above average pick-and-roll defender, good on switches, can sometimes be beaten to spots when covering the roll man
- Fairly solid team defender that will consistently close out on perimeter shooters

Lauri Markkanen	Height	Weight	Cap #	Years Left
	7'0"	240	$6.732M	RFA

Similar at Age 22

		Season	SIMsc
1	Frank Kaminsky	2015-16	935.1
2	Andrea Bargnani	2007-08	921.0
3	Charlie Villanueva	2006-07	918.9
4	Trey Lyles	2017-18	918.0
5	Dirk Nowitzki	2000-01	915.5
6	Kelly Olynyk	2013-14	905.7
7	Ryan Anderson	2010-11	904.9
8	Oleksiy Pecherov	2007-08	904.0
9	Bobby Portis	2017-18	902.9
10	Yi Jianlian	2009-10	902.0

Baseline Basic Stats

MPG	PTS	AST	REB	BLK	STL
25.5	12.6	1.4	5.8	0.6	0.6

Advanced Metrics

USG%	3PTA/FGA	FTA/FGA	TS%	eFG%	3PT%
22.4	0.408	0.264	0.564	0.520	0.366
AST%	**TOV%**	**OREB%**	**DREB%**	**STL%**	**BLK%**
8.5	9.8	5.0	20.9	1.3	1.7
PER	**ORTG**	**DRTG**	**WS/48**	**VOL**	
16.67	110.4	109.4	0.118	0.273	

- Regular starter for Chicago in his third season, missed over month with a stress reaction in his pelvis
- Efficiency declined, had trouble adjusting to a lower usage role
- Three-Point Percentage dropped to just above break-even last season, still excellent at making corner threes, made over 42% of his corner threes last season
- Solid spot-up shooter, good as the screener on pick-and-pop plays
- Did not roll to the rim as frequently last season, still an effective cutter off the ball
- Selectively hits the offensive boards to score on put-backs, improving passer that limits turnovers
- 2019-20 Defensive Degree of Difficulty: 0.432
- Tends to guard starting level players
- Improved his rim protecting abilities despite not being a real shot blocking threat, stayed vertical to contest shots, solid defensive rebounder
- Average on-ball defender, stronger big man can back him down in the post, has some with shiftier guards
- Played effective pick-and-roll defense, good in drop coverages, also showed enough mobility to capably defend on switches
- Not always disciplined when closing out on perimeter shooters, can sometimes get caught on screens off the ball

Tomáš Satoranský

Height	Weight	Cap #	Years Left
6'7"	198	$10.000M	1

Similar at Age **28**

		Season	SIMsc
1	Marko Jaric	2006-07	922.1
2	Anfernee Hardaway	1999-00	918.2
3	Brian Shaw	1994-95	917.2
4	Eric Piatkowski	1998-99	916.0
5	Keyon Dooling	2008-09	909.5
6	Evan Turner	2016-17	909.3
7	Derek Anderson	2002-03	908.0
8	Ricky Davis	2007-08	907.8
9	Gordon Hayward	2018-19	907.2
10	Greivis Vasquez	2014-15	907.1

Baseline Basic Stats

MPG	PTS	AST	REB	BLK	STL
27.1	9.7	3.2	3.5	0.3	1.0

Advanced Metrics

USG%	3PTA/FGA	FTA/FGA	TS%	eFG%	3PT%
16.3	0.359	0.241	0.543	0.500	0.360
AST%	**TOV%**	**OREB%**	**DREB%**	**STL%**	**BLK%**
20.9	15.9	3.5	11.1	1.8	0.7
PER	**ORTG**	**DRTG**	**WS/48**	**VOL**	
13.06	110.7	110.9	0.081	0.311	

- Regular starter for Chicago last season
- Lower volume, pass-first, playmaker, good at kicking the ball out to shooters, somewhat turnover prone
- Struggled to shoot efficiently from outside, made threes at a below break-even rate last season
- Better shooter in his years with Washington, made 40% of his threes in three seasons as a Wizard
- Historically has been better in the corners, has made over 40% of his corner threes throughout his career
- Could get to the rim as an isolation player and pick-and-roll ball handler, defenders had success sagging off him on pick-and-rolls last season
- Still a solid transition player, effective cutter in previous seasons
- 2019-20 Defensive Degree of Difficulty: 0.438
- Typically guards starting level players
- Solid on-ball defender that can capably guard multiple positions
- Fairly good at guarding pick-and-rolls, fights over screens, improved his ability to switch onto different players
- Can gamble a bit too much, can allow his man to get open by trying to shoot the gap when chasing shooters off screens
- Tends to be too aggressive when closing out, can give his man easy driving lanes to the rim
- Fairly solid on the defensive boards, posted a career high in Steal Percentage last season

Otto Porter	Height	Weight	Cap #	Years Left
	6'8"	198	$28.489M	UFA

	Similar at Age	**26**	
		Season	**SIMsc**
1	Gerald Green	2011-12	946.6
2	Francisco Garcia	2007-08	922.0
3	Chandler Parsons	2014-15	920.4
4	Terrence Ross	2017-18	918.0
5	C.J. Miles	2013-14	912.2
6	Dorell Wright	2011-12	912.1
7	Sasha Vujacic	2010-11	911.4
8	Gus Gerard	1979-80	907.3
9	Lloyd Daniels	1993-94	906.8
10	Jarvis Hayes	2007-08	904.6

Baseline Basic Stats

MPG	PTS	AST	REB	BLK	STL
25.7	11.3	1.6	3.6	0.5	0.9

Advanced Metrics

USG%	3PTA/FGA	FTA/FGA	TS%	eFG%	3PT%
20.3	0.458	0.186	0.559	0.532	0.394
AST%	**TOV%**	**OREB%**	**DREB%**	**STL%**	**BLK%**
11.0	8.5	3.2	13.6	2.0	1.6
PER	**ORTG**	**DRTG**	**WS/48**	**VOL**	
15.40	110.8	109.8	0.105	0.457	

- Missed most of last season due to a sprained left foot
- Started a majority of his games last season for Chicago, Minutes per Game was reduced from previous seasons
- Took on a moderate volume role with increased ball handling responsibility
- Effective as a pick-and-roll ball handler, posted the highest Assist Percentage of his career, good at limiting turnovers
- Very good outside shooter that can knock down spot-up threes and come off screens, made almost 39% of his threes last season
- 2019-20 Defensive Degree of Difficulty: 0.401
- Took on lower leverage assignments due to his injury, has handled tougher matchups in the past
- Solid on-ball defender that can guard both forward spots when healthy
- Very good pick-and-roll defender that can capably switch or fight over screens
- Consistently closes out on perimeter shooters, can occasionally get caught on screens off the ball
- Maintained his Steal and Block Percentage from a season ago, fairly solid defensive rebounder

Coby White

	Height	Weight	Cap #	Years Left
	6'4"	185	$5.573M	2 Team Options

	Similar at Age	19	
		Season	SIMsc
1	Jamal Murray	2016-17	929.9
2	D'Angelo Russell	2015-16	917.3
3	Zach LaVine	2014-15	910.3
4	Bradley Beal	2012-13	906.9
5	Malik Monk	2017-18	900.3
6	Dajuan Wagner	2002-03	896.7
7	Anfernee Simons	2018-19	894.9
8	J.R. Smith	2004-05	880.9
9	Devin Booker	2015-16	879.1
10	Jrue Holiday	2009-10	876.4

Baseline Basic Stats

MPG	PTS	AST	REB	BLK	STL
29.3	14.9	3.5	3.3	0.2	0.9

Advanced Metrics

USG%	3PTA/FGA	FTA/FGA	TS%	eFG%	3PT%
25.5	0.380	0.209	0.544	0.511	0.383
AST%	**TOV%**	**OREB%**	**DREB%**	**STL%**	**BLK%**
21.0	11.8	2.1	13.1	1.6	0.5
PER	**ORTG**	**DRTG**	**WS/48**	**VOL**	
15.19	106.1	112.3	0.067	0.366	

- Regular rotation player in his rookie season with Chicago, played much better in the second half of last season
- Mostly used as a scoring guard off the bench, took on considerable volume
- Showed that he could score in volume, could drive by defenders on isolation plays and make pull-up jumpers off pick-and-rolls
- More of a jump shooter at this stage, shot around the league average on threes, had some trouble finishing around the rim
- Can be wild and out of control at times, rated as average in most offensive situations last season
- Decent playmaker, did a better job of limiting turnover than he did at the college level
- 2019-20 Defensive Degree of Difficulty: 0.311
- Typically guarded lower leverage second unit players
- Below average on-ball defender, had the quickness to prevent drives to the rim, gave his man extra space to clean looks from the perimeter
- Fairly good pick-and-roll defender, can funnel his man into help, has some trouble handling bigger players on switches
- Gambles a bit too much, can get burned when trying to shoot the gap while chasing shooters off screens, undisciplined when closing out on perimeter shooters
- Good defensive rebounding guard, posts a middling steals rate

Thaddeus Young

Height	Weight	Cap #	Years Left
6'8"	220	$13.545M	1

Similar at Age 31

		Season	SIMsc
1	Andrei Kirilenko	2012-13	910.6
2	Boris Diaw	2013-14	910.5
3	Jason Richardson	2011-12	906.9
4	Chuck Person	1995-96	905.9
5	Shawn Marion	2009-10	902.5
6	Ken Norman	1995-96	901.9
7	Tracy McGrady*	2010-11	901.4
8	Scottie Pippen*	1996-97	899.9
9	Rashard Lewis	2010-11	899.6
10	Eric Williams	2003-04	899.6

Baseline Basic Stats

MPG	PTS	AST	REB	BLK	STL
25.7	9.2	1.8	5.1	0.4	0.9

Advanced Metrics

USG%	3PTA/FGA	FTA/FGA	TS%	eFG%	3PT%
18.4	0.285	0.163	0.521	0.506	0.322
AST%	**TOV%**	**OREB%**	**DREB%**	**STL%**	**BLK%**
10.9	13.2	6.7	15.5	2.1	1.2
PER	**ORTG**	**DRTG**	**WS/48**	**VOL**	
13.30	103.7	106.4	0.078	0.375	

- Regular rotation player for Chicago, moved into a bench role after serving as a starter for Indiana in previous seasons
- Production declined, slotted into a different role as a lower volume, spot-up shooter
- Shot around league average on threes, shooting percentages from ten feet and in all dropped significantly
- Average or worse in most offensive situations, still can post up smaller player, will crash the offensive boards to score on put-backs
- Decent passer that tends to limit turnovers
- 2019-20 Defensive Degree of Difficulty: 0.405
- Usually defends higher end second unit players or lower leverage starters
- Fairly good on-ball defender that can guard multiple positions
- Pretty good pick-and-roll defender, good on switches, can contain ball handlers and cover roll men
- Very good team defender, stay attached to shooters off the ball, will close out in spot-up situations
- Can protect the rim, Block and Steal Percentages were above his career averages, good defensive rebounder

Garrett Temple

	Height	Weight	Cap #	Years Left
	6'5"	195	$4.767M	UFA

	Similar at Age	33	
		Season	SIMsc
1	Brent Barry	2004-05	932.4
2	Eddie Jones	2004-05	921.4
3	Trent Tucker	1992-93	915.9
4	Trevor Ariza	2018-19	909.0
5	Ron Harper	1996-97	907.0
6	Courtney Lee	2018-19	905.7
7	Anthony Peeler	2002-03	905.7
8	Lucious Harris	2003-04	905.5
9	John Salmons	2012-13	903.3
10	Willie Green	2014-15	902.6

Baseline Basic Stats

MPG	PTS	AST	REB	BLK	STL
23.3	7.7	1.8	2.5	0.2	0.8

Advanced Metrics

USG%	3PTA/FGA	FTA/FGA	TS%	eFG%	3PT%
15.1	0.557	0.174	0.529	0.500	0.356
AST%	**TOV%**	**OREB%**	**DREB%**	**STL%**	**BLK%**
10.7	10.8	1.9	10.6	1.7	1.1
PER	**ORTG**	**DRTG**	**WS/48**	**VOL**	
10.20	105.4	109.3	0.072	0.401	

- Regular rotation player for Brooklyn last season, was in and out of the starting lineup throughout 2019-20
- Predominantly a low volume spot-up shooter, shot below break-even on threes last season
- Better at making long twos last season, more effective at getting to the rim against aggressive close-outs
- Very good in transition at setting up for trail threes or attacking the basket for layups
- Solid on dribble hand-off plays, fairly good secondary playmaker that avoids turnovers
- 2019-20 Defensive Degree of Difficulty: 0.470
- Guards starting level players, will take on tougher perimeter assignments
- Still a good on-ball defender that can guard multiple positions
- Average pick-and-roll defender, can be too aggressive when fighting over the screen
- Fairly solid team defender, consistently closes out in spot-up situations, occasionally will get caught on screens off the ball
- Solid on the defensive boards, more of a stay-at-home defender, Steal Percentage has been in decline for the last three seasons

Denzel Valentine

	Height	Weight	Cap #	Years Left
Denzel Valentine	6'4"	210	$4.698M	UFA

Similar at Age 26

		Season	SIMsc
1	Voshon Lenard	1999-00	924.0
2	Anthony Peeler	1995-96	918.6
3	C.J. Miles	2013-14	918.0
4	O.J. Mayo	2013-14	917.7
5	Gary Neal	2010-11	913.5
6	J.R. Smith	2011-12	912.4
7	Marcus Thornton	2013-14	907.4
8	Dion Waiters	2017-18	905.6
9	Charlie Bell	2005-06	904.7
10	Kent Bazemore	2015-16	902.6

Baseline Basic Stats

MPG	PTS	AST	REB	BLK	STL
25.9	11.8	2.2	2.8	0.3	0.9

Advanced Metrics

USG%	3PTA/FGA	FTA/FGA	TS%	eFG%	3PT%
21.4	0.495	0.128	0.521	0.500	0.363

AST%	TOV%	OREB%	DREB%	STL%	BLK%
14.6	10.4	2.1	13.0	1.8	0.9

PER	ORTG	DRTG	WS/48	VOL
13.00	103.0	110.0	0.064	0.425

- Fringe rotation player for Chicago when healthy, missed parts of the season due to a left hamstring injury
- Had his most productive season as a pro, used as a higher volume, ball handler off the bench
- Very effective as a pick-and-roll ball handler, solid playmaking skills, great at limiting turnovers
- Pretty good spot-up shooter, Three-Point Percentage dropped to just above break-even, made almost 55% of his shots from mid-range last season
- Not used much off the ball, flashed some ability to cut in a small sample of possessions
- 2019-20 Defensive Degree of Difficulty: 0.309
- Tended to guard lower leverage second unit players
- Played below average on-ball defense, struggled to stay with quicker perimeter players on isolations
- Below average pick-and-roll defender, tends to allow his man to turn the corner, decent on switches
- Can get caught on screens off the ball, can be late to close out in spot-up situations, gambled a bit more last season
- Steal and Block Percentage went up significantly to career highs, solid defensive rounder throughout his career

Daniel Gafford

Height	Weight	Cap #	Years Left
6'10"	234	$1.518M	1 + TO

Similar at Age		21 Season	SIMsc
1	Sean Williams	2007-08	905.5
2	Robert Williams	2018-19	881.1
3	Jelani McCoy	1998-99	873.8
4	Steven Hunter	2002-03	868.7
5	Kevon Looney	2017-18	858.5
6	Jermaine O'Neal	1999-00	856.1
7	Cedric Simmons	2006-07	853.5
8	Deyonta Davis	2017-18	848.3
9	Bismack Biyombo	2013-14	848.3
10	Ante Zizic	2017-18	843.9

Baseline Basic Stats

MPG	PTS	AST	REB	BLK	STL
18.1	5.8	0.6	4.5	1.4	0.4

Advanced Metrics

USG%	3PTA/FGA	FTA/FGA	TS%	eFG%	3PT%
13.7	0.003	0.445	0.620	0.610	0.045
AST%	**TOV%**	**OREB%**	**DREB%**	**STL%**	**BLK%**
5.9	15.5	9.9	13.4	1.1	5.9
PER	**ORTG**	**DRTG**	**WS/48**	**VOL**	
14.87	117.9	107.4	0.128	0.415	

- Fringe rotation player for Chicago in his rookie season
- Mainly played as a low volume, rim runner, made almost 77% of his shots inside of three feet last season
- Athletic big man that can be a vertical threat on lobs, good roll man, scores on a high volume of cuts off the ball
- Actively crashes the offensive board to score on put-backs
- Runs hard down the floor in transition, can be a bit wild, prone to committing turnovers
- Not really a passer, no real shooting range outside of three feet, makes less than 55% of his free throws
- 2019-20 Defensive Degree of Difficulty: 0.336
- Typically guards second unit level players, plays a rim protector role
- Good rim protector due to excellent shot blocking skills, highly foul prone, tends to be out of position, below average defensive rebounder
- Average post defender, can be backed inside by stronger players, struggles to defend in space on isolation plays
- Effective pick-and-roll defender, mobile enough to switch onto ball handlers for a few dribbles, good at covering roll men on drop coverages
- Will aggressively close out on perimeter shooters in spot-up situations

Ryan Arcidiacono	**Height**	**Weight**	**Cap #**	**Years Left**
	6'3"	195	$3.000M	Team Option

	Similar at Age	**25**	
		Season	**SIMsc**
1	Damon Jones	2001-02	931.8
2	Daniel Gibson	2011-12	930.4
3	Matt Maloney	1996-97	919.8
4	Luther Head	2007-08	917.0
5	Steve Nash*	1999-00	914.6
6	Chasson Randle	2018-19	910.5
7	Langston Galloway	2016-17	906.0
8	Chris Quinn	2008-09	905.4
9	Seth Curry	2015-16	903.9
10	Chris Herren	2000-01	902.1

Baseline Basic Stats

MPG	PTS	AST	REB	BLK	STL
20.9	7.4	2.8	1.9	0.1	0.6

Advanced Metrics

USG%	3PTA/FGA	FTA/FGA	TS%	eFG%	3PT%
15.0	0.540	0.206	0.546	0.512	0.363
AST%	**TOV%**	**OREB%**	**DREB%**	**STL%**	**BLK%**
20.0	13.9	1.8	9.5	1.5	0.2
PER	**ORTG**	**DRTG**	**WS/48**	**VOL**	
11.51	111.3	112.0	0.085	0.409	

- Regular rotation player for Chicago in his third year in the NBA
- Filled a role as a very low volume, pass-first, backup point guard
- Fairly solid playmaker that tends to make safe passes and rarely turns the ball over
- Mostly a spot-up shooter on offense, made over 39% of his threes last season, excellent corner three-point shooter
- Limited as a stationary shooter, does not really run off screens, good at making backdoor cuts if defenders overplay his shot
- Below average as a pick-and-roll ball handler, doesn't have the quickness to attack the rim, much more effective on dribble hand-offs
- 2019-20 Defensive Degree of Difficulty: 0.337
- Usually guards second unit level players
- Solid on-ball defender that plays with a high effort level, can capably defend both guard spots
- Fairly good pick-and-roll defender, funnels his man into help, will fight over screens, solid on switches
- Consistently will close out on perimeter shooters, tends to get caught on screens off the ball
- Solid defensive rebounder for his size, more of a stay-at-home defender
- Steal Percentage has dropped over the last couple of seasons

Chandler Hutchison

Height	Weight	Cap #	Years Left
6'7"	196	$2.443M	Team Option

Similar at Age 23

		Season	SIMsc
1	Wesley Iwundu	2017-18	924.7
2	James Wilkes	1981-82	908.3
3	Bryce Dejean-Jones	2015-16	907.0
4	Doug West	1990-91	906.1
5	Rodney Carney	2007-08	905.9
6	John Salmons	2002-03	903.6
7	Jeryl Sasser	2002-03	900.1
8	Nicolas Brussino	2016-17	899.4
9	Zoran Planinic	2005-06	899.0
10	Tyrone Wallace	2017-18	898.1

Baseline Basic Stats

MPG	PTS	AST	REB	BLK	STL
19.3	6.8	1.4	2.5	0.3	0.6

Advanced Metrics

USG%	3PTA/FGA	FTA/FGA	TS%	eFG%	3PT%
17.4	0.287	0.287	0.522	0.488	0.345
AST%	**TOV%**	**OREB%**	**DREB%**	**STL%**	**BLK%**
10.2	10.1	3.3	14.5	1.7	1.0
PER	**ORTG**	**DRTG**	**WS/48**	**VOL**	
11.96	105.2	110.8	0.064	0.403	

- Missed most of last season due to a right shoulder injury that required surgery
- Regular rotation player for Chicago when healthy, played as a low volume, spot-up shooter
- Has been a below break-even three-point shooter over his two season in the NBA
- Much more effective when attacking aggressive close-outs, drew fouls at a high rate, solid finisher at the rim
- Still learning to play off the ball at the NBA level, struggled in almost every other situation last season
- Does not shoot well off the dribble, primarily a catch-and-shoot player, limited passing abilities but does not really turn the ball over
- 2019-20 Defensive Degree of Difficulty: 0.391
- Tends to guard higher end second unit players or lower leverage starters
- Below average on-ball defender, struggled to keep opposing perimeter players in front of him in isolation situations
- Average pick-and-roll defender, fairly good on switches, can be too aggressive when fighting over the screen
- Consistently closes out on perimeter shooters, can get caught out of position trying to shoot the gap when chasing shooters off screens
- Very good defensive rebounder, active help defender, increased his Steal and Block Percentages significantly

Luke Kornet	Height	Weight	Cap #	Years Left
	7'2"	240	$2.250M	UFA

Similar at Age 24

		Season	SIMsc
1	Meyers Leonard	2016-17	882.2
2	Mike Muscala	2015-16	881.8
3	Luke Babbitt	2013-14	869.0
4	Wang Zhizhi	2001-02	866.2
5	Jarell Martin	2018-19	862.8
6	Kelly Olynyk	2015-16	857.1
7	Frank Kaminsky	2017-18	855.2
8	Brian Cook	2004-05	850.9
9	Darko Milicic	2009-10	847.9
10	Austin Daye	2012-13	847.6

Baseline Basic Stats

MPG	PTS	AST	REB	BLK	STL
18.9	7.7	1.2	3.8	0.6	0.4

Advanced Metrics

USG%	3PTA/FGA	FTA/FGA	TS%	eFG%	3PT%
17.9	0.505	0.199	0.546	0.517	0.339
AST%	**TOV%**	**OREB%**	**DREB%**	**STL%**	**BLK%**
10.6	9.5	4.5	15.7	1.1	3.5
PER	**ORTG**	**DRTG**	**WS/48**	**VOL**	
13.81	110.6	109.9	0.097	0.370	

- Fringe rotation player for Chicago when healthy, missed the end of last season due to a sprained left ankle and fractured left foot
- Primarily utilized as a low volume, stretch big
- League average three-point shooter in previous seasons with the Knicks, shot below 30% on threes last season
- Better from 10 to 16 feet, average on spot-up jumpers, good as the screener on pick-and-pop plays
- Improved as a rim runner, good cutter off the ball, finished shots more efficiently on rolls to the rim
- Made over 74% of his shots from inside of three feet, fairly solid passer that limits turnovers
- 2019-20 Defensive Degree of Difficulty: 0.379
- Tends to guard second unit level players
- Below average rim protector, blocks shots at a high rate, undisciplined with his positioning
- Defensive Rebound Percentage has continued to drop over his three seasons in the league
- Below average on-ball defender, can be pushed around in the post, struggles to stay with quicker players in space
- Decent pick-and-roll defender, mobile enough to switch onto ball handlers, has some trouble covering roll men inside
- Tends to close out on perimeter shooters, can sometimes be too aggressive, will occasionally give up driving lanes to the rim

Cristiano Felício	Height	Weight	Cap #	Years Left
	6'10"	270	$7.529M	UFA

	Similar at Age	27	
		Season	SIMsc
1	Vitaly Potapenko	2002-03	894.6
2	Marc Jackson	2001-02	887.0
3	Dragan Tarlac	2000-01	881.1
4	Mike Brown	1990-91	881.1
5	Jeff Ayres	2014-15	873.7
6	Eric Leckner	1993-94	871.2
7	Kendrick Perkins	2011-12	868.5
8	Melvin Ely	2005-06	868.5
9	Aaron Gray	2011-12	867.6
10	Brian Grant	1999-00	866.6

Baseline Basic Stats

MPG	PTS	AST	REB	BLK	STL
16.4	5.3	0.6	4.2	0.4	0.3

Advanced Metrics

USG%	3PTA/FGA	FTA/FGA	TS%	eFG%	3PT%
13.8	0.020	0.428	0.585	0.547	0.010
AST%	**TOV%**	**OREB%**	**DREB%**	**STL%**	**BLK%**
6.3	16.8	11.8	17.6	1.0	1.1
PER	**ORTG**	**DRTG**	**WS/48**	**VOL**	
13.07	116.7	110.8	0.097	0.384	

- Fringe rotation player for Chicago in previous seasons, playing time reduced significantly last season
- Almost exclusively a low volume, rim runner, usage decreased significantly in 2019-20
- Below average as a roll man, does not have the lift to finish in traffic, good off-ball cutter
- Very good offensive rebounder that scores on put-backs, posted the highest Offensive Rebound Percentage of his career last season
- No real shooting range outside of three feet, will draw fouls at a high rate, made over 78% of his free throws last season
- Not really much of a passer, can be a bit turnover prone
- 2019-20 Defensive Degree of Difficulty: 0.344
- Generally guarded second unit level players, served as a rim protector when he was on the floor
- Below average rim protector, no longer a shot blocking threat, Block Percentage has continued to decline
- Below average defensive rebounder, Defensive Rebound Percentage was at a career low last season
- Lacks ideal mobility for the modern NBA, was effective against pick-and-rolls in drop coverages
- Willing to close out on perimeter shooters, but can give up driving lanes to the rim due to a lack of foot speed

Newcomers

Patrick Williams	**Height**	**Weight**	**Cap #**	**Years Left**
	6'8"	225	$7.068M	1 + 2 TO

Baseline Basic Stats

MPG	PTS	AST	REB	BLK	STL
24.4	9.4	1.6	4.2	0.7	0.8

Advanced Metrics

USG%	3PTA/FGA	FTA/FGA	TS%	eFG%	3PT%
18.8	0.258	0.269	0.502	0.461	0.296

AST%	TOV%	OREB%	DREB%	STL%	BLK%
11.2	12.8	4.8	13.3	1.7	2.1

PER	ORTG	DRTG	WS/48	VOL
13.21	99.7	102.7	0.068	N/A

- Drafted by Chicago with the 4th overall pick
- Made the ACC All-Freshman team last season, named ACC Sixth Man of the Year
- Unpolished offensively, non-dribbling plays accounted for 88.8% of his offense in 2019-20
- Lacks dynamic ball handling skills, limited playmaking skills, not likely to be a shot creator at the NBA level
- Great athlete, explosive finisher inside, great at running down the wings in transition
- Lob threat, will make hard cuts off the ball, good at crashing the offensive glass to score on put-backs
- Below break-even three-point shooter, shooting motion is rather slow, needs to be wide open to make shots
- Great physical tools on defense, can potentially guard multiple positions, solid on-ball defender in college
- Mainly used as a roamer, disruptive help defender at Florida State
- Excellent weak side shot blocker, can jump passing lanes to get steals, solid defensive rebounder
- Solid pick-and-roll defender, fights over screens to contain ball handlers, has some trouble defending bigger players on switches
- Great recovery speed allows him to close out on perimeter shooters
- Will gamble a bit too much, can get caught out of position when going through screens off the ball

CLEVELAND CAVALIERS

Last Season: 19 – 46, Missed the Playoffs

Offensive Rating: 107.5, 25th in the NBA

Defensive Rating: 115.4, 29th in the NBA

Primary Executive: Koby Altman, General Manager

Head Coach: J.B. Bickerstaff

Key Roster Changes

Subtractions
Alfonzo McKinnie, trade
Jordan Bell, trade
Tristan Thompson, free agency
Ante Zizic, free agency

Additions
Isaac Okoro, draft
JaVale McGee, trade
Damyean Dotson, free agency

Roster

Likely Starting Five

1. *Darius Garland*
2. *Collin Sexton*
3. Isaac Okoro
4. *Kevin Love*
5. *Andre Drummond*

Other Key Rotation Players
Cedi Osman
Larry Nance, Jr.
Kevin Porter, Jr.
JaVale McGee
Dante Exum

* Italics denotes that a player is likely to be on the floor to close game

Remaining Roster

- Damyean Dotson
- Matthew Dellavedova
- Dylan Windler
- Dean Wade
- Lamar Stevens, 23, 6'8", 225, Penn State (Two-Way)
- Matt Mooney, 23, 6'3", 199, Texas Tech (Two-Way)
- Charles Matthews, 24, 6'6", 205, Michigan (Exhibit 10)
- Marques Bolden, 22, 6'11", 245, Duke (Exhibit 10)
- Thon Maker, 23, 7'0", 221, Australia (Exhibit 10)

SCHREMPF Base Rating: 31.6 (72-game season)

Strengths

- Deep rotation of effective rebounding big men should make them a factor on the glass at both ends

Question Marks

- Inefficiency on offense due to a lack of consistent shooting and a reliable playmaker
- Below average performance on defense due to an ill-fitting roster that is deficient in length or versatility
- No established core player to build around for the future

Outlook

- Still rebuilding, will likely be a lottery team in the 2020-21 season

Veterans

Kevin Love	Height	Weight	Cap #	Years Left
	6'8"	251	$31.258M	2

	Similar at Age	31 Season	SIMsc
1	Wally Szczerbiak	2008-09	875.6
2	Chris Bosh	2015-16	870.7
3	Paul Millsap	2016-17	866.9
4	Anthony Tolliver	2016-17	862.8
5	Austin Croshere	2006-07	855.8
6	Luis Scola	2011-12	855.2
7	Carlos Boozer	2012-13	854.1
8	Al Harrington	2011-12	853.9
9	DeMarre Carroll	2017-18	852.5
10	Walt Williams	2001-02	850.2

Baseline Basic Stats

MPG	PTS	AST	REB	BLK	STL
23.8	11.6	1.5	5.5	0.4	0.6

Advanced Metrics

USG%	3PTA/FGA	FTA/FGA	TS%	eFG%	3PT%
22.3	0.452	0.309	0.582	0.530	0.392
AST%	**TOV%**	**OREB%**	**DREB%**	**STL%**	**BLK%**
11.6	11.6	4.9	26.3	1.1	1.1
PER	**ORTG**	**DRTG**	**WS/48**	**VOL**	
17.28	113.3	111.0	0.114	0.486	

- Mostly healthy for the first time in several seasons, regular starter for Cleveland in 2019-20
- Production has been in decline for the last two or three seasons, still fairly effective in his early 30's
- Mainly a moderate volume stretch big, consistent three-point shooter during his time in Cleveland
- Good spot-up shooter, excels as the screener on pick-and-pop plays, can shoot off screens
- Playing away from the basket more often, doesn't go to the offensive boards as frequently as he once did, draws fewer fouls
- Good post-up player, does most of his damage from the left block
- Very good passing big man, good on dribble hand-offs, does not really turn the ball over
- 2019-20 Defensive Degree of Difficulty: 0.374
- Tends to be hidden in favorable matchups against lower leverage offensive players
- Below average rim protector, not really a shot blocker at this stage, still an excellent defensive rebounder
- Below average on-ball defender, not quite long enough to contest shots in the post, lacks lateral quickness to stay with quicker players in space
- Fairly good pick-and-roll defender, solid in drop coverages, can have trouble defending guards on switches
- Consistently closes out on perimeter shooters, will fight through screens off the ball

Andre Drummond	Height	Weight	Cap #	Years Left
	6'10"	279	$28.752M	UFA

	Similar at Age	26	
		Season	SIMsc
1	Greg Monroe	2016-17	855.3
2	Oliver Miller	1996-97	846.5
3	Al Jefferson	2010-11	845.8
4	Emeka Okafor	2008-09	845.7
5	Dwight Howard	2011-12	844.3
6	Hakeem Olajuwon*	1988-89	842.8
7	Kenyon Martin	2003-04	841.5
8	Elton Brand	2005-06	841.3
9	Robert Traylor	2003-04	839.5
10	Enes Kanter	2018-19	838.1

Baseline Basic Stats

MPG	PTS	AST	REB	BLK	STL
31.5	15.8	2.0	10.5	1.6	1.1

Advanced Metrics

USG%	3PTA/FGA	FTA/FGA	TS%	eFG%	3PT%
24.2	0.026	0.385	0.554	0.523	0.139
AST%	**TOV%**	**OREB%**	**DREB%**	**STL%**	**BLK%**
11.7	15.0	13.2	31.2	2.2	4.2
PER	**ORTG**	**DRTG**	**WS/48**	**VOL**	
21.85	108.8	102.7	0.145	0.510	

- Regular starter for Detroit and Cleveland last season, traded to Cleveland in February 2020
- One of the most productive big men, maintained his efficiency in a high usage role with both teams
- Athletic rim runner, vertical threat to catch lobs, effective as a roll man and cutter off the ball
- Above average post-up player, draws fouls at a high rate
- Mainly looks to use his strength to bully defenders inside, more effective after the trade to Cleveland
- Has become a decent passing big man, a bit turnover prone last season
- 2019-20 Defensive Degree of Difficulty: 0.414
- Guards starting level big men, played as his team's primary rim protector
- Blocks shots in a high volume, limitations in mobility hurt his ability to protect the rim, somewhat foul prone
- Arguably the best rebounder in the NBA, has the highest Total Rebound Percentage among active players
- Average pick-and-roll defender, better on switches last season, can be late to cover roll men at the rim
- Does not always come out to contest perimeter shots

Collin Sexton

	Height	Weight	Cap #	Years Left
Collin Sexton	6'1"	190	$4.992M	Team Option

Similar at Age **21**

		Season	SIMsc
1	Brandon Knight	2012-13	917.7
2	Tony Parker	2003-04	911.0
3	Trey Burke	2013-14	910.2
4	Kyrie Irving	2013-14	907.3
5	Ben Gordon	2004-05	906.8
6	Derrick Rose	2009-10	906.6
7	Rex Chapman	1988-89	903.6
8	Mike Conley	2008-09	902.4
9	Bradley Beal	2014-15	899.1
10	Jamal Murray	2018-19	898.2

Baseline Basic Stats

MPG	PTS	AST	REB	BLK	STL
31.6	16.4	4.4	3.0	0.2	1.0

Advanced Metrics

USG%	3PTA/FGA	FTA/FGA	TS%	eFG%	3PT%
24.8	0.199	0.256	0.541	0.497	0.369
AST%	**TOV%**	**OREB%**	**DREB%**	**STL%**	**BLK%**
20.3	13.5	2.5	7.6	1.5	0.3
PER	**ORTG**	**DRTG**	**WS/48**	**VOL**	
15.00	106.1	113.3	0.074	0.314	

- Regular starter for Cleveland in his second season, led the team in scoring last season
- Improved his efficiency in a high usage role as one of the team's main ball handlers
- Good isolation player and pick-and-roll ball handler, better at attacking the rim, can shoot off the dribble
- Took fewer long twos, good three-pointer shooter that can knock down spot-up jumpers, good at shooting off screens last season
- Also made almost 54% of his corner threes last season
- Cut his turnover rate in 2019-20, solid playmaking skills, but plays with more a score-first mindset
- 2019-20 Defensive Degree of Difficulty: 0.447
- Tends to guard starter level players on the defensive end
- Below average on-ball defender, gives up too much space for his man to take outside shots, has trouble keeping opposing players in front of him
- Below average pick-and-roll defender, indecisive when making rotations
- Not especially disciplined when closing out on perimeter shooters
- Can get caught out of position when chasing shooters off screens, tends to gamble too much
- Middling defensive rebounder, Steal Percentage increased significantly last season

Darius Garland

Height	Weight	Cap #	Years Left
6'1"	175	$6.721M	2 Team Options

Similar at Age 20

		Season	SIMsc
1	Brandon Knight	2011-12	903.1
2	Mike Conley	2007-08	902.4
3	Tony Parker	2002-03	890.8
4	Jonny Flynn	2009-10	890.7
5	Jordan Farmar	2006-07	888.9
6	Collin Sexton	2018-19	886.4
7	De'Aaron Fox	2017-18	878.5
8	Monta Ellis	2005-06	876.0
9	Dennis Schröder	2013-14	875.9
10	Sebastian Telfair	2005-06	875.8

Baseline Basic Stats

MPG	PTS	AST	REB	BLK	STL
26.6	11.7	4.1	2.3	0.1	0.8

Advanced Metrics

USG%	3PTA/FGA	FTA/FGA	TS%	eFG%	3PT%
22.3	0.399	0.163	0.519	0.490	0.366
AST%	**TOV%**	**OREB%**	**DREB%**	**STL%**	**BLK%**
23.2	15.3	1.7	6.3	1.4	0.2
PER	**ORTG**	**DRTG**	**WS/48**	**VOL**	
12.26	102.8	114.4	0.034	0.470	

- Regular starter for Cleveland in his rookie season
- Shared ball handling duties with Collin Sexton, inefficient in a moderate volume as a rookie
- Made threes at around a league average rate, fairly solid spot-up shooter, can make pull-up jumpers off the dribble
- Really struggled to drive and make shots around the rim, made less than 50% of his shots inside of three feet
- Rated as average or worse in most offensive situations last season, also does not really know how to play off the ball
- Fairly solid playmaking skills, but can be a bit turnover prone
- 2019-20 Defensive Degree of Difficulty: 0.426
- Typically defended starter level players last season
- Below average on-ball defender, stronger players can bully him to get to the rim
- Not especially long, taller perimeter players can shoot over him
- Below average pick-and-roll defender, can be too aggressive when fighting over the screen, can struggle to guard bigger players on switches
- Undisciplined when trying to close out on perimeter shooters, can get caught on screens off the ball
- Not very active help defender, below average defensive rebounder, does not really get steals or blocks

Cedi Osman	Height	Weight	Cap #	Years Left
	6'7"	215	$8.841M	3

	Similar at Age	24	
		Season	SIMsc
1	James Anderson	2013-14	954.3
2	Damyean Dotson	2018-19	948.2
3	Denzel Valentine	2017-18	947.3
4	Kyle Korver	2005-06	947.2
5	Scott Burrell	1994-95	945.1
6	Mike Miller	2004-05	937.1
7	Taurean Prince	2018-19	934.1
8	Rodney Hood	2016-17	932.5
9	Hollis Thompson	2015-16	931.7
10	Martell Webster	2010-11	931.2

Baseline Basic Stats

MPG	PTS	AST	REB	BLK	STL
26.2	10.9	1.7	3.5	0.3	0.8

Advanced Metrics

USG%	3PTA/FGA	FTA/FGA	TS%	eFG%	3PT%
18.5	0.474	0.199	0.553	0.523	0.370
AST%	**TOV%**	**OREB%**	**DREB%**	**STL%**	**BLK%**
11.3	11.3	2.4	13.3	1.4	0.8
PER	**ORTG**	**DRTG**	**WS/48**	**VOL**	
12.48	107.6	113.1	0.062	0.425	

- Regular starter for Cleveland in his third season in the NBA
- Mostly used as a low volume shooter off the ball, made over 38% of his threes last season
- Improved as a spot-up shooter, also effective at shooting off screens, good cutter off the ball
- Excellent transition player that will set up trail threes, sprints out to get layups or draw shooting fouls
- Improved pick-and-roll ball handler, can make pull-up jumpers off the dribble, not quite quick enough to get all the way to the rim on drives
- Fairly solid passer, good at avoiding turnovers
- 2019-20 Defensive Degree of Difficulty: 0.466
- Defends starting level players, occasionally is tasked to guard elite perimeter players
- Played solid on-ball defense, capable of guarding multiple positions
- Below average at defending pick-and-rolls, tended be indecisive
- Consistently closed out on perimeter shooters, can get caught on screens off the ball
- Stay-at-home-defender, decent defensive rebounder, but Defensive Rebound Percentage declined last season
- Steal and Block Percentages were slightly above his career averages

Larry Nance, Jr.	Height	Weight	Cap #	Years Left
	6'7"	230	$11.709M	2

	Similar at Age	27 Season	SIMsc
1	JaMychal Green	2017-18	920.2
2	Matt Barnes	2007-08	914.9
3	Rodney Rogers	1998-99	905.6
4	Trevor Booker	2014-15	903.9
5	Luke Walton	2007-08	899.6
6	Marvin Williams	2013-14	898.5
7	Chuck Hayes	2010-11	895.9
8	Jared Dudley	2012-13	892.1
9	Chucky Brown	1995-96	891.2
10	Chase Budinger	2015-16	891.2

Baseline Basic Stats

MPG	PTS	AST	REB	BLK	STL
22.9	8.0	1.5	4.9	0.4	0.8

Advanced Metrics

USG%	3PTA/FGA	FTA/FGA	TS%	eFG%	3PT%
15.5	0.339	0.205	0.568	0.548	0.343
AST%	**TOV%**	**OREB%**	**DREB%**	**STL%**	**BLK%**
11.8	13.1	7.3	20.5	1.8	1.4
PER	**ORTG**	**DRTG**	**WS/48**	**VOL**	
14.83	114.1	109.1	0.109	0.333	

- Regular rotation player for Cleveland, played as the team's sixth man off the bench
- Utilized as a low volume, spot-up shooter and rim runner, took more spot-up threes
- Made threes at almost a league average percentage, shot 41.9% on corner threes last season
- More of a stand-still shooter at this stage, not quite as effective on move as a screener on pick-and-pop plays
- Great athlete, energetic rim runner that is good at cutting off the ball, scores on a lot of rolls to the rim
- Runs hard down the floor in transition, opportunistically crashes the offensive boards to score on put-backs
- Has become a solid passer, cut his turnover rate significantly
- 2019-20 Defensive Degree of Difficulty: 0.364
- Usually guards second unit level players
- Not quite as active at playing help defense as he was in previous seasons, Steal and Block Percentages were at career lows
- Below average rim protector as a result, still a very good defensive rebounder
- Improving as an on-ball defender, very good on the perimeter, still struggled to guard bigger post players inside
- Fairly good pick-and-roll defender, effective at switching onto ball handlers
- Fights through screens off the ball, closes out on perimeter shooters in spot-up situations

Kevin Porter, Jr.	Height	Weight	Cap #	Years Left
	6'4"	216	$2.033M	2 Team Options

Similar at Age 19

		Season	SIMsc
1	Jamal Murray	2016-17	916.7
2	Bradley Beal	2012-13	913.4
3	J.R. Smith	2004-05	900.8
4	Devin Booker	2015-16	883.2
5	Archie Goodwin	2013-14	883.2
6	D'Angelo Russell	2015-16	881.9
7	Frank Ntilikina	2017-18	881.0
8	Zhaire Smith	2018-19	879.5
9	Troy Brown	2018-19	879.3
10	Martell Webster	2005-06	876.9

Baseline Basic Stats

MPG	PTS	AST	REB	BLK	STL
22.5	10.8	1.9	2.5	0.2	0.8

Advanced Metrics

USG%	3PTA/FGA	FTA/FGA	TS%	eFG%	3PT%
22.5	0.357	0.260	0.566	0.529	0.368
AST%	**TOV%**	**OREB%**	**DREB%**	**STL%**	**BLK%**
16.1	14.1	2.4	12.3	2.0	0.8
PER	**ORTG**	**DRTG**	**WS/48**	**VOL**	
14.48	107.2	113.0	0.066	0.400	

- Regular rotation player for Cleveland in his rookie season
- Played as a moderate volume, scoring guard off the bench
- Fairly efficient shooter as a rookie, made almost 72% of his shots inside of three feet
- Good cutter off the ball, great athleticism makes him a dynamic threat to score in transition
- Not quite as effective with the ball in his hands, ball handling needs work, can't drive all the way to the rim
- Inconsistent shooter off the dribble, takes ill-advised threes above the break, slightly above break-even as an overall three-point shooter
- Much better at making spot-up corner threes, made almost 42% of his corner threes last season
- Fairly decent secondary playmaker, can be a bit turnover prone
- 2019-20 Defensive Degree of Difficulty: 0.385
- Tends to guard higher end second unit players or lower leverage starters
- Below average on-ball defender, tends to give his man extra space to take perimeter shots
- Average pick-and-roll defender, can contain ball handlers on drives, tends to go too far under screens to give up open outside shots
- Does not always close out on perimeter shooters, can occasionally get caught on screens off the ball
- Solid defensive rebounder for his size, posted fairly solid Steal and Block Percentages as a rookie

JaVale McGee	Height	Weight	Cap #	Years Left
	7'0"	270	$4.200M	UFA

	Similar at Age	32	
		Season	**SIMsc**
1	Samuel Dalembert	2013-14	879.3
2	Brendan Haywood	2011-12	874.6
3	Chris Kaman	2014-15	870.9
4	Erick Dampier	2007-08	861.9
5	Zeljko Rebraca	2004-05	860.3
6	Salah Mejri	2018-19	847.4
7	Brian Skinner	2008-09	841.0
8	Greg Ostertag	2005-06	834.1
9	Kelvin Cato	2006-07	831.8
10	Aron Baynes	2018-19	830.6

Baseline Basic Stats

MPG	PTS	AST	REB	BLK	STL
18.8	5.6	0.7	5.5	1.1	0.4

Advanced Metrics

USG%	3PTA/FGA	FTA/FGA	TS%	eFG%	3PT%
14.3	0.021	0.293	0.597	0.587	0.261
AST%	**TOV%**	**OREB%**	**DREB%**	**STL%**	**BLK%**
5.2	15.6	11.5	23.8	1.2	5.5
PER	**ORTG**	**DRTG**	**WS/48**	**VOL**	
16.23	115.0	104.0	0.145	0.487	

- Regular rotation player for the Lakers last season, started all of his games
- Highly effective in his role as a low volume, rim runner, posted a True Shooting Percentage above 65% last season
- Vertical lob threat, dives hard to the rim as a cutter off the ball and a roll man
- Good offensive rebounder that scores on a high volume of put-backs, runs hard down the floor in transition
- Limited offensive skill, shooting is inconsistent outside of three feet, not really a passer, solid at avoiding turnovers
- 2019-20 Defensive Degree of Difficulty: 0.450, tends to guard starting level big men
- Good rim protector, excellent shot blocker, very good defensive rebounder
- Played below average on-ball defense, can bite on fakes and be beaten to spots in the post
- Mobile enough to defend in space on isolation, can switch onto ball handlers for a few dribbles on pick-and-rolls
- Tends to sag into the paint, does not always close out on shooters, late to recognize pick-and-pops

Dante Exum	Height	Weight	Cap #	Years Left
	6'5"	190	$9.600M	UFA

	Similar at Age	24 Season	SIMsc
1	Alex Caruso	2018-19	953.1
2	Conner Henry	1987-88	931.1
3	Elliot Williams	2013-14	922.0
4	Ray McCallum	2015-16	922.0
5	Derrick White	2018-19	919.7
6	Cameron Payne	2018-19	918.8
7	Markel Brown	2015-16	918.8
8	Terrel Harris	2011-12	917.5
9	Delon Wright	2016-17	916.3
10	Jordan McRae	2015-16	915.7

Baseline Basic Stats

MPG	PTS	AST	REB	BLK	STL
18.3	7.0	1.9	2.2	0.2	0.7

Advanced Metrics

USG%	3PTA/FGA	FTA/FGA	TS%	eFG%	3PT%
17.8	0.327	0.303	0.543	0.497	0.333
AST%	**TOV%**	**OREB%**	**DREB%**	**STL%**	**BLK%**
15.7	14.4	2.7	11.0	1.6	1.1
PER	**ORTG**	**DRTG**	**WS/48**	**VOL**	
12.05	106.6	110.7	0.075	0.500	

- Missed games for Utah and Cleveland due to a right knee injury and a sprained right ankle
- Was out of Utah's rotation before he was traded to Cleveland, became a regular rotation player for Cleveland when healthy
- Used as a low volume, backup point guard by Cleveland
- Effective pick-and-roll ball handler that could slash to the rim to finish or draw fouls
- Took more of a scoring mindset in Cleveland, solid playmaker in previous seasons, can be turnover prone
- Better at making spot-up jumpers in Cleveland, made threes at almost a league average rate in a small sample of games
- 2019-20 Defensive Degree of Difficulty: 0.341, typically guarded second unit level players
- Solid on-ball defender that can defend smaller guards and taller wing players
- Good pick-and-roll defender that will fight over screens and funnel his man into help
- Good team defender off the ball, stays attached to shooters, consistently closes out in spot-up situations
- Set a career high in Defensive Rebound Percentage last season
- Steal and Block Percentages were above his career averages in a small sample of games with Cleveland

Damyean Dotson

Height	Weight	Cap #	Years Left
6'5"	202	$2.000M	1

Similar at Age **25**

		Season	SIMsc
1	Wayne Ellington	2012-13	944.7
2	Nik Stauskas	2018-19	940.0
3	Kentavious Caldwell-Pope	2018-19	933.4
4	Pat Connaughton	2017-18	931.5
5	Courtney Lee	2010-11	931.1
6	Langston Galloway	2016-17	929.9
7	Von Wafer	2010-11	923.8
8	Reggie Williams	2011-12	923.0
9	Troy Daniels	2016-17	920.9
10	Daequan Cook	2012-13	920.3

Baseline Basic Stats

MPG	PTS	AST	REB	BLK	STL
22.6	8.9	1.4	2.5	0.2	0.6

Advanced Metrics

USG%	3PTA/FGA	FTA/FGA	TS%	eFG%	3PT%
17.2	0.534	0.150	0.543	0.520	0.368

AST%	TOV%	OREB%	DREB%	STL%	BLK%
9.9	8.5	1.6	10.7	1.4	0.6

PER	ORTG	DRTG	WS/48	VOL
11.55	108.5	113.2	0.071	0.313

- Regular rotation player for New York at the start of the season, was inactive several times towards the end of 2019-20
- Mostly a low volume shooter off the ball, made threes at just above the league average last season
- Generally made spot-up jumpers, average at making shots off screens
- Could use an on-ball screen to make outside shots off dribble hand-offs, fairly good at taking quick pull-up jumpers on isolations and pick-and-rolls
- Rarely gets to the ball, finishes inside shots efficiently in limited attempts, made almost 68% of his shots inside of three feet last season
- Mostly a catch-and-shoot, has some passing skills, rarely turns the ball over
- <u>2019-20 Defensive Degree of Difficulty</u>: 0.325, tends to guard second unit level players
- Played decent on-ball defense, could handle bigger players in the post, good against drives
- Sometimes gave up extra space for opponents to take jump shots on isolation plays
- Above average pick-and-roll defender, good at funneling his man into help, had some trouble against bigger players on switches
- Tended to be late when closing out on perimeter shooters, usually could fight through screens away from the ball
- Decent defensive rebounder, consistently posts a middling steals rate

Matthew Dellavedova	Height	Weight	Cap #	Years Left
	6'3"	200	$1.621M	UFA

	Similar at Age	29	
		Season	SIMsc
1	Jerryd Bayless	2017-18	926.8
2	Greivis Vasquez	2015-16	923.8
3	Emanual Davis	1997-98	917.6
4	Erick Strickland	2002-03	915.4
5	Keyon Dooling	2009-10	914.2
6	Rex Walters	1999-00	912.0
7	Sarunas Jasikevicius	2005-06	908.4
8	Charlie Bell	2008-09	903.4
9	Rumeal Robinson	1995-96	902.5
10	Chris Childs	1996-97	901.9

Baseline Basic Stats

MPG	PTS	AST	REB	BLK	STL
20.2	6.7	3.0	1.8	0.1	0.7

Advanced Metrics

USG%	3PTA/FGA	FTA/FGA	TS%	eFG%	3PT%
15.9	0.424	0.221	0.509	0.463	0.318
AST%	**TOV%**	**OREB%**	**DREB%**	**STL%**	**BLK%**
26.2	19.3	2.1	8.8	1.5	0.3
PER	**ORTG**	**DRTG**	**WS/48**	**VOL**	
10.86	104.8	111.9	0.058	0.442	

- Regular rotation player for Cleveland last season
- Used as a low volume, pass-first, backup point guard, good playmaking skills, fairly turnover prone
- Struggled to shoot efficiently, not quite quick enough to get easy shots at the rim
- Outside shooting declined significantly, made less than 25% of his threes
- Most effective as a spot-up shooter in previous seasons, career Three-Point Percentage is 36.8%
- Rated as below average or worse in most offensive situations, only was effective on a small sample of dribble hand-offs
- 2019-20 Defensive Degree of Difficulty: 0.380
- Typically guards second level players, takes on tougher point guard matchups for short stretches
- Decent on-ball defender, can stay with quicker guards on isolations, has a history being an irritant
- Solid pick-and-roll defender that can funnel his man into help
- Will close out on perimeter shooters, sometimes has trouble getting around screens off the ball
- Stay-at-home defender, middling on the defensive boards, does not really get steals or blocks

Dean Wade

Height	Weight	Cap #	Years Left
6'9"	228	$1.518M	1 + TO

Similar at Age **23**

		Season	SIMsc
1	Andris Biedrins	2009-10	841.3
2	Jonah Bolden	2018-19	839.7
3	Erik Murphy	2013-14	838.3
4	Lorenzo Williams	1992-93	825.6
5	Jordan Mickey	2017-18	818.3
6	Jordan Bell	2017-18	816.0
7	Tang Hamilton	2001-02	813.6
8	Joel Bolomboy	2016-17	810.7
9	Keita Bates-Diop	2018-19	809.8
10	Furkan Aldemir	2014-15	807.7

Baseline Basic Stats

MPG	PTS	AST	REB	BLK	STL
16.0	4.7	0.9	4.2	0.7	0.4

Advanced Metrics

USG%	3PTA/FGA	FTA/FGA	TS%	eFG%	3PT%
12.5	0.296	0.216	0.642	0.638	0.408
AST%	**TOV%**	**OREB%**	**DREB%**	**STL%**	**BLK%**
6.9	14.9	7.2	22.6	1.2	3.6
PER	**ORTG**	**DRTG**	**WS/48**	**VOL**	
14.50	119.2	109.2	0.123	0.413	

- Played on a Two-Way contract for most of the season, converted to a standard contract in June 2020
- Spent most of the season in the G-League with the Canton Charge
- Played as a low volume, stretch big at both levels, made almost 40% of his threes in the G-League
- Mostly a spot-up shooter in a small sample of NBA minutes, flashed some ability to be effective as the screener on pick-and-pop plays
- Effective rim runner on a small sample of NBA possessions, good on rolls to the rim and cuts off the ball
- Fairly decent passer in the G-League, good at limiting turnovers
- <u>2019-20 Defensive Degree of Difficulty</u>: 0.217
- Played mostly in garbage time, only played 71 minutes in the NBA
- Played middling on-ball defense, could get pushed around in the post, flashed some mobility to defend in space
- Effective pick-and-roll defender in a small sample of possessions, solid at switching onto ball handlers
- Does not always come out to contest perimeter shots
- Some rim protector potential, good shot blocker at both levels, maintains solid positioning, good defensive rebounder

Newcomers

Isaac Okoro	<u>**Height**</u>	<u>**Weight**</u>	<u>**Cap #**</u>	<u>**Years Left**</u>
	6'6"	225	$6.401M	1 + 2 TO

<u>**Baseline Basic Stats**</u>

MPG	PTS	AST	REB	BLK	STL
22.2	8.9	1.6	3.4	0.4	0.7

<u>**Advanced Metrics**</u>

USG%	3PTA/FGA	FTA/FGA	TS%	eFG%	3PT%
18.4	0.276	0.342	0.524	0.488	0.335

AST%	TOV%	OREB%	DREB%	STL%	BLK%
12.0	13.0	4.5	12.3	1.8	1.5

PER	ORTG	DRTG	WS/48	VOL
13.34	102.6	103.8	0.069	N/A

- Drafted by Cleveland with the 5th overall pick
- Made the SEC All-Defense team last season, named to the All-SEC 2nd Team in 2019-20
- Unpolished offensively, lower usage player for Auburn last season
- Very athletic, will aggressively attack the rim, great finisher in transition, good cutter, can make hard straight-line drives to score inside or draw fouls
- Uncertain if he can be a shot creator, ball handling skills are limited
- Willing passer, not a natural playmaker, can only make simple passes on the perimeter
- Inconsistent outside shooter, made less than 30% of his threes, struggled to make shots against man defense
- Likely a stationary spot-up shooter, shooting motion is slow, needs extra space to get his shot off
- Great on-ball defender that can potentially guard multiple positions in the NBA
- Great combination of length, athleticism and strength allows him to defend bigger wings and quicker guards
- Solid team defender, generally good pick-and-roll defender, stays attached to shooters off the ball
- Active weak side help defender, got steals and blocks at a high rate in college, decent defensive rebounder

Dylan Windler

Height	Weight	Cap #	Years Left
6'6"	196	$2.137M	2 TO

Baseline Basic Stats

MPG	PTS	AST	REB	BLK	STL
21.6	8.0	1.5	3.1	0.3	0.6

Advanced Metrics

USG%	3PTA/FGA	FTA/FGA	TS%	eFG%	3PT%
15.8	0.484	0.229	0.524	0.495	0.345

AST%	TOV%	OREB%	DREB%	STL%	BLK%
9.9	10.3	4.0	12.7	1.4	1.0

PER	ORTG	DRTG	WS/48	VOL
12.64	101.5	98.0	0.086	N/A

- Drafted by Cleveland with the 26th overall pick in 2019
- Missed the entire 2019-20 season due to a stress reaction in his left leg
- Received Standout honors from the 2019 Utah Summer League
- Good all-around shooter coming out of Belmont, can knock down spot-up jumpers, good at running off screens
- Solid secondary playmaker, effective as a pick-and-roll ball handler at the college level
- Not an overwhelmingly explosive athlete, may struggle to create his own offense at the NBA level
- Played adequate on-ball defense when healthy in the two Summer Leagues in 2019
- Plays with a high effort level, more of a team defender, solid pick-and-roll defender that makes sound rotations
- Good defensive rebounder, plays more a stay-at-home style, seldomly got steals or blocks in his Summer League games

DETROIT PISTONS

Last Season: 20 – 46, Missed the Playoffs

Offensive Rating: 109.0, 21st in the NBA

Defensive Rating: 112.7, 22nd in the NBA

Primary Executive: Troy Weaver, General Manager

Head Coach: Dwane Casey

Key Roster Changes

Subtractions
Luke Kennard, trade
Bruce Brown, trade
Tony Snell, trade
Khryi Thomas, trade
Justin Patton, trade
Christian Wood, free agency
Thon Maker, free agency
Brandon Knight, free agency
John Henson, free agency
Langston Galloway, free agency
Jordan McRae, free agency

Additions
Killian Hayes, draft
Isaiah Stewart, draft
Saddiq Bey, draft
Delon Wright, trade
Dzanan Musa, trade
Jerami Grant, free agency
Mason Plumlee, free agency
Josh Jackson, free agency
Wayne Ellington, free agency
Jahlil Okafor, free agency
Deividas Sirvydis, signed 2019 draft pick

Roster

Likely Starting Five

1. *Killian Hayes*
2. *Delon Wright*
3. *Jerami Grant*
4. *Blake Griffin*
5. Mason Plumlee

Other Key Rotation Players
Derrick Rose
Sekou Doumbouya
Svi Mykhailiuk
Isaiah Stewart
Saddiq Bey

* Italics denotes that a player is likely to be on the floor to close games

Remaining Roster

- Josh Jackson
- Wayne Ellington
- Jahlil Okafor
- Dzanan Musa
- Deividas Sirvydis
- Saben Lee, 21, 6'2", 183, Vanderbilt (Two-Way)
- Louis King, 6'7", 205, Oregon (Two-Way)
- Anthony Lamb, 23, 6'6", 225, Vermont (Exhibit 10)
- LiAngelo Ball, 22, 6'5", 230, Chino Hills HS (Exhibit 10)

SCHREMPF Base Rating: 31.3 (72-game season)

Strengths

- Team does not seem to have any discernible strengths at this point

Question Marks

- Health and possible decline of Blake Griffin
- Jerami Grant's ability to ascend into a primary role
- Development of younger players into potential core building blocks

Outlook

- Likely a lottery team, could possibly be one of the NBA's worst teams this coming season

Veterans

Blake Griffin	Height	Weight	Cap #	Years Left
	6'9"	250	$36.811M	Player Option

	Similar at Age	30	
		Season	SIMsc
1	Carmelo Anthony	2014-15	889.8
2	Chris Webber	2003-04	888.0
3	Chris Bosh	2014-15	882.9
4	Jeff Green	2016-17	882.0
5	Tim Thomas	2007-08	871.9
6	Chris Copeland	2014-15	871.1
7	David Lee	2013-14	869.6
8	Mirza Teletovic	2015-16	867.6
9	Luis Scola	2010-11	867.2
10	Al Harrington	2010-11	865.8

Baseline Basic Stats

MPG	PTS	AST	REB	BLK	STL
28.2	15.1	2.7	5.5	0.4	0.7

Advanced Metrics

USG%	3PTA/FGA	FTA/FGA	TS%	eFG%	3PT%
25.6	0.364	0.327	0.533	0.482	0.337
AST%	**TOV%**	**OREB%**	**DREB%**	**STL%**	**BLK%**
18.6	12.2	4.0	17.4	1.0	1.1
PER	**ORTG**	**DRTG**	**WS/48**	**VOL**	
15.63	106.6	109.8	0.068	0.479	

- Missed most of last season due to injuries to his left hamstring and left knee
- Struggled to maintain his All-Star level production from the season before due to the injuries
- Was Detroit's primary scoring option when he was in the lineup
- Good playmaking big man that can find open teammates as a pick-and-roll ball handler
- Struggled to shoot efficiently in a half court set, did not have the lift to finish at the rim
- Outside shooting declined significantly, shot below 25% on threes last season
- Rated as average or worse in most offensive situations last season
- Athletic roll man with the quickness and ball handling skills to beat defenders off the dribble when healthy
- 2019-20 Defensive Degree of Difficulty: 0.382
- Had to be hidden in favorable matchups against lower leverage offensive players
- Injuries limited his mobility, struggled to keep opposing players in front of him on isolation plays
- Decent pick-and-roll defender, can switch onto ball handlers and cover the roll man inside
- Did not have the range to close out on perimeter shooters
- Unable to be active as a help defender or rim protector, Defensive Rebound and Steal Percentage declined significantly
- Block Percentage was still consistent with his career average

Jerami Grant	Height	Weight	Cap #	Years Left
	6'8"	214	$19.050M	2

Similar at Age 25

		Season	SIMsc
1	James Jones	2005-06	922.3
2	Shane Battier	2003-04	921.7
3	Al-Farouq Aminu	2015-16	915.6
4	Kyle Singler	2013-14	913.9
5	Jason Kapono	2006-07	912.2
6	Jared Dudley	2010-11	910.6
7	Brandon Rush	2010-11	908.6
8	T.J. Warren	2018-19	908.5
9	Jumaine Jones	2004-05	907.5
10	Dorian Finney-Smith	2018-19	906.2

Baseline Basic Stats

MPG	PTS	AST	REB	BLK	STL
27.7	10.8	1.5	4.1	0.5	0.8

Advanced Metrics

USG%	3PTA/FGA	FTA/FGA	TS%	eFG%	3PT%
17.4	0.410	0.258	0.577	0.545	0.384
AST%	**TOV%**	**OREB%**	**DREB%**	**STL%**	**BLK%**
7.5	9.2	3.5	12.5	1.3	2.2
PER	**ORTG**	**DRTG**	**WS/48**	**VOL**	
13.89	114.4	109.6	0.111	0.340	

- Regular rotation player for Denver in his first season with the team, started some games in 2019-20
- Mainly used as a low volume, spot-up shooter, made almost 39% of his threes last season
- Very good spot-up shooter, effective screener on pick-and-pop plays
- Moves very well without the ball, very good cutter that also rolls hard to the rim on pick-and-rolls
- Great at running on the wings in transition to get dunks or draw shooting fouls
- Can post up smaller perimeter players, good at using an on-ball screen to get to the rim on dribble hand-offs
- Limited as a shot creator, does not really shoot off the dribble, not a great ball handler
- Catch-and-shoot player, playmaking skills are limited, rarely turns the ball over
- 2019-20 Defensive Degree of Difficulty: 0.424
- Tended to guard starter level players, sometimes took on tougher defensive assignments
- Solid on-ball defender that guards multiple positions, better against perimeter wings, has trouble against bigger post players
- Solid at guarding pick-and-rolls, good at switching, fights over screens to contain ball handlers
- Stays attached to shooters off the ball, good at closing out on perimeter shooters
- Solid defensive rebounder, good weak side shot blocker, Steal Percentage is still consistent with his career average

Delon Wright

	Height	Weight	Cap #	Years Left
	6'5"	183	$9.000M	1

Similar at Age 27

		Season	SIMsc
1	Craig Ehlo	1988-89	923.7
2	Courtney Lee	2012-13	920.1
3	Cory Joseph	2018-19	916.9
4	Kendall Gill	1995-96	915.8
5	Justin Holiday	2016-17	915.7
6	Kerry Kittles	2001-02	914.8
7	Brent Barry	1998-99	913.5
8	Derek Anderson	2001-02	909.9
9	Alvin Williams	2001-02	905.6
10	Delonte West	2010-11	904.9

Baseline Basic Stats

MPG	PTS	AST	REB	BLK	STL
28.3	10.7	3.4	3.6	0.4	1.1

Advanced Metrics

USG%	3PTA/FGA	FTA/FGA	TS%	eFG%	3PT%
17.0	0.340	0.245	0.540	0.502	0.360
AST%	**TOV%**	**OREB%**	**DREB%**	**STL%**	**BLK%**
20.4	12.8	3.7	12.4	2.2	1.1
PER	**ORTG**	**DRTG**	**WS/48**	**VOL**	
14.98	113.5	107.9	0.123	0.343	

- Regular rotation player in his first season with Dallas
- Primarily used as a low volume, secondary ball handler
- Good playmaker, can kick the ball out to shooters and make interior passes, limits turnovers
- Good at making pull-up jumpers on pick-and-rolls, can drive to the rim on isolation plays
- Mostly a spot-up shooter off the ball, made 37% of his threes last season, good at making backdoor cuts if defenders crowd him
- 2019-20 Defensive Degree of Difficulty: 0.387
- Tends to guard higher end second unit players or low end starters, occasionally defends top point guards
- Decent on-ball defender that can guard multiple positions
- Above average pick-and-roll defender, good at fighting over the screens, has some trouble defending the screener on switches
- Fights through screens off the ball, sometimes can be late to close out in spot-up situations
- Active on the weak side, solid defensive rebounder, posts consistently high Steal and Block Percentages for his size

Mason Plumlee	Height	Weight	Cap #	Years Left
	6'11"	238	$8.000M	2

	Similar at Age	29	
		Season	SIMsc
1	Ian Mahinmi	2015-16	931.0
2	Dwight Howard	2014-15	913.6
3	Will Perdue	1994-95	909.1
4	Tiago Splitter	2013-14	906.8
5	Greg Anderson	1993-94	899.2
6	Joakim Noah	2014-15	894.5
7	John Salley	1993-94	890.5
8	Rony Seikaly	1994-95	890.4
9	Dan Gadzuric	2007-08	888.9
10	Zaza Pachulia	2013-14	887.9

Baseline Basic Stats

MPG	PTS	AST	REB	BLK	STL
21.2	7.5	1.3	6.2	1.0	0.6

Advanced Metrics

USG%	3PTA/FGA	FTA/FGA	TS%	eFG%	3PT%
16.3	0.013	0.504	0.586	0.570	0.089
AST%	**TOV%**	**OREB%**	**DREB%**	**STL%**	**BLK%**
14.5	17.5	10.7	22.3	1.6	3.6
PER	**ORTG**	**DRTG**	**WS/48**	**VOL**	
16.71	114.3	105.6	0.130	0.422	

- Regular rotation player for Denver last season, increased his overall effectiveness in 2019-20
- Thrived as a low volume, rim runner, made almost 78% of his shots inside of three feet last season
- High motor, dives hard to the rim, excellent roll man and cutter
- Good offensive rebounder that efficiently scores on put-backs
- Limited as a scorer, below average post player, no real shooting range outside of three feet
- Very good passing man that hits cutters and finds open shooters, can be slightly turnover prone
- 2019-20 Defensive Degree of Difficulty: 0.330, tends to guard second unit big men
- Average rim protector, highly foul prone, good defensive rebounder, solid shot blocker
- Below average on-ball defender, stronger big men can back him down in the post, struggles to guard quicker players on isolation plays
- Solid pick-and-roll defender, good in drop coverages, can switch onto ball handlers for a few dribbles
- Tends to sag into the paint, does not always come out to contest perimeter shots

Derrick Rose

	Height	Weight	Cap #	Years Left
	6'2"	200	$7.683M	UFA

	Similar at Age	31	
		Season	SIMsc
1	Tony Parker	2013-14	905.7
2	Vinnie Johnson	1987-88	899.1
3	World B. Free	1984-85	897.1
4	Jarrett Jack	2014-15	885.8
5	Lou Williams	2017-18	883.6
6	Andre Miller	2007-08	882.2
7	Byron Scott	1992-93	881.6
8	Deron Williams	2015-16	878.7
9	Mike James	2006-07	878.2
10	Ricky Pierce	1990-91	877.5

Baseline Basic Stats

MPG	PTS	AST	REB	BLK	STL
26.6	13.6	4.5	2.7	0.2	0.8

Advanced Metrics

USG%	3PTA/FGA	FTA/FGA	TS%	eFG%	3PT%
26.2	0.209	0.254	0.546	0.499	0.368
AST%	**TOV%**	**OREB%**	**DREB%**	**STL%**	**BLK%**
29.4	13.1	2.3	8.7	1.4	0.7
PER	**ORTG**	**DRTG**	**WS/48**	**VOL**	
17.76	109.2	112.5	0.095	0.473	

- Continued his reinvention as a sixth man for Detroit last season, had his most productive season since 2011-12
- Utilized as a high volume scoring guard off the bench, generally limits turnovers, posted the highest Assist Percentage of his career last season
- Three-point shooting regressed to his career averages, excellent mid-range shooter that make spot-up jumpers or come off screens
- Enough of a threat to make pull-up jumpers to be an effective driver as a pick-and-roll ball handler or isolation player
- 2019-20 Defensive Degree of Difficulty: 0.392
- Tends to guard higher-end second unit players or lower leverage starters
- Middling on-ball defender, has the quickness to stay with smaller guards, taller perimeter players had success shooting over him
- Decent pick-and-roll defender that will funnel his man into help, has trouble defending bigger players on switches
- Fights through screens off the ball, tends to be late when closing out in spot-up situations
- Steal and Block Percentages were slightly higher than his career averages, middling defensive rebounder

Sekou Doumbouya	Height	Weight	Cap #	Years Left
	6'8"	209	$3.449M	2 Team Options

Similar at Age 19

		Season	SIMsc
1	Martell Webster	2005-06	930.8
2	Troy Brown	2018-19	930.0
3	Kevin Knox	2018-19	904.2
4	Aaron Gordon	2014-15	900.7
5	C.J. Miles	2006-07	891.8
6	Ersan Ilyasova	2006-07	889.3
7	Tobias Harris	2011-12	889.0
8	James Young	2014-15	887.2
9	Maurice Harkless	2012-13	885.0
10	Rashad Vaughn	2015-16	880.8

Baseline Basic Stats

MPG	PTS	AST	REB	BLK	STL
24.8	9.6	1.5	4.0	0.4	0.8

Advanced Metrics

USG%	3PTA/FGA	FTA/FGA	TS%	eFG%	3PT%
18.4	0.365	0.224	0.526	0.495	0.347
AST%	**TOV%**	**OREB%**	**DREB%**	**STL%**	**BLK%**
8.5	11.1	3.2	16.1	1.7	1.0
PER	**ORTG**	**DRTG**	**WS/48**	**VOL**	
11.18	102.2	111.3	0.038	0.390	

- Regular rotation player and part-time starter in the second half of his rookie season
- Mainly used as a low volume, spot-up shooter, pretty inefficient in his NBA minutes
- Fairly raw, still learning to play without the ball, average or worse in most off-ball categories
- Showed the most promise as a cutter, has great athleticism to finish plays above the rim
- More effective with the ball in his hands as a pick-and-roll ball handler, isolation and post-up player
- In short bursts, he can post up smaller players, make a few pull-up jumpers, drive to the rim
- Does not turn the ball over, rarely looks to pass, court vision is not really developed at this stage
- 2019-20 Defensive Degree of Difficulty: 0.422, tended to guard starting level players
- Below average on-ball defender, has trouble staying with opposing players on the perimeter, tends to bite on fakes when playing post defense
- Decent pick-and-roll defender that shows an ability to switch and cover multiple positions
- Fights through screens off the ball, tends to be too aggressive when closing out, gives up driving lanes to the basket
- More of a stay-at-home defender at the NBA level, middling steal and block rates, fairly solid defensive rebounder

Svi Mykhailiuk

Height	Weight	Cap #	Years Left
6'7"	205	$1.664M	RFA

Similar at Age 22

		Season	SIMsc
1	Caris LeVert	2016-17	943.6
2	Tony Snell	2013-14	940.0
3	Nik Stauskas	2015-16	936.8
4	Timothe Luwawu-Cabarrot	2017-18	929.3
5	Kyle Korver	2003-04	927.6
6	Reggie Bullock	2013-14	926.5
7	Sasha Vujacic	2006-07	922.4
8	Luke Kennard	2018-19	914.7
9	Darrun Hilliard	2015-16	909.3
10	Rodney Hood	2014-15	907.2

Baseline Basic Stats

MPG	PTS	AST	REB	BLK	STL
21.6	8.0	1.5	2.7	0.2	0.6

Advanced Metrics

USG%	3PTA/FGA	FTA/FGA	TS%	eFG%	3PT%
16.9	0.586	0.167	0.542	0.516	0.379

AST%	TOV%	OREB%	DREB%	STL%	BLK%
12.1	11.8	1.8	9.7	1.6	0.5

PER	ORTG	DRTG	WS/48	VOL
10.60	105.6	112.7	0.065	0.391

- Regular rotation player for Detroit, started some games last season
- Mostly played a role as a low volume, spot-up shooter, made over 40% of his threes last season
- Primarily a spot-up shooter, pretty good at coming off screens last season, will set up for trail threes in transition
- Effective at using an on-ball screen to get an extra step to the rim on dribble hand-offs
- Cannot really create his own shot, struggled to get all the way to the rim on drives
- Decent secondary playmaking skills, usually limits turnovers
- 2019-20 Defensive Degree of Difficulty: 0.360
- Tends to guard second unit level players, sometimes hidden in favorable matchups
- Below average on-ball defender, lacks quickness to stay with perimeter players, can be backed down inside on post-ups
- Below average at guarding pick-and-rolls, has trouble handling switches, tends to allow ball handlers to turn the corner
- Fights through screens off the ball, consistently closes out on perimeter shooters
- Stay-at-home defender, improved his defensive rebounding rate a bit, slightly increased his Steal Percentage last season

Josh Jackson	Height	Weight	Cap #	Years Left
	6'8"	207	$4.767M	1

Similar at Age 22

		Season	SIMsc
1	Taurean Prince	2016-17	924.7
2	Rodney Hood	2014-15	916.1
3	Mickael Pietrus	2004-05	915.5
4	Maurice Harkless	2015-16	913.3
5	Mario Hezonja	2017-18	910.1
6	C.J. Miles	2009-10	909.7
7	Gordon Hayward	2012-13	908.4
8	Darius Miles	2003-04	905.5
9	Mike Dunleavy, Jr.	2002-03	903.1
10	Stephen Jackson	2000-01	902.4

Baseline Basic Stats

MPG	PTS	AST	REB	BLK	STL
25.8	11.8	2.1	4.2	0.5	1.0

Advanced Metrics

USG%	3PTA/FGA	FTA/FGA	TS%	eFG%	3PT%
23.3	0.351	0.277	0.526	0.489	0.336
AST%	**TOV%**	**OREB%**	**DREB%**	**STL%**	**BLK%**
14.5	13.4	3.4	14.6	2.1	1.7
PER	**ORTG**	**DRTG**	**WS/48**	**VOL**	
13.94	100.8	109.0	0.052	0.337	

- Fringe rotation player for Memphis last season, spent some time in the G-League with the Memphis Hustle
- Had his best season in a role as a low volume, spot-up shooter
- Improved his shot selection, took fewer mid-range shots, shot more threes
- Still a below break-even three-point shooter, excellent finisher around the rim last season, made 78% of his shots inside of three feet
- Effective at cutting to the rim off the ball, good at running the floor in transition
- Fairly solid secondary playmaker, cut his turnover rate last season
- 2019-20 Defensive Degree of Difficulty: 0.423, tended to guard starting level players
- Not tested very much on the perimeter, solid post defender that could hold position against bigger players
- Below average pick-and-roll defender, tends to go too far under screens, has trouble on switches
- Stays attached to shooters off the ball, consistently closes out on perimeter shooters
- Active help defender, fairly good defensive rebounder, gets steals and blocks at a fairly high rate

Wayne Ellington

Height	Weight	Cap #	Years Left
6'4"	200	$1.621M	UFA

Similar at Age 32

		Season	SIMsc
1	Willie Green	2013-14	931.2
2	Roger Mason	2012-13	924.1
3	Nick Young	2017-18	923.8
4	Jaren Jackson	1999-00	915.0
5	Wesley Person	2003-04	908.0
6	Anthony Peeler	2001-02	906.9
7	Marco Belinelli	2018-19	902.2
8	Raja Bell	2008-09	899.1
9	Tim Legler	1998-99	898.6
10	Keith Bogans	2012-13	898.1

Baseline Basic Stats

MPG	PTS	AST	REB	BLK	STL
19.4	6.6	1.5	2.0	0.1	0.6

Advanced Metrics

USG%	3PTA/FGA	FTA/FGA	TS%	eFG%	3PT%
14.6	0.738	0.096	0.531	0.515	0.363
AST%	**TOV%**	**OREB%**	**DREB%**	**STL%**	**BLK%**
11.0	10.0	1.2	11.1	1.5	0.6
PER	**ORTG**	**DRTG**	**WS/48**	**VOL**	
9.70	106.1	111.4	0.063	0.422	

- Fringe rotation player for New York last season, missed a few weeks due to a left Achilles injury
- Low volume shooting specialist at this stage of his career, made threes at around the league average last season
- Better at making spot-up jumpers, made over 42% of his corner threes for his career
- Better in previous seasons at shooting off screens, can occasionally use an on-ball screen to make shots on dribble hand-offs
- Not really a shot creator, was effective at making pull-up jumpers as a pick-and-roll ball handler on a small sample of possessions
- Posted the highest Assist Percentage of his career, rarely turns the ball over
- 2019-20 Defensive Degree of Difficulty: 0.332, tends to guard second unit level players
- Hidden a bit in favorable matchups, helped him to play solid on-ball defense in limited situations
- Below average pick-and-roll defender, tends to be too aggressive when fighting over screens, can be targeted by bigger players in the post on switches
- Does not really fight through screens off the ball, tends to be late when closing out on perimeter shooters
- Steal Percentage was below his career average, fairly decent defensive rebounding guard

Jahlil Okafor	Height	Weight	Cap #	Years Left
	6'10"	275	$1.883M	1

Similar at Age **24**

		Season	SIMsc
1	Erick Dampier	1999-00	899.1
2	Todd MacCulloch	1999-00	898.4
3	Melvin Ely	2002-03	896.7
4	Vitaly Potapenko	1999-00	896.7
5	Kevin Seraphin	2013-14	896.6
6	Victor Alexander	1993-94	894.8
7	Cristiano Felicio	2016-17	891.8
8	Isaac Austin	1993-94	888.9
9	Josh Harrellson	2013-14	887.7
10	Robert Traylor	2001-02	886.2

Baseline Basic Stats

MPG	PTS	AST	REB	BLK	STL
18.1	7.1	0.9	4.7	0.7	0.3

Advanced Metrics

USG%	3PTA/FGA	FTA/FGA	TS%	eFG%	3PT%
19.5	0.016	0.316	0.581	0.555	0.207
AST%	**TOV%**	**OREB%**	**DREB%**	**STL%**	**BLK%**
9.4	14.5	10.0	18.6	0.8	3.3
PER	**ORTG**	**DRTG**	**WS/48**	**VOL**	
16.39	111.3	109.4	0.116	0.446	

- Fringe rotation player for New Orleans last season
- Predominantly a low volume, rim runner, made almost 78% of his shots inside of three feet last season
- Good at sliding into open spaces inside as a cutter and roll man
- Good offensive rebounder that can score on put-backs, runs hard down the floor in transition
- Good post-up scorer on the left block, good passing big man that can hit cutters, slightly turnover prone last season
- 2019-20 Defensive Degree of Difficulty: 0.383, tended to guard second unit level big men
- Average rim protector, fairly foul prone, can block shots, solid defensive rebounder
- Decent on-ball defender, strong post defender, limited mobility, struggles to defend in space
- Decent pick-and-roll defender, good in drop coverages, had trouble containing ball handlers on the perimeter
- Does not always come out to contest shots on the perimeter

Džanan Musa

	Height	Weight	Cap #	Years Left
	6'9"	217	$2.003M	Team Option

Similar at Age 20

		Season	SIMsc
1	J.R. Smith	2005-06	885.1
2	Quincy Miller	2012-13	881.9
3	Antonis Fotsis	2001-02	881.7
4	Al-Farouq Aminu	2010-11	874.2
5	Justise Winslow	2016-17	871.2
6	Gerald Green	2005-06	870.3
7	Sasha Pavlovic	2003-04	868.5
8	Rodions Kurucs	2018-19	865.3
9	DerMarr Johnson	2000-01	864.4
10	Quentin Richardson	2000-01	863.4

Baseline Basic Stats

MPG	PTS	AST	REB	BLK	STL
19.1	7.7	1.2	3.0	0.3	0.6

Advanced Metrics

USG%	3PTA/FGA	FTA/FGA	TS%	eFG%	3PT%
21.5	0.466	0.230	0.511	0.481	0.305

AST%	TOV%	OREB%	DREB%	STL%	BLK%
10.1	13.7	3.7	13.2	1.6	0.7

PER	ORTG	DRTG	WS/48	VOL
10.99	97.8	108.5	0.033	0.479

- Fringe rotation player for Brooklyn, spent some time with the Long Island Nets in the G-League
- Mostly used as a lower volume, spot-up shooter in the NBA, took on more volume in the G-League
- Has struggled to shoot efficiently in his NBA minutes, made over 41% of his threes with Long Island
- More comfortable with the ball in his hands, better shooter off the dribble, very good in a small sample of isolation possessions in the NBA
- Still learning to play off the ball, has flashed some promise as a cutter, good in a small sample of NBA possessions
- Decent secondary playmaker in the G-League, but was fairly turnover prone
- 2019-20 Defensive Degree of Difficulty: 0.269
- Mostly played in garbage time or he was tasked to guard second unit level players
- Improved as an on-ball defender, effective in a small sample of isolation possessions
- Solid pick-and-roll defender that could funnel his man into help
- Team defense needs work, gambles a bit too much, can get caught on screens, undisciplined when closing out on perimeter shooters
- Solid defensive rebounder, gets steals at a moderate rate

Newcomers

Killian Hayes	Height	Weight	Cap #	Years Left
	6'5"	216	$5.307M	1 + 2 TO

Baseline Basic Stats

MPG	PTS	AST	REB	BLK	STL
21.5	8.4	2.8	2.6	0.3	0.9

Advanced Metrics

USG%	3PTA/FGA	FTA/FGA	TS%	eFG%	3PT%
19.9	0.286	0.272	0.508	0.467	0.293
AST%	**TOV%**	**OREB%**	**DREB%**	**STL%**	**BLK%**
24.7	17.3	2.7	10.2	2.0	0.7
PER	**ORTG**	**DRTG**	**WS/48**	**VOL**	
12.58	98.3	105.5	0.060	N/A	

- Drafted by Detroit with the 7th overall pick
- Played for Ratiopharm Ulm in the German BBL, had a solid season as the team's starting point guard in 2019-20
- Great playmaking potential, good court vision and passing skills, can be turnover prone, tries to do too much
- Inconsistent when driving to the rim, draws fouls at a solid rate, tends to settle for floaters or tough pull-up jumpers
- Has strong shooting potential, sound repeatable stroke, has made almost 86% of his free throws over the last three seasons
- Shot selection is questionable, tends to force up a lot of tough, contested shots
- Has not been a break-even three-point shooter at any point in his professional career
- Good tools on defense, has solid length, quickness and athleticism, still unpolished at this stage
- Solid weak side help defender, good at playing passing lanes to get steals at a high rate, solid shot blocker for his size, good defensive rebounder
- Undisciplined as a team defender, over-helps in the paint, leaves shooters open, tends to gamble too much
- Active on-ball defender that can pressure opposing guards, may potentially be able to defend both guard spots at the NBA level
- Can be too aggressive on the ball, a little foul prone, sometimes will over-commit to allow an open driving lane

Isaiah Stewart

	Height	Weight	Cap #	Years Left
	6'9"	250	$3.121M	1 + 2 TO

Baseline Basic Stats

MPG	PTS	AST	REB	BLK	STL
19.7	7.3	0.8	5.2	0.8	0.5

Advanced Metrics

USG%	3PTA/FGA	FTA/FGA	TS%	eFG%	3PT%
17.4	0.058	0.381	0.532	0.490	0.228
AST%	**TOV%**	**OREB%**	**DREB%**	**STL%**	**BLK%**
6.4	13.0	8.8	18.7	1.0	2.9
PER	**ORTG**	**DRTG**	**WS/48**	**VOL**	
15.40	105.0	100.1	0.093	N/A	

- Drafted by Portland with the 16th overall pick, traded to Detroit via Houston
- Made the Pac-12's All-Freshman team, named to the All-Pac 12 1st Team in 2019-20
- Good post-up player, gets deep position, bullies weaker defenders inside, struggled to finish against length
- High energy rim runner, rolls hard to the rim on pick-and-rolls, sets solid screens, good offensive rebounder
- Solid passing big man, can kick the ball out to shooters or hit cutters
- Rarely shoots perimeter shots, good free throw shooter, may eventually be able to extend his shooting range
- Defense difficult to project, mostly played in zone at Washington
- Good shot blocker, decent defensive rebounder, middling rim protector, undisciplined with his positioning
- Strong enough to hold position in the post, tends to bite on fakes, quicker players can beat him to spots inside
- May lack the lateral quickness to defend in space, struggled to stay with quicker guards on switches in a small sample of pick-and-roll possessions

Saddiq Bey

Height	Weight	Cap #	Years Left
6'8"	216	$2.690M	1 + 2 TO

Baseline Basic Stats

MPG	PTS	AST	REB	BLK	STL
22.0	8.6	1.3	3.1	0.3	0.7

Advanced Metrics

USG%	3PTA/FGA	FTA/FGA	TS%	eFG%	3PT%
18.4	0.377	0.204	0.514	0.484	0.353
AST%	**TOV%**	**OREB%**	**DREB%**	**STL%**	**BLK%**
10.1	10.4	3.7	11.1	1.5	1.1
PER	**ORTG**	**DRTG**	**WS/48**	**VOL**	
12.33	101.0	104.0	0.067	N/A	

- Drafted by Brooklyn with the 19th overall pick, traded to Detroit
- Named to the All-Big East 1st Team in 2019-20, won The Julius Erving Award
- Excellent shooter at Villanova, made almost 42% of his career threes
- Mostly a spot-up shooter, can sometimes shoot off screens, effective in a small sample of possessions as a screener on pick-and-pops
- Good at making backdoor cuts if defenders try to crowd him, effective at running the floor in transition to get layups or set up for trail threes
- Lacks ideal ball handling skills and quickness, not really able to beat defenders off the dribble
- Willing to make the extra pass, not a natural playmaker, sticks to making safer passes
- Solid position defender that can potentially guard multiple positions
- Quick enough to guard perimeter players, solid functional strength to handle bigger players in the post
- Stays attached to shooters off the ball, good at fighting through screens and closing out
- Solid at going over screens to contain ball handlers, can go too far over the top to allow his man to turn the corner
- Stay-at-home defender, does not really look to go for steals or blocks, fairly solid defensive rebounder

Deividas Sirvydis

	Height	Weight	Cap #	Years Left
	6'8"	190	$0.898M	2

Baseline Basic Stats

MPG	PTS	AST	REB	BLK	STL
17.5	5.3	1.1	1.9	0.2	0.5

Advanced Metrics

USG%	3PTA/FGA	FTA/FGA	TS%	eFG%	3PT%
12.4	0.628	0.125	0.516	0.501	0.352
AST%	**TOV%**	**OREB%**	**DREB%**	**STL%**	**BLK%**
9.0	12.5	2.2	11.4	1.2	0.6
PER	**ORTG**	**DRTG**	**WS/48**	**VOL**	
8.79	94.8	97.8	0.068	N/A	

- Drafted by Dallas with the 37th overall pick in 2019, rights were traded to Detroit
- Split time between Lietuvos Rytas in the Lithuanian LKL and Hapoel Bank Jerusalem in the Israeli BSL
- Utilized in both leagues as a lower volume spot-up shooter, break-even three-point shooter last season
- Primarily a stationary spot-up shooter, prefers to shoot in the corners
- Has limited responsibility with his team, does not really shoot off screens or off the dribble
- Lacks ideal quickness to drive by NBA level defenders, rarely draws fouls
- Catch-and-shoot player, limited playmaking skills, can be somewhat turnover prone
- Does not have ideal physical tools to defend NBA players, has below average lateral quickness and length
- Generally hidden in favorable matchups, did not really defend upper-tier players overseas
- Fairly decent team defender, makes proper rotations, stays attached to shooters off the ball, consistently closes out in spot-up situations
- Stay-at-home defender, does not really get blocks or steals, fairly solid defensive rebounder

CHARLOTTE HORNETS

Last Season: 23 – 42, Missed the Playoffs

Offensive Rating: 106.3, 29th in the NBA

Defensive Rating: 113.3, 24th in the NBA

Primary Executive: Mitch Kupchak, President of Basketball Operations

Head Coach: James Borrego

Key Roster Changes

Subtractions
Dwayne Bacon, free agency
Willy Hernangomez, free agency
Nicolas Batum, waived

Additions
LaMelo Ball, draft
Vernon Carey, Jr., draft
Nick Richards, draft
Gordon Hayward, trade

Roster

Likely Starting Five

1. *LaMelo Ball*
2. *Devonte' Graham*
3. *Gordon Hayward*
4. *P.J. Washington*
5. Cody Zeller

Other Key Rotation Players
Terry Rozier
Miles Bridges
Bismack Biyombo
Malik Monk
Cody Martin

* Italics denotes that a player is likely to be on the floor to close games

Remaining Roster

- Vernon Carey, Jr.
- Caleb Martin
- Jalen McDaniels
- Nick Richards
- Nate Darling, 22, 6'5", 200, Delaware (Two-Way)
- Grant Riller, 23, 6'3", 190, College of Charleston (Two-Way)
- Keandre Cook, 23, 6'5", 187, Missouri State (Exhibit 10)
- Javin DeLaurier, 22, 6'10", 238, Duke (Exhibit 10)
- Xavier Sneed, 23, 6'5", 215, Kansas State (Exhibit 10)
- Kahlil Whitney, 20, 6'6", 210, Kentucky (Exhibit 10)

SCHREMPF Base Rating: 30.6 (72-game season)

Strengths

- The Hornets do not appear to have any distinct strengths right now

Question Marks

- The team's ability to create coherent systems that maximize talent on both ends of the floor
- Negative effects of past injuries and possible decline of Gordon Hayward
- LaMelo Ball's fit within a team structure and his ability to play a style that is conducive to winning basketball

Outlook

- Will probably be a lottery team in the 2020-21 season, could be one of the worst teams in the league

Veterans

Gordon Hayward	Height	Weight	Cap #	Years Left
	6'7"	207	$28.500M	3

	Similar at Age	29 Season	SIMsc
1	Kyle Korver	2010-11	931.7
2	Walt Williams	1999-00	928.3
3	Evan Turner	2017-18	922.0
4	Wilson Chandler	2016-17	921.1
5	Andres Nocioni	2008-09	919.7
6	John Salmons	2008-09	918.6
7	Eric Piatkowski	1999-00	917.9
8	Rod Higgins	1988-89	917.7
9	Chuck Person	1993-94	916.8
10	Gordan Giricek	2006-07	916.6

Baseline Basic Stats

MPG	PTS	AST	REB	BLK	STL
25.3	10.2	1.7	3.6	0.3	0.7

Advanced Metrics

USG%	3PTA/FGA	FTA/FGA	TS%	eFG%	3PT%
18.5	0.377	0.214	0.559	0.522	0.350
AST%	**TOV%**	**OREB%**	**DREB%**	**STL%**	**BLK%**
13.0	10.5	3.0	14.8	1.2	0.9
PER	**ORTG**	**DRTG**	**WS/48**	**VOL**	
14.10	111.7	107.5	0.121	0.279	

- Missed a month due to a fractured left hand, regular starter for Boston when healthy
- Had a bounce-back season in his role as a moderate volume, secondary ball handler and scorer
- Effective one-on-one player that can make pull-up jumpers and get to the rim as a pick-and-roll ball handler and isolation player
- Solid playmaker that can make interior passes or kick the ball out to shooters, avoids turnovers
- Good at using an on-ball screen to get to the rim or make outside shots on dribble hand-offs
- Made over 38% of his threes last season, solid mid-range shooter
- Mainly a spot-up shooter, can sometimes make shots off screens
- 2019-20 Defensive Degree of Difficulty: 0.418, tends to guard starter level players
- Solid on-ball defender that can capably guard multiple positions
- Generally a good team defender that makes sound rotations
- Good pick-and-roll defender that effectively switches, fights through screens off the ball
- Tended to be late when closing out on perimeter shooters last season
- More of a stay-at-home defender last season, did not really get steals, Block Percentage is still consistent with his career average, solid defensive rebounder

Devonte' Graham	Height	Weight	Cap #	Years Left
	6'1"	185	$1.664M	RFA

	Similar at Age	24	
		Season	SIMsc
1	Jordan Farmar	2010-11	939.8
2	Nick Van Exel	1995-96	931.3
3	Chris Duhon	2006-07	927.2
4	D.J. Augustin	2011-12	924.6
5	Isaiah Canaan	2015-16	924.2
6	Fred VanVleet	2018-19	921.9
7	Mike Bibby	2002-03	920.4
8	Jason Williams	1999-00	920.3
9	Shabazz Napier	2015-16	917.4
10	Daniel Gibson	2010-11	916.9

Baseline Basic Stats

MPG	PTS	AST	REB	BLK	STL
25.3	10.2	4.2	2.3	0.1	0.8

Advanced Metrics

USG%	3PTA/FGA	FTA/FGA	TS%	eFG%	3PT%
20.9	0.514	0.243	0.523	0.477	0.352
AST%	**TOV%**	**OREB%**	**DREB%**	**STL%**	**BLK%**
29.6	13.8	1.8	8.7	1.5	0.4
PER	**ORTG**	**DRTG**	**WS/48**	**VOL**	
14.24	108.2	112.9	0.083	0.463	

- Became a full-time starter for Charlotte in his second season in the NBA
- Production improved significantly across the board, led Charlotte in per-game scoring last season
- Split ball handling duties with Terry Rozier, excellent playmaker, finished in the top ten in every assist metric in 2019-20
- Good pick-and-roll ball handler, more of a jump shooter, has some trouble getting to the rim and finishing
- Good at making spot-up threes, excellent in the corners, made almost 43% of his corner threes in his career
- Not as effective off the ball, struggles to shoot off screens, rarely cuts to the basket
- 2019-20 Defensive Degree of Difficulty: 0.389
- Hidden in favorable matchups against lower leverage starters
- Decent as an on-ball defender, could use quickness to stay in front of perimeter players, taller wing players had success shooting over him
- Solid pick-and-roll defender that could fight through screens and capably switch to guard the screener
- Can get caught on screens off the ball, not always disciplined when closing out on perimeter shooters
- Played more of a stay-at-home role, steals rate was slightly down, fairly decent defensive rebounder

P.J. Washington	Height	Weight	Cap #	Years Left
	6'7"	236	$4.024M	2 Team Options

Similar at Age 21

		Season	SIMsc
1	Jaylen Brown	2017-18	937.2
2	Justise Winslow	2017-18	932.2
3	Omri Casspi	2009-10	913.1
4	Donte Greene	2009-10	905.5
5	Stanley Johnson	2017-18	905.5
6	Richard Jefferson	2001-02	904.2
7	Aaron Gordon	2016-17	904.1
8	Kawhi Leonard	2012-13	904.1
9	Lamond Murray	1994-95	904.1
10	OG Anunoby	2018-19	904.0

Baseline Basic Stats

MPG	PTS	AST	REB	BLK	STL
26.4	11.4	1.8	4.8	0.5	1.0

Advanced Metrics

USG%	3PTA/FGA	FTA/FGA	TS%	eFG%	3PT%
18.8	0.267	0.243	0.542	0.515	0.348
AST%	**TOV%**	**OREB%**	**DREB%**	**STL%**	**BLK%**
11.5	13.1	4.3	15.4	1.8	1.6
PER	**ORTG**	**DRTG**	**WS/48**	**VOL**	
13.01	105.7	109.6	0.076	0.263	

- Regular starter for Charlotte in his rookie season
- Mostly utilized as a low volume, spot-up shooter, made more than 50% of his corner threes last season
- Shot higher than the league average on threes overall, stroke still somewhat inconsistent, made less than two-thirds of his free throws
- More of a stationary shooter at this stage, less effective when shooting on the move
- Can post up smaller perimeter players, better on the right block, also runs hard down the floor in transition
- Fairly good passer that can kick the ball out to shooters, good at avoiding turnovers
- 2019-20 Defensive Degree of Difficulty: 0.391
- Primarily guards lower leverage starters to higher-end second unit players
- Fairly solid on-ball defender, better at handling perimeter players in space, less effective against taller post players
- Average pick-and-roll defender, good at covering the screener, has some difficulty containing ball handlers
- Can get caught on screens, not always disciplined when trying to close out on shooters
- Active help defender, solid defensive rebounder, gets blocks and steals at a solid rate

Cody Zeller

Height	Weight	Cap #	Years Left
7'0"	240	$15.416M	UFA

Similar at Age 27

		Season	SIMsc
1	Matt Geiger	1996-97	934.5
2	Will Perdue	1992-93	926.4
3	Dwight Powell	2018-19	917.8
4	Nenad Krstic	2010-11	917.4
5	Stacey King	1993-94	912.6
6	Alton Lister	1985-86	910.6
7	Tiago Splitter	2011-12	908.4
8	Steve Johnson	1984-85	908.2
9	Nikola Pekovic	2012-13	907.2
10	Zaza Pachulia	2011-12	904.5

Baseline Basic Stats

MPG	PTS	AST	REB	BLK	STL
23.0	9.6	1.4	6.1	0.7	0.6

Advanced Metrics

USG%	3PTA/FGA	FTA/FGA	TS%	eFG%	3PT%
18.9	0.105	0.366	0.576	0.535	0.319
AST%	**TOV%**	**OREB%**	**DREB%**	**STL%**	**BLK%**
11.3	13.3	10.1	20.8	1.4	2.1
PER	**ORTG**	**DRTG**	**WS/48**	**VOL**	
17.14	115.1	108.9	0.127	0.376	

- Regularly started for Charlotte last season, played fewer Minutes per Game from the season before
- Had his most productive season in his seventh year, took on a more moderate volume role
- Primarily used as a rim runner, solid roll man and cutter, runs hard down the floor in transition
- Good offensive rebounder that scores on put-backs, set a career high in Offensive Rebound Percentage last season
- Started to shoot more threes, struggled to make them consistently, Three-Point Percentage was below 30%
- Effective passing big man that limits turnovers, fairly good at flashing to the middle on a small sample of post-ups
- 2019-20 Defensive Degree of Difficulty: 0.403
- Typically guarded starting level players, served as Charlotte's primary rim protector
- Struggled to protect the rim, Block Percentage decreased significantly last season
- Solid defensive rebounder, set a career high in Defensive Rebound Percentage last season
- Mixed results as an on-ball defender, effective at playing post defense, struggled to defend in space on isolation plays
- Average pick-and-roll defender, has enough mobility to switch onto ball handlers, had trouble covering roll man at the rim
- Does not always come out to contest shots on the perimeter

Terry Rozier	Height	Weight	Cap #	Years Left
	6'1"	190	$18.900M	1

Similar at Age 25

		Season	SIMsc
1	Mike Bibby	2003-04	926.8
2	Mo Williams	2007-08	924.4
3	Luther Head	2007-08	922.3
4	Jason Williams	2000-01	917.7
5	Dennis Schroder	2018-19	917.0
6	Tyler Johnson	2017-18	915.5
7	Patty Mills	2013-14	914.5
8	Cory Joseph	2016-17	912.8
9	Mario Chalmers	2011-12	912.3
10	Leandro Barbosa	2007-08	910.1

Baseline Basic Stats

MPG	PTS	AST	REB	BLK	STL
28.0	12.2	3.9	2.8	0.2	1.0

Advanced Metrics

USG%	3PTA/FGA	FTA/FGA	TS%	eFG%	3PT%
21.2	0.448	0.201	0.538	0.501	0.382
AST%	**TOV%**	**OREB%**	**DREB%**	**STL%**	**BLK%**
21.7	11.9	2.0	11.4	1.7	0.5
PER	**ORTG**	**DRTG**	**WS/48**	**VOL**	
14.51	108.1	110.0	0.090	0.397	

- Full-time starter in his first season with Charlotte
- Split ball handling duties with Devonte' Graham, used more as a scoring guard
- Good making quick no dribble jumpers, could get to the rim, good on isolation plays
- Average pick-and-roll ball handler, will settle for inefficient mid-range floaters
- Decent playmaker, mainly sticks to making simple passes, typically limits turnovers
- Good shooter off the ball, made over 40% of his threes last season, can knock down spot-up jumpers and can run off screens
- Scores a lot in volume in transition, but tends to be a bit out of control
- 2019-20 Defensive Degree of Difficulty: 0.437
- Generally guards starting level players, occasionally takes on tougher point guard matchups
- Solid on-ball defender that can stay with quicker guards, vulnerable to post-ups inside against taller wing players
- Fairly good pick-and-roll defender, but will occasionally allow his man to turn the corner
- Fights through screens to stay attached to shooters off the ball, sometimes closes out too aggressively to allow driving lanes to the rim
- More of a stay-at-home defender in Charlotte, defensive rebound, steal and block rates are down from his career averages

Miles Bridges	Height	Weight	Cap #	Years Left
	6'6"	225	$3.934M	Team Option

Similar at Age **21**

		Season	SIMsc
1	Quentin Richardson	2001-02	927.3
2	Chase Budinger	2009-10	924.4
3	Martell Webster	2007-08	918.5
4	Jaylen Brown	2017-18	917.7
5	Kawhi Leonard	2012-13	917.3
6	Justise Winslow	2017-18	916.6
7	Wilson Chandler	2008-09	915.4
8	Omri Casspi	2009-10	914.5
9	Aaron Gordon	2016-17	913.1
10	C.J. Miles	2008-09	910.1

Baseline Basic Stats

MPG	PTS	AST	REB	BLK	STL
28.3	12.5	1.9	4.7	0.5	0.8

Advanced Metrics

USG%	3PTA/FGA	FTA/FGA	TS%	eFG%	3PT%
18.9	0.284	0.195	0.531	0.502	0.333
AST%	**TOV%**	**OREB%**	**DREB%**	**STL%**	**BLK%**
10.5	10.8	4.1	14.5	1.4	1.5
PER	**ORTG**	**DRTG**	**WS/48**	**VOL**	
12.87	105.8	111.1	0.068	0.323	

- Became a full-time starter for Charlotte in his second season in the NBA
- Played a moderate volume role, mostly used off the ball as a spot-up shooter
- Break-even three-point shooter overall, much better in the corners, made almost 54% of his long twos
- Stationary shooter at this stage, not as effective when shooting on the move
- Improving with the ball in his hands, can make pull-up jumpers off pick-and-rolls, effective at posting up smaller perimeter players
- Will hit the offensive boards to score on put-backs, solid cutter
- Catch-and-shoot player at this stage, limited passing skills, will avoid turnovers
- 2019-20 Defensive Degree of Difficulty: 0.483
- Usually guards starting level players, will take on tougher defensive assignments
- Very good on-ball defender that can guard multiple positions
- Solid pick-and-roll defender, but can be too aggressive when fighting over screens
- Very good at closing out on perimeter shooters, will sometimes get caught out of position trying to shoot the gap when chasing shooters off screens
- More of a stay-at-home defender last season, steals rate went down, solid defensive rebounder and shot blocker for his size

Bismack Biyombo

Height	Weight	Cap #	Years Left
6'8"	255	$3.500M	UFA

Similar at Age 27

		Season	SIMsc
1	Etan Thomas	2005-06	949.1
2	Jason Caffey	2000-01	910.8
3	Jeff Adrien	2013-14	910.1
4	Don Reid	2000-01	903.0
5	Louis Amundson	2009-10	902.1
6	Brian Grant	1999-00	901.6
7	Gary Trent	2001-02	900.8
8	Brian Skinner	2003-04	896.9
9	Miles Plumlee	2015-16	894.8
10	Shelden Williams	2010-11	894.4

Baseline Basic Stats

MPG	PTS	AST	REB	BLK	STL
19.2	6.9	0.6	5.0	0.8	0.4

Advanced Metrics

USG%	3PTA/FGA	FTA/FGA	TS%	eFG%	3PT%
17.3	0.000	0.436	0.553	0.528	0.000
AST%	**TOV%**	**OREB%**	**DREB%**	**STL%**	**BLK%**
6.5	12.6	11.0	20.7	0.8	3.6
PER	**ORTG**	**DRTG**	**WS/48**	**VOL**	
15.49	111.5	107.9	0.108	0.285	

- Regular rotation player for Charlotte, had his most productive season as a pro in 2019-20
- Predominantly a low volume, rim runner throughout his career
- Draws fouls at a high rate, scores on cuts and rolls to the rim
- Runs hard down the floor in transition, very good offensive rebounder that will score on put-backs
- No real shooting range outside of three feet, traditionally has struggled to make free throws, has made above 60% of his free throw in each of the last three seasons
- Improved as a passer, set a career high in Assist Percentage, cut his Turnover Percentage to a career low as well
- 2019-20 Defensive Degree of Difficulty: 0.405
- Guarded starter level players, served as one of Charlotte's rim protectors
- Solid defensive rebounder and shot blocker, can be out of position at times, highly foul prone
- Good post defender that uses his length to contest shots, has some difficulty staying with quicker players on isolation plays
- Pretty good pick-and-roll defender that can guard the roll man in drop coverage, has enough mobility to switch onto ball handlers for a few dribbles
- Consistently will close out on perimeter shooters

Malik Monk	Height	Weight	Cap #	Years Left
	6'3"	200	$5.346M	RFA

	Similar at Age	21 Season	SIMsc
1	Bradley Beal	2014-15	924.1
2	Rashad McCants	2005-06	917.1
3	Jamal Murray	2018-19	916.7
4	Marcus D. Williams	2006-07	913.0
5	Emmanuel Mudiay	2017-18	911.9
6	Jerryd Bayless	2009-10	908.8
7	Ben Gordon	2004-05	907.7
8	Elie Okobo	2018-19	906.2
9	Archie Goodwin	2015-16	904.5
10	Dennis Smith, Jr.	2018-19	904.3

Baseline Basic Stats

MPG	PTS	AST	REB	BLK	STL
23.5	11.7	2.7	2.5	0.2	0.7

Advanced Metrics

USG%	3PTA/FGA	FTA/FGA	TS%	eFG%	3PT%
22.6	0.304	0.223	0.532	0.493	0.331
AST%	**TOV%**	**OREB%**	**DREB%**	**STL%**	**BLK%**
18.2	12.9	2.1	10.0	1.4	0.8
PER	**ORTG**	**DRTG**	**WS/48**	**VOL**	
13.08	104.0	112.9	0.054	0.483	

- Showed steady improvement in his second year as a regular rotation player for Charlotte
- Utilized as a scoring guard off the bench, mostly played off the ball
- Went to the rim more frequently last season, improved as a mid-range shooter
- 49% of his shots came from inside of ten feet, very good at attacking aggressive close-outs, drew fouls at a high rate
- Rated as average or worse in most offensive situations, less of a threat to make threes
- Three-Point Percentage has decreased in each of his three seasons, shot below 30% from three last season
- Shows decent secondary playmaking skills, solid at limiting turnovers
- 2019-20 Defensive Degree of Difficulty: 0.299
- Usually hidden in lower leverage second unit matchups
- Rarely tested on the ball, played effective on-ball defense in a small sample of isolation possessions
- Fairly solid at defending pick-and-rolls, will funnel his man into help
- Fights through screens to stay attached to shooters, can be undisciplined when trying to close out on perimeter shooters
- Improved as a defensive rebounder, steal and block rates are still consistent with his career averages

Cody Martin	Height	Weight	Cap #	Years Left
	6'5"	205	$1.518M	1

	Similar at Age	24 Season	SIMsc
1	Aaron McKie	1996-97	937.4
2	Kent Bazemore	2013-14	933.9
3	Iman Shumpert	2014-15	927.8
4	Royce O'Neale	2017-18	915.5
5	John Salmons	2003-04	914.7
6	Mitchell Butler	1994-95	914.6
7	MarShon Brooks	2012-13	911.4
8	Fred Jones	2003-04	911.3
9	George McCloud	1991-92	910.8
10	Thabo Sefolosha	2008-09	909.9

Baseline Basic Stats

MPG	PTS	AST	REB	BLK	STL
20.9	6.7	1.7	2.8	0.3	0.9

Advanced Metrics

USG%	3PTA/FGA	FTA/FGA	TS%	eFG%	3PT%
15.2	0.355	0.282	0.515	0.478	0.285
AST%	**TOV%**	**OREB%**	**DREB%**	**STL%**	**BLK%**
14.3	14.7	3.6	13.4	2.1	0.9
PER	**ORTG**	**DRTG**	**WS/48**	**VOL**	
10.98	103.8	109.6	0.057	0.453	

- Regular rotation player for Charlotte in his rookie season
- Primarily used as a very low volume, spot-up shooter, struggled to make shots outside of three feet
- Much more effective when attacking the basket, made over 68% of his shots inside of three feet
- Excelled at running the floor in transition to get layups or draw fouls
- Showed fairly solid playmaking skills, effective as a pick-and-roll ball handler, slightly turnover prone
- Will opportunistically go to the offensive boards to score on put-backs
- 2019-20 Defensive Degree of Difficulty: 0.434
- Tended to guard higher-end second unit players, sometimes was tasked to guard elite perimeter players
- May have been over-extended in his role, below average at defending in isolation situations, committed shooting fouls at a high rate
- Fairly good pick-and-roll defender that could fight through screens and switch to guard multiple positions
- Stayed attached to shooters off the ball, but was sometimes late when closing out in spot-up situations
- Good defensive rebounder, good at using length to force turnovers, gets steals at a high rate

Caleb Martin

	Height	Weight	Cap #	Years Left
Caleb Martin	6'5"	205	$1.518M	1

Similar at Age 24

		Season	SIMsc
1	Kim English	2012-13	926.8
2	Walter Bond	1993-94	924.9
3	Ben McLemore	2017-18	916.0
4	Pat Connaughton	2016-17	913.2
5	Fred Hoiberg	1996-97	911.5
6	Royce O'Neale	2017-18	907.7
7	Stan Pietkiewicz	1980-81	906.3
8	Danny Green	2011-12	905.9
9	Jerian Grant	2016-17	905.4
10	Trajan Langdon	2000-01	905.1

Baseline Basic Stats

MPG	PTS	AST	REB	BLK	STL
22.3	8.1	1.8	2.8	0.3	0.8

Advanced Metrics

USG%	3PTA/FGA	FTA/FGA	TS%	eFG%	3PT%
16.3	0.467	0.215	0.574	0.539	0.454
AST%	**TOV%**	**OREB%**	**DREB%**	**STL%**	**BLK%**
12.5	13.1	2.9	10.3	1.8	1.5
PER	**ORTG**	**DRTG**	**WS/48**	**VOL**	
12.13	110.0	110.6	0.076	0.497	

- Fringe rotation player for Charlotte as a rookie, spend most of the season with the Greensboro Swarm in the G-League
- Used as a low volume, spot-up shooter in the NBA, played a higher volume role in the G-League
- Shot extremely well on a small sample of NBA threes, was an above average three-point shooter in the G-League
- Had some difficulty getting to the basket in the NBA, not likely to be a reliable shot creator
- Below average as the ball handler on a small sample of pick-and-roll possessions
- Solid secondary playmaker in the G-League and the NBA, fairly good at limiting turnovers
- 2019-20 Defensive Degree of Difficulty: 0.341
- Typically defended second unit level players, rarely tested on the ball, held up on a small sample of isolation possessions
- Below average pick-and-roll defender, tended to go too far under screens to allow open perimeter shots
- Generally stayed attached to shooters off the ball, could sometimes be late when closing out in spot-up situations
- Active help defender, posted fairly high Steal and Block Percentages, solid defensive rebounder

Jalen McDaniels

	Height	Weight	Cap #	Years Left
	6'10"	192	$1.518M	1 + TO

Similar at Age 22

		Season	SIMsc
1	Austin Daye	2010-11	896.3
2	Jason Kapono	2003-04	886.1
3	Corey Brewer	2008-09	885.7
4	Chandler Hutchison	2018-19	885.7
5	Cedi Osman	2017-18	883.9
6	Sergei Monia	2005-06	873.9
7	Otto Porter	2015-16	872.9
8	Antoine Wright	2006-07	872.6
9	Gerald Green	2007-08	870.8
10	Hollis Thompson	2013-14	870.2

Baseline Basic Stats

MPG	PTS	AST	REB	BLK	STL
22.4	8.4	1.2	3.4	0.4	0.8

Advanced Metrics

USG%	3PTA/FGA	FTA/FGA	TS%	eFG%	3PT%
16.0	0.360	0.226	0.563	0.529	0.382
AST%	**TOV%**	**OREB%**	**DREB%**	**STL%**	**BLK%**
8.1	10.7	4.4	15.6	1.6	1.1
PER	**ORTG**	**DRTG**	**WS/48**	**VOL**	
12.15	111.5	111.4	0.087	0.433	

- Fringe rotation player for Charlotte as a rookie, spent most of the season with the Greensboro Swarm in the G-League
- Mainly a low volume spot-up shooter in his minutes with Charlotte, took on more volume in the G-League
- Solid three-point shooter in the G-League and the NBA, shot 6-for-14 on corner threes in the NBA
- Flashed some ability to play off the ball, good cutter in a small sample of possessions, willing to crash the offensive glass to score on put-backs
- Mainly a catch-and-shoot player, showed some passing skills in the G-League, good at avoiding turnovers
- 2019-20 Defensive Degree of Difficulty: 0.311
- Usually defended lower leverage second unit players
- Rarely tested on the ball, struggled to stay with opposing players in isolation situations
- Solid in pick-and-roll defense, showed the mobility to switch and guard multiple positions
- Good defender off the ball, stayed attached to shooters, consistently used his length to close out and contest shots
- Stay-at-home defender at the NBA level, good defensive rebounder, can get steals by using his length to play passing lanes

Newcomers

LaMelo Ball	**Height**	**Weight**	**Cap #**	**Years Left**
	6'6"	181	$7.840M	1 + 2 TO

Baseline Basic Stats

MPG	PTS	AST	REB	BLK	STL
23.5	9.4	2.6	3.3	0.3	0.9

Advanced Metrics

USG%	3PTA/FGA	FTA/FGA	TS%	eFG%	3PT%
20.1	0.337	0.215	0.494	0.463	0.300

AST%	TOV%	OREB%	DREB%	STL%	BLK%
22.5	13.8	3.8	13.3	1.8	0.8

PER	ORTG	DRTG	WS/48	VOL
12.65	99.0	108.2	0.053	N/A

- Drafted by Charlotte with the 3rd overall pick
- Played with the Illawarra Hawks in the Australian NBL, named NBL Rookie of the Year in 2019-20
- Missed the second half of 2019-20, chose to sit out the remainder of the season after a foot injury in December 2019
- Great playmaking potential, shows great court vision, dynamic passer in the half court and in transition
- Tends to be careless with the ball, prone to throwing the ball away or over-dribbling into traffic
- Good quickness, athleticism and ball handling skills, can beat defenders off the dribble and make deep threes
- Very questionable shot selection, tends to take rushed early threes, forces up contested step-back jumpers
- True Shooting Percentage was below 50% last season, shooting percentages in his professional stints have been pretty low
- Typically has been a lackadaisical defensive player, effort level is not especially high
- Can be slow to get back on defense, tends to get caught ball watching, gambles too much
- Rarely tasked to take on tougher defensive assignments, usually guards non-shooters off the ball
- Good quickness and length, better as a weak side roamer, good defensive rebounder, jumps passing lanes to get steals

Vernon Carey, Jr.

Height	Weight	Cap #	Years Left
6'10"	270	$1.350M	2 + TO

Baseline Basic Stats

MPG	PTS	AST	REB	BLK	STL
18.7	7.5	0.7	5.4	0.9	0.5

Advanced Metrics

USG%	3PTA/FGA	FTA/FGA	TS%	eFG%	3PT%
19.3	0.026	0.431	0.551	0.519	0.112

AST%	TOV%	OREB%	DREB%	STL%	BLK%
7.4	13.8	9.9	20.9	1.2	3.1

PER	ORTG	DRTG	WS/48	VOL
17.38	106.8	99.5	0.106	N/A

- Drafted by Charlotte with the 32nd overall pick
- Made the All-ACC 1st Team, named USBWA Freshman of the Year in 2019-20
- Highly productive big man, effective low post scorer, great at using size and strength to get deep position and bully defenders around the rim
- Good rim runner, athletic enough to catch lobs, dives hard as a roll man and cutter off the ball
- Very good offensive rebounder, will draw fouls at a high rate
- Flashes some stretch potential, made over 38% of his threes at Duke in a small sample of attempts
- Shooting mechanics need work, slow release, line drive shot, stroke not yet repeatable
- Old school interior defender, stout post defender, size allows him to clog the lane, good defensive rebounder and shot blocker
- Lacks mobility to defend in space, had difficulty guarding pick-and-rolls, tends to get into foul trouble, does not always come out to contest perimeter shots
- Has active hands, can poke balls away from opponents inside, can opportunistically play passing lanes to get steals

Nick Richards	Height	Weight	Cap #	Years Left
	6'11"	247	$1.000M	RFA

Baseline Basic Stats

MPG	PTS	AST	REB	BLK	STL
14.5	5.1	0.6	3.8	0.9	0.3

Advanced Metrics

USG%	3PTA/FGA	FTA/FGA	TS%	eFG%	3PT%
16.2	0.004	0.438	0.540	0.509	0.044

AST%	TOV%	OREB%	DREB%	STL%	BLK%
5.3	14.7	9.8	18.1	0.8	4.4

PER	ORTG	DRTG	WS/48	VOL
14.04	105.8	102.2	0.068	N/A

- Drafted by New Orleans with the 42nd overall pick, traded to Charlotte
- Made the SEC All-Defense team, named to the All-SEC 1st Team
- High motor rim runner, vertical lob threat with great length and leaping ability, draws fouls at a high rate
- Dives hard to the rim as a roll man and cutter, active offensive rebounder that scores on put-backs
- Lacks advanced post moves, limited passing skills, can only make simplified reads
- Has never taken a three in college, more comfortable as a mid-range shooter, still needs to expand his shooting range
- Good rim protector at Kentucky, very good shot blocker, solid defensive rebounder
- Tends to play out of control, can get caught out of position when going for blocks, prone to committing cheap fouls
- Improved post defender due to increased strength, good in drop coverages when guarding pick-and-rolls, consistently closes out on perimeter shooters
- Rarely asked to defend in space, showed decent lateral quickness in a small sample of possessions

NEW YORK KNICKS

Last Season: 21 – 45, Missed the Playoffs

Offensive Rating: 106.5, 28th in the NBA

Defensive Rating: 113.0, 23rd in the NBA

Primary Executive: Leon Rose, Team President

Head Coach: Tom Thibodeau

Key Roster Changes

Subtractions
Bobby Portis, free agency
Damyean Dotson, free agency
Maurice Harkless, free agency
Taj Gibson, waived
Wayne Ellington, waived

Additions
Obi Toppin, draft
Immanuel Quickley, draft
Omari Spellman, trade
Jacob Evans, trade
Alec Burks, free agency
Nerlens Noel, free agency
Austin Rivers, free agency

Roster

Likely Starting Five

1. *Elfrid Payton*
2. *Alec Burks*
3. *R.J. Barrett*
4. Obi Toppin
5. *Julius Randle*

Other Key Rotation Players
Mitchell Robinson
Nerlens Noel
Austin Rivers
Frank Ntilikina
Kevin Knox

* Italics denotes that a player is likely to be on the floor to close games

Remaining Roster

- Reggie Bullock
- Dennis Smith, Jr.
- Immanuel Quickley
- Omari Spellman
- Jacob Evans
- Ignas Brazdeikis
- Theo Pinson, 25, 6'5",'212, North Carolina (Two-Way)
- Jared Harper, 23, 5'11", 175, Auburn (Two-Way)
- Michael Kidd-Gilchrist, 27, 6'6", 232, Kentucky (Exhibit 10)
- Myles Powell, 23, 6'2", 195, Seton Hall (Exhibit 10)
- Skal Labissiere, 24, 6'10", 230, Kentucky (Exhibit 10)

SCHREMPF Base Rating: 30.1 (72-game season)

Strengths

- Potentially a good rebounding team due to a decent big man rotation and solid all-around size

Question Marks

- Team lacks a true foundational talent to build around
- Lack of any coherent structure on either side of the ball at this stage
- Tom Thibodeau is a questionable fit with a younger roster that is more development-oriented

Outlook

- Likely will be headed for the lottery as one of the league's worst teams

Veterans

Julius Randle

Height	Weight	Cap #	Years Left
6'8"	250	$18.900M	1

	Similar at Age	25 Season	SIMsc
1	Blake Griffin	2014-15	913.8
2	Zach Randolph	2006-07	908.3
3	Carlos Boozer	2006-07	906.2
4	Paul Millsap	2010-11	903.1
5	Juwan Howard	1998-99	897.7
6	Jamal Mashburn	1997-98	894.4
7	Craig Smith	2008-09	893.7
8	Popeye Jones	1995-96	892.8
9	Brian Grant	1997-98	892.1
10	Nikola Vucevic	2015-16	888.8

Baseline Basic Stats

MPG	PTS	AST	REB	BLK	STL
33.4	19.3	2.9	8.9	0.5	0.9

Advanced Metrics

USG%	3PTA/FGA	FTA/FGA	TS%	eFG%	3PT%
26.4	0.159	0.338	0.555	0.510	0.295
AST%	**TOV%**	**OREB%**	**DREB%**	**STL%**	**BLK%**
15.6	13.0	7.6	22.6	1.3	1.2
PER	**ORTG**	**DRTG**	**WS/48**	**VOL**	
18.96	108.7	109.6	0.104	0.292	

- Regular starter in his first season with New York, led the team in scoring in 2019-20
- Took on a high usage role as an interior scorer, efficiency decreased in New York
- Effective post-up player that can use his strength bully defenders inside, draws fouls at a high rate
- Good at driving to the rim on isolations, struggled to efficiently make outside shots
- Below 30% on threes last season, mostly effective from 16 feet and in
- Good rim runner that can score on rolls to the rim and cuts off the ball, fairly active offensive rebounder that scores on put-backs
- Good passing big man, effective at limiting turnovers over the last two seasons
- <u>2019-20 Defensive Degree of Difficulty</u>: 0.445, tended to guard starting level players
- Fairly effective at protecting the rim, not really a shot blocker, stays vertical to contest shots, very good defensive rebounder
- Improved his on-ball defense, solid at containing drives on isolations, used his strength to be a more effective post defender
- Fairly solid pick-and-roll defender, good in drop coverages, decent at switching onto ball handlers
- Did not always come out to contest perimeter shots in spot-up situations

RJ Barrett

	Height	Weight	Cap #	Years Left
	6'6"	202	$8.232M	2 Team Options

	Similar at Age	19 Season	SIMsc
1	J.R. Smith	2004-05	927.5
2	Kobe Bryant*	1997-98	926.9
3	Devin Booker	2015-16	921.9
4	Emmanuel Mudiay	2015-16	913.7
5	Bradley Beal	2012-13	904.4
6	D'Angelo Russell	2015-16	901.5
7	Luol Deng	2004-05	899.8
8	Jamal Murray	2016-17	896.7
9	Andrew Wiggins	2014-15	893.6
10	Jayson Tatum	2017-18	891.2

Baseline Basic Stats

MPG	PTS	AST	REB	BLK	STL
28.5	14.8	3.2	3.7	0.4	1.0

Advanced Metrics

USG%	3PTA/FGA	FTA/FGA	TS%	eFG%	3PT%
25.6	0.246	0.335	0.518	0.477	0.375
AST%	**TOV%**	**OREB%**	**DREB%**	**STL%**	**BLK%**
19.6	13.4	2.6	14.6	1.8	0.8
PER	**ORTG**	**DRTG**	**WS/48**	**VOL**	
14.43	101.3	112.9	0.031	0.275	

- Regular starter in his rookie season for New York
- Struggled to score efficiently in a higher usage scoring role
- Could get to the rim on isolation plays, drew fouls at a solid rate, only made around 61% of his free throws
- Inefficient shooter in general, below break-even three-point shooter, tended to settle for contested mid-range shots
- Rated as average or worse in most offensive categories, effective at posting up smaller players
- Decent secondary playmaker, fairly good at limiting turnovers
- 2019-20 Defensive Degree of Difficulty: 0.449, tended to guard starting level players
- Below average on-ball defender, can stay with perimeter players on drives, tends to give up space for opponents to step into jump shots
- Fairly decent pick-and-roll defender, can fight over the screen to guard the ball handler, struggled when asked to switch
- Gets around screens off the ball, tends to be either late or too aggressive when closing out on perimeter shooters
- Fairly solid defensive rebounder, posted a moderate Steal Percentage last season

Elfrid Payton	Height	Weight	Cap #	Years Left
	6'3"	185	$4.760M	UFA

Similar at Age 25

		Season	SIMsc
1	John Starks	1990-91	927.1
2	Anthony Carter	2000-01	914.7
3	Cory Joseph	2016-17	914.5
4	Gary Grant	1990-91	913.2
5	Bobby Jackson	1998-99	911.5
6	Keith McLeod	2004-05	911.1
7	Sam Vincent	1988-89	908.7
8	Alvin Williams	1999-00	908.2
9	Sam Cassell	1994-95	907.6
10	Jay Humphries	1987-88	906.7

Baseline Basic Stats

MPG	PTS	AST	REB	BLK	STL
24.9	9.9	4.7	2.8	0.2	1.1

Advanced Metrics

USG%	3PTA/FGA	FTA/FGA	TS%	eFG%	3PT%
19.4	0.223	0.231	0.510	0.478	0.290
AST%	**TOV%**	**OREB%**	**DREB%**	**STL%**	**BLK%**
31.6	16.6	3.3	11.5	2.3	0.9
PER	**ORTG**	**DRTG**	**WS/48**	**VOL**	
15.22	106.9	109.7	0.088	0.371	

- Regular starter for New York when healthy, missed over a month due to a strained right hamstring
- Utilized as a low volume, pass-first point guard, very good playmaker, fairly turnover prone
- Struggled to score efficiently, has made less than 30% of his threes for his career
- Fairly decent mid-range shooters, tends to settle for contested floaters
- Not really effective with the ball in hands, has not drawn fouls at a high rate in either of the last two seasons
- Better off the ball, good at making backdoor cuts, fairly effective on dribble hand-offs
- 2019-20 Defensive Degree of Difficulty: 0.532
- Tended to take on tougher assignment against elite guards or wing players
- Slightly over-matched in these assignments, played average on-ball defense, better at contesting jump shots
- Good pick-and-roll defender, funnels his man into help, pretty solid on switches
- Stays attached to shooters off screens, consistently closes out in spot-up situations
- Active help defender, consistently gets steals and blocks at a high rate, good defensive rebounding guard

Alec Burks

Height	Weight	Cap #	Years Left
6'6"	214	$6.000M	UFA

Similar at Age **28**

		Season	SIMsc
1	Gerald Henderson	2015-16	936.6
2	Devin Brown	2006-07	936.4
3	Gordon Hayward	2018-19	927.2
4	Jason Richardson	2008-09	924.8
5	Eric Piatkowski	1998-99	923.3
6	Josh Howard	2008-09	922.9
7	Rodney Stuckey	2014-15	921.8
8	Tyreke Evans	2017-18	920.5
9	Stephen Jackson	2006-07	918.7
10	J.R. Smith	2013-14	918.5

Baseline Basic Stats

MPG	PTS	AST	REB	BLK	STL
26.4	12.2	2.0	3.4	0.3	0.8

Advanced Metrics

USG%	3PTA/FGA	FTA/FGA	TS%	eFG%	3PT%
20.9	0.425	0.271	0.545	0.496	0.382
AST%	**TOV%**	**OREB%**	**DREB%**	**STL%**	**BLK%**
13.2	10.1	2.6	13.7	1.5	0.9
PER	**ORTG**	**DRTG**	**WS/48**	**VOL**	
14.14	108.4	111.3	0.078	0.327	

- Regular rotation player for Golden State and Philadelphia last season, traded to Philadelphia in February 2020
- Had his most productive NBA season, used as a higher volume scoring wing off the bench
- Made 38.5% of his threes last season, good spot-up shooter that can also run off screens
- Good at getting to the rim or making outside shots on dribble hand-offs
- Effective pick-and-roll ball handler and isolation player, drew fouls at a high rate, good at making pull-up jumpers
- Fairly good secondary playmaker that can control the ball, set career bests in both Assist and Turnover Percentages last season
- 2019-20 Defensive Degree of Difficulty: 0.413
- Tended to guard lower leverage starters or higher-end second unit players
- Average on-ball defender, has some trouble against quicker guards
- Middling pick-and-roll defender, can funnel ball handlers into help, struggles at containing ball handlers on his own
- Stayed attached to shooters off the ball in Golden State, tended to be late when closing out on perimeter shooters in Philadelphia
- Solid defensive rebounding wing, Steal and Block Percentages were slightly above his career averages

Mitchell Robinson	Height	Weight	Cap #	Years Left
	7'0"	223	$1.664M	Team Option

Similar at Age 21

		Season	SIMsc
1	Steven Hunter	2002-03	866.8
2	Sean Williams	2007-08	863.9
3	Ed Davis	2010-11	859.7
4	Kevon Looney	2017-18	858.9
5	JaVale McGee	2008-09	855.1
6	Jermaine O'Neal	1999-00	848.0
7	Jelani McCoy	1998-99	845.6
8	Serge Ibaka	2010-11	844.8
9	Clint Capela	2015-16	842.2
10	Robert Williams	2018-19	838.1

Baseline Basic Stats

MPG	PTS	AST	REB	BLK	STL
21.4	7.5	0.8	5.8	1.6	0.5

Advanced Metrics

USG%	3PTA/FGA	FTA/FGA	TS%	eFG%	3PT%
14.2	0.012	0.431	0.638	0.630	0.140
AST%	**TOV%**	**OREB%**	**DREB%**	**STL%**	**BLK%**
5.9	11.6	12.5	18.4	1.5	5.9
PER	**ORTG**	**DRTG**	**WS/48**	**VOL**	
18.91	128.1	105.5	0.176	0.373	

- Regular rotation player for New York in his second season in the NBA
- Increased his per-minute production as a low volume, rim runner
- Led the NBA in Field Goal Percentage and True Shooting Percentage last season
- Vertical lob threat that is very good at scoring on rolls to the rim and cuts off the ball
- Excellent at running the floor in transition, great offensive rebounder that scores on put-backs, draws fouls at a high rate
- No real shooting range outside of three feet, strictly a catch-and-finish player at this stage
- Limited passing skills, rarely turns the ball over
- 2019-20 Defensive Degree of Difficulty: 0.355
- Matched up against second unit big men or lower leverage starters
- Very good rim protector, excellent shot blocker, pretty foul prone at this stage, sometimes out of position to get defensive rebounds
- Average on-ball defender, struggled in the post last season, showed more mobility to defend in space
- Above average pick-and-roll defender, fairly good on switches
- Does not always come out to contest perimeter shots

Nerlens Noel

	Height	Weight	Cap #	Years Left
	6'10"	220	$5.000M	UFA

Similar at Age **25**

		Season	SIMsc
1	Edgar Jones	1981-82	907.5
2	Jeff Withey	2015-16	895.2
3	Daniel Theis	2017-18	890.7
4	Richaun Holmes	2018-19	889.3
5	Chris Andersen	2003-04	889.1
6	Aaron Williams	1996-97	885.9
7	Lucas Nogueira	2017-18	885.9
8	Dan Gadzuric	2003-04	884.5
9	Mark Blount	2000-01	875.9
10	Chris Gatling	1992-93	874.5

Baseline Basic Stats

MPG	PTS	AST	REB	BLK	STL
19.8	7.1	0.8	5.3	1.3	0.6

Advanced Metrics

USG%	3PTA/FGA	FTA/FGA	TS%	eFG%	3PT%
15.1	0.015	0.376	0.625	0.594	0.259
AST%	**TOV%**	**OREB%**	**DREB%**	**STL%**	**BLK%**
6.7	15.2	10.1	20.7	1.9	5.2
PER	**ORTG**	**DRTG**	**WS/48**	**VOL**	
17.77	119.4	102.1	0.174	0.451	

- Regular rotation player for Oklahoma City in his second season with the team
- Highly productive in his role as a low volume, rim runner, made over 86% of his shots inside of three feet last season
- Explosive vertical lob threat that excels at rolling to the rim on pick-and-rolls and cutting off the ball
- Active offensive rebounder that score on put-backs, runs the floor hard in transition to get dunks or draw fouls
- Shows some passing ability, slightly turnover prone, has improved his ability to make shots from the three-to-ten foot range
- 2019-20 Defensive Degree of Difficulty: 0.396
- Tended to guard higher-end second unit players or lower leverage starters
- Very good rim protector, excellent shot blocker, solid rebounder, consistently get steals at a high rate
- Good on-ball defender, uses his length to contest shots in the post, good mobility to defend in space
- Solid pick-and-roll defender, good in drop coverages, effective at switching onto ball handlers
- Consistently closes out on spot-up shooters, can sometimes be too aggressive on his close-outs

Austin Rivers

Height	Weight	Cap #	Years Left
6'3"	200	$3.175M	2

Similar at Age 27

		Season	SIMsc
1	Jerryd Bayless	2015-16	956.3
2	Rodney McGruder	2018-19	936.8
3	Langston Galloway	2018-19	932.5
4	Ben Gordon	2010-11	929.4
5	Roger Mason	2007-08	928.8
6	Derek Fisher	2001-02	928.3
7	Voshon Lenard	2000-01	926.0
8	Willie Green	2008-09	925.8
9	Royal Ivey	2008-09	924.2
10	Brandon Knight	2018-19	923.2

Baseline Basic Stats

MPG	PTS	AST	REB	BLK	STL
23.5	8.9	2.0	2.2	0.2	0.7

Advanced Metrics

USG%	3PTA/FGA	FTA/FGA	TS%	eFG%	3PT%
16.7	0.539	0.177	0.529	0.507	0.364
AST%	**TOV%**	**OREB%**	**DREB%**	**STL%**	**BLK%**
13.0	10.2	1.6	9.1	1.4	0.6
PER	**ORTG**	**DRTG**	**WS/48**	**VOL**	
10.63	107.1	112.8	0.058	0.342	

- Regular rotation player in his first full season with Houston in 2019-20
- Primarily utilized as a low volume, spot-up shooter and secondary ball handler
- Increased his overall effectiveness, made threes at around the league average last season
- Better at making corner threes, made over 41% of his corner threes in 2019-20
- Good spot-up shooter that can occasionally make shots off the dribble in isolation situations
- Effective pick-and-roll ball handler, can sometimes get to the rim
- Decent secondary playmaker, cut his Turnover Percentage to a career low last season
- 2019-20 Defensive Degree of Difficulty: 0.392
- Tends to guard higher-end second unit players or lower leverage starters
- Fairly solid on-ball defender, good against quicker guards, can be backed down inside by stronger wing players
- Fairly good pick-and-roll defender, decent at switching, good at going over the screen to contain ball handlers
- Can get caught on screens off the ball, tends to close out too aggressively in spot-up situations
- Stay-at-home defender, steal and block rates are consistent with his career average, posted the highest Defensive Rebound Percentage of his career last season

Frank Ntilikina

Height	Weight	Cap #	Years Left
6'4"	190	$6.177M	RFA

Similar at Age **21**

		Season	SIMsc
1	Elie Okobo	2018-19	948.2
2	Smush Parker	2002-03	923.3
3	Delonte West	2004-05	922.5
4	Dante Exum	2016-17	922.1
5	Cameron Payne	2015-16	912.7
6	Devin Harris	2004-05	912.2
7	Willie Warren	2010-11	907.6
8	Cory Joseph	2012-13	906.4
9	Isaiah Whitehead	2016-17	902.4
10	Manny Harris	2010-11	901.5

Baseline Basic Stats

MPG	PTS	AST	REB	BLK	STL
19.6	7.1	2.4	2.2	0.2	0.7

Advanced Metrics

USG%	3PTA/FGA	FTA/FGA	TS%	eFG%	3PT%
16.6	0.266	0.222	0.495	0.457	0.320
AST%	**TOV%**	**OREB%**	**DREB%**	**STL%**	**BLK%**
20.4	15.5	2.2	9.2	2.0	0.9
PER	**ORTG**	**DRTG**	**WS/48**	**VOL**	
10.45	102.3	111.8	0.041	0.356	

- Regular rotation player for New York in his third season, started some games in 2019-20
- Used as a low volume, secondary ball handler and spot-up shooter
- Efficiency improved to a career best, still fairly inefficient overall, below break-even three-point shooter throughout his career
- Improved his ability to knock down pull-up long twos, made him more effective as a pick-and-roll ball handler
- Increasing threat of a jump shot allowed him to get easier shots at the rim, shooting percentage inside of ten feet improved last season
- Decent secondary playmaker in his three seasons, still a bit turnover prone
- <u>2019-20 Defensive Degree of Difficulty</u>: 0.486
- Mostly guarded second unit players, took on some tough assignments when he started
- Showed the ability to guard multiple positions in previous seasons, played below average on-ball defense last season
- Solid pick-and-roll ball handler, fights over screens to contain ball handlers, solid at switching onto the roll man
- Gambles a bit too much, gets caught out of position when chasing shooters off screens, undisciplined when closing out on perimeter shooters
- More active help defender, got steals and blocks at a higher rate, still a middling defensive rebounder

Kevin Knox	Height	Weight	Cap #	Years Left
	6'7"	215	$4.589M	Team Option

	Similar at Age	**20**	
		Season	**SIMsc**
1	Martell Webster	2006-07	945.1
2	Jaylen Brown	2016-17	927.2
3	Mike Miller	2000-01	921.0
4	Daequan Cook	2007-08	909.4
5	Wilson Chandler	2007-08	907.3
6	Rodions Kurucs	2018-19	907.0
7	Harrison Barnes	2012-13	906.8
8	Miles Bridges	2018-19	906.5
9	Mario Hezonja	2015-16	904.8
10	DeMar DeRozan	2009-10	900.4

Baseline Basic Stats

MPG	PTS	AST	REB	BLK	STL
26.7	11.4	1.6	4.1	0.4	0.8

Advanced Metrics

USG%	3PTA/FGA	FTA/FGA	TS%	eFG%	3PT%
20.7	0.453	0.231	0.512	0.478	0.355
AST%	**TOV%**	**OREB%**	**DREB%**	**STL%**	**BLK%**
8.6	10.0	2.8	13.7	1.3	1.3
PER	**ORTG**	**DRTG**	**WS/48**	**VOL**	
11.41	101.6	112.2	0.039	0.302	

- Regular rotation player for New York last season, playing time reduced significantly after being a starter in 2018-19
- Had difficulty adapting to his role as a low volume, spot-up shooter, efficiency decreased slightly
- Basically a break-even three-point shooter, middling on spot-ups, struggles to shoot on the move or off the dribble
- Rated as average or worse in most offensive situations, inefficient when trying to create his own shot
- Most effective at using an on-ball screen to make shots off dribble hand-offs, could also crash inside to score on put-backs
- Primarily a catch-and-shoot player, limited playmaking skills, cut his turnover rate last season
- 2019-20 Defensive Degree of Difficulty: 0.317, mostly guarded second unit level players
- Effective on-ball defender in lower leverage matchups, can capably defend both forward spots
- Solid pick-and-roll defender, fairly good at switching to cover multiple positions
- Tends to sag into the paint, can be late to close out on perimeter shooters, gets caught on screens off the ball
- More active help defender, became a better weak side shot blocker, fairly solid defensive rebounder

Reggie Bullock	Height	Weight	Cap #	Years Left
	6'6"	200	$4.200M	UFA

Similar at Age 28

		Season	SIMsc
1	Wayne Ellington	2015-16	936.5
2	Wesley Person	1999-00	933.5
3	Jarvis Hayes	2009-10	933.3
4	Marco Belinelli	2014-15	926.7
5	Anthony Morrow	2013-14	923.4
6	Iman Shumpert	2018-19	922.5
7	Dorell Wright	2013-14	922.4
8	Courtney Lee	2013-14	920.9
9	Mickael Pietrus	2010-11	920.3
10	Rasual Butler	2007-08	915.1

Baseline Basic Stats

MPG	PTS	AST	REB	BLK	STL
22.2	8.1	1.4	2.3	0.2	0.6

Advanced Metrics

USG%	3PTA/FGA	FTA/FGA	TS%	eFG%	3PT%
15.8	0.586	0.126	0.530	0.508	0.361
AST%	**TOV%**	**OREB%**	**DREB%**	**STL%**	**BLK%**
9.3	8.7	1.7	9.2	1.5	0.6
PER	**ORTG**	**DRTG**	**WS/48**	**VOL**	
10.29	107.0	111.4	0.069	0.471	

- Missed the first half of last season while recovering from neck surgery, played as a starter for New York when healthy
- Predominantly a low volume, shooting specialist throughout his career
- Made over 41% of his threes with Detroit in the past, break-even three-point shooter with other teams
- Generally effective at making spot-up jumpers, good at coming off screens, could make pull-up jumpers as a pick-and-roll ball handler last season
- Does not really create his own shot, rarely turns the ball over, limited playmaking skills
- 2019-20 Defensive Degree of Difficulty: 0.486
- Usually defends starter level players, will take on tougher assignments
- Good on-ball defender that can guard multiple positions
- Fairly solid at guarding pick-and-rolls, good on switches, occasionally allows ball handlers to turn the corner
- Fights through screens off the ball, tended to be late when closing out on perimeter shooters last season
- Stay-at-home defender, middling defensive rebounder, steals rate increased significantly last season

Dennis Smith, Jr.	Height	Weight	Cap #	Years Left
	6'2"	195	$5.687M	RFA

Similar at Age **22**

		Season	SIMsc
1	Darius Washington	2007-08	919.5
2	Terry Dehere	1993-94	912.6
3	Derek Fisher	1996-97	912.3
4	Jordan Farmar	2008-09	910.0
5	Marcus Banks	2003-04	905.5
6	Luke Ridnour	2003-04	900.9
7	Tony Smith	1990-91	898.8
8	Jeff Teague	2010-11	898.6
9	Jordan Crawford	2010-11	897.2
10	Jerryd Bayless	2010-11	897.0

Baseline Basic Stats

MPG	PTS	AST	REB	BLK	STL
22.3	9.5	3.5	2.3	0.2	0.9

Advanced Metrics

USG%	3PTA/FGA	FTA/FGA	TS%	eFG%	3PT%
22.3	0.285	0.293	0.499	0.463	0.336
AST%	**TOV%**	**OREB%**	**DREB%**	**STL%**	**BLK%**
26.7	16.1	2.7	9.7	2.2	0.9
PER	**ORTG**	**DRTG**	**WS/48**	**VOL**	
13.26	101.2	110.4	0.041	0.531	

- Fringe rotation player for New York when healthy, missed games due to a strained left oblique and a concussion
- Mainly used as a higher volume, scoring point guard off the bench
- Good playmaker, Assist Percentage steadily dropping, has become more turnover prone
- Shooting percentages have fallen to alarming levels, True Shooting Percentage is below 40%, made just over half of his free throws last season
- Rated as average or worse in almost every offensive situation
- Could occasionally use his quickness to drive by defenders on isolation plays
- 2019-20 Defensive Degree of Difficulty: 0.411
- Tended to guard second unit players, occasionally defended top point guards
- Fairly solid on-ball defender, quick enough to stop drives, taller perimeter players could shoot over him in the post
- Solid pick-and-roll defender that can funnel his man into help and fight over the screen
- Can get caught on screens, tends to be late when closing out in spot-up situations
- Active help defender, Steal and Block Percentage have continued to increase, solid defensive rebounder for his size

Omari Spellman

	Height	Weight	Cap #	Years Left
	6'8"	245	$1.988M	Team Option

Similar at Age **22**

		Season	SIMsc
1	Linas Kleiza	2006-07	914.4
2	Danny Granger	2005-06	910.1
3	Markieff Morris	2011-12	908.1
4	Donyell Marshall	1995-96	907.7
5	Taurean Prince	2016-17	906.5
6	Stanley Johnson	2018-19	903.5
7	Jabari Parker	2017-18	899.0
8	Justin Anderson	2015-16	898.1
9	Brandon Bass	2007-08	896.5
10	Dante Cunningham	2009-10	894.5

Baseline Basic Stats

MPG	PTS	AST	REB	BLK	STL
23.4	9.5	1.3	4.5	0.5	0.7

Advanced Metrics

USG%	3PTA/FGA	FTA/FGA	TS%	eFG%	3PT%
18.4	0.400	0.249	0.549	0.514	0.381

AST%	TOV%	OREB%	DREB%	STL%	BLK%
9.2	11.9	7.1	16.1	1.5	1.9

PER	ORTG	DRTG	WS/48	VOL
14.10	109.2	112.0	0.076	0.336

- Regular rotation player for Golden State, traded in February 2020 to Minnesota
- Did not play for Minnesota, spent time in the G-League playing for the Iowa Wolves
- Mainly utilized as a low volume stretch big, made over 39% of his threes last season
- Mostly a stationary spot-up shooter, excellent in the corners, has made almost 47% of his corner threes in two NBA seasons
- Average as a rim runner, does not quite have to lift to finish inside on rolls to the rim or cuts off the ball
- Runs hard down the floor in transition, drew fouls at a higher rate last season
- Primarily a catch-and-shoot player, has some passing skills, generally avoid turnovers
- 2019-20 Defensive Degree of Difficulty: 0.333, tends to guard second unit level big men
- Good rim protector, fairly solid shot blocker and defensive rebounder
- Below average post defender, tends to bite on fakes, shows solid mobility to defend in space on isolations
- Decent pick-and-roll defender, solid on switches, can hedge out too far to allow the ball handler to get a lane to the rim
- Does not always come out to contest perimeter shots

Jacob Evans	Height	Weight	Cap #	Years Left
	6'4"	210	$2.017M	Team Option

Similar at Age 22

		Season	SIMsc
1	Laron Profit	1999-00	926.6
2	Khyri Thomas	2018-19	916.7
3	Nick Johnson	2014-15	907.9
4	D.J. Strawberry	2007-08	907.1
5	Malcolm Lee	2012-13	907.0
6	Isaiah Briscoe	2018-19	904.9
7	Corey Crowder	1991-92	904.3
8	DeAndre' Bembry	2016-17	903.6
9	Thabo Sefolosha	2006-07	902.0
10	Kareem Rush	2002-03	900.4

Baseline Basic Stats

MPG	PTS	AST	REB	BLK	STL
19.1	6.6	1.5	2.3	0.3	0.7

Advanced Metrics

USG%	3PTA/FGA	FTA/FGA	TS%	eFG%	3PT%
16.9	0.282	0.204	0.502	0.463	0.359
AST%	**TOV%**	**OREB%**	**DREB%**	**STL%**	**BLK%**
12.9	13.0	2.4	9.5	1.6	1.5
PER	**ORTG**	**DRTG**	**WS/48**	**VOL**	
9.95	101.5	111.1	0.047	0.426	

- Missed over a month due to a strained left adductor, fringe rotation player for Golden State, traded to Minnesota in February 2020
- Not particularly effective in his role as a low volume backup guard, also struggled in limited action in the G-League
- Rated as below average in most offensive situations last season
- Cut his turnover rate a bit, shows some passing skills
- Most effective at making spot-up jumpers, made threes at a break-even rate
- 2019-20 Defensive Degree of Difficulty: 0.371
- Tended to guard second unit level players or lower leverage starters
- Below average on-ball defender, struggled to stay with perimeter players on drives, more effective in the post against taller wings
- Below average at defending pick-and-rolls, tends to allow his man to turn the corner
- Fights through screens away from the ball, sometimes can be late to close out in spot-up situations
- More than doubled his Block Percentage at the NBA level, middling defensive rebounder
- Generally a stay-at-home defender, does not really get steals

Ignas Brazdeikis

	Height	Weight	Cap #	Years Left
	6'6"	216	$1.518M	Team Option

Similar at Age **21**

		Season	SIMsc
1	James Anderson	2010-11	899.3
2	Allen Crabbe	2013-14	891.1
3	Malachi Richardson	2016-17	880.4
4	John Jenkins	2012-13	869.5
5	Rawle Alkins	2018-19	868.1
6	Nik Stauskas	2014-15	862.1
7	Vincent Askew	1987-88	861.1
8	Mario Hezonja	2016-17	859.7
9	Kenny Green	1985-86	859.6
10	Antonio Blakeney	2017-18	859.5

Baseline Basic Stats

MPG	PTS	AST	REB	BLK	STL
17.0	6.9	1.0	1.8	0.2	0.5

Advanced Metrics

USG%	3PTA/FGA	FTA/FGA	TS%	eFG%	3PT%
19.1	0.338	0.205	0.458	0.416	0.240
AST%	**TOV%**	**OREB%**	**DREB%**	**STL%**	**BLK%**
10.4	9.5	3.4	7.5	0.9	1.0
PER	**ORTG**	**DRTG**	**WS/48**	**VOL**	
7.94	96.6	115.1	-0.005	0.549	

- Spent most of his rookie season with the Westchester Knicks in the G-League
- Took on a higher volume role as an off-ball shooter with Westchester
- Made threes at a rate above break-even in the G-League, made over 58% of his two-point shots last season
- Mostly a spot-up shooter at the NBA level, flashed an ability to cut off the ball and make a few shots off screens
- Displayed solid secondary playmaking skills at Westchester, good at limiting turnovers
- 2019-20 Defensive Degree of Difficulty: 0.164
- Only played 53 NBA minutes, mostly played in garbage time
- Rarely tested on the ball, on-ball defense uncertain at this stage, better against perimeter players in a small sample of NBA possessions
- Had some trouble guarding pick-and-rolls, better on switches, tended to go too far under screens
- Stayed attached to shooters, closed out in spot-up situations
- Stay-at-home defender in the G-League, did not really get steals or blocks, good defensive rebounder

Newcomers

Obi Toppin

Height	Weight	Cap #	Years Left
6'9"	220	$4.862M	1 + 2 TO

Baseline Basic Stats

MPG	PTS	AST	REB	BLK	STL
24.0	9.7	1.4	4.5	0.6	0.7

Advanced Metrics

USG%	3PTA/FGA	FTA/FGA	TS%	eFG%	3PT%
18.5	0.202	0.269	0.508	0.478	0.314
AST%	**TOV%**	**OREB%**	**DREB%**	**STL%**	**BLK%**
9.9	11.4	5.7	14.8	1.5	1.9
PER	**ORTG**	**DRTG**	**WS/48**	**VOL**	
14.07	101.3	98.5	0.082	N/A	

- Drafted by New York with the 8th overall pick
- Consensus 1st Team All-American, winner of the Naismith and Wooden Awards in 2019-20
- High motor rim runner, good roll man and cutter, crashes the offensive glass to score on put-backs
- Physical player that can bully smaller defenders around the rim on post-ups
- Good stationary spot-up shooter, made almost 42% of his career threes at Dayton, struggles to shoot on the move
- Solid passing big man that kicks the ball out to open shooters and hits cutters
- Shows some ball handling skills, more suited to being a complementary player, off ball plays accounted for 97.5% of his offense in 2019-20
- Lacks lateral mobility to defend in space, struggled to defend ball handlers on pick-and-rolls, does not always come out to contest perimeter shots
- Better interior defender, strong post defender that holds position inside
- Shows some rim protector potential, stays vertical to contest shots, good shot blocker and defensive rebounder

Immanuel Quickley	**Height**	**Weight**	**Cap #**	**Years Left**
	6'3"	188	$2.106M	1 + 2 TO

Baseline Basic Stats

MPG	PTS	AST	REB	BLK	STL
18.0	7.1	1.9	1.8	0.1	0.5

Advanced Metrics

USG%	3PTA/FGA	FTA/FGA	TS%	eFG%	3PT%
18.8	0.465	0.244	0.520	0.483	0.365
AST%	**TOV%**	**OREB%**	**DREB%**	**STL%**	**BLK%**
15.1	12.5	1.9	9.2	1.5	0.5
PER	**ORTG**	**DRTG**	**WS/48**	**VOL**	
11.71	102.2	105.9	0.052	N/A	

- Drafted by Oklahoma City with the 25th overall pick, traded to New York via Minnesota
- Made the All-SEC 1st Team, named SEC Co-Player of the Year in 2019-20
- Good three-point shooter at Kentucky, made almost 40% of his career threes
- Mostly a spot-up shooter, can sometimes use an on-ball screen to make jumpers off pick-and-rolls or dribble hand-offs, struggles to shoot on the move
- Lacks ideal ball handling skills to consistently create his own offense
- Mainly a catch-and-shoot player, limited as a playmaker, can only make simple reads, good at avoiding turnovers
- Good length and athleticism, can potentially defend both guard spots in the NBA
- Good on-ball defender, actively pressures ball handlers, has enough strength to handle bigger perimeter players
- Solid pick-and-roll defender, can fight over screens to contain ball handlers or funnel his man into help
- Can be too aggressive when defending shooters off the ball, tends to close out too hard, over-commits when chasing shooters off screens
- Stay-at-home defender, does not really get steals or blocks, pretty good defensive rebounding guard

PREVIEWING THE WESTERN CONFERENCE

<u>SCHREMPF Rankings</u>

1. L.A. Lakers
2. L.A. Clippers
3. Utah Jazz
4. Houston Rockets (6th)
5. Dallas Mavericks (4th)
6. New Orleans Pelicans (5th)
7. Denver Nuggets
8. Phoenix Suns
9. San Antonio Spurs
10. Portland Trail Blazers
11. Memphis Grizzlies
12. Sacramento Kings
13. Golden State Warriors
14. Oklahoma City Thunder
15. Minnesota Timberwolves

Rosters are accurate as of December 2, 2020. For my official 2020-21 NBA predictions, turn to page 500. The SCHREMPF rankings listed above did not account for the trade involving Russell Westbrook and John Wall because the trade happened just as the book was being finalized. The adjustments that reflect this trade are in parentheses.

LOS ANGELES LAKERS

Last Season: 52 – 19, 2019-20 NBA Champions

Offensive Rating: 112.0, 11th in the NBA

Defensive Rating: 106.3, 3rd in the NBA

Primary Executive: Rob Pelinka, Vice President of Basketball Operations

Head Coach: Frank Vogel

Key Roster Changes

Subtractions
Danny Green, trade
JaVale McGee, trade
Avery Bradley, free agency
Dwight Howard, free agency
Rajon Rondo, free agency
J.R. Smith, free agency
Dion Waiters, free agency

Additions
Dennis Schroder, trade
Alfonzo McKinnie, trade
Montrezl Harrell, free agency
Marc Gasol, free agency
Wesley Matthews, free agency

Roster

Likely Starting Five
1. *LeBron James*
2. Wesley Matthews
3. *Kentavious Caldwell-Pope*
4. *Anthony Davis*
5. Marc Gasol

Other Key Rotation Players
Dennis Schroder
Montrezl Harrell
Alex Caruso
Kyle Kuzma
Markieff Morris

* Italics denotes that a player is likely to be on the floor to close games

Remaining Roster

- Alfonzo McKinnie
- Jared Dudley
- Talen Horton-Tucker
- Quinn Cook – not profiled, signed just before the book was finalized
- Kostas Antetokounmpo, 23, 6'10", 200, Dayton (Two-Way)
- Devontae Cacok, 6'7", 240, UNC-Wilmington (Two-Way)
- Zavier Simpson, 23, 6'0", 190, Michigan (Exhibit 10)
- Tres Tinkle, 24, 6'7", 225, Oregon State (Exhibit 10)
- Kevon Harris, 23, 6'6", 216, Stephen F. Austin (Exhibit 10)

SCHREMPF Base Rating: 41.7 (72-game season)

Strengths

- Talented and balanced rotation with elite stars and quality role players to complement their skills
- Versatile defensive unit that can counter differing styles of play
- Efficient offense that can attack the rim, move the ball and spread the floor

Question Marks

- Possible negative effects related to the very shortened offseason

Outlook

- The odds-on favorite to win the 2020-21 NBA title, should finish with one of the top three seeds in the West

Veterans

LeBron James	Height	Weight	Cap #	Years Left
	6'9"	250	$39.220M	2

	Similar at Age	35 Season	SIMsc
1	Karl Malone*	1998-99	872.8
2	Paul Pierce	2012-13	853.2
3	Dirk Nowitzki	2013-14	841.3
4	Larry Bird*	1991-92	834.6
5	Dan Issel*	1983-84	830.9
6	Zach Randolph	2016-17	830.2
7	Luis Scola	2015-16	822.4
8	Bob Lanier*	1983-84	815.6
9	Antawn Jamison	2011-12	814.6
10	Sam Perkins	1996-97	812.9

Baseline Basic Stats

MPG	PTS	AST	REB	BLK	STL
34.5	22.2	5.2	7.9	0.6	1.2

Advanced Metrics

USG%	3PTA/FGA	FTA/FGA	TS%	eFG%	3PT%
29.3	0.218	0.378	0.578	0.538	0.355
AST%	**TOV%**	**OREB%**	**DREB%**	**STL%**	**BLK%**
33.8	14.8	4.0	21.7	1.6	1.5
PER	**ORTG**	**DRTG**	**WS/48**	**VOL**	
23.37	112.9	105.6	0.177	0.607	

- Made his 16th All-Star team, named to the All-NBA 1st Team in 2019-20
- Arguably the NBA's best playmaker, led the league in Assist Percentage and Assists per Game
- Very good pick-and-roll ball handler and isolation player, getting to the rim less frequently, draws fewer fouls than he did in previous seasons
- Taking more threes, makes them at an above break-even rate, better off the catch, less consistent off the dribble
- Dynamic transition player that can push the ball up the floor or run down the wings to score
- Good at posting up smaller players, good cutter off the ball
- 2019-20 Defensive Degree of Difficulty: 0.422, tends to guard starting level players
- Good on-ball defender that can guard multiple positions
- Good at guarding pick-and-rolls, guards screeners or ball handlers, sometimes he can go too far under screens
- Stays attached to shooters off the ball, good at closing out in spot-up situations
- Plays more conservative in the regular season, good defensive rebounder, steal and block rates are down
- Increases his activity on the weak side in the playoffs, good at making chase-down blocks

Anthony Davis

	Height	Weight	Cap #	Years Left
	6'10"	253	$32.742M	3 + PO

	Similar at Age	26	
		Season	SIMsc
1	Tim Duncan*	2002-03	886.4
2	Alonzo Mourning*	1996-97	884.7
3	Chris Webber	1999-00	874.8
4	Dirk Nowitzki	2004-05	872.6
5	Derrick Coleman	1993-94	866.3
6	Nikola Vucevic	2016-17	864.8
7	Gorgui Dieng	2015-16	863.7
8	Hakeem Olajuwon*	1988-89	863.5
9	Elton Brand	2005-06	863.2
10	Amar'e Stoudemire	2008-09	861.8

Baseline Basic Stats

MPG	PTS	AST	REB	BLK	STL
34.9	20.9	3.0	10.1	1.9	1.0

Advanced Metrics

USG%	3PTA/FGA	FTA/FGA	TS%	eFG%	3PT%
28.2	0.129	0.406	0.577	0.519	0.339
AST%	**TOV%**	**OREB%**	**DREB%**	**STL%**	**BLK%**
16.0	11.0	8.1	23.8	1.7	4.8
PER	**ORTG**	**DRTG**	**WS/48**	**VOL**	
25.17	115.1	101.9	0.211	0.388	

- Named to the All-NBA 1st Team, made the All-Defensive 1st Team in 2019-20
- Good isolation player that can drive by defenders to score or draw fouls
- High volume post scorer, most effective at posting up on the left block
- Excellent rim runner that dives hard to the rim as a roll man and cutter, solid offensive rebounder that scores on put-backs
- Below break-even three-point shooter, good at making shorter mid-range shots
- Solid spot-up shooter, effective screener on pick-and-pops
- Good passing big man that can find open shooters, rarely turns the ball over
- 2019-20 Defensive Degree of Difficulty: 0.445
- Handles a variety of matchups against starter level players, draws tougher defensive assignments
- Excellent rim protector, very good shot blocker and defensive rebounder
- Very good on-ball defender that can guard multiple positions
- Fairly good pick-and-roll defender that can guard ball handlers or screeners, occasionally has lapses when defending the roll man
- Stays attached to shooters off the ball, consistently comes out to contest perimeter shots

Marc Gasol	Height	Weight	Cap #	Years Left
	6'11"	255	$2.565M	1

	Similar at Age	35	
		Season	**SIMsc**
1	David West	2015-16	873.5
2	Derrick Coleman	2002-03	871.3
3	Bill Laimbeer	1992-93	870.6
4	Luis Scola	2015-16	869.3
5	Jack Sikma*	1990-91	868.5
6	Bob Lanier*	1983-84	865.9
7	Rasheed Wallace	2009-10	864.3
8	Hakeem Olajuwon*	1997-98	864.1
9	Danny Schayes	1994-95	857.1
10	Matt Barnes	2015-16	856.1

Baseline Basic Stats

MPG	PTS	AST	REB	BLK	STL
21.5	8.5	2.0	4.8	0.7	0.7

Advanced Metrics

USG%	3PTA/FGA	FTA/FGA	TS%	eFG%	3PT%
16.8	0.338	0.234	0.552	0.522	0.368
AST%	**TOV%**	**OREB%**	**DREB%**	**STL%**	**BLK%**
15.2	15.1	4.6	21.1	1.5	3.1
PER	**ORTG**	**DRTG**	**WS/48**	**VOL**	
13.77	108.7	105.0	0.116	0.484	

- Regular starter for Toronto when healthy, missed games due to a left hamstring injury
- Mainly used as a low volume stretch big, made 38.5% of his threes last season
- Mostly a stationary spot-up shooter, less effective at shooting on the move
- Still can score efficiently when rolling to the rim, decent at posting up on the right block
- Runs hard down the floor in transition, can set up for trail threes
- Very good passing big man that can hit cutters or find open shooters, slightly turnover prone last season
- 2019-20 Defensive Degree of Difficulty: 0.427
- Usually guards starting level big men, sometimes takes on tougher big man assignments
- Very good rim protector, solid defensive rebounder and shot blocker
- Good on-ball defender, good post defender that holds position inside, mobile enough to defend in space
- Good at guarding pick-and-rolls, good in drop coverages, can switch onto ball handlers for a few dribbles
- Willing to close out on spot-up shooters, tends to close too aggressively, can allow driving lanes to the rim

Kentavious Caldwell-Pope

	Height	Weight	Cap #	Years Left
	6'5"	205	$12.073M	2

Similar at Age 26

		Season	SIMsc
1	Iman Shumpert	2016-17	954.5
2	Marcus Thornton	2013-14	946.9
3	Courtney Lee	2011-12	946.5
4	Reggie Bullock	2017-18	939.3
5	Sasha Danilovic	1996-97	936.8
6	DeShawn Stevenson	2007-08	936.7
7	Wesley Matthews	2012-13	936.6
8	Anthony Morrow	2011-12	935.8
9	Martell Webster	2012-13	930.2
10	Dorell Wright	2011-12	928.3

Baseline Basic Stats

MPG	PTS	AST	REB	BLK	STL
25.3	10.2	1.6	2.7	0.2	0.8

Advanced Metrics

USG%	3PTA/FGA	FTA/FGA	TS%	eFG%	3PT%
17.2	0.497	0.197	0.558	0.525	0.373

AST%	TOV%	OREB%	DREB%	STL%	BLK%
9.4	9.0	2.1	9.2	1.5	0.7

PER	ORTG	DRTG	WS/48	VOL
12.06	111.1	110.2	0.092	0.369

- Regular rotation player for the Lakers, started some games last season
- Usage was reduced, increased his scoring efficiency in his role as a low volume, spot-up shooter
- Made 38.5% of his threes last season, above break-even career three-point shooter
- Mostly a stationary spot-up shooter, can be streaky, can attack aggressive close-outs if his shot is falling
- Good at running the wings in transition to get layups or draw shooting fouls, good at making backdoor cuts if defenders overplay his shot
- Strictly a catch-and-shoot player, can make the extra pass, rarely turns the ball over
- 2019-20 Defensive Degree of Difficulty: 0.477
- Guards starter level players, will draw tougher defensive assignments
- Played below average on-ball defense, over-matched against top players
- Below average pick-and-roll defender, tends to go too far under screens, has trouble defending bigger screeners on switches
- Stays attached to shooters off the ball, consistently closes out in spot-up situations
- Stay-at-home defender, middling defensive rebounder, Steal Percentage has been below his career average for the last two seasons
- Block Percentage has held fairly steady throughout his career

Wesley Matthews	Height	Weight	Cap #	Years Left
	6'4"	220	$3.623M	UFA

	Similar at Age	33 Season	SIMsc
1	Randy Foye	2016-17	922.8
2	Anthony Peeler	2002-03	911.5
3	Richard Jefferson	2013-14	910.3
4	Chuck Person	1997-98	903.8
5	Dan Majerle	1998-99	903.5
6	John Salmons	2012-13	902.5
7	Eric Piatkowski	2003-04	899.0
8	Jared Dudley	2018-19	890.2
9	Mike Miller	2013-14	888.9
10	Willie Green	2014-15	886.5

Baseline Basic Stats

MPG	PTS	AST	REB	BLK	STL
23.0	7.1	1.7	2.5	0.2	0.7

Advanced Metrics

USG%	3PTA/FGA	FTA/FGA	TS%	eFG%	3PT%
14.3	0.596	0.189	0.531	0.502	0.364
AST%	**TOV%**	**OREB%**	**DREB%**	**STL%**	**BLK%**
9.9	10.5	1.5	9.6	1.5	0.6
PER	**ORTG**	**DRTG**	**WS/48**	**VOL**	
9.26	105.4	107.9	0.070	0.350	

- Regular starter in his first season with Milwaukee
- Utilized as a very low volume, spot-up shooter, solid three-point shooter throughout his career
- Mostly a spot-up shooter, can occasionally shoot off screens, career percentage on corner threes is 42.5%
- Rated as average or worse in every other offensive situation
- Does not really create his own shot at this stage, has some passing skills, rarely turns the ball over
- 2019-20 Defensive Degree of Difficulty: 0.574
- Had the 3rd toughest set of matchups in the NBA, almost always guards the opponent's top perimeter player
- Very good on-ball defender that can guard multiple positions
- Good pick-and-roll defender, effective at containing ball handlers, solid at switching to cover the screener
- Fights through screens off the ball, occasionally can be late to close out on perimeter shooters
- Stay-at-home defender right now, steal rates have been declining for the last two seasons, below average defensive rebounder

Dennis Schröder

Height	Weight	Cap #	Years Left
6'1"	172	$15.500M	UFA

Similar at Age **26**

		Season	SIMsc
1	Kemba Walker	2016-17	936.8
2	Troy Hudson	2002-03	935.2
3	Mo Williams	2008-09	928.4
4	Mike Conley	2013-14	924.4
5	J.J. Barea	2010-11	923.7
6	Nick Van Exel	1997-98	922.4
7	Tyronn Lue	2003-04	922.4
8	Mahmoud Abdul-Rauf	1995-96	921.9
9	Jason Terry	2003-04	914.8
10	D.J. Augustin	2013-14	910.9

Baseline Basic Stats

MPG	PTS	AST	REB	BLK	STL
29.4	14.5	4.8	2.7	0.2	0.9

Advanced Metrics

USG%	3PTA/FGA	FTA/FGA	TS%	eFG%	3PT%
25.1	0.341	0.236	0.539	0.495	0.367
AST%	**TOV%**	**OREB%**	**DREB%**	**STL%**	**BLK%**
25.3	12.8	1.4	10.2	1.3	0.5
PER	**ORTG**	**DRTG**	**WS/48**	**VOL**	
15.73	106.9	110.7	0.087	0.370	

- Finalist for the Sixth Man of the Year award in 2019-20
- Production increased significantly in his role as a high volume scoring guard off the bench
- Good pick-and-roll ball handler and isolation player, better at making quick pull-up jumpers
- More effective at driving by defenders on isolations, drew more fouls last season
- Made a career best 38.5% of his threes last season, good spot-up shooter that can also come off screens
- Effective on dribble hand-offs at getting to the rim and making outside jumpers
- Good at making backdoor cuts, has a slight tendency to rush plays in transition
- Solid playmaker that finds open shooters and hits the roll man, solid at limiting turnovers
- 2019-20 Defensive Degree of Difficulty: 0.400
- Tends to guard higher-end second unit players or lower leverage starters
- Played solid on-ball defense last season, could capably defend both guard spots
- Average pick-and-roll defender, tends to go too far under screens to allow open jump shots
- Stays attached to shooters off the screens, consistently closes out in spot-up situations
- Solid defensive rebounding guard, more of a stay-at-home defender now
- Steal Percentage is declining, tied his career high in Block Percentage last season

Montrezl Harrell	Height	Weight	Cap #	Years Left
	6'7"	240	$9.258M	Player Option

	Similar at Age	26	
		Season	SIMsc
1	David West	2006-07	902.3
2	Amar'e Stoudemire	2008-09	897.3
3	Craig Smith	2009-10	897.3
4	Trevor Booker	2013-14	896.5
5	Kenneth Faried	2015-16	895.8
6	Derrick Favors	2017-18	892.8
7	Matt Harpring	2002-03	890.3
8	Carl Landry	2009-10	889.0
9	Bison Dele	1995-96	888.3
10	Alan Henderson	1998-99	887.1

Baseline Basic Stats

MPG	PTS	AST	REB	BLK	STL
27.4	13.6	1.5	6.8	0.8	0.8

Advanced Metrics

USG%	3PTA/FGA	FTA/FGA	TS%	eFG%	3PT%
24.0	0.041	0.391	0.582	0.548	0.155
AST%	**TOV%**	**OREB%**	**DREB%**	**STL%**	**BLK%**
10.6	11.0	9.4	18.1	1.4	2.9
PER	**ORTG**	**DRTG**	**WS/48**	**VOL**	
20.95	114.5	106.5	0.154	0.335	

- Named Sixth Man of the Year in 2019-20, not quite as effective in the playoffs
- Thrived in his role as a high usage, rim runner off the bench, made 72.5% of his shots inside of three feet for his career
- High energy athlete that efficiently scores on rolls to the rim and cuts off the ball
- Fairly good offensive rebounder that scores on put-backs
- Quick interior player, solid ball handler that can drive by opposing big men on isolations or when facing up in the post
- No real shooting range outside of ten feet, fairly solid passing big man, good at avoiding turnovers
- <u>2019-20 Defensive Degree of Difficulty</u>: 0.378
- Tends to guard higher-end second unit players or lower leverage starters
- Effective at protecting the rim despite being undersized, good shot blocker, solid defensive rebounder
- Middling on-ball defender, struggles in the post against taller big men, better at using his mobility to defend in space
- Middling pick-and-roll defender, decent at switching, less effective in drop coverages, lacks the length to contest lobs inside
- Consistently closes out on perimeter shooters in spot-up situations

Alex Caruso	Height	Weight	Cap #	Years Left
	6'5"	186	$2.750M	UFA

Similar at Age 25

		Season	SIMsc
1	Delon Wright	2017-18	937.8
2	Brent Barry	1996-97	931.4
3	Rex Walters	1995-96	921.6
4	Jon Barry	1994-95	917.3
5	Kent Bazemore	2014-15	916.8
6	Diante Garrett	2013-14	914.8
7	Justin Holiday	2014-15	914.4
8	Shaquille Harrison	2018-19	913.7
9	Nando De Colo	2012-13	913.3
10	Alvin Williams	1999-00	910.8

Baseline Basic Stats

MPG	PTS	AST	REB	BLK	STL
19.6	7.1	2.4	2.4	0.3	0.9

Advanced Metrics

USG%	3PTA/FGA	FTA/FGA	TS%	eFG%	3PT%
16.6	0.364	0.282	0.531	0.490	0.366
AST%	**TOV%**	**OREB%**	**DREB%**	**STL%**	**BLK%**
17.7	14.2	2.5	10.4	2.4	1.2
PER	**ORTG**	**DRTG**	**WS/48**	**VOL**	
12.71	107.1	107.2	0.094	0.405	

- Became a regular rotation player for the Lakers in his third NBA season
- Utilized as a low volume, spot-up shooter and secondary ball handler
- Solid secondary playmaker that can hit cutters or find open shooters, cut his Turnover Percentage significantly last season
- Above average three-point shooter throughout his career, percentages tend to fluctuate from year-to-year
- More of a stationary shooter right now, not effective at shooting on the move or off the dribble
- Good transition player that can push the ball up the floor to get layups or draw fouls, good cutter off the ball
- 2019-20 Defensive Degree of Difficulty: 0.450
- Plays second unit minutes, draws tougher assignments against elite guards
- Good on-ball defender that can defend both guard spots
- Solid pick-and-roll defender, very good at defending ball handlers, can be targeted by bigger screeners on switches
- Tends to be too aggressive when defending off the ball, can be caught on screens, undisciplined with his close-outs
- Active help defender, gets steals at a high rate, posts consistent Block Percentages, decent defensive rebounder

Kyle Kuzma	Height	Weight	Cap #	Years Left
	6'8"	220	$3.562M	RFA

Similar at Age 24

		Season	SIMsc
1	Rodney Hood	2016-17	942.8
2	Al Thornton	2007-08	941.5
3	Tobias Harris	2016-17	935.7
4	Dennis Scott	1992-93	930.5
5	Travis Outlaw	2008-09	926.9
6	Danny Granger	2007-08	925.9
7	Mike Miller	2004-05	925.3
8	Tim Thomas	2001-02	923.6
9	Taurean Prince	2018-19	923.3
10	Tracy Murray	1995-96	923.2

Baseline Basic Stats

MPG	PTS	AST	REB	BLK	STL
29.7	14.0	2.0	4.8	0.4	0.8

Advanced Metrics

USG%	3PTA/FGA	FTA/FGA	TS%	eFG%	3PT%
22.2	0.418	0.224	0.542	0.507	0.342
AST%	**TOV%**	**OREB%**	**DREB%**	**STL%**	**BLK%**
10.6	10.4	3.4	15.2	1.1	1.2
PER	**ORTG**	**DRTG**	**WS/48**	**VOL**	
14.02	106.6	109.6	0.079	0.357	

- Moved into a bench role for the Lakers in 2019-20 after spending his first two NBA seasons as a starter
- Utilized as a moderate volume scorer off the bench, shooting efficiency dropped slightly
- Below break-even three-point shooter overall, has made over 41% of his career corner threes
- Mostly a spot-up shooter, inconsistent at shooting on the move or off the dribble
- Can be streaky with his shot, good at attacking aggressive close-outs if his shot is falling
- Good at posting up smaller players, will crash the offensive glass to score on put-backs
- Decent passer in the past, more of a catch-and-shoot player now, solid at avoiding turnovers
- 2019-20 Defensive Degree of Difficulty: 0.385
- Tends to guard higher-end second unit players or lower leverage starters
- Average on-ball defender, has trouble staying with quicker perimeter players, better against post players
- Solid at guarding pick-and-rolls, can guard ball handlers or screeners, sometimes can go too far under screens to allow open outside shots
- Can get caught on screens off the ball, tends to be late when closing out on perimeter shots
- Stay-at-home defender, solid defensive rebounder, Block Percentage increased to a career high, does not really get steals

Markieff Morris	Height	Weight	Cap #	Years Left
	6'8"	245	$1.621M	UFA

	Similar at Age	30	
		Season	SIMsc
1	Al Harrington	2010-11	929.6
2	Ersan Ilyasova	2017-18	927.4
3	Mirza Teletovic	2015-16	926.9
4	Andres Nocioni	2009-10	921.5
5	Walt Williams	2000-01	919.7
6	Rodney Rogers	2001-02	917.1
7	Mike Scott	2018-19	913.6
8	Brian Cook	2010-11	912.0
9	Nemanja Bjelica	2018-19	909.4
10	Matt Barnes	2010-11	909.2

Baseline Basic Stats

MPG	PTS	AST	REB	BLK	STL
21.3	8.4	1.3	4.1	0.4	0.5

Advanced Metrics

USG%	3PTA/FGA	FTA/FGA	TS%	eFG%	3PT%
18.4	0.455	0.201	0.551	0.523	0.374
AST%	**TOV%**	**OREB%**	**DREB%**	**STL%**	**BLK%**
9.4	11.5	4.6	17.1	1.3	1.4
PER	**ORTG**	**DRTG**	**WS/48**	**VOL**	
12.49	107.9	109.3	0.075	0.375	

- Regular rotation player for Detroit and the Lakers, bought out by Detroit in February 2020, later signed by the Lakers
- Used by the Lakers as a low volume, stretch big, took on a higher volume role in Detroit
- Mostly a spot-up shooter with both teams, made almost 39% of his threes last season, shot better in Detroit
- Effective at making backdoor cuts if defenders aren't paying attention
- Decent passer that can kick the ball out to shooters, solid at limiting turnovers
- 2019-20 Defensive Degree of Difficulty: 0.374
- Tends to guard second unit players, occasionally draws some tougher assignments
- Fairly solid defender that can capably guard multiple positions
- Average pick-and-roll defender, good at guarding the screener, has trouble staying with quicker ball handlers
- Good at closing out on perimeter shooters, can get caught on screens off the ball
- Middling rim protector, does not really block shots, can be foul prone, solid defensive rebounder

Alfonzo McKinnie	Height	Weight	Cap #	Years Left
	6'7"	215	$1.763M	2

	Similar at Age	**27**	
		Season	**SIMsc**
1	Torrey Craig	2017-18	941.1
2	Chase Budinger	2015-16	935.0
3	Stephen Graham	2009-10	931.7
4	Cartier Martin	2011-12	921.9
5	Kyle Singler	2015-16	921.9
6	James Ennis	2017-18	919.8
7	Solomon Hill	2018-19	915.0
8	Jarvis Hayes	2008-09	913.3
9	Joey Graham	2009-10	912.9
10	Sasha Pavlovic	2010-11	912.8

Baseline Basic Stats

MPG	PTS	AST	REB	BLK	STL
18.1	6.0	1.0	2.8	0.3	0.5

Advanced Metrics

USG%	3PTA/FGA	FTA/FGA	TS%	eFG%	3PT%
15.2	0.492	0.172	0.530	0.508	0.322
AST%	**TOV%**	**OREB%**	**DREB%**	**STL%**	**BLK%**
6.3	11.8	5.5	13.9	1.5	1.3
PER	**ORTG**	**DRTG**	**WS/48**	**VOL**	
10.21	105.4	110.0	0.064	0.316	

- Claimed on waivers by Cleveland from Golden State, fringe rotation player for Cleveland last season
- Primarily used as a low volume, spot-up shooter
- Really struggled to make shots from outside, shot below 25% on threes last season
- Almost exclusively a stationary, catch-and-shoot player, does not shoot on the move or off the dribble
- Good cutter off the ball, will opportunistically crash the offensive boards to score on put-backs
- Limited passing skills, will only make safe passes on the perimeter, does not really turn the ball over
- 2019-20 Defensive Degree of Difficulty: 0.324
- Mostly guarded second unit level players last season
- Decent on-ball defender, can capably guard multiple positions, better against bigger wings in the post last season
- Solid pick-and-roll that can contain ball handlers or switch to cover the roll man
- Late to close out on perimeter shooters last season, occasionally gets caught on screens off the ball
- More active as a help defender, steals rate increased significantly, solid defensive rebounder, Block Percentage still consistent with his career average

Jared Dudley

Height	Weight	Cap #	Years Left
6'6"	237	$1.621M	UFA

Similar at Age **34**

		Season	SIMsc
1	Matt Barnes	2014-15	889.8
2	Bryon Russell	2004-05	889.6
3	Brian Cardinal	2011-12	888.2
4	Dan Majerle	1999-00	887.1
5	Mike Miller	2014-15	881.8
6	Eduardo Najera	2010-11	879.6
7	Caron Butler	2014-15	876.3
8	Eric Piatkowski	2004-05	876.0
9	Anthony Parker	2009-10	874.4
10	Rick Fox	2003-04	872.2

Baseline Basic Stats

MPG	PTS	AST	REB	BLK	STL
17.9	4.8	1.3	2.5	0.2	0.6

Advanced Metrics

USG%	3PTA/FGA	FTA/FGA	TS%	eFG%	3PT%
11.0	0.646	0.132	0.522	0.503	0.362
AST%	**TOV%**	**OREB%**	**DREB%**	**STL%**	**BLK%**
10.5	12.8	2.9	13.6	1.7	1.1
PER	**ORTG**	**DRTG**	**WS/48**	**VOL**	
8.62	107.4	108.3	0.081	0.453	

- Played sparingly for the Lakers in his first season with the team, mainly provided veteran leadership
- Utilized as a very low volume, spot-up shooter, made almost 43% of his threes last season
- Almost strictly a stationary spot-up shooter, sometimes effective as a screener on pick-and-pops
- Rarely moves off the ball, can occasionally make backdoor cuts from the weak side
- Not really able to create his own offense, willing to make the extra pass, good at avoiding turnovers
- 2019-20 Defensive Degree of Difficulty: 0.289
- Tends to either guard second unit players or play in garbage time
- Below average on-ball defender, has trouble staying with quicker players on the perimeter
- More foul prone at this stage, can be bullied inside by stronger players in the post
- Decent pick-and-roll defender, solid at preventing ball handlers from turning the corner, tends to go too far under screens
- Tends to be late when closing out on perimeter shooters, has trouble defending dribble hand-off plays
- Solid defensive rebounder, Steal and Block Percentages were slightly above his career averages last season

Talen Horton-Tucker	Height	Weight	Cap #	Years Left
	6'4"	235	$1.518M	RFA

	Similar at Age	19	
		Season	SIMsc
1	Zhaire Smith	2018-19	814.5
2	C.J. Miles	2006-07	812.4
3	Jamal Murray	2016-17	797.1
4	Jabari Parker	2014-15	795.3
5	Stanley Johnson	2015-16	794.1
6	DeShawn Stevenson	2000-01	789.0
7	J.R. Smith	2004-05	787.5
8	Archie Goodwin	2013-14	786.7
9	Ersan Ilyasova	2006-07	783.8
10	Gerald Wallace	2001-02	783.1

Baseline Basic Stats

MPG	PTS	AST	REB	BLK	STL
20.5	8.6	1.5	2.6	0.2	0.9

Advanced Metrics

USG%	3PTA/FGA	FTA/FGA	TS%	eFG%	3PT%
20.8	0.335	0.211	0.569	0.548	0.360
AST%	**TOV%**	**OREB%**	**DREB%**	**STL%**	**BLK%**
12.9	13.3	3.0	9.4	3.6	0.9
PER	**ORTG**	**DRTG**	**WS/48**	**VOL**	
15.01	106.9	106.5	0.098	0.612	

- Played sparingly for the Lakers in his rookie season, spent most of 2019-20 in the G-League with the South Bay Lakers
- Used as a low volume, spot-up shooter in limited NBA action, took on much more volume in the G-League
- Below break-even three-point shooter at both levels, mainly a spot-up shooter at this stage
- Effective at running the wings in transition in a small sample of possessions, not really effective in other situations at the NBA level
- Solid secondary playmaker in the G-League, slightly turnover prone
- 2019-20 Defensive Degree of Difficulty: 0.383, only played 81 NBA minutes
- Played middling on-ball defense, got a few tougher assignments, appeared over-matched against James Harden, Malcolm Brogdon and Buddy Hield
- Below average at guarding pick-and-rolls, struggled to get around the screen to contain ball handlers
- Fights through screens off the ball, tends to be late when closing out on perimeter shooters
- Active help defender in the G-League, solid defensive rebounder, got steals and blocks at a fairly high rate

LOS ANGELES CLIPPERS

Last Season: 49 – 23, Lost 2nd Round to Denver (3 – 4)

Offensive Rating: 113.9, 2nd in the NBA

Defensive Rating: 107.6, 5th in the NBA

Primary Executive: Lawrence Frank, President of Basketball Operations

Head Coach: Tyronn Lue

Key Roster Changes

Subtractions
Landry Shamet, trade
Rodney McGruder, trade
Montrezl Harrell, free agency
JaMychal Green, free agency
Joakim Noah, waived

Additions
Daniel Oturu, draft
Luke Kennard, trade
Serge Ibaka, free agency
Nicolas Batum, free agency

Roster

Likely Starting Five

1. *Patrick Beverley*
2. *Paul George*
3. *Kawhi Leonard*
4. *Marcus Morris*
5. *Serge Ibaka*

Other Key Rotation Players
Lou Williams
Luke Kennard
Ivica Zubac
Patrick Patterson

* Italics denotes that a player is likely to be on the floor to close games

Remaining Roster

- Nicolas Batum
- Reggie Jackson
- Terance Mann
- Mfiondu Kabengele
- Daniel Oturu
- Amir Coffey, 23, 6'7", 210, Minnesota (Two-Way)
- Jay Scrubb, 20, 6'6", 210, John A. Logan College (Two-Way)
- Ky Bowman, 23, 6'1", 187, Boston College (Exhibit 10)
- Malik Fitts, 23, 6'8", 230, St. Mary's (CA) (Exhibit 10)
- Jordan Ford, 22, 6'1", 175, St. Mary's (CA) (Exhibit 10)
- Rayjon Tucker, 23, 6'5", 210, Arkansas-Little Rock (Exhibit 10)

SCHREMPF Base Rating: 41.7 (72-game season)

Strengths

- Potentially dynamic and versatile switching defense from the expected starting unit
- Efficient offense that can spread floor around its star players

Question Marks

- Depth beyond the top eight players
- Combustibility due to past chemistry issues and a lack of vocal leadership

Outlook

- Contender in the West, will probably finish with one of the top four seeds

Veterans

Kawhi Leonard	Height	Weight	Cap #	Years Left
	6'7"	230	$34.379M	Player Option

	Similar at Age	28 Season	SIMsc
1	Jimmy Butler	2017-18	911.4
2	Vince Carter	2004-05	897.7
3	Tyreke Evans	2017-18	894.6
4	Paul Pierce	2005-06	894.4
5	Carmelo Anthony	2012-13	891.6
6	Paul George	2018-19	891.6
7	DeMar DeRozan	2017-18	889.5
8	Glenn Robinson	2000-01	887.7
9	Lamond Murray	2001-02	885.8
10	Caron Butler	2008-09	883.4

Baseline Basic Stats

MPG	PTS	AST	REB	BLK	STL
35.2	21.9	4.1	6.2	0.5	1.3

Advanced Metrics

USG%	3PTA/FGA	FTA/FGA	TS%	eFG%	3PT%
29.0	0.291	0.362	0.575	0.513	0.365
AST%	**TOV%**	**OREB%**	**DREB%**	**STL%**	**BLK%**
21.4	11.2	3.5	17.7	2.3	1.4
PER	**ORTG**	**DRTG**	**WS/48**	**VOL**	
22.72	113.1	104.8	0.176	0.469	

- Made his fourth All-Star team last season, named to the All-NBA 2nd Team in 2019-20
- Sat games for load management reasons, highly effective as the Clippers' primary option when active
- Dramatically improved his playmaking skills, good at finding open shooters, better at hitting cutters inside, rarely turns the ball over
- Excellent pick-and-roll ball handler and isolation player, great mid-range shooter that can knock down pull-up jumpers
- Attacks the rim to score or draw fouls, good at posting up smaller perimeter players
- Good three-point shooter that can spot up or come off screens, excellent at making backdoor cuts if defenders try to crowd him
- 2019-20 Defensive Degree of Difficulty: 0.505, takes on tough assignments against elite level players
- One of the best perimeter defenders in the league, guards multiple positions, had some trouble against bigger post players last season
- Good pick-and-roll defender, contains ball handlers by fighting over screens, effective on switches
- Stays attached to shooters off the ball, great at using his length to contest shots
- Active help defender, has the 3rd highest career Steals Percentage among active players, Block Percentage still consistent with his career average, good defensive rebounder

Paul George

Height	Weight	Cap #	Years Left
6'8"	220	$35.450M	Player Option

Similar at Age **29**

		Season	SIMsc
1	Glenn Robinson	2001-02	917.1
2	Manu Ginobili	2006-07	916.3
3	Stephen Jackson	2007-08	899.6
4	Larry Bird*	1985-86	898.3
5	Al Harrington	2009-10	897.5
6	Tyreke Evans	2018-19	894.3
7	Carmelo Anthony	2013-14	893.8
8	Walt Williams	1999-00	892.8
9	DeMar DeRozan	2018-19	892.7
10	Wilson Chandler	2016-17	892.2

Baseline Basic Stats

MPG	PTS	AST	REB	BLK	STL
32.8	18.9	3.6	5.5	0.5	1.3

Advanced Metrics

USG%	3PTA/FGA	FTA/FGA	TS%	eFG%	3PT%
26.7	0.400	0.297	0.568	0.515	0.387
AST%	**TOV%**	**OREB%**	**DREB%**	**STL%**	**BLK%**
18.4	12.4	2.8	16.3	2.2	1.1
PER	**ORTG**	**DRTG**	**WS/48**	**VOL**	
19.10	110.1	106.7	0.144	0.532	

- Missed the first month of last season while recovering from a right shoulder injury, also missed games due to a strained left hamstring
- Maintained his scoring efficiency in his high volume role as one the Clippers' primary scorers
- Good pick-and-roll ball handler, can attack the rim and make pull-up jumpers
- Good playmaker that can find open shooters and cutters inside, solid at avoiding turnovers
- Not as effective on isolations, had trouble driving by defenders without a screen due to injuries
- Good shooter that made over 41% of his threes, very good at spotting up and coming off screens
- Good at using the screen on dribble hand-offs to make outside shots or go the rim
- 2019-20 Defensive Degree of Difficulty: 0.502
- Takes on tougher defensive assignments against high-end perimeter players
- Good on-ball defender that guards multiple positions, less effective against quicker guards last season
- Fairly solid pick-and-roll defender, good on switches, tends to go too far under screens
- Fights through screens off the ball, tended to be late when closing out, effort level was inconsistent last season
- Solid defensive rebounder, gets steals at a high rate, Block Percentage still consistent with his career average

Serge Ibaka	Height	Weight	Cap #	Years Left
	7'0"	235	$9.258M	Player Option

	Similar at Age	30	
		Season	SIMsc
1	Mehmet Okur	2009-10	919.1
2	Sam Bowie	1991-92	916.3
3	Robert Parish*	1983-84	908.8
4	Jason Smith	2016-17	906.8
5	Marcin Gortat	2014-15	905.1
6	Rasheed Wallace	2004-05	899.0
7	Roy Tarpley	1994-95	898.3
8	Benoit Benjamin	1994-95	897.0
9	LaMarcus Aldridge	2015-16	896.5
10	Mark Blount	2005-06	895.7

Baseline Basic Stats

MPG	PTS	AST	REB	BLK	STL
28.3	13.1	1.4	8.0	1.2	0.6

Advanced Metrics

USG%	3PTA/FGA	FTA/FGA	TS%	eFG%	3PT%
20.6	0.153	0.245	0.566	0.535	0.347
AST%	**TOV%**	**OREB%**	**DREB%**	**STL%**	**BLK%**
7.2	13.2	8.4	23.1	0.9	3.0
PER	**ORTG**	**DRTG**	**WS/48**	**VOL**	
15.82	108.3	104.7	0.099	0.466	

- Regular rotation player for Toronto, started some games last season
- Maintained his usual level of production in his role as a moderate volume rim runner and stretch big
- Solid mid-range shooter throughout his career, made 38.5% of his threes last season
- Decent spot-up shooter, average at being a screener on pick-and-pops
- Good at setting up for trail threes in transition, can occasionally shoot off screens
- Scores on a high volume of cuts off the ball and rolls to the rim on pick-and-rolls
- Solid offensive rebounder that efficiently scores on put-backs, fairly good at posting up smaller players
- Has become a decent passer in recent seasons, good at avoiding turnovers
- 2019-20 Defensive Degree of Difficulty: 0.415, tends to guard starting level big men
- Good rim protector, good defensive rebounder and shot blocker
- Solid on-ball defender, good at using his length to contest shots in the post, mobile enough to defend in space
- Average pick-and-roll defender, tends to sag into the paint to allow open outside shots
- Consistently closes out on perimeter shooters, occasionally will be too aggressive on his close-outs

Patrick Beverley	Height	Weight	Cap #	Years Left
	6'1"	185	$13.333M	1

	Similar at Age	31 Season	SIMsc
1	George Hill	2017-18	905.6
2	Kirk Hinrich	2011-12	904.8
3	Earl Watson	2010-11	897.8
4	Mike Bibby	2009-10	894.3
5	Shammond Williams	2006-07	889.8
6	Devin Harris	2014-15	885.5
7	Scott Skiles	1995-96	880.9
8	Henry Bibby	1980-81	880.7
9	Jason Williams	2006-07	879.3
10	Steve Blake	2011-12	878.1

Baseline Basic Stats

MPG	PTS	AST	REB	BLK	STL
22.4	7.4	2.9	2.5	0.2	0.9

Advanced Metrics

USG%	3PTA/FGA	FTA/FGA	TS%	eFG%	3PT%
14.9	0.544	0.182	0.547	0.522	0.388
AST%	**TOV%**	**OREB%**	**DREB%**	**STL%**	**BLK%**
18.8	15.3	3.6	12.3	2.0	1.2
PER	**ORTG**	**DRTG**	**WS/48**	**VOL**	
12.37	112.0	107.7	0.101	0.402	

- Made the All-Defensive 2nd team in 2019-20, regular starter when healthy, missed games due to a series of minor injuries
- Mostly used as a low volume, spot-up shooter and secondary ball handler
- Good three-point shooter that made almost 39% of his threes last season
- Primarily a stationary spot-up shooter, does not really shoot off the dribble or on the move
- Can occasionally catch defenders off guard on drives in isolation situations
- Decent playmaker that can find open shooters, slightly turnover prone last season
- 2019-20 Defensive Degree of Difficulty: 0.519
- Takes on tough assignments against higher-end ball handlers
- Good on-ball defender that can defend both guard spots, can get into foul trouble at times
- Below average pick-and-roll defender, tends to over-commit when making rotations
- Stays attached to shooters off the ball, good at closing down the air space to contest shots
- Good defensive rebounding guard, Steal and Block Percentages are still consistent with his career averages

Marcus Morris	Height	Weight	Cap #	Years Left
	6'8"	235	$14.884M	3

	Similar at Age	30	
		Season	SIMsc
1	Mirza Teletovic	2015-16	952.9
2	Ersan Ilyasova	2017-18	940.5
3	Andres Nocioni	2009-10	930.6
4	Jeff Green	2016-17	929.1
5	Walt Williams	2000-01	928.7
6	Rodney Rogers	2001-02	927.9
7	Tim Thomas	2007-08	927.8
8	Al Harrington	2010-11	924.8
9	Antawn Jamison	2006-07	922.6
10	Marvin Williams	2016-17	916.6

Baseline Basic Stats

MPG	PTS	AST	REB	BLK	STL
24.8	10.4	1.4	4.5	0.3	0.6

Advanced Metrics

USG%	3PTA/FGA	FTA/FGA	TS%	eFG%	3PT%
19.5	0.441	0.235	0.555	0.518	0.372
AST%	**TOV%**	**OREB%**	**DREB%**	**STL%**	**BLK%**
7.6	10.2	3.8	16.4	1.2	1.2
PER	**ORTG**	**DRTG**	**WS/48**	**VOL**	
13.18	109.2	109.6	0.085	0.298	

- Regular starter for New York and the Clippers last season, traded to the Clippers in February 2020
- More effective in a higher usage role with New York, used by the Clippers as a low volume, spot-up shooter
- Shot unusually well with the Knicks, made almost 44% of his threes, regressed considerably after trade, made threes at a below break-even rate with the Clippers
- Mostly a spot-up shooter, occasionally can come off screens or make pull-up jumpers on pick-and-rolls
- Occasionally can post up smaller players or drive by opposing big men
- Can be a ball stopper on offense, limited passing skills, rarely turns the ball over
- 2019-20 Defensive Degree of Difficulty: 0.464
- Tends to guard starter level players, sometimes takes on tougher defensive assignments
- Fairly decent on-ball defender, good against bigger post players, has some trouble against quicker perimeter players
- Solid pick-and-roll defender, funnels ball handlers into help, good at covering the roll man in drop coverage, can struggle to contain quicker ball handling guards
- Fights through screens off the ball, tends to be late when closing out on perimeter shooters
- Solid defensive rebounder, steal and block rates are still consistent with his career averages

Lou Williams	Height	Weight	Cap #	Years Left
	6'1"	175	$8.000M	UFA

	Similar at Age	33	
		Season	SIMsc
1	Jason Terry	2010-11	904.2
2	Tim Hardaway	1999-00	902.7
3	Tony Parker	2015-16	897.0
4	Allen Iverson*	2008-09	895.1
5	Sam Cassell	2002-03	893.0
6	Nick Van Exel	2004-05	888.4
7	J.J. Barea	2017-18	884.0
8	Mark Price	1997-98	883.4
9	Bobby Jackson	2006-07	880.9
10	John Lucas	1986-87	880.6

Baseline Basic Stats

MPG	PTS	AST	REB	BLK	STL
28.7	15.0	5.0	2.6	0.1	0.8

Advanced Metrics

USG%	3PTA/FGA	FTA/FGA	TS%	eFG%	3PT%
26.7	0.308	0.301	0.532	0.476	0.364
AST%	**TOV%**	**OREB%**	**DREB%**	**STL%**	**BLK%**
27.9	13.4	1.7	8.5	1.3	0.4
PER	**ORTG**	**DRTG**	**WS/48**	**VOL**	
16.78	106.5	109.3	0.099	0.333	

- Finalist for the Sixth Man of the Year award in 2019-20
- Effective in his role as a high volume, scoring guard off the bench, production declined last season
- Good pick-and-roll ball handler that can make pull-up jumpers or floaters in the paint
- Has become a pretty good playmaker that can find open shooters or hit the roll man inside, good at limiting turnovers
- May have lost a step from a quickness standpoint, less effective at driving by defenders on isolation plays
- Around a league average three-point shooter last season, good spot-up shooter that can also come off screens
- <u>2019-20 Defensive Degree of Difficulty</u>: 0.321
- Tends to be hidden in lower leverage matchups against starters or second unit players
- Played solid on-ball defense in these matchups, good at stopping drives, taller wing players could shoot over him
- Solid pick-and-roll defender that could funnel his man into help, effective on switches last season
- Stayed attached to shooters off the ball, consistently closed out in spot-up situations
- Fairly decent defensive rebounder, Steal Percentage has been declining for the last few seasons

Luke Kennard	Height	Weight	Cap #	Years Left
	6'5"	206	$5.274M	RFA

	Similar at Age	23	
		Season	SIMsc
1	Tim Hardaway, Jr.	2015-16	934.3
2	Reggie Williams	2009-10	928.8
3	Chris Carr	1997-98	928.4
4	Anthony Morrow	2008-09	925.8
5	Ben McLemore	2016-17	925.3
6	Buddy Hield	2016-17	920.2
7	Voshon Lenard	1996-97	918.1
8	Nik Stauskas	2016-17	913.4
9	Sasha Vujacic	2007-08	912.8
10	Von Wafer	2008-09	911.6

Baseline Basic Stats

MPG	PTS	AST	REB	BLK	STL
24.2	10.2	1.7	2.8	0.2	0.6

Advanced Metrics

USG%	3PTA/FGA	FTA/FGA	TS%	eFG%	3PT%
19.2	0.528	0.194	0.569	0.535	0.400
AST%	**TOV%**	**OREB%**	**DREB%**	**STL%**	**BLK%**
13.9	9.9	1.6	11.4	1.1	0.6
PER	**ORTG**	**DRTG**	**WS/48**	**VOL**	
13.43	112.6	112.2	0.104	0.391	

- Regular starter for Detroit when healthy, missed most of the season due to knee tendinitis
- Utilized as a lower volume shooter off the ball, has made just over 40% of his threes throughout his career
- Excellent spot-up shooter, good at running off screens, can make backdoor cuts if defenders overplay his shot
- Good at using an on-ball screen to make outside shots as a pick-and-roll ball handler, solid at getting to the rim on hand-offs
- Can occasionally drive past defenders on isolations, has become a good secondary playmaker, tends to avoid turnovers
- 2019-20 Defensive Degree of Difficulty: 0.355
- Tends to be hidden in favorable matchups against lower leverage offensive players
- Not tested very often, average on-ball defender at best, has trouble staying with quicker perimeter players
- Fairly decent pick-and-roll defender, funnels his man into help, has difficulty guarding bigger players on switches
- Consistently fights through screens off the ball, sometimes is late to close out on perimeter shooters
- Stay-at-home defender, got fewer blocks and steals, fairly solid defensive rebounder

Ivica Zubac	Height	Weight	Cap #	Years Left
	7'0"	240	$7.000M	1 + TO

	Similar at Age	22	
		Season	SIMsc
1	Andris Biedrins	2008-09	923.5
2	Jonas Valanciunas	2014-15	919.1
3	Travis Knight	1996-97	918.8
4	Ante Zizic	2018-19	918.5
5	Cody Zeller	2014-15	910.5
6	Willie Cauley-Stein	2015-16	909.9
7	Clint Capela	2016-17	908.9
8	Willy Hernangomez	2016-17	906.1
9	Tim McCormick	1984-85	902.4
10	Nick Fazekas	2007-08	901.4

Baseline Basic Stats

MPG	PTS	AST	REB	BLK	STL
23.3	9.9	1.2	6.9	1.1	0.5

Advanced Metrics

USG%	3PTA/FGA	FTA/FGA	TS%	eFG%	3PT%
18.6	0.018	0.347	0.602	0.564	0.173
AST%	**TOV%**	**OREB%**	**DREB%**	**STL%**	**BLK%**
9.1	12.2	11.8	24.0	0.9	3.9
PER	**ORTG**	**DRTG**	**WS/48**	**VOL**	
19.69	121.2	104.4	0.189	0.469	

- Regular starter for the Clippers in his first full season with the team
- Played a situational role as a low volume, rim runner, made over 68% of his shots inside of three feet last season
- Led the NBA in Offensive Rebound Percentage, high motor player that scores on a high volume of put-backs
- Goes hard to the rim as a cutter off the ball and a roll man on pick-and-rolls, draws fouls at a high rate
- Expanded his shooting range, good at making mid-range shots in a limited number of attempts
- Decent passing big man, good at limiting turnovers
- 2019-20 Defensive Degree of Difficulty: 0.472
- Tends to guard starting level big men, takes on tough assignments against elite big men
- Good rim protector that can block shots, clog the lane and grab defensive rebounds
- Good on-ball defender, stout post defender, has enough mobility to defend big men in space
- Middling pick-and-roll defender, decent in drop coverages, has trouble containing quicker ball handlers on the perimeter
- Good at closing out to contest perimeter shots in spot-up situations

Patrick Patterson	Height	Weight	Cap #	Years Left
	6'8"	230	$3.078M	UFA

Similar at Age 30

		Season	SIMsc
1	Anthony Tolliver	2015-16	936.1
2	Mike Scott	2018-19	934.1
3	Lance Thomas	2018-19	928.7
4	Dennis Scott	1998-99	927.5
5	Dante Cunningham	2017-18	925.2
6	Matt Bonner	2010-11	917.9
7	James Jones	2010-11	914.6
8	Mike Miller	2010-11	911.6
9	Quentin Richardson	2010-11	910.6
10	Wilson Chandler	2017-18	910.5

Baseline Basic Stats

MPG	PTS	AST	REB	BLK	STL
17.2	5.3	0.8	2.6	0.2	0.4

Advanced Metrics

USG%	3PTA/FGA	FTA/FGA	TS%	eFG%	3PT%
13.3	0.682	0.165	0.552	0.529	0.371
AST%	**TOV%**	**OREB%**	**DREB%**	**STL%**	**BLK%**
6.7	9.1	3.9	14.2	0.9	0.9
PER	**ORTG**	**DRTG**	**WS/48**	**VOL**	
10.16	113.0	110.1	0.097	0.402	

- Back-end rotation player for the Clippers in his first season with the team
- Utilized in a role as a low volume, stretch big, made 39% of his threes last season
- Mainly a stationary spot-up shooter, not as effective at shooting on the move
- Good at running the floor to get layups in transition
- Only average as a rim runner, does not have the lift to consistently finish inside, can slide into open spaces down low as a roll man and cutter
- Strictly a catch-and-shoot player, limited passing skills, rarely turns the ball over
- 2019-20 Defensive Degree of Difficulty: 0.383, tended to guard second unit level big men
- Solid on-ball defender that can guard post players or perimeter-oriented fours
- Above average pick-and-roll defender, good in drop coverages, has trouble containing quicker ball handlers on the perimeter
- Generally stays attached to shooters off the ball, occasionally can be late to close out in spot-up situations
- Solid defensive rebounder, Steal and Block Percentages dropped to career lows last season

Nicolas Batum

	Height	Weight	Cap #	Years Left
	6'9"	200	$1.621M	UFA

	Similar at Age	31 Season	SIMsc
1	Sasha Vujacic	2015-16	897.8
2	Wilson Chandler	2018-19	889.1
3	Vladimir Radmanovic	2011-12	886.3
4	Harvey Grant	1996-97	884.5
5	Devean George	2008-09	882.6
6	Wesley Johnson	2018-19	876.7
7	Rashard Lewis	2010-11	876.0
8	Robert Horry	2001-02	875.7
9	Luol Deng	2016-17	874.8
10	Matt Bullard	1998-99	873.6

Baseline Basic Stats

MPG	PTS	AST	REB	BLK	STL
20.7	6.3	1.8	3.5	0.4	0.7

Advanced Metrics

USG%	3PTA/FGA	FTA/FGA	TS%	eFG%	3PT%
13.3	0.477	0.162	0.517	0.486	0.332
AST%	**TOV%**	**OREB%**	**DREB%**	**STL%**	**BLK%**
14.8	16.8	4.5	15.4	1.7	1.4
PER	**ORTG**	**DRTG**	**WS/48**	**VOL**	
11.00	106.5	110.1	0.068	0.408	

- Missed parts of the 2019-20 season due to a fractured finger and a left hand injury
- Moved into a bench role, production declined significantly, had his worst season as a pro last season
- Utilized as a very low volume, spot-up shooter, struggled to make shots last season, Effective Field Goal Percentage was below 45%
- Limited to making open, stand-still threes, decline in athleticism makes him unable to create quality shots in other situations
- Still effective as a cutter, will opportunistically hit the offensive glass to score on put-backs
- Solid playmaking wing player, can be somewhat turnover prone
- 2019-20 Defensive Degree of Difficulty: 0.456
- Usually guarded starter level players in limited minutes, sometimes tasked to take on tougher defensive assignments
- Solid on-ball defender that can guard multiple positions
- Generally a good pick-and-roll defender, sometimes has difficulty containing quicker ball handlers
- Will fight through screens to stay attached to shooters off the ball, will sometimes be late when closing out in spot-up situations
- Solid defensive rebounder, Block and Steal Percentages are still consistent with his career averages

Reggie Jackson	Height	Weight	Cap #	Years Left
	6'3"	208	$1.621M	UFA

Similar at Age 29

		Season	SIMsc
1	Erick Strickland	2002-03	941.8
2	Ben Gordon	2012-13	933.3
3	Gary Neal	2013-14	933.3
4	Jarrett Jack	2012-13	916.9
5	Voshon Lenard	2002-03	913.6
6	Keyon Dooling	2009-10	912.8
7	Deron Williams	2013-14	909.8
8	Charlie Bell	2008-09	906.9
9	Junior Bridgeman	1982-83	906.9
10	Isaiah Rider	2000-01	904.2

Baseline Basic Stats

MPG	PTS	AST	REB	BLK	STL
24.7	10.7	3.3	2.4	0.1	0.7

Advanced Metrics

USG%	3PTA/FGA	FTA/FGA	TS%	eFG%	3PT%
22.2	0.383	0.197	0.523	0.485	0.373
AST%	**TOV%**	**OREB%**	**DREB%**	**STL%**	**BLK%**
23.2	12.9	2.0	9.6	1.1	0.5
PER	**ORTG**	**DRTG**	**WS/48**	**VOL**	
13.30	105.4	111.3	0.074	0.360	

- Missed most of the season due to a back injury, started for Detroit, became a rotation player for the Clippers after he was waived in February 2020
- Used as a lower volume backup point guard with the Clippers, took on a higher usage role in Detroit
- More effective with the Clippers, made over 39% of his threes overall last season
- Good spot-up shooter that can sometimes make pull-up jumpers as a pick-and-roll ball handler
- Effective at using an on-ball screen to make outside shots or get to the rim on dribble hand-offs
- Solid playmaker that can hit the roll man or find open shooters, generally avoids committing turnovers
- 2019-20 Defensive Degree of Difficulty: 0.435, tends to guard starter level guards
- Average on-ball defender, struggled to stay with opposing players in Detroit, more effective with the Clippers
- Below average pick-and-roll defender, tends to allow ball handlers to turn the corner
- Good at closing out on perimeter shooters, tends to get caught on screens off the ball
- Fairly solid defensive rebounding guard, Steal Percentage declined significantly last season

Terance Mann	Height	Weight	Cap #	Years Left
	6'5"	215	$1.518M	1 + TO

	Similar at Age	23	
		Season	SIMsc
1	Sindarius Thornwell	2017-18	928.8
2	John Salmons	2002-03	917.7
3	Tyrone Wallace	2017-18	913.8
4	Arron Afflalo	2008-09	912.6
5	Kelenna Azubuike	2006-07	905.3
6	Marcus Georges-Hunt	2017-18	904.6
7	Alonzo Gee	2010-11	901.9
8	Thabo Sefolosha	2007-08	899.6
9	Kevin Gamble	1988-89	897.8
10	Andrew Harrison	2017-18	897.8

Baseline Basic Stats

MPG	PTS	AST	REB	BLK	STL
19.2	6.5	1.6	2.7	0.3	0.6

Advanced Metrics

USG%	3PTA/FGA	FTA/FGA	TS%	eFG%	3PT%
15.0	0.305	0.285	0.530	0.492	0.323
AST%	**TOV%**	**OREB%**	**DREB%**	**STL%**	**BLK%**
17.0	14.1	3.5	11.9	1.6	1.0
PER	**ORTG**	**DRTG**	**WS/48**	**VOL**	
11.54	110.6	108.7	0.096	0.399	

- Fringe rotation player for the Clippers in his rookie season
- Used as a low volume, energetic backup combo guard
- Good athlete that can push the ball quickly up the floor in transition to get layups or draw fouls
- Decent spot-up shooter that made threes at around the league average last season
- Struggles to shoot on the move or off the dribble
- Rated as average or worse in every half-court offensive situation last season
- Solid playmaker that can find open shooters or cutters inside, slightly turnover prone
- 2019-20 Defensive Degree of Difficulty: 0.302
- Either played in garbage time or defended second unit level players
- Fairly solid on-ball defender that can potentially defend both guard spots
- Solid pick-and-roll defender that fights over screens to contain ball handlers, sometimes allows his man to turn the corner
- Consistently uses his length to contest perimeter shots in spot-up situations, can get caught on screens off the ball
- Stay-at-home defender, posted fairly moderate steal and block rates last season, good defensive rebounding guard

Mfiondu Kabengele	Height	Weight	Cap #	Years Left
	6'9"	250	$2.076M	2 Team Options

Similar at Age 22

		Season	SIMsc
1	Marcus Derrickson	2018-19	865.9
2	D.J. White	2008-09	863.9
3	Ryan Anderson	2010-11	862.8
4	Luke Babbitt	2011-12	850.2
5	Juan Hernangomez	2017-18	846.2
6	Luke Kornet	2017-18	846.2
7	Henry Ellenson	2018-19	843.5
8	Marcus Morris	2011-12	842.2
9	P.J. Hairston	2014-15	842.1
10	Marreese Speights	2009-10	836.0

Baseline Basic Stats

MPG	PTS	AST	REB	BLK	STL
18.6	7.5	0.7	3.9	0.4	0.5

Advanced Metrics

USG%	3PTA/FGA	FTA/FGA	TS%	eFG%	3PT%
20.2	0.505	0.212	0.595	0.558	0.442
AST%	**TOV%**	**OREB%**	**DREB%**	**STL%**	**BLK%**
5.7	7.4	4.4	16.8	1.4	2.1
PER	**ORTG**	**DRTG**	**WS/48**	**VOL**	
16.73	116.9	106.8	0.165	0.751	

- Played sparingly in his rookie season, spent most of 2019-20 in the G-League with the Agua Caliente Clippers
- Used as a moderate volume stretch big in the G-League
- Shot just below break-even on threes in the G-League, went 9-for-20 on threes in the NBA
- Mostly a spot-up shooter, flashed the ability to make shots as the screener on pick-and-pops
- Effective rim runner in a small sample of NBA possessions, good at rolling to the rim and cutting off the ball
- Made over 83% of his shots inside of three feet at the NBA level
- Catch-and-shoot player at this stage, limited passing skills, does not really turn the ball over
- 2019-20 Defensive Degree of Difficulty: 0.208, tended to play in garbage time
- Below average rim protector at the NBA level, undisciplined in his positioning, highly foul prone
- Good defensive rebounder and shot blocker in the G-League
- Mixed results as an on-ball defender, played solid post defense, struggled to defend in space
- Below average pick-and-roll defender, struggled to stay with ball handlers on the perimeter
- Very good at closing out to contest perimeter shots in spot-up situations

Newcomers

Daniel Oturu

Height	Weight	Cap #	Years Left
6'10"	240	$0.898M	1

Baseline Basic Stats

MPG	PTS	AST	REB	BLK	STL
13.5	5.0	0.6	3.5	0.6	0.3

Advanced Metrics

USG%	3PTA/FGA	FTA/FGA	TS%	eFG%	3PT%
17.5	0.092	0.286	0.527	0.501	0.243

AST%	TOV%	OREB%	DREB%	STL%	BLK%
6.9	13.0	9.6	18.4	1.1	3.7

PER	ORTG	DRTG	WS/48	VOL
14.93	104.1	100.1	0.099	N/A

- Drafted by Minnesota with the 33rd overall pick, traded to the L.A. Clippers via New York
- Made the Big Ten All-Defense team, named to the All-Big Ten 2nd Team in 2019-20
- High motor rim runner, dives hard to the rim as a cutter off the ball or roll man, aggressive offensive rebounder
- Showed stretch potential, made 37% of his career threes at Minnesota, stroke still inconsistent, middling free throw shooter
- Lacks advanced post moves, limited as a passer, effective at avoiding turnovers
- Effective rim protector, good length and timing, very good defensive rebounder and shot blocker
- Strong post defenders that can push opposing big men off the block, showed improving discipline
- Good at taking away the screener in drop coverages in pick-and-roll situations, consistently comes out to contest perimeter shots
- Ability to defend in space is uncertain, rarely asked to switch onto a perimeter player in college
- Flashed decent lateral mobility in a small sample of possessions

UTAH JAZZ

Last Season: 44 – 28, Lost 1st Round to Denver (3 – 4)

Offensive Rating: 112.3, 10th in the NBA

Defensive Rating: 109.9, 13th in the NBA

Primary Executive: Dennis Lindsey, Executive Vice President of Basketball Operations

Head Coach: Quin Snyder

Key Roster Changes

Subtractions
Ed Davis, trade
Tony Bradley, trade
Rayjon Tucker, trade
Emmanuel Mudiay, free agency
Juwan Morgan, free agency

Additions
Udoka Azubuike, draft
Elijah Hughes, draft
Derrick Favors, free agency

Roster

Likely Starting Five

1. *Mike Conley*
2. *Donovan Mitchell*
3. *Joe Ingles*
4. Royce O'Neale
5. *Rudy Gobert*

Other Key Rotation Players
Bojan Bogdanovic
Derrick Favors
Jordan Clarkson

* Italics denotes that a player is likely to be on the floor to close games

Remaining Roster

- Georges Niang
- Udoka Azubuike
- Miye Oni
- Nigel Williams-Goss
- Elijah Hughes
- Jarrell Brantley, 24, 6'5", 250, College of Charleston (Two-Way)
- Trent Forrest, 22, 6'4", 210, Florida State (Two-Way)
- Jake Toolson, 24, 6'5", 205, BYU (Exhibit 10)
- Trevon Bluiett, 26, 6'6", 198, Xavier (Exhibit 10)
- Romaro Gill, 26, 7'2", 255, Seton Hall (Exhibit 10)

SCHREMPF Base Rating: 40.9 (72-game season)

Strengths

- Efficient shooting team that can spread the floor around Mitchell and Gobert
- Elite rim protection and sound defensive structure should allow them to consistently get stops

Question Marks

- Depth beyond their top eight players
- Lacking in quality front-end talent to compete with the other contenders in the West

Outlook

- Strong continuity should allow them to be a solid playoff team, will likely finish with a top four or five seed

Veterans

Donovan Mitchell

Height	Weight	Cap #	Years Left
6'1"	215	$5.196M	5

Similar at Age 23

		Season	SIMsc
1	Isaiah Rider	1994-95	915.9
2	Bradley Beal	2016-17	912.9
3	Ben Gordon	2006-07	910.2
4	Reggie Jackson	2013-14	892.9
5	Jordan Crawford	2011-12	886.6
6	Ray Allen*	1998-99	886.0
7	Rashad McCants	2007-08	884.9
8	Kyrie Irving	2015-16	884.2
9	Gilbert Arenas	2004-05	883.4
10	Damian Lillard	2013-14	882.4

Baseline Basic Stats

MPG	PTS	AST	REB	BLK	STL
33.2	20.6	4.1	3.6	0.3	1.0

Advanced Metrics

USG%	3PTA/FGA	FTA/FGA	TS%	eFG%	3PT%
29.5	0.365	0.266	0.566	0.518	0.379
AST%	**TOV%**	**OREB%**	**DREB%**	**STL%**	**BLK%**
22.2	11.2	2.4	10.4	1.6	0.7
PER	**ORTG**	**DRTG**	**WS/48**	**VOL**	
19.36	111.0	110.1	0.115	0.290	

- Made his first All-Star team in his third NBA season
- Production increased, excelled as Utah's primary scorer and ball handler
- Good isolation player and pick-and-roll handler, can create offense for himself and others
- Good at making pull-up jumpers and getting to the rim to get layups or draw fouls
- Solid playmaker that hits the roll man and finds outside shooters, consistently limits turnovers
- Solid three-point shooter that makes spot-up jumpers, can also shoot off screens
- Gets to the rim on dribble hand-offs, good at making backdoor cuts to catch defenders off guard
- 2019-20 Defensive Degree of Difficulty: 0.414, tends to guard starting level guards
- Solid on-ball defender, good against opposing guards, taller wings can shoot over him in the post
- Average pick-and-roll defender, gets caught on the screen when defending the ball handler
- Also gets caught on screens off the ball, tends to be either late or too aggressive when closing out on perimeter shooters
- Solid defensive rebounder, Steal and Block Percentages were down from his career averages

Rudy Gobert	Height	Weight	Cap #	Years Left
	7'1"	245	$27.525M	UFA

Similar at Age **27**

		Season	SIMsc
1	Dikembe Mutombo*	1993-94	914.0
2	DeAndre Jordan	2015-16	897.4
3	Hassan Whiteside	2016-17	889.7
4	Dwight Howard	2012-13	885.1
5	Alton Lister	1985-86	879.1
6	Timofey Mozgov	2013-14	877.9
7	Emeka Okafor	2009-10	877.7
8	Rasho Nesterovic	2003-04	875.8
9	Vlade Divac*	1995-96	872.0
10	Marcin Gortat	2011-12	860.4

Baseline Basic Stats

MPG	PTS	AST	REB	BLK	STL
31.0	12.1	1.2	11.3	2.1	0.6

Advanced Metrics

USG%	3PTA/FGA	FTA/FGA	TS%	eFG%	3PT%
16.4	0.001	0.652	0.655	0.640	0.129

AST%	TOV%	OREB%	DREB%	STL%	BLK%
7.1	15.1	11.9	30.0	1.0	4.8

PER	ORTG	DRTG	WS/48	VOL
20.77	124.8	102.0	0.207	0.382

- Made his first All-Star team last season, named to the All-Defensive 1st Team and All-NBA 3rd Team in 2019-20
- Maintained his usual level of production in his role as a low volume rim runner
- Draws fouls at a very high rate, made 75.5% of his shot inside of three feet last season
- Vertical lob threat that excels as a roll man and cutter off the ball
- Good offensive rebounder that efficiently scores on put-backs, runs hard down the floor in transition
- Good at flashing to the middle in the post against smaller players
- No real shooting range outside of three feet, limited passing skills, slightly turnover prone
- 2019-20 Defensive Degree of Difficulty: 0.457
- Usually guards other starting big men, takes on tougher big man matchups
- One of the league's best rim protectors, excellent rebounder, great shot blocker, Block Percentage is down from his career average
- Good on-ball defender, holds position inside when playing post defense, mobile enough to defend big men in space
- Solid at guarding pick-and-rolls, good in drop coverages, solid at switching onto ball handlers for a few dribbles
- Generally closed out on perimeter shooters in spot-up situations

Joe Ingles

	Height	Weight	Cap #	Years Left
Joe Ingles	6'7"	226	$10.864M	1

Similar at Age 32

		Season	SIMsc
1	Kyle Korver	2013-14	920.9
2	Rick Fox	2001-02	917.0
3	J.R. Smith	2017-18	912.7
4	Dan Majerle	1997-98	902.9
5	Hedo Turkoglu	2011-12	901.4
6	Anthony Parker	2007-08	898.1
7	Shane Battier	2010-11	888.2
8	Alan Anderson	2014-15	887.5
9	Jose Calderon	2013-14	886.2
10	Wesley Matthews	2018-19	885.4

Baseline Basic Stats

MPG	PTS	AST	REB	BLK	STL
24.9	7.8	2.9	3.5	0.2	0.7

Advanced Metrics

USG%	3PTA/FGA	FTA/FGA	TS%	eFG%	3PT%
14.7	0.629	0.177	0.570	0.548	0.373
AST%	**TOV%**	**OREB%**	**DREB%**	**STL%**	**BLK%**
21.4	18.5	1.7	13.4	1.5	0.6
PER	**ORTG**	**DRTG**	**WS/48**	**VOL**	
11.63	109.6	108.0	0.100	0.462	

- Regular starter for Utah for most of last season
- Maintained his effectiveness as a low volume shooter and ball handler
- Has made almost 41% of his career threes, good spot-up shooter that can also shoot off screens
- Good at making outside shots on dribble hand-offs, can set up for trail threes in transition
- Good pick-and-roll ball handler, makes pull-up jumpers, can occasionally get to the rim
- Very good secondary playmaker that hits cutters and finds open shooters, somewhat turnover prone
- 2019-20 Defensive Degree of Difficulty: 0.450
- Tends to guard starting level players, occasionally takes on tougher defensive assignments
- Solid on-ball defender that can guard multiple positions
- Good team defender that makes sound rotations, stays attached to shooters off the ball, consistently contests perimeter shots
- Good pick-and-roll defender, can guard ball handlers and switch onto screeners
- Solid defensive rebounder, Steal Percentage has been steadily declining for the last few seasons, Block Percentage is still consistent with his career average

Mike Conley	Height	Weight	Cap #	Years Left
	6'1"	175	$34.502M	UFA

Similar at Age 32

		Season	SIMsc
1	Bobby Jackson	2005-06	935.5
2	Mo Williams	2014-15	928.6
3	Goran Dragic	2018-19	920.7
4	Jason Terry	2009-10	918.8
5	John Starks	1997-98	916.1
6	Nick Van Exel	2003-04	915.6
7	Jannero Pargo	2011-12	914.5
8	Chris Paul	2017-18	912.3
9	Mark Price	1996-97	911.0
10	Tony Parker	2014-15	910.4

Baseline Basic Stats

MPG	PTS	AST	REB	BLK	STL
25.3	12.2	4.1	2.5	0.1	0.9

Advanced Metrics

USG%	3PTA/FGA	FTA/FGA	TS%	eFG%	3PT%
23.0	0.434	0.254	0.535	0.489	0.355
AST%	**TOV%**	**OREB%**	**DREB%**	**STL%**	**BLK%**
27.1	12.9	2.1	9.5	1.6	0.5
PER	**ORTG**	**DRTG**	**WS/48**	**VOL**	
15.31	108.1	110.0	0.090	0.386	

- Mostly a starter for Utah when healthy, missed games due to a left hamstring injury and a sore right knee
- Production declined in his role as a moderate volume, secondary ball handler
- Good three-point shooter throughout his career, good spot-up shooter
- Can make pull-up jumpers as a pick-and-roll ball handler and isolation player
- Less effective as a pick-and-roll ball handler overall, couldn't consistently turn the corner, got to the rim less frequently, drew fewer fouls
- Solid at using an on-ball screen to get an extra step to the rim on dribble hand-offs
- Solid playmaker that can find open shooters or hit cutters, good at avoiding turnovers
- 2019-20 Defensive Degree of Difficulty: 0.387
- Tends to guard higher-end second unit players or lower leverage starters
- Solid on-ball defender that can defend both guard spots
- Played below average pick-and-roll defense, had trouble getting around the screen, not really effective when making rotations
- Stays attached to shooters off the ball, good at closing out on spot-up shooters
- Decent defensive rebounder, Steal Percentage has declined sharply

Royce O'Neale

Height	Weight	Cap #	Years Left
6'4"	226	$8.500M	3

Similar at Age **26**

		Season	SIMsc
1	Iman Shumpert	2016-17	911.1
2	Joe Harris	2017-18	903.9
3	Quincy Pondexter	2014-15	895.0
4	Thabo Sefolosha	2010-11	892.5
5	Keith Bogans	2006-07	890.5
6	Kyle Singler	2014-15	890.1
7	Austin Rivers	2018-19	887.9
8	Pat Connaughton	2018-19	886.5
9	Eric Gordon	2014-15	884.3
10	Morris Peterson	2003-04	879.4

Baseline Basic Stats

MPG	PTS	AST	REB	BLK	STL
24.9	8.3	1.7	3.4	0.2	0.8

Advanced Metrics

USG%	3PTA/FGA	FTA/FGA	TS%	eFG%	3PT%
12.9	0.568	0.193	0.571	0.541	0.385

AST%	TOV%	OREB%	DREB%	STL%	BLK%
10.5	12.5	2.3	15.2	1.5	1.0

PER	ORTG	DRTG	WS/48	VOL
10.80	113.2	108.1	0.101	0.337

- Full-time starter for Utah in his third NBA season
- Used on offense as a very low volume, spot-up shooter, made almost 38% of his threes in 2019-20
- Strictly a stationary spot-up shooter, does not shoot on the move or off the dribble
- Good at making back-door cuts to catch defenders off guard
- Not really effective in other offensive situations last season
- Unselfish, will make the extra pass to find open shooters, fairly solid at avoiding turnovers
- 2019-20 Defensive Degree of Difficulty: 0.556
- Had the 8th toughest set of matchups among players that played 500 or more minutes
- Good on-ball defender that has the versatility to guard multiple positions
- Fairly solid at guarding pick-and-rolls, good at guarding ball handlers, tends to be late to rotate back to cover the roll man
- Stays attached to shooters off the ball, consistently contests shots in spot-up situations
- Good defensive rebounder, Steal and Block Percentages are consistent with his career averages

Bojan Bogdanović	Height	Weight	Cap #	Years Left
	6'8"	216	$17.850M	2

Similar at Age 30

		Season	SIMsc
1	Eric Piatkowski	2000-01	933.8
2	Joe Johnson	2011-12	924.7
3	Peja Stojakovic	2007-08	919.1
4	Chuck Person	1994-95	914.2
5	Richard Jefferson	2010-11	914.1
6	Glen Rice	1997-98	912.7
7	Walt Williams	2000-01	911.8
8	Eddie A. Johnson	1989-90	911.2
9	Rashard Lewis	2009-10	910.7
10	Luol Deng	2015-16	910.1

Baseline Basic Stats

MPG	PTS	AST	REB	BLK	STL
30.3	14.2	2.0	4.0	0.2	0.7

Advanced Metrics

USG%	3PTA/FGA	FTA/FGA	TS%	eFG%	3PT%
22.0	0.411	0.258	0.577	0.534	0.398
AST%	**TOV%**	**OREB%**	**DREB%**	**STL%**	**BLK%**
9.7	10.8	2.4	12.4	1.1	0.4
PER	**ORTG**	**DRTG**	**WS/48**	**VOL**	
14.85	110.8	109.4	0.100	0.296	

- Regular starter for Utah in his first season with the team, missed the Orlando restart due to right wrist surgery
- Effective in his role as a fairly high volume shooter off the ball, has made over 40% of his threes in each of the last three seasons
- Very good spot-up shooter that can also shoot off screens, solid at making no dribble jumpers on isolation plays
- Moves well off the ball, excels as a roll man and cutter, occasionally crashes the offensive glass to score on put-backs
- Can post-up smaller players, decent passer, consistently limits turnovers
- 2019-20 Defensive Degree of Difficulty: 0.393
- Tends to be hidden in favorable matchups against lower leverage players
- Played fairly solid on-ball defense, good against perimeter players, bigger post players could back him down inside
- Average pick-and-roll defender, good at containing ball handlers, tended to late to rotate back to the roll man
- Good at closing out on perimeter shooters, tends to get caught on screens off the ball
- Stay-at-home defender, does not really get steals or blocks, fairly solid defensive rebounder

Derrick Favors

	Height	Weight	Cap #	Years Left
Derrick Favors	6'9"	265	$9.258M	1 + PO

	Similar at Age	28 Season	SIMsc
1	Nick Collison	2008-09	903.8
2	Kosta Koufos	2017-18	900.5
3	Jason Maxiell	2011-12	897.3
4	Brian Skinner	2004-05	895.5
5	Kris Humphries	2013-14	892.4
6	Emeka Okafor	2010-11	891.4
7	Etan Thomas	2006-07	890.4
8	Erick Dampier	2003-04	888.6
9	Gary Trent	2002-03	883.3
10	Marcin Gortat	2012-13	882.0

Baseline Basic Stats

MPG	PTS	AST	REB	BLK	STL
21.9	7.0	0.8	6.2	0.8	0.5

Advanced Metrics

USG%	3PTA/FGA	FTA/FGA	TS%	eFG%	3PT%
14.9	0.032	0.288	0.579	0.564	0.173

AST%	TOV%	OREB%	DREB%	STL%	BLK%
7.4	13.2	11.7	23.5	1.1	3.3

PER	ORTG	DRTG	WS/48	VOL
15.98	116.7	105.6	0.139	0.292

- Regular starter for New Orleans when healthy, missed some games due to lower back spasms
- Primarily a lower volume rim runner, made over 70% of his shots inside of three feet last season
- Good at sliding into open spaces inside as a cutter and roll man
- Great offensive rebounder that can score on put-backs, high motor, runs hard down the floor in transition
- Decent post-up player on a small sample of possessions, can back down weaker defenders on the left block
- Decent passing big man, consistently limits turnovers
- 2019-20 Defensive Degree of Difficulty: 0.459
- Tends to guard starting level big men, draws tougher assignments against top centers
- Very good rim protector, fairly good shot blocker, excellent defensive rebounder
- Fairly solid on-ball defender, good at defending in space on isolations, average post defender, stronger big men can get deep position on him
- Solid pick-and-roll defender, good in drop coverages, effective at switching onto ball handlers
- Fairly good at coming out to contest perimeter shots

Jordan Clarkson	Height	Weight	Cap #	Years Left
	6'4"	194	$11.500M	2 + PO

	Similar at Age	27 Season	SIMsc
1	CJ McCollum	2018-19	954.1
2	Dell Curry	1991-92	935.0
3	Marco Belinelli	2013-14	930.7
4	Voshon Lenard	2000-01	926.7
5	J.J. Redick	2011-12	926.2
6	Ben Gordon	2010-11	925.8
7	Gary Neal	2011-12	922.0
8	E'Twaun Moore	2016-17	921.6
9	Rex Chapman	1994-95	919.4
10	Terrence Ross	2018-19	917.6

Baseline Basic Stats

MPG	PTS	AST	REB	BLK	STL
28.0	13.6	2.5	2.9	0.2	0.8

Advanced Metrics

USG%	3PTA/FGA	FTA/FGA	TS%	eFG%	3PT%
24.0	0.446	0.186	0.546	0.513	0.360
AST%	**TOV%**	**OREB%**	**DREB%**	**STL%**	**BLK%**
14.8	10.0	2.8	9.4	1.4	0.6
PER	**ORTG**	**DRTG**	**WS/48**	**VOL**	
15.40	108.0	112.5	0.079	0.288	

- Traded from Cleveland to Utah in December 2019, regular rotation player for both teams
- Had a career best season in a role as a high volume, scoring guard off the bench
- Good three-point shooter, makes spot-up jumpers, can shoot off screens
- Effective at creating his own offense as a pick-and-roll ball handler and isolation player
- Good at using an on-ball screen to get to the rim or make outside shots on dribble hand-offs
- Does not really move off the ball when he's not directly involved in the play, rarely looks to cut off the ball
- Decent secondary playmaker that can hit cutters, good at avoiding turnovers
- 2019-20 Defensive Degree of Difficulty: 0.340, tends to guard second unit players
- Below average on-ball defender, has trouble staying with quicker guards in isolation situations
- Average at guarding pick-and-rolls, tends to go too far under screens to allow open shots
- Fairly good at closing out on perimeter shooters, sometimes gets caught on screens off the ball
- Stay-at-home defender, decent defensive rebounder, Steal Percentage has been below his career average for the last three seasons

Georges Niang

	Height	Weight	Cap #	Years Left
	6'7"	230	$1.784M	UFA

Similar at Age **26**

		Season	SIMsc
1	Sam Mack	1996-97	929.0
2	Cartier Martin	2010-11	920.1
3	Quincy Acy	2016-17	917.9
4	Joe Harris	2017-18	915.9
5	Dennis Scott	1994-95	913.3
6	Mike Scott	2014-15	912.9
7	Kyle Singler	2014-15	911.2
8	Chase Budinger	2014-15	909.4
9	Allen Crabbe	2018-19	909.0
10	Luke Babbitt	2015-16	908.3

Baseline Basic Stats

MPG	PTS	AST	REB	BLK	STL
20.4	7.6	1.1	2.9	0.2	0.5

Advanced Metrics

USG%	3PTA/FGA	FTA/FGA	TS%	eFG%	3PT%
17.1	0.590	0.136	0.559	0.539	0.370
AST%	**TOV%**	**OREB%**	**DREB%**	**STL%**	**BLK%**
8.6	10.5	2.9	13.6	1.2	0.8
PER	**ORTG**	**DRTG**	**WS/48**	**VOL**	
11.48	108.0	109.9	0.086	0.323	

- Regular rotation player for Utah in his fourth NBA season
- Used as a low volume, spot-up shooter, made 40% of his threes last season
- Mostly a stationary spot-up shooter, can occasionally shoot off screens
- Rated as average or worse in the other offensive categories last season
- Does not really create his own offense or move off the ball
- Flashed some passing skills in previous seasons, rarely turned the ball over in 2019-20
- 2019-20 Defensive Degree of Difficulty: 0.275
- Tended to be hidden in favorable matchups against lower leverage second unit players
- Below average on-ball defender, struggles to stay with quicker perimeter players, better against bigger players in the post
- Below average when guarding pick-and-rolls, has trouble defending in space against ball handlers, decent in drop coverages
- Gets caught on screens off the ball, good at closing out on perimeter shooters in spot-up situations
- Stay-at-home defender, fairly solid defensive rebounder, does not really get steals or blocks

Miye Oni	Height	Weight	Cap #	Years Left
	6'5"	206	$1.518M	1

Similar at Age 22

		Season	SIMsc
1	Donte DiVincenzo	2018-19	941.2
2	Davon Reed	2017-18	926.5
3	Shake Milton	2018-19	926.3
4	Malachi Richardson	2017-18	924.8
5	R.J. Hunter	2015-16	922.8
6	Reggie Bullock	2013-14	921.6
7	Iman Shumpert	2012-13	921.3
8	Danny Green	2009-10	920.9
9	Malcolm Lee	2012-13	916.7
10	Sterling Brown	2017-18	913.3

Baseline Basic Stats

MPG	PTS	AST	REB	BLK	STL
19.2	7.1	1.2	2.7	0.2	0.6

Advanced Metrics

USG%	3PTA/FGA	FTA/FGA	TS%	eFG%	3PT%
16.2	0.543	0.189	0.547	0.515	0.375

AST%	TOV%	OREB%	DREB%	STL%	BLK%
7.2	11.0	3.8	12.0	1.8	1.0

PER	ORTG	DRTG	WS/48	VOL
11.26	107.8	109.6	0.092	0.497

- Saw limited action in his rookie season with Utah, spent most of 2019-20 in the G-League with the Salt Lake City Stars
- Used as a low volume, spot-up shooter in the NBA, played a slightly higher volume role in the G-League
- Above average three-point shooter at both levels, mainly a spot-up shooter at this stage
- Effective at getting to the rim or making outside shots on dribble hand-offs in a small sample of possessions
- Struggles to shoot on the move or off the dribble, flashes some ability to cut off the ball
- Fairly good secondary playmaker in the G-League, slightly turnover prone
- 2019-20 Defensive Degree of Difficulty: 0.352, mostly guarded second unit level players
- Played below average on-ball defense, struggled to stay with quicker guards, bigger wings could post him up inside
- Struggled to make rotations when guarding pick-and-rolls, allowed 23 points in 20 possessions
- Sometimes got caught on screens off the ball, solid at closing out on perimeter shooters
- Fairly good defensive rebounder, got steals and blocks at a decent rate in limited NBA minutes

Nigel Williams-Goss	Height	Weight	Cap #	Years Left
	6'2"	190	$1.518M	1

	Similar at Age	25	
		Season	SIMsc
1	Ronnie Price	2008-09	904.2
2	Toney Douglas	2011-12	898.2
3	Lester Hudson	2009-10	897.5
4	Rusty LaRue	1998-99	892.8
5	Jimmer Fredette	2014-15	890.9
6	Sedric Toney	1987-88	887.5
7	Jaren Jackson	1992-93	885.2
8	Dan Dickau	2003-04	883.8
9	A.J. Price	2011-12	883.1
10	Anthony Johnson	1999-00	882.6

Baseline Basic Stats

MPG	PTS	AST	REB	BLK	STL
14.1	4.8	1.7	1.4	0.1	0.7

Advanced Metrics

USG%	3PTA/FGA	FTA/FGA	TS%	eFG%	3PT%
17.1	0.447	0.158	0.479	0.442	0.342
AST%	**TOV%**	**OREB%**	**DREB%**	**STL%**	**BLK%**
17.3	14.7	3.8	8.3	2.5	1.0
PER	**ORTG**	**DRTG**	**WS/48**	**VOL**	
10.24	100.5	109.1	0.046	0.425	

- Played sparingly for Utah in his rookie season, spent most of 2019-20 in the G-League with the Salt Lake City Stars
- Utilized as a lower volume, secondary ball handler at the NBA level, used in a higher usage role in the G-League
- Solid playmaker at both levels, slightly turnover prone in limited NBA action
- Made just over 35% of his threes in the G-League, posted a True Shooting Percentage over 61%, struggled to shoot efficiently at the NBA level
- Not yet proven to be effective in any particular situation in limited NBA minutes
- 2019-20 Defensive Degree of Difficulty: 0.163, only played 50 NBA minutes
- Allowed four points in four one-on-one situations, better against guards in isolation situations, had trouble guarding a bigger wing in his only post-up possession
- Struggled to make rotations when guarding pick-and-rolls, allowed 13 points in nine possessions
- Allowed two made threes and forced a miss in three spot-up possessions
- Forced a miss in his only possession when guarding a shooter coming off a screen
- Steal rates were pretty high at both levels, solid defensive rebounder in the G-League, recorded one block in 50 minutes at the NBA level

Newcomers

Udoka Azubuike

Height	Weight	Cap #	Years Left
7'0"	270	$1.977M	1 + 2 TO

Baseline Basic Stats

MPG	PTS	AST	REB	BLK	STL
18.7	6.2	0.6	4.9	1.1	0.3

Advanced Metrics

USG%	3PTA/FGA	FTA/FGA	TS%	eFG%	3PT%
16.1	0.005	0.409	0.534	0.513	0.137

AST%	TOV%	OREB%	DREB%	STL%	BLK%
4.9	15.9	10.6	18.9	0.9	4.7

PER	ORTG	DRTG	WS/48	VOL
14.09	101.9	97.0	0.070	N/A

- Drafted by Utah with the 27th overall pick
- Consensus 2nd Team All-American, named Big 12 Player of the Year in 2019-20
- Good rim runner, plays with a high motor, has good hands, dives hard to the rim as a roll man and cutter
- Led the NCAA in Effective Field Goal Percentage last season, very good offensive rebounder
- Big body center, gets deep position on post-ups, bullies weaker defender inside
- Lacks advanced post moves, fairly turnover prone, has limited passing skills
- Has no shooting range beyond the immediate basket area, poor free throw shooter throughout his career at Kansas
- Space eating big man, wide body allows him to clog the lane, keeps opponents off the block as a post defender
- Solid rim protector, has great length and solid timing, great shot blocker, good defensive rebounder
- Somewhat immobile, struggles to defend in space, not really effective at guarding pick-and-rolls
- Tends to stay in the paint, does not always come out to contest perimeter shots

Elijah Hughes

Height	Weight	Cap #	Years Left
6'6"	215	$0.898M	1

Baseline Basic Stats

MPG	PTS	AST	REB	BLK	STL
18.7	6.7	1.4	2.5	0.2	0.6

Advanced Metrics

USG%	3PTA/FGA	FTA/FGA	TS%	eFG%	3PT%
17.3	0.363	0.220	0.507	0.475	0.325

AST%	TOV%	OREB%	DREB%	STL%	BLK%
12.9	12.2	2.9	11.1	1.6	1.0

PER	ORTG	DRTG	WS/48	VOL
11.43	100.4	105.8	0.022	N/A

- Drafted by New Orleans with the 39th overall pick, traded to Utah
- Made the All-ACC 1st Team in 2019-20
- Above average shooter at Syracuse, mainly a spot-up shooter, less effective when shooting on the move
- Good at making backdoor cuts when defenders try to crowd him
- Does not quite have the quickness or ball handling skills to create his own offense at the NBA level
- Drew more fouls as a junior, tended to struggle to get all the way to the rim, average shooter off the dribble
- More of a secondary playmaker, better at making simple reads, does not really see the whole floor
- Defense tougher to project, played mostly zone defense in two seasons at Syracuse
- Solid on-ball defender in his freshman year at East Carolina, showed decent length and quickness to stay with opposing perimeter players
- Middling team defender, tends to get caught ball watching, gambles too much when going for steals
- Solid help defender, gets steals and blocks at a high rate, pretty good defensive rebounder for his size

HOUSTON ROCKETS

Last Season: 44 – 28, Lost 2nd Round to L.A. Lakers (1 – 4)

Offensive Rating: 112.9, 6th in the NBA

Defensive Rating: 110.1, 14th in the NBA

Primary Executive: Rafael Stone, General Counsel and General Manager

Head Coach: Stephen Silas

Key Roster Changes

Subtractions
Robert Covington, trade
Russell Westbrook, trade
Austin Rivers, sign-and-trade
Jeff Green, free agency
Tyson Chandler, free agency
Thabo Sefolosha, free agency
DeMarre Carroll, free agency
Luc Mbah a Moute, free agency

Additions
Kenyon Martin, Jr., draft
John Wall, trade
Christian Wood, trade
Sterling Brown, free agency
DeMarcus Cousins, free agency
Jae'Sean Tate, free agency
Gerald Green, free agency

Roster

Likely Starting Five

1. *John Wall*
2. *James Harden*
3. Danuel House
4. *P.J. Tucker*
5. *Christian Wood*

Other Key Rotation Players
Eric Gordon
Ben McLemore
Sterling Brown
DeMarcus Cousins

* Italics denotes that a player is likely to be on the floor to close games

Remaining Roster

- David Nwaba
- Bruno Caboclo
- Gerald Green
- Chris Clemons
- Jae'Sean Tate
- Kenyon Martin, Jr.
- Mason Jones, 22, 6'5", 200, Arkansas (Two-Way)
- Kenny Wooten, 22, 6'9", 235, Oregon (Two-Way)
- Jerian Grant, 28, 6'4", 205, Notre Dame (Exhibit 10)
- Brodric Thomas, age unknown, 6'5", 185, Truman State (Exhibit 10)
- Trevelin Queen, 23, 6'6", 190, New Mexico State (Exhibit 10)

SCHREMPF Base Rating: 39.3 (72-game season)

Strengths

- High-powered offense that features the dominant scoring of Harden and solid complementary shooting
- Improved ability to match up with opponents with differing style with the addition of Christian Wood

Question Marks

- The capacity for the team to balance their typical isolation-heavy offense with more movement
- Depth beyond their top seven players and ability to manage distractions related to internal issues

Outlook

- Top eight seed in the West as currently constructed, could be headed for the lottery if the Harden is traded

Veterans

James Harden	Height	Weight	Cap #	Years Left
	6'5"	220	$41.255M	1 + PO

	Similar at Age	30 Season	SIMsc
1	Manu Ginobili	2007-08	882.8
2	LeBron James	2014-15	860.3
3	Mitch Richmond	1995-96	857.6
4	Paul Pierce	2007-08	852.2
5	Vince Carter	2006-07	837.3
6	Kobe Bryant*	2008-09	836.8
7	Baron Davis	2009-10	833.2
8	Magic Johnson*	1989-90	833.2
9	Dwyane Wade	2011-12	830.3
10	Ray Allen*	2005-06	827.8

Baseline Basic Stats

MPG	PTS	AST	REB	BLK	STL
35.8	24.7	5.8	5.4	0.6	1.5

Advanced Metrics

USG%	3PTA/FGA	FTA/FGA	TS%	eFG%	3PT%
33.6	0.421	0.443	0.598	0.526	0.352
AST%	**TOV%**	**OREB%**	**DREB%**	**STL%**	**BLK%**
32.9	13.7	3.0	15.6	2.2	1.6
PER	**ORTG**	**DRTG**	**WS/48**	**VOL**	
26.19	116.1	106.7	0.207	0.349	

- Led the NBA in Win Shares in five of the last six seasons, named to the All-NBA 1st team last season
- Excelled in his role as Houston's primary ball handler, great playmaker, good at limiting turnovers
- Led the NBA in points scored on isolation plays by a wide margin, arguably the NBA's best isolation player
- Very good pick-and-roll ball handler, draws fouls at a high rate, excellent at scoring on dribble hand-offs
- Good spot-up shooter that made threes at around the league average, led the NBA in Three-Point Attempts for the last three seasons
- Rarely moves without the ball, good cutter off the ball in a small sample of possessions
- 2019-20 NBA Degree of Difficulty: 0.423, tends to guard starter level players
- Improved to become a solid on-ball defender, defends both guard spots, can handle taller wings
- Solid pick-and-roll defender, can fight over screens to contain ball handlers, fairly good at switching
- Closes out on perimeter shooters, sometimes can get caught on screens off the ball
- Solid defensive rebounder, consistently gets steals at a high rate, posted a career high in Block Percentage last season

John Wall	Height	Weight	Cap #	Years Left
	6'4"	195	$41.255M	1 + PO

	Similar at Age	29	
		Season	SIMsc
1	Jamaal Tinsley	2007-08	901.3
2	Baron Davis	2008-09	877.4
3	Flip Murray	2008-09	875.1
4	Gilbert Arenas	2010-11	873.6
5	Jason Kidd*	2002-03	868.8
6	Paul Westphal*	1979-80	868.7
7	Ben Gordon	2012-13	868.3
8	Darrell Griffith	1987-88	866.0
9	Rod Strickland	1995-96	863.9
10	Aaron McKie	2001-02	860.7

Baseline Basic Stats

MPG	PTS	AST	REB	BLK	STL
30.8	15.4	6.2	3.4	0.4	1.3

Advanced Metrics

USG%	3PTA/FGA	FTA/FGA	TS%	eFG%	3PT%
26.1	0.278	0.310	0.514	0.468	0.320
AST%	**TOV%**	**OREB%**	**DREB%**	**STL%**	**BLK%**
35.7	16.0	2.0	10.1	2.1	1.6
PER	**ORTG**	**DRTG**	**WS/48**	**VOL**	
16.94	104.2	109.0	0.087	0.564	

- Missed most of the last two seasons due to a torn left Achilles tendon
- Missed most of 2017-18 due to a left knee injury that required surgery
- Dynamic, All-Star level, high volume ball handler if healthy
- Great playmaker that can find open shooters or make interior passes, slightly turnover prone
- Uses quickness to drive by defenders on isolation plays or on pick-and-rolls, draw fouls at a fairly high rate
- Below break-even three-point shooter throughout his career, percentages tend to fluctuate from year-to-year
- 2018-19 Defensive Degree of Difficulty: 0.504
- Took on tougher defensive assignments when he last played in the NBA
- Solid on-ball defender that can defend both guard spots, sometimes gives up too much space for his man to take jump shots
- Middling pick-and-roll defender, decent at switching onto screeners, has trouble defending opposing ball handlers
- Fights through screens off the ball, tends to be late when closing out on perimeter shooters
- Active help defender, solid defensive rebounder, gets steals and blocks at a fairly high rate

Christian Wood	Height	Weight	Cap #	Years Left
	6'10"	214	$13.016M	2

Similar at Age 24

		Season	SIMsc
1	Jon Leuer	2013-14	888.3
2	Carlos Rogers	1995-96	883.6
3	Keith Lee	1986-87	877.7
4	Tyrus Thomas	2010-11	876.8
5	Derrick Coleman	1991-92	876.3
6	Brad Branson	1982-83	873.9
7	Travis Outlaw	2008-09	873.4
8	Pervis Ellison	1991-92	872.1
9	Ed Davis	2013-14	870.6
10	James Bailey	1981-82	870.3

Baseline Basic Stats

MPG	PTS	AST	REB	BLK	STL
23.9	10.7	1.3	5.9	0.8	0.7

Advanced Metrics

USG%	3PTA/FGA	FTA/FGA	TS%	eFG%	3PT%
21.5	0.223	0.381	0.591	0.551	0.349
AST%	**TOV%**	**OREB%**	**DREB%**	**STL%**	**BLK%**
8.4	11.5	7.9	22.3	1.4	2.7
PER	**ORTG**	**DRTG**	**WS/48**	**VOL**	
19.21	114.8	107.2	0.154	0.408	

- Regular rotation player for Detroit last season, became a starter after Andre Drummond was traded in February 2020
- Thrived as a moderate volume, rim runner and stretch big, had his most productive season in the NBA
- Provides a vertical threat to catch lobs, effective at rolling to the rim and cutting off the ball
- Runs hard down the floor in transition, good at crashing the offensive boards to score on put-backs
- Became a good spot-up shooter, effective as the screener on pick-and-pop plays, made almost 39% of his threes last season
- Improved as a passer, set a career high in Assist Percentage, solid at limiting turnovers
- 2019-20 Defensive Degree of Difficulty: 0.373
- Guarded higher-end second unit players or lower leverage starters, played a rim protector role
- Good at protecting the rim, good shot blocker and rebounder
- Fairly solid on-ball defender, good at using his length to contest shots in the post
- Can be too aggressive when defending in space on isolations, can give up driving lanes to the rim
- Solid pick-and-roll defender, good in drop coverages, mobile enough to switch onto ball handlers
- Tends to sag into the paint, does not always come out to contest perimeter shots

P.J. Tucker

Height	Weight	Cap #	Years Left
6'5"	245	$7.970M	UFA

Similar at Age **34**

		Season	SIMsc
1	Matt Barnes	2014-15	893.1
2	Dan Majerle	1999-00	887.2
3	Anthony Parker	2009-10	866.8
4	Kyle Korver	2015-16	853.1
5	Caron Butler	2014-15	837.6
6	Wes Unseld*	1980-81	835.9
7	Brian Cardinal	2011-12	832.3
8	Raja Bell	2010-11	832.2
9	Shane Battier	2012-13	831.3
10	Bryon Russell	2004-05	830.6

Baseline Basic Stats

MPG	PTS	AST	REB	BLK	STL
25.8	7.2	1.7	4.1	0.3	0.9

Advanced Metrics

USG%	3PTA/FGA	FTA/FGA	TS%	eFG%	3PT%
10.8	0.693	0.132	0.546	0.526	0.363
AST%	**TOV%**	**OREB%**	**DREB%**	**STL%**	**BLK%**
7.4	12.4	4.3	15.6	1.7	1.3
PER	**ORTG**	**DRTG**	**WS/48**	**VOL**	
9.42	111.4	109.2	0.084	0.488	

- Full-time starter for Houston last season, posted the highest True Shooting Percentage of his career in 2019-20
- Utilized as a very low volume spot-up shooter, made threes at just above the league average last season
- Much better at shooting in the corners, has made 38% of his corner threes in his career
- Limited to being a stationary spot-up shooter, rated as average or worse in every other offensive situation
- Has limited passing skills, sticks to making safe passes on the perimeter, does not really turn the ball over
- 2019-20 Defensive Degree of Difficulty: 0.471
- Tends to guard starting level players, will take on tougher defensive assignments
- Good on-ball defender that can guard big men and perimeter players
- Average pick-and-roll defender, good at guarding the screener, has some trouble staying with ball handlers on the perimeter
- Good at closing out on shooters in spot-up situations, tends to get caught on screens off the ball
- Block Percentage has held steady, Steal Percentage dropped last season, fairly solid defensive rebounder

Danuel House

Height	Weight	Cap #	Years Left
6'6"	215	$3.717M	1

Similar at Age **26**

		Season	SIMsc
1	Iman Shumpert	2016-17	936.5
2	Mickael Pietrus	2008-09	936.0
3	Quincy Pondexter	2014-15	934.6
4	Danny Green	2013-14	934.1
5	Allen Crabbe	2018-19	933.6
6	Joe Harris	2017-18	923.7
7	Pat Connaughton	2018-19	922.5
8	Kyle Korver	2007-08	920.4
9	James Anderson	2015-16	917.8
10	Brandon Rush	2011-12	917.2

Baseline Basic Stats

MPG	PTS	AST	REB	BLK	STL
23.1	8.4	1.3	3.2	0.3	0.6

Advanced Metrics

USG%	3PTA/FGA	FTA/FGA	TS%	eFG%	3PT%
15.3	0.627	0.194	0.572	0.542	0.373

AST%	TOV%	OREB%	DREB%	STL%	BLK%
8.0	9.7	2.8	12.9	1.4	1.3

PER	ORTG	DRTG	WS/48	VOL
11.78	112.8	110.4	0.095	0.358

- Played his first season as a regular starter for Houston in 2019-20
- Primarily a low volume, spot-up shooter, made threes at just above the league average last season
- Mostly a spot-up shooter, can occasionally come off screens
- Good at running the floor in transition to either get layups or set up for trail threes
- Can occasionally get to the rim on dribble hand-offs, not really a playmaker, rarely turns the ball over
- 2019-20 Defensive Degree of Difficulty: 0.448
- Tends to guard starting level players, occasionally takes on tougher defensive assignments
- Solid on-ball defender that can capably defend multiple positions
- Average pick-and-roll defender, good at fighting over the screen to contain ball handler, has some trouble handling bigger players on switches
- Can be undisciplined when closing out on perimeter shooters, tends to be either late or too aggressive, can get caught on screens off the ball
- Steal and Block Percentage both increased to career highs last season, fairly solid defensive rebounder

Eric Gordon

Height	Weight	Cap #	Years Left
6'3"	215	$16.869M	3

	Similar at Age	**31**	
		Season	**SIMsc**
1	Randy Foye	2014-15	912.6
2	Ben Gordon	2014-15	902.1
3	Glen Rice	1998-99	901.5
4	Gary Neal	2015-16	898.1
5	Arron Afflalo	2016-17	897.8
6	Roger Mason	2011-12	894.5
7	J.J. Redick	2015-16	894.2
8	C.J. Miles	2018-19	892.6
9	Wesley Matthews	2017-18	892.3
10	Devin Brown	2009-10	888.9

Baseline Basic Stats

MPG	PTS	AST	REB	BLK	STL
24.1	10.6	1.8	2.2	0.2	0.6

Advanced Metrics

USG%	3PTA/FGA	FTA/FGA	TS%	eFG%	3PT%
20.5	0.599	0.229	0.534	0.494	0.347
AST%	**TOV%**	**OREB%**	**DREB%**	**STL%**	**BLK%**
9.7	9.7	1.2	7.9	1.0	1.0
PER	**ORTG**	**DRTG**	**WS/48**	**VOL**	
11.04	104.7	112.8	0.055	0.511	

- Missed games in 2019-20 due to right knee surgery and a bruised left leg
- Regular rotation player when healthy, started towards the end of last season
- Mostly used as a higher volume, spot-up shooter
- Three-Point Percentage fell to below break-even last season, above three-point shooter in his career
- Good at making pull-up jumpers as a pick-and-roll ball handler and isolation player
- Occasionally got to the rim to draw fouls, good at making shots off screens in a small sample of possessions
- More of a catch-and-shoot player now, has some passing skills, rarely turns the ball over
- 2019-20 Defensive Degree of Difficulty: 0.414
- Tended to guard starter level players or higher-end second unit players
- Solid on-ball defender that can guard multiple positions, fairly good against taller wing players
- Good pick-and-roll defender, good at switching, fights over screens to guard ball handlers
- Great at closing out on perimeter shooters, sometimes gets caught on screens away from the ball
- Stay-at-home defender, does not really get steals, Block Percentage is slightly above his career average, below average defensive rebounder

Ben McLemore	Height	Weight	Cap #	Years Left
	6'3"	195	$2.283M	UFA

	Similar at Age	26	
		Season	SIMsc
1	Troy Daniels	2017-18	923.5
2	Charlie Bell	2005-06	910.1
3	Daniel Gibson	2012-13	907.1
4	E'Twaun Moore	2015-16	905.2
5	Allen Crabbe	2018-19	902.2
6	Mike Penberthy	2000-01	902.1
7	Damon Jones	2002-03	902.1
8	Langston Galloway	2017-18	898.2
9	Rex Walters	1996-97	897.3
10	Marcus Banks	2007-08	896.0

Baseline Basic Stats

MPG	PTS	AST	REB	BLK	STL
21.6	8.1	2.1	1.9	0.1	0.6

Advanced Metrics

USG%	3PTA/FGA	FTA/FGA	TS%	eFG%	3PT%
17.1	0.657	0.136	0.558	0.538	0.367
AST%	**TOV%**	**OREB%**	**DREB%**	**STL%**	**BLK%**
11.7	9.3	1.6	8.5	1.3	0.8
PER	**ORTG**	**DRTG**	**WS/48**	**VOL**	
11.42	110.3	114.7	0.062	0.462	

- Regular rotation player for Houston in 2019-20, had the most productive season of his NBA career
- Mainly used as a low volume, spot-up shooter, made 40% of his threes last season
- Very good in the corners throughout his career, career percentage on corner threes in almost 42%
- Mostly a spot-up shooter, can occasionally shoot off screens, better at coming off screens to his left
- Good at running the floor in transition to set up for trail threes or to get layups, good at cutting off the ball
- Strictly a catch-and-shoot player, limited as a playmaker, rarely turns the ball over
- 2019-20 Defensive Degree of Difficulty: 0.377
- Usually guards higher end second unit players or lower leverage starters
- Below average on-ball defender, struggles to stay with his man in isolation situations
- Average pick-and-roll defender, fairly good at fighting over the screen to contain ball handlers, has trouble guarding bigger players on switches
- Generally stays attached to shooters off the ball, occasionally gets caught on screens
- Stay-at-home defender, steal and block rates were consistent with his career averages, fairly decent defensive rebounder

Sterling Brown	Height	Weight	Cap #	Years Left
	6'5"	232	$1.621M	UFA

	Similar at Age	24	
		Season	**SIMsc**
1	Carlos Delfino	2006-07	940.1
2	Wayne Selden	2018-19	930.3
3	Quincy Pondexter	2012-13	926.2
4	Justin Anderson	2017-18	923.6
5	Henry (Bill) Walker	2011-12	916.3
6	Royce O'Neale	2017-18	911.8
7	Abdel Nader	2017-18	910.1
8	Solomon Hill	2015-16	910.0
9	Norman Powell	2017-18	909.5
10	James Anderson	2013-14	907.9

Baseline Basic Stats

MPG	PTS	AST	REB	BLK	STL
21.3	7.6	1.3	3.3	0.3	0.6

Advanced Metrics

USG%	3PTA/FGA	FTA/FGA	TS%	eFG%	3PT%
16.5	0.502	0.174	0.534	0.506	0.360
AST%	**TOV%**	**OREB%**	**DREB%**	**STL%**	**BLK%**
9.5	11.3	3.6	15.3	1.4	0.9
PER	**ORTG**	**DRTG**	**WS/48**	**VOL**	
11.19	105.8	108.6	0.080	0.431	

- Fringe rotation player for Milwaukee in his third NBA season
- Predominantly a low volume, spot-up shooter on offense, above break-even three-point for his career
- Much better in the corners, career percentage on corner threes is just over 45%
- Good spot-up shooter that can sometimes shoot off screens, effective at going to the basket on dribble hand-offs
- Good at making backdoor cuts, opportunistically crashes the offensive boards to score on put-backs
- Strictly a catch-and-shoot player, shows some passing skills, fairly effective at limiting turnovers
- 2019-20 Defensive Degree of Difficulty: 0.326, tends to guard second unit players
- Played solid on-ball defense against perimeter players, has some trouble against stronger post players
- Average pick-and-roll defender, tends to go too far under screens to allow open outside shots
- Closes out on perimeter shooters in spot-up situations, can get caught on screens off the ball
- Solid defensive rebounder, posts a moderately high steals rate, Block Percentage is still consistent with his career average

DeMarcus Cousins

	Height	Weight	Cap #	Years Left
DeMarcus Cousins	6'11"	270	$1.621M	UFA

Similar at Age **29**

		Season	SIMsc
1	Nene	2011-12	870.7
2	Gorgui Dieng	2018-19	852.8
3	Chris Kaman	2011-12	851.2
4	Zeljko Rebraca	2001-02	843.5
5	Tim Duncan*	2005-06	839.7
6	Al Jefferson	2013-14	835.0
7	Dewayne Dedmon	2018-19	833.5
8	Kevin Love	2017-18	828.9
9	Marc Gasol	2013-14	827.8
10	Brook Lopez	2017-18	826.6

Baseline Basic Stats

MPG	PTS	AST	REB	BLK	STL
26.9	15.1	2.4	7.8	1.1	0.9

Advanced Metrics

USG%	3PTA/FGA	FTA/FGA	TS%	eFG%	3PT%
27.5	0.220	0.385	0.552	0.504	0.334
AST%	**TOV%**	**OREB%**	**DREB%**	**STL%**	**BLK%**
18.5	15.1	6.7	26.5	1.9	3.8
PER	**ORTG**	**DRTG**	**WS/48**	**VOL**	
20.00	104.8	102.0	0.123	0.469	

- Missed the entire 2019-20 season due to a torn ACL
- Missed parts of the 2017-18 and 2018-19 seasons due to a torn left Achilles
- Good post-up player that can get deep position inside, better from the left block, draws fouls at a high rate
- Solid rim runner when healthy, will run the floor in transition
- Not as active on the offensive glass as he was in his younger years in Sacramento
- Struggled with his outside shot in Golden State, career Three-Point Percentage is around break-even
- Very good passing big man that can find open shooters and hit cutters
- 2018-19 Defensive Degree of Difficulty: 0.458, typically guarded starting level centers
- Solid rim protector in his last healthy season in Golden State, good rebounder and shot blocker, uses size to eat up space and clog the lane
- Stout post defender that holds position inside, defended well on isolation plays against opposing big men
- Played decent pick-and-roll defense in 2018-19, held up well on switches against ball handlers
- Quicker screeners could beat him to the rim, late to recognize pick-and-pop plays
- Tended to stay in the paint, did not always come out to contest perimeter shots

David Nwaba	Height	Weight	Cap #	Years Left
	6'5"	219	$1.824M	UFA

	Similar at Age	27	
		Season	SIMsc
1	Michael Curry	1995-96	922.5
2	Maurice Evans	2005-06	908.1
3	Torrey Craig	2017-18	907.1
4	Stephen Graham	2009-10	906.2
5	C.J. Williams	2017-18	901.7
6	Sam Young	2012-13	895.9
7	Chase Budinger	2015-16	895.3
8	Alonzo Gee	2014-15	894.7
9	Thabo Sefolosha	2011-12	889.5
10	Iman Shumpert	2017-18	888.2

Baseline Basic Stats

MPG	PTS	AST	REB	BLK	STL
19.0	5.8	1.0	2.6	0.3	0.6

Advanced Metrics

USG%	3PTA/FGA	FTA/FGA	TS%	eFG%	3PT%
14.0	0.385	0.287	0.562	0.534	0.381
AST%	**TOV%**	**OREB%**	**DREB%**	**STL%**	**BLK%**
7.4	9.6	3.8	12.4	1.6	1.9
PER	**ORTG**	**DRTG**	**WS/48**	**VOL**	
11.63	113.7	110.2	0.088	0.536	

- Fringe rotation player for Brooklyn when healthy, missed most of the season due to a torn right Achilles tendon, signed with Houston in June 2020
- Primarily a lower volume spot-up shooter, made almost 43% of his threes in a limited number of attempts
- Almost strictly a stationary shooter, does not really shoot on the move or off the dribble
- Active player off the ball, great cutter and transition finisher, crashes the offensive glass to score on put-backs, drew fouls at a fairly high rate
- Not really a passer, sticks to making safer passes, does not turn the ball over
- 2019-20 Defensive Degree of Difficulty: 0.367
- Tended to guard higher end second unit players, drew some tougher assignments in previous seasons
- Solid on-ball defender that can capably defend multiple positions
- Good pick-and-roll defender, solid at containing ball handlers, can switch to cover the screener
- Gambles a bit too much, can be out of position when chasing shooters off screens or closing out in spot-up situations
- Very effective as a weak side shot blocker, Block Percentage spiked significantly, good defensive rebounding guard, Steal Percentage has slightly risen each year

Bruno Caboclo	Height	Weight	Cap #	Years Left
	6'9"	218	$2.029M	Team Option

	Similar at Age	24	
		Season	SIMsc
1	Al-Farouq Aminu	2014-15	903.5
2	Jumaine Jones	2003-04	894.6
3	Johnny Taylor	1998-99	894.2
4	Shawne Williams	2010-11	891.4
5	Omri Casspi	2012-13	889.0
6	Luke Babbitt	2013-14	885.4
7	Troy Williams	2018-19	882.7
8	James Michael McAdoo	2016-17	880.6
9	Josh Davis	2004-05	880.4
10	Brian Evans	1997-98	879.6

Baseline Basic Stats

MPG	PTS	AST	REB	BLK	STL
21.0	7.3	1.2	4.1	0.5	0.7

Advanced Metrics

USG%	3PTA/FGA	FTA/FGA	TS%	eFG%	3PT%
17.0	0.495	0.165	0.532	0.503	0.314
AST%	**TOV%**	**OREB%**	**DREB%**	**STL%**	**BLK%**
9.0	11.4	6.9	16.4	1.7	3.1
PER	**ORTG**	**DRTG**	**WS/48**	**VOL**	
13.62	108.7	108.9	0.103	0.634	

- Played sparingly for Memphis and Houston, traded to Houston in February 2020
- Primarily a low volume, spot-up shooter, took slightly more volume in Houston
- Had trouble shooting efficiently last season, made less than 20% of his threes
- Most effective at attacking the rim, drew fouls at a decent rate, made almost 66% of his shots inside of three feet
- Actively ran the floor in transition, good roll man on pick-and-rolls, can crash the offensive boards to score on put-backs
- Strictly a catch-and-shoot or catch-and-finish player, limited playmaking skills, does not really turn the ball over
- 2019-20 Defensive Degree of Difficulty: 0.267
- Tended to play against second unit players or in garbage time
- Middling on-ball defender, had some trouble staying with perimeter players in isolation situations
- Below average pick-and-roll defender, struggled to contain ball handlers in space, better at covering the roll man inside
- Can get caught on screens, generally too aggressive when closing out on perimeter shooters
- Solid defensive rebounder, good shot blocker, posted the highest Steal Percentage of his career last season
- Tends to undisciplined with his positioning, below average rim protector, fouls at a fairly high rate

Gerald Green

	Height	Weight	Cap #	Years Left
Gerald Green	6'8"	200	$1.621M	UFA

	Similar at Age	34 Season	SIMsc
1	Jalen Rose	2006-07	902.7
2	Dale Ellis	1994-95	898.9
3	Chuck Person	1998-99	891.3
4	James Jones	2014-15	891.1
5	Rasual Butler	2013-14	890.0
6	James Posey	2010-11	881.4
7	Shane Battier	2012-13	880.6
8	Kyle Korver	2015-16	878.4
9	Steve Smith	2003-04	877.8
10	Mike Dunleavy, Jr.	2014-15	875.6

Baseline Basic Stats

MPG	PTS	AST	REB	BLK	STL
19.6	7.6	1.1	2.4	0.2	0.5

Advanced Metrics

USG%	3PTA/FGA	FTA/FGA	TS%	eFG%	3PT%
17.8	0.706	0.149	0.563	0.540	0.366

AST%	TOV%	OREB%	DREB%	STL%	BLK%
6.4	8.6	2.2	12.7	1.2	1.5

PER	ORTG	DRTG	WS/48	VOL
11.94	109.1	111.2	0.081	0.512

- Missed the entire 2019-20 season due to a left foot injury
- Traded to Denver in February 2020, then waived
- Used by Houston as a moderate volume, spot-up shooter for the previous two seasons
- Around a league average three-point shooter for his career, has made over 39% of his career corner threes
- Mainly a stationary spot-up shooter, only average at shooting off screens
- Can use an on-ball screen to make threes off pick-and-rolls and hand-offs
- Strictly a catch-and-shoot player, limited playmaking skills, does not really create his own shot
- 2018-19 Defensive Degree of Difficulty: 0.336, tended to guard second unit level players
- Effective on-ball defender against perimeter players, stronger players could overpower him in the post
- Below average pick-and-roll defender, tended to go too far under screens to allow open outside shots
- Consistently closes out on perimeter shooters, can sometimes get caught on screens off the ball
- More of a stay-at-home defender in Houston, solid defensive rebounder, does not really get steals, good at using his length to block shots

Chris Clemons	Height	Weight	Cap #	Years Left
	5'9"	180	$1.518M	RFA

Similar at Age 22

		Season	SIMsc
1	Nate Robinson	2006-07	878.7
2	Aaron Holiday	2018-19	877.5
3	Joe Crispin	2001-02	876.2
4	Isaiah Canaan	2013-14	867.7
5	Kay Felder	2017-18	854.4
6	Isaiah Thomas	2011-12	845.6
7	Patty Mills	2010-11	844.4
8	Eddie House	2000-01	841.2
9	Rodrigue Beaubois	2010-11	837.5
10	A.J. Guyton	2000-01	836.8

Baseline Basic Stats

MPG	PTS	AST	REB	BLK	STL
22.0	10.3	2.7	2.1	0.1	0.7

Advanced Metrics

USG%	3PTA/FGA	FTA/FGA	TS%	eFG%	3PT%
22.8	0.565	0.142	0.545	0.517	0.355
AST%	**TOV%**	**OREB%**	**DREB%**	**STL%**	**BLK%**
18.1	11.0	1.6	9.1	1.6	1.0
PER	**ORTG**	**DRTG**	**WS/48**	**VOL**	
14.35	107.0	111.3	0.085	0.655	

- Fringe rotation player for Houston in his rookie season, spent some time in the G-League with the Rio Grande Valley Vipers
- Utilized as a higher volume, scoring guard off the bench at the NBA level
- Above break-even three-point shooter in the NBA, effective at making pull-up jumpers as the pick-and-roll ball handler
- Mostly a stationary spot-up shooter off the ball, only average at shooting off screens
- Can occasionally use his quickness to get to the rim on isolations, rarely looks to cut off the ball
- More scoring minded, decent secondary playmaker, good at avoiding turnovers
- Hits the roll man inside, has some trouble locating open shooters on the perimeter
- 2019-20 Defensive Degree of Difficulty: 0.296
- Tended to hidden in favorable matchups against lower leverage second unit players
- Not tested much on the ball, showed decent quickness to stay in front of opposing players, taller players could shoot over him due to his smallish stature
- Below average pick-and-roll defender, tended to allow ball handlers to turn the corner, sometimes was targeted by bigger players on switches
- Good at staying attached to shooters off the ball, consistently closed out in spot-up situations
- Solid defensive rebounder for his size, posted a pretty high Block Percentage for a sub-six footer, gets steals at a moderate rate

Newcomers

Jae'Sean Tate		Height	Weight	Cap #	Years Left
		6'4"	230	$1.446M	1 + TO

Baseline Basic Stats

MPG	PTS	AST	REB	BLK	STL
17.7	6.3	1.0	3.0	0.3	0.6

Advanced Metrics

USG%	3PTA/FGA	FTA/FGA	TS%	eFG%	3PT%
16.0	0.240	0.314	0.541	0.514	0.320
AST%	**TOV%**	**OREB%**	**DREB%**	**STL%**	**BLK%**
9.0	11.3	6.2	13.1	1.7	1.3
PER	**ORTG**	**DRTG**	**WS/48**	**VOL**	
12.78	106.7	103.2	0.089	N/A	

- Undrafted in the 2018 NBA Draft out of Ohio State, played for the Sydney Kings in the Australian NBL last season
- Moderate volume, undersized power forward overseas
- High energy player with good athleticism, runs hard down the floor in transition
- Will crash the offensive glass to score on put-back dunks, good cutter off the ball, draws fouls at a high rate
- Good three-point shooter overseas, has made over 40% of his threes in each of the last two seasons in Australia and Belgium
- Mostly a spot-up shooter at this stage, stroke may still be inconsistent, has made less than 60% of his free throws as a pro
- Shows some secondary playmaking skills, has improved his ability to limit turnovers
- Has a thicker build and a low center of gravity, may be capable of defending bigger players at the NBA level
- Solid perimeter defender at Ohio State, strong enough to hold position in the post, lacks ideal length to contest shots from taller players
- Better pick-and-roll defender overseas, capable of switching onto ball handlers or defending screeners
- Will aggressively close out to contest perimeter shots in spot-up situations, can occasionally get caught on screens
- Solid help defender, good defensive rebounder, consistently gets steals and blocks at a solid rate

Kenyon Martin, Jr.	Height	Weight	Cap #	Years Left
	6'6"	215	$0.898M	2 + TO

Baseline Basic Stats

MPG	PTS	AST	REB	BLK	STL
18.5	6.8	1.0	3.1	0.4	0.6

Advanced Metrics

USG%	3PTA/FGA	FTA/FGA	TS%	eFG%	3PT%
12.8	0.193	0.386	0.429	0.397	0.301
AST%	**TOV%**	**OREB%**	**DREB%**	**STL%**	**BLK%**
6.6	9.9	2.5	15.8	1.4	1.8
PER	**ORTG**	**DRTG**	**WS/48**	**VOL**	
13.80	79.7	74.1	0.123	N/A	

- Drafted by Sacramento with the 52nd overall pick, traded to Houston
- Originally expected to play at Vanderbilt, elected to spend last season at the IMG Academy
- Projection uses translated high school stats
- Skill level is raw, great athleticism, vertical lob threat, powerful finisher in transition, good cutter and offensive rebounder
- Lacks ball handling skills to regularly create offense off the dribble, rarely goes to his right
- Didn't look to take perimeter shots in games, shooting stroke is still inconsistent
- Had some issues making free throws, more of a spot-up shooter at this stage, struggles to shoot off screens
- Long and athletic defender, shows promise due to his athleticism, may potentially be able to guard multiple positions
- Solid on-ball defender at the high school level, stays with his man and contests shots
- Active help defender, will rotate inside to block shots, plays passing lanes to get steals, solid defensive rebounder
- Generally stays attached to shooters off the ball, not challenged enough in high school, prone to losing his focus

DALLAS MAVERICKS

Last Season: 43 – 32, Lost 1st Round to L.A. Clippers (2 – 4)

Offensive Rating: 116.7, 1st in the NBA

Defensive Rating: 111.7, 18th in the NBA

Primary Executive: Donnie Nelson, General Manager and President of Basketball Operations

Head Coach: Rick Carlisle

Key Roster Changes

Subtractions
Seth Curry, trade
Delon Wright, trade
Justin Jackson, trade
Courtney Lee, free agency
Michael Kidd-Gilchrist, free agency

Additions
Josh Green, draft
Tyrell Terry, draft
Josh Richardson, trade
James Johnson, trade
Wesley Iwundu, free agency

Roster

Likely Starting Five
1. *Luka Doncic*
2. *Tim Hardaway, Jr.*
3. *Josh Richardson*
4. *Dorian Finney-Smith*
5. *Kristaps Porzingis*

Other Key Rotation Players
Maxi Kleber
Dwight Powell
Trey Burke
Jalen Brunson
Willie Cauley-Stein

* Italics denotes that a player is likely to be on the floor to close games

Remaining Roster

- Boban Marjanovic
- Wesley Iwundu
- Josh Green
- Tyrell Terry
- J.J. Barea
- James Johnson – not profiled, book was finalized before he could be included
- Tyler Bey, 22, 6'7", 216, Colorado (Two-Way)
- Nate Hinton, 21, 6'5", 210, Houston (Two-Way)
- Freddie Gillespie, 23, 6'9", 245, Baylor (Exhibit 10)
- Devonte Patterson, 24, 6'7", 205, Prairie View A&M (Exhibit 10)

SCHREMPF Base Rating: 39.6 (72-game season)

Strengths

- Highly efficient offense that can space the floor around Luka Doncic
- Solid depth allows them to manage the potentially compressed schedule

Question Marks

- Health and durability of Kristaps Porzingis
- Ability to make the right plays in critical situations

Outlook

- Solid playoff team in the West, a notch below the elite contenders, probably will be a top six seed

Veterans

Luka Dončić	Height	Weight	Cap #	Years Left
	6'7"	218	$8.049M	1

	Similar at Age	20	
		Season	SIMsc
1	Tyreke Evans	2009-10	864.2
2	Kevin Durant	2008-09	839.1
3	Devin Booker	2016-17	837.2
4	Carmelo Anthony	2004-05	837.0
5	LeBron James	2004-05	833.6
6	Tony Wroten	2013-14	827.8
7	D'Angelo Russell	2016-17	827.3
8	Cliff Robinson	1980-81	825.9
9	Mike Miller	2000-01	825.6
10	Dennis Smith, Jr.	2017-18	821.0

Baseline Basic Stats

MPG	PTS	AST	REB	BLK	STL
36.5	24.5	4.7	5.7	0.6	1.2

Advanced Metrics

USG%	3PTA/FGA	FTA/FGA	TS%	eFG%	3PT%
33.1	0.374	0.376	0.571	0.517	0.337
AST%	**TOV%**	**OREB%**	**DREB%**	**STL%**	**BLK%**
32.0	13.1	3.6	18.1	1.6	0.8
PER	**ORTG**	**DRTG**	**WS/48**	**VOL**	
23.65	112.6	108.9	0.173	0.519	

- Was named an All-Star in his second season in the NBA, led the NBA with 17 triple-doubles in 2019-20
- Excelled as the team's primary ball handler and scoring option
- Excellent pick-and-roll ball handler that can make shots off the dribble, get to the rim and find open teammates
- Good at attacking defenders on isolation plays, can post up smaller guards, draws fouls at a high rate
- Improving as an off-ball player, showed an ability to cut and make off shots off screens in a small sample of possessions
- More of a volume three-point shooter at this stage, Three-Point Percentage is below break-even for his career
- 2019-20 Defensive Degree of Difficulty: 0.389
- Hidden in favorable matchups against lower leverage offensive players
- Average on-ball defender, can stay with perimeter players on drives, tends to give up extra space for opponents to take jumpers
- Fairly solid pick-and-roll defender that can funnel his man into help, decent when switching onto the screener
- Closes out on perimeter shooters, can sometimes get caught on screens off the ball
- Excellent defensive rebounder, gets steals at a moderate rate

Kristaps Porziņģis	Height	Weight	Cap #	Years Left
	7'3"	240	$29.468M	2 + PO

	Similar at Age	24	
		Season	SIMsc
1	Charlie Villanueva	2008-09	870.5
2	Raef LaFrentz	2000-01	861.2
3	Patrick Ewing*	1986-87	857.6
4	Rik Smits	1990-91	856.9
5	Brook Lopez	2012-13	849.6
6	Ralph Sampson*	1984-85	846.7
7	Frank Kaminsky	2017-18	845.8
8	Pau Gasol	2004-05	841.1
9	Spencer Hawes	2012-13	839.2
10	Willie Cauley-Stein	2017-18	839.0

Baseline Basic Stats

MPG	PTS	AST	REB	BLK	STL
28.9	15.6	1.6	7.1	1.8	0.7

Advanced Metrics

USG%	3PTA/FGA	FTA/FGA	TS%	eFG%	3PT%
26.5	0.267	0.308	0.551	0.507	0.382
AST%	**TOV%**	**OREB%**	**DREB%**	**STL%**	**BLK%**
9.1	9.7	6.5	21.1	1.2	5.1
PER	**ORTG**	**DRTG**	**WS/48**	**VOL**	
19.91	109.3	106.3	0.133	0.372	

- Regular starter in his first season playing for Dallas, tore the meniscus in his right knee in the playoffs against the Clippers
- Maintained an All-Star level of play in a new role as a high volume, stretch big
- Good three-point shooter that can make spot-up jumpers, effective as the screener on pick-and-pop plays, can knock down trail threes in transition
- Very good rim runner that can score on rolls to the rim and cuts off the ball, good at crashing the offensive glass to score on put-backs
- Not quite as effective on post-ups as he had been in New York, lack of lower body strength did not allow him to get deep position against opposing big men
- Mainly a catch-and-shoot player, has some passing skills, rarely turns the ball over
- 2019-20 Defensive Degree of Difficulty: 0.420
- Guarded starting level big men, served as Dallas' primary rim protector
- Excellent rim protector due his great shot blocking abilities, very good defensive rebounder
- Decent on-ball defender, good at using his considerable length to contest shots in the post, has some trouble defending in space on isolations
- Good pick-and-roll defender, solid in drop coverages, can capably switch onto ball handlers for a few dribbles
- Does not always come out to contest perimeter shots

Tim Hardaway, Jr.	Height	Weight	Cap #	Years Left
	6'5"	205	$18.975M	UFA

	Similar at Age	27	
		Season	**SIMsc**
1	Voshon Lenard	2000-01	940.5
2	Arron Afflalo	2012-13	933.9
3	C.J. Miles	2014-15	933.0
4	Terrence Ross	2018-19	932.8
5	Wesley Matthews	2013-14	931.1
6	CJ McCollum	2018-19	930.8
7	Gary Neal	2011-12	929.2
8	Roger Mason	2007-08	929.1
9	Marco Belinelli	2013-14	927.8
10	Nick Young	2012-13	927.0

Baseline Basic Stats

MPG	PTS	AST	REB	BLK	STL
26.5	12.3	1.9	2.7	0.2	0.7

Advanced Metrics

USG%	3PTA/FGA	FTA/FGA	TS%	eFG%	3PT%
21.4	0.545	0.214	0.547	0.510	0.377
AST%	**TOV%**	**OREB%**	**DREB%**	**STL%**	**BLK%**
11.6	8.5	1.5	10.1	1.2	0.4
PER	**ORTG**	**DRTG**	**WS/48**	**VOL**	
13.51	109.2	112.7	0.083	0.287	

- Regular starter for Dallas in his first full season with the team
- Improved his efficiency in a role as a moderate volume secondary scorer
- Made almost 40% of his threes last season, excelled as a spot-up shooter, also good at making pull-up jumpers off the dribble
- Effective pick-and-roll player last season, made outside shots as the ball handler and as the screener on pick-and-pop plays
- Movement off the ball needs work, can make backdoor cuts, struggles to shoot off screens
- Fairly decent playmaker in previous seasons, rarely turns the ball over
- 2019-20 Defensive Degree of Difficulty: 0.496
- Usually guards starting level players, takes on a lot of tougher assignments as well
- Fairly solid on-ball defender last year, good at taking away the drive, backed off a little too much, prone to giving up outside shots
- Fairly effective pick-and-roll defender, good on switches, sometimes prone to allowing ball handlers to turn the corner
- Will usually stay attached to shooters off the ball, closes out consistently, sometimes can get caught on screens away from the ball
- Stay-at-home defender, rarely gets steals or blocks, decent defensive rebounder

Josh Richardson	Height	Weight	Cap #	Years Left
	6'5"	200	$10.866M	Player Option

	Similar at Age	26	
		Season	SIMsc
1	Sasha Danilovic	1996-97	949.7
2	Kent Bazemore	2015-16	949.0
3	Courtney Lee	2011-12	946.2
4	Bogdan Bogdanovic	2018-19	942.0
5	Bob Sura	1999-00	939.8
6	Voshon Lenard	1999-00	939.5
7	Marco Belinelli	2012-13	932.6
8	Bryant Stith	1996-97	931.7
9	Nick Young	2011-12	929.7
10	Gordan Giricek	2003-04	929.0

Baseline Basic Stats

MPG	PTS	AST	REB	BLK	STL
27.1	12.1	2.4	2.8	0.3	0.9

Advanced Metrics

USG%	3PTA/FGA	FTA/FGA	TS%	eFG%	3PT%
20.9	0.380	0.231	0.534	0.494	0.359
AST%	**TOV%**	**OREB%**	**DREB%**	**STL%**	**BLK%**
15.1	11.8	2.3	9.0	1.7	1.3
PER	**ORTG**	**DRTG**	**WS/48**	**VOL**	
13.15	105.5	109.8	0.071	0.232	

- Regular starter for Philadelphia last season, missed games due to a right hamstring injury and a concussion
- Maintained his scoring efficiency in a moderate volume role as a shooter off the ball
- Made threes at a rate just above break-even last season, better at making corner threes
- Solid spot-up shooter, good at running off screens, effective at making quick pull-up jumpers as a pick-and-roll ball handler and isolation player
- Can use an on-ball screen to make outside shots on dribble hand-offs
- Good secondary playmaker that can find open shooters, good at avoiding turnovers
- 2019-20 Defensive Degree of Difficulty: 0.515
- Takes on tougher defensive assignments against top perimeter players
- Fairly solid on-ball defender, good at stopping drives, tends to give up space for his man to take jump shots
- Effective pick-and-roll defender, fights over screens to contain ball handlers, can be targeted by bigger screeners on switches
- Can be caught on screens off the ball, tends to be late when closing out on perimeter shooters
- Gets blocks and steals at a solid rate, middling defensive rebounder for his size

Dorian Finney-Smith	Height	Weight	Cap #	Years Left
	6'7"	220	$4.000M	1

	Similar at Age	26	
		Season	SIMsc
1	Quincy Pondexter	2014-15	935.2
2	Wilson Chandler	2013-14	931.0
3	Kyle Singler	2014-15	927.3
4	Morris Peterson	2003-04	923.9
5	Martell Webster	2012-13	923.2
6	James Ennis	2016-17	921.8
7	Iman Shumpert	2016-17	921.2
8	Mickael Pietrus	2008-09	920.8
9	Kyle Korver	2007-08	919.6
10	Joe Harris	2017-18	918.1

Baseline Basic Stats

MPG	PTS	AST	REB	BLK	STL
23.5	8.5	1.3	3.4	0.3	0.6

Advanced Metrics

USG%	3PTA/FGA	FTA/FGA	TS%	eFG%	3PT%
15.3	0.526	0.195	0.560	0.533	0.368
AST%	**TOV%**	**OREB%**	**DREB%**	**STL%**	**BLK%**
8.1	10.8	5.1	13.0	1.3	1.2
PER	**ORTG**	**DRTG**	**WS/48**	**VOL**	
11.87	112.5	111.0	0.091	0.366	

- Played his first year as a full-time starter for Dallas last season
- Mainly used as a very low volume, spot-up shooter
- Became an above average three-point shooter last season, also made almost 44% of his corner threes
- Primarily a stand-still shooter, does not really shoot on the move or off the dribble
- Good cutter off the ball, runs hard down the floor in transition
- Generally avoids turnovers, limited playmaking skills at this stage
- 2019-20 Defensive Degree of Difficulty: 0.596
- Usually guards the opponent's top perimeter player, had the 2nd toughest set of matchups in the NBA last season
- Good on-ball defender that guards multiple positions
- Fairly solid pick-and-roll defender, good at switching, prone to bouts of miscommunication, can allow ball handlers to turn the corner
- Good at staying attached to shooters off the ball, fights through screens, closes out on perimeter shooters
- Steal Percentage dropped last season, block rate improved, better at using his length to challenge shots, fairly solid defensive rebounder

Maxi Kleber	Height	Weight	Cap #	Years Left
	6'10"	240	$8.325M	2

	Similar at Age	28	
		Season	SIMsc
1	Matt Bonner	2008-09	919.4
2	Raef LaFrentz	2004-05	916.0
3	Ryan Anderson	2016-17	908.3
4	Serge Ibaka	2017-18	901.8
5	Jonas Jerebko	2015-16	894.6
6	Nemanja Bjelica	2016-17	891.7
7	Marvin Williams	2014-15	891.0
8	Brad Lohaus	1992-93	889.6
9	Scott Padgett	2004-05	889.6
10	Walter McCarty	2002-03	887.6

Baseline Basic Stats

MPG	PTS	AST	REB	BLK	STL
21.7	8.2	1.2	4.6	0.6	0.4

Advanced Metrics

USG%	3PTA/FGA	FTA/FGA	TS%	eFG%	3PT%
14.6	0.613	0.166	0.585	0.563	0.370
AST%	**TOV%**	**OREB%**	**DREB%**	**STL%**	**BLK%**
7.8	10.0	6.3	16.8	0.8	3.3
PER	**ORTG**	**DRTG**	**WS/48**	**VOL**	
13.44	117.7	109.2	0.109	0.391	

- Regular rotation player for Dallas last season, started in the playoffs against the Clippers
- Mostly used as a low volume, stretch big, made over 37% of his threes last season
- Solid spot-up shooter, excellent as the screener on pick-and-pop plays
- Good rim runner that plays with a high motor, good at rolling to the rim and cutting off the ball, runs the floor hard in transition
- Strictly a catch-and-shoot or catch-and-finish player, limited ball handling and passing skills, rarely turns the ball over
- 2019-20 Defensive Degree of Difficulty: 0.425
- Guards starter level players, occasionally takes on tougher assignments
- Good rim protector, has been a consistently good shot blocker, will block his man out but is a middling defensive rebounder
- Solid on-ball defender, good strength to play post defense, solid mobility to guard perimeter players in space
- Fairly good pick-and-roll defender, good on hard switches, can sometimes be late to cover the roll man at the rim
- Usually closes out on perimeter shooters, can sometimes get out of position by wandering too far into the paint off the ball

Dwight Powell	Height	Weight	Cap #	Years Left
	6'10"	240	$11.080M	2

Similar at Age **28**

		Season	SIMsc
1	Gorgui Dieng	2017-18	906.3
2	Scott Hastings	1988-89	902.4
3	Cherokee Parks	2000-01	901.3
4	Tiago Splitter	2012-13	897.9
5	Corie Blount	1996-97	895.8
6	Anderson Varejao	2010-11	895.0
7	Mark Bryant	1993-94	894.2
8	Matt Bonner	2008-09	893.2
9	Rick Mahorn	1986-87	893.1
10	Nemanja Bjelica	2016-17	892.9

Baseline Basic Stats

MPG	PTS	AST	REB	BLK	STL
19.6	7.1	1.2	4.8	0.5	0.6

Advanced Metrics

USG%	3PTA/FGA	FTA/FGA	TS%	eFG%	3PT%
14.8	0.212	0.400	0.626	0.596	0.344
AST%	**TOV%**	**OREB%**	**DREB%**	**STL%**	**BLK%**
9.2	12.7	8.0	17.4	1.4	1.9
PER	**ORTG**	**DRTG**	**WS/48**	**VOL**	
15.72	123.4	107.6	0.152	0.290	

- Regular starter for Dallas when healthy, missed the second half of the season due to a torn right Achilles
- Utilized as a low volume, rim runner, made over 81% of his shots inside of three feet
- Excellent roll man and cutter, plays with high energy, runs hard down the floor in transition
- Will opportunistically crash the offensive boards to score on put-backs
- Trying to shoot threes, still not a reliable shooter at this stage, career Three-Point Percentage is below 30%
- Mainly a catch-and-finish player, limited passing skills, does not really commit turnovers
- 2019-20 Defensive Degree of Difficulty: 0.473
- Defended starter level players, sometimes tasked to guard tougher matchups on the interior
- Fairly solid on-ball defender, has good mobility to defend in space, has some trouble in the post against stronger players
- Above average pick-and-roll defender, good at guarding the screener, has some difficulty defending guards on switches
- Consistently comes out to contest perimeter shots
- Below average rim protector, somewhat foul prone, occasionally can block shots
- Defensive Rebound Percentage declined last season, solid rebounder in the past

Trey Burke	Height	Weight	Cap #	Years Left
	6'0"	175	$3.000M	1 + PO

	Similar at Age	27	
		Season	SIMsc
1	Brian Roberts	2012-13	933.9
2	Troy Hudson	2003-04	924.6
3	Jannero Pargo	2006-07	920.3
4	Patty Mills	2015-16	913.2
5	Lynn Greer	2006-07	911.8
6	J.J. Barea	2011-12	911.2
7	Jameer Nelson	2009-10	910.9
8	Chris Whitney	1998-99	910.6
9	Eddie House	2005-06	908.8
10	Negele Knight	1994-95	906.9

Baseline Basic Stats

MPG	PTS	AST	REB	BLK	STL
20.6	8.9	3.2	1.8	0.1	0.6

Advanced Metrics

USG%	3PTA/FGA	FTA/FGA	TS%	eFG%	3PT%
21.2	0.379	0.182	0.535	0.503	0.391
AST%	**TOV%**	**OREB%**	**DREB%**	**STL%**	**BLK%**
25.7	10.9	2.2	7.8	1.4	0.3
PER	**ORTG**	**DRTG**	**WS/48**	**VOL**	
15.04	111.3	112.9	0.092	0.346	

- Waived by Philadelphia in February 2020, signed by Dallas in July 2020 as a substitute for Willie Cauley-Stein for the Orlando restart
- Regular rotation player for Dallas during the seeding games and playoffs in Orlando
- Used as a moderate volume, backup scoring guard off the bench
- Made almost 43% of his threes last season, fairly good spot-up shooter
- Average effectiveness as a pick-and-roll ball handler, could make tough pull-up jumpers off the dribble, struggled to finish at the rim in Dallas
- Better at taking no dribble jumpers on isolation plays, fairly solid playmaker, great at limiting turnovers
- 2019-20 Defensive Degree of Difficulty: 0.370
- Generally defended second unit level players or lower leverage starters, hidden somewhat in favorable matchups
- Not tested very frequently, played below average on-ball defense, taller perimeter players could shoot over him due to his smallish stature
- Fairly effective pick-and-roll defender that can funnel his man into help, can be targeted on switches against bigger players in the post
- Can get caught on screens off the ball, undisciplined when closing out on perimeter shooters
- Steal and Block Percentages are still consistent with his career averages, below average defensive rebounder for his size

Jalen Brunson

Height	Weight	Cap #	Years Left
6'1"	190	$1.664M	1

	Similar at Age	23 Season	SIMsc
1	Mo Williams	2005-06	939.7
2	Yogi Ferrell	2016-17	927.3
3	Steve Nash*	1997-98	927.2
4	Trey Burke	2015-16	921.6
5	Ray McCallum	2014-15	920.9
6	Salim Stoudamire	2005-06	920.7
7	Mike Bibby	2001-02	920.4
8	Troy Hudson	1999-00	920.3
9	Toney Douglas	2009-10	919.5
10	Fred VanVleet	2017-18	918.5

Baseline Basic Stats

MPG	PTS	AST	REB	BLK	STL
23.4	9.7	3.4	2.2	0.1	0.8

Advanced Metrics

USG%	3PTA/FGA	FTA/FGA	TS%	eFG%	3PT%
20.4	0.366	0.215	0.547	0.510	0.358
AST%	**TOV%**	**OREB%**	**DREB%**	**STL%**	**BLK%**
24.9	12.7	1.9	9.9	1.4	0.3
PER	**ORTG**	**DRTG**	**WS/48**	**VOL**	
14.82	111.5	111.6	0.103	0.409	

- Regular rotation player for Dallas in his second season, missed the end of the 2019-20 season due to a torn labrum in his right shoulder
- Played a moderate usage role as a secondary ball handler and playmaker
- Showed improving passing skills, good at finding the roll man on pick-and-rolls, tends to avoid turnovers
- Solid pick-and-roll ball handler that can get to the rim or make quick pull-up jumpers, also effective on dribble hand-offs
- Made threes at just above the league average last season, fairly solid on spot-up jumpers, good at coming off screens
- 2019-20 Defensive Degree of Difficulty: 0.370
- Typically guarded higher-end second unit players or lower leverage starters
- Below average on-ball defender, has trouble against taller perimeter players, had difficulty staying in front of his man on isolations
- Below average at guarding pick-and-rolls, can be targeted in the post on switches, has trouble going over the screen, can allow ball handlers to turn the corner
- Fights through screens to stay attached to shooters off the ball, generally closes out on perimeter shooters
- Can be too aggressive when closing out, prone to giving up driving lanes to the rim
- Improving defensive rebounder, rarely gets blocks or steals

Willie Cauley-Stein

Height	Weight	Cap #	Years Left
7'0"	240	$4.100M	1

Similar at Age **26**

		Season	SIMsc
1	Cody Zeller	2018-19	925.7
2	Marcin Gortat	2010-11	919.1
3	Gustavo Ayon	2011-12	915.3
4	Gorgui Dieng	2015-16	914.9
5	Clemon Johnson	1982-83	914.6
6	Dwight Powell	2017-18	911.5
7	Will Perdue	1991-92	908.6
8	Alton Lister	1984-85	907.7
9	Rasho Nesterovic	2002-03	907.5
10	Vladimir Stepania	2002-03	906.8

Baseline Basic Stats

MPG	PTS	AST	REB	BLK	STL
22.9	8.6	1.2	6.4	1.0	0.6

Advanced Metrics

USG%	3PTA/FGA	FTA/FGA	TS%	eFG%	3PT%
16.9	0.018	0.289	0.560	0.541	0.260
AST%	**TOV%**	**OREB%**	**DREB%**	**STL%**	**BLK%**
9.7	11.7	9.1	22.5	1.6	3.5
PER	**ORTG**	**DRTG**	**WS/48**	**VOL**	
16.63	113.0	106.4	0.131	0.397	

- Regular starter for Golden State, became a fringe rotation player for Dallas after he was traded in January 2020
- Utilized as a low volume, rim runner with both teams, per-minute effective increased significantly with Dallas
- Very athletic vertical lob threat, good finisher on rolls to the rim and cuts off the ball
- Runs hard down the floor in transition, will hit the offensive boards to score on put-backs
- Decent passing big man, does not really turn the ball over, no real shooting range outside of three feet
- 2019-20 Defensive Degree of Difficulty: 0.464
- Typically guarded starting level big men, played a rim protector role
- Increased his Block Percentage significantly, became a good rim protector as a result, good defensive rebounder
- Played solid on-ball defender, good at using length to contest shots in the post, showed good mobility to defend in space
- Fairly solid at guarding pick-and-rolls, good at switching onto ball handlers
- Does not always come out to contest perimeter shots, will give up a lot of open outside shots

Boban Marjanović	Height	Weight	Cap #	Years Left
	7'4"	290	$3.500M	UFA

	Similar at Age	31	
		Season	**SIMsc**
1	Arvydas Sabonis*	1995-96	880.8
2	Chris Kaman	2013-14	831.7
3	Rik Smits	1997-98	822.2
4	James Donaldson	1988-89	811.0
5	Luc Longley	1999-00	791.8
6	Zydrunas Ilgauskas	2006-07	790.3
7	Timofey Mozgov	2017-18	787.8
8	Marc Gasol	2015-16	783.0
9	Zeljko Rebraca	2003-04	782.0
10	Al Jefferson	2015-16	780.8

Baseline Basic Stats

MPG	PTS	AST	REB	BLK	STL
22.6	11.4	1.3	6.3	0.9	0.4

Advanced Metrics

USG%	3PTA/FGA	FTA/FGA	TS%	eFG%	3PT%
24.8	0.043	0.352	0.588	0.545	0.277
AST%	**TOV%**	**OREB%**	**DREB%**	**STL%**	**BLK%**
10.0	13.7	11.8	26.3	1.0	2.6
PER	**ORTG**	**DRTG**	**WS/48**	**VOL**	
21.51	113.2	104.6	0.170	0.674	

- Fringe rotation player for Dallas last season, got steady playing time during the playoffs against the Clippers
- Very efficient in his role as a higher volume post-up player and rim runner
- Excellent at flashing to the middle on post-ups to score over his left shoulder
- Made over 83% of his shots inside of three feet, good cutter off the ball, solid at rolling to the rim on pick-and-rolls
- Very active offensive rebounder that will efficiently finish his put-back attempts
- Decent passing big man, good at avoiding turnovers
- 2019-20 Defensive Degree of Difficulty: 0.332
- Usually defends second unit level big men, utility is limited due to his lack of ideal mobility
- Very good rim protector, good at staying vertical to contest shots
- Solid shot blocker despite a decreased Block Percentage last season, excellent defensive rebounder
- Stout post defender that push opposing players off the block, surprisingly effective on-ball defender in space last season
- Above average pick-and-roll defender, solid in drop coverages, does not always come out to contest perimeter shots

Wesley Iwundu

Height	Weight	Cap #	Years Left
6'6"	195	$1.679M	1

Similar at Age **25**

		Season	SIMsc
1	Martell Webster	2011-12	922.7
2	Alec Burks	2016-17	922.5
3	Francisco Garcia	2006-07	917.6
4	Oscar Torres	2001-02	915.5
5	Rod Higgins	1984-85	913.6
6	Quinton Ross	2006-07	913.5
7	Chris Johnson	2015-16	913.0
8	Courtney Lee	2010-11	908.9
9	Rasual Butler	2004-05	908.2
10	Jordan McRae	2016-17	907.7

Baseline Basic Stats

MPG	PTS	AST	REB	BLK	STL
20.8	7.7	1.5	2.8	0.3	0.7

Advanced Metrics

USG%	3PTA/FGA	FTA/FGA	TS%	eFG%	3PT%
15.8	0.373	0.302	0.542	0.491	0.359
AST%	**TOV%**	**OREB%**	**DREB%**	**STL%**	**BLK%**
10.3	10.2	2.9	12.2	1.4	1.1
PER	**ORTG**	**DRTG**	**WS/48**	**VOL**	
11.34	109.1	110.8	0.082	0.473	

- Regular rotation player for Orlando in his third NBA season
- Played a role as a low volume, spot-up shooter, above break-even three-point shooter over the last two seasons
- Mostly a stationary spot-up shooter, can attack aggressive close-outs if his shot is falling
- Moves very well without the ball, fairly solid cutter that goes hard to the rim, draws fouls at a high rate
- Picks his spots to aggressively hit the offensive glass to score on put-backs
- Good at running the floor in transition to get dunks or draw shooting fouls
- Slightly improving as a passer, cut his Turnover Percentage to a career low last season
- 2019-20 Defensive Degree of Difficulty: 0.387
- Tends to guard higher-end second unit players or lower leverage starters
- Middling on-ball defender, has trouble staying with quicker perimeter players
- Decent pick-and-roll defender, good at containing ball handler, struggles to guard bigger screeners on switches
- Stays attached to shooters off the ball, good at closing out in spot-up situations
- Stay-at-home defender, Block and Steal Percentages are still consistent with his career averages, solid defensive rebounder

J.J. Barea

Height	Weight	Cap #	Years Left
5'10"	185	$1.621M	UFA

Similar at Age 35

		Season	SIMsc
1	Darrick Martin	2006-07	888.9
2	Sam Cassell	2004-05	862.2
3	Tim Hardaway	2001-02	861.7
4	Jameer Nelson	2017-18	854.2
5	Tony Parker	2017-18	849.3
6	Avery Johnson	2000-01	846.3
7	Anthony Johnson	2009-10	843.2
8	Bobby Jackson	2008-09	842.0
9	Mark Jackson	2000-01	836.5
10	Chauncey Billups	2011-12	835.9

Baseline Basic Stats

MPG	PTS	AST	REB	BLK	STL
22.8	9.8	4.2	2.3	0.1	0.7

Advanced Metrics

USG%	3PTA/FGA	FTA/FGA	TS%	eFG%	3PT%
23.2	0.356	0.171	0.513	0.485	0.367

AST%	TOV%	OREB%	DREB%	STL%	BLK%
32.6	15.7	1.9	10.4	1.2	0.2

PER	ORTG	DRTG	WS/48	VOL
14.13	105.0	112.4	0.058	0.737

- Fringe rotation player for Dallas in his age-35 season
- Operated as a higher volume, offensive guard off the bench, good playmaker, rarely commits turnovers
- Does not quite have the quickness to drive by defenders on isolations, better at making pull-up jumpers as a pick-and-roll ball handler
- Made almost 38% of his threes last season, effective at making spot-up threes above the break
- Age-related decline has limited his ability to play off the ball, does not really move on the weak side
- 2019-20 Defensive Degree of Difficulty: 0.348
- Guarded second unit level players, sometimes hidden in favorable matchups against lower leverage players
- Not tested very frequently, played good on-ball defense in a small sample of possessions
- Average pick-and-roll defender, can prevent drives to the rim, can be targeted on switches, taller players can shoot over him
- High effort player, generally closes out on perimeter shooters, does not have the length to disrupt shots from longer players
- Steal Percentage dropped off significantly, fairly solid defensive rebounder for his size

Newcomers

Josh Green	**Height**	**Weight**	**Cap #**	**Years Left**
	6'6"	210	$2.817M	1 + 2 TO

Baseline Basic Stats

MPG	PTS	AST	REB	BLK	STL
19.8	7.7	1.8	2.7	0.3	0.7

Advanced Metrics

USG%	3PTA/FGA	FTA/FGA	TS%	eFG%	3PT%
18.4	0.262	0.263	0.496	0.459	0.336

AST%	TOV%	OREB%	DREB%	STL%	BLK%
14.6	12.2	3.9	11.4	1.8	1.0

PER	ORTG	DRTG	WS/48	VOL
12.25	99.3	102.4	0.059	N/A

- Drafted by Dallas with the 18th overall pick
- Solid spot-up shooter, made over 36% of his threes at Arizona, struggles to shoot on the move
- Unselfish player that will make the extra pass, solid secondary playmaker, limits turnovers
- Aggressively attacks the rim to draw fouls, very good athlete, explosive finisher inside
- Lacks ideal ball handling skills to be a shot creator at the NBA level
- Limited basketball experience, started playing basketball full-time at age 15, doesn't know how to move off the ball at this stage
- Great athletic tools, can potentially defend multiple positions, still unpolished right now
- Usually a solid defender, actively contests shots, good quickness to stay in front of his man
- Tends to be too aggressive, can commit cheap fouls on the ball, undisciplined when closing out on perimeter shooters
- Good help defender, uses length to play passing lanes to get steals, can rotate inside to block shots, solid defensive rebounder

Tyrell Terry

Height	Weight	Cap #	Years Left
6'1"	160	$1.290M	2 + TO

Baseline Basic Stats

MPG	PTS	AST	REB	BLK	STL
18.1	6.7	2.8	1.7	0.1	0.7

Advanced Metrics

USG%	3PTA/FGA	FTA/FGA	TS%	eFG%	3PT%
18.6	0.350	0.234	0.504	0.468	0.355
AST%	**TOV%**	**OREB%**	**DREB%**	**STL%**	**BLK%**
23.7	15.5	2.0	9.3	2.1	0.4
PER	**ORTG**	**DRTG**	**WS/48**	**VOL**	
12.87	99.8	101.9	0.061	N/A	

- Drafted by Dallas with the 31st overall pick
- Named to the Pac-12's All-Freshman team last season
- Great all-around shooter at Stanford, made almost 41% of his threes in 2019-20
- Very good spot-up shooter that can also run off screens, good at making side-step threes off a pump fake
- Can use the threat of his shot to drive by defenders, effective pick-and-roll ball handler that can knock down pull-up jumpers or get to the rim
- More of a secondary playmaker, better at making simple reads, does not quite see the whole floor, somewhat turnover prone
- Limited defensive versatility, small frame may not allow him to defend taller players, lacks ideal length to contest shots
- Good lateral quickness, solid on-ball defender against smaller guards
- Solid pick-and-roll defender, good at preventing ball handlers from turning the corner
- Willing to fight through screens off the ball, consistently plays with high effort to close out on perimeter shooters
- Great at playing passing lanes to get steals, fairly good defensive rebounding guard

NEW ORLEANS PELICANS

Last Season: 30 – 42, Missed the Playoffs

Offensive Rating: 110.7, 17th in the NBA

Defensive Rating: 111.9, 19th in the NBA

Primary Executive: David Griffin, Executive Vice President of Basketball Operations

Head Coach: Stan Van Gundy

Key Roster Changes

Subtractions
Jrue Holiday, trade
Darius Miller, trade
Kenrich Williams, trade
Derrick Favors, free agency
E'Twaun Moore, free agency
Frank Jackson, free agency
Jahlil Okafor, free agency

Additions
Kira Lewis, Jr., draft
Eric Bledsoe, trade
Steven Adams, trade
Wenyen Gabriel, free agency
Willy Hernangomez, free agency

Roster

Likely Starting Five
1. *Eric Bledsoe*
2. *Lonzo Ball*
3. *Brandon Ingram*
4. *Zion Williamson*
5. Steven Adams

Other Key Rotation Players
J.J. Redick
Josh Hart
Nicolo Melli
Jaxson Hayes

* Italics denotes that a player is likely to be on the floor to close games

Remaining Roster

- Nickeil Alexander-Walker
- Wenyen Gabriel
- Kira Lewis, Jr.
- Sindarius Thornwell
- Willy Hernangomez
- Naji Marshall, 23, 6'7", 220, Xavier (Two-Way)
- Will Magnay, 22, 6'10", 234, Australia (Two-Way)
- Jarrod Uthoff, 27, 6'9", 221, Iowa (Exhibit 10)
- Tony Carr, 23, 6'5", 204, Penn State (Exhibit 10)
- Ike Anigbogu, 22, 6'10", 250, UCLA (Exhibit 10)

SCHREMPF Base Rating: 39.5 (72-game season)

Strengths

- Efficient shooting team that can attack the rim and spread the floor with credible three-point shooters
- Active group of big men that can generate plenty of second chance opportunities on the offensive glass

Question Marks

- Zion Williamson's ability to play starter level minutes for an entire season
- Potential for defensive improvement as a result of the coaching change

Outlook

- Could be greatly improved with a full season of Zion Williamson, could be in the mix for a playoff spot

Veterans

Brandon Ingram

Height	Weight	Cap #	Years Left
6'7"	190	$27.285M	4

	Similar at Age	**22** **Season**	**SIMsc**
1	Alec Burks	2013-14	921.9
2	Gordon Hayward	2012-13	913.1
3	Ricky Davis	2001-02	913.0
4	Rolando Blackman	1981-82	907.8
5	Emmanuel Mudiay	2018-19	905.8
6	Reggie Miller*	1987-88	905.0
7	Kevin Martin	2005-06	898.8
8	Richard Hamilton	2000-01	897.8
9	Michael Carter-Williams	2013-14	895.8
10	Evan Fournier	2014-15	893.8

Baseline Basic Stats

MPG	PTS	AST	REB	BLK	STL
33.4	18.5	3.6	4.3	0.4	1.0

Advanced Metrics

USG%	3PTA/FGA	FTA/FGA	TS%	eFG%	3PT%
25.5	0.282	0.354	0.564	0.509	0.380
AST%	**TOV%**	**OREB%**	**DREB%**	**STL%**	**BLK%**
19.3	13.0	2.3	13.8	1.4	1.2
PER	**ORTG**	**DRTG**	**WS/48**	**VOL**	
17.10	109.2	111.5	0.103	0.250	

- Named Most Improved Player in 2019-20, made his first All-Star team in his first season with New Orleans
- Thrived in his high volume role as New Orleans' primary scoring option
- Very good pick-and-roll ball handler and isolation player, can get to the rim and make pull-up jumpers
- Made over 39% of his threes, good spot-up shooter, good screener on pick-and-pops
- Still needs to improve his ability to shoot off screens, only about average last season
- Great cutter off the ball, selectively crashes the offensive boards to score on put-backs
- Very good secondary playmaker, can hit roll men inside, good at limiting turnovers
- 2019-20 Defensive Degree of Difficulty: 0.426, tends to guard starter level players
- Below average on-ball defender, can be bullied by stronger post players, gives up too much space for his man to take jump shots
- Below average pick-and-roll defender, tends to go too far under screens, not as effective at guarding switches
- Fights through screens off the ball, tends to be late when closing out on perimeter shooters
- Solid defensive rebounder, posts a middling steals rate, occasionally rotates from the weak side to block shots

Zion Williamson	Height	Weight	Cap #	Years Left
	6'6"	285	$10.245M	2 Team Options

	Similar at Age	19	
		Season	SIMsc
1	Eddy Curry	2001-02	810.0
2	Jabari Parker	2014-15	797.0
3	Kwame Brown	2001-02	793.4
4	Kendrick Perkins	2003-04	780.3
5	Tobias Harris	2011-12	774.9
6	Maciej Lampe	2004-05	773.9
7	Enes Kanter	2011-12	773.4
8	Carmelo Anthony	2003-04	772.5
9	Kris Humphries	2004-05	766.2

Baseline Basic Stats

MPG	PTS	AST	REB	BLK	STL
24.9	11.9	1.3	5.7	0.7	0.6

Advanced Metrics

USG%	3PTA/FGA	FTA/FGA	TS%	eFG%	3PT%
26.5	0.028	0.487	0.608	0.572	0.375
AST%	**TOV%**	**OREB%**	**DREB%**	**STL%**	**BLK%**
12.4	12.5	9.3	17.0	1.3	1.5
PER	**ORTG**	**DRTG**	**WS/48**	**VOL**	
22.70	114.8	110.3	0.149	0.423	

- Missed most of his rookie season due to a torn meniscus in his right knee
- Regular starter when healthy, named to the All-Rookie 1st team in 2019-20
- Unique body type, tough to find comps, highly efficient in his role as a high volume rim runner
- Explosive athleticism makes him a vertical threat to catch lobs, good roll man and cutter
- Aggressive offensive rebounder that scores on put-backs, runs hard down the floor in transition
- Good at using his wide frame to get deep position to score on post-ups
- Good at driving by slower big men on isolations, draws fouls at a high rate
- Went 6-for-14 (42.9%) on threes, solid passing big man that limits turnovers
- 2019-20 Defensive Degree of Difficulty: 0.388
- Tended to be hidden in lower leverage matchups, utilized as a roamer off the ball
- Above average on-ball defender, strong post defender, tended to give his man space to take jump shots on the perimeter
- Average pick-and-roll defender, solid in drop coverages, struggled to contain ball handlers on switches
- Stays attached to shooters off the ball, good at closing out in spot-up situations
- Below average rim protector, undisciplined with his positioning
- Did not really get steals or blocks at a high rate, middling defensive rebounder, struggled at times with his conditioning

Eric Bledsoe

Height	Weight	Cap #	Years Left
6'1"	205	$16.875M	2

Similar at Age 30

		Season	SIMsc
1	Terry Porter	1993-94	923.0
2	Derek Fisher	2004-05	916.9
3	Deron Williams	2014-15	915.6
4	Baron Davis	2009-10	906.3
5	Jeremy Lin	2018-19	902.6
6	George Hill	2016-17	899.2
7	Jameer Nelson	2012-13	898.9
8	Mike Bibby	2008-09	897.2
9	Mike James	2005-06	896.3
10	Earl Watson	2009-10	894.7

Baseline Basic Stats

MPG	PTS	AST	REB	BLK	STL
28.7	12.9	4.9	3.2	0.2	1.0

Advanced Metrics

USG%	3PTA/FGA	FTA/FGA	TS%	eFG%	3PT%
22.4	0.339	0.254	0.556	0.519	0.357
AST%	**TOV%**	**OREB%**	**DREB%**	**STL%**	**BLK%**
27.4	14.4	2.7	11.6	1.8	1.0
PER	**ORTG**	**DRTG**	**WS/48**	**VOL**	
16.91	111.2	107.0	0.132	0.341	

- Regular starter for Milwaukee last season, production closer to his career average in 2019-20
- Moderately high usage playmaker that excels with the ball in his hands, still posted a good Assist Percentage, slightly turnover prone last season
- Most effective as a pick-and-roll ball handler and isolation player, drew a few more fouls in 2019-20
- Average in other offensive situations, just above break-even on threes last season
- Does not shoot well on the move or off the dribble, opponents had success sagging off him in the playoffs in each of the last two seasons
- 2019-20 Defensive Degree of Difficulty: 0.470, made the All-Defensive 2nd team last season
- Defending starter level guards, took on tougher point guard matchups
- Solid on-ball defender that can stay with quicker guards
- Good pick-and-roll defender that can switch onto screener and contain ball handlers
- Consistently closes out on perimeter shooters, sometimes gets caught on screens off the ball
- Block Percentage is still consistent with his career average, Steal Percentage dropped considerably, solid defensive rebounder

Steven Adams	Height	Weight	Cap #	Years Left
	6'11"	265	$29.593M	2

	Similar at Age	26	
		Season	SIMsc
1	Nene	2008-09	930.8
2	Scot Pollard	2001-02	924.4
3	Derrick Favors	2017-18	905.2
4	Marc Gasol	2010-11	905.1
5	Gorgui Dieng	2015-16	903.2
6	Felton Spencer	1993-94	900.0
7	Kosta Koufos	2015-16	899.4
8	Joakim Noah	2011-12	896.0
9	Clemon Johnson	1982-83	895.7
10	Omer Asik	2012-13	894.5

Baseline Basic Stats

MPG	PTS	AST	REB	BLK	STL
30.1	12.3	1.9	7.8	1.2	1.0

Advanced Metrics

USG%	3PTA/FGA	FTA/FGA	TS%	eFG%	3PT%
17.6	0.019	0.378	0.584	0.563	0.242
AST%	**TOV%**	**OREB%**	**DREB%**	**STL%**	**BLK%**
10.9	12.8	11.1	20.9	1.6	3.2
PER	**ORTG**	**DRTG**	**WS/48**	**VOL**	
18.73	118.0	105.1	0.159	0.299	

- Regular starter for Oklahoma City in his seventh season in the NBA
- Consistently effective in his role as a low volume rim runner, made over 74% of his shots inside of three feet last season
- Good at rolling to the rim on pick-and-rolls, scores on a high volume of cuts off the ball
- Very good offensive rebounder that scores on a high volume of put-backs
- Runs hard down the floor in transition, has developed an effective short flip shot from around ten feet
- Has become a solid passing big man, set a career high in Assist Percentage, fairly solid at avoiding turnover
- 2019-20 Defensive Degree of Difficulty: 0.432, tends to guard starting level big men
- Average rim protector, opponents can exploit his limitations in mobility
- Active weak side defender, good defensive rebounder and shot blocker, gets steals at a high rate for a center
- Played below average on-ball defense, struggles to defend in space, tends to bite on fakes in the post
- Below average pick-and-roll defender, decent in drop coverages, has trouble containing ball handlers out on the perimeter
- Willing to close out on perimeter shooters, tends to be too aggressive, can allow driving lanes to the rim

Lonzo Ball

Height	Weight	Cap #	Years Left
6'6"	190	$11.004M	RFA

	Similar at Age	22 Season	SIMsc
1	Jamal Crawford	2002-03	895.6
2	Terrence Ross	2013-14	887.5
3	Brian Shaw	1988-89	885.0
4	Kyle Weaver	2008-09	880.5
5	Nik Stauskas	2015-16	874.2
6	Ben McLemore	2015-16	871.5
7	Delonte West	2005-06	871.0
8	Latrell Sprewell	1992-93	870.5
9	Chris Robinson	1996-97	870.4
10	Evan Fournier	2014-15	870.3

Baseline Basic Stats

MPG	PTS	AST	REB	BLK	STL
25.6	9.8	3.1	3.1	0.4	1.0

Advanced Metrics

USG%	3PTA/FGA	FTA/FGA	TS%	eFG%	3PT%
18.5	0.494	0.164	0.517	0.496	0.358
AST%	**TOV%**	**OREB%**	**DREB%**	**STL%**	**BLK%**
23.0	16.6	2.9	12.9	2.1	1.4
PER	**ORTG**	**DRTG**	**WS/48**	**VOL**	
12.91	103.7	109.1	0.065	0.339	

- Regular starter in his first season with New Orleans in 2019-20
- Had his most productive season in a low volume role as an additional ball handler
- Excellent playmaker that can throw accurate lobs and kick the ball out to shooters, fairly turnover prone
- Improved to become a good spot-up shooter, made 37.5% of his threes last season
- Struggles to shoot off the dribble, not really effective as a pick-and-roll ball handler or isolation player
- Good at using the screen to make outside jumpers on dribble hand-offs
- Below 50% free throw shooter in his career, improved his Free Throw Percentage to almost 57% last season
- 2019-20 Defensive Degree of Difficulty: 0.467
- Tends to guard starting level players, occasionally takes on tougher assignments
- Good on-ball defender against perimeter players, can get backed down in the post by stronger players
- Below average pick-and-roll defender, tends to go too far under screens, has trouble against bigger players on switches
- Good at closing out on spot-up shooters, occasionally is caught gambling when chasing shooters off screens
- Active help defender, gets steals and blocks at a fairly high rate, good defensive rebounding guard

J.J. Redick

Height	Weight	Cap #	Years Left
6'3"	200	$13.014M	UFA

Similar at Age **35**

		Season	SIMsc
1	Joe Dumars*	1998-99	916.7
2	Chauncey Billups	2011-12	909.3
3	Ray Allen*	2010-11	902.1
4	Byron Scott	1996-97	902.0
5	Dell Curry	1999-00	895.8
6	Terry Porter	1998-99	891.4
7	Chris Mullin*	1998-99	887.1
8	Jason Terry	2012-13	886.7
9	Brent Barry	2006-07	875.2
10	Jon Barry	2004-05	873.0

Baseline Basic Stats

MPG	PTS	AST	REB	BLK	STL
25.4	11.6	2.2	2.3	0.1	0.6

Advanced Metrics

USG%	3PTA/FGA	FTA/FGA	TS%	eFG%	3PT%
19.4	0.507	0.277	0.615	0.570	0.433
AST%	**TOV%**	**OREB%**	**DREB%**	**STL%**	**BLK%**
11.9	10.9	1.0	9.1	0.9	0.5
PER	**ORTG**	**DRTG**	**WS/48**	**VOL**	
14.35	116.5	111.4	0.126	0.467	

- Regular rotation player for New Orleans when healthy, missed a few games due to a strained left hamstring
- Maintained his effectiveness in his role as a moderate volume shooter off the ball
- Excellent all-around shooter, made over 45% of his threes last season
- Very good at coming off screens and making spot-up jumpers, good screener on a small sample of pick-and-pop plays
- Good at using an on-ball screen to make pull-up jumpers on pick-and-rolls or score on dribble hand-offs
- Fairly solid secondary playmaker that rarely turns the ball over
- 2019-20 Defensive Degree of Difficulty: 0.314
- Tends to hidden in favorable matchups against lower leverage second unit players
- Average on-ball defender, quick enough to prevent drives to the rim, taller wings can shoot over him
- Middling pick-and-roll defender, can be targeted by bigger players on switches, decent at fighting over screens to contain ball handlers
- Can get caught on screens off the ball, tended to be late when closing out in spot-up situations
- Stay-at-home defender, does not really get steals or blocks, decent defensive rebounder

Josh Hart

	Height	Weight	Cap #	Years Left
	6'5"	215	$3.491M	RFA

Similar at Age **24**

		Season	SIMsc
1	Arron Afflalo	2009-10	931.6
2	James Anderson	2013-14	930.3
3	Royce O'Neale	2017-18	925.4
4	Kelenna Azubuike	2007-08	923.8
5	Danny Green	2011-12	921.3
6	Anthony Morrow	2009-10	918.4
7	Denzel Valentine	2017-18	917.7
8	Kentavious Caldwell-Pope	2017-18	913.8
9	Scott Burrell	1994-95	910.7
10	Quincy Pondexter	2012-13	910.6

Baseline Basic Stats

MPG	PTS	AST	REB	BLK	STL
25.1	9.0	1.5	3.6	0.3	0.8

Advanced Metrics

USG%	3PTA/FGA	FTA/FGA	TS%	eFG%	3PT%
15.8	0.590	0.204	0.558	0.530	0.361
AST%	**TOV%**	**OREB%**	**DREB%**	**STL%**	**BLK%**
9.1	10.7	3.0	16.0	1.6	1.2
PER	**ORTG**	**DRTG**	**WS/48**	**VOL**	
11.94	110.0	110.4	0.090	0.375	

- Regular rotation player in his first season with New Orleans
- Mostly a low volume, spot-up shooter, made threes at just over a break-even rate last season
- Around a league average three-point shooter for his career, has made over 42% of his corner threes in three NBA seasons
- Good spot-up shooter that can also shoot off screens
- Moves well without the ball, good cutter, can occasionally crash the offensive glass to score on put-backs
- Mainly a catch-and-shoot player, passing improved slightly, good at avoiding turnovers
- 2019-20 Defensive Degree of Difficulty: 0.448
- Tends to guard starting level players, sometimes is tasked to guard elite perimeter players
- Solid on-ball defender that can guard multiple positions, occasionally can have trouble in the post against stronger players
- Fairly solid pick-and-roll defender, fairly good at switching, sometimes allows ball handlers to turn the corner
- Consistently closes out on perimeter shooters, gambles a bit too much when chasing shooters off screens
- Fairly active help defender, good defensive rebounder, gets steals and blocks at a moderate rate

Nicolò Melli

Height	Weight	Cap #	Years Left
6'9"	235	$3.897M	RFA

	Similar at Age	**29**	
		Season	**SIMsc**
1	Matt Bonner	2009-10	941.5
2	Pat Garrity	2005-06	930.2
3	Scott Padgett	2005-06	926.3
4	Anthony Tolliver	2014-15	924.2
5	Walter McCarty	2003-04	918.5
6	Nemanja Bjelica	2017-18	918.1
7	Patrick Patterson	2018-19	915.3
8	Pete Chilcutt	1997-98	912.4
9	Matt Bullard	1996-97	911.7
10	Jonas Jerebko	2016-17	910.5

Baseline Basic Stats

MPG	PTS	AST	REB	BLK	STL
19.1	6.9	1.1	3.6	0.3	0.5

Advanced Metrics

USG%	3PTA/FGA	FTA/FGA	TS%	eFG%	3PT%
16.1	0.569	0.215	0.547	0.517	0.345
AST%	**TOV%**	**OREB%**	**DREB%**	**STL%**	**BLK%**
9.8	10.8	4.4	15.4	1.4	1.6
PER	**ORTG**	**DRTG**	**WS/48**	**VOL**	
11.87	109.9	109.7	0.090	0.309	

- Regular rotation player for New Orleans in his rookie season
- Utilized as a low volume, stretch big, very good mid-range shooter, made threes at a rate just above break-even
- Good spot-up shooter, effective as a pick-and-pop screener, can occasionally shoot off screens
- Can post up smaller players, does most of his damage on the left block, better on the right block
- Above average rim runner, not overwhelmingly athletic, can slide into open spaces as the roll man or as an off-ball cutter
- Fairly solid passing big man that usually limits turnovers
- 2019-20 Defensive Degree of Difficulty: 0.332, tends to guard second unit level big men
- Below average rim protector, not really a shot blocker, middling defensive rebounder
- Below average on-ball defender, can be backed down inside by stronger post players, fairly foul prone
- Slightly better in space against isolations, contests jump shots, lacks lateral quickness to stay with opponents on a regular basis
- Average pick-and-roll defender, decent on switches, can allow ball handlers to turn the corner
- Tends to be late when closing out on perimeter shooters
- Has active hands, good at stripping the ball away to occasionally get steals

Jaxson Hayes	Height	Weight	Cap #	Years Left
	6'11"	220	$5.105M	2 Team Options

	Similar at Age	19	
		Season	SIMsc
1	Tyson Chandler	2001-02	890.3
2	Jarrett Allen	2017-18	887.5
3	Jermaine O'Neal	1997-98	881.8
4	Andris Biedrins	2005-06	870.0
5	Kevin Garnett*	1995-96	863.7
6	Derrick Favors	2010-11	859.8
7	Dwight Howard	2004-05	851.7
8	Thon Maker	2016-17	847.8
9	Chris Bosh	2003-04	846.2
10	Anthony Randolph	2008-09	843.6

Baseline Basic Stats

MPG	PTS	AST	REB	BLK	STL
23.7	8.5	1.1	6.5	1.4	0.5

Advanced Metrics

USG%	3PTA/FGA	FTA/FGA	TS%	eFG%	3PT%
16.3	0.015	0.583	0.647	0.624	0.235
AST%	**TOV%**	**OREB%**	**DREB%**	**STL%**	**BLK%**
8.8	13.5	10.2	19.8	1.3	3.8
PER	**ORTG**	**DRTG**	**WS/48**	**VOL**	
18.86	125.3	107.8	0.178	0.413	

- Regular rotation player for New Orleans in his rookie season
- Primarily a low volume, rim runner, made over 75% of his shots inside of three feet last season
- Excellent athleticism makes him a vertical lob threat, very good roll man and cutter off the ball
- Active offensive rebounder that scores on a high volume of put-backs
- Great at running the floor in transition to get dunks or draw shooting fouls
- No real shooting range outside of three feet, flashes some passing skills, solid at limiting turnovers
- 2019-20 Defensive Degree of Difficulty: 0.345, tended to guard second unit level big men
- Good rim protector, blocks shots at a high rate, fairly solid defensive rebounder
- Below average on-ball defender, can be bullied inside by stronger post players, has trouble defending in space against isolations, highly foul prone
- Decent pick-and-roll defender, can switch and cover roll men, does not always come out to guard perimeter ball handlers
- Tends to be too aggressive when closing out on perimeter shooters, can allow driving lanes to the rim

Nickeil Alexander-Walker	Height	Weight	Cap #	Years Left
	6'5"	205	$3.113M	2 Team Options

	Similar at Age	21	
		Season	SIMsc
1	Emmanuel Mudiay	2017-18	919.7
2	Archie Goodwin	2015-16	916.7
3	Malik Beasley	2017-18	907.9
4	Shannon Brown	2006-07	905.0
5	Chris Carr	1995-96	901.4
6	Malachi Richardson	2016-17	899.3
7	Rashad McCants	2005-06	898.7
8	D'Angelo Russell	2017-18	897.6
9	Corey Benjamin	1999-00	895.1
10	Tyler Dorsey	2017-18	895.0

Baseline Basic Stats

MPG	PTS	AST	REB	BLK	STL
20.1	8.8	1.5	2.2	0.1	0.6

Advanced Metrics

USG%	3PTA/FGA	FTA/FGA	TS%	eFG%	3PT%
20.6	0.384	0.173	0.532	0.508	0.374
AST%	**TOV%**	**OREB%**	**DREB%**	**STL%**	**BLK%**
16.4	12.6	1.6	10.2	1.5	0.7
PER	**ORTG**	**DRTG**	**WS/48**	**VOL**	
11.38	105.2	112.1	0.041	0.504	

- Fringe rotation player for New Orleans when healthy, missed games due to a fractured right wrist
- Used as a moderate volume, secondary ball handler off the bench
- Fairly good playmaking skills, can make interior passes and kick the ball out to shooters, a bit turnover prone last season
- Can make spot-up jumpers, made threes at a rate just above break-even, better as a corner three-point shooter
- Effective in a small sample of possessions at getting to the rim on dribble hand-offs
- Stationary shooter at this point, struggles to shoot off the dribble or on the move
- Can occasionally drive by defenders to get to the rim on isolations
- 2019-20 Defensive Degree of Difficulty: 0.303, tended to guard second unit level players
- Solid on-ball defender that can capably guard multiple positions
- Below average pick-and-roll defender, indecisive when making rotations, not especially effective on switches
- Fights through screens off the ball, tends to be late when closing out on perimeter shooters
- Solid defensive rebounder, got steals and blocks at a moderate rate

Wenyen Gabriel	Height	Weight	Cap #	Years Left
	6'9"	220	$1.621M	RFA

Similar at Age 22

		Season	SIMsc
1	Bill Curley	1994-95	900.6
2	Viktor Khryapa	2004-05	896.7
3	Taurean Prince	2016-17	889.4
4	Andre Roberson	2013-14	886.9
5	Mark Hendrickson	1996-97	886.6
6	A.C. Green	1985-86	885.1
7	Bill Garnett	1982-83	883.2
8	Pete Verhoeven	1981-82	879.8
9	Andrew DeClercq	1995-96	878.2
10	Brandon Davies	2013-14	877.7

Baseline Basic Stats

MPG	PTS	AST	REB	BLK	STL
18.8	6.2	1.0	4.1	0.5	0.6

Advanced Metrics

USG%	3PTA/FGA	FTA/FGA	TS%	eFG%	3PT%
14.8	0.319	0.381	0.556	0.513	0.359
AST%	**TOV%**	**OREB%**	**DREB%**	**STL%**	**BLK%**
6.9	16.7	8.3	15.8	1.7	1.9
PER	**ORTG**	**DRTG**	**WS/48**	**VOL**	
11.97	108.6	110.7	0.077	0.476	

- Traded to Portland from Sacramento in January 2020, became a rotation player near the end of last season
- Productive after the trade, had success in his role as a low volume, rim runner and stretch big
- Energetic athlete, made 70% of his shots inside of three feet, draws fouls at a high rate
- Good cutter off the ball, active offensive rebounder that scores on put-backs
- Flashed some stretch potential in Portland, went 5-for-12 (41.7%) on threes
- Strictly a catch-and-shoot or catch-and-finish player, limited playmaking skills, fairly turnover prone
- 2019-20 Defensive Degree of Difficulty: 0.287
- Played in garbage time early in the season, guarded second unit players when he played regular minutes
- Not tested often on the ball, played middling on-ball defense
- Solid against drives on the perimeter, tended to sag off his man, could backed down in the post by stronger players
- Decent pick-and-roll defender, good mobility to guard ball handlers for a few dribbles
- Tends to be either late or too aggressive when closing out on perimeter shooters
- Active help defender, gets steals and blocks at a high rate, fairly solid defensive rebounder

Sindarius Thornwell	Height	Weight	Cap #	Years Left
	6'5"	215	$1.621M	Team Option

	Similar at Age	25	
		Season	SIMsc
1	Kent Bazemore	2014-15	905.9
2	Von Wafer	2010-11	893.2
3	Mitchell Butler	1995-96	892.8
4	Luke Jackson	2006-07	889.7
5	Norman Powell	2018-19	888.9
6	Keith Bogans	2005-06	888.3
7	Sasha Danilovic	1995-96	887.7
8	Walter Bond	1994-95	886.2
9	Jeffery Taylor	2014-15	886.0
10	Scott Burrell	1995-96	885.8

Baseline Basic Stats

MPG	PTS	AST	REB	BLK	STL
19.5	7.0	1.3	2.8	0.2	0.7

Advanced Metrics

USG%	3PTA/FGA	FTA/FGA	TS%	eFG%	3PT%
15.9	0.413	0.319	0.564	0.533	0.374
AST%	**TOV%**	**OREB%**	**DREB%**	**STL%**	**BLK%**
10.7	13.9	2.0	12.4	1.7	1.5
PER	**ORTG**	**DRTG**	**WS/48**	**VOL**	
11.67	107.1	109.1	0.076	0.673	

- Spent most of the season in the G-League with the Rio Grande Valley Vipers, signed in July 2020 as a substitute for Josh Gray
- Used as a low volume, spot-up shooter and secondary ball handler in the G-League
- Made less than 30% of his threes in the G-League last season
- Mainly a spot-up shooter, struggles to shoot on the move or off the dribble
- Better as an off-ball player, effective cutter in previous NBA seasons
- Increased his Assist Percentage considerably in the G-League, fairly turnover prone last season
- 2019-20 Defensive Degree of Difficulty: 0.257
- Tended to play against other non-starters on the Magic and Kings in two games in Orlando
- Committed a shooting foul against Harrison Barnes in his only isolation possession
- Struggled in four pick-and-roll possessions, allowed five points, likely to D.J. Augustin
- Better at closing out in spot-up situations, forced threes misses, allowed one three to Melvin Frazier
- Solid defensive rebounder in his NBA career, gets steals and blocks at a fairly high rate

Willy Hernangómez	Height	Weight	Cap #	Years Left
	6'11"	240	$1.621M	UFA

	Similar at Age	25	
		Season	**SIMsc**
1	Scott Williams	1993-94	912.4
2	Cody Zeller	2017-18	902.0
3	J.J. Hickson	2013-14	901.2
4	Rony Seikaly	1990-91	899.1
5	Marty Conlon	1992-93	895.2
6	Rick Robey	1980-81	894.6
7	Joffrey Lauvergne	2016-17	893.7
8	Jonas Valanciunas	2017-18	893.3
9	Alaa Abdelnaby	1993-94	893.2
10	Thomas Robinson	2016-17	893.0

Baseline Basic Stats

MPG	PTS	AST	REB	BLK	STL
22.1	9.7	1.1	6.7	0.6	0.6

Advanced Metrics

USG%	3PTA/FGA	FTA/FGA	TS%	eFG%	3PT%
20.9	0.105	0.403	0.566	0.526	0.285
AST%	**TOV%**	**OREB%**	**DREB%**	**STL%**	**BLK%**
10.5	13.2	12.2	24.4	1.4	1.9
PER	**ORTG**	**DRTG**	**WS/48**	**VOL**	
18.61	113.5	108.0	0.135	0.599	

- Fringe rotation player for Charlotte last season
- Mainly used as a rim runner that took on moderately high volume against non-starters
- Mostly scored as the roll man on pick-and-rolls or as a cutter
- Very effective offensive rebounder that actively crashed the glass to score on put-backs
- Solid passing big man, was a little turnover prone last season
- Took threes at a higher rate in limited minutes, outside shot is still inconsistent, percentage declined significantly
- Below break-even three-point shooter for his career, slightly better in the corners
- 2019-20 Defensive Degree of Difficulty: 0.284
- Usually plays in garbage time or against second unit level players
- Below average rim protector, shot blocking rate declined significantly, still a very good defensive rebounder
- Struggles on defense in general due to a lack of mobility, has difficulty defending in space
- Below average at defending isolation plays and pick-and-rolls
- Will consistently close out on perimeter shooters in spot-up situations

Newcomers

Kira Lewis, Jr.	Height	Weight	Cap #	Years Left
	6'3"	165	$3.640	1 + 2 TO

Baseline Basic Stats

MPG	PTS	AST	REB	BLK	STL
20.8	8.4	3.3	2.1	0.1	0.8

Advanced Metrics

USG%	3PTA/FGA	FTA/FGA	TS%	eFG%	3PT%
20.6	0.327	0.228	0.508	0.471	0.321
AST%	**TOV%**	**OREB%**	**DREB%**	**STL%**	**BLK%**
27.4	15.6	1.8	8.8	1.7	0.6
PER	**ORTG**	**DRTG**	**WS/48**	**VOL**	
13.27	99.6	105.8	0.064	N/A	

- Drafted by New Orleans with the 13th overall pick
- Led Alabama in scoring, named to the All-SEC 1st Team in 2019-20
- Has great speed, dynamic transition player, blows by defenders when he has the ball in his hands
- Above average outside shooter, good stand-still spot-up shooter, struggles to shoot on the move or off the dribble
- Not really a natural playmaker, does not really see the whole floor, can be careless with the ball
- Great quickness and athleticism, unpolished as an overall defender
- Effective weak side defender, plays passing lanes to get steals, solid defensive rebounder
- Middling on-ball defender, can stay with opposing guards, tends to give up too much space for his man to take jump shots
- Average pick-and-roll defender, tends to go too far under screens
- Gambles too much off the ball, can get caught out of position trying to shoot the gap, tends to close out too aggressively

DENVER NUGGETS

Last Season: 46 – 27, Lost in Conference Finals to L.A. Lakers (1 – 4)

Offensive Rating: 113.1, 5th in the NBA

Defensive Rating: 111.0, 16th in the NBA

Primary Executive: Tim Connelly, President of Basketball Operations

Head Coach: Mike Malone

Key Roster Changes

Subtractions
Jerami Grant, free agency
Torrey Craig, free agency
Mason Plumlee, free agency
Troy Daniels, free agency
Noah Vonleh, free agency
Keita Bates-Diop, waived

Additions
Zeke Nnaji, draft
R.J. Hampton, draft
JaMychal Green, free agency
Facundo Campazzo, free agency
Isaiah Hartenstein, free agency

Roster

Likely Starting Five
1. *Jamal Murray*
2. *Gary Harris*
3. *Will Barton*
4. *Paul Millsap*
5. *Nikola Jokic*

Other Key Rotation Players
Michael Porter, Jr.
Monte Morris
JaMychal Green
P.J. Dozier

* Italics denotes that a player is likely to be on the floor to close games

Remaining Roster

- Bol Bol
- Zeke Nnaji
- Facundo Campazzo
- R.J. Hampton
- Vlatko Cancar
- Isaiah Hartenstein
- Markus Howard, 21, 5'11", 180, Marquette (Two-Way)
- Greg Whittington, 27, 6'8", 212, Georgetown (Two-Way)

SCHREMPF Base Rating: 38.7 (72-game season)

Strengths

- Efficient offense that utilizes lots of effective ball movement
- Excellent chemistry between Nikola Jokic and Jamal Murray

Question Marks

- Lack of a true defensive stopper or reliable scheme
- Limited depth beyond their top eight players

Outlook

- Solid playoff team, could be on the borderline between the top six seeds and the play-in tournament

Veterans

Nikola Jokić	Height	Weight	Cap #	Years Left
	7'0"	253	$29.542M	2

	Similar at Age	24	
		Season	SIMsc
1	Dirk Nowitzki	2002-03	880.0
2	Greg Monroe	2014-15	879.7
3	Blake Griffin	2013-14	872.6
4	Julius Randle	2018-19	872.6
5	Charlie Villanueva	2008-09	869.7
6	Nikola Vucevic	2014-15	861.2
7	Markieff Morris	2013-14	861.1
8	Chris Webber	1997-98	859.9
9	Andray Blatche	2010-11	859.4
10	Christian Laettner	1993-94	858.3

Baseline Basic Stats

MPG	PTS	AST	REB	BLK	STL
31.7	17.9	3.4	8.9	0.8	1.0

Advanced Metrics

USG%	3PTA/FGA	FTA/FGA	TS%	eFG%	3PT%
25.6	0.200	0.296	0.580	0.536	0.347
AST%	**TOV%**	**OREB%**	**DREB%**	**STL%**	**BLK%**
27.6	13.5	7.5	25.3	1.7	1.8
PER	**ORTG**	**DRTG**	**WS/48**	**VOL**	
23.14	116.0	106.2	0.186	0.412	

- Made his second All-Star team, named to the All-NBA 2nd Team in 2019-20
- One of the NBA best offensive centers, elite playmaker that has excellent court vision to create offense for his teammates
- Excellent post-up player that can score with a variety of moves
- Consistently good mid-range shooter, more effective three-point shooter in the playoffs, has made almost 42% of his threes over the last two post-seasons
- Better at shooting on the move, good screener on pick-and-pops, can also shoot off screens
- Decent rim runner, good cutter off the ball, crashes the offensive boards to score on put-backs, does not really roll hard to the rim on pick-and-rolls
- 2019-20 Defensive Degree of Difficulty: 0.420, tends to guard starting level big men
- Solid rim protector, stays vertical to contest shots, not really a shot blocker, great defensive rebounder
- Played effective on-ball defender, good at holding position in the post, mobile enough to defend in space
- Solid pick-and-roll defender, more engaged when switching on the perimeter, tended to lose track of screeners in drop coverages
- Usually came out to contest perimeter shots in spot-up situations

Jamal Murray

Height	Weight	Cap #	Years Left
6'4"	201	$27.285M	4

Similar at Age 22

		Season	SIMsc
1	Marcus Thornton	2009-10	943.8
2	Bradley Beal	2015-16	940.2
3	Emmanuel Mudiay	2018-19	936.8
4	Ben Gordon	2005-06	936.1
5	Dion Waiters	2013-14	932.4
6	Brandon Knight	2013-14	925.2
7	O.J. Mayo	2009-10	919.7
8	Damian Lillard	2012-13	917.4
9	Eric Gordon	2010-11	915.0
10	Jordan Clarkson	2014-15	914.0

Baseline Basic Stats

MPG	PTS	AST	REB	BLK	STL
31.3	16.9	3.5	3.5	0.2	1.0

Advanced Metrics

USG%	3PTA/FGA	FTA/FGA	TS%	eFG%	3PT%
24.7	0.346	0.225	0.557	0.515	0.369

AST%	TOV%	OREB%	DREB%	STL%	BLK%
21.0	11.5	2.5	10.5	1.6	0.8

PER	ORTG	DRTG	WS/48	VOL
17.28	110.9	110.7	0.118	0.309

- Missed games due to a sprained left ankle and a left hamstring injury, broke out with an excellent performance in the 2020 NBA Playoffs
- Highly effective as Denver's lead ball handling guard, continued to increase his production
- Developed outstanding chemistry with Nikola Jokic to be dynamic on dribble hand-offs and pick-and-rolls
- Good at attacking the basket and shooting off the dribble, not quite as effective in isolation situations
- Solid three-point shooter for his career, good spot-up shooter that can also run off screens
- Fairly solid playmaker that can hit open shooters and avoid turnovers
- Good cutter off the ball, shows some ability to post up smaller guards
- 2019-20 Defensive Degree of Difficulty: 0.419, tends to defend starting level guards
- Middling on-ball defender, struggles to stay with quicker guards, strong enough to handle bigger perimeter players in the post
- Average pick-and-roll defender, fights over screens to chase ball handlers off the three-point line, tends to allow ball handlers to turn the corner
- Stays attached to shooters off the ball, consistently closes out in spot-up situations
- Fairly solid defensive rebounding guard, posted a career high in Steal Percentage last season

Will Barton

Height	Weight	Cap #	Years Left
6'5"	175	$13.723M	Player Option

Similar at Age 29

		Season	SIMsc
1	Rex Chapman	1996-97	926.4
2	Cuttino Mobley	2004-05	909.8
3	Kerry Kittles	2003-04	909.7
4	Marco Belinelli	2015-16	903.5
5	Larry Hughes	2007-08	901.2
6	Danny Ainge	1988-89	900.0
7	Vernon Maxwell	1994-95	898.1
8	Goran Dragic	2015-16	895.7
9	George Hill	2015-16	894.4
10	Derek Anderson	2003-04	894.3

Baseline Basic Stats

MPG	PTS	AST	REB	BLK	STL
30.0	13.0	3.0	3.8	0.3	1.0

Advanced Metrics

USG%	3PTA/FGA	FTA/FGA	TS%	eFG%	3PT%
19.9	0.371	0.197	0.531	0.497	0.354
AST%	**TOV%**	**OREB%**	**DREB%**	**STL%**	**BLK%**
15.2	10.9	3.2	14.4	1.6	1.1
PER	**ORTG**	**DRTG**	**WS/48**	**VOL**	
13.91	107.1	109.1	0.082	0.290	

- Had a bounce-back year in 2019-20, regular starter when healthy, missed the Orlando bubble due to a sore right knee
- Increased his effectiveness as a moderate volume shooter off the ball
- Made 37.5% of his threes last season, good spot-up shooter, could make quick, no dribble jumpers on isolation plays
- Good on dribble hand-offs at getting to the rim or using the screen to make outside shots
- Excellent cutter off the ball, ranked in the 98th percentile at per-possession scoring off cuts
- Solid secondary playmaker that can hit cutters, very good at avoiding turnovers
- <u>2019-20 Defensive Degree of Difficulty</u>: 0.457
- Usually guards starter level players, sometimes takes on tougher defensive assignments
- Good on-ball defender, solid perimeter defender, can be backed down in the post by stronger players
- Solid pick-and-roll defender, good at switching, sometimes has trouble containing elite ball handlers
- Fights through screens off the ball, tends to be too aggressive when closing out on perimeter shooters
- Good defensive rebounder, Steal and Block Percentages are still consistent with his career averages

Paul Millsap

Height	Weight	Cap #	Years Left
6'7"	250	$10.000M	UFA

Similar at Age **34**

		Season	SIMsc
1	Shawn Marion	2012-13	888.6
2	Luis Scola	2014-15	886.4
3	Nick Collison	2014-15	883.4
4	Sam Perkins	1995-96	882.8
5	Frank Brickowski	1993-94	875.8
6	David West	2014-15	873.0
7	Charles Barkley*	1997-98	871.9
8	Anthony Mason	2000-01	870.4
9	Bob Lanier*	1982-83	868.4
10	Robert Horry	2004-05	865.9

Baseline Basic Stats

MPG	PTS	AST	REB	BLK	STL
22.5	8.8	1.7	4.6	0.5	0.8

Advanced Metrics

USG%	3PTA/FGA	FTA/FGA	TS%	eFG%	3PT%
18.1	0.311	0.287	0.570	0.532	0.366
AST%	**TOV%**	**OREB%**	**DREB%**	**STL%**	**BLK%**
10.6	13.3	7.6	18.1	1.7	2.4
PER	**ORTG**	**DRTG**	**WS/48**	**VOL**	
15.26	111.8	107.5	0.120	0.405	

- Missed games due to a bruised left knee, sprained right ankle and a sprained right quadriceps
- Regular starter when healthy, effective in a moderate volume role as a spot-up shooter and interior player
- Made 43.5% of his threes last season, good spot-up shooter and screener on pick-and-pops
- Average post-up player at this stage of his career, good against smaller players, has trouble finishing against longer big men
- Average rim runner, does not have the lift to finish in traffic
- Very good transition player, runs hard to beat his man down the floor, can set up for trail threes
- Fairly solid passing big man that kicks the ball out to shooters, good at limiting turnovers
- 2019-20 Defensive Degree of Difficulty: 0.439
- Guards starting level players, sometimes takes on tougher defensive assignments
- Solid on-ball defender that can guard perimeter and post players
- Decent pick-and-roll defender, solid in drop coverages, has trouble staying with quicker ball handlers in space
- Fights through screens off the ball, can be too aggressive when closing out on perimeter shooters
- Good defensive rebounder, Steal and Block Percentages are down from his career averages

Gary Harris

Height	Weight	Cap #	Years Left
6'4"	205	$19.611M	1

Similar at Age 25

		Season	SIMsc
1	Courtney Lee	2010-11	949.6
2	Shannon Brown	2010-11	948.5
3	Wayne Ellington	2012-13	945.6
4	Jodie Meeks	2012-13	945.4
5	Kentavious Caldwell-Pope	2018-19	941.6
6	Anthony Peeler	1994-95	941.1
7	Marcus Thornton	2012-13	940.0
8	Austin Rivers	2017-18	936.0
9	Fred Jones	2004-05	934.8
10	Von Wafer	2010-11	934.0

Baseline Basic Stats

MPG	PTS	AST	REB	BLK	STL
25.4	10.7	1.9	2.6	0.2	0.9

Advanced Metrics

USG%	3PTA/FGA	FTA/FGA	TS%	eFG%	3PT%
18.4	0.419	0.203	0.534	0.498	0.353
AST%	**TOV%**	**OREB%**	**DREB%**	**STL%**	**BLK%**
11.3	10.1	1.9	8.6	1.9	0.7
PER	**ORTG**	**DRTG**	**WS/48**	**VOL**	
11.97	106.9	111.2	0.061	0.200	

- Regular starter for Denver for the last five seasons, missed games due to a strained right adductor and right hip
- Shifted to a role as a low volume, spot-up shooter, shot a break-even percentage on threes last season
- Has made 40% of his corner threes in his career, mainly a spot-up shooter at this stage
- Handling the ball less, not as effective on pick-and-rolls or driving on isolation plays
- Rated as average or worse in most half-court offense situations last season
- Now a catch-and-shoot player, showed decent passing skills in previous years, good at avoiding turnovers
- 2019-20 Defensive Degree of Difficulty; 0.532
- Usually takes on tougher assignments against top guards or wing players
- Fairly good on-ball defender that guards multiple positions, taller wing players have some success shooting over the top of him
- Solid pick-and-roll defender, good at switching, occasionally will go too far under screens
- Good at closing out on perimeter shooters, gambles a bit too much when chasing shooters off screens
- Has active hands, good at playing passing lanes, gets steals at a high rate, middling defensive rebounder

Michael Porter, Jr.	Height	Weight	Cap #	Years Left
	6'10"	215	$3.551M	Team Option

Similar at Age 21

		Season	SIMsc
1	Austin Daye	2009-10	910.5
2	Shawne Williams	2007-08	902.5
3	Ryan Anderson	2009-10	892.7
4	Marquese Chriss	2018-19	890.5
5	Trey Lyles	2016-17	890.2
6	Andrea Bargnani	2006-07	889.3
7	Rashard Lewis	2000-01	889.2
8	Ivan Rabb	2018-19	889.0
9	Quincy Miller	2013-14	888.2
10	Bobby Portis	2016-17	885.6

Baseline Basic Stats

MPG	PTS	AST	REB	BLK	STL
22.9	10.1	1.3	5.1	0.6	0.7

Advanced Metrics

USG%	3PTA/FGA	FTA/FGA	TS%	eFG%	3PT%
20.4	0.260	0.220	0.569	0.536	0.373
AST%	**TOV%**	**OREB%**	**DREB%**	**STL%**	**BLK%**
9.4	10.8	7.3	19.9	1.6	1.9
PER	**ORTG**	**DRTG**	**WS/48**	**VOL**	
16.74	113.1	108.2	0.134	0.449	

- Regular rotation player for Denver as a rookie, made the All-Seeding Games 2nd Team in the Orlando restart
- Highly productive in his role as a moderate volume scorer off the bench
- Made over 42% of his threes in 2019-20, great spot-up shooter, good at making quick no dribble jumpers in isolation situations
- Inconsistent shooter off the dribble, not really able to shoot on the move
- Good at using a screen to get to the rim or make outside shots on dribble hand-offs
- Good cutter off the ball, can post up smaller players
- Struggles to make reads as a pick-and-roll ball handler, limited playmaking skills
- 2019-20 Defensive Degree of Difficulty: 0.323
- Hidden in favorable matchups against lower leverage second unit players
- Middling on-ball defender, struggles to stay with opposing perimeter players, better against bigger post players
- Below average pick-and-roll defender, struggled to make solid rotations
- Tends to ball-watch or gamble to make plays on the ball, usually is out of position to contest perimeter shots
- Active help defender, good defensive rebounder and weak side shot blocker, gets steals at a moderate rate

Monte Morris	Height	Weight	Cap #	Years Left
	6'2"	175	$1.724M	3

	Similar at Age	24 Season	SIMsc
1	Steve Kerr	1989-90	934.7
2	B.J. Armstrong	1991-92	929.6
3	Chris Quinn	2007-08	927.8
4	C.J. Watson	2008-09	924.1
5	Steve Alford	1988-89	918.8
6	Norris Cole	2012-13	917.3
7	Sedale Threatt	1985-86	916.0
8	George Hill	2010-11	915.9
9	Kyle Macy	1981-82	913.2
10	Luke Ridnour	2005-06	907.7

Baseline Basic Stats

MPG	PTS	AST	REB	BLK	STL
25.5	9.7	3.6	2.2	0.1	0.9

Advanced Metrics

USG%	3PTA/FGA	FTA/FGA	TS%	eFG%	3PT%
17.9	0.302	0.190	0.552	0.516	0.359
AST%	**TOV%**	**OREB%**	**DREB%**	**STL%**	**BLK%**
23.8	10.5	1.6	8.1	1.9	0.5
PER	**ORTG**	**DRTG**	**WS/48**	**VOL**	
15.31	116.4	110.8	0.125	0.306	

- Maintained his effectiveness in his second full season as a regular rotation player for Denver
- Used as a low volume, pass-first backup point guard, rarely turns the ball over, solid overall playmaker
- Has made almost 40% of his career threes, very good spot-up shooter that can shoot off screens
- Good at making outside shots or getting to the rim on dribble hand-offs
- Can make pull-up jumpers as a pick-and-roll ball handler, effective cutter without the ball
- Can occasionally sneak by defenders on isolations, not really a threat to score off the dribble
- 2019-20 Defensive Degree of Difficulty: 0.335, tends to guard second unit level players
- Fairly solid on-ball defender, stays with quicker guards on the perimeter, has trouble against bigger perimeter players in the post
- Solid pick-and-roll defender, effective on switches, occasionally allows ball handlers to turn the corner
- Fights through screens off the ball, sometimes can be late to close out on perimeter shooters
- Middling defensive rebounder, posts a solid Steal Percentage, Block Percentage increased significantly last season

JaMychal Green

Height	Weight	Cap #	Years Left
6'8"	227	$7.200M	1

Similar at Age **29**

		Season	SIMsc
1	Devean George	2006-07	915.5
2	Anthony Tolliver	2014-15	910.1
3	Jonas Jerebko	2016-17	905.8
4	Lance Thomas	2017-18	905.3
5	Mirza Teletovic	2014-15	904.7
6	Pete Chilcutt	1997-98	904.6
7	Marvin Williams	2015-16	904.6
8	Andres Nocioni	2008-09	904.6
9	David Benoit	1997-98	902.3
10	Scott Burrell	1999-00	900.0

Baseline Basic Stats

MPG	PTS	AST	REB	BLK	STL
18.8	6.8	0.9	4.0	0.3	0.4

Advanced Metrics

USG%	3PTA/FGA	FTA/FGA	TS%	eFG%	3PT%
15.9	0.534	0.168	0.558	0.534	0.376
AST%	**TOV%**	**OREB%**	**DREB%**	**STL%**	**BLK%**
6.3	11.1	5.6	21.3	1.1	1.5
PER	**ORTG**	**DRTG**	**WS/48**	**VOL**	
11.98	109.7	107.6	0.104	0.292	

- Regular rotation player for the Clippers in his first full season with the team
- Mainly used as a low volume, stretch big, made almost 39% of his threes last season
- Primarily a stationary spot-up shooter, effective as a screener on pick-and-pops last season
- Not quite as effective as a rim runner, does not have the lift to finish efficiently at the rim
- Rated as average or worse in every offensive situation except spot-up shooting
- Catch-and-shoot player, limited passing skills, good at avoiding turnovers
- 2019-20 Defensive Degree of Difficulty: 0.347, tended to guard second unit level players
- Very good defensive rebounder, average rim protector, not really a shot blocker
- Middling on-ball defender, does not have the length to contest shots in the post, better at guarding quicker big men in space
- Below average pick-and-roll defender, limited mobility, late to cover roll men, has trouble keeping up with ball handlers on the perimeter
- Consistently comes out to contest shots on the perimeter in spot-up situations

PJ Dozier

	Height	Weight	Cap #	Years Left
PJ Dozier	6'6"	205	$1.763M	1

	Similar at Age	**23**	
		Season	**SIMsc**
1	Chris Robinson	1997-98	916.8
2	Darrun Hilliard	2016-17	916.6
3	Conner Henry	1986-87	915.9
4	Damyean Dotson	2017-18	915.7
5	Kevin Loder	1982-83	909.8
6	George McCloud	1990-91	907.6
7	Dillon Brooks	2018-19	906.1
8	Chris Carr	1997-98	905.0
9	Daniel Hamilton	2018-19	902.2
10	Terrence Williams	2010-11	901.1

Baseline Basic Stats

MPG	PTS	AST	REB	BLK	STL
18.7	8.1	1.7	2.6	0.2	0.6

Advanced Metrics

USG%	3PTA/FGA	FTA/FGA	TS%	eFG%	3PT%
22.3	0.357	0.176	0.503	0.474	0.320
AST%	**TOV%**	**OREB%**	**DREB%**	**STL%**	**BLK%**
16.4	12.1	4.2	14.7	1.6	0.8
PER	**ORTG**	**DRTG**	**WS/48**	**VOL**	
12.21	102.4	110.4	0.041	0.376	

- Started on a Two-Way contract, converted to a standard contract in June 2020
- Became a rotation player for Denver in the playoffs, used as a secondary ball handler off the bench
- Struggles to score efficiently, settles for a lot of tough floaters in the paint
- Rated as average or worse in most half-court situations on offense
- Inconsistent shooter off the dribble, above average at making long twos, above break-even three-point shooter last season
- Excellent transition player and cutter off the ball, made almost 68% of his shots inside of three feet in 2019-20
- Solid secondary playmaker that can find open shooters or cutters inside, good at avoiding turnovers
- 2019-20 Defensive Degree of Difficulty: 0.332, mostly guarded second unit players
- Played good on-ball defense, could capably defend multiple positions, drew some tough assignments in the playoffs
- Average pick-and-roll defender, fought over screens to take away the outside shots, tended to allow ball handlers to turn the corner
- Tended to be late when closing out on perimeter shooters, sometimes gets caught on screens off the ball
- Solid defensive rebounder, gets steals and blocks at a fairly solid rate

Bol Bol

	Height	Weight	Cap #	Years Left
	7'2"	235	$2.058M	1

	Similar at Age	20 Season	SIMsc
1	Mohamed Bamba	2018-19	857.6
2	Kristaps Porzingis	2015-16	850.4
3	Darko Milicic	2005-06	845.5
4	Tyson Chandler	2002-03	832.5
5	Andray Blatche	2006-07	831.7
6	Myles Turner	2016-17	830.9
7	Dirk Nowitzki	1998-99	827.5
8	Isaiah Hartenstein	2018-19	825.5
9	Skal Labissiere	2016-17	824.3
10	Zach Collins	2017-18	822.4

Baseline Basic Stats

MPG	PTS	AST	REB	BLK	STL
22.4	9.4	1.0	5.4	1.4	0.5

Advanced Metrics

USG%	3PTA/FGA	FTA/FGA	TS%	eFG%	3PT%
20.4	0.287	0.315	0.591	0.552	0.431
AST%	**TOV%**	**OREB%**	**DREB%**	**STL%**	**BLK%**
8.3	17.3	7.2	18.2	1.1	5.2
PER	**ORTG**	**DRTG**	**WS/48**	**VOL**	
15.70	107.0	107.5	0.104	0.406	

- Played on a Two-Way contract, missed most of 2019-20 due to a left foot injury
- Used in the Orlando seeding games as a moderate volume, stretch big and rim runner
- Went 4-for-9 (44.4%) on threes, most effective as a screener on pick-and-pops, could set up for trail threes in transition
- Flashed an ability to shoot off screens, not as effective as a stationary shooter
- Made almost 78% of his shots inside of three feet, scores on put-backs, runs the floor hard in transition
- Can shoot over players in the post, does not hold position well due to his thin frame
- Shows some passing skills, pretty turnover prone at this stage
- 2019-20 Defensive Degree of Difficulty: 0.311, only played 87 NBA minutes
- Tended to guard second unit level players
- Below average rim protector, highly foul prone, great shot blocker, decent defensive rebounder
- Forced one miss and allowed made basket in his only two post-up possessions
- Struggled to stay with quicker players on the perimeter
- Played solid pick-and-roll defense, effective at baiting ball handlers into taking contested jumpers
- Tended to be either late or too aggressive when closing out on perimeter shooters, still learning NBA defensive schemes and rotations

Vlatko Čančar

Height	Weight	Cap #	Years Left
6'8"	210	$1.518M	1

Similar at Age **22**

		Season	SIMsc
1	Charlie Sitton	1984-85	904.8
2	K.J. McDaniels	2015-16	901.4
3	Devean George	1999-00	895.6
4	Donyell Marshall	1995-96	891.7
5	Sergei Monia	2005-06	887.1
6	Bobby Simmons	2002-03	886.6
7	Jason Kapono	2003-04	885.0
8	Joe Alexander	2008-09	882.6
9	Quincy Lewis	1999-00	881.7
10	Gerald Green	2007-08	880.6

Baseline Basic Stats

MPG	PTS	AST	REB	BLK	STL
18.7	6.9	1.1	3.9	0.4	0.6

Advanced Metrics

USG%	3PTA/FGA	FTA/FGA	TS%	eFG%	3PT%
18.3	0.334	0.266	0.537	0.483	0.300
AST%	**TOV%**	**OREB%**	**DREB%**	**STL%**	**BLK%**
9.4	13.6	9.2	15.9	1.5	1.6
PER	**ORTG**	**DRTG**	**WS/48**	**VOL**	
13.24	109.2	110.4	0.087	0.587	

- Played sparingly for Denver in his rookie season, spent some time in the G-League with the Erie BayHawks
- Used as a low volume, spot-up shooter in limited NBA minutes, took on more volume with Erie
- Made over 39% of his threes in the G-League, mainly a spot-up shooter, flashed some ability to shoot off screens
- Has not yet shown that he can be effective in on-ball situations at the NBA level
- Mainly a catch-and-shoot player right now, shows fairly solid secondary playmaking skills, a bit turnover prone in the G-League
- 2019-20 Defensive Degree of Difficulty: 0.247, only played 45 NBA minutes
- Struggled to play on-ball defense, allowed two made threes and committed two shooting fouls in three isolation possessions and one post-up possession
- Decent at playing pick-and-roll defense, forced eight misses in 12 possessions, sometimes allowed ball handlers to turn the corner to get easy layups
- Tended to be late when closing out on perimeter shooters, allowed three made threes in six spot-up possessions
- Solid defensive rebounder in the G-League, got steals at a moderate rate

Isaiah Hartenstein	Height	Weight	Cap #	Years Left
	7'0"	249	$1.621M	Player Option

	Similar at Age	21	
		Season	SIMsc
1	Jakob Poeltl	2016-17	912.7
2	Steven Adams	2014-15	889.2
3	Dalibor Bagaric	2001-02	882.5
4	Greg Oden	2008-09	879.2
5	Josh McRoberts	2008-09	878.7
6	Patrick O'Bryant	2007-08	877.9
7	DeAndre Jordan	2009-10	876.8
8	Alex Len	2014-15	875.8
9	Damian Jones	2016-17	875.8
10	Robin Lopez	2009-10	875.4

Baseline Basic Stats

MPG	PTS	AST	REB	BLK	STL
16.6	5.2	0.6	4.4	0.9	0.4

Advanced Metrics

USG%	3PTA/FGA	FTA/FGA	TS%	eFG%	3PT%
13.8	0.044	0.339	0.593	0.564	0.189

AST%	TOV%	OREB%	DREB%	STL%	BLK%
8.4	16.7	11.0	19.4	1.5	3.4

PER	ORTG	DRTG	WS/48	VOL
14.46	117.8	106.6	0.142	0.495

- Played sparingly for Houston in 2019-20, waived right before the Orlando restart
- Utilized as a low volume, rim runner, plays with a high motor, will draw fouls at a high rate
- Dives hard to the rim as a roll man and cutter off the ball, active offensive rebounder
- Mainly sticks to scoring in the immediate basket area, flashed some ability to make shorter mid-range shots
- Fairly decent passer that can find open shooters, somewhat turnover prone in his limited minutes
- 2019-20 Defensive Degree of Difficulty: 0.316, mostly guarded second unit level big men
- Middling rim protector, highly foul prone, good defensive rebounder and shot blocker
- Strong post defender that holds position inside, defended well against opposing big men in isolation situations
- Mixed results as a pick-and-roll defender, tended to be late to rotate back to the screener, was better at switching out on ball handlers
- Tended to stay in the paint, did not really come out to contest perimeter shots

Newcomers

Zeke Nnaji	**Height**	**Weight**	**Cap #**	**Years Left**
	6'11"	240	$2.380M	1 + 2 TO

Baseline Basic Stats

MPG	PTS	AST	REB	BLK	STL
19.3	6.7	0.9	4.7	0.6	0.5

Advanced Metrics

USG%	3PTA/FGA	FTA/FGA	TS%	eFG%	3PT%
17.2	0.086	0.383	0.515	0.475	0.307
AST%	**TOV%**	**OREB%**	**DREB%**	**STL%**	**BLK%**
6.9	13.8	8.9	18.5	1.3	2.5
PER	**ORTG**	**DRTG**	**WS/48**	**VOL**	
13.96	101.9	99.3	0.071	N/A	

- Drafted by Denver with the 22nd overall pick
- Made the All-Pac 12 1st Team, named Pac-12 Rookie of the Year in 2019-20
- High motor rim runner, has good hands, great athleticism and length makes him a vertical lob threat
- Rolls hard to the rim on pick-and-rolls, effective cutter off the ball, crashes the offensive glass to score on put-backs
- Lacks advanced post moves, limited as a passer, solid at avoiding turnovers
- May have some shooting potential, good free throw shooter, range doesn't extend beyond the paint right now
- Effective rim protector at Arizona, good defensive rebounder and shot blocker
- Frame is somewhat thin, has solid functional strength, good at holding position when playing post defense
- Mixed results when defending in space, good lateral quickness to defend big men on isolations, good at closing out on perimeter shooters
- Struggled to defend pick-and-rolls, tended to be indecisive when making rotations

R.J. Hampton

Height	Weight	Cap #	Years Left
6'5"	185	$2.193M	1 + 2 TO

Baseline Basic Stats

MPG	PTS	AST	REB	BLK	STL
14.8	5.4	1.6	2.0	0.2	0.6

Advanced Metrics

USG%	3PTA/FGA	FTA/FGA	TS%	eFG%	3PT%
18.8	0.336	0.178	0.483	0.456	0.296

AST%	TOV%	OREB%	DREB%	STL%	BLK%
18.4	14.1	3.3	11.7	1.9	0.8

PER	ORTG	DRTG	WS/48	VOL
10.92	96.4	106.8	0.043	N/A

- Drafted by Milwaukee with the 24th overall pick, traded to Denver via New Orleans
- Played for the New Zealand Breakers in the Australian NBL, missed a month due to a hip injury
- Great athlete, explosive finisher around the basket, dynamic transition player, aggressive slasher that will absorb contact to draw fouls
- Solid ball handler, fairly good secondary playmaker that makes simple reads, limits turnovers
- Not a consistent outside shooter, made less than 30% of his threes last season, more comfortable from mid-range
- Rarely moves off the ball, flashed potential to be an effective cutter in a small sample of possessions
- Good lateral quickness, potentially can guard multiple positions, good at defending quicker guards in Australia
- Thin frame, lacks strength, stronger perimeter players can overpower him on drives to the basket
- Decent team defender, fights through screens, tends to sag into the paint, can allow open perimeter shots
- Active weak side defender, gets steals and blocks at a high rate, solid defensive rebounder
- Tends to gamble a bit too much, will get caught out of position at times

Facundo Campazzo		Height	Weight	Cap #	Years Left
		5'11"	165	$3.200M	1

Baseline Basic Stats

MPG	PTS	AST	REB	BLK	STL
18.2	7.3	3.5	1.6	0.1	0.9

Advanced Metrics

USG%	3PTA/FGA	FTA/FGA	TS%	eFG%	3PT%
19.0	0.567	0.326	0.560	0.503	0.344
AST%	**TOV%**	**OREB%**	**DREB%**	**STL%**	**BLK%**
36.1	21.3	2.2	9.2	2.7	0.1
PER	**ORTG**	**DRTG**	**WS/48**	**VOL**	
14.09	113.0	113.9	0.094	N/A	

- Undrafted in the 2013 NBA Draft out of Argentina, has played for Real Madrid since the 2017-18 season
- Excellent playmaking point guard with great court vision to find open teammates all over the floor
- Capable of making flashy, highlight-reel passes, can also throw the ball away and turn the ball over
- Good pick-and-roll ball handler, crafty enough to get to his spots, does not have explosive quickness to regularly beat NBA defenders off the dribble
- Solid three-point shooter over the last three seasons, Three-Point Percentage tends to fluctuate from year-to-year
- Better as a stand-still spot-up shooter, struggles to make shots off the dribble or on the move
- Has physical limitations on defense, sub-six footer with relatively short arms, lacks ideal lateral quickness
- Fairly solid position and team defender with Real Madrid, tends to be in the right spots defensively
- Might be effective if he's hidden in favorable matchups
- Active weak side defender, can be a pest, consistently gets steals at a high rate, fairly solid defensive rebounder for his size

PHOENIX SUNS

Last Season: 34 – 39, Missed the Playoffs

Offensive Rating: 111.7, 12th in the NBA

Defensive Rating: 111.4, 17th in the NBA

Primary Executive: James Jones, General Manager

Head Coach: Monty Williams

Key Roster Changes

Subtractions
Ricky Rubio, trade
Kelly Oubre, Jr., trade
Ty Jerome, trade
Jalen Lecque, trade
Frank Kaminsky, free agency
Cheick Diallo, free agency
Aron Baynes, free agency
Elie Okobo, waived

Additions
Jalen Smith, draft
Chris Paul, trade
Abdel Nader, trade
Jae Crowder, free agency
E'Twaun Moore, free agency
Langston Galloway, free agency
Damian Jones, free agency

Roster

Likely Starting Five

1. *Chris Paul*
2. *Devin Booker*
3. *Jae Crowder*
4. Dario Saric
5. *Deandre Ayton*

Other Key Rotation Players
Mikal Bridges
Cameron Johnson
Cameron Payne
Jevon Carter
Jalen Smith

* Italics denotes that a player is likely to be on the floor to close games

Remaining Roster

- E'Twaun Moore
- Langston Galloway
- Abdel Nader
- Damian Jones
- Ty-Shon Alexander, 22, 6'4", 195, Creighton (Two-Way)
- Johnathan Motley, 25, 6'8", 230, Baylor (Exhibit 10)

SCHREMPF Base Rating: 38.7 (72-game season)

Strengths

- Effective offense that uses great ball movement to generate open looks or free throw opportunities
- Improved complementary shooting around Devin Booker and Chris Paul

Question Marks

- Durability and potential age-related decline of Chris Paul
- Depth beyond their top seven or eight players

Outlook

- Phoenix should be an improved unit, will likely be in the mix for one of the lower playoff seeds

Veterans

Devin Booker	Height	Weight	Cap #	Years Left
	6'5"	210	$29.468M	3

	Similar at Age	23	
		Season	SIMsc
1	Isaiah Rider	1994-95	922.4
2	Ben Gordon	2006-07	917.0
3	Ray Allen*	1998-99	907.5
4	Zach LaVine	2018-19	907.1
5	James Harden	2012-13	899.7
6	Mitch Richmond*	1988-89	899.3
7	Rodney Stuckey	2009-10	890.8
8	Randy Foye	2006-07	890.2
9	Brandon Roy	2007-08	889.5
10	Kobe Bryant*	2001-02	889.0

Baseline Basic Stats

MPG	PTS	AST	REB	BLK	STL
34.2	21.4	4.7	4.3	0.3	1.1

Advanced Metrics

USG%	3PTA/FGA	FTA/FGA	TS%	eFG%	3PT%
29.5	0.348	0.362	0.596	0.530	0.369
AST%	**TOV%**	**OREB%**	**DREB%**	**STL%**	**BLK%**
27.6	13.4	2.0	11.9	1.3	0.7
PER	**ORTG**	**DRTG**	**WS/48**	**VOL**	
20.93	113.9	113.1	0.148	0.400	

- Made his first All-Star team last season, named to the All-Seeding Games 1st Team in the Orlando bubble
- Continued his upward trajectory in his role as Phoenix's primary ball handler and scorer
- Very good pick-and-roll ball handler and isolation player, gets to the rim, draws fouls at a high rate, makes pull-up jumpers
- Good playmaker that can find open shooters, fairly good at limiting turnovers
- Excellent all-around shooter, good mid-range shooter, makes threes at a league average rate for his career
- Good spot-up shooter that also shoots off screens, can also post-up smaller guards
- 2019-20 Defensive Degree of Difficulty: 0.446, tends to guard starting level players
- Below average on-ball defender, struggles to stay with quicker guards, bigger wings can score on him in the post
- Decent pick-and-roll defender, could funnel ball handlers into help with non-shooters on the floor, struggled to contain ball handlers with a spread floor
- Tends to be late when closing out on perimeter shooters, can get caught on screens off the ball
- Solid defensive rebounder, does not really get blocks or steals

Chris Paul	Height	Weight	Cap #	Years Left
	6'1"	175	$41.359M	Player Option

Similar at Age **34**

		Season	SIMsc
1	Tim Hardaway	2000-01	914.8
2	Jason Terry	2011-12	902.0
3	John Lucas	1987-88	901.1
4	Mark Jackson	1999-00	893.5
5	Darrell Armstrong	2002-03	893.4
6	Greg Anthony	2001-02	892.6
7	Sam Cassell	2003-04	878.4
8	John Stockton*	1996-97	878.3
9	Maurice Cheeks*	1990-91	877.3
10	Jeff Hornacek	1997-98	875.8

Baseline Basic Stats

MPG	PTS	AST	REB	BLK	STL
29.2	12.9	5.8	3.3	0.2	1.3

Advanced Metrics

USG%	3PTA/FGA	FTA/FGA	TS%	eFG%	3PT%
21.3	0.458	0.262	0.568	0.520	0.352
AST%	**TOV%**	**OREB%**	**DREB%**	**STL%**	**BLK%**
32.4	14.7	1.8	13.5	2.3	0.6
PER	**ORTG**	**DRTG**	**WS/48**	**VOL**	
18.70	114.7	106.3	0.159	0.401	

- Made his tenth All-Star team last season, named to the All-NBA 2nd Team in 2019-20
- Excelled in his first season as Oklahoma City's primary ball handler
- Excellent playmaker that controls the tempo and avoids turnovers
- One of the league's best mid-range shooters, good at making pull-up jumpers as a pick-and-roll ball handler and isolation player
- Had some trouble driving by defenders on isolations, may be losing a step due to age
- Consistently good three-point shooter throughout his career, most effective at making spot-up jumpers
- 2019-20 Defensive Degree of Difficulty: 0.384
- Load managed a bit on the defensive end, hidden in lower leverage matchups against spot-up wing players
- Played solid on-ball defense, still good on the perimeter, has some trouble against bigger players in the post
- Good pick-and-roll defender, fights over screens to contain ball handlers, good at switching
- Closes out on spot-up shooters, tends to get caught on screens off the ball
- Good defensive rebounding point guard, Steal Percentage was down from his career average but was still fairly high

Deandre Ayton	Height	Weight	Cap #	Years Left
	6'11"	250	$10.018M	Team Option

	Similar at Age	**21**	
		Season	**SIMsc**
1	Mike Gminski	1980-81	934.8
2	Domantas Sabonis	2017-18	921.1
3	Marreese Speights	2008-09	913.9
4	Enes Kanter	2013-14	907.9
5	Thomas Bryant	2018-19	904.9
6	Spencer Hawes	2009-10	901.5
7	LaMarcus Aldridge	2006-07	900.7
8	Andris Biedrins	2007-08	899.4
9	Greg Monroe	2011-12	898.6
10	Tim Duncan*	1997-98	895.1

Baseline Basic Stats

MPG	PTS	AST	REB	BLK	STL
26.7	13.5	1.5	8.0	1.0	0.6

Advanced Metrics

USG%	3PTA/FGA	FTA/FGA	TS%	eFG%	3PT%
22.4	0.027	0.245	0.570	0.539	0.278
AST%	**TOV%**	**OREB%**	**DREB%**	**STL%**	**BLK%**
10.3	12.2	11.4	24.0	1.2	2.6
PER	**ORTG**	**DRTG**	**WS/48**	**VOL**	
19.10	112.6	108.6	0.135	0.376	

- Served a 25-game suspension for testing positive for a diuretic, regular starter for Phoenix when active
- Maintained his production in his role as Phoenix's primary interior scorer
- Good rim runner, made 72.5% of his shots inside of three feet, good at rolling to the basket, scores on a high volume of cuts off the ball
- Good offensive rebounder that scores on a high volume of put-backs, great at beating his man down-court to get dunks in transition
- Below average efficiency on post-ups, struggles to score efficiently against opposing big men
- Outside shooting is still a work-in-progress, decent passing big man, good at avoiding turnovers
- 2019-20 Defensive Degree of Difficulty: 0.448, tends to guard starting level big men
- Very good shot blocker and defensive rebounder, average rim protector, can be undisciplined with his positioning
- Average on-ball defender, tends to commit shooting fouls in the post, tends to back off when defending on the perimeter
- Below average pick-and-roll defender, struggles to guard ball handlers on switches, tends to be late when covering the screener inside
- Consistently come out to contest perimeter shots in spot-up situations

Jae Crowder

Height	Weight	Cap #	Years Left
6'6"	235	$9.258M	2

	Similar at Age	29 Season	SIMsc
1	Quentin Richardson	2009-10	944.2
2	Matt Barnes	2009-10	933.8
3	Carlos Delfino	2011-12	919.9
4	J.R. Smith	2014-15	914.9
5	Morris Peterson	2006-07	908.1
6	Andres Nocioni	2008-09	907.2
7	P.J. Tucker	2014-15	905.8
8	Wesley Matthews	2015-16	905.4
9	Cartier Martin	2013-14	904.0
10	Ersan Ilyasova	2016-17	903.8

Baseline Basic Stats

MPG	PTS	AST	REB	BLK	STL
25.3	9.2	1.5	4.0	0.3	0.8

Advanced Metrics

USG%	3PTA/FGA	FTA/FGA	TS%	eFG%	3PT%
16.2	0.597	0.197	0.537	0.508	0.345
AST%	**TOV%**	**OREB%**	**DREB%**	**STL%**	**BLK%**
9.2	9.7	3.4	15.1	1.7	1.1
PER	**ORTG**	**DRTG**	**WS/48**	**VOL**	
11.72	108.1	107.7	0.091	0.354	

- Traded from Memphis to Miami in February 2020, started for Memphis, moved to a bench role for Miami
- Used by both teams as a low volume, spot-up shooter
- Made threes at an above break-even rate overall, made 44.5% of his threes with Miami
- Mainly a spot-up shooter throughout his career, could make pull-up jumpers on pick-and-rolls in a small sample of possessions with Miami
- Effective transition player, good at running down the wing to get layups, can set up for trail threes
- Catch-and-shoot player, will make the extra pass, rarely turns the ball over
- 2019-20 Defensive Degree of Difficulty: 0.508
- Draws tough assignments against guards, wings and some big men
- Solid on-ball defender that guards multiple positions, better perimeter defender in Miami
- Good pick-and-roll defender that can guard ball handlers or switch onto screeners
- Generally stays attached to shooters off the ball, tended to be late in his close-outs in Miami, better at closing out in Memphis
- Good defensive rebounder, Steal and Block Percentages are still consistent with his career averages

Dario Šarić

	Height	Weight	Cap #	Years Left
	6'10"	225	$9.250M	2

Similar at Age 25

		Season	SIMsc
1	Vladimir Radmanovic	2005-06	951.2
2	Matt Bullard	1992-93	932.0
3	Omri Casspi	2013-14	929.7
4	Keith Van Horn	2000-01	926.9
5	Earl Clark	2012-13	918.8
6	Marvin Williams	2011-12	916.8
7	Marcus Morris	2014-15	916.8
8	Al-Farouq Aminu	2015-16	913.8
9	Ersan Ilyasova	2012-13	912.2
10	Nikola Mirotic	2016-17	911.5

Baseline Basic Stats

MPG	PTS	AST	REB	BLK	STL
23.8	9.8	1.5	4.3	0.3	0.6

Advanced Metrics

USG%	3PTA/FGA	FTA/FGA	TS%	eFG%	3PT%
18.6	0.437	0.215	0.560	0.524	0.364
AST%	**TOV%**	**OREB%**	**DREB%**	**STL%**	**BLK%**
10.7	11.7	5.5	17.5	1.2	0.9
PER	**ORTG**	**DRTG**	**WS/48**	**VOL**	
13.82	110.6	110.2	0.092	0.300	

- Regular starter for Phoenix in his first season with the team
- Had his most efficient shooting season in a role as a low volume, spot-up shooter
- Around a league average three-point shooter throughout his career
- Better shooter on the move, effective screener on pick-and-pops, can shoot off screens
- Good pick-and-roll player, can make pull-up jumpers as a ball handler, can roll to the rim as the screener
- Can post up smaller players, scores on a high volume of off-ball cuts
- Fairly good secondary playmaker in his early years in Philadelphia, good at avoiding turnovers
- 2019-20 Defensive Degree of Difficulty: 0.417, tends to guard starting level players
- Good at protecting the rim, not really a shot blocker, stays vertical when contesting shots, solid defensive rebounder
- Decent on-ball defender, better against bigger post players, has some trouble staying with quicker perimeter players
- Decent pick-and-roll defender, good at covering the screener, tends to go too far under screens when guarding the ball handler
- Sometimes can be late to close out on spot-up shooters

Mikal Bridges

Height	Weight	Cap #	Years Left
6'6"	210	$4.359M	Team Option

Similar at Age **23**

		Season	SIMsc
1	Allen Crabbe	2015-16	924.7
2	James Posey	1999-00	919.7
3	Iman Shumpert	2013-14	919.0
4	Josh Hart	2018-19	918.2
5	Kyle Korver	2004-05	910.7
6	Josh Richardson	2016-17	910.0
7	Courtney Lee	2008-09	909.1
8	Martell Webster	2009-10	908.5
9	Nik Stauskas	2016-17	907.1
10	Maurice Harkless	2016-17	905.8

Baseline Basic Stats

MPG	PTS	AST	REB	BLK	STL
28.1	10.8	1.8	3.6	0.4	0.9

Advanced Metrics

USG%	3PTA/FGA	FTA/FGA	TS%	eFG%	3PT%
15.5	0.469	0.240	0.577	0.539	0.360
AST%	**TOV%**	**OREB%**	**DREB%**	**STL%**	**BLK%**
10.1	10.7	2.8	11.3	2.0	1.5
PER	**ORTG**	**DRTG**	**WS/48**	**VOL**	
13.07	113.5	110.4	0.101	0.213	

- Regular rotation player for Phoenix in his second NBA season, started some games in 2019-20
- Increased his efficiency in a role as a low volume, spot-up shooter
- Above league average three-point shooter last season, made over 41% of his corner threes in 2019-20
- Mainly a spot-up shooter, sets up for trail three in transition, occasionally makes pull-up jumpers on pick-and-rolls
- Moves well without the ball, very good cutter, selectively crashes the offensive glass to score on put-backs
- Made almost 75% of his shots inside of three feet last season, drew fouls at a higher rate
- Catch-and-shoot player, shows some passing skills, good at avoiding turnovers
- 2019-20 Defensive Degree of Difficulty: 0.480
- Guards starter level players, takes on tougher defensive assignments against top perimeter players
- Fairly solid on-ball defender that can guard multiple positions, tends to back off too much when guarding perimeter players
- Average pick-and-roll defender, tends to allow ball handlers to turn the corner
- Stays attached to shooters off the ball, good at closing out in spot-up situations
- Active help defender, gets blocks and steals at a high rate, solid defensive rebounder

Cameron Johnson

Height	Weight	Cap #	Years Left
6'8"	205	$4.235M	2 Team Options

	Similar at Age	23	
		Season	SIMsc
1	Hollis Thompson	2014-15	944.0
2	Justin Jackson	2018-19	936.8
3	Tony Snell	2014-15	931.2
4	Harrison Barnes	2015-16	920.5
5	Martell Webster	2009-10	914.7
6	Dorian Finney-Smith	2016-17	914.3
7	Sasha Vujacic	2007-08	913.5
8	Tim Hardaway, Jr.	2015-16	911.4
9	Wesley Johnson	2010-11	906.3
10	Chris Johnson	2013-14	904.4

Baseline Basic Stats

MPG	PTS	AST	REB	BLK	STL
24.9	9.8	1.4	3.3	0.4	0.7

Advanced Metrics

USG%	3PTA/FGA	FTA/FGA	TS%	eFG%	3PT%
17.4	0.604	0.166	0.565	0.538	0.380
AST%	**TOV%**	**OREB%**	**DREB%**	**STL%**	**BLK%**
8.3	7.7	3.4	12.4	1.4	1.3
PER	**ORTG**	**DRTG**	**WS/48**	**VOL**	
13.11	113.1	112.1	0.105	0.347	

- Regular rotation player for Phoenix in his rookie season, missed some games due to a bruised right quadriceps
- Used as a low volume, spot-up shooter, made 39% of his threes last season
- Mostly a stationary spot-up shooter, can sometimes shoot off screens or set up for trail threes in transition
- Decent at cutting to the rim off the ball, good at running the wings to get layups in transition
- Not really able to create his own offense, strictly a catch-and-shoot player
- Limited as a playmaker, rarely turns the ball over
- 2019-20 Defensive Degree of Difficulty: 0.336, tends to guard second unit players
- Played below average on-ball defense, struggled to stay with perimeter players, had more success guarding bigger post players
- Average pick-and-roll defender, decent at switching, tends to go too far under screens
- Tends to be late when closing out on perimeter shooters, gets caught on screens off the ball
- Stay-at-home defender, gets steals and blocks at a moderate rate, solid defensive rebounder

Cameron Payne

	Height	Weight	Cap #	Years Left
	6'3"	190	$1.977M	UFA

	Similar at Age	25	
		Season	SIMsc
1	Vonteego Cummings	2001-02	926.6
2	Trajan Langdon	2001-02	921.4
3	Luther Head	2007-08	916.2
4	Rex Walters	1995-96	908.3
5	Ian Clark	2016-17	907.5
6	Seth Curry	2015-16	906.5
7	Jorge Gutierrez	2013-14	904.9
8	Ronnie Price	2008-09	902.9
9	Toney Douglas	2011-12	902.2
10	A.J. Price	2011-12	902.0

Baseline Basic Stats

MPG	PTS	AST	REB	BLK	STL
19.3	6.9	2.4	1.9	0.1	0.7

Advanced Metrics

USG%	3PTA/FGA	FTA/FGA	TS%	eFG%	3PT%
17.8	0.406	0.152	0.539	0.513	0.382
AST%	**TOV%**	**OREB%**	**DREB%**	**STL%**	**BLK%**
20.1	13.9	2.2	11.2	1.9	0.8
PER	**ORTG**	**DRTG**	**WS/48**	**VOL**	
12.58	106.0	110.9	0.071	0.406	

- Spent most of 2019-20 in the G-League with the Texas Legends, signed by Phoenix in June 2020
- Productive as a low volume, backup point guard in the seeding games in the Orlando bubble
- Effective as a pick-and-roll ball handler, could make pull-up jumpers and floaters in the lane
- Fairly solid playmaker that could find open shooters, good at controlling the ball to avoid turnovers
- Made over half of his threes in the bubble, an above break-even three-point shooter in his career, better in the corners
- Mostly a spot-up shooter, shot better off the dribble in the restart
- Good transition player that can push the ball up court and set up for trail threes
- 2019-20 Defensive Degree of Difficulty: 0.247
- Tended to be hidden in favorable matchups against lower leverage second unit players
- Not tested very much on the ball, played solid on-ball defense in a small sample of possessions
- Below average pick-and-roll defender, tends to go too far under screens, can be targeted by bigger screeners on switches
- Stays attached to shooters off the ball, good at closing out on spot-up shooters
- Solid defensive rebounder for his size, Steal and Block Percentages are still consistent with his career averages

Jevon Carter	Height	Weight	Cap #	Years Left
	6'1"	195	$3.925M	2

	Similar at Age	24	
		Season	SIMsc
1	Mario Chalmers	2010-11	932.1
2	Shawn Respert	1996-97	923.7
3	Jerian Grant	2016-17	914.8
4	Patrick Beverley	2012-13	912.6
5	Markel Brown	2015-16	902.9
6	Trajan Langdon	2000-01	902.3
7	Charles R. Jones	1999-00	899.3
8	Patty Mills	2012-13	899.0
9	Raul Neto	2016-17	898.5
10	Toney Douglas	2010-11	897.6

Baseline Basic Stats

MPG	PTS	AST	REB	BLK	STL
22.0	8.0	2.7	2.3	0.2	0.9

Advanced Metrics

USG%	3PTA/FGA	FTA/FGA	TS%	eFG%	3PT%
16.8	0.523	0.175	0.511	0.481	0.361
AST%	**TOV%**	**OREB%**	**DREB%**	**STL%**	**BLK%**
17.4	11.9	2.6	9.6	2.1	1.0
PER	**ORTG**	**DRTG**	**WS/48**	**VOL**	
11.30	106.1	109.7	0.065	0.435	

- Regular rotation player for Phoenix in his first season with the team
- Utilized in a very low volume role as a spot-up shooter and secondary ball handler
- Made 42.5% of his threes last season, mainly a stationary spot-up shooter
- Occasionally makes pull-up jumpers on pick-and-rolls or no dribble jumpers on isolations, does not really get to the rim
- Rarely looks to cut or move off the ball, can selectively crash inside to score on put-backs
- Decent secondary playmaker, solid at controlling the ball to avoid turnovers
- 2019-20 Defensive Degree of Difficulty: 0.371
- Tends to guard second unit players or lower leverage starters
- Played middling on-ball defense, good at containing perimeter players on drives, gave up extra space for his man to take jump shots
- Below average pick-and-roll defender, struggled to guard opposing ball handlers, could be targeted by bigger screeners on switches
- Tends to get caught on screens off the ball, can be too aggressive when closing out on spot-up shooters
- Active help defender, solid defensive rebounder, gets steals and blocks at a fairly high rate

E'Twaun Moore

Height	Weight	Cap #	Years Left
6'3"	191	$1.621M	UFA

	Similar at Age	**30**	
		Season	**SIMsc**
1	Eldridge Recasner	1997-98	948.1
2	Willie Green	2011-12	938.4
3	Charlie Bell	2009-10	936.9
4	Dell Curry	1994-95	924.6
5	Flip Murray	2009-10	921.8
6	Jaren Jackson	1997-98	921.2
7	Trent Tucker	1989-90	919.8
8	Anthony Peeler	1999-00	919.2
9	Derek Anderson	2004-05	917.2
10	Kirk Hinrich	2010-11	915.9

Baseline Basic Stats

MPG	PTS	AST	REB	BLK	STL
23.4	9.5	2.0	2.2	0.2	0.7

Advanced Metrics

USG%	3PTA/FGA	FTA/FGA	TS%	eFG%	3PT%
18.5	0.372	0.136	0.533	0.512	0.384
AST%	**TOV%**	**OREB%**	**DREB%**	**STL%**	**BLK%**
11.7	10.0	2.5	8.8	1.5	0.6
PER	**ORTG**	**DRTG**	**WS/48**	**VOL**	
11.71	106.3	111.4	0.063	0.394	

- Regular rotation player for New Orleans last season
- Utilized as a low volume, spot-up shooter, made almost 38% of his threes last season
- Good at making shooting corner threes, career percentage on corner threes is almost 42%
- Primarily a spot-up shooter, struggled to shoot on the move or off the dribble
- Moves fairly well off the ball, very good at making backdoor cuts, selectively crashes the offensive boards to score on put-backs
- Decent secondary playmaker, good at avoiding turnovers
- 2019-20 Defensive Degree of Difficulty: 0.355, tended to guard second unit level players
- Below average on-ball defender last season, struggled to stay with quicker guards, better in the post against taller wing players
- Solid pick-and-roll defender, good at containing ball handlers
- Good at closing out on shooters in spot-up situations, tends to get caught on screens away from the ball
- Stay-at-home defender, Steal and Block Percentages are still consistent with his career averages, decent defensive rebounder

Langston Galloway

Height	Weight	Cap #	Years Left
6'1"	200	$1.621M	UFA

	Similar at Age	28	
		Season	SIMsc
1	Seth Curry	2018-19	923.2
2	Wayne Ellington	2015-16	921.2
3	Derek Fisher	2002-03	906.0
4	Charlie Bell	2007-08	903.6
5	Craig Hodges	1988-89	897.9
6	Avery Bradley	2018-19	895.2
7	Eldridge Recasner	1995-96	894.6
8	Patty Mills	2016-17	894.3
9	Courtney Lee	2013-14	893.7
10	Rex Chapman	1995-96	890.2

Baseline Basic Stats

MPG	PTS	AST	REB	BLK	STL
22.0	8.5	1.8	1.9	0.1	0.7

Advanced Metrics

USG%	3PTA/FGA	FTA/FGA	TS%	eFG%	3PT%
16.4	0.636	0.157	0.550	0.523	0.375
AST%	**TOV%**	**OREB%**	**DREB%**	**STL%**	**BLK%**
9.9	6.8	2.1	7.9	1.5	0.5
PER	**ORTG**	**DRTG**	**WS/48**	**VOL**	
11.60	112.8	112.4	0.086	0.243	

- Regular rotation player for Detroit last season
- Had his most effective season since his rookie year in 2019-20, excelled as a low volume, spot-up shooter
- Made almost 40% of his threes, mostly a catch-and-shoot player, very good spot-up shooter, can make shots off screens
- Good mid-range shooter, not as effective at creating his own shot
- Led the NBA with the lowest Turnover Percentage in each of the last two seasons
- Has some playmaking skills, sticks to make safe passes around the perimeter
- 2019-20 Defensive Degree of Difficulty: 0.408
- Tends to guard lower leverage starters or higher end second unit players
- Played below average on-ball defense, solid against drives, gave up too much space for opponents to get outside shots
- Fairly solid pick-and-roll defender that can funnel his man into help, solid at switching to cover multiple positions
- Fights through screens off the ball, tends to be late when closing out on perimeter shooters
- More of a stay-at-home defender, Steal Percentage increased last season, middling as a defensive rebounder

Abdel Nader

	Height	Weight	Cap #	Years Left
Abdel Nader	6'5"	225	$1.753M	UFA

	Similar at Age	**26**	
		Season	**SIMsc**
1	Keith Bogans	2006-07	931.8
2	Mickael Pietrus	2008-09	926.4
3	James Anderson	2015-16	921.3
4	Quincy Acy	2016-17	917.8
5	Cartier Martin	2010-11	916.2
6	Sam Mack	1996-97	914.4
7	Allen Crabbe	2018-19	914.1
8	Quincy Pondexter	2014-15	913.1
9	Maurice Evans	2004-05	912.5
10	Iman Shumpert	2016-17	912.3

Baseline Basic Stats

MPG	PTS	AST	REB	BLK	STL
20.2	7.3	1.0	2.9	0.3	0.6

Advanced Metrics

USG%	3PTA/FGA	FTA/FGA	TS%	eFG%	3PT%
16.5	0.479	0.200	0.553	0.525	0.372
AST%	**TOV%**	**OREB%**	**DREB%**	**STL%**	**BLK%**
7.0	11.2	2.8	12.0	1.4	1.5
PER	**ORTG**	**DRTG**	**WS/48**	**VOL**	
10.98	106.2	109.7	0.069	0.374	

- Became a regular rotation player for Oklahoma City in his third season in the NBA
- Mainly a low volume, spot-up shooter, made 37.5% of his threes last season
- Solid spot-up shooter that improved his ability to shoot off screens
- Good at making backdoor cuts off the ball, can run the floor in transition to get layups or draw shooting fouls
- Predominantly a catch-and-shoot player, limited playmaking skills, good at avoiding turnovers
- 2019-20 Defensive Degree of Difficulty: 0.322, tends to guard second unit level players
- Played below average on-ball defense, had trouble staying with opposing perimeter players
- Better team defender, good at guarding pick-and-rolls, effective at switching, good at containing ball handlers
- Stays attached to shooters off the ball, consistently closes out in spot-up situations
- Fairly solid defensive rebounder, set a career high in Block Percentage last season, steals rate is still consistent with his career average

Damian Jones

	Height	Weight	Cap #	Years Left
	6'11"	245	$1.737M	1

Similar at Age 24

		Season	SIMsc
1	Semih Erden	2010-11	916.0
2	Dan Gadzuric	2002-03	914.1
3	Cherokee Parks	1996-97	913.0
4	Duane Causwell	1992-93	912.9
5	Don Reid	1997-98	910.6
6	Ozell Jones	1984-85	909.0
7	Hilton Armstrong	2008-09	908.9
8	Tarik Black	2015-16	908.8
9	Solomon Jones	2008-09	908.7
10	Eric Mobley	1994-95	899.4

Baseline Basic Stats

MPG	PTS	AST	REB	BLK	STL
18.0	5.3	0.5	4.5	0.9	0.5

Advanced Metrics

USG%	3PTA/FGA	FTA/FGA	TS%	eFG%	3PT%
13.2	0.022	0.461	0.617	0.584	0.155
AST%	**TOV%**	**OREB%**	**DREB%**	**STL%**	**BLK%**
5.8	12.1	9.3	17.4	1.3	3.9
PER	**ORTG**	**DRTG**	**WS/48**	**VOL**	
14.82	123.5	108.7	0.136	0.390	

- Regular rotation player and occasional starter for Atlanta last season
- Almost exclusively a low volume, rim runner
- Has posted a True Shooting Percentage above 70% in each of the last two seasons
- Excels at rolling to the rim on pick-and-rolls, leaping ability makes him a lob threat
- Scores on a high volume of cuts, effective offensive rebounder that scores on put-backs
- No shooting range outside of three feet, limited passing skills
- Will draw fouls at a high rate, made over 70% of his free throws last season, cut his turnover rate significantly as well
- 2019-20 Defensive Degree of Difficulty: 0.411
- Usually guards starting level players, serves as a rim protector on defense
- Very good shot blocker that effectively contests shots inside
- Will sometimes sacrifice some positioning to go for blocks, highly foul prone, middling defensive rebounder
- Below average post defender due to a lack of strength
- Has some trouble grasping defensive rotation concepts, struggled to guard pick-and-rolls last season
- Doesn't always close out on perimeter shooters
- Flashed the necessary mobility to switch out on opposing ball handlers in previous seasons in Golden State

Newcomers

Jalen Smith

Height	Weight	Cap #	Years Left
6'10"	225	$4.246M	1 + 2 TO

Baseline Basic Stats

MPG	PTS	AST	REB	BLK	STL
19.6	7.2	0.9	4.6	0.9	0.5

Advanced Metrics

USG%	3PTA/FGA	FTA/FGA	TS%	eFG%	3PT%
17.5	0.196	0.314	0.512	0.477	0.296

AST%	TOV%	OREB%	DREB%	STL%	BLK%
7.2	12.5	8.6	18.8	1.4	3.8

PER	ORTG	DRTG	WS/48	VOL
14.90	102.3	99.1	0.079	N/A

- Drafted by Phoenix with the 10th overall pick
- Made the Big Ten All-Defense team, named to the All-Big Ten 1st Team in 2019-20
- High motor rim runner, sets solid screens, dives hard to the rim as a roll man and cutter
- Good offensive rebounder, runs hard to fill a lane in transition, draws fouls at a fairly high rate
- Shows stretch potential, made almost 37% of his threes as a sophomore
- Mainly a spot-up shooter, flashed some ability to shoot off screens, can occasionally make shots as the screener on pick-and-pops
- Limited as a passer, does not have advanced post moves, lacks ideal ball handling skills
- Good rim protector at Maryland, very good defensive rebounder and shot blocker
- Effective at keeping his blocks in play to allow teammates to recover the ball
- Strong post defender that holds position inside, shows enough mobility to defend in space
- Solid pick-and-roll defender, good in drop coverages, can switch onto ball handlers for a few dribbles
- Usually good at closing out on perimeter shooters, can occasionally be too aggressive with his close-outs

SAN ANTONIO SPURS

Last Season: 32 – 39, Missed the Playoffs

Offensive Rating: 112.4, 9th in the NBA

Defensive Rating: 113.5, 25th in the NBA

Primary Executive: R.C. Buford, CEO of Spurs Sports and Entertainment

Head Coach: Gregg Popovich

Key Roster Changes

Subtractions
Marco Belinelli, free agency
Bryn Forbes, free agency
Chimezie Metu, free agency

Additions
Devin Vassell, draft
Tre Jones, draft

Roster

Likely Starting Five
1. *Dejounte Murray*
2. Lonnie Walker
3. *Derrick White*
4. *DeMar DeRozan*
5. *LaMarcus Aldridge*

Other Key Rotation Players
Patty Mills
Rudy Gay
Trey Lyles
Jakob Poeltl

* Italics denotes that a player is likely to be on the floor to close games

Remaining Roster

- Devin Vassell
- Keldon Johnson
- Tre Jones
- Drew Eubanks
- Luka Samanic
- Quinndary Weatherspoon, 24, 6'3", 205, Mississippi State (Two-Way)
- Keita Bates-Diop, 25, 6'8", 229, Ohio State (Two-Way)
- Cameron Reynolds, 25, 6'7", 225, Tulane (Exhibit 10)

SCHREMPF Base Rating: 38.2 (72-game season)

Strengths

- Efficient offense that can play different styles depending on personnel
- Strong continuity and organizational infrastructure that can build on their success in the Orlando bubble

Question Marks

- Lack of a distinct defensive identity
- Uncertain balance between established veterans and developing young talents

Outlook

- Could be better than expected, might be a team that stays in the playoff picture for most of the season

Veterans

DeMar DeRozan	Height	Weight	Cap #	Years Left
	6'6"	220	$27.740M	UFA

	Similar at Age	30	
		Season	SIMsc
1	Kelly Tripucka	1989-90	930.0
2	Paul Pierce	2007-08	921.2
3	Corey Maggette	2009-10	920.9
4	Vince Carter	2006-07	919.5
5	Glenn Robinson	2002-03	909.3
6	Manu Ginobili	2007-08	906.7
7	Stephen Jackson	2008-09	906.7
8	Jerry Stackhouse	2004-05	906.1
9	Tom Chambers	1989-90	904.8
10	Kobe Bryant*	2008-09	898.3

Baseline Basic Stats

MPG	PTS	AST	REB	BLK	STL
32.1	17.7	3.3	4.6	0.3	1.0

Advanced Metrics

USG%	3PTA/FGA	FTA/FGA	TS%	eFG%	3PT%
25.2	0.128	0.360	0.559	0.497	0.296
AST%	**TOV%**	**OREB%**	**DREB%**	**STL%**	**BLK%**
20.5	12.0	2.4	15.0	1.5	0.8
PER	**ORTG**	**DRTG**	**WS/48**	**VOL**	
17.91	110.6	109.6	0.122	0.352	

- Regular starter for San Antonio, has continued to produce at an All-Star level
- Had his most efficient shooting season in his role as San Antonio's main scoring option
- Rarely shoots threes, one of the league's most consistent mid-range shooters
- Excellent one-on-one player that can score at the rim, draw fouls or make pull-up jumpers
- Good at getting to the rim on dribble hand-offs, can make mid-range shots off screens
- Can post up smaller players, good playmaker that can find open shooters, good at avoiding turnovers
- Effective cutter off the ball, good at running the wing to score in transition
- 2019-20 Defensive Degree of Difficulty: 0.456
- Tends to guard starting level players, sometimes takes on tougher defensive assignments
- Below average on-ball defender, has trouble staying with quicker perimeter players
- Middling pick-and-roll defender, tends to go too far under screens to allow open outside shots
- Fights through screens off the ball, tends to close out too aggressively on perimeter shooters
- Fairly good defensive rebounder, Steal and Block Percentages are still consistent with his career averages

LaMarcus Aldridge

	Height	Weight	Cap #	Years Left
LaMarcus Aldridge	6'11"	260	$24.000M	UFA

Similar at Age 34

		Season	SIMsc
1	Tim Duncan*	2010-11	907.4
2	Zach Randolph	2015-16	894.2
3	Dirk Nowitzki	2012-13	881.7
4	Hakeem Olajuwon*	1996-97	878.2
5	Bill Laimbeer	1991-92	877.1
6	Pau Gasol	2014-15	875.8
7	Derrick Coleman	2001-02	875.3
8	Dan Issel*	1982-83	861.4
9	Elvin Hayes*	1979-80	860.2
10	Marc Gasol	2018-19	859.4

Baseline Basic Stats

MPG	PTS	AST	REB	BLK	STL
28.4	14.9	2.4	7.7	1.2	0.7

Advanced Metrics

USG%	3PTA/FGA	FTA/FGA	TS%	eFG%	3PT%
23.2	0.131	0.285	0.563	0.519	0.362
AST%	**TOV%**	**OREB%**	**DREB%**	**STL%**	**BLK%**
12.8	9.4	8.2	21.8	1.1	4.3
PER	**ORTG**	**DRTG**	**WS/48**	**VOL**	
20.66	114.2	107.2	0.135	0.385	

- Regular starter for San Antonio when healthy, missed the Orlando restart due to a right shoulder injury that required surgery
- Production declined in his age-34 season, still effective as San Antonio's main interior scorer
- Very good post-up player from the left block, fairly solid passing big man, rarely turns the ball over
- Slides into open spaces inside as a roll man and cutter, selective offensive rebounder that scores on put-backs
- Expanded his range to the three-point line, made almost 39% of his threes in 2019-20
- Good spot-up shooter, effective screener on pick-and-pops
- 2019-20 Defensive Degree of Difficulty: 0.502
- Takes on tough defensive assignments against top big men
- Good rim protector that still blocks shots at a high rate, decent defensive rebounder
- Fairly solid on-ball defender, mobile enough to defend in space on isolations, tends to be late to contest shots in the post
- Good pick-and-roll defender, good in drop coverages, solid at switching out onto ball handlers
- Tends to be late to close out on perimeter shooters in spot-up situations

Dejounte Murray

	Height	Weight	Cap #	Years Left
	6'4"	170	$14.286M	3

	Similar at Age	23	
		Season	SIMsc
1	Fat Lever	1983-84	921.0
2	Steve Colter	1985-86	908.1
3	Darwin Cook	1981-82	906.9
4	Vernon Maxwell	1988-89	906.2
5	Vonteego Cummings	1999-00	905.3
6	Elfrid Payton	2017-18	904.5
7	Larry Hughes	2001-02	904.4
8	Rod Strickland	1989-90	901.0
9	Derek Harper	1984-85	900.6
10	Winston Garland	1987-88	899.9

Baseline Basic Stats

MPG	PTS	AST	REB	BLK	STL
28.6	11.5	5.1	3.2	0.3	1.7

Advanced Metrics

USG%	3PTA/FGA	FTA/FGA	TS%	eFG%	3PT%
19.9	0.117	0.230	0.513	0.480	0.327
AST%	**TOV%**	**OREB%**	**DREB%**	**STL%**	**BLK%**
24.5	15.5	4.4	15.2	2.8	0.9
PER	**ORTG**	**DRTG**	**WS/48**	**VOL**	
15.94	105.0	104.9	0.097	0.336	

- Regular starter for San Antonio last season after missing the previous year due to a torn ACL in his right knee
- Had his most productive season in his role as a moderate volume ball handler
- Solid playmaker that can hit cutters and find open shooters, slightly turnover prone
- Great at using his quickness to push the ball up court in transition to get layups or draw shooting fouls
- Made threes at a rate above the league average last season, made 39% of his corner threes in 2019-20
- More of stand-still spot-up shooter, inconsistent at shooting off the dribble or on the move
- 2019-20 Defensive Degree of Difficulty: 0.524
- Tends to take on tough defensive assignments against top perimeter players
- Good on-ball defender that can defend guards and wing players
- Solid pick-and-roll defender, good at containing ball handlers, effective at switching onto the screener
- Tends to close out too aggressively, gambles too much when chasing shooters off screens
- Active help defender, good defensive rebounder, ranked 2nd in the NBA in Steal Percentage last season

Derrick White

	Height	Weight	Cap #	Years Left
Derrick White	6'4"	190	$3.516M	RFA

	Similar at Age	25 Season	SIMsc
1	Delon Wright	2017-18	933.4
2	Tyler Johnson	2017-18	927.2
3	Jerian Grant	2017-18	922.1
4	Antonio Daniels	2000-01	918.2
5	George Hill	2011-12	917.8
6	Fred Jones	2004-05	916.1
7	J.J. Redick	2009-10	913.2
8	Doug Overton	1994-95	908.2
9	Jeremy Lin	2013-14	907.4
10	Shaquille Harrison	2018-19	906.7

Baseline Basic Stats

MPG	PTS	AST	REB	BLK	STL
23.1	9.2	2.5	2.7	0.3	0.8

Advanced Metrics

USG%	3PTA/FGA	FTA/FGA	TS%	eFG%	3PT%
18.2	0.379	0.300	0.564	0.517	0.370

AST%	TOV%	OREB%	DREB%	STL%	BLK%
17.6	12.0	2.3	11.9	1.7	1.8

PER	ORTG	DRTG	WS/48	VOL
14.70	113.1	110.2	0.111	0.365

- Regular rotation player for San Antonio in his third NBA season, started some games in 2019-20
- Had his most productive season, solid in his role as a low volume, secondary playmaker
- Good pick-and-roll ball handler, makes pull-up jumpers, can get to the rim, draws fouls at a high rate
- Solid playmaker that can find open shooters and hit the roll man, consistently limits turnovers
- Good at using an on-ball screen to go the basket or make outside shots on dribble hand-offs
- Solid three-point shooter, mostly makes spot-up jumpers, effective screener on pick-and-pops in a small sample of possessions
- 2019-20 Defensive Degree of Difficulty: 0.517
- Takes on tough defensive assignments against elite perimeter players
- Good on-ball defender that can guard multiple positions
- Solid at guarding pick-and-rolls, makes solid rotations, can switch or go over the screen to contain ball handlers
- Decent at getting through screens, has some trouble guarding dribble hand-offs, sometimes can be late to close out on perimeter shooters
- Solid defensive rebounder, gets steals at a moderate rate, very good at rotating from the weak side to block shots

Lonnie Walker

	Height	Weight	Cap #	Years Left
Lonnie Walker	6'5"	205	$2.892M	Team Option

	Similar at Age	21	
		Season	SIMsc
1	Christian Eyenga	2010-11	935.0
2	Shannon Brown	2006-07	921.0
3	Malachi Richardson	2016-17	917.0
4	DeShawn Stevenson	2002-03	914.4
5	Malik Beasley	2017-18	914.0
6	Manny Harris	2010-11	908.7
7	Terrence Ross	2012-13	908.4
8	Chris Carr	1995-96	907.3
9	Kentavious Caldwell-Pope	2014-15	907.2
10	Rashad McCants	2005-06	904.7

Baseline Basic Stats

MPG	PTS	AST	REB	BLK	STL
21.9	9.3	1.5	2.5	0.2	0.7

Advanced Metrics

USG%	3PTA/FGA	FTA/FGA	TS%	eFG%	3PT%
19.0	0.247	0.211	0.517	0.482	0.375

AST%	TOV%	OREB%	DREB%	STL%	BLK%
10.8	10.4	2.2	10.9	1.9	0.9

PER	ORTG	DRTG	WS/48	VOL
11.58	103.4	111.7	0.067	0.455

- Regular rotation player for San Antonio in his second NBA season
- Improved his shooting efficiency, used as a low volume, spot-up shooter
- Has made over 40% of his threes in two NBA seasons, good at making spot-up jumpers
- Unpolished, not as effective in other situations, rated as average or worse in most offensive situations last season
- Good at getting to the rim on dribble hand-offs, can sometimes make no dribble jumpers on isolation plays
- Mainly a catch-and-shoot player, shows some passing ability, rarely turns the ball over
- 2019-20 Defensive Degree of Difficulty: 0.390
- Tends to guard higher-end second unit players or lower leverage starters
- Fairly solid on-ball defender, good at guarding perimeter players, can be backed down in the post by stronger wing players
- Below average against pick-and-rolls, has trouble containing ball handlers on the perimeter
- Fights through screens off the ball, tends to be late when closing out on perimeter shooters
- Fairly good defensive rebounder, gets steals and blocks at a fairly solid rate

Patty Mills	Height	Weight	Cap #	Years Left
	6'1"	180	$13.536M	UFA

	Similar at Age	31	
		Season	SIMsc
1	Eddie House	2009-10	944.3
2	Mike Bibby	2009-10	921.8
3	George Hill	2017-18	918.9
4	Jason Williams	2006-07	916.8
5	Mo Williams	2013-14	908.8
6	Marco Belinelli	2017-18	902.5
7	D.J. Augustin	2018-19	901.7
8	Tony Delk	2004-05	900.7
9	Jason Terry	2008-09	900.6
10	Mike Evans	1986-87	899.6

Baseline Basic Stats

MPG	PTS	AST	REB	BLK	STL
24.1	10.2	3.1	2.1	0.1	0.8

Advanced Metrics

USG%	3PTA/FGA	FTA/FGA	TS%	eFG%	3PT%
19.3	0.568	0.201	0.573	0.536	0.389
AST%	**TOV%**	**OREB%**	**DREB%**	**STL%**	**BLK%**
17.1	10.6	1.6	7.6	1.5	0.4
PER	**ORTG**	**DRTG**	**WS/48**	**VOL**	
14.09	112.9	113.4	0.092	0.294	

- Regular rotation player for San Antonio last season
- Increased his efficiency in a moderate volume role as a shooter off the bench
- Good three-point shooter throughout his career, has made almost 39% of his career threes
- Good spot-up shooter that also run off screens, can make outside shots on dribble hand-offs
- Effective pick-and-roll ball handler that can make pull-up jumpers, occasionally can use the screen to get to the rim
- Not really able to drive by defenders on isolations at this stage, more of a catch-and-shoot player now
- Solid playmaker in previous seasons, cut his Turnover Percentage to a career low last season
- 2019-20 Defensive Degree of Difficulty: 0.374, tends to guard second unit players
- Average on-ball defender, quick enough to stay with perimeter players, taller guards can shoot over him
- Average pick-and-roll defender, tends to allow ball handlers to turn the corner, sometimes goes too far under screens
- Fights through screens off the ball, tends to be late when closing out on perimeter shooters
- Middling defensive rebounder, Steal and Block Percentages are still consistent with his career averages

Rudy Gay	Height	Weight	Cap #	Years Left
	6'8"	230	$14.500M	UFA

	Similar at Age	33	
		Season	SIMsc
1	Carmelo Anthony	2017-18	922.4
2	Antawn Jamison	2009-10	902.2
3	David West	2013-14	901.6
4	Joe Johnson	2014-15	897.5
5	Rodney Rogers	2004-05	896.9
6	Paul Millsap	2018-19	895.9
7	Mike Dunleavy, Jr.	2013-14	894.9
8	Glen Rice	2000-01	894.2
9	Caron Butler	2013-14	894.1
10	Paul Pierce	2010-11	893.9

Baseline Basic Stats

MPG	PTS	AST	REB	BLK	STL
28.8	12.6	2.2	5.1	0.5	0.8

Advanced Metrics

USG%	3PTA/FGA	FTA/FGA	TS%	eFG%	3PT%
20.2	0.345	0.221	0.548	0.512	0.358
AST%	**TOV%**	**OREB%**	**DREB%**	**STL%**	**BLK%**
11.5	11.8	4.3	19.0	1.4	1.7
PER	**ORTG**	**DRTG**	**WS/48**	**VOL**	
14.82	107.4	109.3	0.092	0.378	

- Regular rotation player for San Antonio in his age-33 season
- Overall production declined, still effective in his role as a moderate volume scorer off the bench
- Above break-even three-point shooter, can be a streaky spot-up shooter
- Effective as a screener on pick-and-pops, good at making pull-up jumpers as a pick-and-roll ball handler
- Moves well without the ball, can shoot off screens, good cutter off the ball, runs the floor in transition to get layups or draw fouls
- Decent secondary playmaker that can make interior passes, good at avoiding turnovers
- 2019-20 Defensive Degree of Difficulty: 0.389
- Tends to guard second unit level players or lower leverage starters
- Solid on-ball defender that can guard multiple positions
- Fairly solid at guarding pick-and-rolls, good at containing ball handlers, tends to be late to rotate back to the screener
- Fights through screens off the ball, usually is late to close out on perimeter shooters
- Good defensive rebounder, Block Percentage is still consistent with his career average, Steal Percentage has been declining for the last three seasons

Trey Lyles

	Height	Weight	Cap #	Years Left
	6'9"	234	$5.500M	UFA

	Similar at Age	24	
		Season	SIMsc
1	Patrick Patterson	2013-14	941.6
2	Brian Cook	2004-05	940.7
3	Anthony Tolliver	2009-10	933.1
4	Jake Layman	2018-19	922.0
5	Marcus Morris	2013-14	921.4
6	Luke Babbitt	2013-14	919.4
7	Shawne Williams	2010-11	918.8
8	Ersan Ilyasova	2011-12	915.3
9	James Jones	2004-05	914.3
10	Vladimir Radmanovic	2004-05	913.8

Baseline Basic Stats

MPG	PTS	AST	REB	BLK	STL
21.3	8.2	1.2	4.2	0.4	0.6

Advanced Metrics

USG%	3PTA/FGA	FTA/FGA	TS%	eFG%	3PT%
17.4	0.448	0.205	0.546	0.517	0.360
AST%	**TOV%**	**OREB%**	**DREB%**	**STL%**	**BLK%**
9.3	10.0	5.1	19.9	1.2	1.5
PER	**ORTG**	**DRTG**	**WS/48**	**VOL**	
13.50	110.3	109.7	0.094	0.328	

- Regular starter for San Antonio when healthy, missed the Orlando restart due to appendicitis
- Mainly used as a low volume, stretch big, made almost 39% of his threes last season
- Very good at making corner threes in his career, made almost 46% of his corner threes in 2019-20
- Strictly a stationary spot-up shooter, does not really shoot on the move or off the dribble
- Middling rim runner, does not have the lift to finish in traffic, does not really draw fouls
- Good transition player that can run the floor and set up for trail threes
- Showed decent passing skills in previous seasons, good at avoiding turnovers
- 2019-20 Defensive Degree of Difficulty: 0.438, tended to guard starting level players
- Below average rim protector, not really a shot blocker, good defensive rebounder
- Decent on-ball defender, can be bullied inside by stronger post players, good mobility to defend big men in space on isolations
- Average pick-and-roll defender, good in drop coverages, has trouble staying with quicker ball handlers
- Fights through screens off the ball, tends to be late when closing out on perimeter shooters

Jakob Poeltl

	Height	Weight	Cap #	Years Left
Jakob Poeltl	7'1"	230	$8.102M	2

Similar at Age 24

		Season	SIMsc
1	Tree Rollins	1979-80	907.8
2	JaVale McGee	2011-12	897.6
3	Tony Battie	2000-01	896.7
4	Eric Mobley	1994-95	893.1
5	Tyson Chandler	2006-07	890.3
6	Sam Bowie	1985-86	889.5
7	Steven Hunter	2005-06	886.4
8	Marcus Camby	1998-99	884.8
9	Marcin Gortat	2008-09	883.4
10	Nerlens Noel	2018-19	882.9

Baseline Basic Stats

MPG	PTS	AST	REB	BLK	STL
23.4	7.9	0.9	7.3	1.7	0.6

Advanced Metrics

USG%	3PTA/FGA	FTA/FGA	TS%	eFG%	3PT%
14.5	0.007	0.387	0.600	0.590	0.169
AST%	**TOV%**	**OREB%**	**DREB%**	**STL%**	**BLK%**
9.7	14.0	12.6	22.6	1.2	5.3
PER	**ORTG**	**DRTG**	**WS/48**	**VOL**	
18.47	122.2	104.9	0.170	0.247	

- Regular rotation player for San Antonio in his second season with the team
- Utilized as a low volume rim runner, has made 70% of his shots inside of three feet in his career
- Dives hard to the rim, good roll man and cutter, draws fouls, makes less than 55% of his free throws
- Good offensive rebounder that gets second chances opportunities, has some trouble finishing put-back attempts
- Shooting range is limited to 16 feet and in, solid at making shorter mid-range spot-up jumpers
- Solid passing big man, set a career high in Assist Percentage, slightly turnover prone last season
- 2019-20 Defensive Degree of Difficulty: 0.367, tends to guard second unit big men
- Great rim protector, good defensive rebounder, excellent shot blocker, somewhat foul prone
- Plays good on-defense, strong post defender, shows enough mobility to defend big men in space
- Fairly solid pick-and-roll defender, can switch onto ball handlers for a few dribbles, sometimes can be a step slow to cover the roll man
- Consistently comes out to close out on perimeter shooters in spot-up situations

Keldon Johnson	Height	Weight	Cap #	Years Left
	6'5"	211	$2.048M	2 Team Options

	Similar at Age	20 Season	SIMsc
1	C.J. Miles	2007-08	898.4
2	Martin Lewis	1995-96	889.0
3	Hamidou Diallo	2018-19	875.1
4	Paul George	2010-11	872.7
5	Xavier Henry	2011-12	871.8
6	James Harden	2009-10	871.8
7	Javaris Crittenton	2007-08	869.4
8	Malik Beasley	2016-17	867.1
9	J.R. Smith	2005-06	867.0
10	Kelly Oubre	2015-16	864.4

Baseline Basic Stats

MPG	PTS	AST	REB	BLK	STL
20.8	7.6	1.5	2.9	0.2	0.7

Advanced Metrics

USG%	3PTA/FGA	FTA/FGA	TS%	eFG%	3PT%
17.5	0.260	0.351	0.621	0.578	0.473
AST%	**TOV%**	**OREB%**	**DREB%**	**STL%**	**BLK%**
9.6	11.2	3.7	13.3	2.0	0.6
PER	**ORTG**	**DRTG**	**WS/48**	**VOL**	
15.70	119.3	111.4	0.136	0.456	

- Fringe rotation player for San Antonio in his rookie season, spent most of 2019-20 in the G-League with the Austin Spurs
- Used by San Antonio as a low volume, slashing wing player, took on more volume in the G-League
- Made less than 30% of his threes in the G-League, went 13-for-22 (59.1%) on threes in the NBA
- Mainly a spot-up shooter, occasionally can make pull-up jumpers on pick-and-rolls
- Good at attacking aggressive close-outs if his shot is falling, effective cutter off the ball, drew fouls at a very high rate in the NBA
- Predominantly a catch-and-shoot, showed some passing skills in the G-League, good at avoiding turnovers
- 2019-20 Defensive Degree of Difficulty: 0.340, tends to guard second unit players
- Rarely tested on the ball, solid on-ball defender in a small sample of possessions, flashes the potential to guard multiple positions
- Below average at guarding pick-and-rolls, tended to go too far under screens
- Good at closing out on perimeter shooters, sometimes got caught on screens off the ball
- Solid defensive rebounder, got steals at a high rate at the NBA level

Drew Eubanks	Height	Weight	Cap #	Years Left
	6'9"	245	$1.621M	2

	Similar at Age	22	
		Season	SIMsc
1	Jelani McCoy	1999-00	911.2
2	Jeff Ayres	2009-10	892.2
3	Jordan Mickey	2016-17	889.3
4	James Johnson	2009-10	885.2
5	Clint Capela	2016-17	885.0
6	Greg Smith	2012-13	884.6
7	Jeremy Tyler	2013-14	883.7
8	Adonal Foyle	1997-98	883.6
9	Richaun Holmes	2015-16	881.8
10	Montrezl Harrell	2015-16	880.0

Baseline Basic Stats

MPG	PTS	AST	REB	BLK	STL
16.2	6.0	0.7	4.4	0.7	0.4

Advanced Metrics

USG%	3PTA/FGA	FTA/FGA	TS%	eFG%	3PT%
16.6	0.021	0.380	0.624	0.587	0.469
AST%	**TOV%**	**OREB%**	**DREB%**	**STL%**	**BLK%**
8.0	16.6	9.7	23.3	1.1	3.8
PER	**ORTG**	**DRTG**	**WS/48**	**VOL**	
17.04	116.1	107.4	0.146	0.518	

- Played on a Two-Way contract, became a fringe rotation player for San Antonio towards the end of last season
- Mostly used as a low volume rim runner, made 75% of his shots inside of three feet last season
- Very good at rolling to the rim, scores on a high volume of cuts off the ball, draws fouls at a solid rate
- Good offensive rebounder that efficiently scores on put-backs
- Can post-up smaller players, flashed some outside shooting ability
- Fairly good at making mid-range shots in a small sample of attempts, made his only three-point attempt last season
- Has some passing ability, pretty turnover prone at the NBA level
- 2019-20 Defensive Degree of Difficulty: 0.376, tended to guard second unit level big men
- Good defensive rebounder and shot blocker, average rim protector, highly foul prone
- Middling on-ball defender, strong post defender that holds position inside
- Lacking in mobility, struggles to defender quicker big men in space
- Decent at guarding pick-and-rolls, effective at switching onto ball handlers for a few dribbles, tended to be late to rotate back to the screener in other coverages
- Does not always come out to contest perimeter shots

Luka Šamanić	Height	Weight	Cap #	Years Left
	6'10"	227	$2.824M	2 Team Options

	Similar at Age	20	
		Season	SIMsc
1	Thomas Bryant	2017-18	885.9
2	Donte Greene	2008-09	868.0
3	Marquese Chriss	2017-18	865.5
4	Zach Collins	2017-18	854.4
5	Trey Lyles	2015-16	851.9
6	Andray Blatche	2006-07	848.3
7	Danilo Gallinari	2008-09	847.2
8	Jonathan Bender	2000-01	847.1
9	Jermaine O'Neal	1998-99	844.2
10	Christian Wood	2015-16	840.0

Baseline Basic Stats

MPG	PTS	AST	REB	BLK	STL
18.5	7.2	0.9	4.0	0.7	0.4

Advanced Metrics

USG%	3PTA/FGA	FTA/FGA	TS%	eFG%	3PT%
18.6	0.406	0.263	0.527	0.488	0.390
AST%	**TOV%**	**OREB%**	**DREB%**	**STL%**	**BLK%**
12.3	11.1	4.4	18.4	0.7	3.0
PER	**ORTG**	**DRTG**	**WS/48**	**VOL**	
12.93	107.3	112.0	0.070	0.633	

- Played sparingly for San Antonio in his rookie season, spent most of 2019-20 in the G-League with the Austin Spurs
- Used in the G-League as a higher volume, stretch big, went 3-for-8 (37.5%) on threes in the NBA
- Below break-even three-point shooter in the G-League, more of a mid-range shooter at this stage
- Effective in a very small sample of possessions as the screener on pick-and-pops in the NBA
- Middling rim runner, does not have the lift or explosiveness to finish in traffic, does not really draw fouls
- Catch-and-shoot player at this stage, passing skills are limited, fairly turnover prone in the G-League
- 2019-20 Defensive Degree of Difficulty: 0.135, only played 48 NBA minutes
- Allowed a made three and forced three misses in four isolation possessions in the NBA
- Committed a shooting foul, forced a turnover and two misses in four pick-and-roll possessions
- Allowed two made threes and forced six misses in eight spot-up possessions
- Forced two misses in two possessions when guarding shooters off screens
- Allowed two made two-pointers in two possessions when defending a dribble hand-off
- Good rebounder and solid shot blocker in the G-League, gets steals at a decent rate for a big man

Newcomers

Devin Vassell	Height	Weight	Cap #	Years Left
	6'6"	180	$4.033M	1 + 2 TO

Baseline Basic Stats

MPG	PTS	AST	REB	BLK	STL
21.2	8.3	1.6	2.5	0.3	0.8

Advanced Metrics

USG%	3PTA/FGA	FTA/FGA	TS%	eFG%	3PT%
18.1	0.349	0.197	0.524	0.496	0.353

AST%	TOV%	OREB%	DREB%	STL%	BLK%
12.2	10.7	3.2	11.0	2.0	1.6

PER	ORTG	DRTG	WS/48	VOL
12.91	104.4	103.7	0.063	N/A

- Drafted by San Antonio with the 11th overall pick
- Made the All-ACC 2nd Team, led Florida State in scoring and rebounding as a sophomore
- Good shooter in college, made almost 42% of his career threes
- Mostly a stationary spot-up shooter, effective at shooting off screens in a small sample of possessions
- Good at making backdoor cuts if defenders try to crowd him, good athlete, explosive finisher in transition
- Willing to make the extra pass, rarely turns the ball over, led the ACC in Turnover Percentage in 2019-20
- Ball handling still needs work, does not get all the way to the rim on drives, likely to be a complementary player at the NBA level
- Great length and athleticism, can potentially guard multiple positions in the NBA
- Good on-ball defender in college, can defend bigger wings in the post and quicker guards on the perimeter
- Very good help defender, got steals and blocks at a high rate, solid defensive rebounder
- Gambles a bit too much, tends to get caught out of position, undisciplined when making rotations off the ball or on pick-and-rolls

Tre Jones

Height	Weight	Cap #	Years Left
6'3"	185	$0.898M	2

Baseline Basic Stats

MPG	PTS	AST	REB	BLK	STL
16.5	5.6	2.4	1.7	0.1	0.7

Advanced Metrics

USG%	3PTA/FGA	FTA/FGA	TS%	eFG%	3PT%
17.7	0.270	0.244	0.483	0.445	0.315

AST%	TOV%	OREB%	DREB%	STL%	BLK%
23.3	15.8	2.2	8.8	2.1	0.5

PER	ORTG	DRTG	WS/48	VOL
12.00	99.7	104.1	0.052	N/A

- Drafted by San Antonio with the 41st overall pick
- Made the All-ACC 1st Team last season, named ACC Player of the Year in 2019-20, younger brother of Memphis' Tyus Jones
- Solid ball control point guard, good pass-first playmaker, can find open shooters and make interior passes
- Good natural speed, great at pushing the ball in transition, can blow by defenders in half court situations
- Below break-even three-point shooter in two seasons at Duke, improved as a sophomore
- Showed better shot selection, stuck to his strengths, can make open spot-up jumpers, struggles to shoot on the move or off the dribble
- Excellent defensive guard, named ACC Defensive Player of the Year last season
- Very good on-ball defender, actively pressures opposing ball handlers, good at taking away air space to contest shots
- Good pick-and-roll defender, good at containing ball handlers, also can funnel his man into help
- Stays attached to shooters off the ball, fights through screens off the ball and closes out
- Good at taking the ball away from careless ball handlers, can play passing lanes to get steals, solid rebounder for his size

PORTLAND TRAIL BLAZERS

Last Season: 35 – 39, Lost 1st Round to L.A. Lakers (1 – 4)

Offensive Rating: 113.7, 3rd in the NBA

Defensive Rating: 114.8, 28th in the NBA

Primary Executive: Neil Olshey, President of Basketball Operations and General Manager

Head Coach: Terry Stotts

Key Roster Changes

Subtractions
Trevor Ariza, trade
Mario Hezonja, trade
Hassan Whiteside, free agency
Caleb Swanigan, free agency
Wenyen Gabriel, free agency

Additions
C.J. Elleby, draft
Robert Covington, trade
Enes Kanter, trade
Derrick Jones, Jr., free agency
Harry Giles, free agency

Roster

Likely Starting Five

1. *Damian Lillard*
2. *C.J. McCollum*
3. Rodney Hood
4. *Robert Covington*
5. *Jusuf Nurkic*

Other Key Rotation Players
Carmelo Anthony
Derrick Jones, Jr.
Gary Trent, Jr.
Anfernee Simons
Zach Collins
Enes Kanter

* Italics denotes that a player is likely to be on the floor to close games

Remaining Roster

- Nassir Little
- Harry Giles
- C.J. Elleby
- Keljin Blevins, 25, 6'6", 200, Montana State (Two-Way)

SCHREMPF Base Rating: 37.1 (72-game season)

Strengths

- Efficient offense that can attack the rim and spread the floor to complement Lillard and McCollum
- Deep rotation that features 11 quality NBA players

Question Marks

- Limited defensive versatility and uncertain ability to make lineup adjustments on the fly
- No established defensive stopper outside of Robert Covington

Outlook

- Deeper unit that could out-perform the projection, should be in the playoff mix in the 2020-21 season

Veterans

Damian Lillard	Height	Weight	Cap #	Years Left
	6'2"	195	$31.627M	4

	Similar at Age	29	
		Season	SIMsc
1	Mike Conley	2016-17	917.2
2	Chauncey Billups	2005-06	906.2
3	Terry Porter	1992-93	898.8
4	Steve Nash*	2003-04	893.0
5	Stephon Marbury	2006-07	889.6
6	Paul Westphal*	1979-80	886.9
7	Tony Parker	2011-12	886.1
8	Jason Terry	2006-07	884.8
9	Stephen Curry	2017-18	884.2
10	Jeff Hornacek	1992-93	882.9

Baseline Basic Stats

MPG	PTS	AST	REB	BLK	STL
32.9	20.9	6.3	3.7	0.2	1.0

Advanced Metrics

USG%	3PTA/FGA	FTA/FGA	TS%	eFG%	3PT%
27.7	0.437	0.366	0.597	0.530	0.375
AST%	**TOV%**	**OREB%**	**DREB%**	**STL%**	**BLK%**
31.5	11.9	1.9	10.8	1.4	0.8
PER	**ORTG**	**DRTG**	**WS/48**	**VOL**	
23.27	120.6	113.3	0.205	0.500	

- Made the All-NBA 2nd Team in 2019-20, named Player of the Seeding Games in the Orlando bubble
- Had his most productive season as Portland's primary ball handler
- Excellent scorer in one-on-one situations, draws fouls at a high rate, regularly gets to the rim
- Great overall shooter, made over 40% of his threes last season
- Great shooter off the dribble, has very deep range, excellent spot-up shooter that also can run off screens
- Great playmaker that can find open shooter, consistently good at avoiding turnovers
- 2019-20 Defensive Degree of Difficulty: 0.407
- Tends to be hidden in favorable matchups against lower leverage starters
- Played solid on-ball defense in these situations, occasionally allowed his man to get clean looks from outside
- Solid team defender that makes sound rotations, good at guarding pick-and-rolls, funnels ball handlers into help
- Usually stays attached to shooters off the ball and contests perimeter shots, occasionally allow his man to get to the rim on dribble hand-offs
- Solid defensive rebounder, Steal and Block Percentages are still consistent with his career averages

CJ McCollum

	Height	Weight	Cap #	Years Left
	6'3"	197	$29.354M	3

	Similar at Age	28 Season	SIMsc
1	Byron Scott	1989-90	934.3
2	Damian Lillard	2018-19	918.1
3	Reggie Jackson	2018-19	918.0
4	Ben Gordon	2011-12	914.7
5	Voshon Lenard	2001-02	912.3
6	Dell Curry	1992-93	910.3
7	Klay Thompson	2018-19	905.8
8	Derrick Rose	2016-17	905.1
9	Terry Porter	1991-92	901.9
10	Cuttino Mobley	2003-04	900.4

Baseline Basic Stats

MPG	PTS	AST	REB	BLK	STL
30.7	16.0	3.3	3.1	0.3	0.9

Advanced Metrics

USG%	3PTA/FGA	FTA/FGA	TS%	eFG%	3PT%
23.9	0.408	0.187	0.542	0.511	0.375

AST%	TOV%	OREB%	DREB%	STL%	BLK%
17.4	9.9	2.1	9.7	1.2	1.0

PER	ORTG	DRTG	WS/48	VOL
15.67	109.0	113.5	0.082	0.339

- Led the NBA in total minutes played in 2019-20
- Provided reliable production in his role as the second scoring option and secondary ball handler
- Good three-point shooter throughout his career, made almost 40% of his career threes
- Good shooter off the dribble, very good spot-up shooter that can also come off screens
- Good one-on-one player that can make pull-up jumpers from mid-range, very consistent mid-range shooter throughout his career
- Solid playmaker that can hit the roll man or find open shooters as a pick-and-roll ball handler, rarely turns the ball over
- 2019-20 Defensive Degree of Difficulty: 0.451
- Usually guards starting level players, occasionally takes on tougher defensive assignments
- Played fairly good on-ball defense, could capably defend both guard spots
- Average pick-and-roll defender, decent at switching, tended to go too far under screens when guarding ball handlers
- Tended to get caught on screens off the ball, could be late to close out on perimeter shooters
- Posted career highs in Defensive Rebound and Block Percentage, Steal Percentage dropped to a career low in 2019-20

Jusuf Nurkić	Height	Weight	Cap #	Years Left
	7'0"	280	$14.139M	1

	Similar at Age	25	
		Season	SIMsc
1	Stanley Roberts	1995-96	877.5
2	Chris Kaman	2007-08	870.8
3	Chris Anstey	1999-00	870.1
4	Elmore Spencer	1994-95	868.9
5	Roy Hibbert	2011-12	867.8
6	Kyle O'Quinn	2015-16	865.6
7	Aaron Gray	2009-10	863.4
8	Kosta Koufos	2014-15	861.0
9	Luc Longley	1993-94	858.2
10	Hakeem Olajuwon*	1987-88	857.8

Baseline Basic Stats

MPG	PTS	AST	REB	BLK	STL
23.3	10.3	1.4	6.7	1.4	0.6

Advanced Metrics

USG%	3PTA/FGA	FTA/FGA	TS%	eFG%	3PT%
23.1	0.039	0.319	0.546	0.501	0.101
AST%	**TOV%**	**OREB%**	**DREB%**	**STL%**	**BLK%**
13.9	13.9	10.7	22.9	1.5	4.5
PER	**ORTG**	**DRTG**	**WS/48**	**VOL**	
19.75	110.0	105.0	0.139	0.642	

- Missed most of last season while recovering from a fractured left leg, recovered in time for the Orlando restart
- Excelled in his role as Portland's primary interior scorer
- Good at bullying weaker defenders in the post, most effective from the left block
- Solid rim runner, made 68.5% of his shot inside of three feet in Orlando, better at cutting off the ball
- Forced to set screens from further away due to Damian Lillard's range, struggled to get to the rim as a roll man
- Very good passing big man, set a career high in Assist Percentage, good at limiting turnovers
- 2019-20 Defensive Degree of Difficulty: 0.453
- Defends opposing starting big men, will take on tougher assignments when necessary
- Great shot blocker and defensive rebounder, middling rim protector, lacks mobility, fairly foul prone
- Played solid on-ball defense, strong post defender that holds position inside, effective at guarding opposing big men on isolations in a small sample of possessions
- Middling pick-and-roll defender, solid in drop coverages, struggles to stay with quicker ball handlers in space
- Has trouble closing out on perimeter shooters, sometimes is late to contest, quicker players can blow by him if he's too aggressive

Robert Covington

Height	Weight	Cap #	Years Left
6'7"	211	$12.138M	1

Similar at Age 29

		Season	SIMsc
1	Scott Burrell	1999-00	920.0
2	Danny Green	2016-17	907.9
3	James Posey	2005-06	898.7
4	Quentin Richardson	2009-10	897.8
5	Shawn Marion	2007-08	892.0
6	Francisco Garcia	2010-11	891.5
7	Morris Peterson	2006-07	891.2
8	C.J. Miles	2016-17	888.7
9	Greg Buckner	2005-06	888.1
10	Trevor Ariza	2014-15	887.7

Baseline Basic Stats

MPG	PTS	AST	REB	BLK	STL
25.2	8.6	1.4	4.3	0.7	1.0

Advanced Metrics

USG%	3PTA/FGA	FTA/FGA	TS%	eFG%	3PT%
15.9	0.627	0.179	0.555	0.528	0.358

AST%	TOV%	OREB%	DREB%	STL%	BLK%
7.1	11.5	2.9	17.5	2.1	2.8

PER	ORTG	DRTG	WS/48	VOL
12.18	105.8	106.5	0.090	0.398

- Regular starter for Minnesota and Houston in 2019-20, traded to Houston in February 2020
- Mostly used as a low volume spot-up shooter, made threes at just above a break-even rate last season
- Mainly a stationary shooter, does not really run off screens or shoot on the move
- Good off the ball, can make backdoor cuts, will crash the offensive glass to score on put-backs
- Solid transition player, runs hard down the floor to get layups, can set up trail threes
- Does not really create his own shot, strictly a catch-and-shoot player, limited playmaking skills, good at avoiding turnovers
- 2019-20 Defensive Degree of Difficulty: 0.470
- Tends to guard starting level players, will take on tougher defensive assignments
- Fairly solid on-ball defender, effective at guarding bigger players in the post, quicker guards could sometimes drive by him in isolation situations
- Solid at guarding pick-and-rolls, good at switching onto ball handlers, can drop to take away the roll man inside
- Good at fighting through screens off the ball, sometimes can be late to close out on perimeter shooters
- Active help defender, solid at protecting the rim, good defensive rebounder and shot blocker, gets steals at a high rate, good at staying vertical to contest shots

Rodney Hood

Height	Weight	Cap #	Years Left
6'8"	208	$10.047M	1

Similar at Age 27

		Season	SIMsc
1	Doug McDermott	2018-19	940.1
2	Jason Kapono	2008-09	931.9
3	Mindaugas Kuzminskas	2016-17	930.7
4	James Ennis	2017-18	929.3
5	Sean Higgins	1995-96	927.4
6	Matt Carroll	2007-08	926.7
7	Chris Douglas-Roberts	2013-14	926.2
8	Eric Piatkowski	1997-98	925.8
9	Martell Webster	2013-14	924.1
10	Reggie Bullock	2018-19	921.8

Baseline Basic Stats

MPG	PTS	AST	REB	BLK	STL
21.4	8.1	1.2	2.5	0.2	0.6

Advanced Metrics

USG%	3PTA/FGA	FTA/FGA	TS%	eFG%	3PT%
16.2	0.507	0.174	0.575	0.547	0.415

AST%	TOV%	OREB%	DREB%	STL%	BLK%
8.5	9.0	1.9	10.0	1.3	0.6

PER	ORTG	DRTG	WS/48	VOL
12.08	114.0	113.2	0.092	0.451

- Missed of 2019-20 due to a torn left Achilles tendon, regular starter for Portland when healthy
- Effective in his role as a low volume, spot-up shooter, solid three-point shooter throughout his career
- Made over 49% of his threes before his injury, very good spot-up shooter that can sometimes shoot off screens
- Can make pull-up jumpers on pick-and-rolls, sometimes can drive by defenders on isolations if they try to crowd him
- Good at running down the wings in transition for layups, solid secondary playmaker, rarely turns the ball over
- 2019-20 Defensive Degree of Difficulty: 0.551
- Had the 10th toughest set of matchups among players that played 500 or more minutes
- Average on-ball defender that can capably defend multiple positions, slightly over-matched against top perimeter players
- Solid pick-and-roll defender, can contain ball handlers or funnel them into help
- Fights through screens off the ball, tended to be late when closing out on perimeter shooters
- Fairly solid defensive rebounder, Steal and Block Percentages are still consistent with his career averages

Carmelo Anthony	Height	Weight	Cap #	Years Left
	6'8"	240	$1.621M	UFA

Similar at Age 35

		Season	SIMsc
1	Luis Scola	2015-16	932.4
2	Joe Johnson	2016-17	912.0
3	Sam Perkins	1996-97	903.1
4	Matt Barnes	2015-16	894.6
5	Rasual Butler	2014-15	888.3
6	Grant Hill*	2007-08	885.5
7	Antawn Jamison	2011-12	883.9
8	Rasheed Wallace	2009-10	883.6
9	David West	2015-16	882.5
10	Vince Carter	2011-12	879.8

Baseline Basic Stats

MPG	PTS	AST	REB	BLK	STL
21.7	8.3	1.3	3.8	0.4	0.6

Advanced Metrics

USG%	3PTA/FGA	FTA/FGA	TS%	eFG%	3PT%
18.4	0.346	0.225	0.534	0.499	0.369
AST%	**TOV%**	**OREB%**	**DREB%**	**STL%**	**BLK%**
6.7	10.6	3.8	16.5	1.1	1.6
PER	**ORTG**	**DRTG**	**WS/48**	**VOL**	
11.77	105.8	110.5	0.058	0.601	

- Signed with Portland in November 2019, started all of his games last season
- Had a bounce-back season in his role as a secondary scorer and floor spacer
- Made 38.5% of his threes last season, became a good spot-up shooter
- Good at posting up smaller players on the left block, effective isolation player that can make shorter mid-range pull-up jumpers and get to the rim
- Strictly a catch-and-shoot player at this stage, solid playmaker in previous seasons, does not really turn the ball over
- 2019-20 Defensive Degree of Difficulty: 0.401
- Tended to be hidden in favorable matchups against lower leverage starters
- Played solid on-ball defense, could capably guard both forward positions
- Generally solid at guarding pick-and-rolls, sometimes would go too far under screens when guarding ball handlers
- Can get caught on screens off the ball, tends to be late when closing out on perimeter shooters
- Good defensive rebounder, Block and Steal Percentages are still consistent with his career averages

Derrick Jones, Jr.	Height	Weight	Cap #	Years Left
	6'6"	210	$9.258M	Player Option

	Similar at Age	22	
		Season	SIMsc
1	Maurice Harkless	2015-16	922.9
2	Josh Richardson	2015-16	918.9
3	Jerami Grant	2016-17	909.5
4	Josh Hart	2017-18	902.2
5	Mickael Pietrus	2004-05	901.5
6	Antoine Wright	2006-07	899.8
7	Arron Afflalo	2007-08	899.4
8	Kyle Weaver	2008-09	898.5
9	Paul Thompson	1983-84	894.5
10	Chris Carr	1996-97	894.2

Baseline Basic Stats

MPG	PTS	AST	REB	BLK	STL
22.7	7.8	1.2	3.5	0.6	0.9

Advanced Metrics

USG%	3PTA/FGA	FTA/FGA	TS%	eFG%	3PT%
14.9	0.361	0.314	0.572	0.538	0.297
AST%	**TOV%**	**OREB%**	**DREB%**	**STL%**	**BLK%**
7.2	9.7	5.5	12.3	2.0	2.6
PER	**ORTG**	**DRTG**	**WS/48**	**VOL**	
13.44	115.5	108.4	0.126	0.229	

- Regular rotation player for Miami in his fourth NBA season
- Had his productive season as a pro, used as a low volume, spot-up shooter and energy wing
- Outside shot is still a work-in-progress, has made less than 30% of his career threes
- Excellent athlete, won the 2020 Slam Dunk Contest, dynamic finisher in transition
- Vertical lob threat that can efficiently finish at the rim as a roll man and cutter off the ball
- Solid offensive rebounder that can score on put-backs or create second chance opportunities
- Catch-and-shoot or catch-and-finish player, limited playmaking skills, rarely turns the ball over
- 2019-20 Defensive Degree of Difficulty: 0.494
- Plays second unit minutes, will draw tough assignments against top perimeter players
- Good on-ball defender that can guard multiple positions
- Middling pick-and-roll defender, struggles to get around the screen, more effective on hard switches
- Generally stays attached to shooters off the ball, consistently contest shots, had some trouble defending dribble hand-offs last season
- Active help defender, good on the defensive boards, can rotate from the weak side to block shots
- Set a career high in Steal Percentage last season, fairly good at using his length to play passing lanes

Gary Trent Jr.	Height	Weight	Cap #	Years Left
	6'5"	209	$1.664M	RFA

	Similar at Age	21	
		Season	SIMsc
1	Daequan Cook	2008-09	933.6
2	Malik Beasley	2017-18	933.3
3	Tim Hardaway, Jr.	2013-14	920.9
4	Allen Crabbe	2013-14	920.1
5	Christian Eyenga	2010-11	919.4
6	Nik Stauskas	2014-15	914.9
7	Rashad Vaughn	2017-18	914.4
8	John Jenkins	2012-13	914.3
9	Kentavious Caldwell-Pope	2014-15	910.3
10	Casey Jacobsen	2002-03	906.9

Baseline Basic Stats

MPG	PTS	AST	REB	BLK	STL
21.9	8.5	1.3	2.5	0.2	0.6

Advanced Metrics

USG%	3PTA/FGA	FTA/FGA	TS%	eFG%	3PT%
17.3	0.393	0.169	0.527	0.502	0.352
AST%	**TOV%**	**OREB%**	**DREB%**	**STL%**	**BLK%**
8.5	8.7	1.8	8.6	1.2	0.8
PER	**ORTG**	**DRTG**	**WS/48**	**VOL**	
10.02	106.8	114.1	0.061	0.397	

- Regular rotation player for Portland in his second NBA season
- Productive in his role as a low volume, spot-up shooter, made almost 42% of his threes in 2019-20
- Primarily a stand-still spot-up shooter, average at making shot off screens
- Can knock down pull-up jumpers as a pick-and-roll ball handler, good at getting to the rim on dribble hand-offs
- Occasionally can sneak by defenders on isolations, rarely gets to the rim
- Catch-and-shoot player at this stage, limited playmaking skills, very rarely turns the ball over
- 2019-20 Defensive Degree of Difficulty: 0.403
- Usually defended second unit players, drew some tough matchups against top guards
- Good on-ball defender that can guard multiple positions
- Fairly solid pick-and-roll defender, good when defending ball handlers, can be targeted on switches by bigger screeners
- Tends to be late when closing out on perimeter shooters, gets caught on screens off the ball
- Below average defensive rebounder, gets steals and blocks at a moderate rate

Anfernee Simons

Height	Weight	Cap #	Years Left
6'3"	181	$2.252M	Team Option

	Similar at Age	20 Season	SIMsc
1	Frank Jackson	2018-19	925.0
2	Monta Ellis	2005-06	922.1
3	Daniel Gibson	2006-07	906.0
4	Brandon Knight	2011-12	901.7
5	Jordan Farmar	2006-07	901.4
6	Malik Monk	2018-19	897.3
7	Jeremy Lamb	2012-13	890.9
8	Daequan Cook	2007-08	889.7
9	Zach LaVine	2015-16	888.8
10	Collin Sexton	2018-19	887.9

Baseline Basic Stats

MPG	PTS	AST	REB	BLK	STL
24.7	11.0	3.0	2.4	0.1	0.8

Advanced Metrics

USG%	3PTA/FGA	FTA/FGA	TS%	eFG%	3PT%
22.1	0.421	0.224	0.536	0.503	0.360
AST%	**TOV%**	**OREB%**	**DREB%**	**STL%**	**BLK%**
16.7	11.7	1.9	8.1	1.3	0.3
PER	**ORTG**	**DRTG**	**WS/48**	**VOL**	
12.82	106.6	115.1	0.048	0.350	

- Played his first season as a regular rotation player for Portland
- Showed promise in his role as a low volume shooter and secondary playmaker
- Break-even three-point shooter overall, better from the corners
- Slightly better at shooting on the move off screens, inconsistent in spot-up situations, can sometimes make pull-up jumpers on pick-and-rolls
- Has good quickness to drive by defenders on isolations, good cutter off the ball in a small sample of possessions
- Flashes some secondary playmaking skills, cut his Turnover Percentage significantly last season
- 2019-20 Defensive Degree of Difficulty: 0.333, tends to guard second unit level players
- Played solid on-ball defense in lower leverage matchups
- Middling pick-and-roll defender, tends to go too far under screens, decent at switching
- Stays attached to shooters off the ball, consistently contests perimeter shots in spot-up situations
- Stay-at-home defender, rarely gets blocks or steals, fairly decent defensive rebounder

Zach Collins	Height	Weight	Cap #	Years Left
	6'11"	232	$5.406M	RFA

Similar at Age 22

		Season	SIMsc
1	Perry Jones	2013-14	937.4
2	Jon Leuer	2011-12	923.7
3	D.J. Wilson	2018-19	921.6
4	Ryan Kelly	2013-14	910.7
5	Hilton Armstrong	2006-07	904.7
6	Raef LaFrentz	1998-99	904.6
7	Greg Foster	1990-91	903.7
8	Noah Vonleh	2017-18	902.3
9	Zarko Cabarkapa	2003-04	901.6
10	Lavoy Allen	2011-12	898.8

Baseline Basic Stats

MPG	PTS	AST	REB	BLK	STL
17.1	6.3	1.0	4.0	0.6	0.4

Advanced Metrics

USG%	3PTA/FGA	FTA/FGA	TS%	eFG%	3PT%
15.9	0.283	0.223	0.542	0.513	0.343
AST%	**TOV%**	**OREB%**	**DREB%**	**STL%**	**BLK%**
9.1	14.5	7.6	16.7	1.1	2.6
PER	**ORTG**	**DRTG**	**WS/48**	**VOL**	
12.50	108.4	110.7	0.086	0.292	

- Missed most of last season due to injuries to his left shoulder and left ankle, regular starter when healthy
- Less effective in his role as a lower volume, stretch big and rim runner
- Made almost 37% of his threes last season, effective screener on pick-and-pops, had some trouble knocking down spot-up jumpers
- Decent rim runner, good at rolling to the rim, scores on a high volume of cuts off the ball
- Fairly good offensive rebounder, has some trouble finishing his put-back attempts
- Can post up smaller players, middling as a passer, slightly turnover prone
- 2019-20 Defensive Degree of Difficulty: 0.448, tended to guard starter level players
- Fairly good rim protector, solid shot blocker, decent defensive rebounder, somewhat foul prone
- Solid on-ball defender in limited action, good at holding position in the post, mobile enough to defend big men in space
- Below average pick-and-roll defender, struggles to guard ball handlers on switches, tends to be late when rotating back to cover the screener
- Does not always come out to contest perimeter shots in spot-up situations

Enes Kanter	Height	Weight	Cap #	Years Left
	6'10"	262	$5.005M	UFA

	Similar at Age	27	
		Season	SIMsc
1	Melvin Ely	2005-06	915.7
2	Brian Skinner	2003-04	904.9
3	Carlos Boozer	2008-09	895.2
4	Nick Collison	2007-08	893.8
5	Isaac Austin	1996-97	892.7
6	Kevin Seraphin	2016-17	892.1
7	Kosta Koufos	2016-17	890.1
8	Greg Monroe	2017-18	889.8
9	Derrick Favors	2018-19	884.9
10	Jordan Hill	2014-15	883.8

Baseline Basic Stats

MPG	PTS	AST	REB	BLK	STL
23.7	10.7	1.4	7.5	0.7	0.5

Advanced Metrics

USG%	3PTA/FGA	FTA/FGA	TS%	eFG%	3PT%
20.3	0.021	0.294	0.579	0.546	0.173

AST%	TOV%	OREB%	DREB%	STL%	BLK%
10.8	12.6	14.4	26.4	1.1	2.4

PER	ORTG	DRTG	WS/48	VOL
20.49	117.9	106.0	0.173	0.514

- Regular rotation player for Boston in his first season with the team
- Highly efficient on a per-minute basis, used as a low volume rim runner
- Made almost 64% of his shots inside of three feet last season, good at bullying smaller defenders on post-ups
- Good at sliding into open spaces inside to score on rolls to the rim or cuts off the ball
- One of the NBA's best offensive rebounders, scores on a high volume of put-backs
- Has no real shooting range outside of ten feet, decent passer in recent seasons, fairly good at avoiding turnovers
- 2019-20 Defensive Degree of Difficulty: 0.370
- Tends to guard second unit level big men or lower leverage starters
- Good at protecting the rim last season, below average protector throughout his career
- Block Percentage spiked upwards in 2019-20, not a great shot blocker throughout his career, excellent defensive rebounder
- Middling on-ball defender, strong post defender, struggles to defend in space on isolations
- Passable pick-and-roll defender at times, good in drop coverages, has trouble staying with quicker ball handlers on switches
- Consistently comes out to contest perimeter shots in spot-up situations

Nassir Little	Height	Weight	Cap #	Years Left
	6'5"	220	$2.211M	2 Team Options

Similar at Age 19

		Season	SIMsc
1	Xavier Henry	2010-11	897.9
2	Aaron Gordon	2014-15	894.0
3	James Young	2014-15	890.3
4	Troy Brown	2018-19	887.4
5	Archie Goodwin	2013-14	877.8
6	Martell Webster	2005-06	872.7
7	Zhaire Smith	2018-19	865.1
8	Justise Winslow	2015-16	862.3
9	Derrick Jones, Jr.	2016-17	860.3
10	Rashad Vaughn	2015-16	859.6

Baseline Basic Stats

MPG	PTS	AST	REB	BLK	STL
22.2	8.7	1.3	3.6	0.3	0.6

Advanced Metrics

USG%	3PTA/FGA	FTA/FGA	TS%	eFG%	3PT%
16.7	0.344	0.271	0.548	0.520	0.335

AST%	TOV%	OREB%	DREB%	STL%	BLK%
8.7	9.2	4.9	14.6	1.4	1.5

PER	ORTG	DRTG	WS/48	VOL
12.86	111.8	113.2	0.069	0.544

- Missed some games due to a sprained ankle, back spasms and dehydration, fringe rotation player in his rookie season when healthy
- Used as a low volume, spot-up shooter, had trouble making shots from outside of three feet
- Made less than 25% of his threes, limited ability to create his own offense, strictly a stationary shooter
- Energetic athlete, more effective off the ball, excels as a cutter, good at crashing the offensive glass to score on put-backs,
- Fairly effective at running down the wings to get dunks in transition, draws fouls at a solid rate
- Catch-and-shoot player, limited playmaking skills, rarely turns the ball over
- 2019-20 Defensive Degree of Difficulty: 0.343, tends to guard second unit level players
- Below average on-ball defender, good against drives, gives up space to allow clean looks from the outside
- Has trouble handling stronger post players inside, foul prone in one-on-one situations
- Middling pick-and-roll defender, tends to go too far under screens
- Gambles too much off the ball, tends to be out of position to contest perimeter shots
- Fairly active help defender, good at rotating from the weak side to block shots, fairly good defensive rebounder

Harry Giles	Height	Weight	Cap #	Years Left
	6'11"	240	$1.621M	UFA

	Similar at Age	21	
		Season	SIMsc
1	Domantas Sabonis	2017-18	917.6
2	Samaki Walker	1997-98	905.1
3	Johan Petro	2006-07	904.4
4	Tony Battie	1997-98	901.8
5	Cody Zeller	2013-14	896.9
6	Marquese Chriss	2018-19	896.9
7	Nikola Vucevic	2011-12	894.7
8	Deyonta Davis	2017-18	892.1
9	Andray Blatche	2007-08	890.4
10	Jan Vesely	2011-12	889.8

Baseline Basic Stats

MPG	PTS	AST	REB	BLK	STL
20.0	8.5	1.3	5.4	0.8	0.5

Advanced Metrics

USG%	3PTA/FGA	FTA/FGA	TS%	eFG%	3PT%
20.6	0.023	0.268	0.533	0.501	0.142
AST%	**TOV%**	**OREB%**	**DREB%**	**STL%**	**BLK%**
12.9	15.3	7.9	21.5	1.4	2.2
PER	**ORTG**	**DRTG**	**WS/48**	**VOL**	
14.42	103.8	106.8	0.091	0.484	

- Fringe rotation player for Sacramento last season, started a few games in 2019-20
- Effective in his role as a moderate volume rim runner, made over 80% of his shots inside of three feet last season
- Good at rolling to the rim and cutting off the ball, runs hard down the floor in transition
- Fairly good passing big man, cut his Turnover Percentage a bit last season
- Not really a consistent outside shooter, below average post player
- Can use his quickness to beat slower big men off the dribble on isolations
- 2019-20 Defensive Degree of Difficulty: 0.375, tends to guard second unit players
- Below average rim protector, undisciplined with positioning, fairly foul prone
- Decent shot blocker, good defensive rebounder
- Below average on-ball defender, can be bullied inside by stronger post players, struggles to defend in space on isolations
- Decent pick-and-roll defender, solid in drop coverages, mobile enough to switch onto ball handlers for a few dribbles
- Willing to close out on perimeter shooters, tends to be too aggressive on his close-outs

Newcomers

C.J. Elleby

Height	Weight	Cap #	Years Left
6'6"	200	$0.898M	1

Baseline Basic Stats

MPG	PTS	AST	REB	BLK	STL
15.7	5.9	1.0	2.1	0.2	0.5

Advanced Metrics

USG%	3PTA/FGA	FTA/FGA	TS%	eFG%	3PT%
18.6	0.351	0.237	0.496	0.463	0.337
AST%	**TOV%**	**OREB%**	**DREB%**	**STL%**	**BLK%**
10.8	11.5	3.6	12.9	1.8	1.1
PER	**ORTG**	**DRTG**	**WS/48**	**VOL**	
11.71	98.2	101.6	0.055	N/A	

- Drafted by Portland with the 46th overall pick
- Named to the All-Pac 12 1st Team as a sophomore at Washington State
- Solid three-point shooter, mostly a stationary spot-up shooter right now, occasionally knocks down shots as the screener on pick-and-pops
- Struggles to shoot on the move or off the dribble, shooting percentages dropped due to increased volume
- Lacks ideal quickness and ball handling skills to create shots, average isolation player and pick-and-roll ball handler in college
- Decent secondary playmaker that can find open shooters, cut his turnover rates significantly last season
- Needs to improve his ability to play without the ball, only average as a cutter at this stage
- Effective on-ball defender in a small sample of isolation possessions last season
- Struggled to contain pick-and-roll ball handlers, better at switching onto screeners
- Stayed attached to shooters off the ball, solid at fighting through screens, good at closing out on perimeter shooters
- Active weak side defender, gets steals and blocks at a high rate, good defensive rebounder

MEMPHIS GRIZZLIES

Last Season: 34 – 39, Missed the Playoffs

Offensive Rating: 109.2, 20th in the NBA

Defensive Rating: 110.3, 15th in the NBA

Primary Executive: Zach Kleiman, Executive Vice President of Basketball Operations

Head Coach: Taylor Jenkins

Key Roster Changes

Subtractions
Josh Jackson, free agency
Anthony Tolliver, free agency

Additions
Desmond Bane, draft
Xavier Tillman, draft
Mario Hezonja, trade

Roster

Likely Starting Five
1. *Ja Morant*
2. *Dillon Brooks*
3. Kyle Anderson
4. *Jaren Jackson, Jr.*
5. Jonas Valanciunas

Other Key Rotation Players
Brandon Clarke
De'Anthony Melton
Tyus Jones
Grayson Allen
Justise Winslow

* Italics denotes that a player is likely to be on the floor to close games

Remaining Roster

- Gorgui Dieng
- Mario Hezonja
- Desmond Bane
- Xavier Tillman
- Marko Guduric
- John Konchar
- Jontay Porter
- Sean McDermott, 24, 6'6", 195, Butler (Two-Way)
- Killian Tillie, 22, 6'10", 220, Gonzaga (Two-Way)
- Jahlil Tripp, 23, 6'5", 215, Pacific (Exhibit 10)

SCHREMPF Base Rating: 36.8 (72-game season)

Strengths

- Deep roster with a minimum of ten solid NBA players
- Youth and depth could allow them to play an effective, high energy brand of defense

Question Marks

- Lacking in ideal front-end talent to compete with the contenders in the West
- Team does not have adequate spacing to complement the talents of Ja Morant

Outlook

- Competitive but will not surprise opponents like last season, could push for a spot in the play-in tournament

Veterans

Ja Morant

	Height	Weight	Cap #	Years Left
Ja Morant	6'3"	175	$9.167M	2 Team Options

	Similar at Age	20 Season	SIMsc
1	Trae Young	2018-19	933.9
2	De'Aaron Fox	2017-18	929.6
3	Tony Parker	2002-03	919.3
4	Jrue Holiday	2010-11	915.3
5	Kyrie Irving	2012-13	914.2
6	Stephon Marbury	1997-98	911.8
7	Russell Westbrook	2008-09	904.1
8	Derrick Rose	2008-09	897.7
9	Brandon Knight	2011-12	897.4
10	Zach LaVine	2015-16	897.4

Baseline Basic Stats

MPG	PTS	AST	REB	BLK	STL
33.8	18.7	6.3	3.6	0.3	1.3

Advanced Metrics

USG%	3PTA/FGA	FTA/FGA	TS%	eFG%	3PT%
27.5	0.218	0.321	0.560	0.510	0.349

AST%	TOV%	OREB%	DREB%	STL%	BLK%
34.4	14.9	2.5	9.5	1.8	0.6

PER	ORTG	DRTG	WS/48	VOL
19.62	111.1	109.9	0.130	0.167

- Named Rookie of the Year in 2019-20
- Excelled in his role as Memphis' primary ball handler
- Great playmaker that can find the open man, can sometimes be a bit wild, a little bit turnover prone
- Has great quickness to drive by defenders on isolations or as a pick-and-roll ball handler
- Ability to shoot off the dribble and off screens is inconsistent, can be streaky at times, made threes at a rate just above break-even
- Better as a spot-up shooter, made half of his corner threes last season
- Excellent speed and leaping ability makes him a dynamic threat in transition
- 2019-20 Defensive Degree of Difficulty: 0.428, tended to guard starting level players
- Good on-ball defender, great in isolation situations against quicker guards, help up well in the post against bigger guards despite his relatively thin frame
- Average pick-and-roll defender, funnels his man into help, can be targeted by bigger screeners on switches
- Fights through screens and contests perimeter shots, can be too aggressive when closing out, can give up driving lanes to the basket
- Stay-at-home defender, does not really get blocks or steals, decent defensive rebounder for his size

Jaren Jackson, Jr.	Height	Weight	Cap #	Years Left
	6'11"	242	$7.257M	Team Option

	Similar at Age	20	
		Season	SIMsc
1	Myles Turner	2016-17	898.1
2	Marquese Chriss	2017-18	886.9
3	Kristaps Porzingis	2015-16	886.2
4	Dirk Nowitzki	1998-99	883.9
5	Domantas Sabonis	2016-17	878.9
6	Tim Thomas	1997-98	872.7
7	John Collins	2017-18	868.0
8	Ryan Anderson	2008-09	867.3
9	Karl-Anthony Towns	2015-16	867.0
10	Yi Jianlian	2007-08	857.5

Baseline Basic Stats

MPG	PTS	AST	REB	BLK	STL
25.8	12.1	1.3	5.7	1.1	0.7

Advanced Metrics

USG%	3PTA/FGA	FTA/FGA	TS%	eFG%	3PT%
23.5	0.331	0.266	0.577	0.541	0.394
AST%	**TOV%**	**OREB%**	**DREB%**	**STL%**	**BLK%**
8.4	11.0	5.2	15.7	1.4	3.6
PER	**ORTG**	**DRTG**	**WS/48**	**VOL**	
16.87	109.7	108.8	0.118	0.384	

- Regular starter for Memphis in his second season, tore the meniscus in his left knee in the Orlando bubble
- Efficient in his role as a higher volume, stretch big, made over 39% of his threes last season
- Very good spot-up shooter, also effective as the screener on pick-and-pop plays
- Good rim runner that provides a vertical threat when healthy, good at rolling to the rim and cutting off the ball
- Good at running the floor in transition, selectively crashes the offensive boards to score on put-backs
- Average post-up player, can occasionally drive past slower big men
- Mostly a catch-and-shoot player, has some passing skills, cut his turnover rate last season
- 2019-20 Defensive Degree of Difficulty: 0.427, tended to guard starting level big men
- Solid rim protector, great shot blocker, not always in position to grab defensive rebounds
- Average on-ball defender, tends to commit fouls in the post, struggled to defend in space on isolations
- Average pick-and-roll defender, decent in drop coverages, has trouble defending out on the perimeter against ball handlers
- Usually comes out to contest perimeter shots, tends to be too aggressive, will allow driving lanes to the rim

Jonas Valančiūnas

Height	Weight	Cap #	Years Left
6'11"	265	$15.000M	1

Similar at Age 27

		Season	SIMsc
1	Brook Lopez	2015-16	884.2
2	Benoit Benjamin	1991-92	883.7
3	Al Jefferson	2011-12	883.5
4	Chris Kaman	2009-10	881.9
5	Derrick Favors	2018-19	880.1
6	Kosta Koufos	2016-17	874.8
7	Erick Dampier	2002-03	874.1
8	Timofey Mozgov	2013-14	873.2
9	Greg Monroe	2017-18	871.3
10	Isaac Austin	1996-97	871.0

Baseline Basic Stats

MPG	PTS	AST	REB	BLK	STL
26.5	13.3	1.4	8.2	1.1	0.5

Advanced Metrics

USG%	3PTA/FGA	FTA/FGA	TS%	eFG%	3PT%
22.8	0.090	0.277	0.593	0.563	0.334

AST%	TOV%	OREB%	DREB%	STL%	BLK%
10.9	12.5	11.0	28.4	0.9	3.3

PER	ORTG	DRTG	WS/48	VOL
20.95	115.1	106.3	0.158	0.430

- Regular starter for Memphis is his first full season with the team
- Highly efficient scoring big man in a moderate volume role, posted the highest True Shooting Percentage of his career last season
- Very good post player that can quickly face up to get to the rim, does most of his damage from the left block
- Good rim runner that can roll to the rim and cut off the ball, good offensive rebounder that scores on put-backs
- Can space the floor, made threes at around the league average, mainly a stand-still spot-up shooter
- Runs hard down the floor in transition, solid passing big man that doesn't really commit turnovers
- 2019-20 Defensive Degree of Difficulty: 0.413, tends to guard starting level big men
- Very good defensive rebounder and shot blocker, average rim protector, not especially mobile, can be a bit foul prone
- Below average on-ball defender, tends to foul when playing post defense, struggles to defend in space due to his limited mobility
- Average pick-and-roll defender, decent in drop coverages, has trouble staying with quicker guards on switches
- Willing to come out to contest perimeter shots, tends to close out too aggressively to allow driving lanes to the rim

Dillon Brooks

	Height	Weight	Cap #	Years Left
	6'7"	220	$11.400M	2

	Similar at Age	24	
		Season	SIMsc
1	Eric Piatkowski	1994-95	941.3
2	Dennis Scott	1992-93	937.8
3	Morris Peterson	2001-02	936.3
4	Tracy Murray	1995-96	934.0
5	Antoine Wright	2008-09	932.2
6	Tyrone Nesby	1999-00	931.6
7	Rodney Hood	2016-17	931.3
8	Chase Budinger	2012-13	926.9
9	C.J. Miles	2011-12	926.2
10	Calbert Cheaney	1995-96	923.6

Baseline Basic Stats

MPG	PTS	AST	REB	BLK	STL
26.1	11.4	1.5	3.6	0.3	0.8

Advanced Metrics

USG%	3PTA/FGA	FTA/FGA	TS%	eFG%	3PT%
21.5	0.377	0.202	0.520	0.486	0.362
AST%	**TOV%**	**OREB%**	**DREB%**	**STL%**	**BLK%**
9.5	10.0	3.4	10.8	1.5	0.9
PER	**ORTG**	**DRTG**	**WS/48**	**VOL**	
11.82	103.0	110.6	0.054	0.376	

- Full-time starter for Memphis in his third year in the NBA
- Per-minute effectiveness increased in a higher volume role as a shooter off the ball
- Consistently has made threes around the league average in three seasons
- Good spot-up shooter, average at making shots off screens, can make pull-up jumpers off pick-and-rolls
- Does not frequently get to the rim, takes a lot of mid-range shots, makes them at an average rate
- Mostly a catch-and-shoot player, passing skills improved, cut his Turnover Percentage to a career low last season
- 2019-20 Defensive Degree of Difficulty: 0.549, usually guards top perimeter players
- Had the 9th toughest set of matchups among all players that played at least 1000 minutes last season
- Fairly good on-ball defender that can guard multiple positions
- Above average pick-and-roll defender, good at switching, tends to go too far under screens
- Stays attached to shooters off the ball, sometimes can close too aggressively and commit shooting fouls
- Stay-at-home defender, fairly decent defensive rebounder, Steal and Block Percentages are still consistent with his career averages

Kyle Anderson

	Height	Weight	Cap #	Years Left
	6'9"	230	$9.505M	1

	Similar at Age	26	
		Season	SIMsc
1	Dominic McGuire	2011-12	930.7
2	Larry Nance	2018-19	924.4
3	Robert Horry	1996-97	922.5
4	Pete Chilcutt	1994-95	915.2
5	Lavoy Allen	2015-16	911.9
6	Danny Ferry	1992-93	909.3
7	Ben Poquette	1981-82	908.9
8	Major Jones	1979-80	907.4
9	Brian Scalabrine	2004-05	904.7
10	Omri Casspi	2014-15	904.3

Baseline Basic Stats

MPG	PTS	AST	REB	BLK	STL
22.1	7.2	1.8	4.4	0.6	0.8

Advanced Metrics

USG%	3PTA/FGA	FTA/FGA	TS%	eFG%	3PT%
14.3	0.261	0.229	0.544	0.522	0.316
AST%	**TOV%**	**OREB%**	**DREB%**	**STL%**	**BLK%**
13.6	13.9	5.0	16.6	1.9	2.2
PER	**ORTG**	**DRTG**	**WS/48**	**VOL**	
13.11	109.5	106.8	0.104	0.345	

- Regular rotation player for Memphis, started some games last season
- Utilized in a role as a low volume, secondary ball handler
- Good pick-and-roll ball handler, solid playmaker that can find the open man, effective at driving into the mid-range area to make runners and floaters
- Rated as average or worse in every other offensive situation
- Did not really get to the rim, struggled to make shots from outside, Three-Point Percentage has been below 30% in two season with Memphis
- Cut his Turnover Percentage a bit, still somewhat prone to turning the ball over
- 2019-20 Defensive Degree of Difficulty: 0.412
- Typically guarded second unit level players, occasionally got tougher defensive assignments
- Average on-ball defender, quicker guards can beat him off the dribble, has trouble in the post against stronger players
- Excellent pick-and-roll defender, great at switching to defend multiple positions
- Great at closing out to contest perimeter shots, gambles too much when defending off-ball screens, can get caught trying to shoot the gap
- Active help defender, gets steals and blocks at a high rate, good defensive rebounder

Brandon Clarke

	Height	Weight	Cap #	Years Left
Brandon Clarke	6'8"	210	$2.603M	2 Team Options

	Similar at Age	23 Season	SIMsc
1	Jerami Grant	2017-18	908.4
2	Josh Howard	2003-04	905.7
3	Mark Alarie	1986-87	903.7
4	Kenny Williams	1992-93	903.1
5	Eddie Robinson	1999-00	902.1
6	Josh Childress	2006-07	900.0
7	T.J. Warren	2016-17	898.2
8	David Benoit	1991-92	897.2
9	Amir Johnson	2010-11	897.1
10	Brandan Wright	2010-11	895.6

Baseline Basic Stats

MPG	PTS	AST	REB	BLK	STL
23.5	9.9	1.1	4.9	0.8	0.7

Advanced Metrics

USG%	3PTA/FGA	FTA/FGA	TS%	eFG%	3PT%
19.4	0.128	0.244	0.609	0.581	0.366
AST%	**TOV%**	**OREB%**	**DREB%**	**STL%**	**BLK%**
8.7	10.4	7.5	17.4	1.5	2.6
PER	**ORTG**	**DRTG**	**WS/48**	**VOL**	
18.99	118.8	106.2	0.164	0.467	

- Regular rotation player for Memphis in rookie season, made the All-Rookie 1st Team in 2019-20
- Highly effective in his role as a lower volume, rim runner
- Energetic big man that actively scores on rolls to the rim and cuts off the ball
- Fairly solid offensive rebounder that efficiently scores on put-backs, high motor, runs hard down the floor in transition
- Flashed some stretch potential, made threes at just above the league average on less than 100 attempts
- Good at making spot-up jumpers, effective as the screener on pick-and-pop plays
- Mainly a catch-and-shoot player, shows solid passing skills, great at limiting turnovers
- 2019-20 Defensive Degree of Difficulty: 0.357, mostly guarded second unit level players
- Fairly solid on-ball defender, great mobility to defend perimeter players in space, vulnerable against stronger post players inside
- Solid against pick-and-rolls, shows the ability to switch to guard multiple positions
- Fights through screens off the ball, can be too aggressive when closing out on perimeter shooters
- Solid rebounder and shot blocker, average at protecting the rim, does not always stay vertical to contest shots

De'Anthony Melton	Height	Weight	Cap #	Years Left
	6'2"	200	$9.572M	3

	Similar at Age	21	
		Season	SIMsc
1	Devin Harris	2004-05	923.1
2	Tyus Jones	2017-18	909.4
3	Jay Williams	2002-03	897.7
4	Elie Okobo	2018-19	897.5
5	Eric Bledsoe	2010-11	895.1
6	William Avery	2000-01	893.7
7	Reggie Jackson	2011-12	893.6
8	Jeff Teague	2009-10	889.9
9	Tyler Ennis	2015-16	887.7
10	Cameron Payne	2015-16	887.4

Baseline Basic Stats

MPG	PTS	AST	REB	BLK	STL
20.1	7.3	3.1	2.3	0.2	0.9

Advanced Metrics

USG%	3PTA/FGA	FTA/FGA	TS%	eFG%	3PT%
17.3	0.241	0.260	0.504	0.462	0.316
AST%	**TOV%**	**OREB%**	**DREB%**	**STL%**	**BLK%**
23.6	16.5	3.0	11.7	2.5	1.0
PER	**ORTG**	**DRTG**	**WS/48**	**VOL**	
12.67	104.7	109.1	0.075	0.289	

- Regular rotation player for Memphis in his second season in the NBA
- Showed improvement in his role as a lower volume, backup point guard
- Decent playmaker that can hit the roll man inside, cut his Turnover Percentage, still somewhat turnover prone
- Energetic guard that has quickness to get to the rim, made almost 63% of his shots inside of three feet last season
- Still inefficient as a scorer, inconsistent outside shooter, has made less than 30% of his threes in two NBA seasons
- Rated as average or worse in almost every offensive situation last season
- 2019-20 Defensive Degree of Difficulty: 0.468
- Drew a lot of tough assignments against top guards, tended to guard starter level players
- Slightly over-matched in these assignments, above average on-ball defender
- Good at taking away air space on jump shots, had some trouble containing top guards on drives to the rim
- Good pick-and-roll defender, funnels his man into help, solid on switches
- Gambles a bit too much, tries to shoot the gap when chasing shooters off screens, undisciplined when closing out on shooters
- Active help defender, gets steals and blocks at a high rate, good defensive rebounder for his size

Tyus Jones

Height	Weight	Cap #	Years Left
6'0"	196	$8.817M	1

Similar at Age 23

		Season	SIMsc
1	Fred VanVleet	2017-18	926.5
2	Earl Watson	2002-03	908.7
3	Trey Burke	2015-16	904.7
4	Ty Lawson	2010-11	904.5
5	Derek Fisher	1997-98	904.3
6	Steve Nash*	1997-98	903.4
7	Raul Neto	2015-16	903.1
8	Jameer Nelson	2005-06	900.1
9	Mo Williams	2005-06	900.0
10	Yogi Ferrell	2016-17	900.0

Baseline Basic Stats

MPG	PTS	AST	REB	BLK	STL
26.2	10.6	4.4	2.7	0.1	1.0

Advanced Metrics

USG%	3PTA/FGA	FTA/FGA	TS%	eFG%	3PT%
18.1	0.340	0.195	0.534	0.501	0.361
AST%	**TOV%**	**OREB%**	**DREB%**	**STL%**	**BLK%**
28.8	12.3	1.5	9.0	2.1	0.4
PER	**ORTG**	**DRTG**	**WS/48**	**VOL**	
15.40	113.2	110.5	0.106	0.294	

- Regular rotation player for Memphis last season, missed the Orlando restart due to a sore right knee
- Used as a low volume, pass-first, backup point guard
- Good playmaker, set a career high in Assist Percentage, good at limiting turnovers
- Effective at getting to the rim as a pick-and-roll ball handler, made over 65% of his shots inside of three feet last season
- Good spot-up shooter, solid from mid-range, made almost 38% of his threes last season
- Flashed some ability to move without the ball, good at making shots off screens and cutting off the ball in a small sample of possessions
- 2019-20 Defensive Degree of Difficulty: 0.341, tended to guard second unit level players
- Not tested frequently on the ball, solid against isolations last season, bigger perimeter players could shoot over him in the post
- Solid pick-and-roll defender that can funnel his man into help, can sometimes be targeted by taller players on switches
- Good at closing out on perimeter players, tends to gamble a bit too much, tries to shoot the gap when chasing shooters off screens
- Active hands, plays passing lanes, gets steals at a high rate, middling defensive rebounder

Grayson Allen

	Height	Weight	Cap #	Years Left
	6'4"	198	$2.545M	Team Option

	Similar at Age	**24**	
		Season	**SIMsc**
1	J.J. Redick	2008-09	927.9
2	Troy Daniels	2015-16	924.7
3	Austin Rivers	2016-17	923.9
4	Marco Belinelli	2010-11	919.3
5	Willie Green	2005-06	915.3
6	Trajan Langdon	2000-01	913.2
7	Jerian Grant	2016-17	911.1
8	Nik Stauskas	2017-18	910.0
9	Rex Walters	1994-95	907.7
10	John Jenkins	2015-16	907.5

Baseline Basic Stats

MPG	PTS	AST	REB	BLK	STL
22.5	9.7	1.7	2.1	0.1	0.6

Advanced Metrics

USG%	3PTA/FGA	FTA/FGA	TS%	eFG%	3PT%
20.2	0.508	0.236	0.560	0.521	0.376
AST%	**TOV%**	**OREB%**	**DREB%**	**STL%**	**BLK%**
12.5	11.1	1.4	9.0	1.1	0.5
PER	**ORTG**	**DRTG**	**WS/48**	**VOL**	
12.04	108.6	112.1	0.062	0.415	

- Regular rotation player for Memphis when healthy, missed games last season due to injuries to both ankles and his left hip
- Effectiveness increased in his role as a low volume, spot-up shooter, made over 40% of his threes last season
- Very good spot-up shooter that can also run off screens
- Good at using an on-ball screen to make shots or get an extra step to the rim on dribble hand-offs
- Struggles to create his own shot, rarely gets to the rim, does not shoot well off the dribble
- Catch-and-shoot player at this stage, some secondary playmaking skills, rarely turns the ball over
- 2019-20 Defensive Degree of Difficulty: 0.380
- Tends to guard higher-end second unit players, occasionally takes on tougher point guard matchups
- Decent on-ball defender, help up in the post against bigger wing players, sometimes struggles against quicker guards
- Fairly solid pick-and-roll defender, prevents ball handlers from getting to the rim, has some trouble on switches against bigger players
- Closes out on perimeter shooters, can get caught on screens off the ball
- Stay-at-home defender, decent defensive rebounder, does not really get blocks or steals

Justise Winslow	Height	Weight	Cap #	Years Left
	6'6"	225	$13.000M	Team Option

Similar at Age 23

		Season	SIMsc
1	Carlos Delfino	2005-06	941.6
2	Dion Glover	2001-02	919.0
3	Justin Anderson	2016-17	918.6
4	Morris Almond	2008-09	916.7
5	Alan Anderson	2005-06	915.5
6	Kirk Snyder	2006-07	915.2
7	Andrew Harrison	2017-18	915.0
8	Tariq Abdul-Wahad	1997-98	911.1
9	Desmond Mason	2000-01	910.3
10	Mickael Pietrus	2005-06	907.9

Baseline Basic Stats

MPG	PTS	AST	REB	BLK	STL
21.4	8.4	1.6	3.2	0.3	0.7

Advanced Metrics

USG%	3PTA/FGA	FTA/FGA	TS%	eFG%	3PT%
20.1	0.290	0.228	0.511	0.480	0.324
AST%	**TOV%**	**OREB%**	**DREB%**	**STL%**	**BLK%**
15.9	13.4	4.3	14.9	1.5	1.1
PER	**ORTG**	**DRTG**	**WS/48**	**VOL**	
12.44	103.1	108.8	0.059	0.394	

- Missed most of last season due to a lower back and left hip injury, traded from Miami to Memphis in February 2020
- Regular part of Miami's rotation when healthy, used as a moderate volume, secondary ball handler
- Solid secondary playmaker that can make interior passes and kick the ball out to shooters, good at limiting turnovers
- Struggled to score efficiently last season, rated as below average or worse in every offensive situation
- Good spot-up shooter in the past, made almost 38% of his threes in the previous two seasons
- 2019-20 Defensive Degree of Difficulty: 0.460
- Tended to guard starter level players, occasionally took on tougher defensive assignments
- Playing middling on-ball defense last season, good against drives, tended to give up space for his man to take jump shots
- Good pick-and-roll defender that can switch screens and fight over screens to contain ball handlers
- Stayed attached to shooters off the ball, sometimes closed out too aggressively, gave up a few driving lanes to the rim
- Good defensive rebounder, Steal Percentage took a hit due to his injuries, Block Percentage increased a bit

Gorgui Dieng	Height	Weight	Cap #	Years Left
	6'10"	252	$17.288M	UFA

	Similar at Age	30	
		Season	SIMsc
1	Sean Rooks	1999-00	900.7
2	Mehmet Okur	2009-10	898.1
3	Nemanja Bjelica	2018-19	894.4
4	Kelvin Cato	2004-05	887.9
5	LaSalle Thompson	1991-92	886.1
6	Emeka Okafor	2012-13	884.6
7	Samuel Dalembert	2011-12	882.9
8	Kris Humphries	2015-16	882.4
9	Aron Baynes	2016-17	880.1
10	Matt Barnes	2010-11	879.9

Baseline Basic Stats

MPG	PTS	AST	REB	BLK	STL
19.2	7.4	1.3	5.1	0.7	0.5

Advanced Metrics

USG%	3PTA/FGA	FTA/FGA	TS%	eFG%	3PT%
17.8	0.301	0.242	0.553	0.518	0.398
AST%	**TOV%**	**OREB%**	**DREB%**	**STL%**	**BLK%**
10.3	13.0	8.0	23.6	1.6	3.4
PER	**ORTG**	**DRTG**	**WS/48**	**VOL**	
15.43	110.2	105.9	0.118	0.360	

- Regular rotation player for Minnesota and Memphis last season, traded to Minnesota in February 2020
- Used by both teams as a low volume, stretch big, outside shot more consistent in Minnesota
- Made threes at around the league average overall, good spot-up shooter, fairly effective as a pick-and-pop screener
- More active rim runner in Memphis, drew fouls at a much higher rate, good roll man and cutter off the ball
- Runs the floor in transition, can go to the offensive glass to score on put-backs
- Decent passing big man that usually limits turnovers
- 2019-20 Defensive Degree of Difficulty: 0.382, tended to guard second unit big men
- Good rim protector in Memphis, very good rebounder and shot blocker overall
- Solid post defender due to his length, shows enough mobility to defend in space on isolations
- Fairly good at guarding pick-and-rolls, good on switches, sometimes can be late when rotating back to cover the screener
- Consistently closes out on perimeter shooters in spot-up situations

Mario Hezonja	Height	Weight	Cap #	Years Left
	6'8"	201	$1.977M	UFA

	Similar at Age	**24**	
		Season	**SIMsc**
1	DerMarr Johnson	2004-05	940.0
2	John Salmons	2003-04	927.1
3	James Posey	2000-01	923.5
4	Devean George	2001-02	921.5
5	Kim English	2012-13	919.1
6	Dorell Wright	2009-10	918.9
7	Ricky Berry	1988-89	917.6
8	Martell Webster	2010-11	917.5
9	Francisco Garcia	2005-06	915.6
10	Chris Douglas-Roberts	2010-11	914.7

Baseline Basic Stats

MPG	PTS	AST	REB	BLK	STL
24.0	8.8	1.8	3.7	0.4	0.9

Advanced Metrics

USG%	3PTA/FGA	FTA/FGA	TS%	eFG%	3PT%
17.8	0.415	0.241	0.525	0.485	0.338
AST%	**TOV%**	**OREB%**	**DREB%**	**STL%**	**BLK%**
11.6	13.3	3.1	16.0	1.9	0.9
PER	**ORTG**	**DRTG**	**WS/48**	**VOL**	
11.64	103.3	110.3	0.053	0.443	

- Regular rotation player for Portland in his first season with the team
- Shooting efficiency increased in a very low volume role as a spot-up shooter
- Below break-even three-point shooter, streaky spot-up shooter, good at attacking aggressive close-outs if his shot is falling
- Struggled in most half-court situations on offense, inconsistent shooter off the dribble and on the move
- Good transition player that can run down the wing to get dunks or draw shooting fouls
- Catch-and-shoot player, showed some passing skills with Orlando and New York, solid at avoiding turnovers
- 2019-20 Defensive Degree of Difficulty: 0.381
- Tends to guard higher-end second unit players or lower leverage starters
- Middling on-ball defender, struggles against quicker perimeter players, effective last season against bigger post players
- Average pick-and-roll defender, can switch out on ball handlers for a few dribbles, tends to go too far under screens
- Fairly good at closing out on perimeter shooters, tends to get caught on screens off the ball
- Good defensive rebounder, gets steals at a fairly high rate, Block Percentage is still consistent with his career average

Marko Guduric	Height	Weight	Cap #	Years Left
	6'6"	201	$2.750M	RFA

	Similar at Age	**24**	
		Season	**SIMsc**
1	Nik Stauskas	2017-18	926.6
2	Greivis Vasquez	2010-11	914.9
3	Mickael Gelabale	2007-08	914.6
4	George McCloud	1991-92	913.4
5	Danuel House	2017-18	912.7
6	Chris Johnson	2014-15	911.6
7	Reggie Bullock	2015-16	911.0
8	Kim English	2012-13	910.2
9	Damyean Dotson	2018-19	908.4
10	Ben McLemore	2017-18	907.7

Baseline Basic Stats

MPG	PTS	AST	REB	BLK	STL
21.2	8.1	1.6	2.6	0.3	0.6

Advanced Metrics

USG%	3PTA/FGA	FTA/FGA	TS%	eFG%	3PT%
17.8	0.539	0.180	0.543	0.508	0.344
AST%	**TOV%**	**OREB%**	**DREB%**	**STL%**	**BLK%**
12.5	14.0	2.5	11.6	1.4	1.2
PER	**ORTG**	**DRTG**	**WS/48**	**VOL**	
11.07	104.4	112.0	0.048	0.460	

- Fringe rotation player for Memphis in his rookie season
- Mostly used as a low volume, spot-up shooter, shot below break-even on threes last season
- Struggled to adapt to the level of play in the NBA after spending the previous seasons in Europe
- Rated as average or worse in every half court situation last season, mainly a spot-up shooter
- Could occasionally get to the rim, made over 60% of his shots inside of three feet last season
- High effort player that runs hard down the floor in transition to get layups or draw shooting fouls
- Decent secondary playmaker, a bit turnover prone last season
- 2019-20 Defensive Degree of Difficulty: 0.294
- Tended to hidden in favorable matchups against lower leverage second unit players
- Below average on-ball defender, struggled to stay with perimeter players in isolation situations
- Average pick-and-roll defender, funnels his man into help, had trouble with bigger players on switches
- Stays attached to shooters off the ball, closes out in spot-up situations
- Stay-at-home defender, solid defensive rebounder, got steals at a fairly low rate, posted a fairly solid Block Percentage for his size

John Konchar

Height	Weight	Cap #	Years Left
6'5"	210	$2.100M	3

	Similar at Age	**23**	
		Season	**SIMsc**
1	Bryce Dejean-Jones	2015-16	862.8
2	Jabari Bird	2017-18	852.3
3	Sindarius Thornwell	2017-18	847.9
4	Andre Roberson	2014-15	847.9
5	James Anderson	2012-13	845.5
6	Jemerrio Jones	2018-19	844.4
7	John Salmons	2002-03	841.9
8	Davon Reed	2018-19	841.8
9	Thabo Sefolosha	2007-08	839.9
10	DeAndre' Bembry	2017-18	838.6

Baseline Basic Stats

MPG	PTS	AST	REB	BLK	STL
22.5	6.9	2.0	3.7	0.4	0.8

Advanced Metrics

USG%	3PTA/FGA	FTA/FGA	TS%	eFG%	3PT%
12.9	0.331	0.138	0.628	0.613	0.417
AST%	**TOV%**	**OREB%**	**DREB%**	**STL%**	**BLK%**
15.5	13.8	7.0	15.4	1.8	1.4
PER	**ORTG**	**DRTG**	**WS/48**	**VOL**	
15.66	124.9	108.7	0.151	0.687	

- Played on a Two-Way contract, spent most of last season in the G-League with the Memphis Hustle
- Effective in the G-League as a low volume shooter and secondary ball handler, ranked 3rd in the G-League in Offensive Rating last season
- Excellent finisher at both levels, made two-thirds of his two-pointers in the G-League, made 75% of his shots inside of three feet in the NBA
- Decent spot-up shooter, made threes at a break-even rate in the G-League
- Moves well without the ball, very effective cutter in a small sample of NBA possessions, good at crashing the offensive boards to score on put-backs
- Solid secondary playmaker that limits turnovers
- 2019-20 Defensive Degree of Difficulty: 0.228, usually played in garbage time
- Not tested often on the ball, struggled in his limited minutes, tended to give up extra space for his man to take jump shots
- Solid at guarding pick-and-rolls, fairly good at funneling his man into help
- Tended to be late when closing out on shooters in spot-up situations
- Active help defender, solid on the defensive boards, got steals and blocks at a fairly solid rate

Newcomers

Desmond Bane	<u>**Height**</u>	<u>**Weight**</u>	<u>**Cap #**</u>	<u>**Years Left**</u>
	6'6"	215	$1.936M	1 + 2 TO

<u>**Baseline Basic Stats**</u>

MPG	PTS	AST	REB	BLK	STL
18.9	7.1	1.4	2.4	0.3	0.5

<u>**Advanced Metrics**</u>

USG%	3PTA/FGA	FTA/FGA	TS%	eFG%	3PT%
16.8	0.370	0.178	0.523	0.497	0.355
AST%	**TOV%**	**OREB%**	**DREB%**	**STL%**	**BLK%**
12.8	12.6	3.3	11.3	1.5	1.0
PER	**ORTG**	**DRTG**	**WS/48**	**VOL**	
11.55	100.7	103.7	0.063	N/A	

- Drafted by Boston with the 30th overall pick, traded to Memphis
- Led the Big 12 in Three-Point Percentage, made the All-Big 12 1st Team in 2019-20
- Great all-around shooter at TCU, made over 43% of his career threes
- Has deep range, knocks down spot-up jumpers, can run off screens, improved ability to shoot off the dribble
- Decent secondary playmaker, finds open shooters, hits the roll man on pick-and-rolls, avoids turnovers
- Not overwhelmingly quick, needs to improve ball handling skills, may struggle to create his own shot in the NBA
- Less than ideal physical tools, solid position defender in on-ball situations, can guard multiple positions
- Consistently closes out on perimeter shooters, can get caught on screens off the ball
- Average pick-and-roll defender, good at preventing ball handlers from turning the corner, tends to go too far under screens
- Good at playing passing lanes to get deflections or steals, solid defensive rebounder

Xavier Tillman

Height	Weight	Cap #	Years Left
6'8"	245	$1.300M	2 + TO

Baseline Basic Stats

MPG	PTS	AST	REB	BLK	STL
17.1	6.0	1.0	4.1	0.6	0.6

Advanced Metrics

USG%	3PTA/FGA	FTA/FGA	TS%	eFG%	3PT%
15.9	0.098	0.376	0.505	0.470	0.244
AST%	**TOV%**	**OREB%**	**DREB%**	**STL%**	**BLK%**
9.6	13.6	9.3	17.8	1.6	2.8
PER	**ORTG**	**DRTG**	**WS/48**	**VOL**	
13.51	102.5	97.9	0.087	N/A	

- Drafted by Sacramento with the 35th overall pick, traded to Memphis
- Made the All-Big Ten 2nd Team, named Big Ten Defensive Player of the Year in 2019-20
- Good passer that hits cutters, can kick the ball out to open shooters
- Sets solid screens, high motor rim runner, makes sharp cuts off the ball, rolls hard to the rim on pick-and-rolls
- Lacks advanced post moves, inconsistent outside shooter that struggles to repeat his stroke
- Has limited ball handling skills, non-dribbling plays accounted for almost 98% of his offense last season
- Excellent all-around defensive player at Michigan State, potential small-ball center that can guard big men and wing players
- Solid interior defender, good at holding position in the post, good rim protector, great shot blocker and defensive rebounder
- Defends well in space, good defender against isolation plays, good at switching onto ball handlers on pick-and-rolls
- Fights through screens off the ball, consistently closes out on perimeter shooters
- Has active hands, rips the ball away from opponents inside, can jump passing lanes, gets steals at a high rate

Jontay Porter

Height	Weight	Cap #	Years Left
6'11"	240	$1.900M	2

Baseline Basic Stats

MPG	PTS	AST	REB	BLK	STL
14.5	5.3	0.8	3.5	0.7	0.4

Advanced Metrics

USG%	3PTA/FGA	FTA/FGA	TS%	eFG%	3PT%
16.3	0.224	0.327	0.530	0.492	0.272

AST%	TOV%	OREB%	DREB%	STL%	BLK%
8.6	14.9	8.2	17.0	1.3	3.1

PER	ORTG	DRTG	WS/48	VOL
12.72	102.9	102.9	0.057	N/A

- Not selected in the 2019 NBA Draft, signed with Memphis in March 2020
- Has not played since 2018, tore his ACL and MCL in his sophomore season at Missouri, tore his ACL again while rehabbing in 2019
- Stretch big potential, above average three-point shooter in college
- Mainly a stationary shooter, good at making spot-up jumpers, effective screener on pick-and-pops
- Can bully smaller defenders in the post, good passing big man at the college level, hits cutters and finds open shooters
- Limited ball handling skills, does not really move off the ball, does not run well, non-factor in transition
- Athleticism likely to be diminished, good shot blocker in college, solid at contesting shots around the basket, very good defensive rebounder
- Effective on-ball defender, strong post defender that holds positions, showed solid mobility to defend big men in isolation situations
- Struggled to defend pick-and-rolls, had trouble guarding quicker ball handlers, tended to be late to cover the screener, highly foul prone

SACRAMENTO KINGS

Last Season: 31 – 41, Missed the Playoffs

Offensive Rating: 110.2, 18th in the NBA

Defensive Rating: 112.2, 20th in the NBA

Primary Executive: Monte McNair, General Manager

Head Coach: Luke Walton

Key Roster Changes

Subtractions
Bogdan Bogdanovic, free agency
Kent Bazemore, free agency
Alex Len, free agency
Yogi Ferrell, free agency
Harry Giles, free agency
Corey Brewer, free agency

Additions
Tyrese Haliburton, draft
Robert Woodard, draft
Jahmi'us Ramsey, draft
Hassan Whiteside, free agency
Frank Kaminsky, free agency
Glenn Robinson III, free agency

Roster

Likely Starting Five
1. *De'Aaron Fox*
2. *Buddy Hield*
3. *Harrison Barnes*
4. Nemanja Bjelica
5. *Richaun Holmes*

Other Key Rotation Players
Tyrese Haliburton
Cory Joseph
Marvin Bagley III
Hassan Whiteside
Jabari Parker

* Italics denotes that a player is likely to be on the floor to close games

Remaining Roster

- Glenn Robinson III
- Frank Kaminsky
- DaQuan Jeffries
- Robert Woodard
- Jahmi'us Ramsey
- Justin James
- Kyle Guy, 23, 6'1", 167, Virginia (Two-Way)
- Vince Edwards, 24, 6'8", 225, Purdue (Exhibit 10)
- Chimezie Metu, 23, 6'9", 225, USC (Exhibit 10)
- Quinton Rose, 23, 6'8", 195, Temple (Exhibit 10)

SCHREMPF Base Rating: 36.8 (72-game season)

Strengths

- Solid shooting team that can utilize the speed of De'Aaron Fox to create effective transition offense

Question Marks

- Lacks ideal front-end talent to create quality half-court offense against good defensive teams
- Expected primary rotation does not have many proven defensive players
- Coaching staff's ability to place players in optimal roles or create positive team chemistry

Outlook

- Competitive but not quite talented enough to make the playoffs in a deep Western Conference

Veterans

De'Aaron Fox	Height	Weight	Cap #	Years Left
	6'3"	185	$8.100M	5

	Similar at Age	22	
		Season	SIMsc
1	Gilbert Arenas	2003-04	933.5
2	Jrue Holiday	2012-13	923.2
3	Brandon Knight	2013-14	922.4
4	Elfrid Payton	2016-17	918.6
5	Stephen Curry	2010-11	918.5
6	Steve Francis	1999-00	917.9
7	Ramon Sessions	2008-09	917.7
8	Tony Parker	2004-05	915.7
9	Stephon Marbury	1999-00	914.1
10	Lou Williams	2008-09	911.9

Baseline Basic Stats

MPG	PTS	AST	REB	BLK	STL
32.9	17.8	5.9	3.8	0.3	1.4

Advanced Metrics

USG%	3PTA/FGA	FTA/FGA	TS%	eFG%	3PT%
26.7	0.231	0.363	0.552	0.502	0.344
AST%	**TOV%**	**OREB%**	**DREB%**	**STL%**	**BLK%**
32.8	14.7	2.3	10.5	2.3	1.0
PER	**ORTG**	**DRTG**	**WS/48**	**VOL**	
19.48	109.9	109.3	0.122	0.400	

- Missed games in 2019-20 due to a sprained left ankle and sore left shoulder
- Had his most productive NBA season when healthy as a high usage, primary ball handler
- Most effective at driving to the rim as a pick-and-roll ball handler and isolation player
- Made 66.5% of his shots inside of three feet, drew fouls at a high rate
- Good at using his great speed to push the ball in transition, good at getting to the basket on dribble hand-offs
- Solid mid-range shooter, Three-Point Percentage fell below 30% last season
- Long range shot can be streaky, can attack aggressive close-outs if his shot is falling
- Good playmaker that finds open shooters, Turnover Percentage has decreased each season
- 2019-20 Defensive Degree of Difficulty: 0.455
- Defends starting level players, takes on some tough assignments against top point guards
- Solid on-ball defender that can capably defend both guard spots
- Below average pick-and-roll defender, tends to allow ball handlers to turn the corner, can be targeted by bigger screeners on switches
- Gambles too much away from the ball, can be out of position to contest perimeter shots
- Active help defender, gets steals and blocks at high rate for his size, solid defensive rebounder

Buddy Hield	Height	Weight	Cap #	Years Left
	6'4"	220	$24.932M	3

	Similar at Age	**27**	
		Season	**SIMsc**
1	CJ McCollum	2018-19	926.5
2	Wesley Matthews	2013-14	914.0
3	Jason Richardson	2007-08	913.3
4	J.R. Smith	2012-13	911.0
5	Eric Gordon	2015-16	908.7
6	Voshon Lenard	2000-01	907.3
7	Sean Kilpatrick	2016-17	907.1
8	Khris Middleton	2018-19	904.6
9	Gary Neal	2011-12	904.0
10	O.J. Mayo	2014-15	902.9

Baseline Basic Stats

MPG	PTS	AST	REB	BLK	STL
30.4	15.9	2.7	3.5	0.3	0.9

Advanced Metrics

USG%	3PTA/FGA	FTA/FGA	TS%	eFG%	3PT%
24.2	0.561	0.142	0.563	0.539	0.400
AST%	**TOV%**	**OREB%**	**DREB%**	**STL%**	**BLK%**
14.3	10.5	2.8	12.0	1.3	0.8
PER	**ORTG**	**DRTG**	**WS/48**	**VOL**	
15.69	109.2	112.6	0.091	0.313	

- Starter for most of his fourth NBA season, moved into a sixth man role at the end of 2019-20
- Played to his normal level of effectiveness in his role as a high volume scoring guard
- Good three-point shooter, has made over 41% of his career threes, made just over half of his career corner threes
- Very good spot-up shooter that can run off screens, good at making pull-up jumpers as a pick-and-roll ball handler and isolation player
- Effective at using an on-ball screen to get to the rim on dribble hand-offs
- Solid secondary playmaker, set a career high in Assist Percentage, consistently limits turnovers
- 2019-20 Defensive Degree of Difficulty: 0.435, usually guards starting level players
- Below average on-ball defender, struggles to stay with opposing guards on isolations, effective against taller wings in the post
- Middling pick-and-roll defender, solid at switching onto the screener, had trouble guarding ball handlers
- Fights through screens off the ball, tends to close out too aggressively in spot-up situations
- Good defensive rebounder, Steal and Block Percentages are consistent with his career averages

Harrison Barnes

Height	Weight	Cap #	Years Left
6'8"	225	$22.216M	2

	Similar at Age	27 Season	SIMsc
1	Marcus Morris	2016-17	938.0
2	Wilson Chandler	2014-15	933.9
3	Morris Peterson	2004-05	930.7
4	Peja Stojakovic	2004-05	927.9
5	Lance Thomas	2015-16	925.8
6	Jeff Green	2013-14	923.1
7	Luol Deng	2012-13	923.1
8	Dennis Scott	1995-96	922.8
9	Mike Miller	2007-08	922.0
10	Tayshaun Prince	2007-08	920.8

Baseline Basic Stats

MPG	PTS	AST	REB	BLK	STL
31.7	14.5	2.2	4.8	0.3	0.8

Advanced Metrics

USG%	3PTA/FGA	FTA/FGA	TS%	eFG%	3PT%
19.5	0.393	0.269	0.558	0.516	0.385

AST%	TOV%	OREB%	DREB%	STL%	BLK%
10.0	9.4	3.1	13.9	1.0	0.6

PER	ORTG	DRTG	WS/48	VOL
13.83	111.2	112.4	0.090	0.330

- Full-time starter for Sacramento in his first full season with the team
- Performed at his normal level in his role as a low volume, spot-up shooter
- Made over 38% of his threes last season, has made over 40% of his career corner threes
- Mostly a spot-up shooter, can set up for trail threes in transition, effective screener on pick-and-pops
- Can make pull-up jumpers on pick-and-rolls, good at posting up smaller players to score on flashes to the middle or draw fouls
- Can't reliably create his own offense, limited playmaking skills, rarely turns the ball over
- 2019-20 Defensive Degree of Difficulty: 0.469
- Tends to guard starter level players, will take on tougher defensive assignments
- Fairly solid on-ball defender, good at guarding bigger post players, has some trouble with quicker perimeter players
- Decent pick-and-roll defender, effective at switching to cover screeners, tends to allow ball handlers to turn the corner
- Will get caught on screens off the ball, tends to either be late or too aggressive when closing out on perimeter shooters
- Stay-at-home defender, does not really get steals or blocks, solid defensive rebounder

Nemanja Bjelica	Height	Weight	Cap #	Years Left
	6'10"	235	$7.150M	UFA

	Similar at Age	31	
		Season	SIMsc
1	Jonas Jerebko	2018-19	932.0
2	Marvin Williams	2017-18	923.6
3	Rashard Lewis	2010-11	917.7
4	Ersan Ilyasova	2018-19	911.7
5	Matt Barnes	2011-12	910.8
6	Vladimir Radmanovic	2011-12	906.9
7	Al Horford	2017-18	903.9
8	Donyell Marshall	2004-05	902.8
9	Hedo Turkoglu	2010-11	900.4
10	Danny Ferry	1997-98	900.0

Baseline Basic Stats

MPG	PTS	AST	REB	BLK	STL
22.8	8.5	1.5	4.4	0.5	0.6

Advanced Metrics

USG%	3PTA/FGA	FTA/FGA	TS%	eFG%	3PT%
16.4	0.481	0.157	0.571	0.547	0.389
AST%	**TOV%**	**OREB%**	**DREB%**	**STL%**	**BLK%**
11.3	11.7	5.4	17.4	1.4	1.9
PER	**ORTG**	**DRTG**	**WS/48**	**VOL**	
13.75	113.5	109.4	0.109	0.351	

- Regular starter for Sacramento last season, had his most productive NBA season
- Utilized as a low volume stretch big, made almost 42% of his threes in 2019-20
- Mostly a stand-still spot-up shooter, effective screener on pick-and-pops, can hit trail threes in transition
- Good at making backdoor cuts when defenders try to crowd him
- Can occasionally post up smaller players on the right block
- Solid passing big man, set a career high in Assist Percentage last season, good at avoiding turnovers
- 2019-20 Defensive Degree of Difficulty: 0.376
- Tends to be hidden in favorable matchups against lower leverage starters or higher end second unit players
- Below average on-ball defender, struggles to defend in space, stronger post players can back him down in the post
- Middling pick-and-roll defender, decent in drop coverages, has trouble guarding quicker ball handlers
- Consistently closes out on perimeter shooters in spot-up situations
- Decent defensive rebounder, not really a shot blocker, gets steals at a fairly high rate for a big man

Richaun Holmes

	Height	Weight	Cap #	Years Left
Richaun Holmes	6'10"	240	$5.005M	UFA

	Similar at Age	26 Season	SIMsc
1	Cody Zeller	2018-19	923.6
2	Clemon Johnson	1982-83	916.5
3	Jordan Hill	2013-14	912.2
4	Kyle O'Quinn	2016-17	909.2
5	LaSalle Thompson	1987-88	907.5
6	Charles D. Smith	1991-92	906.2
7	Dan Gadzuric	2004-05	905.7
8	Dwight Powell	2017-18	905.2
9	John Henson	2016-17	905.1
10	Chris Andersen	2004-05	905.1

Baseline Basic Stats

MPG	PTS	AST	REB	BLK	STL
21.4	8.3	1.1	6.1	1.0	0.6

Advanced Metrics

USG%	3PTA/FGA	FTA/FGA	TS%	eFG%	3PT%
17.0	0.021	0.358	0.612	0.582	0.136
AST%	**TOV%**	**OREB%**	**DREB%**	**STL%**	**BLK%**
7.5	13.0	10.2	21.2	1.4	3.6
PER	**ORTG**	**DRTG**	**WS/48**	**VOL**	
17.57	119.0	107.8	0.143	0.383	

- Missed games in 2019-20 due to a sprained right shoulder and sore right hip
- Effective in his role as a low volume, rim running starting center
- Posted a True Shooting Percentage over 68% last season, efficient finisher at the rim, good at making shorter mid-range shots
- Athletic big man that can be a vertical lob threat, very good roll man and cutter
- Good offensive rebounder that scores on put-backs, runs hard down the floor in transition, draws fouls at a high rate
- Can post up smaller players, shows some passing skills, good at avoiding turnovers
- 2019-20 Defensive Degree of Difficulty: 0.439, guards starting level big men
- Good rim protector, good shot blocker, solid defensive rebounder, fairly foul prone
- Below average on-ball defender, can be backed down inside by stronger post players, has trouble defending in space on isolations
- Middling pick-and-roll defender, tends to be late to rotate back to the screener, decent at switching onto ball handlers for a few dribbles
- Consistently comes out to contest perimeter shots in spot-up situations

Cory Joseph

	Height	Weight	Cap #	Years Left
	6'3"	200	$12.600M	1

Similar at Age 28

		Season	SIMsc
1	Charlie Bell	2007-08	952.8
2	Keyon Dooling	2008-09	939.9
3	Derek Fisher	2002-03	922.6
4	Fred Jones	2007-08	921.9
5	Courtney Lee	2013-14	918.1
6	Bryant Stith	1998-99	916.0
7	Beno Udrih	2010-11	913.9
8	Ben Gordon	2011-12	911.2
9	Erick Strickland	2001-02	910.4
10	Fred Hoiberg	2000-01	910.4

Baseline Basic Stats

MPG	PTS	AST	REB	BLK	STL
24.3	8.7	3.0	2.4	0.2	0.8

Advanced Metrics

USG%	3PTA/FGA	FTA/FGA	TS%	eFG%	3PT%
15.2	0.375	0.169	0.512	0.481	0.346
AST%	**TOV%**	**OREB%**	**DREB%**	**STL%**	**BLK%**
19.5	14.1	2.1	10.0	1.8	0.8
PER	**ORTG**	**DRTG**	**WS/48**	**VOL**	
11.28	106.5	109.6	0.067	0.322	

- Regular rotation player for Sacramento in his first season with the team
- Maintained his typical level of scoring efficiency in his role as a very low volume, spot-up shooter and secondary ball handler
- Made threes at around the league average last season, mostly a stationary spot-up shooter, can sometimes set up for trail threes in transition
- Solid playmaker on pick-and-rolls, can find open shooters and hit cutters, slightly turnover prone
- Good at making backdoor cuts to catch defenders off guard, selectively crashes inside to score on put-backs
- Does not really create his own offense, does not frequently get to the rim
- 2019-20 Defensive Degree of Difficulty: 0.515
- Takes on tougher defensive assignments against top perimeter players
- Solid on-ball defender that can guard multiple positions, stays with opposing players on drives
- Good at holding position in the post, taller wings can shoot over him on the perimeter
- Middling pick-and-roll defender, better at guarding side pick-and-rolls, struggled to make rotations in the middle of the floor
- Can get caught on screens off the ball, sometimes was late to close out on perimeter shooters
- Fairly solid defensive rebounder, Steal Percentage was slightly down, Block Percentage was above his career average

Marvin Bagley III

Height	Weight	Cap #	Years Left
6'11"	240	$8.964M	Team Option

Similar at Age 20

		Season	SIMsc
1	Bobby Portis	2015-16	909.1
2	Skal Labissiere	2016-17	904.0
3	Andray Blatche	2006-07	900.7
4	J.J. Hickson	2008-09	893.9
5	Harry Giles	2018-19	893.9
6	Samaki Walker	1996-97	892.0
7	Spencer Hawes	2008-09	891.6
8	Yi Jianlian	2007-08	891.2
9	Michael Beasley	2008-09	891.0
10	Karl-Anthony Towns	2015-16	890.8

Baseline Basic Stats

MPG	PTS	AST	REB	BLK	STL
25.7	11.4	1.2	6.3	1.0	0.6

Advanced Metrics

USG%	3PTA/FGA	FTA/FGA	TS%	eFG%	3PT%
24.0	0.143	0.235	0.528	0.493	0.315
AST%	**TOV%**	**OREB%**	**DREB%**	**STL%**	**BLK%**
7.4	10.0	8.5	20.4	1.1	2.8
PER	**ORTG**	**DRTG**	**WS/48**	**VOL**	
16.53	106.4	109.4	0.096	0.440	

- Missed most of last season due to a fractured right thumb and a sprained left foot
- Used as a higher volume rim runner when he was healthy
- Made over 68% of his shots inside of three feet last season, athletic roll man that also scores on a high volume of cuts off the ball
- Good offensive rebounder that scores on put-backs, runs hard down the floor in transition
- Struggled to shoot efficiently last season, made less than 20% of his threes, below average on post-ups and isolation plays
- Not really a passer, rarely turns the ball over
- 2019-20 Defensive Degree of Difficulty: 0.401
- Tended to guard higher-end second unit player or lower leverage starters
- Good defensive rebounder and shot blocker, below average rim protector, fairly foul prone, undisciplined with positioning
- Below average on-ball defender, struggled to defend in space on isolation plays
- Not tested often in the post, defended well in a small sample of possessions
- Played solid pick-and-roll defense, good in drop coverage, could switch onto ball handlers for a few dribbles
- Consistently closed out on perimeter shooters in spot-up situations

Hassan Whiteside

	Height	Weight	Cap #	Years Left
	7'0"	235	$1.621M	UFA

Similar at Age 30

		Season	SIMsc
1	Alton Lister	1988-89	887.3
2	JaVale McGee	2017-18	880.4
3	Marcus Camby	2004-05	873.4
4	Robert Parish*	1983-84	869.7
5	Dale Davis	1999-00	865.7
6	Will Perdue	1995-96	864.0
7	Samuel Dalembert	2011-12	861.4
8	Jermaine O'Neal	2008-09	859.0
9	Marcin Gortat	2014-15	858.8
10	Sam Bowie	1991-92	856.9

Baseline Basic Stats

MPG	PTS	AST	REB	BLK	STL
25.0	10.7	1.0	8.6	1.7	0.6

Advanced Metrics

USG%	3PTA/FGA	FTA/FGA	TS%	eFG%	3PT%
18.9	0.010	0.329	0.599	0.582	0.376
AST%	**TOV%**	**OREB%**	**DREB%**	**STL%**	**BLK%**
6.0	13.1	12.8	30.9	1.0	6.3
PER	**ORTG**	**DRTG**	**WS/48**	**VOL**	
21.20	117.3	103.0	0.176	0.477	

- Starter for most of last season while Jusuf Nurkic was recovering from a broken left leg
- Highly effective in his role as a low volume rim runner on offense
- Made 74% of his shots inside of three feet last season, excels as a roll man and cutter off the ball
- Good offensive rebounder that scores on put-backs, draws fouls at a high rate
- Became a solid mid-range shooter, good at making spot-up jumpers, effective at posting up shorter big men
- Strictly a catch-and-finish player, limited passing skills, solid at avoiding turnovers
- 2019-20 Defensive Degree of Difficulty: 0.423, tends to guard starting level big men
- Good rim protector, led the NBA in Block Percentage and Blocks per Game
- Does not always keep his blocks in play for teammates to recover the ball, excellent defensive rebounder
- Strong post defender that holds position inside, has trouble defending quicker big men on the perimeter
- Below average pick-and-roll defender, struggles to guard ball handlers in space, can be late to recognize pick-and-pops
- Will come out to contest perimeter shots, sometimes closes out too aggressively

Jabari Parker	Height	Weight	Cap #	Years Left
	6'8"	245	$6.500M	UFA

	Similar at Age	24	
		Season	SIMsc
1	Anthony Tolliver	2009-10	905.2
2	Patrick Patterson	2013-14	905.1
3	Markieff Morris	2013-14	904.3
4	John Williams	1990-91	904.2
5	Henry Sims	2014-15	904.0
6	Derrick Williams	2015-16	903.8
7	Rodney White	2004-05	901.0
8	Marcus Morris	2013-14	899.5
9	Rodney Rogers	1995-96	898.8
10	Carlos Boozer	2005-06	896.0

Baseline Basic Stats

MPG	PTS	AST	REB	BLK	STL
23.0	10.0	1.5	4.8	0.4	0.8

Advanced Metrics

USG%	3PTA/FGA	FTA/FGA	TS%	eFG%	3PT%
21.7	0.317	0.212	0.546	0.514	0.304
AST%	**TOV%**	**OREB%**	**DREB%**	**STL%**	**BLK%**
12.0	11.7	5.8	18.3	1.8	1.4
PER	**ORTG**	**DRTG**	**WS/48**	**VOL**	
15.48	107.1	110.0	0.078	0.403	

- Missed over a month due to a right shoulder injury, starter for Atlanta, traded to Sacramento in February 2020
- Productive in his role as a high volume scorer, efficient finisher around the basket last season
- Made almost 73% of his shots inside of three feet, good at running down the wings to get layups in transition
- Scores on a high volume of cuts off the ball, solid offensive rebounders that scores on put-backs
- Good at posting up smaller players, gets to the rim on dribble hand-offs
- Not really an outside shooter, made less than 30% of his threes last season
- Fairly solid passer that can find open shooters, good at limiting turnovers
- 2019-20 Defensive Degree of Difficulty: 0.399
- Tended to be hidden in favorable matchups against lower leverage starters
- Average on-ball defender, more effective against post players, struggled to guard perimeter players
- Below average pick-and-roll defender, decent in drop coverages, has trouble defending ball handlers in space
- Stays attached to shooters off the ball, solid at closing out on spot-up shooters
- More active as a help defender, posted career highs in Steal and Block Percentages, fairly good defensive rebounder

Glenn Robinson III	Height	Weight	Cap #	Years Left
	6'6"	222	$1.621M	UFA

	Similar at Age	26	
		Season	SIMsc
1	Chase Budinger	2014-15	948.1
2	Maurice Evans	2004-05	937.1
3	Quincy Pondexter	2014-15	927.3
4	Mickael Pietrus	2008-09	927.2
5	Sam Mack	1996-97	926.4
6	Jared Dudley	2011-12	923.8
7	Doug McDermott	2017-18	922.9
8	Devin Brown	2004-05	922.8
9	Joe Harris	2017-18	922.0
10	Matt Carroll	2006-07	919.5

Baseline Basic Stats

MPG	PTS	AST	REB	BLK	STL
23.1	9.2	1.3	3.2	0.2	0.6

Advanced Metrics

USG%	3PTA/FGA	FTA/FGA	TS%	eFG%	3PT%
16.8	0.399	0.181	0.561	0.532	0.392
AST%	**TOV%**	**OREB%**	**DREB%**	**STL%**	**BLK%**
8.4	9.0	3.6	11.8	1.4	0.8
PER	**ORTG**	**DRTG**	**WS/48**	**VOL**	
12.55	111.2	111.9	0.086	0.417	

- Starter for Golden State last season, traded to Philadelphia in February 2020, came off the bench after the trade
- Used mostly as a low volume, spot-up shooter, made over 39% of his threes last season, shot better with Golden State
- Good at making spot-up jumpers and running off screens, can make outside shots on dribble hand-off plays
- Moves well without the ball, effective cutter off the ball, good at running the wings in transition to get dunks or draw fouls
- Mainly a catch-and-shoot player, has limited playmaking skills, rarely turns the ball over
- 2019-20 Defensive Degree of Difficulty: 0.542
- Had the 13th toughest set of matchups among players that played 500 or more minutes
- Played below average on-ball defense, over-matched against top perimeter players
- Average pick-and-roll defender, tends to go too far under screens to allow open jump shots
- Tends to get caught on screens off the ball, generally closes out on spot-up shooters
- Fairly solid defensive rebounder, Steal and Block Percentages are still fairly consistent with his career averages

Frank Kaminsky	Height	Weight	Cap #	Years Left
	7'0"	240	$1.621M	UFA

Similar at Age 26

		Season	SIMsc
1	Matt Bonner	2006-07	912.3
2	Charlie Villanueva	2010-11	911.1
3	Kelly Olynyk	2017-18	911.1
4	Troy Murphy	2006-07	902.7
5	Spencer Hawes	2014-15	902.4
6	Earl Barron	2007-08	901.0
7	Mike Scott	2014-15	900.9
8	Joffrey Lauvergne	2017-18	899.4
9	Austin Croshere	2001-02	898.2
10	Mike Muscala	2017-18	894.7

Baseline Basic Stats

MPG	PTS	AST	REB	BLK	STL
20.4	8.7	1.6	5.0	0.4	0.5

Advanced Metrics

USG%	3PTA/FGA	FTA/FGA	TS%	eFG%	3PT%
19.4	0.449	0.269	0.584	0.551	0.371

AST%	TOV%	OREB%	DREB%	STL%	BLK%
13.2	11.0	5.2	21.4	1.0	1.3

PER	ORTG	DRTG	WS/48	VOL
15.60	114.8	109.5	0.124	0.307

- Regular rotation player for Phoenix when healthy, missed most of last season due to a sore right knee
- Used as a moderate volume stretch big, shot around break-even on threes last season
- Above break-even three-point shooter throughout his career, percentages fluctuate from year-to-year
- Primarily a spot-up shooter, effective screener on pick-and-pops, occasionally shoots off screens
- Not really an effective rim runner, lacks the lift to finish in traffic
- Pretty good passing big man, rarely turns the ball over
- 2019-20 Defensive Degree of Difficulty: 0.366, tends to guard second unit big men
- Below average rim protector, does not really block shots, fairly solid defensive rebounder
- Played decent on-ball defense, decent post defender that has enough strength to hold position
- Shows some mobility to defend big men in space on isolations
- Middling pick-and-roll defender, struggles to cover roll men at the rim, better at switching on the perimeter
- Does not always come out to contest perimeter shots in spot-up situations

DaQuan Jeffries

	Height	Weight	Cap #	Years Left
	6'5"	216	$1.446M	Team Option

Similar at Age 22

		Season	SIMsc
1	Henry (Bill) Walker	2009-10	917.5
2	Corey Crowder	1991-92	912.3
3	Allen Crabbe	2014-15	909.9
4	Iman Shumpert	2012-13	909.3
5	Shake Milton	2018-19	907.5
6	Sterling Brown	2017-18	907.3
7	Josh Hart	2017-18	906.8
8	Malachi Richardson	2017-18	901.1
9	Quincy Pondexter	2010-11	899.2
10	Chris Carr	1996-97	898.4

Baseline Basic Stats

MPG	PTS	AST	REB	BLK	STL
20.8	7.1	1.3	2.8	0.2	0.6

Advanced Metrics

USG%	3PTA/FGA	FTA/FGA	TS%	eFG%	3PT%
14.9	0.460	0.146	0.571	0.548	0.332
AST%	**TOV%**	**OREB%**	**DREB%**	**STL%**	**BLK%**
9.1	8.8	2.7	11.8	1.5	0.7
PER	**ORTG**	**DRTG**	**WS/48**	**VOL**	
11.22	114.1	112.5	0.084	0.422	

- Played on a Two-Way contract, spent most of 2019-20 in the G-League with the Stockton Kings
- Used as a low volume, spot-up shooter in the NBA, took on more volume in the G-League
- Mostly a stationary spot-up shooter, below break-even three-point shooter in the G-League
- More effective off the ball, good cutter, runs the floor in transition, made over 68% of his two-pointers at the NBA level
- Strictly a catch-and-shoot player, limited playmaking skills, rarely turns the ball over
- 2019-20 Defensive Degree of Difficulty: 0.198, only played 141 NBA minutes
- Played solid on-ball defense in a small sample of possessions, can potentially guard multiple positions
- Solid pick-and-roll defender, good at containing ball handlers, effective at switching onto screeners
- Fights through screens off the ball, tended to be late when closing out on perimeter shooters
- Solid defensive rebounder, gets steals at a moderate rate, good weak side shot blocker in the G-League

Justin James

	Height	Weight	Cap #	Years Left
Justin James	6'7"	190	$1.518M	1

	Similar at Age	23 Season	SIMsc
1	Justin Holiday	2012-13	904.8
2	K.J. McDaniels	2016-17	891.0
3	Conner Henry	1986-87	885.7
4	Rodney Carney	2007-08	884.6
5	Daniel Hamilton	2018-19	884.2
6	Keith Askins	1990-91	882.5
7	Buck Johnson	1986-87	879.9
8	Damyean Dotson	2017-18	878.7
9	Dwayne Morton	1994-95	878.6
10	Axel Toupane	2015-16	878.5

Baseline Basic Stats

MPG	PTS	AST	REB	BLK	STL
17.3	6.6	1.0	2.3	0.3	0.5

Advanced Metrics

USG%	3PTA/FGA	FTA/FGA	TS%	eFG%	3PT%
17.8	0.417	0.214	0.530	0.513	0.368

AST%	TOV%	OREB%	DREB%	STL%	BLK%
9.7	10.2	2.9	11.2	1.4	2.3

PER	ORTG	DRTG	WS/48	VOL
11.79	104.6	111.2	0.055	0.840

- Played sparingly for Sacramento in his rookie season, missed games due to a right knee injury
- Mainly used as a low volume, spot-up shooter, struggled to shoot efficiently last season
- Rated as average or worse in most offensive situations in 2019-20
- Below break-even three-point shooter, better at shooting off screens, below average spot-up shooter
- Most effective as a cutter off the ball that can draw fouls and finish at the rim
- Made almost 74% of his shots inside of three feet last season
- Rarely turns the ball over, decent secondary playmaker
- 2019-20 Defensive Degree of Difficulty: 0.295
- Tended to either guard second unit players or play in garbage time
- Played average on-ball defense, good at stopping drives, gave up too much space for his man to take jump shots
- Below average at guarding pick-and-rolls, tended to allow ball handlers to turn the corner
- Good at closing out on perimeter shooters, sometimes gets caught on screens off the ball
- Active help defender, very good at rotating from the weak side to block shots, solid defensive rebounder, gets steals at a moderate rate

Newcomers

Tyrese Haliburton

Height	Weight	Cap #	Years Left
6'5"	175	$3.832M	1 + 2 TO

Baseline Basic Stats

MPG	PTS	AST	REB	BLK	STL
23.6	9.0	3.5	2.7	0.3	1.0

Advanced Metrics

USG%	3PTA/FGA	FTA/FGA	TS%	eFG%	3PT%
17.8	0.385	0.198	0.530	0.502	0.358
AST%	**TOV%**	**OREB%**	**DREB%**	**STL%**	**BLK%**
24.4	15.4	2.7	10.2	2.4	0.9
PER	**ORTG**	**DRTG**	**WS/48**	**VOL**	
14.06	103.2	103.9	0.070	N/A	

- Drafted by Sacramento with the 12th overall pick
- Named to the All-Big 12 2nd Team in 2019-20, fractured his left wrist in February 2020
- Has great playmaking and ball control skills, great court vision, career Assist-to-Turnover Ratio is 3-to-1
- Good catch-and-shoot player, made almost 43% of his career threes at Iowa State
- Good spot-up shooter that can also shoot off screens, good at attacking aggressive close-outs
- Not likely to be a high volume scorer, heavy pass-first mentality, struggles to shoot off the dribble
- Less effective on isolations, lacks explosive quickness, rarely drives left
- Can potentially defend multiple positions, great length and athleticism
- Great weak side defender in college, got steals and blocks at a high rate, good defensive rebounding guard
- Good on-ball defender that can defend bigger wings and quicker guards
- Tended to go too far under screens when chasing shooters or guarding pick-and-rolls, would gamble too much to try to force turnovers

Robert Woodard

Height	Weight	Cap #	Years Left
6'7"	230	$1.500M	2 + TO

Baseline Basic Stats

MPG	PTS	AST	REB	BLK	STL
20.1	7.0	1.2	3.6	0.4	0.7

Advanced Metrics

USG%	3PTA/FGA	FTA/FGA	TS%	eFG%	3PT%
16.1	0.297	0.227	0.513	0.488	0.349

AST%	TOV%	OREB%	DREB%	STL%	BLK%
8.4	12.5	5.5	13.5	1.6	1.5

PER	ORTG	DRTG	WS/48	VOL
12.08	102.2	103.6	0.039	N/A

- Drafted by Memphis with the 40th overall pick, traded to Sacramento
- Lower usage player at Mississippi State, non-dribbling plays accounted for 92.1% of his offense in 2019-20
- Moves well without the ball, good cutter, can crash the offensive boards to score on put-backs
- Improving three-point shooter, shooting stroke still inconsistent, made less than 62% of his free throws in college
- Mostly a spot-up shooter, flashed some ability to make shots off screens
- Limited as a ball handler and playmaker
- Great physical tools on defense, has the length and athleticism to guard multiple positions
- Good on-ball defender, strong enough to defend bigger players, actively contests shots and pressures ball handlers
- Solid team defender, good in all pick-and-roll situations, stays attached to shooters off the ball
- Active help defender, good weak side shot blocker, will jump passing lanes to get steals, good defensive rebounder

Jahmi'us Ramsey

	Height	Weight	Cap #	Years Left
	6'4"	195	$1.000M	2

Baseline Basic Stats

MPG	PTS	AST	REB	BLK	STL
18.4	7.0	1.8	2.1	0.2	0.7

Advanced Metrics

USG%	3PTA/FGA	FTA/FGA	TS%	eFG%	3PT%
18.6	0.379	0.207	0.513	0.483	0.333

AST%	TOV%	OREB%	DREB%	STL%	BLK%
17.0	12.3	2.5	9.1	1.7	0.9

PER	ORTG	DRTG	WS/48	VOL
12.66	99.6	101.9	0.060	N/A

- Drafted by Sacramento with the 43rd overall pick
- Made the All-Big 12 2nd Team, named Big 12 Rookie of the Year in 2019-20
- Good speed and athleticism, can blow by defenders on isolation plays, dynamic transition player
- Knocks down deep threes, made almost 43% of his threes at Texas Tech
- Good spot-up shooter, can also shoot off screens, stroke somewhat inconsistent, made less than 65% of his free throws
- Not really a natural playmaker, does not see the whole floor, can only make simple reads
- Good physical tools, has great length and lateral quickness
- Effective weak side defender, gets steals and blocks at a high rate, good defensive rebounder
- Middling on-ball defender, tends to back off his man to give up perimeter shots, lacks strength to guard taller wing players
- Better team defender, solid pick-and-roll defender that contains ball handlers, stays attached to shooters off the ball

GOLDEN STATE WARRIORS

Last Season: 15 – 50, Missed the Playoffs

Offensive Rating: 105.2, 30th in the NBA

Defensive Rating: 113.8, 26th in the NBA

Primary Executive: Bob Myers, President of Basketball Operations

Head Coach: Steve Kerr

Key Roster Changes

Subtractions
Ky Bowman, waived

Additions
James Wiseman, draft
Kelly Oubre, Jr., trade
Brad Wanamaker, free agency
Kent Bazemore, free agency

Roster

Likely Starting Five

1. *Stephen Curry*
2. *Kelly Oubre, Jr.*
3. *Andrew Wiggins*
4. *Draymond Green*
5. *James Wiseman*

Other Key Rotation Players
Eric Paschall
Kevon Looney
Damion Lee
Brad Wanamaker
Kent Bazemore

* Italics denotes that a player is likely to be on the floor to close games

Remaining Roster

- Marquese Chriss
- Jordan Poole
- Alen Smailagic
- Juan Toscano-Anderson
- Mychal Mulder
- Klay Thompson (recovering from a torn Achilles, likely to miss the entire season)
- Nico Mannion, 19, 6'3", 190, Arizona (Two-Way)
- Dwayne Sutton, 23, 6'5", 220, Louisville (Exhibit 10)
- Axel Toupane, 28, 6'7", 197, France (Exhibit 10)
- Justinian Jessup, 22, 6'7", 202, Boise State (Exhibit 10)
- Kaleb Wesson, 21, 6'9", 270, Ohio State (Exhibit 10)

SCHREMPF Base Rating: 34.0 (72-game season)

Strengths

- Offense that uses movement to generate open looks by leveraging the threat of Curry's shooting

Question Marks

- Lack of a proven defensive player outside Draymond Green
- Durability, health and possible age-related decline of Stephen Curry
- Depth beyond the starting five

Outlook

- Outside chance of reaching the play-in tournament if Curry stays healthy, likely will miss the playoffs

Veterans

Stephen Curry

Height	Weight	Cap #	Years Left
6'3"	190	$43.006M	1

	Similar at Age	**31**	
		Season	**SIMsc**
1	Terry Porter	1994-95	865.7
2	John Starks	1996-97	858.3
3	Mike Conley	2018-19	851.8
4	Devin Harris	2014-15	851.0
5	Sam Cassell	2000-01	850.1
6	Manu Ginobili	2008-09	849.4
7	Charlie Ward	2001-02	849.0
8	Kevin Edwards	1996-97	848.2
9	Lou Williams	2017-18	846.6
10	Chauncey Billups	2007-08	846.5

Baseline Basic Stats

MPG	PTS	AST	REB	BLK	STL
29.2	16.7	4.7	3.4	0.2	1.1

Advanced Metrics

USG%	3PTA/FGA	FTA/FGA	TS%	eFG%	3PT%
27.9	0.507	0.286	0.586	0.528	0.357
AST%	**TOV%**	**OREB%**	**DREB%**	**STL%**	**BLK%**
29.6	13.3	2.5	13.3	1.8	0.9
PER	**ORTG**	**DRTG**	**WS/48**	**VOL**	
20.38	113.2	111.4	0.148	0.649	

- Missed most of last season due to a fractured left hand, only played in five games
- Also missed parts of the previous two seasons due to multiple ankle sprains, a strained MCL in his left knee and a strained groin
- The NBA's best all-around shooter when healthy, shooting percentages were down in a small sample of minutes
- Has made over 41% of his threes in each of the previous 11 seasons, also has posted a True Shooting Percentage above 61% in each of the previous six seasons
- Excellent at coming off screens and making spot-up jumpers, great at shooting off the dribble
- Very good pick-and-roll ball handler that can finish at the rim, excellent playmaker that generally limits turnovers
- 2019-20 Defensive Degree of Difficulty: 0.364
- Generally hidden in more favorable matchups against lower leverage offensive players
- Played solid on-ball defense in these situations, stayed with opposing perimeter players on isolations
- Fairly good team defender, funnels his man into help on pick-and-rolls, stays attached to shooters off the ball
- Gambling less, becoming more of a position defender, steals rate has gone down
- Has become a better defensive rebounder, posted a career high in Block Percentage

Draymond Green	Height	Weight	Cap #	Years Left
	6'6"	230	$22.247M	2 + PO

	Similar at Age	29 Season	SIMsc
1	Carlos Delfino	2011-12	877.9
2	Matt Barnes	2009-10	873.7
3	P.J. Tucker	2014-15	872.6
4	Boris Diaw	2011-12	870.3
5	Jared Dudley	2014-15	864.2
6	Devin Brown	2007-08	862.1
7	Tyreke Evans	2018-19	861.7
8	Rick Fox	1998-99	859.4
9	Pete Chilcutt	1997-98	858.1
10	Clarence Weatherspoon	1999-00	857.8

Baseline Basic Stats

MPG	PTS	AST	REB	BLK	STL
24.6	8.0	2.7	4.5	0.5	0.9

Advanced Metrics

USG%	3PTA/FGA	FTA/FGA	TS%	eFG%	3PT%
15.6	0.396	0.238	0.518	0.481	0.315
AST%	**TOV%**	**OREB%**	**DREB%**	**STL%**	**BLK%**
22.0	19.1	3.5	18.5	2.1	2.0
PER	**ORTG**	**DRTG**	**WS/48**	**VOL**	
12.84	105.2	107.1	0.091	0.344	

- Missed several games last season due to injuries to his right heel, right ankle, left finger, left knee, lower back and pelvis
- One of the top playmaking big men in the league, set a career high in Assist Percentage last season
- Excels at hitting the roll man on pick-and-rolls, can be fairly turnover prone
- Scoring efficiency decreased, True Shooting Percentage was below 50%
- Had difficulty making shots outside of three feet, still a good finisher at the rim
- Rated as below average or worse in almost every offensive situation last season
- 2019-20 Defensive Degree of Difficulty: 0.466
- Typically guarded starting level players, would sometimes handle tougher assignments
- Solid on-ball defender that has the versatility to defend perimeter players or big men in the post
- Excellent pick-and-roll defender that can switch onto ball handlers and cover the roll man
- Consistently stays attached to shooters off the ball, will fight through screens and close out
- Effective rim protector that will actively contest shots inside
- Very good defensive rebounder, still posts high steal and block rates

Kelly Oubre, Jr.	**Height**	**Weight**	**Cap #**	**Years Left**
	6'7"	205	$14.375M	UFA

	Similar at Age	**24**	
		Season	**SIMsc**
1	Travis Outlaw	2008-09	932.9
2	Rodney Carney	2008-09	921.4
3	C.J. Miles	2011-12	918.5
4	Scott Burrell	1994-95	918.4
5	Danny Green	2011-12	918.0
6	Dale Ellis	1984-85	916.1
7	Ricky Berry	1988-89	916.1
8	Dorell Wright	2009-10	915.8
9	Calbert Cheaney	1995-96	915.7
10	Tracy Murray	1995-96	914.8

Baseline Basic Stats

MPG	PTS	AST	REB	BLK	STL
28.3	13.4	1.8	4.0	0.5	1.0

Advanced Metrics

USG%	3PTA/FGA	FTA/FGA	TS%	eFG%	3PT%
22.1	0.404	0.273	0.553	0.509	0.350
AST%	**TOV%**	**OREB%**	**DREB%**	**STL%**	**BLK%**
9.2	9.6	3.4	14.7	1.8	1.7
PER	**ORTG**	**DRTG**	**WS/48**	**VOL**	
15.26	108.4	110.0	0.093	0.378	

- Regular starter for Phoenix when healthy, missed the Orlando restart due to a right knee injury
- Maintained his effectiveness as a moderate volume shooter off the ball
- Made threes at around the league average last season, mostly a spot-up shooter, can also make pull-up jumpers on pick-and-rolls
- Good transition player that can run down the wing to get dunks or draw shooting fouls
- Good at getting to the rim on dribble hand-offs, can occasionally drive by defenders on isolations
- Primarily a catch-and-shoot player, limited as a playmaker, rarely turns the ball over
- 2019-20 Defensive Degree of Difficulty: 0.489
- Tends to guard starting level players, will take on tougher defensive assignments
- Fairly solid on-ball defender, good against perimeter players, can be bullied inside by stronger post players
- Average pick-and-roll defender, can be too aggressive when fighting over the screen
- Good at closing out on perimeter shooters, can sometimes get caught on screens off the ball
- Good defensive rebounder, Steal and Block Percentages are still consistent with his career averages

Andrew Wiggins

Height	Weight	Cap #	Years Left
6'7"	194	$29.542M	2

Similar at Age **24**

		Season	SIMsc
1	Klay Thompson	2014-15	919.0
2	Reggie Lewis	1989-90	916.6
3	Evan Fournier	2016-17	916.4
4	Kevin Martin	2007-08	912.9
5	Caris LeVert	2018-19	911.6
6	Ricky Davis	2003-04	910.8
7	Travis Outlaw	2008-09	910.0
8	Xavier McDaniel	1987-88	909.6
9	Allan Houston	1995-96	908.3
10	Jordan Clarkson	2016-17	907.9

Baseline Basic Stats

MPG	PTS	AST	REB	BLK	STL
30.7	16.6	2.4	3.6	0.4	0.9

Advanced Metrics

USG%	3PTA/FGA	FTA/FGA	TS%	eFG%	3PT%
25.2	0.329	0.249	0.536	0.499	0.351

AST%	TOV%	OREB%	DREB%	STL%	BLK%
14.1	10.1	3.3	10.7	1.3	1.5

PER	ORTG	DRTG	WS/48	VOL
15.38	106.5	112.5	0.071	0.275

- Regular starter for Minnesota and Golden State last season
- Has traditionally been a high usage player that scores with middling efficiency
- Efficiency increased in Golden State after moving into a slightly lower volume role
- Utilized more off the ball, effective at cutting to the rim and shooting off screens
- Excellent at using his athleticism to run the floor in transition and finish plays above the rim
- Middling success as a pick-and-roll ball handler or isolation player, struggles to shoot off the dribble
- Three-Point Percentage has hovered around break-even for his career, only an average spot-up shooter
- Playmaking skills improved last season, set a career high in Assist Percentage, good at avoiding turnovers
- 2019-20 Defensive Degree of Difficulty: 0.463
- Usually guards starting level players, occasionally handles tougher defensive assignments
- Fairly decent on-ball defender throughout his career, can guard multiple positions
- Solid team defender that will fight through screens and funnel his man into help on pick-and-rolls
- Occasionally has lapses, doesn't always close out on perimeter shooters
- More active as a help defender last season, set career highs in Defensive Rebound and Block Percentages
- Got steals at a much higher rate in a small sample of games with Golden State

Eric Paschall

Height	Weight	Cap #	Years Left
6'6"	255	$1.518M	1

Similar at Age **23**

		Season	SIMsc
1	Linas Kleiza	2007-08	915.8
2	Larry Johnson	1992-93	912.2
3	Shabazz Muhammad	2015-16	907.8
4	Wally Szczerbiak	2000-01	907.3
5	Kenny Thomas	2000-01	894.1
6	Ryan Gomes	2005-06	889.8
7	Tyreke Evans	2012-13	889.5
8	Corliss Williamson	1996-97	887.3
9	Jason Caffey	1996-97	887.1
10	Dion Glover	2001-02	884.5

Baseline Basic Stats

MPG	PTS	AST	REB	BLK	STL
32.3	15.0	2.6	5.6	0.3	0.7

Advanced Metrics

USG%	3PTA/FGA	FTA/FGA	TS%	eFG%	3PT%
21.9	0.222	0.320	0.571	0.525	0.350
AST%	**TOV%**	**OREB%**	**DREB%**	**STL%**	**BLK%**
13.3	10.9	5.5	13.6	1.0	0.6
PER	**ORTG**	**DRTG**	**WS/48**	**VOL**	
16.35	112.6	113.3	0.094	0.336	

- Regular rotation player for Golden State in his rookie season
- Mostly used as a scorer off the bench in a moderate usage role
- Excelled at attacking the rim, made 72.5% of his shots inside of three feet
- Great at driving by opposing big men on isolation plays, very good cutter off the ball
- Effective at scoring on put-backs, good at using his size to bully smaller defenders on post-ups
- Very good pick-and-roll player that can roll to the rim as the screener and occasionally make plays as the ball handler
- Fairly solid passer that can kick the ball out to shooters, good at avoiding turnovers
- Outside shot is a work-in-progress, made less than 30% of his threes, much more comfortable when taking mid-range shots
- 2019-20 Defensive Degree of Difficulty: 0.400
- Mostly guarded lower leverage starters to higher-end second unit players
- Played solid on-ball defense in space on isolation plays, traditional big men had success shooting over him in post-up situations
- Above average pick-and-roll defender, had some difficulty containing quicker ball handlers on drives
- Stays attached to perimeter shooters, will fight through screens, can sometimes by late to close out in spot-up situations
- Stay-at-home defender, does not really get blocks or steals, fairly solid defensive rebounder

Kevon Looney	Height	Weight	Cap #	Years Left
	6'9"	220	$4.821M	Player Option

	Similar at Age	23	
		Season	SIMsc
1	Brian Cook	2003-04	927.6
2	Terry Mills	1990-91	925.8
3	Viktor Khryapa	2005-06	923.5
4	Bostjan Nachbar	2003-04	913.7
5	Lavoy Allen	2012-13	913.6
6	Earl Cureton	1980-81	913.6
7	David West	2003-04	912.8
8	Donnell Harvey	2003-04	912.3
9	Chris Singleton	2012-13	911.5
10	Scooter McCray	1983-84	910.5

Baseline Basic Stats

MPG	PTS	AST	REB	BLK	STL
18.0	6.1	0.9	4.0	0.5	0.6

Advanced Metrics

USG%	3PTA/FGA	FTA/FGA	TS%	eFG%	3PT%
15.9	0.152	0.248	0.519	0.491	0.219
AST%	**TOV%**	**OREB%**	**DREB%**	**STL%**	**BLK%**
9.5	12.4	9.8	15.8	1.8	2.2
PER	**ORTG**	**DRTG**	**WS/48**	**VOL**	
13.22	109.6	108.8	0.084	0.406	

- Missed most of the 2019-20 season due to a neuropathic condition as well as injuries to his abdominal and left hip
- Typically used as a low volume rim runner when healthy, no real shooting range outside of three feet
- Most effective as a cutter and roll man on pick-and-rolls, runs hard in transition to score or draw fouls
- Active offensive rebounder, has become a solid passing big man, good at limiting turnovers
- 2019-20 Defensive Degree of Difficulty: 0.365
- Generally defends second unit players, mostly deployed as a rim protector
- Solid shot blocker, decent defensive rebounder, will sometimes sacrifice positioning to go for blocks
- Has active hands to strip the ball from opponents inside, set a career high in Steal Percentage last season
- Fairly solid on-ball defender that can play post defense and guard players in space
- Effective pick-and-roll defender that can switch onto ball handlers or drop back to cover the roll man
- Is also consistent to close out on perimeter shooters

Damion Lee	Height	Weight	Cap #	Years Left
	6'5"	210	$1.763M	1

	Similar at Age	27	
		Season	SIMsc
1	Richie Frahm	2004-05	941.1
2	Kareem Rush	2007-08	922.0
3	Kyle Korver	2008-09	921.3
4	Jodie Meeks	2014-15	920.3
5	Maurice Evans	2005-06	918.9
6	Bobby Simmons	2007-08	918.6
7	Roger Mason	2007-08	917.8
8	Eric Piatkowski	1997-98	917.1
9	Gary Neal	2011-12	916.9
10	Fred Jones	2006-07	916.8

Baseline Basic Stats

MPG	PTS	AST	REB	BLK	STL
21.2	8.3	1.4	2.5	0.2	0.6

Advanced Metrics

USG%	3PTA/FGA	FTA/FGA	TS%	eFG%	3PT%
18.0	0.502	0.200	0.538	0.504	0.368
AST%	**TOV%**	**OREB%**	**DREB%**	**STL%**	**BLK%**
11.2	10.1	2.3	13.6	1.5	0.5
PER	**ORTG**	**DRTG**	**WS/48**	**VOL**	
11.67	106.7	111.2	0.074	0.400	

- Started the season on a Two-Way contract but was later signed to a standard contract with Golden State
- Became a regular starter for Golden State from December 2019 to the end of the season
- Mostly used as a lower volume, spot-up shooter
- Has been an above average three-point shooter in his two years with Golden State, excellent at making corner threes
- Not as effective at shooting on move or creating his own shot
- Can occasionally make quick pull-up jumpers on pick-and-rolls, can get to the rim on dribble hand-offs
- Decent secondary playmaker that rarely turns the ball over
- 2019-20 Defensive Degree of Difficulty: 0.433, usually guards starting level players
- Below average on-ball defender, struggled to stay in front of his man on isolation plays, could be overpowered by taller wings on post-ups
- Better as a team defender, fights through screens to stay attached to shooters off the ball
- Effective pick-and-roll defender that will funnel his man into help, sometimes can be late to close out on perimeter shooters
- Good defensive rebounder, can play passing lanes to get steals at a fairly high rate

Brad Wanamaker

Height	Weight	Cap #	Years Left
6'3"	210	$2.250M	UFA

Similar at Age **30**

		Season	SIMsc
1	Mario Elie	1993-94	926.5
2	Jeremy Lin	2018-19	922.4
3	Erick Strickland	2003-04	921.2
4	Kirk Hinrich	2010-11	916.7
5	Chris Childs	1997-98	913.6
6	Jon Barry	1999-00	909.5
7	Jarrett Jack	2013-14	906.2
8	Anthony Johnson	2004-05	905.3
9	Deron Williams	2014-15	904.9
10	John Crotty	1999-00	904.0

Baseline Basic Stats

MPG	PTS	AST	REB	BLK	STL
23.5	8.0	3.1	2.5	0.1	0.8

Advanced Metrics

USG%	3PTA/FGA	FTA/FGA	TS%	eFG%	3PT%
15.8	0.332	0.283	0.568	0.514	0.367
AST%	**TOV%**	**OREB%**	**DREB%**	**STL%**	**BLK%**
20.4	15.7	1.7	10.4	1.9	0.6
PER	**ORTG**	**DRTG**	**WS/48**	**VOL**	
12.82	111.9	107.9	0.112	0.389	

- Played his first full season as a regular rotation player for Boston in 2019-20
- Used as a low volume, pass-first backup point guard
- Decent playmaker that can kick the ball out to shooters, slightly turnover prone last season
- Solid three-point shooter in his two NBA seasons, led the NBA in Free Throw Percentage last season
- Good spot-up shooter that can sometimes shoot off screens, very good at making backdoor cuts if defenders overplay his shot
- Not a dynamic threat in on-ball situations, does not really shoot off the dribble, willing to draw contact to get to the foul line
- 2019-20 Defensive Degree of Difficulty: 0.347, tends to guard second unit level players
- Played good on-ball defense, capable of defending both guard spots
- Decent pick-and-roll defender, good on hard switches, tended to allow ball handlers to turn the corner in other coverages
- Fights through screens off the ball, tends to close out too aggressively in spot-up situations
- Decent defensive rebounding guard, posts fairly high steal rates

Kent Bazemore	**Height**	**Weight**	**Cap #**	**Years Left**
	6'4"	195	$1.621M	UFA

	Similar at Age	**30**	
		Season	**SIMsc**
1	Blue Edwards	1995-96	919.1
2	George McCloud	1997-98	911.3
3	Jaren Jackson	1997-98	910.8
4	Trent Tucker	1989-90	907.6
5	Larry Hughes	2008-09	905.5
6	Flip Murray	2009-10	905.5
7	Todd Day	1999-00	904.6
8	Derek Anderson	2004-05	899.7
9	Marco Belinelli	2016-17	898.6
10	Garrett Temple	2016-17	897.8

Baseline Basic Stats

MPG	PTS	AST	REB	BLK	STL
22.8	8.5	1.9	2.8	0.3	0.9

Advanced Metrics

USG%	3PTA/FGA	FTA/FGA	TS%	eFG%	3PT%
18.4	0.434	0.241	0.506	0.466	0.349
AST%	**TOV%**	**OREB%**	**DREB%**	**STL%**	**BLK%**
11.9	13.5	2.1	14.1	2.0	1.6
PER	**ORTG**	**DRTG**	**WS/48**	**VOL**	
10.47	98.9	109.4	0.041	0.146	

- Regular rotation player for Portland and Sacramento, traded to Sacramento in January 2020
- Low volume, spot-up shooter in Portland, more effective in Sacramento in a slightly higher volume role
- Above break-even three-point shooter last season, made over 38% of his threes with the Kings
- Mostly a stationary spot-up shooter, can attack aggressive close-outs if his shot is falling
- Effective at making backdoor cuts to either score at the rim or draw fouls
- Can occasionally post up smaller guards, solid secondary playmaker in past years, good at avoiding turnovers
- 2019-20 Defensive Degree of Difficulty: 0.486
- Took on tougher defensive assignments in Portland, moved to easier assignments in Sacramento
- Decent on-ball defender that can guard multiple positions, over-matched against top players
- Decent pick-and-roll defender, solid in his rotations in Portland, struggled to guard pick-and-rolls in Sacramento
- Fights through screens off the ball, sometimes can be late to close out on spot-up shooters
- Active help defender, good defensive rebounder, gets steals and blocks at a fairly high rate

Marquese Chriss

Height	Weight	Cap #	Years Left
6'9"	240	$1.824M	UFA

Similar at Age 22

		Season	SIMsc
1	James Johnson	2009-10	923.0
2	Richaun Holmes	2015-16	916.2
3	Thomas Robinson	2013-14	912.3
4	Kris Humphries	2007-08	908.9
5	Derrick Favors	2013-14	908.1
6	Markieff Morris	2011-12	907.8
7	Willy Hernangomez	2016-17	907.8
8	Andray Blatche	2008-09	906.8
9	Raef LaFrentz	1998-99	906.7
10	Kyle O'Quinn	2012-13	905.8

Baseline Basic Stats

MPG	PTS	AST	REB	BLK	STL
20.2	8.6	1.1	5.2	0.8	0.6

Advanced Metrics

USG%	3PTA/FGA	FTA/FGA	TS%	eFG%	3PT%
20.3	0.150	0.320	0.552	0.515	0.291

AST%	TOV%	OREB%	DREB%	STL%	BLK%
11.0	14.1	8.5	21.6	1.6	3.3

PER	ORTG	DRTG	WS/48	VOL
16.36	107.1	107.0	0.099	0.402

- Regular rotation player for Golden State last season, played on a Two-Way contract for a week before it was converted to a standard contract
- Had his best season as a pro in 2019-20, mainly utilized as a low volume rim runner
- Excelled as a cutter and roll man, great athleticism makes him a threat to catch lobs above the rim
- Runs hard down the floor in transition, very active offensive rebounder, has some trouble converting on put-back attempts
- Greatly improved as a passer, Assist Percentage increased significantly last season
- Effective at hitting cutters inside or kicking the ball out to shooters, improved his ability to limit turnovers
- 2019-20 Defensive Degree of Difficulty: 0.393
- Typically guarded higher-end second unit players or lower leverage starters, served as an interior rim protector
- Good defensive rebounder and shot blocker, posted fairly high Steal Percentage for a big man
- Can be overpowered inside due to a lack of strength, has been highly foul prone throughout his career
- Mobile big man that flashed an ability to defend in space, effective on-ball defender in isolation situations
- Mixed results as a pick-and-roll defender, good at covering the roll man, struggled when tasked to switch onto ball handlers, doesn't always close out on perimeter shooters

Jordan Poole

	Height	Weight	Cap #	Years Left
	6'4"	195	$2.063M	2 Team Options

	Similar at Age	20	
		Season	SIMsc
1	Malik Monk	2018-19	929.4
2	Emmanuel Mudiay	2016-17	926.9
3	Austin Rivers	2012-13	915.3
4	Ben McLemore	2013-14	915.0
5	Daequan Cook	2007-08	909.9
6	Jamal Murray	2017-18	904.4
7	Frank Ntilikina	2018-19	899.4
8	Frank Jackson	2018-19	898.3
9	Brandon Knight	2011-12	898.3
10	D'Angelo Russell	2016-17	895.8

Baseline Basic Stats

MPG	PTS	AST	REB	BLK	STL
22.8	10.3	2.1	2.5	0.2	0.7

Advanced Metrics

USG%	3PTA/FGA	FTA/FGA	TS%	eFG%	3PT%
22.1	0.472	0.208	0.498	0.458	0.331
AST%	**TOV%**	**OREB%**	**DREB%**	**STL%**	**BLK%**
15.7	11.1	1.4	9.5	1.5	0.6
PER	**ORTG**	**DRTG**	**WS/48**	**VOL**	
10.60	99.0	114.1	0.012	0.244	

- Regular rotation player for Golden State in his rookie season
- Utilized in a combo guard role with moderate usage
- More effective off the ball, good at cutting and coming off screens, could also run the break to score in transition
- Struggled with the ball in his hands, below average pick-and-roll ball handler and isolation player
- Could use quickness to drive to the rim, but struggled to make jump shots in almost every offensive situation
- True Shooting Percentage was below 50%, made less than 30% of his threes but shot more efficiently from the corners
- More of a secondary playmaker at this stage, decent passing skills, good at limiting turnovers
- 2019-20 Defensive Degree of Difficulty: 0.340, generally defends second unit players
- Struggled as an on-ball defender to stay in front of his man
- Better as a team defender, effective on pick-and-rolls, fights through screens and can funnel his man into help
- Stays attached to shooters and usually will close out in spot-up situations
- More of a stay-at-home defender, did not really get blocks or steals, fairly decent defensive rebounder for his size

Alen Smailagić

Height	Weight	Cap #	Years Left
6'10"	215	$1.518M	2

Similar at Age **19**

		Season	SIMsc
1	Giannis Antetokounmpo	2013-14	881.2
2	Aaron Gordon	2014-15	879.5
3	Thon Maker	2016-17	865.3
4	Tobias Harris	2011-12	863.0
5	Al Harrington	1999-00	856.8
6	Troy Brown	2018-19	853.0
7	Noah Vonleh	2014-15	851.2
8	Nikoloz Tskitishvili	2002-03	848.4
9	Marquese Chriss	2016-17	844.4
10	Jarrett Allen	2017-18	844.3

Baseline Basic Stats

MPG	PTS	AST	REB	BLK	STL
23.3	8.7	1.5	4.7	0.6	0.7

Advanced Metrics

USG%	3PTA/FGA	FTA/FGA	TS%	eFG%	3PT%
18.5	0.198	0.408	0.593	0.539	0.282
AST%	**TOV%**	**OREB%**	**DREB%**	**STL%**	**BLK%**
14.5	16.0	7.2	16.2	1.4	2.1
PER	**ORTG**	**DRTG**	**WS/48**	**VOL**	
16.17	112.5	109.3	0.109	0.738	

- Played only 139 minutes for Golden State, spent most of the season with the Santa Cruz Warriors in the G-League
- Utilized as a stretch big in the G-League, made threes at an above break-even rate last season
- Jump shot is still inconsistent, made less than 60% of his free throws in the G-League
- Showed promise as a rim runner in a small sample of NBA minutes
- Made almost 85% of his shots inside of three feet, effective as a cutter, actively crashed the offensive boards to score on put-backs
- Effective in a small sample of post-ups, particularly on the left block
- Displayed some passing skills, but was a bit turnover prone in the NBA
- 2019-20 Defensive Degree of Difficulty: 0.326, typically guarded second unit level players
- Blocked shots at a fairly high rate in the G-League and NBA
- Still learning defensive concepts, struggled to protect the rim at the NBA level, middling defensive rebounder
- Rated as poor in most defensive situations in his limited number of NBA minutes
- Gets lost in pick-and-roll coverages, struggles to defend in space, does not always close out on perimeter shooters
- Showed increased strength to be more effective when guarding opposing big men on post-ups

Juan Toscano-Anderson	Height	Weight	Cap #	Years Left
	6'6"	215	$1.518M	1

Similar at Age 26

		Season	SIMsc
1	Jud Buechler	1994-95	915.2
2	James Anderson	2015-16	900.9
3	Kyle Collinsworth	2017-18	900.8
4	Alonzo Gee	2013-14	898.4
5	Adrian Griffin	2000-01	894.4
6	Solomon Hill	2017-18	892.1
7	Garrett Temple	2012-13	889.9
8	Coby Karl	2009-10	888.3
9	Carlos Terry	1982-83	885.9
10	Kasib Powell	2007-08	885.1

Baseline Basic Stats

MPG	PTS	AST	REB	BLK	STL
17.8	4.9	1.4	2.6	0.3	0.7

Advanced Metrics

USG%	3PTA/FGA	FTA/FGA	TS%	eFG%	3PT%
12.9	0.390	0.143	0.533	0.512	0.357
AST%	**TOV%**	**OREB%**	**DREB%**	**STL%**	**BLK%**
12.3	15.6	3.5	14.5	2.1	1.4
PER	**ORTG**	**DRTG**	**WS/48**	**VOL**	
10.06	104.8	111.1	0.056	0.627	

- Spent most of the season with the Santa Cruz Warriors in the G-League, later signed to a standard contract with Golden State in February 2020
- Played limited minutes in the NBA, primarily used as a very low volume, spot-up shooter
- Above break-even three-point shooter in a small sample of NBA attempts, shot less efficiently in the G-League in the last two seasons
- May be more of a mid-range shooter, made almost 59% of his two-point attempts in the G-League last season
- Has not shown that he can be effective off the ball, rarely drew fouls at either level
- Displays some playmaking skills, but he can be fairly turnover prone
- 2019-20 Defensive Degree of Difficulty: 0.463
- Guarded starting level players and occasionally took on tougher assignments in a small sample of NBA minutes
- Fairly effective as an on-ball defender in isolation situations, flashed the potential to guard multiple positions
- Needs to improve as a team defender, average pick-and-roll defender
- Could get caught ball watching on the weak side, prone to being late to close out on perimeter shooters
- Active help defender that posts fairly high steal and block rates, good defensive rebounder

Mychal Mulder

Height	Weight	Cap #	Years Left
6'4"	185	$1.518M	1

Similar at Age 25

		Season	SIMsc
1	Troy Daniels	2016-17	902.6
2	Damon Jones	2001-02	899.5
3	Alex Abrines	2018-19	895.4
4	Ben McLemore	2018-19	892.8
5	Joe Young	2017-18	882.4
6	Voshon Lenard	1998-99	882.3
7	Jordan McRae	2016-17	881.5
8	Joe Hassett	1980-81	881.1
9	Chris Quinn	2008-09	880.6
10	Seth Curry	2015-16	873.4

Baseline Basic Stats

MPG	PTS	AST	REB	BLK	STL
19.9	7.7	1.6	1.9	0.1	0.4

Advanced Metrics

USG%	3PTA/FGA	FTA/FGA	TS%	eFG%	3PT%
16.5	0.680	0.161	0.552	0.527	0.362
AST%	**TOV%**	**OREB%**	**DREB%**	**STL%**	**BLK%**
10.5	8.0	1.3	10.1	0.8	0.3
PER	**ORTG**	**DRTG**	**WS/48**	**VOL**	
10.57	108.9	114.9	0.054	0.608	

- Signed by Golden State to a standard contract just before the season was suspended in March 2020
- Spent most of the 2019-20 season with the Sioux Falls Skyforce in the G-League
- Used almost exclusively as a low volume, spot-up shooter in limited minutes in the NBA
- Has made 40.5% of his threes over his last two seasons in the G-League
- Flashed some potential to be effective off the ball in limited minutes with Golden State
- Good at setting up for trail threes in transition, had trouble running off screens in a half court set
- Solid at using an on-ball screen to get an extra step to the rim on dribble hand-offs
- Almost strictly a catch-and-shoot player, rarely gets to the rim, not really a playmaker, great at limiting turnovers
- 2019-20 Defensive Degree of Difficulty: 0.438
- Guarded starting level players in a small sample of NBA minutes
- Not tested much on the ball, had success guarding isolations in a very small sample of possessions
- Solid pick-and-roll defender that could fight through screens or funnel his man into help
- Generally stayed attached to shooters off the ball, but could be late to close out in spot-up situations
- Stay-at-home defender, doesn't look to get blocks or steals, solid defensive rebounder for his size

Klay Thompson	Height	Weight	Cap #	Years Left
	6'6"	215	$35.361M	3

	Similar at Age	29	
		Season	SIMsc
1	Jason Richardson	2009-10	939.3
2	Bojan Bogdanovic	2018-19	934.2
3	Michael Finley	2002-03	927.4
4	Jim Jackson	1999-00	914.3
5	Glen Rice	1996-97	912.5
6	Dan Majerle	1994-95	910.2
7	Michael Redd	2008-09	909.1
8	Arron Afflalo	2014-15	908.6
9	Rasual Butler	2008-09	908.0
10	Stephen Jackson	2007-08	906.8

Baseline Basic Stats

MPG	PTS	AST	REB	BLK	STL
32.1	15.3	2.3	3.7	0.3	0.9

Advanced Metrics

USG%	3PTA/FGA	FTA/FGA	TS%	eFG%	3PT%
22.7	0.415	0.158	0.560	0.533	0.399
AST%	**TOV%**	**OREB%**	**DREB%**	**STL%**	**BLK%**
11.3	9.0	1.9	10.3	1.4	1.0
PER	**ORTG**	**DRTG**	**WS/48**	**VOL**	
14.96	108.3	109.9	0.090	0.331	

- Missed the entire 2019-20 season while recovering from a torn ACL in his left knee
- Tore his right Achilles tendon in November 2020, will miss the entire 2020-21 season
- Named as an All-Star in the previous five seasons, also was named to the All-Defensive Second Team in 2018-19
- One of the NBA's most effective shooters when healthy, has made over 40% of his threes in each of his previous eight seasons in the league
- Led the NBA in points scored off screens for fourth straight seasons from 2015-16 to 2018-19
- Consistently makes spot-up jumpers, pretty effective as a cutter, great at running the floor in transition to get layups or knock down trail threes
- Good isolation player that will post up smaller guards, good at getting to the rim on dribble hand-off plays, decent playmaking skills, rarely turns the ball over
- 2018-19 Defensive Degree of Difficulty: 0.531
- Typically guards the opponent's top perimeter player, good on-ball defender that guards multiple positions
- Very good pick-and-roll defender, consistently closes out on perimeter shooters, can occasionally get caught on screens away from the ball
- Solid defensive rebounder, more active as a help defender in 2018-19, Steal and Block Percentages were slightly above his career averages

Newcomers

James Wiseman

Height	Weight	Cap #	Years Left
7'1"	240	$8.730M	1 + 2 TO

Baseline Basic Stats

MPG	PTS	AST	REB	BLK	STL
22.2	8.4	0.8	6.2	1.4	0.6

Advanced Metrics

USG%	3PTA/FGA	FTA/FGA	TS%	eFG%	3PT%
18.1	0.029	0.462	0.551	0.521	0.157

AST%	TOV%	OREB%	DREB%	STL%	BLK%
6.0	11.4	11.1	20.0	1.1	4.6

PER	ORTG	DRTG	WS/48	VOL
19.23	108.9	93.6	0.135	N/A

- Drafted by Golden State with the 2nd overall pick
- Only played in three games at Memphis due an NCAA suspension
- Overwhelmed opponents in college with his excellent athleticism, great at bullying weaker defenders in the post
- Dynamic vertical threat, has great length and explosive leaping ability, great roll man and cutter off the ball
- Great at running the floor in transition, actively crashes the offensive glass to get second chance opportunities or score on put-backs
- Skill level is limited, not really a passer, does not have much range on his outside shot, flashed mid-range shooting potential in college
- Good rim protector at Memphis, excellent shot blocker and defensive rebounder
- Somewhat foul prone, can be too aggressive when going for blocks, tends to bite on fakes
- Mobile big man, uncomfortable when defending in space, struggled to defend guards on switches

OKLAHOMA CITY THUNDER

Last Season: 44 – 28, Lost 1st Round to Houston (3 – 4)

Offensive Rating: 110.8, 16th in the NBA

Defensive Rating: 108.8, 7th in the NBA

Primary Executive: Sam Presti, Executive Vice President of Basketball Operations and General Manager

Head Coach: Mark Daigneault

Key Roster Changes

Subtractions
Chris Paul, trade
Steven Adams, trade
Dennis Schroder, trade
Terrance Ferguson, trade
Abdel Nader, trade
Danilo Gallinari, sign-and-trade
Nerlens Noel, free agency
Andre Roberson, free agency
Deonte Burton, free agency
Devon Hall, free agency

Additions
Aleksej Pokusevski, draft
Al Horford, trade
Trevor Ariza, trade
George Hill, trade
Justin Jackson, trade
Ty Jerome, trade
T.J. Leaf, trade
Vincent Poirier, trade
Darius Miller, trade
Kenrich Williams, trade
Frank Jackson, free agency

Roster

Likely Starting Five
1. *George Hill*
2. *Shai Gilgeous-Alexander*
3. *Luguentz Dort*
4. *Trevor Ariza*
5. *Al Horford*

Other Key Rotation Players
Justin Jackson
Darius Bazley
Hamidou Diallo

* Italics denotes that a player is likely to be on the floor to close games

Note: training camp roster had more than 20 players at this time, rest of roster continues on next page

Remaining Roster

- Ty Jerome
- T.J. Leaf
- Kenrich Williams
- Mike Muscala
- Frank Jackson
- Darius Miller
- Vincent Poirier, traded to Philadelphia right before the book was finalized
- Aleksej Pokusevski
- Isaiah Roby
- Admiral Schofield
- Zylan Cheatham (waived right before the book was finalized)
- Moses Brown, 21, 7'2", 245, UCLA (Two-Way)
- Josh Hall, 20, 6'8", 200, Moravian Prep – Hickory, NC (Two-Way)
- Omer Yurtseven, 22, 7'0", 264, Georgetown (Exhibit 10)

SCHREMPF Base Rating: 33.1 (72-game season)

Strengths

- Collection of assets gained from the last two years to build for the future

Question Marks

- Shai Gilgeous-Alexander's transition from a secondary player to a primary scoring option
- Implementation of structure on both ends to develop the other young players

Outlook

- Beginning a full-scale rebuild, could trade more veterans, likely will be in the lottery this upcoming season

Veterans

Shai Gilgeous-Alexander	Height	Weight	Cap #	Years Left
	6'5"	181	$4.141M	Team Option

	Similar at Age	21	
		Season	SIMsc
1	Jeremy Lamb	2013-14	919.2
2	Ray Allen*	1996-97	914.2
3	Zach LaVine	2016-17	912.5
4	Larry Hughes	1999-00	909.2
5	Jrue Holiday	2011-12	908.2
6	Monta Ellis	2006-07	906.0
7	Manny Harris	2010-11	906.0
8	Kobe Bryant*	1999-00	900.7
9	Mike Conley	2008-09	895.5
10	Tony Parker	2003-04	894.0

Baseline Basic Stats

MPG	PTS	AST	REB	BLK	STL
33.0	16.4	3.7	4.2	0.4	1.3

Advanced Metrics

USG%	3PTA/FGA	FTA/FGA	TS%	eFG%	3PT%
21.9	0.179	0.317	0.542	0.491	0.338
AST%	**TOV%**	**OREB%**	**DREB%**	**STL%**	**BLK%**
17.6	12.6	2.9	11.8	1.9	1.0
PER	**ORTG**	**DRTG**	**WS/48**	**VOL**	
15.43	108.0	109.9	0.091	0.322	

- Full-time starter in his first season with Oklahoma City in 2019-20
- Production increased in his role as a higher volume scoring guard and secondary ball handler
- Effective as a pick-and-roll ball handler and isolation player, can make pull-up jumpers and drive to the rim, drew fouls at a higher rate
- Great quickness makes him a threat to push the ball in transition
- Made threes at an above break-even rate last season, much better in the corners, career percentage on corner threes is almost 42%
- Still learning to move without the ball, not really effective as a cutter, does not really shoot off screens
- Solid secondary playmaker, cut his turnover rate significantly last season
- 2019-20 Defensive Degree of Difficulty: 0.422, tends to defend starter level guards
- Fairly solid on-ball defender, stays with opposing perimeter players, can be bullied inside by stronger players in the post
- Average pick-and-roll defender, tends to go too far under screens to allow open jump shots
- Closes out on perimeter shooters, gambles a bit too much when chasing shooters off screens
- Active help defender, good defensive rebounder, can rotate inside to block shots on the weak side, gets steals at a fairly good rate

Luguentz Dort	Height	Weight	Cap #	Years Left
	6'3"	215	$1.518M	2

	Similar at Age	20	
		Season	SIMsc
1	Gary Harris	2014-15	912.5
2	Frank Jackson	2018-19	908.0
3	Josh Okogie	2018-19	907.2
4	Kentavious Caldwell-Pope	2013-14	907.2
5	J.R. Smith	2005-06	887.9
6	Daniel Gibson	2006-07	886.7
7	Marcus Smart	2014-15	886.7
8	C.J. Miles	2007-08	878.5
9	Daequan Cook	2007-08	876.3
10	Dajuan Wagner	2003-04	871.2

Baseline Basic Stats

MPG	PTS	AST	REB	BLK	STL
23.2	8.4	1.5	2.7	0.2	0.8

Advanced Metrics

USG%	3PTA/FGA	FTA/FGA	TS%	eFG%	3PT%
16.1	0.506	0.232	0.547	0.507	0.355
AST%	**TOV%**	**OREB%**	**DREB%**	**STL%**	**BLK%**
7.9	10.3	2.9	8.5	1.7	0.5
PER	**ORTG**	**DRTG**	**WS/48**	**VOL**	
10.33	108.1	111.3	0.071	0.404	

- Spent most of the season in G-League with the Oklahoma City Blue, became a regular starter after he was called up in January 2020
- Used on offense as a low volume, spot-up shooter
- Inconsistent outside shooter, struggled to efficiently makes shots outside of three feet, made less than 30% of his threes in his rookie season
- More effective at going to the rim, drew fouls at a decent rate, made 60.5% of his shots inside of three feet
- Best at cutting off the ball and driving to the rim as a pick-and-roll ball handler
- More of a catch-and-shoot player at the NBA level, showed some passing skills in the G-League, rarely turns the ball over
- 2019-20 Defensive Degree of Difficulty: 0.572
- Had the 4th toughest set of matchups in the NBA among players that played 500 minutes or more
- Solid on-ball defender that can guard multiple positions
- Held James Harden to a 40.7% Effective Field Goal Percentage in the playoffs
- Decent pick-and-roll defender, good at switching, can be too aggressive when going over the screen
- Good at closing out on perimeter shooters, can sometimes get caught on screens off the ball
- Stay-at-home defender at the NBA level, gets steals at a fairly solid rate, below average defensive rebounder

Al Horford

Height	Weight	Cap #	Years Left
6'9"	245	$27.500M	2

Similar at Age **33**

		Season	SIMsc
1	David West	2013-14	910.1
2	Sam Perkins	1994-95	899.1
3	Paul Millsap	2018-19	897.0
4	Chris Webber	2006-07	887.3
5	Herb Williams	1991-92	887.2
6	Brad Miller	2009-10	886.2
7	Mike Dunleavy, Jr.	2013-14	884.0
8	David Lee	2016-17	881.3
9	Rasheed Wallace	2007-08	877.0
10	Channing Frye	2016-17	873.6

Baseline Basic Stats

MPG	PTS	AST	REB	BLK	STL
23.9	9.6	2.4	4.8	0.7	0.7

Advanced Metrics

USG%	3PTA/FGA	FTA/FGA	TS%	eFG%	3PT%
17.3	0.373	0.161	0.557	0.535	0.363
AST%	**TOV%**	**OREB%**	**DREB%**	**STL%**	**BLK%**
17.4	11.6	5.3	18.0	1.5	2.6
PER	**ORTG**	**DRTG**	**WS/48**	**VOL**	
15.64	114.4	106.8	0.138	0.356	

- Regular starter for Philadelphia in his first season with the team
- Overall production declined after moving into a role as a lower volume, stretch big
- Made threes at around the league average last season, solid at making long twos
- Better shooter as the screener on pick-and-pops, average spot-up shooter
- Effective as a rim runner, can slide into open spaces inside as a roll man and cutter off the ball
- Now only about an average post-up player overall, still effective on the right block
- Good passing big man that rarely turns the ball over
- 2019-20 Defensive Degree of Difficulty: 0.429
- Tends to guard starting level big men, sometimes takes on tougher big man assignments
- Good rim protector that can clog the lane and block shots, solid defensive rebounder
- Solid on-ball defender, strong post defender that holds position inside, still mobile enough to defend in space
- Good pick-and-roll defender, effective in drop coverages, good at switching onto ball handlers
- Consistently closes out on perimeter shooters in spot-up situations

George Hill	Height	Weight	Cap #	Years Left
	6'3"	188	$9.591M	1

	Similar at Age	33	
		Season	SIMsc
1	Hersey Hawkins	1999-00	928.0
2	Mike James	2008-09	922.2
3	Anthony Johnson	2007-08	921.9
4	Danny Ainge	1992-93	919.7
5	Jon Barry	2002-03	919.6
6	Brad Davis	1988-89	917.8
7	Devin Harris	2016-17	916.8
8	Trent Tucker	1992-93	915.6
9	Leandro Barbosa	2015-16	915.4
10	Kirk Hinrich	2013-14	915.0

Baseline Basic Stats

MPG	PTS	AST	REB	BLK	STL
20.6	7.3	2.5	2.0	0.1	0.7

Advanced Metrics

USG%	3PTA/FGA	FTA/FGA	TS%	eFG%	3PT%
15.9	0.452	0.246	0.579	0.542	0.390
AST%	**TOV%**	**OREB%**	**DREB%**	**STL%**	**BLK%**
17.2	12.7	2.8	8.9	1.8	0.5
PER	**ORTG**	**DRTG**	**WS/48**	**VOL**	
13.67	116.0	107.0	0.135	0.343	

- Missed almost a month due to a strained left hamstring, regular rotation player when healthy
- Had his most efficient shooting season in the NBA, led the NBA in Three-Point Percentage
- Excelled as a lower volume, stationary spot-up shooter
- Good at making shots off the dribble as an isolation player and pick-and-roll ball handler
- Effective at using an on-ball screen to get to the rim or make outside shots on dribble hand-offs
- Good cutter away from the ball, solid secondary playmaker, limits turnovers consistently
- 2019-20 Defensive Degree of Difficulty: 0.450
- Usually took on tougher point guard matchups when he was on the floor as a second unit player
- Played average on-ball defense, good against drives, gave up extra space for his man to take jump shots
- Average pick-and-roll defender, tended to go too far under screens
- Tended to get caught on screens off the ball, closed out too aggressively, gave up driving lanes to the rim
- Fairly solid defensive rebounding guard, Steal Percentage is still consistent with his career average, Block Percentage dropped to a career low

Trevor Ariza

	Height	Weight	Cap #	Years Left
	6'8"	215	$12.800M	UFA

	Similar at Age	34	
		Season	SIMsc
1	Mike Dunleavy, Jr.	2014-15	940.0
2	Dan Majerle	1999-00	934.6
3	Anthony Parker	2009-10	929.2
4	Caron Butler	2014-15	926.7
5	Kyle Korver	2015-16	926.2
6	Chuck Person	1998-99	920.1
7	Eric Piatkowski	2004-05	915.5
8	Bryon Russell	2004-05	909.7
9	Rashard Lewis	2013-14	908.2
10	Stephen Jackson	2012-13	908.2

Baseline Basic Stats

MPG	PTS	AST	REB	BLK	STL
24.5	7.4	1.7	3.5	0.3	0.7

Advanced Metrics

USG%	3PTA/FGA	FTA/FGA	TS%	eFG%	3PT%
13.5	0.621	0.210	0.558	0.526	0.361
AST%	**TOV%**	**OREB%**	**DREB%**	**STL%**	**BLK%**
10.4	11.9	2.5	15.4	1.7	1.0
PER	**ORTG**	**DRTG**	**WS/48**	**VOL**	
11.17	110.2	109.9	0.078	0.430	

- Regular rotation player for Sacramento, traded to Portland in January 2020
- Became a starter for Portland, opted out of the Orlando restart
- Effective in his role as a very low volume, spot-up shooter, league average three-point shooter throughout his career
- Almost strictly a stationary spot-up shooter, career percentage on corner threes is over 40%
- Used more in transition and as a pick-and-roll ball handler in Portland, drew shooting fouls at a higher rate
- Solid secondary playmaker in the past, catch-and-shoot player now, tends to avoid turnovers
- 2019-20 Defensive Degree of Difficulty: 0.559
- Had the 7th toughest set of matchups among players that played 500 or more minutes
- Good on-ball defender that guards multiple positions
- Solid team defender that makes sound rotations, good at guarding ball handlers or switching onto screeners on pick-and-rolls
- Fights through screens off the ball, sometimes can be late to close out on perimeter shooters
- Good defensive rebounder, gets steals at a fairly high rate, Block Percentage is still consistent with his career average

Justin Jackson	Height	Weight	Cap #	Years Left
	6'7"	210	$5.030M	RFA

	Similar at Age	24	
		Season	SIMsc
1	Danuel House	2017-18	939.8
2	Tony Snell	2015-16	937.5
3	Hollis Thompson	2015-16	931.6
4	Allen Crabbe	2016-17	927.6
5	Antoine Wright	2008-09	923.7
6	Damyean Dotson	2018-19	923.4
7	James Ennis	2014-15	923.3
8	Martell Webster	2010-11	923.1
9	Reggie Williams	2010-11	921.5
10	Wesley Johnson	2011-12	919.0

Baseline Basic Stats

MPG	PTS	AST	REB	BLK	STL
22.9	8.7	1.2	2.9	0.3	0.5

Advanced Metrics

USG%	3PTA/FGA	FTA/FGA	TS%	eFG%	3PT%
16.7	0.491	0.169	0.544	0.514	0.355
AST%	**TOV%**	**OREB%**	**DREB%**	**STL%**	**BLK%**
8.3	7.1	2.6	12.3	1.0	0.8
PER	**ORTG**	**DRTG**	**WS/48**	**VOL**	
11.73	110.7	113.2	0.074	0.327	

- Lower-end rotation player for Dallas last season
- Struggled to shoot efficiently in his role as a low volume, spot-up shooter
- Three-Point Percentage dropped to below 30%, posted a True Shooting Percentage below 50% last season
- Good at attacking the rim against aggressive close-outs, can curl into the paint to get floaters off screens
- Effective at making long pull-up twos on pick-and-rolls, pretty good cutter off the ball
- Mainly a catch-and-shoot player, sticks to making safe passes on the perimeter, posted an extremely low Turnover Percentage last season
- 2019-20 Defensive Degree of Difficulty: 0.335, tends to guard second unit level players
- Solid on-ball defender, good against perimeter players on isolation plays, can be backed down inside by stronger players in the post
- Fairly solid pick-and-roll defender, can switch to guard multiple positions
- Excellent at staying attached to shooters off the ball, consistently closes out in spot-up situations
- Plays a stay-at-home style, does not really get steals or blocks, solid defensive rebounder

Darius Bazley	Height	Weight	Cap #	Years Left
	6'8"	208	$2.399M	2 Team Options

	Similar at Age	19	
		Season	SIMsc
1	Martell Webster	2005-06	903.6
2	Maurice Harkless	2012-13	890.9
3	Aaron Gordon	2014-15	885.7
4	Troy Brown	2018-19	885.5
5	Giannis Antetokounmpo	2013-14	879.5
6	Kevin Knox	2018-19	876.3
7	Jayson Tatum	2017-18	875.1
8	Eddie Griffin	2001-02	869.6
9	Rashad Vaughn	2015-16	866.1
10	Brandon Ingram	2016-17	859.1

Baseline Basic Stats

MPG	PTS	AST	REB	BLK	STL
25.5	9.5	1.5	4.3	0.6	0.9

Advanced Metrics

USG%	3PTA/FGA	FTA/FGA	TS%	eFG%	3PT%
17.2	0.343	0.247	0.541	0.510	0.368
AST%	**TOV%**	**OREB%**	**DREB%**	**STL%**	**BLK%**
8.9	11.1	3.7	19.0	1.6	2.3
PER	**ORTG**	**DRTG**	**WS/48**	**VOL**	
13.35	105.5	107.5	0.089	0.496	

- Regular rotation player for Oklahoma City in his rookie season
- Mainly used as a low volume, spot-up shooter, made threes at a rate just above break-even
- Took a lot of mid-range shots, didn't make them at a high rate, hurt his overall scoring efficiency
- Most effective as the screener on pick-and-pops, could occasionally make no dribble jumpers on isolations
- High motor player with great athleticism, good at running the floor to get dunks in transition, can crash the offensive boards to score on put-backs
- Catch-and-shoot player at this stage, limited playmaking skills, good at avoiding turnovers
- 2019-20 Defensive Degree of Difficulty: 0.288
- Tended to be hidden in favorable matchups against lower leverage second unit players
- Decent on-ball defender, flashes potential to guard both forward spots, better in the post against bigger fours
- Below average pick-and-roll defender, tends to go too far under screens, can be too late to cover the roll man
- Stays attached to shooters off the ball, closes out in spot-up situations
- Good defensive rebounder, active help defender, very good weak side shot blocker

Hamidou Diallo	Height	Weight	Cap #	Years Left
	6'5"	202	$1.664M	RFA

	Similar at Age	21	
		Season	SIMsc
1	Christian Eyenga	2010-11	927.9
2	Chris Carr	1995-96	917.2
3	Mickael Pietrus	2003-04	915.7
4	Bobby Simmons	2001-02	912.8
5	Javaris Crittenton	2008-09	911.2
6	Alec Burks	2012-13	907.9
7	Corey Benjamin	1999-00	907.8
8	DeShawn Stevenson	2002-03	907.5
9	Malik Beasley	2017-18	904.4
10	Shannon Brown	2006-07	903.8

Baseline Basic Stats

MPG	PTS	AST	REB	BLK	STL
20.2	8.3	1.5	2.7	0.2	0.7

Advanced Metrics

USG%	3PTA/FGA	FTA/FGA	TS%	eFG%	3PT%
18.3	0.137	0.280	0.513	0.480	0.289
AST%	**TOV%**	**OREB%**	**DREB%**	**STL%**	**BLK%**
10.0	12.7	5.2	11.0	2.0	0.8
PER	**ORTG**	**DRTG**	**WS/48**	**VOL**	
11.31	102.7	109.5	0.057	0.402	

- Regular rotation player for Oklahoma City when healthy, missed over a month due to a sprained right elbow
- Used as low volume, energy guard off the bench, has struggled to score efficient in two NBA seasons
- Career True Shooting Percentage is below 50%, shot just above break-even on corner threes last season
- Rated as average or worse in every offensive situation last season
- Most effective at opportunistically crashing the offensive glass to score on put-backs
- Slightly improving as a passer, still a limited playmaker overall, fairly effective at avoiding turnovers
- 2019-20 Defensive Degree of Difficulty: 0.401
- Tends to guard second unit players, sometimes draws tougher defensive assignments
- Fairly solid on-ball defender that can guard multiple positions, highly foul prone at this stage
- Good pick-and-roll defender that can switch or fight over screens to contain ball handlers
- Stays attached to shooters off the ball, good at closing out in spot-up situations
- Active help defender, solid defensive rebounder, gets steals at a fairly high rate, can occasionally rotate inside to block shots

Ty Jerome	Height	Weight	Cap #	Years Left
	6'5"	195	$2.303M	2 Team Options

	Similar at Age	22	
		Season	SIMsc
1	Chris Robinson	1996-97	929.1
2	Marco Belinelli	2008-09	927.9
3	Davon Reed	2017-18	923.4
4	E'Twaun Moore	2011-12	921.7
5	Gabe Pruitt	2008-09	920.1
6	Adam Harrington	2002-03	917.7
7	Damon Jones	1998-99	915.6
8	Iman Shumpert	2012-13	915.5
9	Ben McLemore	2015-16	911.4
10	Daequan Cook	2009-10	910.5

Baseline Basic Stats

MPG	PTS	AST	REB	BLK	STL
18.6	7.1	2.0	2.2	0.2	0.7

Advanced Metrics

USG%	3PTA/FGA	FTA/FGA	TS%	eFG%	3PT%
18.1	0.383	0.182	0.493	0.463	0.326
AST%	**TOV%**	**OREB%**	**DREB%**	**STL%**	**BLK%**
18.0	12.8	2.7	11.6	2.1	0.8
PER	**ORTG**	**DRTG**	**WS/48**	**VOL**	
11.35	101.8	110.9	0.046	0.481	

- Missed over a month due to a sprained right ankle, played limited minutes for Phoenix as a rookie
- Mainly used as a low volume, spot-up shooting backup point guard
- Struggled to shoot efficiently, True Shooting Percentage was below 45%
- Rated as below average or worse in every offensive situation last season
- Mostly used as a pick-and-roll ball handler and spot-up shooter
- Fairly solid playmaker that can find open shooters, good at controlling the ball to avoid turnovers
- 2019-20 Defensive Degree of Difficulty: 0.301
- Tended to be hidden in favorable matchups against lower leverage second unit players
- Played below average on-ball defense, struggled to defend quicker guards on the perimeter
- Middling pick-and-roll defender, tends to go too far under screens, can be targeted by bigger screeners on switches
- Fights through screens off the ball, tends to be late on his close-outs
- Fairly active help defender, solid defensive rebounder, gets steals at a pretty high rate

T.J. Leaf

Height	Weight	Cap #	Years Left
6'10"	225	$4.327M	RFA

	Similar at Age	22	
		Season	SIMsc
1	Charles Shackleford	1988-89	940.5
2	Jon Leuer	2011-12	923.4
3	Josh McRoberts	2009-10	907.8
4	Scott Williams	1990-91	906.8
5	Greg Stokes	1985-86	906.4
6	Chris Washburn	1987-88	905.2
7	Andrew DeClercq	1995-96	902.3
8	Donyell Marshall	1995-96	900.7
9	Jordan Hill	2009-10	900.6
10	Dante Cunningham	2009-10	899.5

Baseline Basic Stats

MPG	PTS	AST	REB	BLK	STL
16.6	6.4	0.8	4.4	0.5	0.4

Advanced Metrics

USG%	3PTA/FGA	FTA/FGA	TS%	eFG%	3PT%
19.1	0.139	0.222	0.521	0.499	0.331
AST%	**TOV%**	**OREB%**	**DREB%**	**STL%**	**BLK%**
6.9	11.1	10.4	20.2	1.4	2.1
PER	**ORTG**	**DRTG**	**WS/48**	**VOL**	
14.65	107.0	105.5	0.098	0.370	

- Played sparingly for Indiana last season, fringe rotation player in the previous two seasons
- Effectiveness decreased significantly in his role as a moderate volume, rim runner and stretch big off the bench
- Rated as below average or worse in every half court offensive situation last season
- Struggled to make shots outside of three feet, inconsistent outside shooter throughout his career, still an above break-even three-point shooter
- Better at finishing at the rim, shooting percentage inside of three feet fell significantly last season
- Still made over 58% of his shots inside of three feet, only effective at running the floor in transition
- Very good offensive rebounder, Offensive Rebound Percentage steadily rising
- Mainly a catch-and-shoot player, limited passing skills, rarely turns the ball over
- 2019-20 Defensive Degree of Difficulty: 0.253, only really played in garbage time
- Below average rim protector, not really a consistent shot blocker, good defensive rebounder last season
- Rarely tested on the ball, played solid on-ball defense in the post and on the perimeter in a small sample of possessions
- Below average pick-and-roll defender, tends to sag too far into the paint to give up open outside to either the ball handler or screener
- Tends to be late when closing out on perimeter shooters in spot-up situations

Kenrich Williams	Height	Weight	Cap #	Years Left
	6'6"	210	$2.000M	2

Similar at Age 25

		Season	SIMsc
1	Chris Johnson	2015-16	911.1
2	Iman Shumpert	2015-16	905.6
3	Royce O'Neale	2018-19	905.3
4	Treveon Graham	2018-19	898.5
5	Rodney Carney	2009-10	890.2
6	Andre Roberson	2016-17	890.1
7	Hollis Thompson	2016-17	888.3
8	John Salmons	2004-05	888.3
9	Antoine Wright	2009-10	888.1
10	Keith Askins	1992-93	887.9

Baseline Basic Stats

MPG	PTS	AST	REB	BLK	STL
23.0	6.9	1.5	3.7	0.4	0.7

Advanced Metrics

USG%	3PTA/FGA	FTA/FGA	TS%	eFG%	3PT%
12.5	0.563	0.183	0.506	0.490	0.326
AST%	**TOV%**	**OREB%**	**DREB%**	**STL%**	**BLK%**
9.7	11.4	5.0	15.1	1.5	1.5
PER	**ORTG**	**DRTG**	**WS/48**	**VOL**	
10.11	108.6	110.9	0.072	0.492	

- Regular rotation player when healthy, missed games due to a sore lower back
- Utilized as a very low volume, spot-up shooter
- Struggled to shoot efficiently, made less than 30% of his threes last season
- Rated as average or worse in every offensive situation last season
- Most effective at going to the rim in transition or off the ball as a cutter, shot better from 16 feet and in
- Strictly a catch-and-shoot player, limited playmaking skills, generally good at limiting turnovers
- 2019-20 Defensive Degree of Difficulty: 0.409
- Tended to guard second unit level players, occasionally drew tougher assignments
- Good on-ball defender that can guard multiple positions
- Solid pick-and-roll defender, fights over screens to contain ball handler, occasionally has trouble on switches
- Good at closing out on perimeter shooters, sometimes gets caught on screens off the ball
- Active help defender, good at rotating from the weak side to block shots, posts a solid Steal Percentage
- Generally boxes out, good defensive rebounding wing player

Mike Muscala	Height	Weight	Cap #	Years Left
	6'10"	240	$2.283M	UFA

	Similar at Age	28	
		Season	SIMsc
1	Nemanja Bjelica	2016-17	921.5
2	Shawne Williams	2014-15	917.1
3	Pat Garrity	2004-05	915.8
4	Scott Padgett	2004-05	914.4
5	Luke Babbitt	2017-18	912.0
6	Mirza Teletovic	2013-14	909.3
7	Ryan Anderson	2016-17	908.8
8	Richard Anderson	1988-89	907.1
9	Anthony Tolliver	2013-14	902.9
10	Matt Bonner	2008-09	902.9

Baseline Basic Stats

MPG	PTS	AST	REB	BLK	STL
17.8	5.9	1.0	3.3	0.3	0.4

Advanced Metrics

USG%	3PTA/FGA	FTA/FGA	TS%	eFG%	3PT%
14.6	0.738	0.155	0.562	0.540	0.373
AST%	**TOV%**	**OREB%**	**DREB%**	**STL%**	**BLK%**
8.7	9.6	4.3	16.2	1.1	1.7
PER	**ORTG**	**DRTG**	**WS/48**	**VOL**	
11.68	112.9	108.8	0.101	0.322	

- Fringe rotation player for Oklahoma City in his first season with the team
- Has been a low volume stretch big throughout his career, made almost 38% of his threes last season
- Mostly a stationary spot-up shooter, also effective as a screener on pick-and-pops
- Not as effective as a rim runner, does not have the lift to finish in traffic, can sometimes slide into open spots inside as a roll man
- Fairly decent passing big man that cut his Turnover Percentage to a career low last season
- 2019-20 Defensive Degree of Difficulty: 0.314
- Tended to be hidden in matchups against lower leverage second unit players
- Fairly effective rim protector, blocking fewer shots, solid at staying vertical to contest shots, decent defensive rebounder
- Below average on-ball defender, can be backed down by stronger post players, shows enough mobility to defend in space
- Decent pick-and-roll defender, effective at switching, good in drop coverages
- Tends to be late to close out on perimeter shooters in spot-up situations

Frank Jackson	Height	Weight	Cap #	Years Left
	6'3"	205	$1.621M	UFA

	Similar at Age	21	
		Season	SIMsc
1	John Jenkins	2012-13	924.8
2	Rashad McCants	2005-06	919.1
3	Bradley Beal	2014-15	918.0
4	Malachi Richardson	2016-17	915.3
5	Shannon Brown	2006-07	912.5
6	Antonio Blakeney	2017-18	911.2
7	Marco Belinelli	2007-08	908.8
8	Doron Lamb	2012-13	907.9
9	Bracey Wright	2005-06	907.5
10	Tyler Dorsey	2017-18	907.5

Baseline Basic Stats

MPG	PTS	AST	REB	BLK	STL
22.0	9.6	2.0	2.3	0.1	0.6

Advanced Metrics

USG%	3PTA/FGA	FTA/FGA	TS%	eFG%	3PT%
19.8	0.303	0.212	0.528	0.495	0.338
AST%	**TOV%**	**OREB%**	**DREB%**	**STL%**	**BLK%**
13.4	11.7	2.3	8.6	1.3	0.3
PER	**ORTG**	**DRTG**	**WS/48**	**VOL**	
11.03	104.5	114.3	0.044	0.421	

- Fringe rotation player for New Orleans in his second season in the NBA
- Mainly used as a low volume, spot-up shooting backup point guard
- Struggled in most half-court situations, rated as average or worse in most offensive situations last season
- Has trouble shooting consistently from outside, below break-even three-point shooter in his two seasons
- Quick enough to drive by defenders on isolations to get to the rim or draw fouls
- Good cutter off the ball in a small sample of possessions
- Decent secondary playmaker, kicks the ball out to shooters, hits the roll man, good at avoiding turnovers
- 2019-20 Defensive Degree of Difficulty: 0.370
- Tends to guard second unit level players or lower leverage starters
- Below average on-ball defender, contests jump shots, has trouble keeping opposing players in front of him
- Below average at guarding pick-and-rolls, allows ball handlers to turn the corner, can be targeted by bigger players on switches
- Fights through screens off the ball, tends to be late when closing out on perimeter shooters
- Stay-at-home defender, does not really get blocks or steals, middling defensive rebounder

Darius Miller

Height	Weight	Cap #	Years Left
6'8"	235	$7.000M	UFA

	Similar at Age	**29** Season	SIMsc
1	Anthony Tolliver	2014-15	947.9
2	James Jones	2009-10	922.7
3	James Posey	2005-06	921.4
4	Ryan Anderson	2017-18	911.3
5	Walter McCarty	2003-04	909.3
6	Pat Garrity	2005-06	907.0
7	Lance Thomas	2017-18	903.5
8	Dennis Scott	1997-98	896.9
9	Patrick Patterson	2018-19	896.8
10	Dante Cunningham	2016-17	895.2

Baseline Basic Stats

MPG	PTS	AST	REB	BLK	STL
19.7	6.0	1.0	2.8	0.3	0.5

Advanced Metrics

USG%	3PTA/FGA	FTA/FGA	TS%	eFG%	3PT%
13.0	0.686	0.162	0.567	0.542	0.374
AST%	**TOV%**	**OREB%**	**DREB%**	**STL%**	**BLK%**
8.2	9.9	2.1	10.5	1.1	1.1
PER	**ORTG**	**DRTG**	**WS/48**	**VOL**	
9.55	111.9	112.3	0.067	0.261	

- Missed the entire 2019-20 season due to a ruptured right Achilles tendon
- Regular rotation player for New Orleans in the past two seasons, mainly a low volume, spot-up shooter
- Has made over 38% of his threes in his career, career percentage on corner threes is almost 44%
- Very good spot-up shooter that can also come off screens
- Solid at using on-ball screen to get to the rim on dribble hand-offs
- Effective at making pull-up jumpers as a pick-and-roll ball handler, occasionally can drive by defenders on isolations if they try to crowd him
- Mainly a catch-and-shoot player, has some passing skills, good at limiting turnovers
- 2018-19 Defensive Degree of Difficulty: 0.402
- Tended to guard higher-end second unit players or lower leverage starters
- Below average on-ball defender, struggled to stay with opposing perimeter players
- Decent pick-and-roll defender, good at fighting over the screen to contain ball handlers, has trouble against bigger players on switches
- Closes out on perimeter shooters, tends to get caught on screens off the ball
- Stay-at-home defender, below average defensive rebounder, does not really get blocks or steals at a high rate

Vincent Poirier

	Height	Weight	Cap #	Years Left
	7'0"	235	$2.619M	RFA

	Similar at Age	**26**	
		Season	**SIMsc**
1	JaVale McGee	2013-14	892.0
2	Kevin Salvadori	1996-97	886.7
3	Jeff Withey	2016-17	881.0
4	Jawann Oldham	1983-84	879.8
5	Larry Sanders	2014-15	879.3
6	Kyle O'Quinn	2016-17	876.4
7	Jason Smith	2012-13	874.8
8	Uwe Blab	1988-89	874.4
9	Timofey Mozgov	2012-13	873.5
10	John Henson	2016-17	873.5

Baseline Basic Stats

MPG	PTS	AST	REB	BLK	STL
13.7	4.4	0.6	4.0	1.0	0.3

Advanced Metrics

USG%	3PTA/FGA	FTA/FGA	TS%	eFG%	3PT%
15.4	0.039	0.319	0.539	0.491	0.374
AST%	**TOV%**	**OREB%**	**DREB%**	**STL%**	**BLK%**
6.9	16.5	10.0	24.4	0.8	5.8
PER	**ORTG**	**DRTG**	**WS/48**	**VOL**	
13.82	107.9	102.4	0.124	0.453	

- Missed a month due to a fractured finger, played sparingly for Boston in his rookie season
- Traded to Philadelphia in December 2020, just before the book was finalized
- Mainly used as a low volume rim runner, decent from ten feet and in
- Does not have the lift to finish in traffic, had some trouble making the first shot off a cut or roll to the rim
- Active offensive rebounder that can get second chances and score on put-backs
- High effort player, runs hard down the floor in transition
- Flashes some stretch potential, went 3-for-5 on long twos and 1-for-2 on threes last season
- Shows some passing ability, slightly turnover prone in his rookie season
- 2019-20 Defensive Degree of Difficulty: 0.295
- Tended to either guard second unit player or play in garbage time
- Good rim protector in limited minutes, grabs defensive rebounds and blocks shots at a high rate
- Middling on-ball defender, highly foul prone, struggled to defend opposing big men in the post
- May have some mobility limitations, had trouble defending ball handlers in space on pick-and-rolls
- Tended to be late to contest perimeter shots in spot-up situations

Isaiah Roby	Height	Weight	Cap #	Years Left
	6'8"	230	$1.518M	1 + TO

	Similar at Age	21	SIMsc
		Season	SIMsc
1	Ben Bentil	2016-17	866.3
2	Chinanu Onuaku	2017-18	809.8
3	Tyler Lydon	2017-18	798.5
4	Pete Williams	1986-87	795.3
5	Brandon Bass	2006-07	726.2
6	Kyle Anderson	2014-15	718.1
7	Antoine Wright	2005-06	717.6
8	Luke Babbitt	2010-11	717.6
9	Kobi Simmons	2018-19	716.2
10	Jacob Evans	2018-19	715.8

Baseline Basic Stats

MPG	PTS	AST	REB	BLK	STL
10.4	2.7	0.4	2.4	0.3	0.2

Advanced Metrics

USG%	3PTA/FGA	FTA/FGA	TS%	eFG%	3PT%
13.8	0.041	0.256	0.409	0.386	0.268
AST%	**TOV%**	**OREB%**	**DREB%**	**STL%**	**BLK%**
5.8	28.5	8.5	18.4	0.3	1.7
PER	**ORTG**	**DRTG**	**WS/48**	**VOL**	
6.00	82.1	114.7	-0.017	0.074	

- Traded from Dallas to Oklahoma City in January 2020, missed most of the season due to a right foot injury
- When healthy spent most of last season in the G-League with the Texas Legends and Oklahoma City Blue
- Used as a low volume shooter off the ball, went 10-for-25 (40%) on threes in the G-League
- Mostly a stationary shooter, does not shoot off the dribble or on the move
- Shooting stroke is still inconsistent, made less than 60% of his free throws in the G-League
- Energetic athlete that can cut off the ball and crash the offensive boards to score on put-backs
- Shows some passing skills, fairly turnover prone in the G-League
- 2019-20 Defensive Degree of Difficulty: 0.104, played only 11 minutes of garbage time at the NBA level
- Forced a miss in his only NBA possession when defending an isolation
- Forced a miss in his only pick-and-roll possession at the NBA level
- Forced two misses, allowed Marco Belinelli to make a three in his only three spot-up possessions in the NBA
- Very active help defender in the G-League, good defensive rebounder, excellent shot blocker, posted a high Steal Percentage

Admiral Schofield	Height	Weight	Cap #	Years Left
	6'5"	241	$1.518M	1

	Similar at Age	22	
		Season	SIMsc
1	Quincy Pondexter	2010-11	888.5
2	Juan Hernangomez	2017-18	887.9
3	Wayne Selden	2016-17	884.9
4	Allen Crabbe	2014-15	883.9
5	Sterling Brown	2017-18	879.6
6	Jae Crowder	2012-13	878.4
7	P.J. Hairston	2014-15	877.4
8	DaJuan Summers	2009-10	870.5
9	Donte DiVincenzo	2018-19	868.4
10	Darius Miller	2012-13	866.8

Baseline Basic Stats

MPG	PTS	AST	REB	BLK	STL
16.1	5.4	0.9	2.4	0.2	0.5

Advanced Metrics

USG%	3PTA/FGA	FTA/FGA	TS%	eFG%	3PT%
13.8	0.549	0.188	0.533	0.509	0.338
AST%	**TOV%**	**OREB%**	**DREB%**	**STL%**	**BLK%**
6.8	9.2	2.7	12.3	1.3	0.8
PER	**ORTG**	**DRTG**	**WS/48**	**VOL**	
8.64	107.0	113.4	0.052	0.409	

- Fringe rotation player for Washington in his rookie season, spent some time in the G-League with the Capital City Go-Go
- Below break-even three-point shooter in the NBA, made 37% of his threes in the G-League
- Mostly a stationary spot-up shooter, solid mid-range shooter in a small sample of attempts
- Effective at rolling to the rim and cutting off the ball, good at running the floor in transition to get layups
- Strictly a catch-and-shoot player at the NBA level, not really a passer, rarely turns the ball over
- 2019-20 Defensive Degree of Difficulty: 0.321, tends to guard second unit players
- Rarely tested on the perimeter in isolation situations, struggled in the post against bigger players
- Below average when guarding pick-and-rolls, tended to go too far under screens
- Very good at closing out on perimeter shooters, had trouble defending dribble hand-offs in a small sample of possessions
- Stay-at-home defender, fairly solid defensive rebounder, does not really get steals or blocks

Zylan Cheatham	Height	Weight	Cap #	Years Left
	6'5"	220	$1.446M	2

Similar at Age 24

		Season	SIMsc
1	Joe Cooper	1981-82	836.3
2	Dominic McGuire	2009-10	835.1
3	Jordan Hamilton	2014-15	831.0
4	Andrae Patterson	1999-00	830.1
5	Sam Worthen	1981-82	829.1
6	Alex Poythress	2017-18	824.0
7	Antonio Anderson	2009-10	822.0
8	Jeff Sanders	1989-90	821.7
9	Steve Lingenfelter	1982-83	812.7
10	Pat Connaughton	2016-17	810.6

Baseline Basic Stats

MPG	PTS	AST	REB	BLK	STL
14.2	4.1	0.8	2.5	0.4	0.3

Advanced Metrics

USG%	3PTA/FGA	FTA/FGA	TS%	eFG%	3PT%
13.2	0.208	0.185	0.582	0.556	0.141
AST%	**TOV%**	**OREB%**	**DREB%**	**STL%**	**BLK%**
8.2	19.0	6.9	12.9	1.0	2.6
PER	**ORTG**	**DRTG**	**WS/48**	**VOL**	
9.37	106.0	110.7	0.065	0.219	

- Played on a Two-Way contract, spent most of the season in the G-League with the Erie BayHawks
- Waived by Oklahoma City in December 2020, just before this book was finalized
- Used in the G-League as a low volume, rim runner and stretch big
- Active rim runner that can cut off the ball and roll to the rim, posted a True Shooting Percentage of almost 65% with Erie last season
- Great at running the floor in transition, good offensive rebounder that can score on put-backs
- Flashed some stretch potential, break-even three-point shooter in the G-League, mainly a spot-up shooter at this stage
- Shows solid secondary playmaking skills, slightly turnover prone
- 2019-20 Defensive Degree of Difficulty: 0.232, mostly played in garbage time
- Not really tested on the ball, forced a miss in his only possession when guarding post-ups
- Struggled in eight pick-and-roll possessions, allowed 10 points, better at guarding the roll man, struggled to stay with ball handlers
- Fairly good at forcing misses in spot-up situations, allowed one made three on six shot attempts
- Great defensive rebounder, fairly active help defender, got steals and blocks at a solid rate in the G-League

Newcomers

Aleksej Pokusevski

Height	Weight	Cap #	Years Left
7'0"	201	$2.965M	1 + 2 TO

Baseline Basic Stats

MPG	PTS	AST	REB	BLK	STL
13.2	4.8	0.6	2.9	0.5	0.5

Advanced Metrics

USG%	3PTA/FGA	FTA/FGA	TS%	eFG%	3PT%
19.6	0.126	0.369	0.525	0.488	0.197

AST%	TOV%	OREB%	DREB%	STL%	BLK%
7.4	16.6	6.7	14.5	1.6	2.1

PER	ORTG	DRTG	WS/48	VOL
13.96	98.4	109.5	0.189	N/A

- Drafted by Minnesota with the 17th overall pick, traded to Oklahoma City
- Played for Olympiakos in two minutes of EuroLeague action, spent most of 2019-20 in the Greek A2 League
- Good playmaking potential, good at using his height to scan defense to find open teammates
- Tends to be careless with the ball, fairly turnover prone, often tries to do too much
- Above average ball handler, shifty player that can get to his spots, tends to over-dribble into traffic
- Can post up smaller players, good footwork, has soft touch inside
- Below break-even three-point shooter, can be streaky, mechanics are inconsistent, prone to taking questionable shots
- Great length, solid quickness, fairly good athlete, good shot blocker and defensive rebounder
- More of a project defensively, still learning to make proper rotations, effort level is inconsistent
- Can lose focus off the ball, tends to get caught ball watching, will leave shooters open on the perimeter
- Not always engaged, slow to get back on defense, does not always pressure his man on the ball
- If engaged, shows good quickness to stay with opponents, good at using length to contest shots
- Thin frame, needs to add strength, could benefit by staying overseas to get additional seasoning and fill out more physically

MINNESOTA TIMBERWOLVES

Last Season: 19 – 45, Missed the Playoffs

Offensive Rating: 108.1, 24th in the NBA

Defensive Rating: 112.2, 21st in the NBA

Primary Executive: Gersson Rosas, President of Basketball Operations

Head Coach: Ryan Saunders

Key Roster Changes

Subtractions
Jacob Evans, trade
Omari Spellman, trade
James Johnson, trade
Evan Turner, free agency

Additions
Anthony Edwards, draft
Jaden McDaniels, draft
Ricky Rubio, trade
Ed Davis, trade

Roster

Likely Starting Five
1. *Ricky Rubio*
2. *DeAngelo Russell*
3. *Anthony Edwards*
4. Juan Hernangomez
5. *Karl-Anthony Towns*

Other Key Rotation Players
Malik Beasley
Josh Okogie
Jarrett Culver
Jake Layman
Jaden McDaniels

* Italics denotes that a player is likely to be on the floor to close games

Remaining Roster

- Ed Davis
- Naz Reid
- Jarred Vanderbilt
- Jaylen Nowell
- Ashton Hagans, 21, 6'3", 198, Kentucky (Two-Way)
- Rondae Hollis-Jefferson, 26, 6'6", 217, Arizona (Exhibit 10)
- Tyler Cook, 23, 6'8", 255, Iowa (Exhibit 10)
- Ade Murkey, 23, 6'5", 201, Denver (Exhibit 10)

SCHREMPF Base Rating: 32.3 (72-game season)

Strengths

- Potentially dynamic individual talents in Karl-Anthony Towns, DeAngelo Russell and Anthony Edwards

Question Marks

- Have not implemented a distinct system to be effective on either side of the ball
- Uncertain ability of the coaching staff to develop the other players around Towns
- Lots of new pieces or inexperience on the team, may not be conducive to a cohesive rotation

Outlook

- Still in a rebuilding stage, likely to be a lottery team in the 2020-21 season

Veterans

Karl-Anthony Towns

Height	Weight	Cap #	Years Left
6'11"	248	$29.468M	3

Similar at Age 24

		Season	SIMsc
1	Charlie Villanueva	2008-09	905.4
2	Joel Embiid	2018-19	894.4
3	Julius Randle	2018-19	893.2
4	Tim Duncan*	2000-01	884.5
5	Mehmet Okur	2003-04	884.0
6	Enes Kanter	2016-17	878.5
7	Markieff Morris	2013-14	872.7
8	Al Jefferson	2008-09	869.6
9	Amar'e Stoudemire	2006-07	869.5
10	Blake Griffin	2013-14	867.4

Baseline Basic Stats

MPG	PTS	AST	REB	BLK	STL
31.4	18.6	3.1	9.8	1.2	0.8

Advanced Metrics

USG%	3PTA/FGA	FTA/FGA	TS%	eFG%	3PT%
26.8	0.299	0.349	0.607	0.559	0.384
AST%	**TOV%**	**OREB%**	**DREB%**	**STL%**	**BLK%**
19.4	12.6	8.4	27.7	1.3	3.0
PER	**ORTG**	**DRTG**	**WS/48**	**VOL**	
24.49	117.8	107.5	0.194	0.318	

- Missed most of the season due to a sprained left knee and fractured left wrist
- Posted highest per-minute efficiency last season, one of the top centers in the NBA when healthy
- Good post-up player that can score on either block, excellent face-up game to score on isolations
- Excellent stretch big that has made over 40% of his threes in each of the last three seasons
- Mostly a stand-still shooter, great at making spot-up jumpers, average at shooting on the move
- Excellent rim runner that can cut off the ball and roll to the rim on pick-and-rolls, solid offensive rebounder that scores on put-backs
- Great passing big man, set a career high in Assist Percentage last season, good at limiting turnovers
- 2019-20 Defensive Degree of Difficulty: 0.440
- Tended to guard starter level big men, served as Minnesota's primary rim protector
- Good shot blocker and defensive rebounder, solid rim protector last season, fairly good at staying vertical to contest shots
- Above average on-ball defender, good at using his length to contest shots in the post, backs off too much when defending in space
- Average pick-and-roll defender, inconsistent when making rotations, either sags too far into the paint to allow jump shots or is late to cover the roll man
- Does not always come out to contest perimeter shots

D'Angelo Russell

Height	Weight	Cap #	Years Left
6'4"	198	$28.649M	2

Similar at Age 23

		Season	SIMsc
1	Jordan Crawford	2011-12	910.9
2	Derrick Rose	2011-12	909.4
3	Brandon Knight	2014-15	898.5
4	Rashad McCants	2007-08	897.9
5	Jerryd Bayless	2011-12	893.7
6	Zach LaVine	2018-19	893.0
7	Marcus Thornton	2010-11	891.9
8	John Wall	2013-14	891.8
9	Kyrie Irving	2015-16	888.9
10	Ben Gordon	2006-07	886.1

Baseline Basic Stats

MPG	PTS	AST	REB	BLK	STL
30.3	18.6	5.0	3.6	0.3	1.0

Advanced Metrics

USG%	3PTA/FGA	FTA/FGA	TS%	eFG%	3PT%
29.7	0.438	0.229	0.559	0.519	0.369

AST%	TOV%	OREB%	DREB%	STL%	BLK%
33.3	13.4	1.9	11.5	1.6	0.8

PER	ORTG	DRTG	WS/48	VOL
19.23	108.8	112.0	0.102	0.423

- Regular starter for Golden State and Minnesota last season, traded to Minnesota in February 2020
- In-and-out of Golden State's lineup due to a series of minor injuries
- Maintained his effective in his role as a primary ball handler, very good playmaker, consistently avoided turnovers
- Took threes at a higher rate, above average three-point shooter overall, good at making spot-up jumpers and coming off screens
- Good pick-and-roll ball handler and isolation player, can make shots off the dribble, got to the rim with more frequency, drew more fouls last season
- 2019-20 Defensive Degree of Difficulty: 0.408
- Hidden a bit in favorable matchups against lower leverage starters
- Below average on-ball defender, has the quickness to stay with perimeter players on drives, gives up too much space for his man to take jump shots
- Below average at guarding pick-and-rolls, does not look to take any specific action away, not especially effective at switching
- Tends to late when closing out on perimeter shooters, does not always fight through screens off the ball
- Solid on the defensive glass, Steal and Block Percentages are still consistent with his career averages

Ricky Rubio

Height	Weight	Cap #	Years Left
6'3"	190	$17.000M	1

Similar at Age 29

		Season	SIMsc
1	Jay Humphries	1991-92	932.1
2	Jamaal Tinsley	2007-08	931.0
3	Jeff Teague	2017-18	930.8
4	Jeff Hornacek	1992-93	929.0
5	Chris Childs	1996-97	928.9
6	Deron Williams	2013-14	927.7
7	Steve Nash*	2003-04	920.9
8	Gilbert Arenas	2010-11	920.8
9	Anthony Johnson	2003-04	916.2
10	Mike James	2004-05	913.3

Baseline Basic Stats

MPG	PTS	AST	REB	BLK	STL
29.7	12.5	5.5	2.9	0.2	1.1

Advanced Metrics

USG%	3PTA/FGA	FTA/FGA	TS%	eFG%	3PT%
20.6	0.309	0.299	0.530	0.473	0.346
AST%	**TOV%**	**OREB%**	**DREB%**	**STL%**	**BLK%**
31.8	16.4	2.1	11.3	2.0	0.5
PER	**ORTG**	**DRTG**	**WS/48**	**VOL**	
15.16	108.8	108.9	0.109	0.346	

- Solid starter for Phoenix in his first season with the team
- Increased his production in a moderate volume role as a ball handling distributor
- Excellent playmaker with great court vision to find open teammates, somewhat turnover prone
- Made threes at above the league average last season, usually better at making corner threes
- Mainly a stationary spot-up shooter, effective at making outside shots on dribble hand-offs last season
- Occasionally can sneak by defender on isolations, can get into the lane for floaters on pick-and-rolls
- Not a dynamic scorer, struggles to shoot on the move or off the dribble
- 2019-20 Defensive Degree of Difficulty: 0.420
- Tends to defend starting level guards, sometimes takes on tougher guard assignments
- Played middling on-ball defense last season, good against taller perimeter players in the post, struggled to stay with elite guards on the perimeter
- Good pick-and-roll defender, effective on switches, fights over screens to contain ball handlers
- Tends to gamble for steals off the ball, can be out of position to contest perimeter shots
- Active help defender, solid defensive rebounder, gets steals at a high rate, but Steal Percentage has been declining for the last two or three seasons

Juan Hernangómez	Height	Weight	Cap #	Years Left
	6'9"	220	$6.493M	2

	Similar at Age	24	
		Season	SIMsc
1	Dorian Finney-Smith	2017-18	930.4
2	James Jones	2004-05	924.9
3	Jake Layman	2018-19	922.8
4	Luke Babbitt	2013-14	921.5
5	Shawne Williams	2010-11	919.6
6	Bostjan Nachbar	2004-05	917.3
7	Qyntel Woods	2005-06	915.9
8	Victor Claver	2012-13	913.3
9	Matt Bullard	1991-92	907.5
10	James Ennis	2014-15	907.3

Baseline Basic Stats

MPG	PTS	AST	REB	BLK	STL
19.1	6.6	1.0	3.4	0.3	0.5

Advanced Metrics

USG%	3PTA/FGA	FTA/FGA	TS%	eFG%	3PT%
15.4	0.513	0.247	0.535	0.504	0.346
AST%	**TOV%**	**OREB%**	**DREB%**	**STL%**	**BLK%**
7.3	10.2	5.0	17.2	1.2	1.2
PER	**ORTG**	**DRTG**	**WS/48**	**VOL**	
11.10	108.5	111.5	0.062	0.315	

- Fringe rotation for Denver, became a starter for Minnesota after the trade in February 2020
- Played a role for both teams as a low volume, spot-up shooter, more effective with Minnesota
- Just above break-even on threes overall, made 42% of his threes in Minnesota
- Good spot-up shooter, also effective as the screener on pick-and-pop plays
- Solid at using the on-ball screen to get an extra step to the rim on dribble hand-offs
- Does not really create his own shot, fairly decent cutter off the ball, runs the floor in transition to get layups
- Catch-and-shoot player, limited passing skills, rarely turns the ball over
- 2019-20 Defensive Degree of Difficulty: 0.371
- Tends to guard second unit level players or lower leverage starters
- Not tested very often on the ball, decent at defending perimeter players on isolations, can be bullied inside by stronger post players
- Below average pick-and-roll defender, can allow ball handlers to turn the corner, better at switching
- Generally fights through screens away from the ball, tends to be either late or too aggressive when closing out on perimeter shooters
- Good defensive rebounder, Steal and Block Percentages are still consistent with his career averages

Malik Beasley	Height	Weight	Cap #	Years Left
	6'4"	198	$13.326M	2 + TO

	Similar at Age	23	
		Season	SIMsc
1	Austin Rivers	2015-16	941.9
2	Ben McLemore	2016-17	934.8
3	Buddy Hield	2016-17	932.9
4	C.J. McCollum	2014-15	931.7
5	Sasha Vujacic	2007-08	930.3
6	Terrence Ross	2014-15	930.3
7	Wayne Ellington	2010-11	928.6
8	Voshon Lenard	1996-97	925.4
9	Tony Snell	2014-15	922.5
10	Wesley Person	1994-95	918.0

Baseline Basic Stats

MPG	PTS	AST	REB	BLK	STL
23.9	9.9	1.7	2.5	0.2	0.8

Advanced Metrics

USG%	3PTA/FGA	FTA/FGA	TS%	eFG%	3PT%
19.9	0.516	0.152	0.552	0.527	0.390
AST%	**TOV%**	**OREB%**	**DREB%**	**STL%**	**BLK%**
10.5	8.9	1.8	10.6	1.6	0.6
PER	**ORTG**	**DRTG**	**WS/48**	**VOL**	
13.26	109.0	111.4	0.075	0.277	

- Fringe rotation player for Denver, became a starter after the trade to Minnesota in February 2020
- Used as a higher volume scoring guard, much more effective in Minnesota with more playing time
- Has made almost 40% of his threes over the last two seasons, better in the corners, has made almost 43% of his career corner threes
- Excellent spot-up shooter, good at making pull-up jumpers as the pick-and-roll ball handler
- Better at making shots off screens in previous seasons, good cutter off the ball
- Below average effectiveness on isolation plays, doesn't handle the ball well enough to get all the way to the rim
- More of a catch-and-shoot player, limited playmaker skills, rarely turns the ball over
- 2019-20 Defensive Degree of Difficulty: 0.368
- Hidden in favorable matchups against lower leverage offensive players
- Rarely tested on the ball, played solid on-ball defense in a small sample of possessions, good quickness to stop opponents from driving
- Below average pick-and-roll defender, tends to go too far under screens, has trouble guarding bigger players on switches
- Tends to get caught on screens, good at closing out on perimeter shooters
- Posted the highest Defensive Rebound Percentage of his career, steal and block rates are still consistent with his career averages

Josh Okogie

	Height	Weight	Cap #	Years Left
	6'4"	212	$2.651M	Team Option

	Similar at Age	21 Season	SIMsc
1	Marcus Smart	2015-16	925.3
2	Gary Harris	2015-16	911.6
3	James Harden	2010-11	905.6
4	Isaiah Whitehead	2016-17	904.2
5	Christian Eyenga	2010-11	903.3
6	Kelly Oubre	2016-17	900.8
7	Rashad McCants	2005-06	900.4
8	Mickael Pietrus	2003-04	897.9
9	Casey Jacobsen	2002-03	895.3
10	Timothe Luwawu-Cabarrot	2016-17	891.8

Baseline Basic Stats

MPG	PTS	AST	REB	BLK	STL
23.6	9.2	1.9	3.1	0.2	1.0

Advanced Metrics

USG%	3PTA/FGA	FTA/FGA	TS%	eFG%	3PT%
17.1	0.309	0.380	0.531	0.472	0.293
AST%	**TOV%**	**OREB%**	**DREB%**	**STL%**	**BLK%**
11.4	14.1	3.7	10.9	2.1	1.0
PER	**ORTG**	**DRTG**	**WS/48**	**VOL**	
11.28	105.0	111.6	0.069	0.396	

- Regular rotation player for Minnesota in his second season, started some games in 2019-20
- Predominantly a low volume, spot-up shooter, increased his effectiveness last season
- Took fewer long twos, got to the rim more frequently, drew fouls at a higher rate
- Better off the ball, very good cutter, good at crashing the offensive glass to score on put-backs
- Not as effective with the ball in his hands, can drive to the rim, struggles to make shots off the dribble
- Below average spot-up shooter, has made less than 30% of his threes in his two seasons in the league
- Slightly improving as a passer, a bit more turnover prone
- 2019-20 Defensive Degree of Difficulty: 0.525
- Tends to take on tougher assignments against top perimeter players
- Good on-ball defender that can guard multiple positions
- Good pick-and-roll defender, can switch to cover the roll man, fights over screens to contain ball handlers
- Gambles a bit too much, gets caught out of position trying to shoot the gap when chasing shooters off screens, not always disciplined when closing out on perimeter shooters
- Active help defender, gets steals and blocks at a fairly high rate, good defensive rebounder for his size

Jarrett Culver	Height	Weight	Cap #	Years Left
	6'6"	195	$6.104M	2 Team Options

Similar at Age **20**

		Season	SIMsc
1	Ben McLemore	2013-14	901.6
2	Lonzo Ball	2017-18	900.8
3	Rashad Vaughn	2016-17	900.4
4	DerMarr Johnson	2000-01	895.5
5	Alec Burks	2011-12	894.7
6	Nicolas Batum	2008-09	892.8
7	Kevin Huerter	2018-19	887.7
8	Shai Gilgeous-Alexander	2018-19	887.6
9	J.R. Smith	2005-06	883.2
10	Maurice Harkless	2013-14	881.0

Baseline Basic Stats

MPG	PTS	AST	REB	BLK	STL
25.0	10.1	2.0	3.1	0.4	0.8

Advanced Metrics

USG%	3PTA/FGA	FTA/FGA	TS%	eFG%	3PT%
19.9	0.440	0.201	0.514	0.496	0.344
AST%	**TOV%**	**OREB%**	**DREB%**	**STL%**	**BLK%**
11.9	11.6	3.3	10.6	1.7	1.4
PER	**ORTG**	**DRTG**	**WS/48**	**VOL**	
11.73	101.1	111.7	0.046	0.423	

- Regular rotation player for Minnesota in his rookie season, starter for most of 2019-20
- Struggled to shoot efficiently in his role as a low volume, spot-up shooter
- Had difficulty adjusting to analytic-style shot selection, almost avoided the mid-range entirely
- Made less than 30% of his threes, drew fouls but shot below 50% on free throws, could make shots inside of three feet
- Most effective at using an on-ball screen to get an extra step to the rim on dribble hand-offs
- Solid at moving off the ball, can make shots off screens, decent cutter, can crash the offensive glass to score on put-backs
- Shown some decent secondary playmaking skills, good at limiting turnovers
- <u>2019-20 Defensive Degree of Difficulty</u>: 0.377
- Tended to guard second unit level players or lower leverage starters
- Played fairly solid on-ball defense, good at taking away air space to guard jump shots, occasionally can be beat off the dribble by quicker guards
- Above average pick-and-roll defender, good on switches, tends to go too far under screens
- Fights through screens off the ball, sometimes can be late when closing out on perimeter shooters
- Fairly active help defender, got blocks and steals at a fairly high rate, decent defensive rebounder

Jake Layman

	Height	Weight	Cap #	Years Left
Jake Layman	6'8"	209	$3.761M	1

	Similar at Age	25	
		Season	**SIMsc**
1	Rodney Carney	2009-10	938.0
2	DerMarr Johnson	2005-06	936.4
3	Hollis Thompson	2016-17	931.0
4	Antoine Wright	2009-10	930.2
5	Martell Webster	2011-12	926.0
6	Travis Outlaw	2009-10	925.8
7	Chase Budinger	2013-14	925.1
8	Wesley Johnson	2012-13	924.4
9	Brandon Rush	2010-11	924.2
10	Sam Mack	1995-96	924.0

Baseline Basic Stats

MPG	PTS	AST	REB	BLK	STL
21.1	8.1	1.0	2.9	0.3	0.6

Advanced Metrics

USG%	3PTA/FGA	FTA/FGA	TS%	eFG%	3PT%
17.2	0.398	0.184	0.546	0.520	0.340
AST%	**TOV%**	**OREB%**	**DREB%**	**STL%**	**BLK%**
6.7	10.4	3.5	11.1	1.4	1.4
PER	**ORTG**	**DRTG**	**WS/48**	**VOL**	
11.56	106.2	111.5	0.063	0.421	

- Missed most of last season due to a toe injury, regular rotation player for Minnesota when healthy
- Mainly used as a low volume spot-up shooter
- Made threes at a break-even rate last season, below break-even three-point shooter for his career
- Good at attacking aggressive close-outs, can use an on-ball screen to get to the rim on dribble hand-offs
- Effective at making backdoor cuts off the ball, does not really create his own shot at this stage
- Catch-and-shoot player, limited as a playmaker, good at avoiding turnovers
- 2019-20 Defensive Degree of Difficulty: 0.374
- Tended to guard second unit level players or lower leverage starters
- Average on-ball defender, quick enough to take away the drives
- Can be backed up down in the post by stronger players, tends to give up space for his man to take jump shots
- Below average pick-and-roll defender, struggles to handle bigger players on switches, can allow ball handlers to turn the corner
- Consistently closes out on perimeter shooters, can get caught on screens off the ball
- Decent on the defensive boards, steal and block rates are still consistent with his career averages

Ed Davis

	Height	Weight	Cap #	Years Left
	6'9"	225	$5.005M	UFA

	Similar at Age	**30**	
		Season	**SIMsc**
1	Major Jones	1983-84	919.4
2	Adam Keefe	2000-01	918.0
3	Darnell Hillman	1979-80	912.4
4	Sam Pellom	1981-82	909.7
5	Terry Davis	1997-98	909.2
6	Kermit Washington	1981-82	907.5
7	Andrew DeClercq	2003-04	904.4
8	Greg Anderson	1994-95	903.2
9	Ray Tolbert	1988-89	902.4
10	Louis Amundson	2012-13	900.7

Baseline Basic Stats

MPG	PTS	AST	REB	BLK	STL
14.0	3.9	0.4	4.6	0.4	0.4

Advanced Metrics

USG%	3PTA/FGA	FTA/FGA	TS%	eFG%	3PT%
11.8	0.003	0.414	0.540	0.517	0.000
AST%	**TOV%**	**OREB%**	**DREB%**	**STL%**	**BLK%**
4.8	18.0	13.4	27.3	1.5	2.2
PER	**ORTG**	**DRTG**	**WS/48**	**VOL**	
12.34	112.6	104.1	0.114	0.243	

- Fringe rotation player for Utah last season, missed games due to a fractured fibula in his left leg, back spasms and a left knee injury
- Production declined sharply, primarily a low volume rim runner throughout his career
- Has made almost 68% of his shots inside of three feet in his career
- Struggled to finish shots inside, did not have the lift to finish in traffic, had trouble scoring as a roll man and cutter
- Highly active big man, still a good offensive rebounder, efficiently finishes his put-back attempts
- No real shooting range outside of ten feet, not really a passer, fairly turnover prone last season
- 2019-20 Defensive Degree of Difficulty: 0.329, tended to guard second unit big men
- Average rim protector, good defensive rebounder, solid shot blocker, highly foul prone
- Solid on-ball defender, good at contesting shots in the post, mobile enough to defend big men in space
- Middling pick-and-roll defender, good in drop coverages, struggles to stay with quicker ball handlers
- Does not always come out to contest perimeter shots in spot-up situations

Naz Reid

	Height	Weight	Cap #	Years Left
Naz Reid	6'9"	264	$1.518M	1 + TO

	Similar at Age	20 Season	SIMsc
1	Jeremy Tyler	2011-12	874.1
2	Zach Randolph	2001-02	869.7
3	Harry Giles	2018-19	867.6
4	Al Jefferson	2004-05	863.2
5	Marquese Chriss	2017-18	851.0
6	Samaki Walker	1996-97	846.2
7	Ryan Anderson	2008-09	845.1
8	Jackie Butler	2005-06	843.3
9	Jared Sullinger	2012-13	842.6
10	Tobias Harris	2012-13	841.7

Baseline Basic Stats

MPG	PTS	AST	REB	BLK	STL
20.7	9.1	1.2	5.6	0.7	0.6

Advanced Metrics

USG%	3PTA/FGA	FTA/FGA	TS%	eFG%	3PT%
22.6	0.253	0.240	0.532	0.503	0.344
AST%	**TOV%**	**OREB%**	**DREB%**	**STL%**	**BLK%**
11.0	9.7	8.1	20.4	1.6	2.6
PER	**ORTG**	**DRTG**	**WS/48**	**VOL**	
16.76	108.5	107.9	0.107	0.627	

- Split time between Minnesota and the Iowa Wolves in the G-League
- Used as a stretch big off the bench in a higher volume role
- Made almost 39% of his threes in the G-League, shot just below break-even on threes at the NBA level
- More of a stand-still spot-up shooter at this stage, much better in the corners, made almost 47% of his corner threes at the NBA level
- Solid rim runner, effective at scoring on rolls to the rim or cuts off the ball
- Limited as a post-up player, solid passing big man that rarely turns the ball over
- 2019-20 Defensive Degree of Difficulty: 0.383, tended to guard second unit big men
- Good shot blocker and solid defensive rebounder, active hands, gets steals at a high rate
- Below average rim protector, tends to be undisciplined with his positioning, highly foul prone
- Below average post defender, can be baited into committing shooting fouls, shows some mobility to defend in space on isolations
- Below average at guarding pick-and-rolls, decent on switches, tends to late when rotating to cover the roll man
- Consistently comes out to contest perimeter shots

Jarred Vanderbilt	Height	Weight	Cap #	Years Left
	6'9"	214	$1.664M	RFA

	Similar at Age	**20**	
		Season	**SIMsc**
1	Julian Wright	2007-08	854.8
2	Gerald Wallace	2002-03	848.6
3	Kevon Looney	2016-17	846.4
4	Ivan Rabb	2017-18	842.9
5	Al-Farouq Aminu	2010-11	842.2
6	Antonis Fotsis	2001-02	839.4
7	Chris Wilcox	2002-03	835.5
8	Paul George	2010-11	831.7
9	Trevor Ariza	2005-06	828.8
10	Chinanu Onuaku	2016-17	828.1

Baseline Basic Stats

MPG	PTS	AST	REB	BLK	STL
18.7	6.6	1.1	4.2	0.5	0.8

Advanced Metrics

USG%	3PTA/FGA	FTA/FGA	TS%	eFG%	3PT%
17.0	0.110	0.319	0.586	0.541	0.149
AST%	**TOV%**	**OREB%**	**DREB%**	**STL%**	**BLK%**
8.3	24.7	8.2	17.6	2.7	1.5
PER	**ORTG**	**DRTG**	**WS/48**	**VOL**	
12.70	98.5	106.4	0.070	0.712	

- Did not play much for Denver and Minnesota, spent most of the season in the G-League with three different teams
- Mostly a low volume rim runner at the NBA level, took on more volume in the G-League
- Has made 65% of his shots inside of three feet in two NBA seasons
- Can score on cuts off the ball, rolls to the rim, very active offensive rebounder
- Energetic player with great athleticism, runs hard down the floor in transition
- Trying to shoot threes, shooting is still inconsistent, improving as a passer, highly turnover prone at this stage
- 2019-20 Defensive Degree of Difficulty: 0.247
- Only played 46 NBA minutes, tends to play in garbage time
- Some potential to protect the rim, great shot blocker and defensive rebounder in the G-League
- Has been undisciplined as a position defender in limited NBA minutes, highly foul prone
- Flashed the ability to be solid on-ball defender, quick enough to stay with perimeter players, shows solid strength to play post defense
- Effective at guarding pick-and-roll in a small sample of possessions, potential to switch and guard multiple positions
- Not particularly disciplined when closing out on perimeter shooters, tends to be either late or too aggressive

Jaylen Nowell	Height	Weight	Cap #	Years Left
	6'4"	196	$1.518M	1 + TO

	Similar at Age	20	
		Season	SIMsc
1	Austin Rivers	2012-13	888.6
2	Sasha Vujacic	2004-05	887.4
3	Cory Joseph	2011-12	882.7
4	Jeremy Lamb	2012-13	878.9
5	Frank Ntilikina	2018-19	878.0
6	Ben McLemore	2013-14	877.7
7	Malik Beasley	2016-17	874.4
8	Frank Jackson	2018-19	873.6
9	Gary Harris	2014-15	868.4
10	Emmanuel Mudiay	2016-17	866.4

Baseline Basic Stats

MPG	PTS	AST	REB	BLK	STL
18.8	7.2	1.5	1.9	0.2	0.6

Advanced Metrics

USG%	3PTA/FGA	FTA/FGA	TS%	eFG%	3PT%
17.5	0.501	0.247	0.529	0.472	0.258
AST%	**TOV%**	**OREB%**	**DREB%**	**STL%**	**BLK%**
15.2	8.3	1.7	7.7	1.4	0.6
PER	**ORTG**	**DRTG**	**WS/48**	**VOL**	
11.92	111.3	114.3	0.073	0.430	

- Spent most of last season playing in the G-League for the Iowa Wolves
- Low volume, spot-up shooter at the NBA level, took on more volume in the G-League
- Ranked in the top ten in Three-Point Percentage last season in the G-League, made over 44% of his threes
- Flashed some ability to be effective as a pick-and-roll ball handler at the NBA level, could finish at the rim, solid secondary playmaker that limits turnovers
- Moved off the ball in a small sample of NBA possessions, fairly good at making backdoor cuts and shooting off screens
- 2019-20 Defensive Degree of Difficulty: 0.313, tended to guard second unit level players
- Rarely tested on the ball, played below average on-ball defense in a small sample of possessions
- Fairly solid pick-and-roll defender that could funnel his man into help or switch to guard the screener
- Solid at closing out on perimeter shooters, tended to get caught on screens off the ball
- Solid defensive rebounding guard in the G-League, did not really get steals, posted a fairly high Block Percentage for his size

Newcomers

Anthony Edwards

	Height	Weight	Cap #	Years Left
	6'5"	225	$9.757M	1 + 2 TO

Baseline Basic Stats

MPG	PTS	AST	REB	BLK	STL
21.2	9.0	1.6	2.6	0.2	0.6

Advanced Metrics

USG%	3PTA/FGA	FTA/FGA	TS%	eFG%	3PT%
20.7	0.402	0.229	0.504	0.470	0.311

AST%	TOV%	OREB%	DREB%	STL%	BLK%
14.3	11.7	2.4	10.7	1.5	0.8

PER	ORTG	DRTG	WS/48	VOL
12.38	98.6	106.4	0.060	N/A

- Drafted by Minnesota with the 1st overall pick
- Named SEC Rookie of the Year in 2019-20, made the All-SEC 2nd Team last season
- Explosive athlete, can potentially be a primary ball handler at the NBA level
- Good isolation player and pick-and-roll ball handler at Georgia, regularly beats his man off the dribble, willing to absorb contact inside to draw fouls
- Dynamic transition player, good at making backdoor cuts off the ball
- Has decent playmaking skills, still not a natural passer, does not always spot open teammates, can hold the ball too long
- Not a consistent outside shooter at Georgia, made less than 30% of his threes, mechanics are inconsistent
- Good defensive potential, great athletic tools, rarely challenged in college
- Used as a weak side roamer, good at playing passing lanes to get steals, can occasionally block shots, good defensive rebounder
- Tends to ball watch, can his lose track of his man off the ball, gambles a bit too much
- Effort level was inconsistent, not active in pressuring ball handlers, did not really fight through screens in pick-and-roll situations

Jaden McDaniels

	Height	Weight	Cap #	Years Left
	6'9"	200	$1.965M	1 + 2 TO

Baseline Basic Stats

MPG	PTS	AST	REB	BLK	STL
22.9	8.9	1.4	4.0	0.6	0.7

Advanced Metrics

USG%	3PTA/FGA	FTA/FGA	TS%	eFG%	3PT%
18.7	0.262	0.314	0.514	0.474	0.317

AST%	TOV%	OREB%	DREB%	STL%	BLK%
10.8	14.3	5.0	14.3	1.5	2.3

PER	ORTG	DRTG	WS/48	VOL
12.68	98.3	101.0	0.078	N/A

- Drafted by the L.A. Lakers with the 28th overall pick, traded to Minnesota via Oklahoma City
- Still unpolished on offense, flashes many skills, production inconsistent at Washington
- Great athlete, fluidly glides into open spaces, explosive finisher at the rim
- Decent ball handler that can make long jumpers, doesn't always go strong to the rim, better with an on-ball screen
- Above break-even three-point shooter, better as a stationary spot-up shooter, mechanics can be thrown off when he has to shoot on the move
- Willing to make the extra pass, can be careless with the ball, rarely looks to move off the ball
- Defense tough to project, played almost exclusively in a zone defense at Washington
- Great physical tools, has long arms, solid lateral quickness, great leaping ability, a bit thin, can be pushed around by bigger players inside
- Effective roamer, good weak side shot blocker, can play passing lanes to get steals, solid defensive rebounder
- Tended to give man too much space to shoot in a small sample of isolation possessions when playing man defense
- Solid at staying attached to shooters off the ball, going at using length to contest shots

My 2020-21 NBA Projections

By now, you have seen how the SCHREMPF forecasting system has projected the performance of every team and player, or you may have just skipped ahead. Even so, these are just my personal thoughts on how the season might play out, based on the information from the system and my own eye test. With that in mind, I took some potentially common real world factors into consideration to adjust the rankings accordingly. As a quick note, the most recent trade involving Russell Westbrook and John Wall is accounted for in this section. With that being said, here are my rankings and predictions from this upcoming 2020-21 season, beginning with the Eastern Conference.

Eastern Conference

	SCHREMPF Rankings		My Rankings
1	Brooklyn	1	**Philadelphia**
2	Philadelphia	2	**Milwaukee**
3	Milwaukee	3	**Brooklyn**
4	Toronto	4	**Boston**
5	Boston	5	**Miami**
6	Miami	6	**Toronto**
7	Indiana	7	Indiana
8	Atlanta	8	**Washington**
9	Washington	9	**Atlanta**
10	Orlando	10	Orlando
11	Chicago	11	Chicago
12	Cleveland	12	Cleveland
13	Detroit	13	Detroit
14	Charlotte	14	Charlotte
15	New York	15	New York

When I looked at the system's projections, I mostly agreed with the rankings of the bottom nine teams. The top six teams in the East are a level above everyone else in the conference, but I felt adjustments needed to made because I have them in a different order than the system. First off, Brooklyn has the most talent and upside in the East. However, they are more likely to rest their stars throughout the season because Kevin Durant is coming back from a serious Achilles tear and Kyrie Irving has also had some injuries. They also have a new coaching staff and are breaking in some new players, so they might drop some games early. This will open the door for some other teams to get some wins early. Most likely, Milwaukee and Philadelphia will finish at the top of the East because both of these teams are expected to play a simplistic style that will allow them to get off to a faster start. I project Philadelphia to come out ahead of Milwaukee because they have fewer new pieces to break into their lineup. From there, I rated Boston and Miami ahead of Toronto because they are well coached teams that have the talent to out-perform their projections. Also, Toronto lost some significant contributors when Marc Gasol and Serge Ibaka left to play for the Lakers and Clippers, respectively. They could feel that loss early, but they are still talented enough to find their footing and finish with a top six seed this coming season. Finally, the Wizards' trade for Russell Westbrook gives them an upgrade over John Wall that should bump them up a few wins and put them solidly in a top eight seed this season.

Western Conference

	SCHREMPF Rankings		My Rankings
1	L.A. Lakers	1	L.A. Lakers
2	L.A. Clippers	2	L.A. Clippers
3	Utah	3	Utah
4	Dallas	4	**Dallas**
5	New Orleans	5	**Denver**
6	Houston	6	**New Orleans**
7	Denver	7	**Houston**
8	Phoenix	8	**Portland**
9	San Antonio	9	**Phoenix**
10	Portland	10	**San Antonio**
11	Memphis	11	**Golden State**
12	Sacramento	12	**Memphis**
13	Golden State	13	**Sacramento**
14	Oklahoma City	14	**Minnesota**
15	Minnesota	15	**Oklahoma City**

In the West, the system has a lot of teams clustered together. However, I have slight disagreements with the order within these clusters. To start off, I agree with the top of the standings because the two teams in Los Angeles are the best teams in the conference, with the Lakers as a heavy favorite. Utah's combination of talent and continuity should allow them to consistently win in the regular season to fall just behind the two main contenders. As you can see from the table above, I have Dallas, Denver and New Orleans as the fourth, fifth and sixth seeds, respectively. I rated Dallas as the best of these three because they made solid moves to improve their defense without weakening their elite offense. Denver lost a couple of their better perimeter defenders, but their continuity and offense should get them a few more wins. The system is pretty bullish on New Orleans, but I knocked them down a spot because it's not certain that Zion Williamson can get through an entire season with a clean bill of health, based on his injury history. Houston drops a bit with their current roster because it's uncertain if Wall return to this previous level of production. Portland usually gets projected lower by my system because they don't usually have great defensive players on paper. Even so, they made some considerable upgrades this offseason to add some quality depth and as a result, I bumped them up a couple of spots. Of the bottom five teams, I have Golden State as the best of this group because last season was a bit of an aberration. Though there's risk that Curry could decline due to his age and injury history, he still is an elite player when he's healthy. If he's anywhere close to his usual self, he could keep Golden State on the fringes of the playoff picture. Finally, I expect Oklahoma City to go to the bottom of the standings because they are now in a full-scale rebuild. Therefore, they will likely sell off some more veterans like George Hill or Trevor Ariza later in the season and take some more losses.

Playoffs

Play-In Tournament

- (E) 7/8 Matchup: Washington beats Indiana (Washington gets the 7th seed)
- (E) 9/10 Matchup: Atlanta beats Orlando
- (E) 7/8 Loser v. 9/10 Winner: Indiana beats Atlanta (Indiana gets the 8th seed)
- (W) 7/8 Matchup: Portland beats Houston (Portland gets the 7th seed)
- (W) 9/10 Matchup: San Antonio beats Phoenix
- (W) 7/8 Loser v. 9/10 Winner: San Antonio beats Houston (San Antonio gets the 8th seed)

First Round

- (E) 1. Philadelphia over 8. Indiana (4 – 2)
- (E) 2. Milwaukee over 7. Washington (4 – 2)
- (E) 3. Brooklyn over 6. Toronto (4 – 2)
- (E) 5. Miami over 4. Boston (4 – 3)
- (W) 1. L.A. Lakers over 8. San Antonio (4 – 1)
- (W) 2. L.A. Clippers over 7. Portland (4 – 2)
- (W) 3. Utah over 6. New Orleans (4 – 2)
- (W) 4. Dallas over 5. Denver (4 – 3)

Second Round

- (E) 5. Miami over 1. Philadelphia (4 – 3)
- (E) 3. Brooklyn over 2. Milwaukee (4 – 2)
- (W) 1. L.A. Lakers over 4. Dallas (4 – 1)
- (W) 2. L.A. Clippers over 3. Utah (4 – 3)

Conference Finals

- (E) 3. Brooklyn over 5. Miami (4 – 3)
- (W) 1. L.A. Lakers over L.A. Clippers (4 – 2)

NBA Finals

- (W) L.A. Lakers over (E) Brooklyn (4 – 2)

THANK YOU

I thank everybody that made this new edition of the preview almanac possible, especially considering the circumstances of this year. I truly appreciate all of my readers and the support that you have given me throughout my years of writing these books. I hope all of you enjoyed reading this book and I look forward to producing more content in the future. If you liked this book and want to read past editions or find out about any future releases, please follow me on my Amazon Author page, which is listed below in the following link:

www.amazon.com/author/rvlhoops

If you have any additional comments or questions, please feel free to contact me using the email address that's listed in the credits section at the beginning of this book. For further updates on any new releases, you can also follow me on Twitter, where my username is @rvlhoops. Once again, thank you to all of my readers for supporting my work. Stay safe and enjoy the 2020-21 NBA season.

Player Index

Dallas Mavericks	
Luka Doncic	321
Kristaps Porzingis	322
Tim Hardaway, Jr.	323
Josh Richardson	324
Dorian Finney-Smith	325
Maxi Kleber	326
Dwight Powell	327
Trey Burke	328
Jalen Brunson	329
Willie Cauley-Stein	330
Boban Marjanovic	331
Wesley Iwundu	332
J.J. Barea	333
Josh Green	334
Tyrell Terry	335
Denver Nuggets	
Nikola Jokic	352
Jamal Murray	353
Will Barton	354
Paul Millsap	355
Gary Harris	356
Michael Porter, Jr.	357
Monte Morris	358
JaMychal Green	359
P.J. Dozier	360
Bol Bol	361
Vlatko Cancar	362
Isaiah Hartenstein	363
Zeke Nnaji	364
R.J. Hampton	365
Facundo Campazzo	366
Detroit Pistons	
Blake Griffin	213
Jerami Grant	214
Delon Wright	215
Mason Plumlee	216
Derrick Rose	217
Sekou Doumbouya	218
Svi Mykhailiuk	219
Josh Jackson	220
Wayne Ellington	221
Jahlil Okafor	222
Dzanan Musa	223
Killian Hayes	224
Isaiah Stewart	225
Saddiq Bey	226
Deividas Sirvydis	227

Orlando Magic	
Nikola Vucevic	150
Aaron Gordon	151
Evan Fournier	152
Markelle Fultz	153
James Ennis	154
Terrence Ross	155
Gary Clark	156
Al-Farouq Aminu	157
Mo Bamba	158
Khem Birch	159
Michael Carter-Williams	160
Dwayne Bacon	161
Jonathan Isaac	162
Chuma Okeke	163
Cole Anthony	164
Philadelphia 76ers	
Ben Simmons	39
Joel Embiid	40
Tobias Harris	41
Danny Green	42
Matisse Thybulle	43
Seth Curry	44
Dwight Howard	45
Shake Milton	46
Furkan Korkmaz	47
Terrance Ferguson	48
Mike Scott	49
Tony Bradley	50
Ryan Broekhoff	51
Derrick Walton, Jr.	52
Tyrese Maxey	53
Isaiah Joe	54
Phoenix Suns	
Devin Booker	368
Chris Paul	369
Deandre Ayton	370
Jae Crowder	371
Dario Saric	372
Mikal Bridges	373
Cameron Johnson	374
Cameron Payne	375
Jevon Carter	376
E'Twaun Moore	377
Langston Galloway	378
Abdel Nader	379
Damian Jones	380
Jalen Smith	381

<u>Portland Trail Blazers</u>	
Damian Lillard	398
C.J. McCollum	399
Jusuf Nurkic	400
Robert Covington	401
Rodney Hood	402
Carmelo Anthony	403
Derrick Jones, Jr.	404
Gary Trent, Jr.	405
Anfernee Simons	406
Zach Collins	407
Enes Kanter	408
Nassir Little	409
Harry Giles	410
C.J. Elleby	411
<u>Sacramento Kings</u>	
De'Aaron Fox	431
Buddy Hield	432
Harrison Barnes	433
Nemanja Bjelica	434
Richaun Holmes	435
Cory Joseph	436
Marvin Bagley III	437
Hassan Whiteside	438
Jabari Parker	439
Glenn Robinson III	440
Frank Kaminsky	441
DaQuan Jeffries	442
Justin James	443
Tyrese Haliburton	444
Robert Woodard	445
Jahmi'us Ramsey	446
<u>San Antonio Spurs</u>	
DeMar DeRozan	383
LaMarcus Aldridge	384
Dejounte Murray	385
Derrick White	386
Lonnie Walker	387
Patty Mills	388
Rudy Gay	389
Trey Lyles	390
Jakob Poeltl	391
Keldon Johnson	392
Drew Eubanks	393
Luka Samanic	394
Devin Vassell	395
Tre Jones	396

Toronto Raptors	
Pascal Siakam	71
Kyle Lowry	72
Fred VanVleet	73
OG Anunoby	74
Aron Baynes	75
Norman Powell	76
Terence Davis	77
Chris Boucher	78
Patrick McCaw	79
Alex Len	80
DeAndre' Bembry	81
Matt Thomas	82
Stanley Johnson	83
Malachi Flynn	84
Utah Jazz	
Donovan Mitchell	291
Rudy Gobert	292
Joe Ingles	293
Mike Conley	294
Royce O'Neale	295
Bojan Bogdanovic	296
Derrick Favors	297
Jordan Clarkson	298
Georges Niang	299
Miye Oni	300
Nigel Williams-Goss	301
Udoka Azubuike	302
Elijah Hughes	303
Washington Wizards	
Bradley Beal	166
Russell Westbrook	167
Thomas Bryant	168
Rui Hachimura	169
Davis Bertans	170
Robin Lopez	171
Troy Brown, Jr.	172
Ish Smith	173
Jerome Robinson	174
Isaac Bonga	175
Moritz Wagner	176
Raul Neto	177
Anzejs Pasecniks	178
Deni Avdija	179
Anthony Gill	180

Printed in Great Britain
by Amazon

55536456R00292